Psychology

REVISED
EDITION

Delos D. Wickens
Donald R. Meyer

The Ohio State University

PSYCHOLOGY

Holt,
Rinehart
and
Winston

The illustrations accompanying the chapter titles are used by permission of the following:
Chapter 1, Black Star, N. Y.; **Chapter 2,** A. Devaney, Inc., N. Y.; **Chapters 3 and 4,** Department of Photography, The Ohio State University; **Chapter 5,** Black Star, N. Y.; **Chapter 6,** Department of Photography, The Ohio State University; **Chapter 7,** Foto-Find Picture Agency, Cleveland, Ohio; **Chapters 8 and 9,** Ewing Galloway, N. Y.; **Chapter 10,** Black Star, N. Y.; **Chapter 11,** Photograph by Harold M. Lambert (from Frederick Lewis); **Chapter 12,** Monkmeyer Press Photo Service, N. Y.; **Chapter 13,** Black Star, N. Y.; **Chapter 14,** Department of Photography, The Ohio State University; **Chapter 15,** A. Devaney, Inc., N. Y.; **Chapter 16,** Ewing Galloway, N. Y.; **Chapter 18,** Monkmeyer Press Photo Service, N. Y.; **Chapter 19,** James C. Mitchell; **Chapter 20,** Ewing Galloway, N. Y.; **Chapter 21,** Black Star, N. Y.

PREFACE

THIS BOOK IS AN ATTEMPT TO PRESENT a systematic and consistent description and interpretation of behavior. As in the original text, the approach emphasizes the importance of learning, and an effort is made to employ learning concepts in the analysis of complex forms of behavior—as, for example, in the chapters devoted to social behavior and to personality.

The effort to achieve a systematic position in which an understanding of the principles of learning is prerequisite to the understanding of other forms of behavior has to a great extent dictated the organization of the book and the sequence of the chapters. The early chapters are devoted to the basic concepts in the areas of learning, motivation, and perception; the later chapters employ these concepts for the analysis and explanation of more complex behavior.

It is the conviction of the authors that the stress upon learning has been justified by the outcomes of research which have appeared since

v

the first edition was prepared. The contemporary trend appears to be toward an increasing emphasis upon the importance of environmental forces as a determinant of behavior. This is more true today than it was a decade ago.

We have continued to make a clear differentiation—both in presentation and authorship—between the molar and the molecular, or the psychological and the general biological approaches to behavior. Although an analysis at the molar level—Chapters 1 through 16—constitutes the major portion of the book, Chapters 17 through 20, on the biological approach, are by no means an afterthought. They serve, we hope, to extend the student's understanding of the behavior of the organism. Throughout these later chapters an attempt is made not merely to differentiate the general biological from the behavioral concepts but also to show how the two are, or may be, related. In this latter aspect, the establishment of relationships between physiological and psychological data, great progress has been made since the original manuscript was completed. These exciting findings have been responsible for a very complete revision of the later chapters.

We continue in our feeling of indebtedness to our graduate advisors, J. F. Dashiell and Harry F. Harlow, for the stimulation they gave to us as graduate students, and we deeply appreciate the assistance that has been afforded to us by many of our colleagues.

There are a number of others who have aided us in specific ways. Frank J. Vattano, Charles K. Allen, Gunther J. Herrmann, James C. Mitchell, and David A. Yutzey have assisted us in obtaining photographs; David I. Suchman and Paul M. Bassett have helped with the compilation of the Glossary. We are most grateful to Lois Q. Fletcher and Diana B. Kreiling, not only for their typing, but for their able and generous assistance with the many other details involved in completing the manuscript.

Finally, we express our great appreciation to our wives, Carol D. Wickens and Patricia M. Meyer, for their help, both direct and indirect, in making the completion of the book possible.

The Ohio State University D.D.W.
January, 1961 D.R.M.

CONTENTS

Chapter One

THE
METHOD
OF
PSYCHOLOGY

IN THE AUTUMN OF 1941, SEVERAL psychologists were commissioned into the U.S. Army and directed to develop a testing program that would increase the efficiency of selection of pilot trainees. Experience had taught the Air Forces Training Command that, although a man may be young, in fine physical condition, and imbued with the ambition of becoming a pilot, he might, nevertheless, fail during one phase or another of the training program. The Air Forces wanted the psychologists to help avoid a waste of money and man-hours by eliminating those men who were likely to fail, before they went into pilot training. These psychologists, and others who joined them later, developed a test battery that became one of the first hurdles the aspiring air cadet had to surmount.

The predicting value of this test battery was demonstrated by an experiment conducted in 1943.[1]* For a group of more than 1000 men, the usual passing requirements on the test battery were waived. These men were given all the tests but were admitted to pilot training *regardless of their test scores.* They immediately entered the regular air-cadet training program, and none of their instructors knew the scores they had received on the test battery. The purpose of the experiment was, thus, to determine the precise relationship between test score and ability to learn to fly a plane.

This degree of relationship is illustrated in Figure 1.1. The length of each bar represents the percentage of candidates who obtained their wings; the others were eliminated for academic deficiency, for deficiency in flying, because of fear, or at their own request. It is apparent that there is a close relationship between test scores achieved by the candidates and their abilities to learn to fly as indicated by their performances in training. The psychologists had obviously succeeded in developing a test battery that was

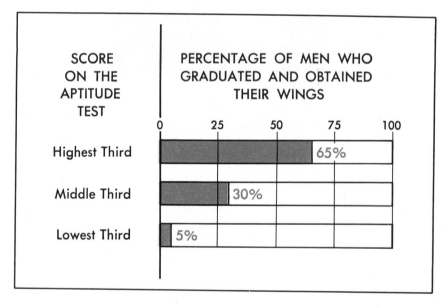

Fig. 1.1 The relationship between scores attained on the AAF Aircrew Classification Test and the percentage of cadets who obtained their wings. (After Du Bois[1])

* Footnotes citing bibliographic sources will be found at the end of each chapter.

very useful in predicting whether or not a young man had the ability to complete the air-cadet training program. The value of the tests was widely recognized, and as a result the Air Forces Training Command required that an individual obtain a certain minimum score on the test before he could be admitted into the training program.

The Army Air Forces selection program is not an isolated case of the successful work of the psychologist. During World War II, many other psychologists worked in various branches of the Army, the Navy, the Marines, and the Maritime Service, developing selection programs and training programs, evaluating morale, diagnosing and correcting problems of personality adjustment, and aiding in the design of more effective weapons. Similar work has long been carried on by psychologists in industry, in retail establishments, in schools and colleges, and in mental hospitals.

The psychologist can do such work, and do it successfully, not because he is gifted with an ability to read minds or possesses an inborn and unusual capacity to understand his fellow men but because of his training in the science of psychology. The student of psychology today falls heir to a vast number of carefully conducted experiments that throw light on the way we behave and the reasons for our behavior. He can learn of tests that have been made and of techniques for making other tests; he also can learn methods of investigation that have been fruitful when applied to the study of the living organism; lastly, and by no means least, he can learn which concepts, which ways of thinking about the behavior of his fellow men, are useful now and promise to be more so as our information grows. With this reservoir of scientific knowledge available, the modern psychologist is in a position to begin to understand himself and others, and he starts out on a level of understanding that far surpasses that of the most brilliant psychologist of fifty years ago.

It is the primary purpose of this textbook to present some information about the subject matter and methods of psychology. In the process of learning this subject matter, the student will inevitably become acquainted with concepts that will make it easier for him to understand himself and his fellow men. Yet even if he learns the subject matter with perfect accuracy, it does not follow that he will automatically become better adjusted and more discerning of social relations than he would be without such knowledge. There is a vast difference between understanding the theory of internal-combustion engines and being able to build an auto-mobile or to repair one. Knowledge of any kind does not guarantee its appropriate application—in psychology or in any other subject. To obtain the greatest value from a course in psychology, the student must do more than simply learn the facts and basic principles of psychology; he must also be motivated to recognize their operation in himself and in others.

THE AIM OF PSYCHOLOGY

The ultimate aim of the psychologist is to make predictions about behavior. This was the goal of the psychologists when they developed the battery of tests to predict the success or failure of the air cadets. It is what the psychologist is attempting to do in many, many areas of behavior; for example, when he suggests to the student who is not doing well in his courses what steps he might take to improve his grades, he is making a prediction. He is saying that if such and such steps are taken, then such and such accomplishments will result. When he advises a parent of procedures that will forestall temper tantrums in his child, he is predicting behavior. He is saying that if the parent behaves in a certain fashion, then the child will react to frustrations by some mode of behavior other than temper tantrums. When the psychologist redesigns the cockpit controls of an airplane in order to reduce accidents, he is predicting. He is saying that if we supply a certain kind of environment, then pilot errors—errors arising from the confusion of one signal with another, or of one control handle with another—will be minimized.

The psychologist can predict that learning in one situation will be better than in another; that this physical stimulus will be noticed and that that one will not; that the people will vote for Mr. Jones and not for Mr. Smith; that one may overcome a fear by acting in a certain way; and that a certain kind of behavior must arise from a particular injury to the brain.

The predictions that the psychologist makes today are, of course, by no means completely accurate. The data on the air-cadet test battery predicted that certain persons would complete their training successfully, but nevertheless some of them failed. Conversely, some who were expected to fail succeeded in passing. In still other areas of behavior, we do not do even so well as in the prediction of pilot success and our errors are greater. This failure to predict with complete accuracy is no cause for alarm; on the contrary, it is a challenge for the future. The modern psychologist who looks back at the great progress his science has made in the past fifty years can look forward hopefully to even greater progress in the next fifty.

THE SCIENTIFIC METHOD IN
PSYCHOLOGY

The world—be it the physical or the social world—presents itself to us in a highly complex manner. The operation of the law of gravity is not immediately seen by a naive observer in such diverse events as the falling of an apple, the downward drifting of a dead leaf in autumn, and the flight of a bird. Each one of these events is complex and appears to be quite different from each of the others. Accepted at face value, the events are different. But the science of physics will tell us that the basic principle of gravity is operating in each case.

In the social world, one may, offhand, see no rhyme or reason behind a man's choices in his clothes, his wife, the location of his home, his occupation, the college fraternity he joined, and the fact that he committed suicide. Nevertheless, a basic motivational law may be operating throughout this series of events, and each event may be as clearly related to the others as the behavior of the apple, the leaf, and the bird are to one another.

Now this very complexity of nature means that the world cannot be understood by simple observation of each of its many events. It means that an understanding can be achieved only if man uses methods which analyze these complex situations and, by eliminating nonessential aspects of the situation, arrives at some description of a basic, underlying mechanism. Thus, science developed as a way of understanding a marvelously complex natural world and of perceiving its infinite variety of events as examples of the operation of a limited number of basic principles.

The methods of scientific inquiry were not suddenly invented by some individual on a certain day. As man began to inquire into the operation of the physical world, he came to learn that some methods of investigation were profitable, whereas others were not. He learned, for example, the simple fact that in order to understand a certain event, he himself had to observe that event. It was not enough to read what Aristotle or some other revered ancient said about it. Furthermore, he learned that he had to prepare in advance for the observation. If he was concerned about the size of an object, or the length of time a certain event took, he could not merely estimate size or time; he had to use instruments for measuring them. He learned also that events occurring in their "natural" state were often so complicated by irrelevant factors that the operation of the single factor he wished to study was obscured. This difficulty he solved by bringing the event into the laboratory and controlling the conditions under which it occurred so that the obscuring factors were eliminated. There, he could vary the specific factors in which he was interested. In other words, he was performing an experiment.

Because the results of the application of experimental methods were very fruitful in the investigation of the physical world, the methods were inevitably applied to other fields. The nineteenth century saw them vigorously introduced into the biological areas, and great advances were made in zoology, physiology, and medicine. A little later, but still in the nineteenth century, some bold spirits began to apply the same methods of science to psychological problems. Thus, experimental psychology began. The kinds of experiments performed were frequently crude; many of them were neither well designed nor adequately evaluated according to present standards; and most of the early workers had a very narrow conception of the range of psychological problems to which scientific methods could be applied. But today our methods have become more refined, the experiments are usually better controlled, and the area of human behavior to which the scientific method is applied has become steadily broader.

Some objections to psychology's program

Sometimes the objection is raised that it is impossible to build a science of behavior. The objectors seem to believe that it is the *material* with which one is working that determines whether or not the discipline is a science and that the *method* of working is unimportant. Actually, it is the method we use in dealing with our materials, and not the kind of material with which we deal, that determines whether or not we are working scientifically. Although they were working with the materials of chemistry, the early alchemists were not scientists; neither were the Romans who collected stories about natural history, although they were interested in the subject matter that later formed the field of biology. When certain methods were applied to these fields, they developed into the science of chemistry and biology as we know them today. There is nothing intrinsic in living organisms that makes it impossible to build a science of behavior. The science of psychology has come into being because man began to apply the basic methods of science to the examination of his own behavior.

But there are some who would assert that the behavior of organisms is not lawful, and therefore it is useless to search for behavioral laws and vain to believe that behavior can be predicted. Obviously this is only an assertion, and not a valid criticism of the program which the psychologist has set for himself. The only way that this criticism could become valid is by establishing, after many years of careful and imaginative research, that efforts to establish laws of behavior did indeed meet with continual failure. Of course the reverse statement—that behavior is lawful—is not proven. All the modern psychologist can state is that we have not, during psychology's admittedly short history as a science, found convincing reasons to give up the assumption that behavior is lawful and predictable.

One other objection to the scientific status of psychology is frequently heard. It is that living organisms are so complex, and their behavior is determined by so large a number of forces, that any effort to analyze and identify these forces is doomed to failure. Admittedly our task is a difficult one, but it speaks ill of man to say that he must admit failure before he tries, and a feeling of defeatism on the part of some onlookers is no valid argument against the worth and eventual success of an endeavor.

THE EXPERIMENT IN PSYCHOLOGY

Let us now examine a typical psychological experiment in which the psychologist, in attempting to analyze a complex behavior, eliminates one complication after another until he discovers the single condition or the complex of conditions that governs the behavior.

Some persons who are totally blind are quite skilled in moving about in their environment—even in a strange environment.[2] There are various theories that attempt to account for this skill. Some hold it as due to an unexplained condition involving magnetism or electricity or to the development of a "sixth," or extra, sense. Others hold that these blind people are guided by a feeling of pressure or temperature on the exposed areas of the skin, especially on the face. Others assume that the blind are guided by pressures in the passages leading to the eardrums. Still others believe that the guiding cues are noises which stimulate the auditory mechanisms. Whatever the cues may be, they are so weak that the blind themselves cannot specify accurately the types of stimuli they are using; their conscious experience offers nothing that explains their behavior. To try to determine the cause of the behavior in this situation, it was necessary, consequently, to conduct a controlled experiment.

As a first step, the ability of blind subjects to perform this type of discrimination was determined in a laboratory situation. The laboratory was a large room equipped with a movable screen or "wall." The subject began walking from one end of the room; he signaled when he first noticed the wall, and again when he thought he had come as close as possible without touching the wall. The distance from the wall to the starting point was varied from trial to trial so that the subject could not count his steps and use the number as a cue. In this first stage of the experiment, the subjects showed considerable skill and were able, on the average, to stop within less than a foot of the wall.

All that this part of the experimental program indicated was that the subjects could guide themselves without the use of vision and without such intellectual aids as knowing the number of steps to take. It did not indicate which sense field was being used for this purpose. The determination of the sense field necessary to make this discrimination was accomplished by eliminating the use of one sense field after another and measuring the effect on the subjects' performance.

First, the subjects' hands and faces were covered with material so heavy that any pressure waves reflected from the wall could not reach the skin. Since this experimental variation failed to change the subjects' performance to any great extent, the experimenter concluded that sensitivity in the skin is not a determining factor.

In the next stage of the experiment, the subjects' ears were plugged, but the material covering the face and hands was removed. Under these conditions, all the subjects collided with the wall on each of the 400 trials. The evidence therefore pointed to the ear mechanism as the sensory area that supplies the necessary cues for obstacle perception. This evidence was now tested further by placing the subjects in a soundproof room with a pair of earphones on their heads. The earphones were connected with a portable microphone which the experimenter held at his own ear level. The experimenter then walked toward the wall at an even speed carrying the microphone while the subjects in the soundproof room tried to judge when he was approaching the wall. Performance under this condition was good, although not quite so good as under normal conditions, when the subjects themselves walked toward the wall.

The results of these experiments seem clear-cut in their indication that the sensory mechanism which guides the blind under these conditions lies in the ear. There are, however, several theories as to precisely how the ear structure is involved. Some hold that hearing, or audition, is the key factor; others hold that the skill is dependent on some sense organ located in the passage leading to the eardrum or, at least, in some portion of the ear structure other than that involved in hearing. The latter—the non-auditory— theory seems to be supported by the fact that there are some persons both deaf and blind who give the impression of being quite capable of getting around by themselves. Apparently they guide themselves without the use of either the visual or the auditory sense, without making physical contact with the objects about them.

The next step in the psychological investigation was, then, to analyze the performance of these deaf-blind persons. Several of them were brought to the laboratory and tested in the same fashion as the subjects in the preceding experimental series.[3] Their performance, however, was markedly inferior to that of the subjects who were blind but not deaf. The deaf-blind either collided with the wall frequently or thought they were close to the wall when they were some distance off. The experimenters decided that, all in all, the performance of these subjects was little better than one would expect under the laws of chance. These data, gathered in a carefully controlled situation, imply that the success of the deaf-blind persons in moving about is either due to the fact that they

9

Fig. 1.2 The streak of light indicates the path of a blind man in an experimental situation designed to discover how such handicapped persons are able to detect and avoid obstacles. In the photograph at the right, the subject, his face partly covered

have learned the locations of the various obstacles in an environment which is familiar to them or because in a strange environment they do indeed make actual physical contacts with obstructing objects through such a medium as a sensitively probing cane.

The conclusion thus seems warranted that true auditory stimuli—sounds made by the subjects themselves, reflected back to them from the obstacle, and received by the hearing mechanism in the ear—were the cues used by the blind in finding their way about. Since the behavior of the subjects can be adequately accounted for by means of the sense of hearing, there is no need for theories that imply a mysterious extra sense, magnetism, or electricity. To presume the existence of some unprovable other sense if we can account for behavior by one of the known senses is unrealistic as well as unscientific.

It will be well now to convert this experiment to a more general and abstract form. We begin with the fact that the behavior occurs. Then we find that some persons say that it is due to one kind of sense organ or cause, whereas others say that it is due to other organs or causes. If we wished to be abstract about it, we

with a masking substance, raises his hand as a signal that he is approaching an obstacle. The subject is transported in a wheeled cart to prevent him from measuring the distance to the obstacle by counting his own paces. (Courtesy *LIFE* Magazine, © TIME, Inc.)

might call the sense organ in the skin of the face, *V;* those in the hand, *W;* the nonauditory sense organs in the ear, *X;* the auditory sense organs, *Y;* and the purely speculative "extra sense," *Z.* Now, in the ordinary daily environment, all of these—*V, W, X, Y,* and *Z* —or any combination of two or more of them—can be operating and no one can tell which one of them is responsible for the behavior. In the experimental situation, each of these factors can be eliminated, one at a time, and we can then determine the importance of each for the behavior. In our experiment it turned out that the behavior was disturbed only when *Y* was removed, and thus the conclusion was reached that it alone was required for adequate performance. For many other behavioral events, a similar method may be used. The *V*'s, *W*'s, *X*'s, *Y*'s, and *Z*'s will stand for something different in each case, but they are handled experimentally in the same manner. It is the major purpose in scientific psychological experimentation to break down the complex situation and to discover the important factors or causes behind the behavior.

In the experiment just described, the conclusion concerning the importance of hearing and the unimportance of the other senses was made possible because the same subject failed to perform adequately when his hearing was impaired but continued to perform adequately if it was present even if other sensory areas were impaired.

Suppose, however, that we had been interested in finding out whether a certain condition improved our ability to learn some material. It is apparent that the experiment could not be conducted in the same manner; we could not have our subjects or groups of subjects learn the materials under this condition and then learn it under the usual conditions, since it would already have been learned when we began testing under the second condition. In these circumstances, experimentation is made possible by use of a *control group.* Two groups of subjects are chosen that are as nearly as possible identical; one, the *experimental group,* learns under the experimental conditions, and the other, the *control group,* under the usual conditions. The averages of the two groups in learning under the two conditions are compared to determine whether or not the new condition is more efficient than the old condition.

This procedure sounds simple and foolproof, but in actual operation it often is neither, and great care must be taken in composing our two groups. We must be certain that the act of including a subject in the experimental group does not introduce some new condition—quite apart from the condition we wish to study—that will influence our results. Perhaps an example will be useful in stressing this point.

A few years ago, some psychologists and sociologists working in a large industrial firm were interested in finding out how certain environmental conditions, such as illumination or layout of the workbench, might influence production.[4] A small group of workers was chosen to serve as experimental subjects, and their production was measured as they worked under the varied environmental conditions that the experimenters arranged. Striking improvements in production were noted, but it was soon discovered that these improvements could not be attributed to the changes in physical environment. Production continued high when the workers were placed under environmental conditions like those used before the experiment was begun and even under conditions which should have been markedly detrimental to efficiency.

The experimenters concluded that the increase in production was the result of social forces which arose as a result of inclusion of the subjects in the experimental group. The subjects were now no longer anonymous workers in a large industrial organization; they were special persons in a special group. This feeling of individuality resulting from being members of the experimental group seemed to be the major reason for the increase in production. Had the experimenters been less careful, they might have concluded, and probably erroneously, that certain physical environmental conditions had had a profound influence upon production; as it was, their conclusions dealt with the importance of human relations as a factor in production in a highly industrialized society.

Problems in human relations lie in the area of social psychology, which we shall discuss later in the text; for the present we wish to re-emphasize the significance of this study as regards the composition of experimental and control groups. *We must be absolutely certain that in setting up our experimental group we do not introduce some other important condition that might influence our results and that will not be present in the control group.*

There is yet another important pitfall that may trap an unwary experimenter as he selects subjects for his control and experimental group. Let us suppose that the experimenter wishes to find out whether a course that is ordinarily given during the freshman year might be mastered better if students were not permitted to take it until their sophomore year. Perhaps the reasoning behind this proposed change is that during the freshman year a number of background courses are given which help to mature the students, and that with this higher level of maturity they can better assimilate the course in question. Arrangements may then be made to have a group of freshmen postpone the course until they are sophomores, at which time they take it under the same instructor, with the same textbook, and with other conditions as much the same as possible. Their mastery of the material as determined by scores on an objective examination may then be compared with that of the freshmen taking the course (the control group).

Now, such a comparison assumes that the ability of the freshmen as a group is equal to the ability of the sophomores as a group except for what the extra year of learning has done for the sophomores. But such is not the case. A very large percentage of the students who enter as freshmen do not return as sophomores, and many studies have shown that those who fail to return score lower as a group on the college-entrance intelligence tests than do those who return. Thus, the ability of the sophomore population is above that of the freshman population even if the effects of an extra year of schooling are eliminated. Our study would almost certainly show that if the course is given in the sophomore year, the performance is higher than if it is given in the freshman year. But we should not be justified in concluding that this difference resulted from the background courses taken during the freshman year. The point of this example is that *we must be certain that our control and experimental subjects are alike in all important respects other than in the experimental condition that we are testing.*

It is probable that many judgments about relationships between causes and events have arisen and have been perpetuated because of the failure to observe that the proper controls are lacking. We blame a political party for a depression or a war because it began during the party's years in office. Who can say with certainty that the calamity was not the result of forces against which both parties would be powerless? We classify a racial group or a sex group as being inferior in some respect, and we assume that the inferiority is inherited. We neglect to note that the environmental opportunities for this racial or sex group are different from what they are for another group. One could compile long lists of follies of reasoning and baseless conclusions that have arisen because appropriate control groups were not available. Obviously it is not always possible to introduce a control group, and this fact need not prevent us from guessing at causes, but it should prevent us from being dogmatic and certain that we know the right answers.

STATISTICS IN PSYCHOLOGY

Most psychological investigations take the form of experiments in which the performance of one group of subjects is compared with that of another group. Such comparisons always involve the risk that one group may be different from the other for reasons other than the experimental condition that has been carefully introduced. Thus we may be led to a false conclusion. How can we minimize the possibility of this kind of error?

Our first step is to use care in selecting subjects for the experimental and the control groups and to be as certain as possible that no conditions are present that will bias our selections. But, even with these dangers eliminated, the risk is not completely avoided, for there is always the possibility that by mere chance the members selected for one group will be different from those selected for another.

Suppose we have two drawers filled with socks. In one drawer half the socks are white and half are black and in the other, one third are white and two thirds are black. However, we do not know these facts but we wish to find out the proportion of black socks to white socks in each of the two drawers. How many socks must we take from each drawer before the proportions in our samples closely approximate the proportions in the drawers themselves? If we take only a few, we may be totally wrong, since by chance we might select socks all of one color from each drawer or obtain proportions which are in some other way quite out of line with reality. As we chose more and more socks, however, our proportions would come closer and closer to the proportions found in the drawers.

The parallel between this situation and that of the public-opinion pollster who wishes to find the ratio of Republican voters to Democratic voters is obvious. The parallel is less obvious, but nevertheless present, when we test one method or condition against another by comparing the performance of one group with that of another.

In order to avoid errors due to chance selection in our groups, the psychologist tends to use a fairly large number of subjects in his groups. Furthermore, he employs certain statistical procedures that aid him in simplifying his data. In addition to using statistics which boil the data down to understandable forms, he uses a special kind of statistics which tells him what the probability is that any difference he obtained might be due to chance selection. Chance factors can never be eliminated completely, but the next best thing to eliminating them is to know what the probability is that they have determined the results. And statistics can tell us this probability quite accurately.

MEASUREMENT IN PSYCHOLOGY

In psychology, as in physics or chemistry, it is necessary to develop exact devices of measurement. The experiment on the deaf-blind (see p. 8) illustrates how an inexact method of measurement may lead one astray. A number of the deaf-blind subjects seemed quite capable of finding their way without help. In other words, general and haphazard observations indicated that the loss of hearing did not affect their ability to sense the presence of obstacles. But in the controlled laboratory situation, where exact methods of testing and measuring were employed, it was discovered that the deaf-blind were actually not capable of making good obstacle discriminations. Conclusions drawn from the laboratory results would consequently have to be quite different from conclusions drawn from the field results.

The assertion has frequently been made that women, as a group, are less intelligent than men. The proud male points to the fact that women, in general, have not achieved as much in the world as men have. Achievement in the world, however, is not a valid measure of intelligence, because there are many factors beside intelligence that make for worldly success. After psychologists had developed valid tests for measuring intelligence and had measured comparable groups of each sex, no marked difference between the two sexes in over-all ability was discovered. Here is a case in which apparently major differences faded when rigorous methods of measurements were employed.

Fig. 1.3 A contrast in the complexity of psychological measurement. The child in the picture above is being given an intelligence test. His score will be determined partly by whether or not he reaches for and grasps the block. The picture below shows some equipment used for measuring the learning of perceptual and motor activities. The subject (with his back to the viewer) must learn certain responses to tones and to visual stimuli projected on the oscilloscope screen before him. The equipment generates the stimuli and records his response. (Courtesy Conrad Kraft)

Is one advertisement more effective than another? Does learning proceed more rapidly under one condition than another? Does a background of loud noise disturb the worker's performance? Does inconsistent treatment make for personality difficulties in the child? These are only a few of the questions we wish to answer. To do so, we must be able to measure the effectiveness of the advertisement, the speed of learning, the efficiency of the worker's performance, and the degree of inconsistency in the child's upbringing, together with the degree of personality maladjustment. If any one of the conditions is not measured with exactness, the error that creeps into our measurement will surely make itself felt in the conclusions we draw from our experimental data. If two things are related to each other in a certain way, but we fail to measure one of these with accuracy, then we cannot identify the true relationship. Thus, the importance of careful measurement in determining the relationships between different aspects of behavior and between the environment and behavior cannot be overstressed.

THE HYPOTHESIS IN PSYCHOLOGY

Ordinarily, the first step in performing an experiment is to begin with a hypothesis that there is a meaningful relationship between one condition and another. Thus, one might hypothesize that speed of learning will be related to the attitude one holds toward the material he is learning, or that frequency of aggression among children will vary with the kind of play equipment available. The hypothesis is something of a shrewd guess derived from isolated items of information: a fact collected here or an observation there.

Usually, the hypothesis has some basis in factual observation. Sometimes, however, it has no such factual basis, but for various reasons it may nevertheless be worth testing experimentally. There were no factual reasons for believing that the Nazi-inspired idea of Nordic superiority was valid; this idea was a statement of opinion rather than a guess made from available facts. But because of the tremendous social significance involved, and because the psychologist is a citizen of the world as well as a professional scientist, he was willing to test the hypothesis, even though it seemed to contradict many well-established facts. In an experiment which compared what were considered to be "purely Nordic" individuals with other individuals of European ancestry, no genetically determined differences in intellectual performance could be discovered. These results, needless to say, disproved the Nazi hypothesis. (The relationship between racial background and intelligence is discussed further in Chapter 13.)

In the ordinary course of scientific work, however, we do not depend upon the mere opinion of some authority or expert as a source of a hypothesis. We demand that the opinion be based on some kind of acceptable factual data. Such demands do not restrict imagination, for imagination plays an important part in scientific thinking; the demands simply require that there be some factual foundation to the imagining. Once the hypothesis is concretely formulated, we design an experimental situation that will put it to test. If there is no way of testing the hypothesis now and no reason to believe that it can be tested—directly or indirectly—in the future, then it is scientifically unacceptable and it must be discarded. We try to design our experiment so that if results point clearly in one direction, the hypothesis is clearly substantiated; if the results point in other directions, they oppose the hypothesis and refute it.

If the hypothesis has been successful in predicting the experimental results—in other words, if it seems to be true—then as a next step it is tested in other experimental situations. Unless the hypothesis is extremely limited in scope, applying to only a very narrow segment of behavior, the work of testing the hypothesis is an almost continuous process.

THE PSYCHOLOGICAL APPROACH
TO BEHAVIOR

Some years ago psychologists were stirred by a very profound controversy over a definition of the aims of psychology. One group of psychologists maintained that the purpose of psychology was to understand and describe states of consciousness. Aligned against them was a group that held that psychology should be concerned with why people act as they do and that the purpose of psychology

19

was to understand and predict behavior. The controversy was a bitter one and lasted for a number of years, but eventually the group that believed that the aim of psychology should be to predict behavior won. Today there are few American psychologists who do not accept this as the purpose of their science.

Having agreed on aims, we must then find a means of fulfilling these aims, and we must decide upon ways of thinking that will aid us most effectively in doing so. Perhaps the most obvious approach is to use the data of conscious experience to explain why a specific kind of behavior occurs. Certainly this is the approach that most people have been using since childhood. They say that they made this choice rather than that because, having considered all possibilities, they liked it better; or they made up their minds that something had to be done, and so they did it. There are, however, a number of difficulties with this method for predicting.

We might at this time perform an experiment. Below you will find a list of words. Look at them one at a time and give the *opposite* of each word you see.

Long	Boy
Sweet	Good
Black	Big

It is almost certain that you responded to these words by thinking of the words *short, sour* or *bitter, white, girl, bad* or *evil,* and *little;* in that order. Now let us examine your performance. Did you, after reading one of these words, think of all the words you know and out of this large group select the one that was appropriate? Most certainly you did not; the response came tumbling out without any consciousness on your part of sorting and selecting. In other words, there is little in your conscious experience that explains your behavior.

This is not an isolated and special case. Many studies have been made of the individual's conscious experience as he reached decisions, and almost all of them indicate that there is little in the conscious experience of the individual that truly explains why a specific choice was made.

In situations far more complex than this we often find that reports of conscious experience fail to provide an adequate explanation. Toward the end of the nineteenth century, Sigmund Freud, the father of psychoanalysis, began his work with abnormal and maladjusted persons. It did not take him long to discover that his patients were frequently—in fact, almost constantly—doing things for which they could find nothing in their consciousness which seemed to offer an adequate explanation. They might find themselves hating a certain person, or fearing a certain place, for no good reason, or they might repeat some purposeless movement again and again without ever knowing why. Not only was consciousness often mute as to cause; frequently it was utterly wrong and deceptive; for Freud found that patients might confidently state a certain reason for their behavior, and believe this reason, whereas the real cause might be quite different. To handle these paradoxes Freud hypothesized the unconscious, and it became, in his system of explaining behavior, even more important than consciousness.

One may question the validity of Freud's device of postulating an unconscious to explain the behavior that could not be explained by the contents of consciousness. The use of the unconscious was made necessary because of the inadequacy and unreliability—and sometimes deceitfulness—of the conscious states. But perhaps we should completely abandon this way of trying to explain our actions and seek some other general method. Let us try to apply such a general method to the experiment on word associations that you have just performed.

To explain your responses to the list of words, we must consider things that happened to you many years ago. One of these is that you were brought up in a certain kind of environment which developed in you certain language habits: you speak and understand English. Reared in Tibet without contact with the English language, you would not have responded as you did. You attended schools and learned to read, and because of these experiences, you had the capacity to answer as you did. Also, because of groups of experiences you have had, you have learned to do at least some of the things that teachers and textbooks ask of you. Then, there was a sentence just preceding the list in which the word "opposite" was emphasized; and lastly there was the list itself. It would appear that we could have predicted your behavior by knowing something about the habits you have acquired (the language you know), the kind of motives under which you operate (such as accepting the task requested by the textbook), general biasing conditions (directions to give opposites), and the stimuli that are striking your sense organs (the printed words that you saw). If this analysis is correct, a person who knew all these things about you—things that he could learn without knowing anything about your consciousness—could have predicted your behavior in response to these stimuli, as, indeed, we have done on the preceding page.

In this book we shall view behavior as responses made to stimuli acting on the individual at the particular moment. Because of the individual's biological structure and the nature of his past experiences, these stimuli will evoke certain psychological mechanisms—such as habits and motives, to mention only two—and certain kinds of responses will follow. We shall devote most of the text to considering the psychological mechanisms that operate and the influence of the individual's past experience upon the development of these mechanisms, which will function throughout his life.

What, if we follow this approach, becomes of consciousness? Obviously the approach does not deny conscious experience; it simply states that it will not use conscious experience as the main source of explanation. Furthermore, although the approach may employ conscious experience as an aid in identifying mechanisms of behavior which might be operating at a given time, it will assume that this behavior occurred *because these mechanisms were operating* and not because the individual was aware of his feelings. And since the individual's awareness or unawareness of his feelings is irrelevant to an explanation of his behavior, clearly there is no need to postulate the existence of an unconscious.

Actually this approach is both contradictory to and consonant with methods of explanation that most students have developed by the time they take a course in psychology. You may refer to someone who "had a rough time in childhood," or who "was born with a silver spoon in his mouth," and you thus imply that these past experiences have developed certain habits which persist and which determine the way in which he will react at some later date. When you do this, you are attempting to explain an individual's behavior in the very sort of terms we shall use in this text.

There are, however, many times when you resort to explanations which imply that some present conscious state is the determinant of behavior. You will say, perhaps, that you did something because you *made up your mind* to do it, or that you *willed* to act in one way rather than in another. Here you are implying that your conscious experience is the cause of your behavior rather than that certain motives and habits are operating to determine your actions and that you are aware of at least some of them. In this text we shall attempt to be consistent and not resort to explanations which are at one time based upon the nature of the past experience and the present environment and at another time based upon some conscious feeling. If you will remember that this is the approach being used consistently, you will be able to understand certain ideas in this book that may puzzle you on the basis of your present thinking.

STIMULUS AND RESPONSE

Our first task is to understand behavior, and if we pause to consider what is meant by behavior we shall see that we can think of it as a response or series of responses that the individual makes.

There are all kinds of responses. Swinging a tennis racket in the direction of an approaching ball is obviously a response; so is jumping out of your chair to answer the telephone. There are other kinds of behavior which you may not have thought of as responses. When you are asked to recall to yourself what you did yesterday, and you do so, this recalling is a response; when you reason out exactly why your car fails to start, you are making a series of responses. A daydream is a response, and so is your feeling of love or hatred for someone. When you estimate that one car is closer to you than another, you are responding, and your solution to a problem in algebra is the end product of a series of responses.

In the final analysis, responses are movements of muscles. Swinging at a tennis ball consists of an extremely complex series of muscular actions. However, with all the help of the anatomist and the physiologist, we cannot state why certain muscles which make the act possible were selected for use rather than others. At the present state of knowledge, we must be content to think of a response not in terms of specific muscular movements but as a total act—such as running, or throwing, or driving a car, or reciting a poem, or thinking about a certain thing.

Responses do not simply occur in and of themselves. They are evoked by stimuli or by a stimulus situation. Stimuli are certain actual changes in physical energy that impinge upon the individual —changes in energy that lead to seeing, hearing, smelling, and tasting, to mention only a few of the kinds of experience that are associated with these changes. For the responses that we cited as examples above, we can identify some of the stimuli without much difficulty. The sight of the tennis ball coming over the net determines your responses, and the sound waves produced by the telephone bell fall upon your ear and arouse you from your chair. In the algebra problem the printed words of the problem are stimuli, but as you work on the problem and write x's and y's on your paper, these responses you have made themselves become stimuli for further responses. The stimulus for daydreaming may not be so easy to find, but it is there, nevertheless.

A few words of warning. One does not *explain* behavior by saying that it is a reaction to a stimulus; one simply sets one's house in order so that one can begin to look for an explanation. The basic question that we must answer is why a specific stimulus produces a specific response, and this question is not always an easy one, for we may be faced with the apparently inconsistent facts that the same stimulus produces one response now and a different one a few hours later, or we may find that different individuals will react quite differently to the same stimulus. Also, we must beware of considering the stimulus as a single, isolated change in the environment. It is, rather, a complex interaction of environmental changes.

Most of the chapters in this book will present the concepts that we use to explain how a specific S (stimulus) happens to produce a specific R (response). When, later, we discuss habits or learning, motivation, perception, or intelligence, we shall be talking about some of the most important concepts that psychologists use to predict behavior—that is, to account for the fact that the organism reacts in a specific fashion when confronted with a certain pattern of stimuli.

We can do this without, if you will, going beneath the skin of the individual, without referring to his underlying physiological make-up. Indeed, some psychologists believe that there is no need whatever for them to concern themselves with physiology as a determinant of behavior. But the behavior that we observe is, in the end, the product of our physiological make-up, the result of the actions of our sense organs, our nervous system, our muscles, and other bodily components. A knowledge of the manner in which these structures operate and are reflected in total behavior adds much to our understanding and appreciation of behavior. The physiological basis of behavior is, moreover, a fascinating field of study in and of itself. The latter part of the text will be devoted to a description of how our bodies operate and how their characteristics govern the ways in which we behave.

THE APPLICATIONS OF PSYCHOLOGY

The ultimate aim of experimental methods such as those we have described above is to filter out of the complex environment those factors that are essential for the occurrence of certain kinds of behavior. When we reach the point at which we can say that when a certain factor is present, a certain kind of behavior will occur, then we have explained that behavior in psychological terms. If, furthermore, we can introduce this factor at will, then we can control and predict behavior. This is the task that society sets for the psychologist; it asks him how the parent should guide his child into a happy and psychologically healthy adulthood; how the student who is slow in learning can be aided; how men can be made more efficient in their work; and how society itself can be changed so that races and nations can live together, free from aggression or the fear of aggression.

Society cannot wait until every single and detailed fact of behavior has been determined. If the psychologist already has available some generalizations that can be applied to a certain maladjusted person, or that make for more efficient behavior in the school or in the factory, these generalizations should be used. In fact, there are many psychologists whose foremost aim is to *apply* those principles we already know in order to meet some of the needs of society.

Industrial psychologists are primarily concerned with making for greater efficiency in work situations. Usually working in industry or in the government, they concern themselves with such problems as how to select the best man for the job, how best to train him, how to keep his morale at its optimal level, and what kind of general working environment should be afforded him. They are occupied, also, with the design and selection of the tools and equipment most appropriate to the worker's physical equipment, skills, and general abilities.

Clinical and *counseling psychologists* are concerned with the individual, and primarily in helping him become more adequately adjusted to his environment. Confronted with a client who is behaving in a manner unsatisfactory both to himself and to society, the clinician or counselor, through interviews, tests, and reports of behavior, eventually arrives at a diagnosis of the difficulty. On the basis of the diagnosis, he plans and carries out the treatment or therapy.

The work of these psychologists brings them into contact with many kinds and degrees of maladjustment. They help the child, the adolescent, the adult, and the very aged over various crises. They may work with the slightly maladjusted person in a typical school situation, and the clinical psychologist in particular may be asked to deal with an extreme personality deviate—the hysteric who has lost the ability to move his hand, although bones, nerves, and muscles are in perfect working order, or the unfortunate person who is incapacitated by feelings of guilt, or the religious fanatic who hears voices when there are no voices to be heard.

Educational psychologists, as the title implies, work principally in schools and colleges, applying the principles of psychology to teaching, to learning, to teacher training, and to the adjustment of the individual in the school situation. Their work includes varied tasks, such as organizing a testing program, providing special techniques for teaching handicapped children, pointing out the best method of training in one school subject or another, and training students at the high-school and college levels in efficient . tudy habits.

Social psychologists apply the methods and techniques of psychology to the measurement and the prediction of social phenomena, such as attitude formation, prejudice, and group behavior. Since by their very nature social phenomena must be studied in a social situation, the work-a-day world is for social psychologists often at the same time a laboratory and the place in which to apply previously discovered principles and methods.

Basic research

All these professional fields and others demonstrate the practical application of the principles and methods of psychology. And society as a whole profits from these applications. But at the same time that the applied psychologists are working in the clinic, in industry, in the schools and elsewhere, another large body of psychologists in the laboratories of our colleges and research organizations are performing experiments whose results may add to the core of psychological principles. The research performed by these groups is sometimes referred to as basic research. Research of this type is not oriented toward the solution of some immediate practical problem; instead its most usual aim is to obtain the empirical data that can be used to evaluate or expand various theoretical formulations about behavior. Someday, perhaps, these theoretical formulations may be of the utmost practical value, but the essential aim of basic research is to expand our knowledge and not to apply it in some practical situation.

Because this is his purpose, the basic researcher is not restricted to working only with humans or with materials or activities that are drawn from the daily life of his culture. He uses subhuman subjects and, in particular instances, especially devised tasks, because they afford ways of controlling and analyzing variables that would otherwise be impossible to achieve. Nevertheless, the conclusions that are drawn from this research may be of considerable significance for the understanding of the behavior of the human being in his highly complex culture.

We cannot in reality draw a sharp line of demarcation between the contributions of the basic-research man and those of the applied psychologist—who also, it must be emphasized, is active in research. The basic researcher frequently applies his material, and the applied psychologist not only uses known principles but also adds to theoretical knowledge when, in his activities, he discerns in operation principles that may never have been discovered in the laboratory. Moreover, he may discover that some laboratory-developed principles break down in certain applications. From his observation, then, a reformulation of the old laboratory principle may arise, or his new observation may be tested under controlled laboratory conditions and may form the basis of a new principle. Through these means the science of psychology continues to inch ever closer to a clearer understanding of behavior.

REFERENCES

[1] DuBois, Philip H. (ed.) *Army Air Forces Psychology Program Research Reports. The Classification Program. Report No. 2,* U.S. Government Printing Office, 1947.

[2] Supa, Michael, Catzin, Milton, and Dallenbach, K. M. Facial vision, the perception of obstacles by the blind, *Amer. J. of Psychol.,* 1944, *57,* 133-183.

[3] Worchel, Philip, and Dallenbach, Karl M. Facial vision, perception of obstacles by the deaf-blind, *Amer. J. of Psychol.,* 1947, *60,* 502-533.

[4] Roethlisberger, F. J., and Dickson, W. J. *Management and the Worker,* Harvard, 1940.

LEARNING:

AN

INTRODUCTION

THE DIFFERENCE BETWEEN THE PER-
formance of the novice and that of the expert is great. Awkwardness
contrasts with dexterity, timidity with confidence, and fumbling
incompetence with facile skill. If one were not aware that organisms possess enormous capacity for learning, he might conclude
that these two individuals, the novice and the expert, represent two
separate species. Because our ability to learn is so dependable, and
because we accept the fact that we shall learn, we seldom stop to
marvel at the phenomenon that can produce such drastic changes
in our behavior. Almost always the beginner picks up his golf clubs,
his tennis racket, or his textbook with a feeling that successful performance is largely a matter of time and effort. And usually success
does come with time and effort.

The fruits of learning are ever apparent in our daily behavior. They are present when we walk over and bend down to
pick up the morning's newspaper. We have learned the motor skill
of walking; we have learned that space exists in three dimensions
and that the newspaper is approximately five feet from us and not
at our fingertips; we have learned to reach out our hand to a specific
point in space. When we look at this collection of pages that we
have learned to call a newspaper, we are confronted not with a
conglomeration of black marks on white paper but with meaningful configurations which we have learned to read. These will tell
us about a world of things and people about which we have learned
and about which, by the very act of reading, we shall learn more.
We have learned to enjoy the coffee that we sip as we read our
paper, and we have learned how to shake just the correct amount
of salt on our breakfast eggs. There is no need to carry the description further. Throughout the day we move from one learned activity to another until we close our eyes at night in bed, which we
have learned to prefer to the ground as a place for sleeping.

Because there is little—indeed, perhaps nothing—that the
adult does that is not influenced in some way by what he has learned
from past experience, a knowledge of the principles of learning is
basic to the understanding of behavior. Psychologists have long
recognized this, and the number of research studies and articles on
the topic is as vast as the topic itself—ranging from investigations of
such simple accomplishments as throwing a ball to such complex
phenomena as the acquisition of personality maladjustments. It is
because of the all-pervasiveness of learning that this chapter appears early in this text. Time and time again throughout the book,
the principles of learning will be encountered in one context or
another.

Before we can begin to understand all the many researches
and problems in the field of learning, it is necessary to define the
concept with some precision. Learning is *the more or less permanent modification of the response or responses to a stimulus or to
a pattern of stimuli as a result of experience with this or with similar stimuli.*

It will take several chapters of this text to clarify this definition, but there are several phrases that can profit from amplification at this point. The phrase *more or less permanent* was
introduced to exclude from the concept the changes that could be
attributed to fatigue, or to any other mechanism that produces a

temporary change in responsiveness—a change that can be eliminated by rest. The phrase is also meant to acknowledge the fact that one can forget something which has been learned, and in a later chapter we will identify some of the conditions which produce a greater or lesser amount of forgetting. The phrase *modification of the response . . . to a stimulus* implies that learning may be conceived of as the formation of an association between a stimulus and a response. The phrase *as a result of experience* simply excludes from the province of learning those stimulus-response associations that stem from the basic biological structure of the organism. In a later chapter entitled "Maturation" it will be shown that certain behavioral changes can be accounted for in this fashion. The phrase *or with similar stimuli* refers to the fact that our behavior in one situation—that is, with a certain pattern of stimuli—may undergo modification because of experience with other stimuli. The factors that are responsible for these changes will be described under the topic of "Transfer of Training" in Chapter 3. Perhaps it is enough to add that the concept of learning is a complex one and a single sentence can only point in a very general way to the behavioral phenomena it subsumes.

The concept of the stimulus and the response and the kinds of associations that can be found between them is meant to be broad. It includes the modification of our responses to the stimulus of a tennis ball coming over the net, the modification of our responses to the sound of the word "psychology," the modification of our responses to the stimulus of another person's behavior. The definition of learning points clearly to the fact that we are dealing with stimuli and with responses, and that the basic question is how and why a specific stimulus comes to be associated with a specific response.

The student may be tempted to say that learning to bat a baseball is fundamentally different from learning to recite a poem, and that both are different from learning the principles that govern an internal-combustion engine. Actually these are not basically dissimilar phenomena, and they are probably not acquired in fundamentally different fashions. In all cases, they involve a change in the ways of responding to stimulus situations. There is a change from responding with an "I don't know" to "Well, it's like this . . ." and there is a change from missing the ball to hitting it squarely. They are all encompassed by our definition of learning—behavior modifications that are more or less permanent.

In his investigations of learning, the psychologist is looking for concepts that will have general utility in many aspects of behavior. He is not satisfied to investigate learning in one situation; he studies learning in many situations, for he is seeking the *principles of learning*—principles that operate wherever and whenever learning occurs. Sometimes the principles he derives from one situation do not seem valid in another, and then he is confronted with the necessity of understanding this inconsistency. Was the original principle incorrect, or does some other factor come into the new situation to make the principle inoperative?

To a great extent, however, we have been able to develop concepts of learning that cut across the boundaries of many fields of activity. Often we can generalize from the learning behavior of rats to that of man, or from the learning of a manual task to the memorization of a poem. Much of the research on learning is carried on in laboratory experiments which are artificial in the sense that exactly similar situations do not occur in daily life. By using specific materials in contrived (laboratory) situations, we can control some variable which would otherwise distort the meaning of our results, and once the operation of a principle has been isolated and studied in a laboratory setting, we are better able to observe and predict its operation in daily life. The student will do well, therefore, to think about the principles we shall discuss in terms of his own daily life. After all, the four years of college life are years devoted to the process of learning in many fields and in many situations.

In the following discussion of the psychology of learning we shall not emphasize specifically the many kinds of things that can be learned or the many situations in which our behavior is modified. Our main concern will be to discuss the basic concepts of learning as the psychologist knows them today.

In fairness to the student we should state that the issue of a single kind of learning—that is, whether the same laws or principles operate in the same way in all situations—has not yet been settled in modern psychology. There are many psychologists who believe that certain kinds of learning principles operate in one situation but do not hold in another. No definitive solution to this issue is yet available and no one can say for certain whether this position is right or wrong. It is beyond the scope of an elementary text to confront the student with all the technical aspects of the problem, and so we shall emphasize instead the somewhat simpler

assumption that there are similarities and communalities in learning in many situations. There is no clear evidence at present that
this position is much less adequate for the prediction of behavior
than the more complex one, and certainly it requires the learning
of fewer principles by the student—technically we call it a more
parsimonious solution.

THE NATURE OF THE LEARNING
SITUATION

One of the basic characteristics of life is that the organism
is constantly being required to make adjustments—to itself and to
its environment. Almost continuously it is confronted with situations that differ—sometimes widely, sometimes only slightly—from
previous situations for which it has already established appropriate
ways of acting. In every new situation the organism is required to
modify its responses until at last it achieves one that surmounts the
obstacle that environment has thrown in his way. The tendency
to modify the behavior and to *fixate*—that is, to make relatively
permanent—this behavior modification constitutes the tendency of
the organism to learn.

We may illustrate learning in another way—by a situation
in which the organism is frustrated and then overcomes that difficulty, as shown in Figure 2.1.

In step 1, the organism is progressing toward the goal when
it is confronted by an obstacle (2), which blocks its activity; unsuccessful responses (3) are made to surmount the obstacle, and finally
a successful response (4) occurs. When once again the organism is
confronted with this situation, there are fewer unsuccessful responses and the successful response occurs sooner. Eventually the
unsuccessful responses may be completely eliminated. A new way
of reacting to the obstacle has replaced the older way. The organism has learned.

Perhaps an example will help. A little child who is locked
in the back yard is attracted by some toy outside the fence. He approaches the gate and pushes at it. When it does not give, he pulls
it. Perhaps he pushes and pulls it again. Next he changes his tactics

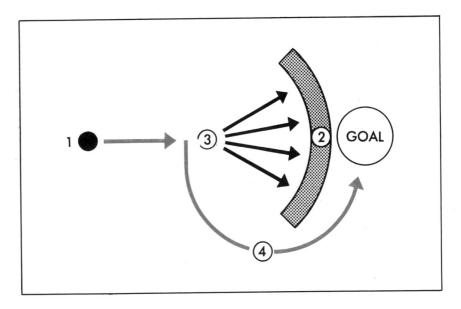

Fig. 2.1 A situation of temporary frustration can give rise to learning. The organism (*1*) is frustrated by a barrier (*2*) in reaching the goal. After several of the responses that it attempts (*3*) prove fruitless, it varies its behavior and discovers a successful response (*4*). (After Dashiell[2])

to a vigorous shaking of the gate. Unmoved, the barrier still stands between him and his goal. Then a pudgy finger probes at the latch and lifts it but releases it before the gate is moved. A moment later the child lifts the latch again, but this time he pushes the gate before releasing the latch and successfully passes through the barrier to gain the toy. A few hours later he may again be locked in the back yard. Again he pushes and pulls the gate a few times and then pokes around at the latch until he releases it. The shaking has been eliminated. Within a few days he dispenses with all preliminary moves and reaches immediately for the latch, pushing the gate as he lifts the latch. The child has learned—and so too has his worried mother.

In the foregoing account, a motivated organism encounters a barrier and, after making a variety of responses, hits upon one that overcomes it. When the situation occurs again, the successful response occurs earlier in the behavior sequence. In the end, the successful response becomes embodied in a well-fixated and smooth sequence of responses. To the stimulus situation of the locked gate, a particular response has become attached.

There is a considerable generality to this pattern. In a similar manner the child may learn a way of getting around his parents or his contemporaries. He may employ tantrums, violence, or social blandishments; and he may fixate these ways of reacting to social barriers. Throughout life we meet barriers that block an easy access to our goals, and when we do so we follow to a greater or less degree the pattern of behavior illustrated in Figure 2.1. The reader will be able to think of many other examples in which the structure of behavior closely fits the structure of this diagram.

There are four highly important aspects of behavior illustrated by the diagram:

1. The organism is *motivated*—that is, its responses are directed toward a certain stimulus pattern which we call the goal.

2. There are barriers that block ready access to the goal.

3. In response to the barrier, the organism *varies its behavior,* and in the process of making the varied responses that are generally appropriate to the particular situation one response may occur which surmounts the difficulty.

4. With continued presentations of the situation, the unsuccessful responses become *eliminated* and a new stimulus-response association is formed and becomes fixated. That is, the response is more and more likely to occur each time the situation is confronted.

Each of these four aspects we shall now consider in some detail, although a complete discussion of them will be given in subsequent chapters of the text.

Motivation

A significant characteristic of the motivational factor in the learning situation is illustrated in Figure 2.2. The diagram shows the way in which our motivational habits serve to direct our behavior toward various areas of the environment. Because Goal 1 and Goal 2 differ from each other, and because the nature of the responses necessary to surmount the two barriers differ, the learnings involved in reaching these goals will differ. The student whose motivation is to become a physician will be confronted by barriers different from those confronting the student who wishes to become

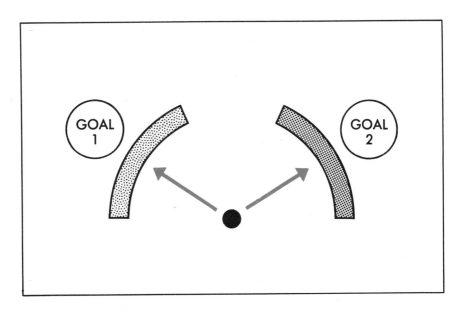

Fig. 2.2 The importance of motivation in the learning responses is indicated here diagrammatically. To reach either Goal 1 or Goal 2, the organism must overcome a specific barrier and make a specific response. The particular response he learns to make will depend largely upon the relative strengths of the organism's motivations toward each of the two goals.

a mechanical engineer, and the responses that the two students learn will differ accordingly. The child whose motivational habits are primarily social will develop a set of learned responses different from those of the youngster whose motivation is directed toward activities that are nonsocial in nature.

When the level of motivation is low, a shift in the direction of the behavior may occur, for if the response to the goal is weakly energized, the organism may, before making a successful response, turn away from the barrier toward some other stimuli. As it withdraws from the situation, it removes itself from the possibility of learning in that situation.

Further consideration of the experimental work dealing with the nature of motivation and the close relationship between motivation and learning will be reserved for Chapter 5. For the present, the student should be aware of the value of motivation in setting a direction to behavior and maintaining this direction until solution is achieved, thus making the discovery and the fixation of the new response possible.

The barriers

The barriers that stand between us and the achievement of our goals are of different sorts. That *physical* structures may serve as barriers is obvious. It is also obvious that there are *social barriers,* for the actions of other people or groups of persons may serve as barrier objects. And social barriers are not only of the face-to-face variety but also the more abstract, yet none the less real, customs, mores, and laws of society. Man finds many ways of circumventing his barriers. The child, forbidden an object by his parents, may still struggle for it and may find ways to obtain it through rational argumentation, coaxing, and even deceit; adults, halted by social barriers, use very much the same techniques to avoid them.

Far less obvious are the barriers that arise from the characteristics of the learner himself. One of these is his own *motive or value system,* for there are many times when we are blocked from ready attainment of a goal object for one class of motive because another personal motive tells us that we would be wrong to do so. This type of situation often leads to personality disorders or discomforts and we will discuss it in some detail in Chapter 6.

Finally, *prior learning* may serve as a barrier to adequate performance in some new situation, and these previously learned habits or ways of reacting must be suppressed before efficient behavior can arise in the new situation. This is called a case of negative transfer and the nature of this phenomenon will be one of our concerns in Chapter 4.

Discovery of the correct response

In an experiment conducted many years ago, cats were placed in a small slatted box with food outside the door.[1] The door was latched but could be opened by the animal itself if it clawed on a string in a downward direction. When the hungry cats were first placed in the box, they responded in many ways. They would mew, scratch at the door, sniff and bite at the slats, and eventually slash at, touch, and pull the cord. When the cord was pulled, the door would swing open and release the cat.

Now, the eventual solution of the problem was made possible by the fact that the animal was capable of varying its behavior in the situation. A continued and stereotyped scratching at the door would have been of no avail. and neither would the continuation

のof any other response that was not oriented about the critical string. The animals shifted from one mode of action to the next, and in the process a response was evoked that was the correct one for the situation. Motives give a direction and persistence to behavior that sustains the reactions until the goal is reached, but the goal could not be achieved if the organism were incapable of varying its reactions to the situation.

The ability of the organism to vary its response makes possible the discovery of the correct response and is a prerequisite of learning. The variety of responses made to a stimulus pattern is not a random selection from all the reactions which the individual has in his behavior repertoire; it is usually limited to the types of reactions that are more or less appropriate to the situation. If, however, this variety is too limited, it may not include the correct response, and solution will then be impossible. The difficulty encountered in the solution of some "trick" problems arises simply because the array of pre-solution acts is too narrow. This aspect of learning—pre-solution variability—is of especial importance in problem solving and in creative thinking.

In most types of learning, pre-solution variability is at a minimum because the objective task is set up in such a way that great variability is not required. If the task is to memorize the trigonometric functions or the first twenty lines of the *Canterbury Tales*, little pre-solution variability is necessary. The correct response does not need to be discovered; it is present and available to the learner in his textbook. In any situation in which the organism can be guided to the correct response, the *discovery* problem does not loom as significant; the task is, rather, to *fixate* that response to the appropriate stimuli. Learning an activity without the aid of a coach involves a double task for the learner: he must *discover* the correct response and, after discovery, he must *fixate* it.

Fixation of the response

The problem as to why certain responses become eliminated and others become fixated has, in all probability, been the subject of as much research as any other single problem in the entire field of psychology. The discovery of the correct response can be explained in terms of the tendency of the organism to vary its behavior (though here, too, many problems arise in accounting for

37

the factors that make for variability); but why the organism, when confronted with the same situation again, is *less* likely to make the incorrect responses and *more* likely to make the correct one is not an easy question to answer. Actually the increasing tendency to make the correct response is a complex process involving many factors. In the next chapter we shall be concerned primarily with the research on the problem of fixation and with the various techniques that have been employed to discover the answers to the questions raised about it.

The nature of learned responses

There is one final characteristic of the total adjustment process that we must mention, and this is the nature of the response which becomes fixated or associated with the stimulus. Psychologists today use the word "response" to refer indiscriminately to many kinds of actions of the organism. They would, for example, use this word for such activities as *walking* or *talking* and also for the more general activities of *wanting something* or *fearing something.* Obviously these two pairs of responses differ from each other in the physiological action systems that make them possible, but this is not of major concern to us at present. We are concerned now with the difference in the psychological significance of these responses. Ordinarily we talk in order to obtain something we want and we walk or run in order to escape from something we fear. Stated simply, one class of response is made for a purpose and the other might be called a purpose itself.

The term *instrumental response* is used to refer to the "for a purpose" class of response, such as walking or talking, the phrase having been chosen because the response is instrumental in attaining some goal. A few examples may make the meaning of the term clearer. Earlier in this chapter we described how a small child may learn to manipulate the lock on a gate to get to something that is outside the yard. The opening of the gate is an instrumental response. A student wishing to become more popular with the opposite sex acquires some technique for keeping the conversation alive or some appealing facial movement. The conversational technique and the facial movement are instrumental responses. Another student desires to obtain a high grade in his psychology examination so he studies his text carefully, and this act of studying is an instrumental response. Finally, a small boy is fearful of a neighborhood

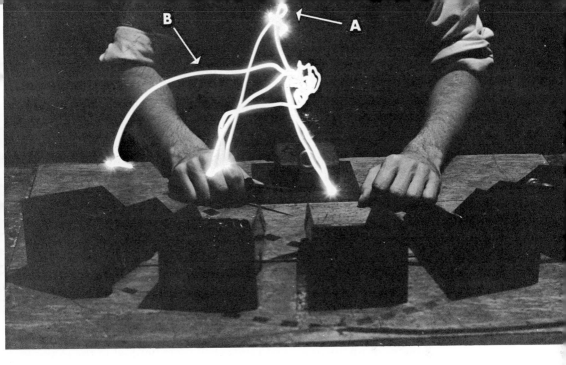

Fig. 2.3 Photographic tracings of the movements made by the same individual during his first (above) and tenth (below) attempts to assemble a faucet. The pictures were taken by attaching a light to the subject's finger, then opening the camera shutter during his attempts. The arrows point to changes in performance resulting from practice. On the tenth attempt, there are fewer movements at point *A,* and the movement traced by line *B* is smoother and more regular. The change in movement pattern was accompanied by a reduction in the time required for completion of the trial. The changes reflect the selection and fixation that are parts of the learning process. (Courtesy of the Departments of Industrial Engineering and Photography, The Ohio State University)

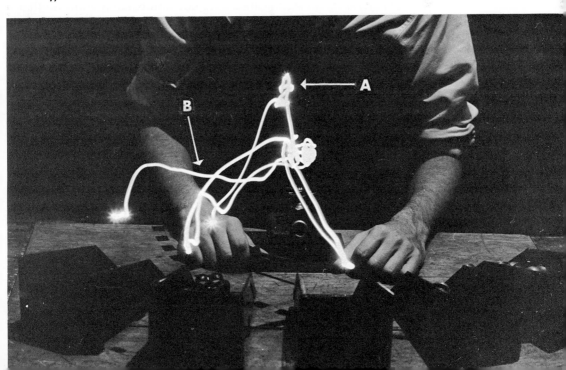

dog and whenever he sees it he runs into the house, slamming the door behind him. It is another instrumental response.

Underlying the performance of these instrumental acts is not only the ability to execute the necessary movements but the fact that they are ways of achieving a goal. They become fixated in the particular situation because they make it possible for the individual to attain the goal; if they failed to do so some different and successful instrumental response would be acquired.

Now consider, for the same examples, the goals themselves. They too are the products of learning. There is no evidence that humans instinctively fear dogs or instinctively demand a certain toy or high grades in psychology examinations—or any other examination. These goals, then, must themselves have been learned. Although the example dealing with interest in the opposite sex would seem to have an obvious biological background, the goal sought is far more likely to be a social than a sexual one, and we have no evidence of instinctive social wants of the sort implied in the example.

It must be obvious that learning of the kind implied in the paragraph above has a psychological significance different from that of the learning of an instrumental act. Since we have given a label, *instrumental learning,* to the learning of one class of response, perhaps the student will feel better if the other class of response is also labeled. For this reason the phrase *motivational learning* will be applied to the fixation of the latter class of response. The fact that these two sorts of learned responses differ from each other in their psychological significance does not immediately indicate that they differ from each other in the way they are learned. There is, in fact, considerable evidence that they have much in common. To avoid confusion it is desirable that the distinction between instrumental learning and motivational learning be remembered.

Although we have drawn a distinction between instrumental and motivational responses, it is not possible to state that a given response is always either instrumental or motivational. An example may be found in smoking cigarettes. It is possible that most beginning smokers find little satisfaction in the act of smoking itself. Indeed, the opposite may be true, and a few drags may leave the beginner dizzy and nauseated. He continues smoking, however, because his friends consider it a smart thing to do and he gains some admiration from them for this demonstration of his manliness. Obviously, the act of smoking is an instrumental response, which is not done for its own sake but because it is a way of satisfying a social motive. Later, smoking becomes an end in itself, and the individual may risk social disapproval by lighting up in a "No Smoking" area. There are undoubtedly many other examples of the shifting of a response from the class of instrumental to motivational.

In many instances a given response partakes of both the instrumental and the motivational simultaneously. The youthful automobile driver is probably learning this skill, not only because it is a way of getting him places and because it gives him prestige with his age mates, but because he enjoys the process of driving itself. Undoubtedly most students hope that their future means of livelihood will satisfy these two goals and that they will find a job which pays well and is intrinsically enjoyable.

Summary

In this section we have been describing the total process of the adjustment of a motivated organism to the barriers it encounters. This total process may be broken down into separate aspects: motivation, the kind of barrier, variability leading to discovery, fixation, and the nature of the response. The extent to which one or another of these processes is involved varies with each situation, but most learning situations include each of these aspects to a greater or less degree.[2] By using this method of analyzing the *total adjustment* process we avoid the task of describing the learning process in this kind of situation, that kind of situation, and the next one, as if they were independent from each other in their underlying psychological processes. We can understand the total adjustment process better if we are careful to determine which aspect predominates in a specific situation. One problem may be difficult to solve because of a failure in the variability process, whereas another is difficult because of factors which slow down fixation; although the end result in each case may be slowness in learning, the psychological situations in the two cases are different.

REFERENCES

[1] Thorndike, E. C. *Animal Intelligence,* Macmillan, 1911.

[2] Dashiell, J. F. Some reapproachments in contemporary psychology, *Psychol. Bull.,* 1939, *36,* 1-24.

Chapter Three

FIXATION

THE PREVIOUS CHAPTER HAS ATTEMPTED
to analyze the complex and recurrent process of psychological adjustment into a limited number of independent psychological processes. We spoke of the different characteristics of adjusting behavior: of variability of response, of motives and goals and barriers, as well as of the fixation of a way of acting. In later chapters we shall concern ourselves specifically with some of these other aspects of behavior, but in the present chapter we shall be interested in the topic of fixation, that is, in the topic of the growth of stimulus → response associations. We shall begin the chapter with the presentation of data that have contributed greatly to the psychologists' understanding of the basic mechanisms involved in the fixation of stimulus → response connections, whether instrumental or motivational in nature. We will then discuss the generalization

of learned responses from one situation to the next, and finally explore the elimination of connections that have once been learned.

But describing the mechanisms involved in the fixation of stimulus → response connections does not completely explain why learning is more rapid in one situation than in another. The achievement of mastery in any environment is the result of more than the simple operation of the principles of fixation. These principles are facilitated or hindered in their operation by other complicating psychological processes that are intrinsic to the act to be learned as well as to the general methods that the learner uses and to the capacities of the learner himself. Because we are interested in predicting the efficiency of behavior in a variety of situations, we shall devote the last section of this chapter to the various psychological processes that complicate the process of fixation. But let us begin with the simple.

The development of the conditioned response

About sixty years ago a physiologist named Ivan Pavlov was investigating the action of the glands that secrete their substances into the stomach and make possible the digestion of food. In some of the dogs that he was using as subjects, Pavlov had severed the esophagus so that food could be injected directly into the stomach without passing through the mouth. In addition, when the passageway from mouth to stomach was interrupted in this way, any food that the dog swallowed would not reach his stomach but would drop into a pan on the floor in front of him.

Now, the adequate stimulus for the secretion of the gastric juices should have been the presence of food in the stomach. But Pavlov discovered that gastric secretion occurred when food was chewed and swallowed, even though the food fell to the floor instead of entering the stomach. Impressed by this fact, he interrupted his research on gastric juices in order to investigate and to discover more about these "psychic secretions." The new research occupied Pavlov's attention for the rest of his life and led to the discovery and the elaboration of the operating characteristics of the *conditioned response.*

The procedures that Pavlov employed in this research were relatively simple. First he operated on the dogs and diverted the duct of one of the salivary glands outward so that the secreted saliva would flow through a tube and into an exterior measuring device. Once these necessary arrangements were made, he was ready to conduct his experiments.

First a stimulus, such as the ringing of a bell or the beating of a metronome, was presented. This stimulus produced a response, such as turning of the head toward the source of the sound, but it *would not produce salivation.* After this fact had been clearly demonstrated, Pavlov subjected the dogs to a series of stimulations consisting of the auditory stimulus—bell or metronome—followed a few seconds later by an offering of food. The food in the mouth would, of course, cause salivation. After a pause of a few minutes, the pair of stimuli—sound and food—would be presented once again. After a few training trials of this sort, salivary secretion began to occur as a response to the sound alone, even though no food was presented. This modification of the usual reaction to the auditory stimulus was the *conditioned response.*[1]

This important process may be understood more easily if we illustrate it by means of the diagram below and present at the same

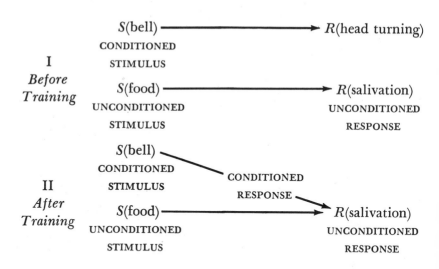

time some of the terminology used in referring to the conditioning process. The situation before the training begins is illustrated in Part I of the diagram. *S*(bell) is referred to as the *conditioned stimulus,* and the response that it produces is a head-turning or *orientation response.* *S*(food) is referred to as the *unconditioned stimulus,* and the response of salivation which it evokes is called the *unconditioned response.* The unconditioned stimulus is also often referred to as a *reinforcement.**

The situation after training—that is, after the bell and the food have been presented together several times—is shown in Part II of the diagram. The original response of the animal to the bell—the head-turning response—has disappeared, and now S(bell) produces the response of salivation. Salivation in response to the bell, or conditioned stimulus, is termed the *conditioned response.* The response of salivating to the stimulus food still remains, of course, and the terminology used in referring to it is the same as before training.

A response evoked by a stimulus before training is called an unconditioned response; the same response evoked after training and as a result of the training is called the conditioned response. The response of salivating is conditioned if it is evoked by the bell, but it is unconditioned if it is evoked by the food. We cannot, then, call a specific response either conditioned or unconditioned until we know the stimulus that is producing it.

Many researches on conditioning conducted by investigators other than Pavlov demonstrate that conditioning has wide applicability. The ability to become conditioned is not, of course, restricted to dogs; it appears in a great range of organisms, from the single-celled to man.

All sorts of stimuli have been used as the conditioned stimulus in various different experiments. More often than not, experimenters use such stimuli as tones, clicks, lights—either white or colored—and the touching of the skin; but they have also used complex patterns of lights or tones and even meaningful words. There is every reason to believe that the input from any of the senses can be used as the conditioned stimulus. All that is needed is for the experimenter to devise a way of controlling the onset and the termination of the stimulus.

Insofar as the response that is to be conditioned is concerned, the latitude is equally great. In all probability, any response can become conditioned if an unconditioned stimulus can be found

---

* Reinforcement is an important term in modern psychology and it will occur again and again in this text, but not always as a synonym for the unconditioned stimulus. A fuller discussion of the modern usage of the word will be presented later in this chapter.

that produces it with regularity and if this unconditioned stimulus is paired with the conditioned stimulus in the appropriate fashion.*

Because of convenience and because the methodology has been carefully worked out, certain kinds of responses are more frequently studied in American laboratories than others. One of these is the conditioning of the response of blinking the eye. The unconditioned stimulus is usually a brief puff of air delivered to the cornea of the eye. The conditioned stimulus is typically the flashing of a light or the onset of a tone (see Figures 3.1 and 3.2). Another fre-

Fig. 3.1 A schematic representation of an eyelid-conditioning apparatus. The conditioned stimulus is the light, located directly in front of the subject. The unconditioned stimulus is a puff of air delivered through the tube directly to the subject's left cornea. Since the blink produced by the stimulus will occur in both eyes, the response can be recorded from the right eye by means of a fine thread attached to the eyelid. The thread actuates a lever which records each response on a tape. On the same tape, the occurrence of the conditioned and unconditioned stimuli is recorded so that all the data shown in Fig. 3.2 appear synchronously. The experimenter produces both the conditioned and the unconditioned stimuli by operating a single master switch. The time interval between the two stimuli is preset and controlled automatically by a timing unit. Recently, electronic equipment has been substituted for the string and lever system for recording the eyelid response, but the essential characteristics of the experimental arrangement is the same as that illustrated below.

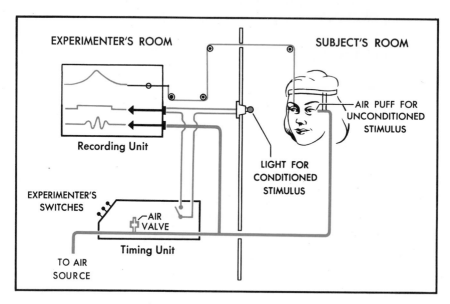

* There seems to be one exception to this statement. Efforts to condition the change in the size of the pupil resulting from shifts in general illumination have usually been unsuccessful. Why this response should behave in a fashion so different from other responses is unknown.[2]

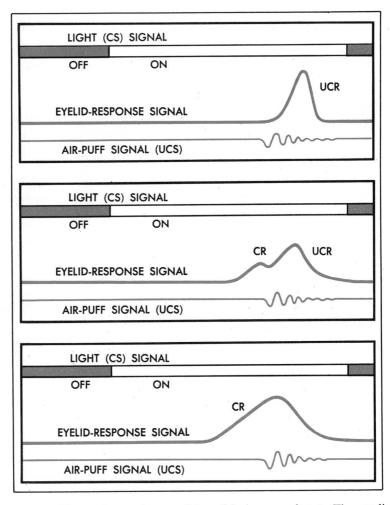

Fig. 3.2 Three phases of an eyelid-conditioning experiment. The conditioned stimulus (*CS*) is a light; the unconditioned stimulus (*UCS*), a puff of air directed to the cornea of the eye. In the first graph (first trial), only the unconditioned response (*UCR*) is obtained. In the second, the conditioned response (*CR*) has begun to develop. The third graph shows response late in training. (After Hilgard and Marquis, *Conditioning and Learning*)

quently conditioned response is a change in the resistance of the skin to the passage of a weak electrical current, a response called the Galvanic Skin Reaction, or GSR. This response arises from the fact that all material offers resistance to the passage of an electrical current; so, of course, the human body does. But since we are living organisms, our resistance is not constant but varies from moment to moment. Any stimulus that produces an emotional reaction,

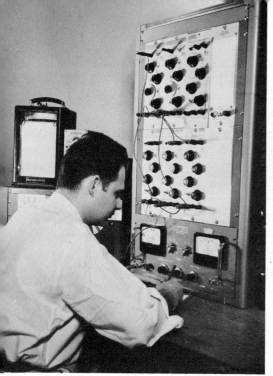

Fig. 3.3 Subject and experimenter in galvanic skin response conditioning experiment. The GSR recording electrodes are on the subject's left hand and the shock will be administered to the right hand. The conditioned stimulus can be a tone delivered through the earphones or the illumination of the small square on the panel in front of the subject. The upper part of the console before the experimenter contains equipment for controlling the time relations of the CS and UCS. The instrument for measuring the GSR is in the lower section of the console and the chart on which the response is recorded is behind the experimenter's head.

such as fear, produces also a marked reduction in skin resistance. A sudden loud noise, or even a mild shock, will elicit such a reaction, therefore these stimuli are often used for unconditioned stimuli in GSR conditioning situations. Actually, many of the principles of fixation which we shall discuss later have been most clearly illustrated in experiments on eyelid or GSR conditioning, but the same principles could have been shown by conditioning of another type of response.

We have stated without example that conditioning is a universal characteristic of the response systems of the body, and it may be well now to give two examples illustrating conditioning in widely different classes of responses:

Conditioning of the heart beat

When a brief electric shock is applied to the skin, one of the many different responses which occur is an acceleration of the heart beat. It is a response that can be recorded accurately by means of a device called the electrocardiograph, and, since it can be elicited regularly, it meets the definition of a response that can become conditioned to some neutral stimulus. In one study of heart-rate conditioning in college students,[3] the experimenters associated a tone with a shock. The tone—or conditioned stimulus—was sounded for one second, and after six seconds a two-second shock (unconditioned stimulus) was administered. During all this time the beating of the heart was recorded by means of an electrocardiograph. Conditioning would be indicated if, following the training, a tendency developed for the tone alone to produce an acceleration of the heart beat. The results of this experiment are presented in Figure 3.4. The first nine points on the curve indicate the response

Fig. 3.4 Results of an experiment on conditioning a change of heart rate. The measure used is the rate after onset of the CS subtracted from the rate just before CS onset. Before conditioning the tone produced a retardation in rate but the CS acquired a tendency to produce an acceleration of heart rate as a result of being paired with the shock. (After Zeaman and Wegner[3])

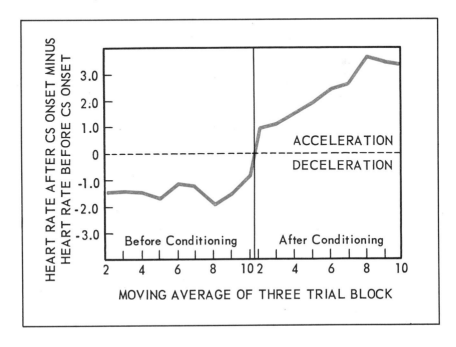

of the heart beat to the tone alone on the nine test trials given before the tone and shock were paired together. The later points on the curve indicate the response of the heart rate to the tone alone during the conditioning training—that is, during the time interval between the tone and the shock. After only two trials, there is clear-cut evidence of conditioning, and in general the amount of acceleration of the heart beat—that is, of conditioning—increases as the number of paired stimulations increases.

Conditioning of word meanings

Another kind of response which we make is one that gives meanings to words. This response is not usually observable, even through the mediation of the finest electronic recording equipment. Nevertheless, the modern psychologist would say that we are responding when we react to a word by thinking and thereby give it meaning and significance. If one is presented with a group of words such as "beauty, win, gift, honest, smart, rich," it is possible to identify not only meanings that are specific to each unit, but a general meaning that is common to all of them, for all of the words refer to a state of affairs that is *pleasant* and *desirable*. One might, therefore, use these words to produce an unconditioned response— call it pleasantness of meaning—and attach this meaning reaction to some neutral word. That is, one could do so if it were possible to condition word-meaning responses.

The experimenters[4] chose two groups of words, one for which the meanings were pleasant for most people, and the other for which the meanings were unpleasant or undesirable. The words of the first group were listed in the previous paragraph; typical words from the undesirable meaning group were: "thief, bitter, ugly, sad, failure." These lists of words were to serve as the unconditioned stimulus in the experiment: the conditioned stimuli consisted of two nonsense words of neutral meaning: YOF and XEH.

During the conditioning training, a nonsense word was flashed on a screen before a group of subjects seated in their college classroom, and then the experimenter called out a meaningful word. The subjects were directed to call out the words that the experimenter announced. Whenever YOF was shown, a pleasant word followed; and whenever XEH was shown, an unpleasant word followed. Mixed in with these critical nonsense and meaningful words were other nonsense and meaningful words. These were introduced simply to prevent the subjects from becoming aware of the purpose of the experiment, which was to condition particular meanings to the two syllables YOF and XEH. Another group of subjects was treated in just the reverse manner, that is, YOF was associated with an unpleasant word and XEH with a pleasant one.

After a number of presentations of the various nonsense words with their appropriate meaningful words or "unconditioned stimuli," a very simple test for the efficacy of the conditioning was conducted. The different nonsense words employed were presented and the subjects were asked to rate them for their degree of pleasantness or unpleasantness on a seven-point scale, with a score of 1 indicating the extreme of pleasantness and 7 the extreme of unpleasantness. A score of 4—the number midway between 1 and 7— would be assigned if the attitude toward the syllable were completely neutral. The subjects could give a word any score from 1 through 7. Conditioning would be demonstrated if the nonsense word that had been consistently associated with pleasant words was considered pleasant, and if the reverse was true for the word associated with the unpleasant words. The results, which consisted simply of the averages of the rating values for the critical words, are given in Table 3.1. The tendency is clear. A nonsense word

TABLE 3.1.

When YOF Was Associated with Words that Were	YOF	XEH	When XEH Was Associated with Words that Were
Pleasant	2.40	4.80	Unpleasant
Unpleasant	4.73	3.17	Pleasant

associated with pleasant words acquired a pleasant meaning (a rating below 4); and a nonsense word associated with unpleasant words acquired mildly unpleasant meanings, that is, ratings slightly above 4. The trend is demonstrated regardless of the word employed.

One other important point should be mentioned. After the experiment had been completed the subjects were asked if they were aware of the relationship between certain meaningful words and the nonsense words, and only a few of them reported that they were. The data for these subjects are not included in the results and therefore the findings presented in the table cannot be attributed to a conscious intent on the part of the subjects to do what they thought the experimenters expected them to do.

These two experiments which we have described in some detail were chosen because they represent two extremes of the different types of learned behavior. One seems to be "mental" in nature and the other "physiological" or "biological." Nevertheless they are both forms of behavior. They both became conditioned by the same general method. And in neither case can the conditioning be accounted for by what might be called some voluntary willing on the part of the subjects, for we cannot readily will our hearts to beat faster, and the subjects in the second experiment were not aware that their ratings had been influenced by the prior conditioning.

Within reasonable limits, these two experiments span the great range of responses that have been conditioned in psychological laboratories, and, for lack of space, we shall not attempt to identify other action systems that have been successfully conditioned. In concluding, it is well to emphasize a statement made earlier: in all probability any response can become conditioned if an unconditioned stimulus can be found that produces it with regularity and if this unconditioned stimulus is paired with the conditioned stimulus.

The relationship of conditioning to learning in general

In relating the data of conditioning to learning in general, the reader should recall that in the previous chapter the total process of adjustment was broken down into a number of different aspects. One of these aspects was *fixation*, the process of attaching a new response to some stimulus. The establishment of the conditioned response is almost solely a problem of fixation. In most conditioning situations the subject does not need to *discover* what response to make; the appropriate response, together with the *motivational source* necessary for eliciting the response, are guaranteed by the mere occurrence of the unconditioned stimulus. The study of behavior in the conditioning situation, then, affords us an opportunity to observe the process and the results of fixation unconfounded by some of the other variables that occur in more complicated situations.

In much of the rest of this chapter we shall be dealing with the general learning process largely in terms of the conditioned response. Consequently, the reader may get the impression that all learning *is* conditioning—or that the only way of learning is through conditioning. This is not true. Actually, conditioning is a laboratory situation in which the general laws of learning operate. The conditioning situation has been used very widely in the study of learning because it is a simple one: the variables are easily isolated and easily controlled. It is important, then, that we recognize that the conditioned response provides us with a *means* of studying learning, but it does not represent learning in totality.

Time relations in conditioning

The ease with which the conditioned response is established depends largely upon the time relation between the conditioned and the unconditioned stimulus. Satisfactory conditioning occurs only if the conditioned stimulus (bell, in Pavlov's experiment) *precedes* the unconditioned stimulus (food). Moreover, the amount of time by which the conditioned stimulus precedes the unconditioned stimulus is extremely important. This fact has been experimentally demonstrated with a variety of both conditioned and unconditioned stimuli. Typical results are presented in Figure 3.5.

Fig. 3.5 A generalized curve showing the relationship between efficiency of conditioning and the amount of time by which the onset of the conditioned and unconditioned stimuli differ.

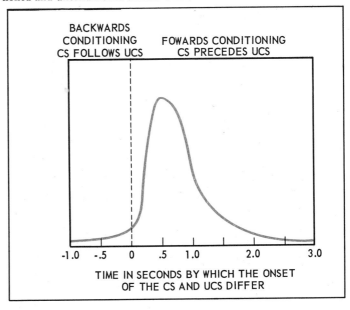

BACKWARDS CONDITIONING CS FOLLOWS UCS

FOWARDS CONDITIONING CS PRECEDES UCS

-1.0   -.5   0   .5   1.0   2.0   3.0

TIME IN SECONDS BY WHICH THE ONSET OF THE CS AND UCS DIFFER

Clearly, the conditioning procedure is more effective at some intervals than at others and, for human subjects, the optimal interval seems to be a little less than one half second.[5] Just why this is so we do not know at the present time, but we do know that it does not depend on the nature of the response being conditioned, for essentially the same results have been obtained for responses as different from each other as the eyelid response and the galvanic skin reaction.

Stimulus generalization

In a typical conditioning experiment, the conditioned stimulus is a particular light or a particular tone, which is repeatedly presented in conjunction with the unconditioned stimulus. However, if, after conditioning has been established, the subject is presented with a light of a different color or a tone of a different pitch, he is likely to give the conditioned response to this new, but similar, stimulus. This is referred to as *stimulus generalization*. In short, the subject has become conditioned not just to a particular stimulus but rather to a class of stimuli. Typically the strength of the response to the new stimulus is determined by the latter's degree of similarity to the original conditioning stimulus; the more similar it is, the greater is the response.

We are not certain at the present time of the exact relationship between the amount of response that will be given to the new stimulus and the latter's degree of similarity to the original conditioned stimulus. Three curves illustrating possible relationships are shown in Figure 3.6. The two red curves are similar in that both of them demonstrate that there is a progressive decline in response strength as the new stimulus becomes more and more dissimilar to the one on which the subjects are trained. They differ in that one curve indicates that the response strength drops off markedly if the new stimulus is even slightly different from the training stimulus, while the dotted curve indicates that minor changes in the stimulus will not result in any considerable decline in the strength of the generalized conditioned response. Neither of these curves is fictitious, for there are experimental data to support both forms.[6, 7] The black curve represents a different interpretation of the same sort of data. It assumes that the subject has a limited number of categories of stimuli that he is capable of making. All stimuli in one category are responded to in the same way.

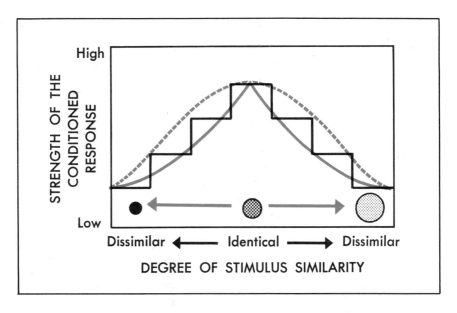

Fig. 3.6 Three possible curves of stimulus generalization. The conditioned stimulus is symbolized by the middle disk. Responses will be made to similar stimuli as well but will decrease in magnitude as these stimuli become more and more unlike the training stimulus. Two of the curves are continuous in nature and they imply that there is a continuous decrease in response with increasing dissimilarity of the test stimulus to the training stimulus. The third curve is discontinuous.

If the new stimulus is classified as being in the same category as the conditioning stimulus, it is reacted to with the same magnitude; declines in response strength will occur only if, for the subject, the new stimulus falls into a category different from that represented by the stimulus to which he was trained.[8]

That stimulus generalization occurs is evident in many ways in our daily life. The reds or greens of traffic lights may vary in their precise hues, but they all mean the same thing to us; a fear of a certain small room may spread to small places in general; and our reactions to our parents are carried over to others in positions of authority.

Stimulus generalization is not restricted in its operation to stimuli such as lights and tones, but operates with language as well. Such stimulus generalization was clearly shown in the following experiment:[9]

A word, the eventual conditioned stimulus, was projected on a screen before the subject and was followed by a loud and unpleasant sound, the unconditioned stimulus. This noise elicited the unconditioned response, the galvanic skin reaction (GSR). As a consequence of the pairing of the word with the unconditioned stimulus, the subjects eventually acquired the tendency to make the galvanic skin response to the word alone, that is, a conditioned response to the verbal stimulus was established. The test for stimulus generalization was conducted by presenting the subject with other words which held certain specified relationships to the word employed as the conditioned stimulus. These generalization test words were homophones (that is, words of the same sound but of different meaning), synonyms, and antonyms. Some examples are given at the top of Table 3.2.

TABLE 3.2. STIMULUS GENERALIZATION TO WORDS

Age of Group	Conditioned Stimulus won whole sea	Homophone one hole see	Antonym lost part land	Synonym beat all ocean
8 yr.	100	72	63	58
11 yr.	100	29	43	26
14 yr.	100	25	32	45
18 yr.	100	19	37	52

One further complication of the experiment was the fact that four groups at different age levels were employed. The average ages for the various groups are identified in the first column of the table. In this table the magnitude of the response to the conditioned stimulus is considered as the point of reference or 100 per cent, and responses to the generalized stimuli are given as percentages of this standard. The table shows that stimulus generalization did occur but that both the magnitude and character of the generalization gradient differed for the various age levels. In the first place the over-all response, regardless of type of word relationship being tested, was greatest for the youngest group. But what is perhaps even more interesting is that this group showed the greatest generalized response to the homophone and the least to the synonym, while this relationship is reversed for the two older groups.

It will be noted that the basis for the judgment of similarity is quite different for the homophones "won" and "one" from what it is for the synonyms "won" and "beat." In one instance the stimuli have a physical similarity to each other—they sound alike. In the other instance the similarity is conceptual. These facts suggest that there may be two quite different kinds of stimulus generalization. One of these may be based upon *physical* similarity of the stimuli, the *psychological* similarity arising because the same sense organs are activated in a similar manner by the different stimuli. This is often referred to as *primary stimulus generalization*. Presumably the Hottentot, the Parisian, the New Englander, and the Eskimo would react in the same fashion when tested for this type of stimulus generalization.

The other type of stimulus generalization is certainly mediated through special processes of learning, and it is referred to as *secondary,* or *mediated, generalization.* Cultural groups would differ quite widely in this kind of generalization, even though the basic learning principles which cause a group of items to be perceived as similar are the same from culture to culture. Obviously, also, individuals from the same culture could, because of their unique backgrounds, show different dimensions of similarity and generalization. To predict both the direction and the amount of secondary generalization, one must know something about the nature of the past learning of the individual.

Response generalization

A counterpart to stimulus generalization is the phenomenon of *response generalization.* Of stimulus generalization we may say that the organism learns to make a certain response to a general class of stimuli, even though he was trained to only one specific stimulus of this class. On the response side, the same is true. A dog that had been trained to lift a certain foot upon the occurrence of the conditioned stimulus lifted another foot when the one normally raised was tied down;[10] college students conditioned to extend their fingers when the hand rested palm down flexed their fingers in just the opposite movement when the hand was turned palm up and the conditioned stimulus sounded.[11] In the area of language usage, response generalization is common. In learning a prose passage, we may substitute synonyms for the exact wording. (A friend of the authors frequently called a Mr. Stubblefield by the name of Mr. Snodgrass, to his own embarrassment.)

Thus it appears that we learn to respond to the stimulus not with a particular response but with a class of responses. If, when the stimulus is presented, the response which was elicited during the training is for any reason blocked, a different response is likely to be elicited, but it will bear some similarity to the originally trained response.

Response generalization, like stimulus generalization, is both an aid and a hindrance to the adjusting individual. If a student is required to learn a prose passage word for word, the substitution of the synonym means that his recitation is wrong. (And it is not likely that the authors' friend endeared himself to Mr. Stubblefield by calling him Snodgrass.) On the other hand, there are many situations in which the similar response is acceptable and serves the same function as the original response. Thus, unless the environment demands a specific response, the occurrence of response generalization is of real adjustment value to the organism.

Extinction and spontaneous recovery

If, after a subject has become conditioned, the conditioned stimulus is presented repeatedly without being reinforced by the unconditioned stimulus, the conditioned response will eventually cease to be given. In the terminology of conditioning, we say that the response has been *extinguished,* and that extinction has resulted from non-reinforcement. If, after a period of extinction, the experimenter suspends further presentations for some time and then presents the conditioned stimulus again, the response is very likely to reoccur. No additional training with the unconditioned stimulus—that is, no reinforcement—is necessary to produce this return of the conditioned response. It occurs quite spontaneously, and for this reason the phenomenon has been termed *spontaneous recovery.*

The reader may have had experiences of his own that demonstrate the principles of extinction and spontaneous recovery. He may have acquired an unreasonable fear of some particular object. As he came into contact with the object (which served as the conditioned stimulus for the fear) and no untoward occurrence resulted to reinforce the fear, the emotional response gradually diminished and eventually disappeared. If then his contacts with the object were terminated for some time, he might have found that when he once again was confronted with the conditioned stimulus the old fear returned. The extinguished response had recovered spontaneously.

The fact that experimental extinction occurs has led some persons to doubt that conditioning is a useful principle for understanding behavior in everyday life. They point out that, whereas some of our laboratory experiments seem to predict that without reinforcement extinction will occur, in daily life habits persist for prolonged periods without reinforcement. Several items of evidence can be offered, however, against the view that conditioned responses in daily life are prone to be lost through extinction.

It has been shown that conditioned responses will not be extinguished if an occasional reinforcement is given among many non-reinforced trials.[12] Furthermore, extinction seems to require that the non-reinforced trials be given within a relatively short span of time. Thus in one experiment no evidence of extinction was found when one trial a day was given for 75 days, but extinction occurred within 60 trials that were presented five minutes apart.[13] In our day-to-day life situations, we probably do not often encounter massed extinction trials. This must be particularly true of conditioned fear reactions, for the very nature of the reaction is such that we avoid coming in contact with the fear-producing situation—the very situation that makes extinction possible.

Further evidence is offered by an experiment in which dogs were conditioned to lift a leg when a tone sounded, the unconditioned stimulus being a shock to the foot. Later the shock was omitted and the dogs were given a pellet of food if they reacted by lifting the foot to the tone. The response to the tone was not extinguished in these circumstances, even though many presentations of the tone without shock were made.[14] In everyday life, there are probably many instances in which conditioned responses learned to one unconditioned stimulus are supported by another.

All in all, these, as well as some other considerations and items of evidence, seem to indicate that conditioned responses, once they are established, would show considerable resistance to extinction in our day-to-day environment.

Counterconditioning

Extinction is accomplished by the mere omission of the unconditioned stimulus. A more active means of eliminating the conditioned response is through the procedure known as counterconditioning. It can best defined by describing one experiment in which this procedure was employed.[15] The subjects were dogs who were trained to make a flexion response of the leg to the sounding of a tone, the unconditioned stimulus being an electric shock applied to the forepaw, which could be avoided by making the conditioned response. After conditioning had been established, the shock electrodes were removed from the paw and placed upon the animal's chest. Following this, the conditioned stimulus was sounded and the animals *received a shock on the chest if they responded, but no shock if they failed to respond.* The number of trials required to eliminate the response under this counterconditioning procedure was compared with the number of trials required under the ordinary extinction regime. Counterconditioning proved to be considerably more efficient, requiring approximately a fifth of the number of trials that were necessary in the simple extinction procedure.

Though this result is scarcely surprising, another experiment in counterconditioning adds some information about the effects of this procedure which are not so intuitively apparent.[16] Again the subjects were dogs; the conditioned stimulus was the sounding of a buzzer, the unconditioned stimulus a shock, and the response foreleg flexion. After the animals had been conditioned to respond by lifting the *right* leg, the electrode was moved to the *left* leg and the shock was applied there following the conditioned stimulus. Since the animals could not readily lift both legs simultaneously, this counterconditioning procedure resulted in their substituting the left leg response for the right leg response. So far we have no more than an example of counterconditioning. The contribution of this experiment lies in the fact that the animals were given no further training for periods of time ranging from one to six months. They were then again placed in the apparatus and the conditioned stimulus was sounded. The question was, with which leg, if any, would the response be made? The question becomes especially significant when one recalls that extinction is usually followed by spontaneous recovery, and the use of this concept alone would lead one to predict that the dogs should return to responding with the right leg. Actually they did not do so. A response was given, even after all this lapse of time, to the conditioned stimulus, but for all but one animal the response was made consistently with the left leg. The exceptional animal gave a few responses of the right leg, but even for him the majority of the responses were made with the left leg. This experiment suggests, then, that counterconditioning *minimizes* the tendency for a previously eliminated response to reoccur, although it does not destroy it completely.

In summary, counterconditioning is another method of eliminating a previously established conditioned response. It is a procedure that involves either (1) punishing the response when it occurs, or (2) rewarding another response that is antagonistic to the original response. It seems likely that the technique of counterconditioning is one which we are more inclined to use in everyday control of behavior than the technique of simple omission of the reinforcement. Certainly it has much to recommend it, for it accomplishes the end more rapidly and its effects are longer lasting.*

Habit as a determinant of response

In Chapter I, we pointed out that a stimulus situation evokes a psychological mechanism and that this mechanism in turn elicits a response—that is, behavior. One kind of psychological mechanism is what we refer to as *habit*. A habit develops when a certain response to a certain stimulus has been reinforced with some consistency, as in the conditioning situation. A psychologist who knows the reinforcement history of an organism can infer the habits of that organism and can therefore predict its behavior in specific situations. A habit, then, is not the same thing as a response. It is, rather, an abstract concept that is of use to us in explaining why a response occurs. In this respect it is like the atom. No one has ever seen or measured an atom—just as no one has ever seen or measured a habit—but the atom is a concept that helps us explain many phenomena, from the action of baking powder to the explosion of a bomb. The atom is not the explosion but does account for it; the habit is not the response but is its determinant. It is, therefore, a purely psychological construct. The strength of a habit is determined by certain environmental events in the organism's past; the consequence of the habit is behavior in a particular situation.

Habit strength in the conditioning situation

We shall have something to say later in this chapter about certain kinds of environmental conditions that produce stronger

---

* Perhaps we should point out, however, that the use of punishment may entail other difficulties, even though it may be a quick way of eliminating a response. The topic of punishment will be discussed more fully in Chapter 5.

or weaker habits. Before we can do so, however, we must describe the specific elements we will record in measuring the strength of conditioned responses or, more broadly, of habits in general.

Magnitude

Perhaps the most obvious reflection of the strength of a conditioned response is its vigor or magnitude. Pavlov measured this aspect of the conditioned response when he counted drops of saliva secreted in response to the conditioned stimulus alone. The distance to which an athlete can put the shot is a measure of magnitude in a different kind of learning situation.

Latency

The time elapsing between the occurrence of the stimulus and the occurrence of the response is referred to as the *latent period*. Ordinarily, the latent period becomes shorter as the conditioned response becomes more firmly established. So, too, we can answer a question more promptly when we know our material well.

Probability of responding

When conditioning is begun, the conditioned response does not, of course, occur to the conditioned stimulus. After a few trials, a conditioned response may occur, but it may fail to occur on the next trial or the next several trials. As training continues, the response occurs with increasing regularity, until finally it is given every time, or almost every time, the conditioned stimulus is presented. The probability of occurrence of the response when the appropriate stimulus is presented is another measure of the strength of the response.

Resistance to extinction

If, after a conditioned response has been established, the unconditioned stimulus is repeatedly omitted, the conditioned response becomes extinguished. Ordinarily the response does not drop out after a single non-reinforced trial; instead, it will persist over a varying span of non-reinforced trials. The number of non-reinforced responses given before extinction is complete indicates the *resistance to extinction*. This, too, is a measure of the strength of the conditioning, and habits in general.

Interrelationship of measures of habit

Although each of the foregoing elements is a measure of the strength of a conditioned response—or, in more general terms, of a habit—they are not always related in the same way to one another. Actually the nature of the response may be such as to require certain special relationships among these measures of strength. Thus, the actor does not speak his lines more and more loudly as he learns his part better. However, his probability of reacting properly each time his cues are presented increases, and he responds with less hesitancy (latency)—unless his part calls for this hesitancy. Yet even when the task itself places no special requirements upon magnitude or latency, we do not find a perfect relationship among all measures of habit strength. This fact means that we cannot use the measures interchangeably but must specify the measure that we are using when we discuss the strength of a particular habit.

Partial reinforcement

It is probable that in everyday life most habits are developed under conditions that do not provide reinforcement with every trial. The child may be punished or rewarded today for an act that tomorrow goes unnoticed. The term *partial reinforcement* is used to refer to conditions of less than 100-percent reinforcement, and the question is how partially reinforced habits differ from responses trained at a level of 100-percent reinforcement.

The typical results of such training are illustrated in Figure 3.7, which demonstrates the learning and extinction of a conditioned eyelid response for two groups of subjects. For one group, 96 paired stimulations by light (the conditioned stimulus) and by puff of air (the unconditioned stimulus) were presented, and then the light alone was presented. For the other group the light was presented 96 times but was followed by reinforcement in only 48 of these trials. The two groups did not differ much from each other during the period of training, as measured by probability of responding, but they differed markedly from each other in their resistance to extinction. The group that was given reinforcement 50 percent of the time showed greater resistance to extinction.[17]

A very large number of studies have dealt with the general problem of partial reinforcement. Different kinds of stimuli and

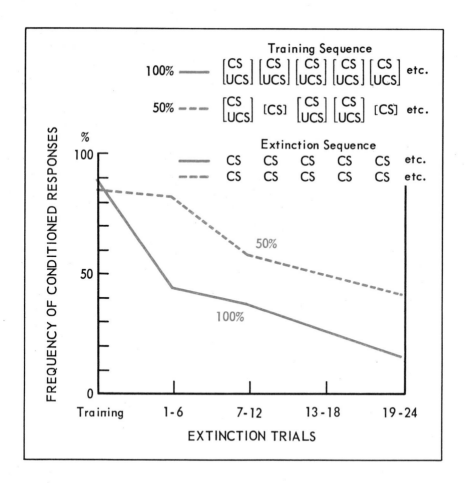

Fig. 3.7 Extinction curves for two groups of subjects. The 100-percent group received both the conditioned and the unconditioned stimuli during every trial. The 50-percent group received the two stimuli together during half the training period and the conditioned stimulus alone during the other half. During the extinction period only the conditioned stimulus was presented for a total of 24 stimulations. The first point on the graph is the average of the last 24 training trials. (After Humphreys[17])

different kinds of responses have been used, and varied ratios of reinforced to non-reinforced trials have been employed, but the studies generally have agreed. The training situation of partial reinforcement leads to the development of conditioned responses that are more resistant to extinction than those developed under 100-percent reinforcement.

There would therefore seem to be some contradiction between an earlier statement that responses will become extinguished if they are not reinforced and the fact that a conditioned response will develop to a high strength under the inconsistent regime characterized by the partial-reinforcement situation. It is obvious that if the proportion of non-reinforced trials to reinforced trials were extremely high, then the conditioned response would not develop. Unfortunately there are no experimental studies available which permit a definitive statement of the proportion of reinforced to non-reinforced trials below which conditioning fails to occur.

The fact of partial reinforcement is of extreme significance, for it indicates a way of developing S-R connections that will be highly resistant to extinction. It is probably accurate to say that the pattern of reinforcement that befalls us in our daily living is more likely to be that of partial than 100 percent reinforcement. The parent attempting to instill some desirable way of reacting in his child reinforces the response, be it with pennies or praises, when it occurs. But it is unlikely that he will reward the response every time. He may be absent when it occurs, preoccupied with the evening paper or the monthly bills, entertaining a guest, or even have wisely decided that "the child has got to learn to do it on his own." Whatever the reason, occasions occur when the response is made and reinforcement does not follow. Thus, the pattern of training is one of partial rather than 100 percent reinforcement. This inconsistency probably characterizes most of our everyday learning situations and is one of the reasons why many of our responses are resistant to extinction.

Differentiation

Because of the operation of stimulus generalization, either primary or secondary, responses learned to a specific stimulus carry over to similar stimuli. From the point of view of efficiency of behavior, this fact may be either good or bad. If the responses learned in one situation are appropriate in a similar situation, generalization makes it possible for the organism to behave appropriately in this similar situation on its first occurrence. Often, however, sharp limits are placed upon the acceptability of transfer. The infant learning his first words is inclined to refer to all men as "Da-da"—a case of generalization. At this early stage of language development, such behavior in the infant is a source of amusement to the fond parents and to other sympathetic adults. But none of this group would be amused if at the age of ten the child continued

65

to react to his parent and to other adults in this fashion either by word or deed. It is not now appropriate to apply to strangers the words of address applied to a parent or to show them the same degree of dependency, intimacy, and affection, and it becomes increasingly inappropriate as the child grows into adulthood. Society demands that we differentiate among different classes of these stimuli, men. Complete generalization from one to another is not permitted.

The process by which differentiation is established in a conditioned response is illustrated by the following extract from the writings of Pavlov:

It was noticed that when, after a conditioned reflex to a definite stimulus (*e.g.*, a definite musical tone) had been firmly established, the effect of another closely allied stimulus (a neighbouring musical tone) was tried for the first time, the conditioned reflex which resulted from the new stimulus was frequently much weaker than that obtained with the original conditioned stimulus. On repetition of the stimulus of the neighbouring tone, always, of course, without reinforcement, the secretory effect . . . began to diminish, falling finally to a permanent zero.[1]

One is tempted to explain the behavior of people in conditioning experiments by reference to the state of their consciousness; we may think that when Pavlov's dog *understands* that one tone will be followed by food and the other will not, he behaves appropriately, salivating to one and not to the other. The following experiment indicates, however, that such an explanation is by no means adequate.[18]

On the first day of the experiment, groups of subjects were conditioned to blink when a light in front of them was turned on. The conditioned response was developed by following the onset of the light (the conditioned stimulus) approximately one half second later with a puff of air to the cornea (the unconditioned stimulus). On the following day, the procedure was changed; a new light was employed, but when it was presented it was never followed by the puff of air. The original conditioned stimulus (that is, the first light) continued to be reinforced with the unconditioned stimulus (the puff of air). The reinforced and nonreinforced lights were presented in a random sequence. The subjects in the several groups were given different directions before the day's procedure was begun. The directions for each group and the

results, stated in terms of frequency of response, are presented in
Table 3.3.

TABLE 3.3.

| Instructions to the Group | Percent Frequency of Response to the | |
	First light (positive— always reinforced)	Second light (negative— never reinforced)
Informed of the positive and negative stimuli	74	26
Informed and told to wink to the positive but not to the negative	90	13
Informed and told to wink to the negative but not the positive	71	94
Informed and told to refrain from winking to either stimulus	55	19

It is apparent from the results of this experiment that the behavior cannot be accounted for entirely by the subjects' understanding of the relationships among the stimuli. Certainly knowledge of relationships plus directions to act in certain ways do influence the behavior. On the other hand, the fact that one stimulus is reinforced and the other is not makes a marked difference.

Compulsiveness of the conditioned stimulus

It is very likely that as the student read about the conditioned response and how it was developed, he was inclined to interpret the behavior in some fashion like the following: The subject knows that the unconditioned stimulus (food, shock, etc.) is going to follow the conditioned stimulus (tone, light, etc.), and he reacts to the conditioned stimulus with the response which he considers appropriate for the unconditioned stimulus. This explanation might be diagramed like this: (1) conditioned stimulus → (2) knowledge that the UCS will follow → (3) tendency to respond to the UCS in a certain way → (4) the making of the conditioned response.

Such an explanation would imply that any break in this chain of psychological events would prevent the conditioned response from occurring. If the subject knew that the unconditioned stimulus would *not* follow the conditioned stimulus he should not respond, or if the tendency to give a certain kind of response to the unconditioned stimulus had been destroyed then that response would not be given to the conditioned stimulus either.

There are, however, several bits of experimental evidence which show this interpretation to be false. The experiment whose results were presented on page 67 shows that being told that the unconditioned stimulus will not occur does not abolish the response, nor does knowledge plus the request not to respond. True, these conditions depress the tendency to respond, but they do not eliminate it. It is probable that complete elimination of a well-established response can be achieved only by the more direct type of experience provided by experimental extinction or counterconditioning.

Another experiment[19] shows rather dramatically that a change in the way of responding to the unconditioned stimulus need not destroy the conditioned response. The subjects of the experiment were monkeys, and the response conditioned was the fear reaction given to the unconditioned stimulus. This unconditioned stimulus was produced by a snake "blowout" of the sort that is often used as a noise-maker at parties. When one blows vigorously into such a toy it rapidly uncurls and extends into a straight tube. The experimenter had discovered that if he stood before the monkeys and blew the toy at the animals' faces, they showed violent fear reactions. The conditioned stimulus was the sounding of a buzzer, a stimulus which did not produce a fear reaction prior to the experiment. First the buzzer was sounded and then the snake blowout was inflated. After a few trials the violent fear reaction was elicited by the buzzer alone; that is, conditioning had been established.

The next portion of the experiment was directed toward eliminating the fear reaction to the unconditioned stimulus. This was done by inflating the toy gradually and by placing a bit of food at the end of the toy. In time this combined extinction and counterconditioning procedure eliminated the fear reaction to the snake blowout, even when it was inflated rapidly. The question was: would the conditioned response to the buzzer be destroyed now that the original unconditioned stimulus no longer produced the fear reaction? The answer was in the negative; the conditioned fear reaction given to the buzzer alone seemed to be undiminished. Additional evidence for the stability of the conditioned response was provided when the experimenter retrained the animals to fear the snake blowout by presenting it first and following it with the buzzer; in other words, by using the buzzer as an unconditioned stimulus.

These experiments, and others as well, indicate that the conditioned response habit acquires a strength and integrity of its own. Once learned, the response shows at least some independence of the events which were necessary for its establishment. Furthermore, the occurrence of the conditioned stimulus seems to have a certain capacity to force a response, even though a rational evaluation of the situation might indicate that such a response is neither sensible nor necessary.* We do not mean to imply that the previously established conditioned response habit is not influenced by subsequent psychological events of various sorts, but only that it is not readily or completely blocked by these later events.

Since we have been so critical of one hypothetical explanation of the conditioning process, the student may well ask how it can be explained. Actually, no completely satisfactory and generally acceptable explanation of conditioning is available, and we shall not attempt one. However, for purposes of predicting behavior, this is not important. We do know that if a conditioned and an unconditioned stimulus have been presented together in a certain time relationship, then one can make certain predictions about the response which is likely to occur when the conditioned stimulus alone is presented. Furthermore, a knowledge of various phenomena of conditioning, such as extinction and generalization permits other reasonably valid predictions to be made. Our objective—an ability to predict behavior—is, therefore, brought nearer

---

* This disparity between what seems rational and what the person seems forced to do in a particular situation is especially noticeable in some individuals who are suffering from *psychoses* or *neuroses*. However, there is nothing abnormal about this disparity itself; it is a characteristic of behavior, and all of us may react this way in one situation or another.

by our knowledge of conditioning, even though there is much more to be learned about the basis for this type of behavior.

The biological value of conditioning

The psychological mechanisms of the conditioning situation are obviously valuable, since an organism must adjust to its environment in order to survive. One can regard the process of conditioning as one in which the organism learns that a specific stimulus (the conditioned stimulus) is a sign for a coming event (the unconditioned stimulus). The organism thus is prepared to deal appropriately with this later event. If, however, the second event fails to occur with any fair degree of consistency, extinction occurs, and the organism has sloughed off a response that is of no use to it.

Stimulus generalization also is of considerable biological utility. The fact that we can interpret two similar but not identical stimuli as having the same meaning implies that learning carried on in conjunction with one stimulus will be carried over to the other. If such were not the case, almost every situation would be completely new to us and would require that we learn what to do all over again.

We have devoted considerable attention to experimental conditioning not because the conditioned response represents a special sort of learning but because it occurs in a relative simple environmental situation in which fairly exact control over the relevant stimuli can be maintained by the experimenter. This environmental simplicity makes it possible for the experimenter to observe and identify some of the basic principles of learning that are often obscured but nevertheless do operate in more complex situations. It will be well to review some of the principles we have identified.

Reinforcement

A previously neutral stimulus will acquire the tendency to elicit a specific response if that stimulus is associated in time with another stimulus which consistently elicits that response. The habit will develop even though reinforcement does not occur on every trial (partial reinforcement).

Time relations

A certain temporal relationship between the onset of the conditioned stimulus and the onset of the unconditioned stimulus seems to be necessary for establishing the conditioned response. Data from several studies indicate that the optimal separation is approximately one half second.

Extinction and spontaneous recovery

Stimulus → response connections learned under conditions of reinforcement will be lost—that is, extinguished—if the stimulus is presented repeatedly and within a relatively short period without reinforcement. Conditioned responses learned under conditions of partial reinforcement will show greater resistance to extinction than responses learned under 100-percent reinforcement. Responses that are extinguished are likely to recover some of their strength without additional training after the passage of time.

Generalization

The organism seems to learn to make a class of responses to a class of stimuli, rather than merely a specific response to a specific stimulus. These tendencies, referred to as *stimulus generalization* and *response generalization,* are not evident during the training period itself but become evident in later situations when different stimuli are used or when the original response is blocked.

Differentiation

The spread of stimulus generalization may be restrained by the process of differential training. It is a process in which reinforcement is not given in association with the generalized stimulus but is given in association with the original conditioned stimulus.

We shall refer to these five important principles repeatedly in our efforts to understand behavior in a wide variety of situations, and it would be well for the student to know them thoroughly.

INSTRUMENTAL RESPONSE LEARNING
IN COMPLEX ENVIRONMENTS

In our description of various conditioning situations we have not been greatly concerned with the question of whether we are dealing with the learning of instrumental or motivational responses. Indeed, it is very likely that in the majority of conditioning situations both these kinds of responses are being acquired by the organism. Thus, in a situation in which the unconditioned stimulus is a shock, the subject probably learns not only to make a particular response to the conditioned stimulus, such as flexing the finger or leg, but also to fear that stimulus. If the experimenter happened to be recording only finger movements, he would be inclined to think of the situation as an example of instrumental learning, but if he were recording other kinds of responses he might believe that he is studying motivational learning. But regardless of what the experimenter records, the subject will learn both kinds of responses. This fact should lead one to suspect that many of the principles which have been identified in conditioning experiments also will be identified in the learning of more complex instrumental responses. In the remainder of this section we shall illustrate some typical instrumental learning situations and then indicate how some of the principles exposed in the conditioning studies aid in understanding the acquisition of some complex instrumental skills.

Experimental apparatus

The pieces of apparatus described below are some of the many that have been employed in experiments on instrumental learning. Researches with such devices have given us great insight into the problem of how we learn.

The Skinner Box

The Skinner box (Figure 3.8), named after its inventor, is a kind of food vendor for rats. It is simply a small cubicle with a lever and food tray at one end. By pressing the lever, the animal closes an electrical circuit, which causes a pellet of food to fall into the near-by tray. It is this response—the pressing of the bar—which is measured. The acquisition of this activity is often referred to as conditioning, but one should note that the behavioral demands for this type of conditioning are different from those for the type described above. There is no clear unconditioned stimulus which from the very beginning forces the organism to make the response (bar pressing) in which the experimenter is interested. The "correct" response must be discovered by the animal in the

Fig. 3.8 Two pieces of apparatus commonly used in the study of learning in rats. The Skinner box (above) is described in the text. The release lever and the food-delivery mechanism are in front of the rat. The panel above the rat contains electrical components used in controlling the equipment. Records of the animals' performances are shown hanging to the right and left of the control panel. The Lashley Discrimination Apparatus (below) has two doors, distinguishable by their patterns. If the rat jumps toward the correct door, it opens and he lands on a platform behind it. If he jumps toward the other door, he finds it locked and he falls into a hammock below.

process of its rovings about the box. Also, the reinforcing stimulus (food pellet) does not occur unless the animal presses the bar—that is, he must make the response which *is* to be reinforced before it *can* be reinforced. There is also no clear-cut conditioned stimulus in this situation. Because of the difference between this and the Pavlovian type of conditioning, the Pavlovian situation is referred to as *classical conditioning* and the Skinner situation as *instrumental conditioning*. The Skinner box is especially useful for investigating such questions as the relationships between levels of motivation and levels of performance during learning and for dealing in general with relationships between response and reinforcement, as in the partial-reinforcement situation.

Discrimination apparatus

Discrimination equipment was first introduced into psychology by comparative psychologists who were interested in finding out how well lower animals could discriminate among stimuli. Could a white rat, for example, tell the difference between a circle and a square? To test this, they required the animal to choose between two doors of a discrimination box, each marked in a distinctive way (Fig. 3.8). Psychologists no longer have a great interest in the discriminative ability of lower animals, but the discrimination box has proved to be an excellent device for investigating certain other problems of learning.

Mazes

Since the very early days of animal psychology, mazes have occupied a dominant position in learning research. A maze is simply a series of pathways along which the subject must pass in order to progress from the starting point to the goal (Fig. 3.9). During his progress, the subject is confronted again and again with choice points. If he turns in one direction. he runs into a blind alley, but if he turns in the other, he goes along the correct pathway until he meets another junction, where another choice must be made. Learning consists of the discovery and fixation of the correct turn at each junction, so that the individual can pass from the start to the end without entering a single blind alley. We can measure the progress of learning by the number of errors made on each trial or by the time taken to go from beginning to end.

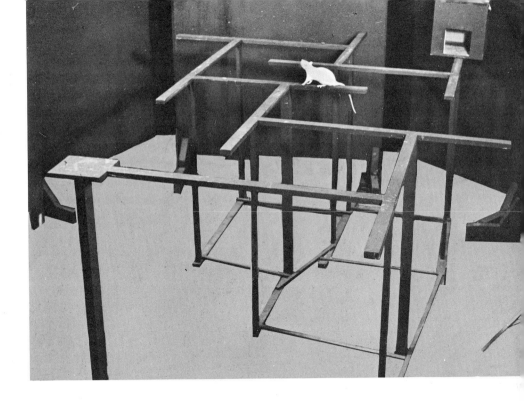

Fig. 3.9 Perhaps the most versatile piece of experimental apparatus used in the study of learning in rats is the maze. Mazes can take numerous forms, such as the elevated maze (above) and the alley maze (below). Like many other types of experimental apparatus, mazes are easily improvised. Careful design of the experiment is usually more important than refinement of the apparatus.

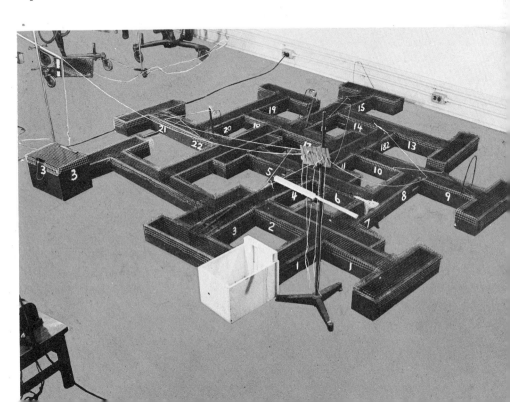

Fig. 3.10 Two kinds of tracking equipment. The female subject stands before a pursuit rotor and attempts to keep her hinged stylus in contact with a small spot on a revolving plate. The recording device to her left measures performance. The other two pictures show a more modern and complicated kind of tracking equipment. The center segment of the line on the oscilloscope screen before the subject will move up and down and he moves the stick held in his right hand forward and backward in an effort to align the center segment with the line on each side. In this illustration he has done so and the photograph gives the impression of a single solid line. The complicated instruments before the experimenter are used to control the movement of the central line segment and to record the subject's performance.

Motor learning devices

Some instruments have been devised to measure the learning of muscular coordination. One of the better-known of these is the pursuit rotor, a device consisting essentially of a phonograph turntable on which is located a small metal spot about the size of a dime (Fig. 3.10). The subject's task is to keep a stylus on the spot while the turntable is rotating. His score is expressed in terms of the number of seconds during a trial of a certain length that he is in contact with the spot. What is being measured is a complex coordination of the subject's hand and eye.

A recent elaboration of this type of task is modeled after the situation in which a pilot of a modern, complex plane may find himself when flying in a fog or pursuing an enemy plane at night. In such a case he is required to fly by instruments, and the instrument he sees is like the face of a television picture tube. On its face there may appear a small dot of light which is an electronic signal, received perhaps by radar, and which indicates the location of the field on which he is to land or of the enemy plane. When the spot is centered exactly in the tube (or *display* as it is usually called), the pilot is flying directly toward his intended target. His task, then, is to keep the spot centered in the display. This type of situation can be readily simulated in the laboratory by means of an oscilloscope (similar to the picture tube of a television set) and various devices which will make the spot rove about. The subject is given controls that he can move in an effort to keep the spot centered on the screen. His score is usually some measure of how long he kept the spot centered during the trial. This kind of task, like the use of the pursuit rotor, is called a *tracking* task. It bears an obvious resemblance to the steering of a car along a highway.

Another standard instrument requires that the subject trace the outline of a star which he can see only in a mirror. The mirror reverses the visual cues we normally use in guiding our movements and as a result the task is quite confusing. The score is determined by the number of times the subject's pencil departs from the outline of the star and by the time he takes to complete the outline. In general motor learning refers to the acquisition of such responses as walking, reaching, throwing, pressing a switch, driving a car and the like. These are responses which move our skeletal framework in space as contrasted with verbal responses.

Memory drum

The standard method of studying verbal learning is by employing a memory drum similar to that shown in Figure 3.11. A list of words or syllables is attached to an inner drum, which is rotated by the action of levers or gears connected with a timing device. As it rotates, the words or syllables appear in the window. The subject's task is to learn the list by rote so that he can call out the next syllable before it appears in the window. The number of trials necessary to learn the list is usually used as a measure of learning speed.

The syllables often employed in such an experiment are called nonsense syllables. Typical syllables are KIF, ZOL, and XIP. They are chosen because the subject is likely to have had no previous experience with them and few of the associations that he would have with meaningful words. There is, however, no reason why meaningful words cannot be used in these memory drum experiments. Indeed, there seems to be a strong trend in modern research to use meaningful rather than nonsense materials.

This is but a very small sample of the material that is used in studies of learning. In addition to using these specially developed tasks psychologists often develop tasks drawn from life situations, which may include such activities as the learning of radio code, the shooting of darts, or the learning of school lessons. The experimenter chooses or devises a task that highlights the particular aspect of the learning process with which he is concerned.

Fig. 3.11 A memory drum (left) as the experimental subject sees it and (right) as a tape of symbols, words, or nonsense syllables is being inserted.

The nature of the experimental tasks

We have referred to experimental tasks in the study of learning as being more complicated than those concerned with classical conditioning. It may be well to consider here what is meant in psychological terms by complication.

One complicating factor is that for most of these tasks the correct response is not immediately available to the subject. In classical conditioning, the unconditioned response is forced to occur by the presentation of the unconditioned stimulus. In many of these tasks, however, the subject must vary his responses during the pre-solution period and must himself discover the correct one —that is, the response that leads to reinforcement. Only after the correct response has been discovered can the fixation process begin.

In the classical conditioning situation there is little possibility for the occurrence of a number of responses that block the conditioned response. In many other experimental situations, on the other hand, psychological complication is introduced because the subject has strong tendencies to make wrong responses and these must be extinguished before the correct one can occur with regularity. Of course, this conflict and the eventual elimination of wrong responses may be a matter of especial interest for the experimenter; he may even have trained his subjects to give these wrong responses in some prior learning situation. The discrimination box and the memory drum are useful in the study of learning that is complicated by conflicting responses.

Another form of psychological complication arises from the amount of material, or the number of different stimulus $\rightarrow$ response units, that must be fixated within a task. In many situations—as in conditioning experiments—a single response to a single stimulus is learned; but other situations involve learning a number of different responses to a number of different stimuli presented over a span of time. An example of this kind of task is the vocabulary list at the end of an assignment in an elementary language course. The foreign word may be considered the stimulus and the English equivalent the response. The student who expects a good grade must know not just a single pair but must master the entire list. This concurrent learning of many units complicates fixation considerably, as a number of studies with memory drums have shown. Learning of this sort, where there are a number of

79

stimulus → response units that can occur in any order, is called *paired associate* learning.

In learning the foreign-language vocabulary, the student is not expected to be able to recite the list in a specific sequence. Many activities, however, such as reciting a poem, singing a song, or driving a car, do require that certain movements precede others. The introduction of the requirement of a serial ordering or unfolding adds another complication. Maze learning is exclusively of this sort. The term *serial learning* is used for such learning.

Finally, of course, we are interested in noting differences among these various kinds of complicated tasks. What, if any, differences exist between the learning or retention of verbal materials and the learning of motor skills, such as riding a bicycle, flying an airplane, or performing on a pursuit rotor? We shall see in a later section of this chapter how these environmental complications may be identified more precisely.

Reinforcement and extinction

With reference to classical conditioning, we defined reinforcement as the occurrence of the unconditioned stimulus, and we pointed out that the development of the conditioned response is dependent upon reinforcement. In more complicated learning situations, we ordinarily cannot identify a specific unconditioned stimulus. Thus, for example, when a rat learns the correct series of turns at the various choice points of the maze, we cannot say that there was some unconditioned stimulus or stimuli that determined its response at the various turns. Nevertheless, something analogous to the unconditioned stimulus must be present if the animal is to perform well in such a situation. There must be food in the end box of the maze if the animal is hungry, or water if it is thirsty. Hungry animals who find no food in the end box will not avoid the blind alleys, and if, after the maze is learned, they no longer discover food at the end of their run, their performance will deteriorate. The presence of food or water in this situation seems to operate to fixate instrumental responses just as the unconditioned stimulus fixates responses in Pavlovian conditioning.

Events that are considered to be reinforcements are not restricted to stimuli of such obvious biological significance as food, water, or avoidance of pain; many other classes of stimuli serve as reinforcements. A word or gesture of approval from parent, teacher, or friend will reinforce the response that preceded it; if the flight of the golf ball is long and straight when a long and straight flight is hoped for, this will serve as a reinforcement of the kind of stroke that propelled it; and, of course, we learn to do things because we are paid for doing them in the coin of the realm.

The discerning student will undoubtedly note that all these reinforcing events share a common characteristic; they all seem to satisfy some wish or desire of the subject, or at least to please him in some way. Although these words undoubtedly give a general notion of what is meant by reinforcement, they themselves need a great deal of explaining. A more technical definition is: *Reinforcement is the occurrence of an event that satisfies a current motivational state of the organism.** (In Chapter 5 we shall discover something of the nature of the various kinds of motivational states that characterize human organisms.)

In summary, we may state that reinforcement is related to learning in that if a stimulus → response event is followed by reinforcement, this stimulus → response connection will be strengthened, and the more frequently reinforcement occurs, the stronger the connection will become. Conversely, if reinforcement is not forthcoming following the response, the tendency to make the response to this stimulus will be decreased.

Principles of conditioning and instrumental learning

This chapter opened with a description of the conditioning situation because it is relatively simple from the point of view of its physical characteristics. This simplicity of the physical surroundings makes for ease in identifying certain important psychological principles and relating them to the specific operations that the experimenter performs in his conditioning experiments. These principles aid us in understanding the behavior that occurs in the conditioning situation. The question is, can we identify these principles in operation in more complex environments, particularly in those that involve the learning of instrumental acts? There seems to be a large amount of evidence supporting the view that

---

* Some psychologists would prefer a more neutral definition of reinforcement and would state simply that reinforcement is *an event which strengthens an* $S \to R$ *connection.* So far as its effect upon fixation is concerned there is no real conflict between such a definition and the one given in the main body of the text.

these same principles which were so clearly illustrated in the conditioning laboratory function also in more complex environments, and in the following paragraphs we shall attempt to illustrate this fact. At this time we shall offer only a few illustrative examples, but we shall refer to the concepts again and again in later chapters of the book.

Experiment I: Reinforcement in verbal behavior[20]

The response that was reinforced in this experiment was the very general one of expressing an opinion. The experimenters were psychology students and the subjects were their friends. The essential plan of the experiment was to engage the subject in conversation, and, without giving reinforcement for any specific kind of response, to count secretly the number of times the subject expressed an opinion. After ten minutes of this conversation, the experimenter began to reinforce any opinion expressing response that the subject made. Opinion-expressing responses were defined as statements that began with: "I think . . . ," "I believe . . . ," "It seems to me . . .," and the like. Two kinds of reinforcement were employed: a paraphrasing of what the subject had just said or a comment such as "You're right," "I agree," or "That's so." This continued for ten minutes. During the next ten minutes the experimenters introduced an extinction procedure for some subjects and for other subjects a kind of counterconditioning procedure. If extinction was being employed, the experimenter simply did not respond to the subjects' comments; while in the counterconditioning procedure he disagreed with the subjects' statements. In all three sessions, which actually flowed into each other without any sharp break as far as the subjects were aware, the experimenters secretly recorded the number of opinion-expressing remarks. These records are the basic data of the experiment. It was predicted that, if the principles of reinforcement and extinction were applicable to such a situation, the frequency of expressed opinions would rise during the reinforcement session and decline during the extinction session. The results, expressed as the percentage of opinion statements to all statements, were as follows: control sessions, 32 percent; conditioning sessions, 56 percent; extinction sessions, 33 percent. The data, therefore, are in accord with predictions made from principles derived from the conditioning situation. No marked differences were found between the effects of the two kinds of reinforcement procedures. The effects of extinction and counterconditioning were essentially the same, though there was a slight tendency for the subjects to argue with the experimenter under counterconditioning and to terminate the session by leaving the room under extinction. Incidentally, none of the subjects was aware that he was the subject of an experiment.

Experiment II: Extinction and spontaneous recovery[21]

This experiment used the Skinner box, which was described and illustrated on page 73. The subjects were white rats who acquired the instrumental response of pressing a bar to obtain the delivery of a pellet of food. Following the learning of the task, during which time each act of pressing the bar resulted in food reward, an extinction session was begun. In this session, pressing the bar no longer caused food to be dropped into the feeding trough. The session was continued until the animal had spent twenty minutes in the box without pressing the bar. On the following day another extinction session was run, and yet another was conducted 55 days later.

The results of this experiment are presented in Figure 3.12. The figure indicates the number of non-reinforced responses which was made during each extinction session. Throughout the sessions, the group that was given the larger number of reinforcements gave more responses than the group with the smaller amount of training. This is to be expected, for the strength of a habit is a function of the number of training trials. Both groups made a larger number of responses during the first extinction session than in any of the other sessions. Even though no further reinforcements were administered, a considerable number of responses were given in the last two extinction periods. This is an illustration of the spontaneous recovery of an instrumental response.

Experiment III: Stimulus generalization[22]

The subjects of this experiment were children of two age ranges: 7 to 9 and 10 to 12 years. The purpose of the investigation was twofold: to determine whether stimulus generalization would occur in this particular task, and to determine whether the amount of generalization would differ for the two age groups. The subjects were seated before a curved panel that contained seven light bulbs, positioned from left to right in a horizontal line and spaced

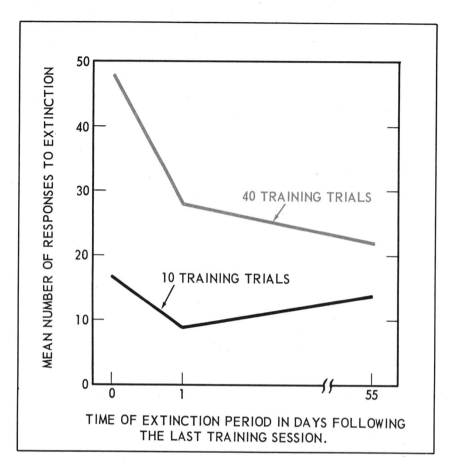

Fig. 3.12 Mean number of responses to extinction of an instrumental response. Since no additional training was given following the first extinction period, the performance on days 1 and 55 are attributed to spontaneous recovery. (After Youtz[21])

eight degrees apart. The arc of the panel was such that all lights were equidistant from the subject's eyes. One light was directly in front of the subject, with three lights to the right and three positioned symmetrically to the left. The subjects were instructed to press a key as rapidly as possible when the center light came on, but *not* to press the key when any other light was illuminated. A small red light above the center light flashed a warning just before any of the test lights (which were white) were lit. After a sequence of ten training trials during which only the center light flashed on, the experimenters introduced occasional trials in which different peripheral lights were lit. Stimulus generalization could be said to have occurred if the subjects responded to the peripheral lights, despite the fact that they had been instructed not to do so.

The results are presented in Figure 3.13. The figure shows the proportion of subjects that responded to each of the lights. The center, or training, light was responded to most often, and in general the tendency to respond to the other lights decreased in proportion to their distances from the center light. Light 2 was an exception, for it was responded to less frequently than the farther removed Light 1. The experimenters felt that this was due to the fact that the bulb in position 2 happened to be dimmer than the rest. If this fact accounts for the anomaly, then the stimulus generalization curve obtained in this situation is essentially similar to that obtained in studies of classical conditioning. It is significant also that the amount of generalization was greater for the younger children than for the older ones.

Fig. 3.13 Generalization gradients of an instrumental response for younger and older subjects. (After Mednick and Lehtinen[22])

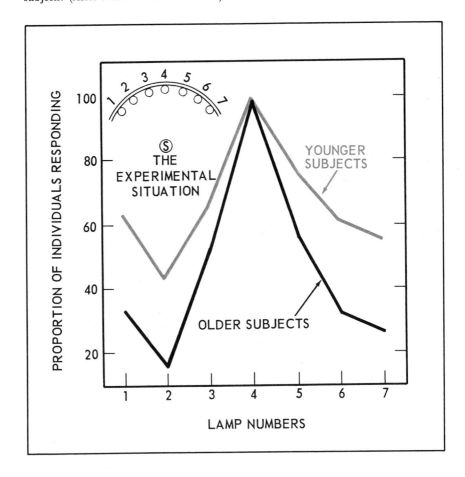

Experiment IV: Response generalization and verbal learning[23]

The term *response generalization* refers to the fact that during the process of learning to make a specific response to a stimulus, the subject is actually learning to make a class of responses, which are similar in some way to the specific response that is required in the particular learning situation. The next experiment demonstrates the occurrence of response generalization in the learning of a verbal task. Ten pairs of items were to be learned by the college student subjects. Each pair consisted of a nonsense syllable stimulus unit and an adjectival response unit. Some examples are: XAN-musty, CEG-horrid, DOP-toilsome, and ZEM-ancient. The materials were presented to the class on slides, with the stimulus unit appearing first for a few seconds, followed by the response unit. After the first trial through the whole list of ten items, the subjects attempted to write down the appropriate response unit during the time the stimulus unit alone was shown on the screen. Obviously the subject might write the correct answer, a wrong answer, or fail to write any answer. The wrong responses were collected and another group of students assessed the degree of similarity of each wrong response to the appropriate correct response. Similarity was judged along four dimensions: homonymity (sounding like the correct response word); synonymity(same meaning); antonymity (opposite meaning); and contextual (for example, the response "laundry" for "toilsome"). They went through the entire list four times, rating each of the 122 errors along one dimension each time.

The results are given in Table 3.4. The table is read in this fashion: When the judges were rating for degree of similarity of sound (homonymity) they estimated that 64 (58 + 4 + 2) of the total of 122 errors sounded more or less like the correct response word, and 58 did not. The results of this experiment demonstrates that response generalization occurs during the learning of verbal habits. It appears also that—at least for college students—the major dimensions of similarity along which response generalization of verbal material occurs are homonymity and synonymity. In this experiment the response generalization tendency results in an error, since the subject's responses are required to be the exact words; but under other circumstances the same tendency may aid the subject. If it were sufficient for the subject to give only the general sense of the correct response word—substance rather than form only—then response generalization tendencies would be helpful.

TABLE 3.4.

Dimension along which similarity is being estimated	Estimated degree of similarity			
	High	Med.	Low	None
Homonymity	58	4	2	58
Synonymity	56	7	5	54
Antonymity	7	0	0	115
Contextual	1	5	7	109

HOW LEARNING PROGRESSES

The initial step in a scientific analysis often consists in obtaining an exact description of the phenomenon to be studied. Once this has been obtained, the research worker is often able to locate certain characteristics that need further study and also to begin to identify the factors that cause the observed variations.

This approach is not difficult to make in the field of learning, and in a somewhat unsystematic manner most of us have followed such a method in observations of ourselves or our associates. We may have noted that with practice the time required to perform a certain task decreases, that we can back a car into a small space with only one false start rather than many, that a child can build a tower of six or seven blocks rather than only of two, or that we can recite the English equivalents of all the French words in our lesson's vocabulary list.

These measures—the amount of time required to perform a task, the rate of elimination of errors, and the frequency of correct responses—are the usual ones employed by the psychologist in plotting the course of learning. His technique differs from the unsystematic efforts of the layman primarily in that he looks for precise and objective ways of measuring the behavior. For example, he uses a stop watch and records the data systematically on every trial rather than merely estimating it on an occasional trial. By such careful means it is possible to obtain an accurate description of the process of learning as it is reflected in the measures being used—time, errors, or correct responses.

Learning curves

When learning data are plotted graphically, they are referred to as learning curves. Three such curves are presented in Figure 3.14. Although each of these curves represents a different measure of behavior in different activities, all of them have one basic characteristic in common; sooner or later the amount of improvement per trial begins to decrease. For one of these curves, the amount of improvement from one trial to the next decreases from the first trial onward. Technically, we say that such a curve is *negatively accelerated*. Most of us are familiar with this phenomenon through observation of our own activities. When we set out to learn a new activity, we often seem to progress by leaps and bounds at the beginning, but gradually our progress slows down until the time comes when there seems to be no real improvement from one session to the next. If, however, we were to use precise measurement, evidence of slight improvement might be perceptible.

So many sorts of activities have produced a negatively accelerated performance curve that psychologists in the past occasionally concluded that this is the typical or "true" learning curve. We

Fig. 3.14 Three kinds of learning curve: the uppermost one is negatively accelerated; the lowest is S-shaped and is positively accelerated during its first portion and negatively accelerated in the last portion.

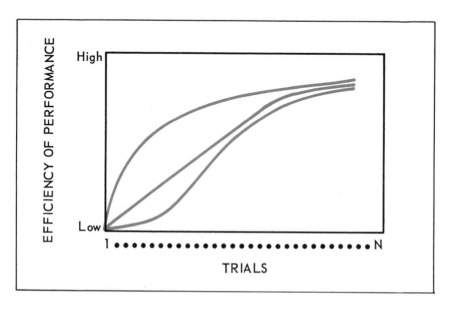

know now, however, that we cannot make such a statement, for learning curves do not always show this form. Some curves show little or no progress during the initial trials and then show negative acceleration. These curves are often called S-shaped curves. Some activities have produced curves that are essentially straight lines. Thus, although the usual curve for learning is negatively accelerated, we cannot say that such a curve is the true curve of learning. It is the most common one, but other kinds of curves will and do occur. One of the basic tasks of the research worker is to identify the factors that cause these variations in the form of the curve.

Our discussion has hitherto been confined to the general trends of the various curves, and it has disregarded the typical fluctuations that give curves a saw-toothed appearance. These variations reflect the fact that the progress of learning is not completely regular. Organisms are not static, and their efficiency fluctuates above and below some average level. Although there may be a trend toward improvement from day to day, there will be occasional recessions that are, in part, the result of lowered general efficiency on a specific trial. Were it possible to control and hold constant all the factors that make for this variation—the level of motivation, the degree of fatigue, the number of distracting stimuli, and other factors—we would expect these fluctuations to disappear almost completely.

The plateau

Although most performance curves show a continuous upward or downward trend, curves of the sort shown in Figure 3.15 are occasionally obtained.[24] The notable features of this curve are that good progress is made until approximately the fourteenth week, that from then to the twenty-fourth week improvement is slight, and that following this period there is once more a spurt in the curve. The period of little progress that is both preceded and followed by periods of marked progress is called a *plateau*. There are a number of possible explanations of its occurrence. It may be associated with a temporary low level of motivation; it may be associated with a shift in the method of performing the task, with the subject moving from a less to a more efficient method; it may be that certain errors have become fixated and the curve cannot rise until they are eliminated; or it may be that the subject is paying

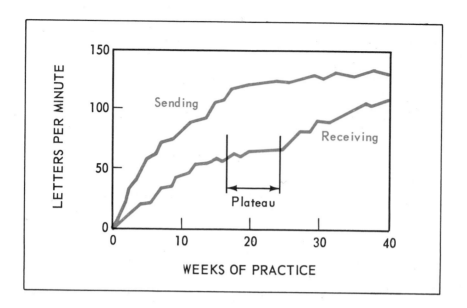

Fig. 3.15 Curves for the learning of a telegraphic code. The receiving curve has a plateau; the sending curve does not, for it shows no steep improvement after leveling off. (After Bryan and Harter[24])

particular attention to one part of the total task and neglecting other parts of it for the time being. The plateau is an interesting phenomenon and has received considerable attention in the psychological literature, although it occurs infrequently and is usually confined to the learning of complex activities.

VARIABLES INFLUENCING THE
RATE OF LEARNING

For almost any task that we are required to learn, we have set for us, or we set for ourselves, some level of proficiency which must be attained before it can be said that the task has been learned. At times the level is achieved with ease, and at other times the most laborious struggles inch us only very slowly toward the goal. At such times we may accuse ourselves of stupidity, consider the task itself to be impossible, or condemn the circumstances within which we must work. These occasional feelings reflect the basic variable factors that influence the ease with which task mastery is attained. We may describe them as *procedural, task,* and *organismic* variables. By *procedural* variables we mean events that are extrinsic to the task itself (the calculus teacher is pleasant and stimulating, or unpleasant and boring). By *task* variables we refer to the psychological process that is intrinsic to the activity itself (calculus has certain characteristics that are different from those involved in driving an automobile). By *organismic* variables we refer to the capabilities and competencies which the particular individual brings to the task. It is not always possible to identify a particular characteristic as falling into one and only one of these three classes, but a recognition of the general differences among these variables should lead to more accurate prediction of the speed of learning in a specific situation.

Procedural variables

Delay of reinforcement

In Chapter 2 we pointed out that there is an intimate relationship between learning and motivation. We can now describe this relationship somewhat more specifically by saying that stimulus → response connections will become fixated if the response is followed by reinforcement, reinforcement being defined as some event that satisfies the organism's current motivational state. Conversely, stimulus → response connections will be extinguished if, once established, they are never followed by reinforcement.

This statement is inadequate because it makes no mention of any time relationship between response and reinforcement. The importance of this relationship is indicated by an experiment in which white rats were required to learn a discrimination problem.[25] The rat was confronted with two doors in the discrimination box, one black and the other white. Food was always hidden behind the door of one color, but never behind the door of the other color. If the rat pushed through the correct door it obtained food; if it entered the incorrect door it was confined in the empty goal box for a few seconds. Six group of rats were put through the experiment, the sole differences in their treatments being in the lengths of time which intervened between the time they passed the door and the time they obtained food. One group received the food immediately after the door was opened, while the other groups experienced some delay before food was obtained. The delays for the different groups were .5, 1.2, 2, 5, and 10 seconds. The question was whether delays as *short* as these would affect the ease with which the problem is learned.

The answer is shown in Figure 3.16. The zero delay group learned readily, while the ten-second groups showed little evidence of learning anything about the problem. The efficiencies of the intermediate groups fell between these two, with longer delays being consistently associated with decreasing learning efficiency.

The same dependence on time interval is found in human subjects; they, too, learn less well if a time delay is introduced between response and reinforcement. We are undoubtedly less time-bound than the lower animals, for we can readily use language to bridge over time, but even with the use of language we do not eliminate this dependency completely. From a practical point of view, the conclusion is clear: learning will be best when reinforcement follows the correct response by the shortest possible time interval.

Knowledge of results

It seems self-evident that if an organism is to learn to make a specific response to a stimulus, it must know during the learning whether it is making a correct or an incorrect response. Without some knowledge of the results of current performance, it is difficult to effect an improvement. Experimental work has provided

Fig. 3.16 The effect of delay of reinforcement on discrimination learning. Delay intervals vary from zero to 10 seconds. (After Grice[25])

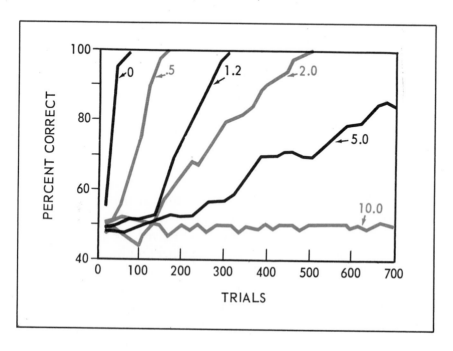

abundant evidence that learning is dependent upon an immediate knowledge of the correctness or incorrectness of our performance. Nevertheless, this principle is frequently violated in our daily living. Almost every student has taken some course in which he did not know his status until he received his final grade. In business organizations, management often establishes policies that undermine the workers' morale and become sources of industrial friction—simply because management is unable to observe the effects of its decisions on the workers. The busy parent often fails to correct or approve a child's act until he discovers that the child has fixated some most undesirable way of acting.

The effects of knowledge of results are dramatically illustrated in the following experiments:[26] A lever arm was shielded from the subject's sight and he was told that if he moved the lever over a certain arc he would score a hit. The arc was actually 33° but the subject was not informed of this. One pull of the lever constituted a trial. Of the three groups of subjects, one was informed of their performances after every trial, another after every fourth trial, and another after every tenth trial. The knowledge given consisted of a statement of the number of degrees too long or too short. Performances for the three groups over the first eleven trials are given in Figure 3.17. Trial 1 is omitted because it was a sheer guess for all subjects, but all were told how they performed on this trial. The group with knowledge after each trial improved steadily throughout the ten trials; the group without knowledge after the first trial showed no improvement; the group which obtained information after every fourth trial improved markedly after each trial on which information was given, but failed to improve following the noninformative trials.

The manner in which knowledge of results operates in order to improve performance is too complicated for discussion here. For the present we shall merely point to its significance, and stress its great importance as a factor in learning.

It is apparent that there is a great deal of similarity in meaning between the terms reinforcement and knowledge of results, but, in fact, they are not synonyms. If the individual is motivated to behave in a certain way—that is, to acquire a particular response—then the information that the appropriate response was made will serve as a reinforcement. However, when the knowledge supplied is to the effect that the response is wrong, this knowledge does not strengthen the response. It does not, in other words, serve

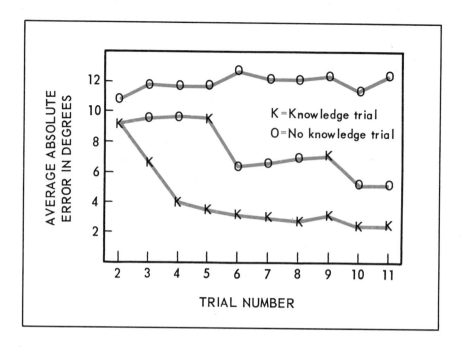

Fig. 3.17 The effect of the relative frequency of knowledge of results upon performance of a motor task. The trials on which knowledge was given are marked *K*; those without knowledge are labeled *0*. The top group obtained no knowledge on any trials; the bottom group obtained knowledge on every trial. (After Bilodeau and Bilodeau[26])

as a reinforcement of the response which it follows. Finally the presentation of knowledge would be ineffective unless there was some motivation to perform in a particular way; the term reinforcement implies that this motivation is present, but knowledge of results does not.

Repetition

The fact that proficiency increases with practice is almost too obvious to mention. It is well illustrated in most of the learning curves that have been presented in this chapter. Sometimes in our eagerness to achieve perfection we forget this fact and become scornful and intolerant of others or disgusted with ourselves if a high level of competence is not soon reached. Like Rome, habits are not built in a day, and we should recognize this fact for ourselves and for others.

By repetition, however, we do not mean simply performing in the situation, but rather performing the appropriate response under conditions that result in at least an occasional reinforcement. This fact is well illustrated in Figure 3.17. Only the group that received information of results after each trial showed consistent improvement with "practice." For the other groups there is even a suggestion of deterioration in performance on the trials following those for which knowledge of results was withheld. The principle of extinction would cause us to predict an actual deterioration of performance if it were "practiced" again and again without at least an occasional reinforcement.

It seems very probable that our continued performance in any situation rises or falls to the level of efficiency that is consonant with the learning principles operating in that situation. If, after having learned in a situation that supplies immediate reinforcement for correct responses and non-reinforcement for incorrect responses, we "practice" again and again in a less optimal situation, then our performance is likely to decline.

Active vs. passive attitude

Learning is work, and many of us, in an effort to lighten the burden, have developed extremely passive habits of study. We choose a comfortable seat, open our textbooks, and read through our assignment from beginning to end. When we finish the last sentence, we close the book with the easy conscience of one who has done his duty and we turn to activities that are more attractive. We have "studied our lesson."

It may be granted that the lesson has been read, but whether this is an effective way to *learn* material is another matter. One study compared a method of this sort with one in which the subjects attempted to recite the material after reading it.[27] The subjects were divided into five groups, and one of the groups devoted all of its time to reading, whereas the other groups devoted part of their time to reading and part to reciting to themselves after each reading. Two types of materials were used: nonsense syllables and short biographies. A recall test was given to the subjects immediately after the last reading and another one four hours later. The results for each of these groups, stated in percentage of the material recalled, are presented in Table 3.5. It is notable that although the time spent was the same for all groups, the level of achievement differed greatly. The trends differ slightly for the nonsense material and for the biographies, but both consistently indicate that a large proportion of time spent in recitation serves to increase efficiency. The implications for study habits are clear: deal actively with the materials to be learned, and begin to recite early in the learning instead of waiting until the learning is almost completed.

TABLE 3.5. MATERIAL RECALLED (%)

METHOD OF STUDY	Nonsense syllables		Biographies	
	Immediate	4 hr. later	Immediate	4 hr. later
All reading	35	15	35	16
20 percent recitation	50	26	37	19
40 percent recitation	54	28	41	25
60 percent recitation	57	37	42	26
80 percent recitation	74	48	42	26

Learning during sleep

Appropriate to the topic of active vs. passive attitude in learning is the question of whether or not we can learn while sleeping. To do so has the appeal of getting something for nothing. How pleasant it would be for a student who must master a vocabulary of foreign words or the trigonometric identities if he could acquire this information while he slept. The technique would not be difficult. The material could be transposed to a record or a tape recorder which could be set to play during the night and the student would awake in the morning with his lesson learned.

A few experiments have indicated that learning during sleep might be possible, but there was always a doubt as to whether the subjects were sleeping soundly when the material was presented to them. Recent work has developed ways of measuring brain activity which permit the experimenter to judge the depth of sleep during the time that material is presented to the subject.[28] The experimenter found that the subjects learned a very small amount if the material was presented during the time they were in a stage of very light sleep (probably what we call being "half awake"), but that they learned nothing if the materials were presented during deep levels of sleep. The experiment would seem to suggest that when the subjects did learn they were really not sleeping. Presumably, if one were willing to spend a restless and unrefreshing night during which time the material was presented to him over and over again, he might get up from the bed in the morning with some knowledge gained. On the other hand, an active half hour of wakeful study followed by undisturbed sleep would almost certainly result in better mastery of the material, together with a feeling of well-being the next day. Apparently the activities of learning and sleeping do not mix either at home or in the classroom.

Massing vs. spacing

If one has decided to budget his time, allotting a certain amount to one learning task and another amount to a different one, the question arises as to how he should distribute the time he has allotted to each. On the one hand, he can work at one task continuously until all the allotted time is exhausted and then do the same with the other task. On the other hand, he can work at a task for a part of the allotted time and then return to it at a later period for the remainder of the time. In the first instance, we would say that he is using the technique of *massed learning*, and in the second instance the technique of *spaced learning*.

This question of how best to distribute one's work efforts in time has been the subject of a great deal of research. For many years it seemed that the answer to the question was a relatively simple one: that distributing one's work in time produced better learning than massing the work periods. But, as is so often true in a science, subsequent research has indicated that the problem and its answer are far more complex than was believed to be the case. Accurate answers to the question can be obtained only if we specify the kind of task being practiced and if we measure the effects of the practice and the characteristics of the subjects. In the following discussion, we shall begin by making a distinction between motor or perceptual motor learning and verbal learning.

The typical perceptual motor situations used for the study of distribution of effort are those employing some tracking task, mirror drawing, solving a maze, or a variant of a task in which one of several lights flash on and the subject must press a different key in order to turn out each light. Usually, except for the maze, each trial lasts for the same length of time; in the massed condition little or no time elapses between the termination of one trial and the beginning of the next, while the distributed condition obviously results from a greater elapsed time between trials and this may be large or small, depending upon the experimenter's wishes. Results typical of such experiments are presented in Figure 3.18. They show that the performance is superior under the distributed conditions; and, at least within the time interval employed, the greater the distribution the higher the performance level.[29]

The conclusion that one is tempted to draw from such an experiment is that distribution results in rather marked superiority in learning. However, the usual definition of "learning"

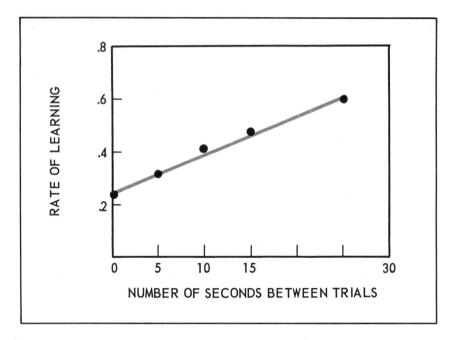

Fig. 3.18 A curve showing the effect of spacing of practice upon performance in a tracking task. The numbers on the Y axis describe the steepness of the performance curve; the higher the number the better the performance. (After Kimble[29])

includes the statement that there will be some permanence to what is learned, and so one more question should be asked before we conclude that distribution has resulted in marked superiority in learning. The question is: how would groups trained under these conditions perform at some later period of time. In one experiment,[30] groups were trained under massed and distributed conditions and then were tested on the task ten minutes after the last training trial and again ten days later. Marked differences were found between the groups during the training, but these differences were greatly reduced on the tests given at the two later times. This work suggests that a large share of the differences in performance between massed and distributed groups which are manifested during practice is not due to true differences in learning. Probably the greatest share of the differences can be attributed to some phenomenon such as fatigue, which lowers the performance level of the massed groups and is eliminated after the subjects rest.*

* In a later chapter we will discuss this phenomenon and point out that here "fatigue" does not refer to the condition produced simply by an accumulation of waste products in the muscles.

On the basis of this study and other data, we conclude that massed practice of perceptual motor tasks results in marked inferiority of performance during practice, but not in much inferiority so far as permanent learning is concerned. In short, if one is learning such an activity for the purpose of using what is learned at some later time, it does not seem to matter greatly whether the practice is massed or distributed, though probably the safest course is to employ some form of spacing.

In the learning of verbal material a distinction must be made between *serial learning* and *paired associate* learning.[31] For paired associate learning there is no clear tendency for the results of distributed practice to be better than those of massed practice, though this difference is generally and rather markedly true for the learning of serial material. With respect to the retention of verbal materials learned under these two conditions, the problem is even more complex. Subjects who have had little experience in learning these lists tend to retain what they have learned somewhat better after massed practice. This is particularly true of slow-learning subjects, whereas for the fast learning subjects the nature of the distribution during training makes little difference. If, on the other hand, the subjects have previously learned a number of similar lists, both learning and retention is facilitated if the practice is distributed.

Cramming

The findings of these studies in learning have implications for the manner in which students prepare for their courses. The studies indicate that the student who devotes, let us say, eight hours of study to a specific subject will probably learn more if his time is spent in several blocks of an hour or two each than if all the study time is spent in a single block of eight hours.

If by cramming we mean that the student does not study the subject at all until the day before the examination and then tries to learn all the material in a single lengthy and intensive study period, we can safely say that cramming is not efficient. Obviously the student will learn by this technique, but he will not learn as much as he would have if he had spaced the same amount of study time over a longer period.

But the word "cramming" is also used to refer to a long and intensive review on the night before the examination. Since the student has studied his material throughout the term, the cram period is not a *learning* period but a review, or *relearning,* period. Obviously a review of the course material the night before the examination will be helpful. The two kinds of situations—the one in which the student meets the materials for the first time in a cram session and tries to learn it, and the one in which the cram session consists in an extensive reviewing of previously learned material—are quite different.

Whole vs. part

If one is given a fairly long assignment to learn—say a passage from Shakespeare, a sonnet, or a vocabulary list—he may proceed in two ways. He may break the material into parts, which he learns separately and integrates later; or he may attempt to learn the material as a whole. These two basically different methods are called *part learning* and *whole learning,* and a considerable amount of research has been conducted to determine their relative efficiency. The research indicates that the problem is not a simple one, for in some instances the whole method excels and in others the part method excels. Such conflicting results are not, however, a matter of chance; they arise from the fact that we are dealing with a phenomenon that is complicated by the operation of other variables. If he examines the factors listed below, the reader may be able to choose the appropriate method for any specific material.[32]

▶ *Intelligence.* There is some evidence that the whole method is more effective than the part method for the more intelligent learners.

▶ *Practice.* With increasing practice in both methods, the whole method becomes more effective.

▶ *Massing and spacing.* Study time may be distributed in any manner regardless of whether the material is being learned by whole or by part. The whole method seems to be especially favored by spacing.

▶ *Type of material learned.* On logical grounds, one might expect that material which fits into a meaningful whole—a sonnet, for example, would be learned much more effectively when the whole method is employed, and that materials composed of independent units—a vocabulary list, for example—would favor the part method. The researchers on this point have not produced findings sufficiently consistent to permit a generalization. It is a point to be cleared up by future research that will adequately control all the other factors that might influence the results.

Thus the relative efficiency of the whole and the part methods is not known conclusively, although findings indicate that certain factors seem to favor one method whereas others favor the other. One investigator has suggested that greatest efficiency will probably be obtained by using the whole method with special emphasis on the more difficult parts of the material.

Guidance

As with knowledge of results, the relationship between the amount of guidance supplied and the efficiency of learning is not a simple one. In some experiments in maze learning in which both rats and humans were used, various numbers of guided trials were given.[33] For some groups these guided trials were introduced early in the series of unguided trials; for others they were introduced toward the middle of the series. The results of these experiments indicated that a moderate amount of guidance introduced very early was most desirable. Larger amounts of guidance, and guidance introduced later, though usually better than no guidance, were not so effective in reducing learning time.

There are several reasons why guidance is effective in speeding up our learning. The total learning process, as we have mentioned in Chapter 2, involves not only fixating the correct response but also discovering it. Guidance early in practice speeds up the discovery of the correct way of acting and paves the way for fixation. Guidance, as the term is used in everyday life, also supplies an evaluation of performance. The good coach or teacher points out to the student his correct and incorrect responses.

In the experiments on guided learning, some of the groups that were given extremely large amounts of guidance had even more difficulty in learning than those that had no guidance at all. Apparently these heavily guided groups were learning to react to the cues afforded by the experimenter and not to cues afforded by the physical environment of the maze. The former interfered with the latter.

The disadvantage of overguidance manifests itself in the rearing of children. The child who is constantly guided by a well-meaning adult does not himself learn the proper modes of behaving in the social and intellectual mazes through which he must move. The excessive guidance given by the apron strings does not permit the child to learn to behave independently. He learns instead to obtain cues for the proper way of behaving from the parent or authority figure, rather than from the structure of the situation itself.

In the present state of psychological knowledge, we cannot state with precision how much or how little guidance should be given in most social and intellectual learning situations; we can only point out to parents the dangers involved in the extremes of too much and too little.

Task variables

Although individuals differ in the ease with which they master tasks, there is undoubtedly a larger ordering of task difficulty, an ordering of difficulty that disregards the special competencies of particular individuals and the particular circumstances in which the individual must work. It is with this problem, the problem of what makes certain tasks difficult or easy for all of us, that we shall concern ourselves in this section. Space will not permit a detailed listing of all identified task variables, and we will consider only some important and basic ones.

The sense used

The stimuli that control or pace our performance in any task may fall within any of our sense fields* without changing the basic nature of the activity. Thus, in a conditioning experiment, one might use a tone, a light, or a touch on the skin as the conditioned stimulus, the unconditioned stimulus in all cases being food. The question we raise is whether the speed of learning of the conditioned response will differ as a result of using one conditioned stimulus rather than another. Again, material could be read to us, or we could read the same material from a printed page. Assuming that the time spent is the same in both cases, do we learn more about the text if we have heard it or if we have seen it? Obviously, the conclusive answer to this question will be obtained only when many careful experiments are conducted which compare learnings to different sensory stimuli when all other potentially relevant fac-

---

* A word about *sense field* is in order at this time, though the topic will be discussed in detail later. We experience qualitative differences when we are stimulated by different kinds of physical stimuli, such as a light, a tone, a pin pressed against the skin, and a heated or cooled object. The qualitative differences are mediated by different senses. Man has many sense fields, more than the traditional five, but for the present the reader needs to know only generally what we mean by senses or sensory fields.

tors (such as intensity and duration) are controlled. On the basis of what is known today, however, we have no reason to predict that the sense fields from which the task stimuli are drawn have any important effect upon the difficulty of the task.

The response system used

The instrumental responses we make to stimuli are of a wide variety, but perhaps the most general classification is between motor and verbal responses. The problem in this case is parallel to the problem of learning in the different sense fields, and here too the answer is probably in the negative. We have no reason to assume at present that, if we equate such factors as the speed or precision of the responses demanded, the learning of verbal responses will differ from the learning of motor responses. Actually, as will become apparent, when we consider the variables which do influence task difficulty, the question of the sensory field employed or the muscle group involved in the response is a meaningless one.

Serial or nonserial task

One basic psychological difference between tasks is whether they demand a consistent and particular ordering of the responses, or whether the nature of the response is dependent simply upon the nature of the stimulus. Tasks that require a particular ordering are called serial, and the others are simply referred to as nonserial. If one learns a poem he is engaging in a serial activity, for there is a correct ordering of each word and line in the poem, and if these are spoken out of turn the recitation is incorrect. On the other hand, learning the vocabulary of a foreign language is nonserial, for one is expected to know the translation of a word regardless of the word that precedes or follows it. Some tasks, such as driving an automobile, combine both these characteristics. The serial characteristic is particularly apparent in driving a car with a standard shift. There is a key to be inserted, the starter to be activated and released, the clutch pedal to be depressed, the gear shift to be inserted into low, the clutch pedal to be released as the accelerator is depressed, and so on through the remaining two gear ratios. If responses do not succeed each other in the sequence prescribed by the mechanical structure of the car, the driver is greeted by the horrible sound of clashing gears, by jerky forward motions, or by the stalling of the car. But as the car moves along the street, even one which has been driven frequently, the driver must be prepared to react appropriately to stimuli that occur in no regular sequence from day to day. Thus, a car backs into the street ahead of the driver, or he observes a plank with a protruding nail in the predicted path of his tires—he swerves to avoid these hazards today, but he may meet quite different ones tomorrow. It is not so with the stimulus and response patterns of operating the gear shift.

A great deal of research has been conducted on the learning of serial activities, and there are several important characteristics of this kind of learning that have been clearly and consistently identified. These characteristics are illustrated in Figure 3.19. The subjects were learning to recite in proper order a list of twelve nonsense syllables, presented to them in a memory drum at the rate of one syllable every two seconds.[34] The list was repeated until the subjects recited it perfectly. The experimenter recorded the failures to respond correctly for each syllable position in the list independently. The figure indicates the average number of failures occurring during the learning of the list for all subjects according to the position of the syllable in the list. The curve has an asymmetrical, bowed form, and demonstrates what is often called the

Fig. 3.19 Curves showing the mean number of errors by position in the list for learning a 12-item serial list of nonsense material. A 6-second interval between trials was used in the massed condition, and a 2-minute, 6-second interval was used for the distributed condition. (After Hovland[34])

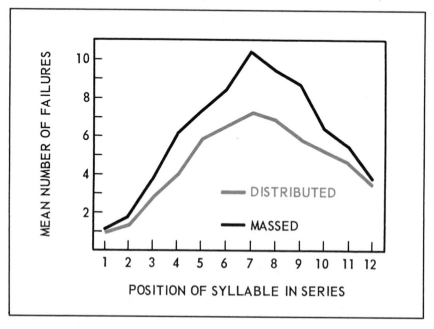

bowing phenomenon of serial learning. The results are quite typical of the serial learning of a list composed of similar items. The most difficult group of syllables is in the middle of the list, with the most difficult single syllable being slightly beyond, not at the middle. The initial item in the list is characteristically the easiest one to learn.

In this text we will not concern ourselves with the problem of how to account for these results; we wish only to acquaint the student with the fact that serial learning involves certain characteristic behaviors.

Discriminability among task stimuli

Performances in most complex tasks are controlled by a large number of stimuli, to each of which a particular response must be made. An obvious example of this kind of task is learning a foreign language. It contains a number of different stimuli (words) to which the student must attach particular responses (the English equivalents of the particular foreign words). An extremely important determinant of difficulty in learning is the degree of similarity among the stimuli of the task. If they are fairly similar to each other, yet with each stimulus requiring a different response, the task becomes a difficult one.

This fact is illustrated indirectly in a study conducted on the learning of Morse code.[35] The degree of similarity of the code signals to each other was determined in the following fashion. Each of the 36 signals of the Morse code was paired with each other signal as well as with itself, and each pair of signals was sounded a short interval of time apart. The subjects, none of whom had received training on Morse code, listened to each pair and simply stated whether the two signals they heard were the same or different. The assumption behind this technique is that if two objectively different physical events are called the same, this is what we mean by psychological similarity. A similarity score for each code signal was derived by averaging the percentage of times it was confused with any of the other 35 code sounds. The experimenter found that though all the sounds were occasionally confused with others in the list, there were some that were confused fairly often and some that were confused infrequently.

Next the experimenter examined the errors that were made by a group of students who were actually learning the Morse code to see if there was any relationship between speed of learning a particular item and its similarity score. The answer was strongly positive; the sounds which were high in similarity to the other sounds were the most difficult to learn, those which were low in similarity were the least difficult.

Although no attempt will be made to give a rigorous explanation of why similarity of the stimuli within a task creates difficulty in learning the task, the thoughtful student will probably note that the underlying mechanism responsible for this difficulty is stimulus generalization. He will recall that this concept states that if a particular stimulus acquires a tendency to elicit a particular response, similar stimuli will elicit the same response. If there are similar stimuli which require a different response in the same task, then a conflict between these different response tendencies will ensue and errors will be made. All these tendencies will sum up to make for difficulty in learning the total task.

Discriminability among task responses

Just as the concept of stimulus generalization enables us to make certain predictions about task difficulty, so also does the concept of response generalization. If the task is one which requires that highly similar though different responses be given to the various stimuli, then response generalization will probably occur and produce errors.[36] It will produce errors because when a particular response is evoked and reinforced there results an increased tendency to give other, similar responses to the same stimulus. When these similar responses occur, they are, of course, errors. If, on the other hand, the responses of the task differ widely from each other, much less of this interference will result.[37]

Meaningfulness

The rate of learning is not the same for a list of nonsense syllables and for a list of disconnected nouns. The learning of the nouns is far more rapid, and passages of prose and poetry are learned with even greater ease. The psychologist knows this, of course, but is likely to be discontent with the simple statement that meaningful material is learned more rapidly than is meaningless. He is likely to ask why this is so and what is meant by the term "meaningful." Neither of these questions can be answered in full at present, but some partial answers are available.

One answer is provided by considering how we compare the amount of meaningless and meaningful material that is to be

learned. We can illustrate this by an example. Suppose we compare
the rate of learning five words forming a meaningful sentence and
five words that form no sentence. The first might be "I heard the
dog bark" and the second "Closed, chair, lake, nose, bark." Consider only the last word in each list, "bark." If the sentence had
stopped after the word "dog" and the subject were asked to supply
the next word, there is a high probability that he would have supplied the right word, but this would not be very likely if the disconnected list were being used. In one case the subject has already
learned, through much past experience, part of the list; and in the
other he has not. Despite the fact that both lists contain five items,
there is really more to be learned in the meaningless than in the
meaningful list. So long as we compare the learning of meaningful
and meaningless lists of the same number of units, there will be a
vast difference in the rate of learning of the two. However, if a
technique is employed which equates the amount of new learning
required of the meaningful and of the meaningless material the
difference in rate of learning is decreased.

A different approach to the problem is concerned with an
effort to determine some of the psychological characteristics of
meaningfulness. One experimenter has suggested that degree of
meaningfulness of a word is directly related to the number of
associations we connect with that word.[38] He therefore presented
various words to subjects and counted the number of associations
they gave to each word in a short, constant period of time. Then
he made out a list of words that had many associations to them
and a list of words with fewer associations and compared the speed
with which these lists were learned by a new group of subjects. The
list composed of words with high association value was learned
with less difficulty that the one with low association value, despite
the fact that the words in each were meaningful to the subjects.
This experiment indirectly suggests that one of the bases for the
idea of meaning is ease and frequency of associations.

The statement that ease of learning is related to meaningfulness undoubtedly comes as no surprise to the reader, but he may
also feel that it is a generalization of no great value to him. If he
is required to learn material that has no meaning for him, what
can he do but struggle? It is probable, however, that many times
he learns materials as if they were nonsense passages, when with a
little effort he could give them meaning. As a result of this effort,

they would become easier to learn. Many times in his college text-books he will encounter materials which he must learn but which seem at first glance to be without meaning. Careful consideration may show that these concepts can be given meaning by associating them with events within his own past experiences and they can then be learned more easily. The good teacher tries to make his materials meaningful, and the good students seek to find meaning in them.

The interrelationship of task and procedural variables

In the section in which the notion of analyzing complex learning activities into task and procedural variables was introduced, it was mentioned in passing that the two kinds of variables cannot be viewed as completely independent of each other. The implication behind this analysis is that procedural variables may be modified at will by the experimenter or teacher, while task variables are inherent in the task itself. In actuality, procedural variables are sometimes inherent in the task itself and contribute to its characteristics; and there are also instances when task variables may be modified without changing the essential purpose of the activity.

That procedural variables may be implicit in the task and vary from task to task is suggested by the following experiment, where the variable of knowledge of results was shown to be different for two components of a single task.[39] The task was aiming a gunsight of the kind used by aerial gunners of World War II. To operate the sight properly, the gunner must keep a small point of light in the center of the sight on the nose of the target plane. That is, he must track the target. In addition to this he must adjust a knob which regulates the diameter of a circle outlined by several diamond-shaped points of light. This is called ranging. The task is performed properly when the center of the circle is on the nose of the plane and the circumference just spans the wing tips. The gunner's task can be imitated on the ground by using the gunsight with a movie screen on which an attacking plane is projected. This device is called a synthetic trainer, and by means of linkages it can be made to indicate when the gunner is tracking and ranging properly.

Characteristically, the subjects were able to track with precision, but ranging errors were rather large. The psychological

mechanism responsible for this seemed to be the difference between
the knowledge of results available in the two activities. It was not
difficult to judge when the single center spot was superimposed on
the nose of the plane, but it was difficult to judge when the
diameter of the broken circle exactly spanned the wings. The training device was then equipped with a red filter which could be
dropped in front of the projector beam when the subject was performing correctly in both parts of his task—thus giving an immediate knowledge of results. One group of subjects was given five
practice periods with this knowledge of results added, while the
control group practiced without it. On the sixth day neither group
was given this aid. The results of this experiment are shown in
Fig. 3.20. Clearly the added knowledge of results facilitated the

Fig. 3.20 The effect of experimentally supplied knowledge of performance on the operation of a gun sight. (After Seashore *et al.*[39])

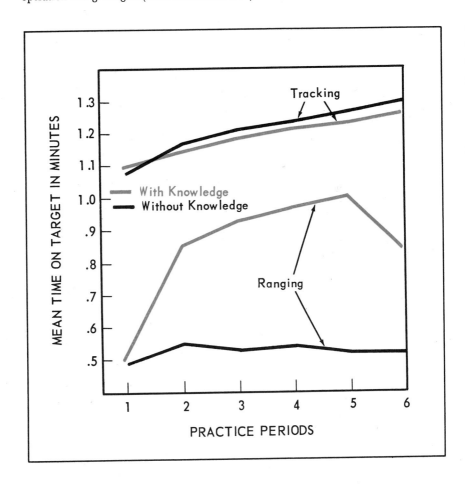

ranging aspect of the total tasks and had no effect upon the tracking. The obvious reason for this is that adequate knowledge of results was implicit in one aspect of the task, but not in the other.

This experiment indicates how an important learning variable may be implicit in a task and may differ for the two aspects of the task. In the present instance some ingenuity made it possible to reduce the detrimental effect of the variable. It must be obvious that this and other procedural variables are imbedded in the very nature of different tasks, sometimes in such a way that they can be modified, but in other instances in such a way that they cannot be.

Although task variables were described as being implicit characteristics of the task, it is often possible to change these variables without changing the essential nature or purpose of the task. A task may be difficult because of similarity among the stimuli of the task. In some instances it is possible to modify these stimuli so as to make them more discriminable. This results in an easier task, but one whose purpose is unchanged. Or, on the response side, means may be found to eliminate responses that are difficult to learn. Thus an automatic gear shift eases the task of the driver, but the automobile serves its same purpose.

Organismic variables

At the beginning of this section it was stated that the rate of learning was a function of the *procedure used*, the *nature of the task*, and the *abilities of the organism*. The first two of these factors have now been discussed, and so the third should be expected to follow. Unfortunately this tidy organization cannot be followed, for to explain completely how the characteristics of the learner affect the rate of acquisition, we must introduce more concepts, and we will turn to them in the following chapter.

REFERENCES

[1] Pavlov, I. P. *Conditioned Reflexes* (trans. G. U. Anrep.) Oxford, 1927.

[2] Young, F. A. An attempt to obtain pupillary conditioning with infrared photography, *J. exper. Psychol.*, 1954, *48*, 62-68.

[3] Zeaman, D., and Wegner N. The role of drive reduction in the classical conditioning of an autonomically mediated response, *J. exper. Psychol.*, 1954, *48*, 349-354.

[4] Staats, C. K., and Staats, A. W. Meaning established by classical conditioning, *J. exper. Psychol.*, 1957, *54*, 74-80.

[5] Wickens, D. D., Gehman, R. S., and Sullivan, S. N. The effect of

differential onset time on the conditioned response strength to elements of a stimulus complex, *J. exper. Psychol.*, 1958, *59*, 85-93.

[6] Hovland, C. I. The generalization of conditioned responses: I. The sensory generalization of conditioned responses with varying frequencies of tone, *J. Gen. Psychol.*, 1937, *17*, 279-291.

[7] Wickens, D. D., Schroder, H. M., and Snide, J. D. Primary stimulus generalization of the GSR under two conditions, *J. exper. Psychol.*, 1954, *47*, 52-56.

[8] Razran, G. H. S. Stimulus generalization of conditioned response, *Psychol. Bull.*, 1949, *46*, 337-365.

[9] Reiss, B. F. Genetic changes in semantic conditioning, *J. exper. Psychol.*, 1946, *36*, 143-152.

[10] Bekhterev, V. M. *General Principles of Human Reflexology*, International, 1932, p. 467.

[11] Wickens, D. D. The transference of conditioned excitation and conditioned inhibition from one muscle group to the antagonistic muscle group, *J. exper. Psychol.*, 1938, *22*, 101-123.

[12] Brogden, W. J. The effect of frequency of reinforcement upon the level of conditioning, *J. exper. Psychol.*, 1939, *14*, 419-431.

[13] Denny, M. R. One bar press per day: Acquisition and extinction, *J. exper. anal. Beh.*, 1959, *2*, 81-85.

[14] Brogden, W. J. Unconditioned stimulus substitution in the conditioning process, *Amer. J. Psychol.*, 1939, *52*, 46-55.

[15] Brogden, W. J., Lipman, E. A., and Culler, Elmer. The role of incentive in conditioning and extinction, *Amer. J. Psychol.*, 1938, *51*, 109-117.

[16] Kellog, W. N., and Wolf, I. S. The nature of the response retained after several varieties of conditioning in the same subject, *J. exper. Psychol.*, 1939, *24*, 366-383.

[17] Humphreys, L. G. The effect of random alteration of reinforcement on the acquisition and extinction of conditioned eye lid reactions, *J. exper. Psychol.*, 1939, *25*, 141-158.

[18] Hilgard, E. R., and Humphreys, L. C. The effect of supporting and antagonistic voluntary instructions on conditioned discrimination, *J. exper. Psychol.*, 1938, *22*, 291-304.

[19] Harlow, H. F. Experimental analysis of the role of the original stimulus in conditioned responses in monkeys, *Psychol. Record*, 1937, *1*, 62-68.

[20] Verplank, W. S. The control of the content of conversation: Reinforcement of statements of opinion, *J. Abn. Soc. Psychol.*, 1955, *51*, 668-676.

[21] Youtz, R. E. P. Reinforcement, extinction, and spontaneous recovery of a non-Pavlovian reaction, *J. exper. Psychol.*, 1938, *22*, 305-318.

[22] Mednick, S. A., and Lehtinen, L. E. Stimulus generalization as a function of age in children, *J. exper. Psychol.*, 1957, *53*, 180-183.

[23] Underwood, B. J., and Hughes, R. H. Gradients of generalized verbal responses, *Amer. J. Psychol.*, 1950, *63*, 422-430.

[24] Bryan, W. L., and Harter, N. Studies in the physiology and psychology of the telegraphic language, *Psychol. Review*, 1897, *4*, 27-53.

[25] Grice, R. G. The relation of secondary reinforcement to delayed reward in visual discrimination learning, *J. exper. Psychol.*, 1948, *38*, 1-16.

[26] Bilodeau, E. A., and Bilodeau, I. McD. Variable frequence of knowledge of results and the learning of a simple skill, *J. exper. Psychol.*, 1958, *55*, 379-383.

27 Gates, A. I. Recitation as a factor in memorizing. *Arch. of Psychol.*, 1917, *6*, No. 4.

28 Simons, C. W. Responses to materials presented during various levels of sleep, *J. exper. Psychol.*, 1956, *51*, 89-97.

29 Kimble, G. A. Performance and reminiscence in motor learning as a function of the degree of distribution of practice, *J. exper. Psychol.*, 1949, *39*, 500-510.

30 Reynolds, B., and Bilodeau, I. McD. Acquisition and retention of three psychomotor tasks as a function of distribution of practice during acquisition, *J. exper. Psychol.*, 1952, *44*, 19-26.

31 Underwood, B. J., and Richardson, J. Studies of distributed practice: XIII. Interlist interference and the retention of serial nonsense lists, *J. exper. Psychol.*, 1955, *50*, 39-46.

32 McGeoch, J. A., and Irion, A. L. *The Psychology of Human Learning*, Longmans, 1952.

33 Carr. H. Teaching and learning, *J. Gen. Psychol.*, 1930, *37*, 189-219.

34 Hovland, C. I. Experimental studies in rote learning theory: III. Distribution of practice with varying speeds of syllable presentation, *J. exper. Psychol.*, 1938, *23*, 172-190.

35 Rothkopf, E. Z. A measure of stimulus similarity and errors in some paired-associate learning tasks, *J. exper. Psychol.*, 1957, *53*, 94-101.

36 Noble, M. E., and Bahrick, H. P. Response generalization as a function of intra-task response similarity, *J. exper. Psychol.*, 1956, *51*, 405-412.

37 Underwood, B. J. Studies of distributed practice: IX. Learning and retention of paired adjectives as a function of intra-list similarity, *J. exper. Psychol.*, 1953, *45*, 143-149.

38 Noble, C. E., and McNeely, D. A. The role of meaningfulness (*m*) in paired-associate learning, *J. exper. Psychol.*, 1957, *53*, 16-22.

39 Seashore, R. H., Underwood, B. J., Houston, R., and Berks, L. The influence of knowledge of results on performance. Cited in Underwood, B. J., *Experimental Psychology*, Appleton, 1949, p. 415.

Chapter
Four

THE
UTILIZATION
OF
LEARNING

IN A BROAD SENSE, THE SIGNIFICANCE
of learning is not so much that new stimulus → response connections are *formed* as that these connections are *available to be
utilized at some later date.* To a greater or less extent, the stimulus
→ response connections that we acquire today will be utilized—
for good or ill—tomorrow.

Institutes of learning represent a formalization of this fact.
Our grade-school system is maintained not to produce learning for
its own sake or to keep young children out of mischief but to develop habits that may be utilized for the learner's and society's
own good at some later date. Purposefulness is so closely associated
with learning that the college student may lose all interest in a
course or in some of its subject matter if it seems to lack potentiali-
ties for later use.

We do not, of course, learn only because we intend to make use of this learning at some later date. We learn because we are placed in a situation that is favorable to the formation of new stimulus → response connections; the intention, or even the possibility, of future use is not necessary. This is especially true of our personality characteristics. As young children we hit upon ways of adjusting to social and work situations; we may fixate these responses, and they may be used again and again. As adults we may be dissatisfied with what we have learned and we may spend a considerable amount of time and money in an effort to unlearn those responses and acquire new ones. Other different responses are acquired just as we acquire personality characteristics; they are fixated because of the momentary situation and not because of a hope that they will be of some value in the future.

Many things that we learn today will help us in our future efforts to adjust; others will be of little value to us one way or another; still others may prove a hindrance to us in the future. Whether or not what we learn will be profitable to us will depend upon the nature of this later situation. The word *potential* implies not only that these habits *can* be used later but also that they *may not* be used. It is the purpose of the present chapter to consider some of the reasons why stimulus → response connections are either not utilized at a later time or are less strong at the later period than they were immediately after the learning period.

There are three basic general conditions—*motivation, transfer* and *forgetting*—that determine whether or not a previously acquired habit will be utilized later. We shall discuss the relationship between the first of these—motivation—and habit utilization in Chapter 5; for the present we shall merely point out that the kind of motive condition that is operating tends to select the class of instrumental responses that may be utilized.

The presence of appropriate motivation is not, however, sufficient. Because of certain events usually associated with the passage of time, losses occur in the ability to utilize habits formed previously. This decrement in retention we call *forgetting,* and in a later section of this chapter we shall concern ourselves with the conditions that influence forgetting.

Lowered efficiency of habit utilization also arises from the fact that the stimulus situation of the present is different from the stimulus situation in which the habit was originally learned. This difference between the learning and the utilization situations is

not an accidental one, for we often train under one situation with
the expectation that if the habits which are learned are ever called
into use it will be in a different situation. Thus, the soldier learns
his skills in a camp in which no gun is fired at him in anger, though
he is expected to use this training in situations in which he is an
intended target; good manners are taught to the child so that he
will be polite not merely at home but elsewhere; and the college
student learns a variety of things which, it is hoped, will make him
a more effective and happier person in a world which differs greatly
from the halls of academia. The term used by the psychologist to
refer to the utilization of old habits in later modified stimulus
situations is *transfer of training*.

In ordinary circumstances, it is extremely difficult to separate two conditions that affect habit utilization: the passage of
time—associated with forgetting—and the modification of the
stimulus situation—associated with transfer. You may learn a poem
in the solitude of your room; the next day you may be asked to
recite it in a crowded classroom. The stimulus situation is slightly
different in the classroom from what it was in your own room and,
of course, it occurs some hours after the learning. In actuality we
deal not with an all-or-none alternative of either change or no-
change in the stimulus situation but with changes of greater or
lesser degree. Sometimes the changes are so minor that we may
disregard them; at other times they are great and have a most
significant effect upon our behavior.

In the second section of this chapter we shall deal with the
phenomenon of forgetting and shall attempt to identify the factors
that are responsible for the loss of retention associated with the
passage of time. In the immediately following section, we shall
investigate the topic of *transfer of training*.

TRANSFER OF TRAINING

Learning, as we have stated earlier, is a modification of our
response to a stimulus or to a configuration of stimuli. After a
course in French, we respond to the pattern *chien* with the English
equivalent *dog* and all that this word implies; after a few trials as
subjects in a memorizing experiment, we may react to the first
nonsense syllable by calling out the second; after a spanking, the

115

child may no longer reach for the fragile vase on the mantelpiece; and after a number of trials in a maze, the rat turns promptly to the right at a certain junction and reaches food. Thus, our responses to certain specific stimuli have become changed.

From a practical point of view, we are concerned with more than modification of responses *in a specific situation;* we are concerned also with the potential modification of responses in a stimulus situation *that is changed to a greater or less degree.* Suppose that we are confronted with a situation involving French people rather than the French language. Will the modification of responses we have learned in the *language* situation be carried over to the *social* situation? If we have enjoyed the language course, will we also like the French people? Will memorizing a list of nonsense syllables enable us to learn better other lists of syllables, or telephone numbers, or the meanings of new words, or the names of new acquaintances? Will the child who has learned to avoid the delicate vase show avoidance of other family knicknacks? Has the rat learned to behave efficiently in mazes in general or has he learned only to make a right turn at a certain point in the maze?

These specific questions may be summarized in a more general form: Will the response learned in one stimulus situation be carried over to new stimulus situations; or, to be more technical, will transfer of training occur?

All of us are aware that our reactions to a new situation are colored by the nature of our previous learning. The student who has a knowledge of one foreign language will react to the learning of another differently from the student who has never before studied a foreign language; skill in badminton will be attained more rapidly by the tennis player than by the novice who has never held a racket in his hand; those whose early learning was acquired in the culture south of the Mason-Dixon line will react differently to many new social situations from those who were reared in the state of Maine.

But the simple statement that previous learning will effect our responses in a new situation is far too general to suffice for a science. *All* of our past learning is not brought to bear in each new situation. The fact that we learned algebra in high school will probably be of no significance to us when we learn to drive an automobile, though it is very likely to effect our performance in college chemistry. Will the algebra, however, aid us in dealing with any type of material that requires a logical approach? The answer to this question involves considerable research.

The utilization of previous learning in later learning situations—that is, the *transfer of training*—is a subject of immense educational significance. Because it is impossible to predict exactly the situation that will confront a student at a later date, good educational training attempts to teach materials that can transfer widely to a number of situations. We are taught that $5 + 5 = 10$ with the expectation that at a later date we shall be able to apply this same relationship to apples, acres, thumbtacks, miles, and money. We are taught how conditioned responses can be developed in dogs with the hope that we shall comprehend this as a principle of learning that can be applied to new situations, involving ourselves, our friends, or our children. All of us feel that some activities influence the learning of some later activities but not of others, and this is certainly true. The psychologist must attempt to predict which will occur.

The method of testing for transfer

Adequate concepts for the prediction of transfer of training cannot be derived from even fairly systematic observations of behavior in a free life situation. They can be developed only as a consequence of careful experimentation directed towards the end of formulating these concepts. Several different methods for the measurement of transfer of training have been developed, and they are applicable either to laboratory activities or to learning situations in the world at large. There are certain advantages and disadvantages inherent in each of these methods, but it will be sufficient for our purpose to describe only one of these.

This experimental design, devised to measure transfer of training, is shown in the table below. The experimenter is interested in the speed with which Activity B is learned by the two groups. If the subjects are selected with some care and in suf-

	STEP I	STEP II
Experimental Group	Training on Activity A	Learning of Activity B
Control Group	No Training	Learning of Activity B

ficient numbers, we may assume that the two groups are identical in the basic ability to learn and in past experiences that might help

117

or hinder their learning of Activity *B*. Then, if the two groups differ in the rate of learning Activity *B*, the difference must be attributed to the fact that the experimental group had previously learned Activity *A* whereas the control group had not. Obviously, we can use the magnitude of the difference between the two groups in the rate of learning of Activity *B* as a measure of the extent to which the experiences gained in Activity *A* can be utilized for the learning of *B*. Thus, we could discover how much the study of Latin aided in the learning of French by selecting Latin as Activity *A* and French as *B*. If Activity *B* were trigonometry, we could measure the effect of learning Latin upon learning trigonometry. Activities *A* and *B* can, of course, be anything we choose. Although the design is a simple one, it is adaptable to a large variety of materials.

The factors resulting in transfer

The problem for the psychologist only begins with the statement that transfer takes place. His principal task is to predict the degree of transfer that is likely to take place between one specific task and another. In attempting to make such a prediction, he must consider the following factors which influence transfer.

Retention

It is obvious that there must be some retention, however small, of the learning in the first situation if it is to affect a later learning activity. This is basic to the entire problem, for if the transferable material of the first activity has been completely forgotten, it cannot possibly affect later learning. This topic will be discussed in detail in the latter portions of the present chapter.

Experience with the stimulus

In the previous chapter, in the section on Task Variables, it was pointed out that the ease of learning a task is a function of the degree of discriminability of the stimuli of the task. If discriminability of the stimuli is poor, the learning is difficult and, other things equal, good discriminability is associated with easy learning. This fact would lead to the prediction that if one were ultimately to be required to attach a number of different responses each to a particular stimulus, then prior practice in discriminating the stimuli to be used would facilitate the learning of the ultimate task. This prediction is confirmed in the following experiment.[1]

Fig. 4.1 In this learning situation, the transfer of training is high enough to justify the expense of the complicated equipment involved. Student drivers seated at simulated automobile steering wheels learn to respond to the constantly changing traffic situations projected on the motion-picture screen. Each response is recorded so that the student can evaluate his own performance. The first part of the total learning task thus takes place in the safety of the classroom, and the transfer of training permits the learner to handle the real automobile adequately. (Courtesy Aetna Casualty and Surety Co.)

The eventual task to be learned consisted of moving a stick in one of six directions when a small window was illuminated. On any given trial, the window was illuminated with one of six different colors, and the subject was required to make a different response to each of the different colors and to do so as rapidly as possible. The six hues ranged from red through yellow. Prior to practice on the task itself, the experimental groups were given training in discriminating the colors. During this session each color appeared in the window, and four seconds later a letter appeared next to it. The subject attempted to learn what letter was associated with each color. A number of these stimulus-discrimination training trials were given. The control groups received the same kind of experience except that the hues which were presented to them during the period were in the blue-green range. In other words, they were given practice in discrimination, but not practice in discriminating among the stimuli which were to be used in the final task. Immediately following the end of the *discrimination training* session, both groups then practiced the perceptual-motor task of moving the stick into the appropriate slot in response to the flashing of the six red-to-yellow stimuli.

The performance of the two groups during the learning of the perceptual motor tasks is presented in Figure 4.2. The graph indicates the number of correct responses and the errors made by both groups for successive blocks of four 20-second trials. The curves for the experimental group are plotted in red, and those for the control group in black. It is apparent that, as measured both by the number of errors committed and by the number of correct responses made, the experimental group excels the control

Fig. 4.2 The effect of pretraining with the task stimuli on performance in a perceptual motor task. (After Cantor[1])

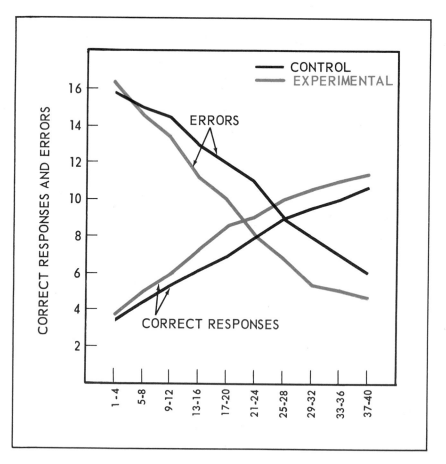

group. Obviously, training in discriminating the particular stimuli that are to be used as cues for particular responses makes it easier to learn those responses. This we have predicted from our knowledge of the importance of discriminability among stimuli as a task variable. This experiment adds further to our knowledge of discriminability and the learning process by showing that degree of discriminability is not solely determined by the nature of the physical stimuli but is determined also by our experience with these stimuli.

Experience with the response

The procedure implied by the title of this section is the inverse of that of the preceding section. Again the ultimate task may be to attach a number of different responses to different stimuli. Will practice with the eventual responses in absence of the appropriate eventual stimuli facilitate the learning of the ultimate task? The answer is that it will do so.[2]

This fact is rather interestingly illustrated in an experiment in which subjects read over a list of words four times and then recalled as many words as they could.[3] There were four groups of subjects and each group read a different list. The words for each list were chosen from *The Teachers' Word Book of 30,000 Words.* This is a book that gives an estimate of the frequency with which each word is used in our culture. Each list was composed by selecting words with different frequency of use, from relatively infrequent to relatively frequent. In Table 4.1 a sample of words from each list is shown, along with the estimated frequency of the words in the list. The average number of words correctly reproduced by the subjects is shown at the bottom of each column.

TABLE 4.1

	Frequency of use per million words			
	1	10	30	50 to 100
Samples from lists	winsome outcrop saddler foolery bagpipe	astound discord positive forlorn esquire	upright immense revenge chimney earnest	forward because destroy special against
Average number remembered	12.04	13.31	15.02	15.04

It is apparent that the amount which is learned from the same length of exposure is related to the degree of familiarity of the words. We can account for this result by reference to the concept of degree of practice with the responses.

Nature of the stimulus-response associations in the two situations

The examples which have been given of stimulus training and response training indicate that training of this nature facilitates the learning of some later activity which employs these stimuli or these responses. We refer to this facilitation as an example of *positive transfer effect*. In instances wherein the prior learning interferes with the performance in the later situation, the term *negative transfer effect* is employed. Lastly, if the earlier learning neither facilitates nor interferes with performance in the later task, we speak of *zero transfer effects*.

It seems very probable that the kind of stimulus training and response training described in the two previous sections will always result in positive transfer effects. That is, they will do so if the two situations employ the same stimuli or the same responses. However, to account for negative transfer effects as well as much of the positive transfer effects to be found in many situations, it is necessary to consider the nature of the stimulus → response associations in the two situations. It is apparent that the relationships of the S-R associations in the two situations may vary widely. The two situations may employ similar stimuli and these stimuli may require responses that are the same, or antagonistic to each other, or neutral to each other. Any variation of degree of similarity of stimuli in the two situations and degree of compatibility of responses to these stimuli is possible. The nature of these relationships will determine the nature of the transfer effects that are obtained.[4]

The direction of transfer

Positive transfer effects

If the stimuli are similar in the new and the old situations and if the responses appropriate in one situation are also appropriate in the other, the transfer effects will be positive. An experienced driver does not need to learn to drive all over again when he buys another make of car. The stimuli afforded by one make

of car are highly similar to those afforded by another, and so also
are the responses required to control the two cars.

This utilization of previously appropriate responses in similar situations is not limited to motor skills. In the social sphere, we
frequently use previously learned techniques or general ways of
reacting in new social settings. In our intellectual life we solve
new problems by using methods and rules that have been successful in other problem-solving situations. The reader will be able
to think of many other instances in which positive transfer has
occurred and previously learned reactions have come to his aid.

Negative transfer effects

Negative transfer effects will occur if in a new situation we
are required to make a response that is antagonistic to the response
previously made to a similar stimulus. It was, for example, noted
during World War II, that a number of accidents occurred during
the landing of a certain type of intermediate training plane. After
investigation, the cause was attributed to the fact that the throttle
on this plane worked in exactly the opposite direction from that
on the primary training planes. In this new situation, past habits
clashed with the execution of the proper response.

Almost all of us have encountered at one time or another an
individual who came from a different social background and who
was forever saying or doing the "wrong" thing. What he had
learned to do or say in one cultural environment interfered with
his adjustment in the new environment. Sometimes a student finds
that he does not do well in a course because in a previous course
quite different answers (responses) were required for similar questions (stimuli). Some students face a difficulty in their psychology
courses because they have learned earlier to "explain" behavior
by such concepts as "mind" or "will," whereas in psychology they
are obliged to think quite differently about behavior.

The two kinds of transfer effects—positive and negative—
sometimes work together in very complicated fashion. Indeed,
both may be operating simultaneously. Frequently, the student
who has learned French in high school and who takes Spanish in
college may experience difficulty in learning the Spanish equivalent of an English word because the French equivalent is recalled.
He may also, however, find it easy to adjust to attaching masculine
or feminine articles to the Spanish nouns because he has learned
to do so in French. This is positive transfer. Or again, if he is a

tennis player and takes up badminton, he will obtain positive transfer effects from such previously acquired skills as handling a racquet and coordinating his movements, and from his knowledge about court strategy. But he will also show some negative transfer effects because in tennis the wrist is held relatively rigid and in badminton it is used extensively.

Zero transfer effects

The conditions which lead to zero transfer effects—that is, effects of previous learning which provide neither facilitation nor retardation in the later situation—are several in nature. If the stimuli of the first and second situations are utterly dissimilar, there will be no transfer, since there will be no tendency for the stimuli in the second situation to evoke the responses that have been learned in the earlier task. That is, no stimulus generalization will occur from the first to the second situation.

Nevertheless, zero transfer effects can result even if the stimuli of the second situation are capable of calling forth the responses acquired during the prior learning. This will be true if the responses of the first task are of no relevance to performance in the second situation. Perhaps this general statement can be clarified by an example: The driver of a car with a conventional gear shift reacts to a stimulus which he interprets as requiring a full stop by pressing downward firmly with both feet. The right foot depresses the brake pedal and the left the clutch pedal. Both must be operated if the car is to be stopped without stalling the motor. For our purposes, let us consider the response of the right and left foot as being independent of each other, as they certainly are in many driving situations. When this driver transfers to a car with an automatic shift, it is most probable that he will react to the same stimulus event by the same two leg responses. While the right leg extension will produce the desired brake result, the response of the left leg will not influence the action of the car. It is a response that has no relevance to performance in the second situation; whether it occurs or whether it does not occur is immaterial. The effect of this response is, in short, zero.

In summary, then, there are two basic causes of zero transfer effect. One is that the responses of one situation have no relevance to the responses of the other situation. The second reason lies in the fact that, as a result of the dissimilarity of the stimuli in the two situations, there is no tendency for the stimulus-attached responses in one situation to be evoked by the stimuli of the next one.

The latter reason is of considerable concern to the educator, be he teacher, parent, or friend. Similarity of stimuli is not solely a matter of physical similarity, it is also a matter of the individual's capacity to perceive similarities among complicated stimuli. The training for effective transfer, therefore, must often follow two courses. One is to establish firmly the appropriate response to the appropriate stimulus. The other is to achieve in the subject a structuring or ordering of stimulus situations such that the relevant stimulus will be reacted to as similar to the training stimulus even if it occurs in a different context and is obscured by other, competing stimuli. Undoubtedly the justified charge that a particular course or program of instruction is "impractical" results from its failure to produce positive transfer effects in some presumably appropriate real life situation. But this "impracticality" may not arise from a failure to teach the correct responses to the appropriate stimuli but from failure to train the student to recognize these stimuli when they are imbedded in other materials.

Learning to learn

The reader's own experience and the data of experimental psychology make it clear that we profit from our past experience, but few of us realize how much we profit and to what extent our present competences depend upon our past learnings. Let us illustrate this point with the findings of an experiment in which monkeys were taught to discover food in a well hidden under one of two objects.[5] A sketch of the apparatus is shown in Figure 4.3. The stimulus tray contains two small food wells, one on the right and one on the left. While an opaque screen is dropped in front of the monkey so that he cannot observe the experimenter, food is placed in one well, and each well is then covered with a different object—such as a plywood triangle and a circle, or a cookie cutter and a match box. The screen is lifted and the monkey tries to find the food. If he picks up the correct object, the reward is his, but if he picks up the wrong object, the tray is withdrawn. In either case the opaque screen is dropped and the tray reloaded for another trial. On each trial the same object is placed over the food, though the food is placed sometimes in the right well of the tray and sometimes in the left one. After each six trials, the experimenter selects a new pair of objects to use, until many, many problems—

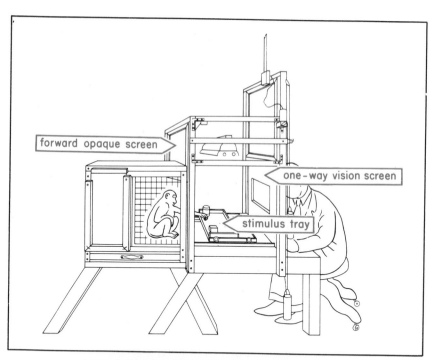

forward opaque screen

one-way vision screen

stimulus tray

Fig. 4.3 The development of learning sets in monkeys. The line drawing shows the apparatus as a whole. The two photographs at the right show the stimulus objects that conceal the food—first at the monkey's left, then at his right. His correct choice depends upon the *shape* and not the *position* of the stimulus object. In the photograph below, the monkey is being presented with a new set of stimulus objects. (Courtesy Harry F. Harlow)

if we can call each new pair of objects a problem—are presented to the monkey.

Now, since each problem uses a new and different set of stimulus objects, and since the correct one in one problem is not necessarily similar to the correct one in the next problem, any improvement from problem to problem may be considered as a general increase in ability to learn in this situation. That such is the case is shown by the curve presented in Figure 4.4. The solid curve shows how the animals performed on each trial during the first eight problems; the curve with short dashes shows performance during problems 25 through 32; the curve with long dashes, during problems 257 through 312. All these curves begin at 50 percent correct responses on the first trial, and this is what is to be expected through chance alone. On the first trial for each problem, the stimulus objects are new, and the animal must guess; half the time

Fig. 4.4 The performances of monkeys on successive sets of discrimination problems. (After Harlow[5])

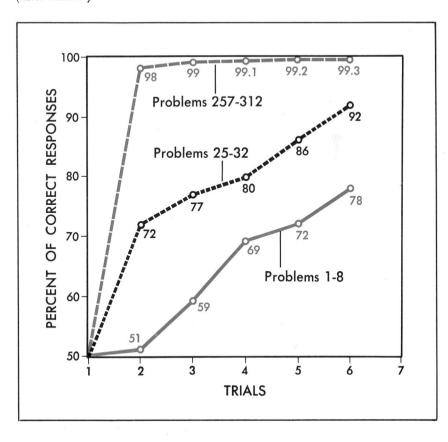

he will guess correctly and half the time incorrectly. A striking difference among the three curves is the level of performance on the second trial. It is on this trial that the animals have an opportunity to make use of the information they obtained from the first trial. The animals change from profiting very little from this single trial in problems 1 through 8 to gaining almost a maximum of information in problems 257 through 312. Clearly the animals are learning how to learn.

A number of other studies with different kinds of subjects and different kinds of materials have corroborated these findings. During the learning of a specific habit, we also learn somewhat more general habits that come into play when we are confronted with a "new" but similar learning situation. These general habits ordinarily support learning in the new task and make for a more rapid rate of learning (see Fig. 4.5).

In the days before experimental psychology the belief was commonly held that the individual possessed certain traits, or faculties, such as Memory, Logical Thought, Concentration, and many others, and that these faculties could, like the muscles of the body, be developed by exercise. Such a view would have explained the results of the experiments we have described on the grounds of

Fig. 4.5 Learning to learn. Twenty different lists of 12 nonsense syllables were presented to a group of college students on 20 successive days. The graph shows their gradual improvement in ability to reproduce the lists even though each of the lists was made up of different syllables. (From Meyer and Miles, *J. exper. Psych.*, 1953, *45*, 109-115)

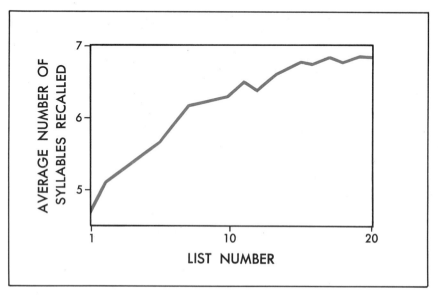

improvement of the faculty of Memory. But numerous experiments in the early days of laboratory psychology failed to support the hypothesis that there were general traits or faculties that could be trained. Time and again it was shown that transfer did not occur unless there was some similarity between the stimuli or the responses in the new and the old situations.

Perhaps the basis for disproving the existence of the general trait can be made clearer if we invert our way of thinking and ask not why the monkeys in the experiment made correct responses but why they made errors. When the tray is pushed forward to the monkey, he finds two objects—say a triangle and a circle—one to the right and one to the left. Suppose that he chooses the circle, which happens to be on the right, and finds food beneath it. The event gives him no clear-cut information as to whether the food is hereafter to be found under any object covering the food well on the *right side* or whether it is to be found under the *circle* regardless of its location. Since the location of the food is varied randomly from trial to trial, errors will arise if the animals respond to the cue of location rather than the cue of shape of the covering object. An analysis of the data from this type of experiment has indicated that one of the major reasons for improvement was the extinction of a tendency to respond to the cue of location.[6] Other, more complicated error-producing tendencies were also extinguished, but we shall not discuss them. For us the significance of this conclusion —that success involves extinction of responses to location—is that it assigns a quite specific reason for the general improvement other than the development of some faculty called *memory*. It would lead us to predict that, in another task which again called for the suppression of tendencies to respond to location, transfer would be great, but if location did not enter into this task at all, transfer might be much less—a prediction quite different from the one we would have made had we assumed that a general faculty of memory had been developed.

FORGETTING: LOSS WITH THE PASSAGE OF TIME

Most of us have had the uncomfortable experience of being asked the name of a person and—try as we might—not being able to recall it. Then our questioner mentioned five or six names and we immediately recognized one as being correct. Had we forgotten the name or had we not forgotten it? Obviously no simple yes-or-no answer can be given to this question. According to one way of testing our memory, the answer is *yes*, but according to another, it is *no*.

The measurement of forgetting

If we are to make any accurate evaluation of how the passage of time is related to forgetting, it is apparent that we cannot talk about forgetting in general. We must discuss forgetting according to the specific measure we are using. It behooves us, therefore, to consider some of the responses currently measured for the assessment of forgetting. These are: free recall, anticipation, recognition, and relearning.

Recall

In the measurement of free recall, the appropriate stimulus is given and the subjects try to make the previously learned response. For example, the subject may have learned a list of nonsense syllables. The experimenter presents him with the first syllable as the starting signal or stimulus, and he attempts to respond with the remainder of the list. His forgetting is measured by the number of syllables he fails to recall. We may also score him as to whether or not he recalls in the proper sequence.

Anticipation

The measurement of anticipation is a more systematic and controlled variation of the measurement of recall. After a list of nonsense syllables or words has been learned, and a forgetting interval introduced, they are presented one at a time through the aperture of the memory drum. Usually one syllable follows the other by two or more seconds. As the subject learns the list, he tries to anticipate during this two-second interval what the next syllable will be, each syllable except the last serving as stimulus for the next one. We can measure his forgetting by presenting the list to him in proper sequence and counting the number of syllables he anticipates correctly on the first presentation following the forgetting interval. In using this method of measuring forgetting, we duplicate almost exactly the stimulus situation used in the original learning. This measure of forgetting is usually called the recall score, but not the free recall score.

Recognition

Recognition can be measured by scoring the subject's attempts to choose the previously learned response from a group of several responses. The multiple-choice examination is an example of this method.

Relearning

Relearning can be measured by comparing the number of trials required to learn the task originally with the number required to relearn it to the same level of mastery at some later time. Suppose that, to learn a list of nonsense syllables to the criterion of one perfect recitation, the subject required eight presentations. A month later, to relearn the list to this same criterion level, the subject requires six presentations. If we convert the difference to percentages, we say of this subject that he has a *savings score* of 25 percent, since the two presentations saved represent 25 percent of the original number of trials required to learn the list. This savings score reflects, of course, the amount of material retained. Subtracting the 25 percent saved, we may say that the forgetting is 75 percent. This method of measuring forgetting is used commonly, for it is convenient, meaningful, and highly sensitive. It may give evidence for some retention that would not otherwise be apparent.

Comparison of methods

The measurement of each of these aspects will produce somewhat different data on what is forgotten. The greatest loss will be shown by the recall methods, whereas the relearning method and the recognition methods will ordinarily show a smaller loss. We are quite likely to find, for example, that although no single syllable in the nonsense list is correctly anticipated, some saving shows up in the number of trials required to relearn the list. Because these various methods produce different forgetting scores, we must be certain to specify the method used in determining the amount of forgetting that has taken place in any given situation. Obviously only results obtained by the same method are comparable. The choice of method will depend largely upon the nature of the experiment.

The curve of forgetting

Just as we have found that it is impossible to say that a single curve of learning is typical of all learning curves, so it is also impossible to say that a single curve of forgetting is the typical forgetting curve. In general, the forgetting curves, if they are plotted on the basis of relearning or recall, follow somewhat the pattern of the curve shown in Figure 4.6. Forgetting seems to be most rapid immediately following the learning period; progressively it becomes less and less.

It is apparent that the curve could be extended to the right for a great distance without ever reaching the point of 100-percent forgetting. This is in accord with the limited experimental data that are available. One experimenter found that passages of Greek that were read to the subject as an infant were learned more easily 10 years later than new passages that were comparable in difficulty.[7] This is evidence of some retention. Another group of experimenters measured the retention of two kinds of perceptual motor skills over a period of two years.[8] One of these was a tracking task (see p. 108); the other was what is called a procedural task. This task required the subject to perform in sequence fifteen different operations, such as inserting a key, flipping a switch or switches, and

Fig. 4.6 A hypothetical forgetting curve. Time units are not specified because they vary with the nature of the task and other conditions.

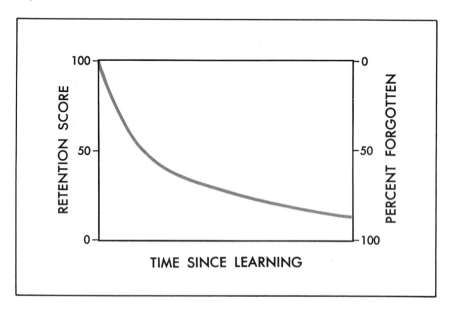

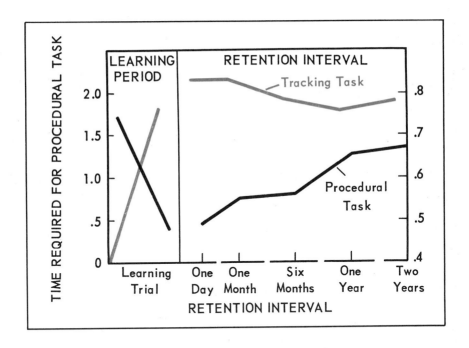

Fig. 4.7 Learning and retention curves for a tracking and a procedural task. A high value on the procedural task and a low value on the tracking task are associated with poorer performances, hence the learning curve rises for one and falls for the other. There is little or no forgetting on the tracking task, whereas the procedural task is forgotten, though performance after two years is still better than performance on the first learning trial. (After Ammons et al.[8])

turning a knob. Performance was measured by the time required to complete the full procedure. Following a relatively brief training period different groups of subjects were tested for retention after various intervals of time. The results are plotted in Figure 4.7. The measure on the Y axis for the tracking task is time on target, and for the procedural task a measure of the speed of performance. The first point on the curve is the score on the first training trial; the next is the score on the last training trial; and the subsequent points indicate the score on the various retention tests. The X axis, it should be noted, is broken after the one-month interval, and again after six months and a year. The reason for this was, of course, to prevent the curve from becoming excessively long. It will be noted that the scores for the first few retention intervals on the tracking task are superior to the performance on the last training trial. This result is not unusual for such tasks and it is a consequence of the same factors that make distributed performance superior to massed performance in motor skill tests. It is apparent that retention of the tracking task is excellent. Forgetting is much greater for the procedural task, but it is not complete even after two years.

This experiment indicated that the effects of a learning period may persist over a long period of time and it has also demonstrated that the rate of forgetting will not be the same for all tasks. This fact points to the need to discover the factors or conditions that influence the rate of forgetting.

It will be noted that no time units have been placed on the horizontal axis of the graph in Figure 4.6, and that only the vague label "Time Since Learning" has been used. This was inevitable, because the time by which, let us say, 50 percent forgetting has occurred varies greatly with a number of factors. For some kinds of material and under certain conditions, it would be 30 minutes; for others it might be 30 days.

FACTORS INFLUENCING FORGETTING

In measuring transfer, we intentionally modify the stimulus from the first to the second situation, and we have learned that the degree to which the stimulus is modified is highly influential in determining the magnitude of transfer. In measuring retention, on the other hand, we are concerned primarily with the influence of the passage of time with no change in the stimulus between its earlier and its later presentation.

Change in the stimulus

Retention is probably always complicated, however, by the fact that the stimuli in the first and second situations are not completely the same. We are often aware of this when, on failing to recall the name of some old friend upon meeting him, we remark that he has changed so much that we did not recognize him. Even when changes in the stimulus are less obvious, they may nevertheless be present. We learn some materials in the quiet of our room and attempt to recall them in some other environment. The general stimulus situations during learning and during recall invariably differ somewhat. The manner in which a change in context or background may influence retention is illustrated in the following experiment.[9]

Four groups of subjects learned a list of nine paired associate terms consisting of a double nonsense-syllable term as the stimulus and a noun as the response. Each paired term was printed on a different colored card. The colored background was considered as the context in which the paired term appears. Twenty-four hours later a recall test was conducted with the conditions of the recall different for various groups. The situation during recall was the same as it was during learning for one group, and the average number of items recalled on the first trial was 7.37. For another group all the items appeared on a gray background; in other words in a changed context. Their recall score was 3.25. For a third group the colored backgrounds remained the same but the stimulus term was changed slightly. For example, the stimulus MOT-FUD became MOT-WID and BIF-JOS became BIF-NES. This group attained a recall score of 5.5. Finally one group was presented with the modified stimuli and the gray background. The recall score for them dropped to an average of 1.37.

In summary, the experiment indicates that recall is depressed not only by a change in what is presumably the major stimulus—the nonsense syllable—but also by a change in the context in which the stimulus occurred. When both of them are changed recall is depressed to an even greater degree. One might be tempted to conclude, on the basis of this experiment, that a change in context is more disturbing than a change in the stimulus itself. This might not have been the case if more distinctive stimuli than nonsense syllables had been employed, and it is safest to conclude only that change in either stimulus or context or both decrease performance in the recall period.

Actually there is very little experimental work dealing specifically with the influence of changes in the general environment on recall, but it is probable that much of our "forgetting" is due to the changes in the stimulus situation between the learning and the recall situations. Thus, some of our loss of efficiency which seems to be associated with the passage of time arises from the fact that there has been a modification of the stimulus situation. The loss is due to the lessening of stimulus generalization between the learning and the retention situations rather than to the passage of time.

Events after and before learning

The amount of forgetting is closely linked to the passage of time. The conscientious student makes a quick review just before the examination so that the time lapse between his study and the test of retention will be minimal. We do not expect to perform well on an activity that we have not practiced for some time; and if we do, we are usually surprised. Time, we say, heals all wounds, and by this we mean that forgetting occurs, our reactions to an unpleasant event becoming less intense with the passage of time.

Because of this close association between the passage of time and the amount of forgetting, it was inevitable that we would try to account for forgetting by the sheer fact of passage of time. This hypothesis was dominant in psychology for many years, but gradually a great deal of experimental evidence has accumulated which has forced us to reject the importance of time in itself as a cause of forgetting. Let us consider some of this evidence.

Retroactive inhibition

One item of evidence is based upon an experiment in which the curve of forgetting of nonsense material was measured under two different conditions.[10] Under one condition, the subjects went to sleep immediately after learning; under the other the subjects continued with their daily activities—activities characteristic of the working day of a college student. These curves are presented in Figure 4.8. For the identical time interval, the amount of material forgotten is greater after wakeful activity condition than after sleep. If the sheer passage of time alone were responsible for our forgetting, this difference could not have been obtained. It is apparent, therefore, that what one does after learning has a considerable influence on how much and how rapidly one forgets.

This influence of later activities upon the retention of previously learned activities is called *retroactive inhibition*. The word *inhibition* is used because the retention of the previously learned material is decreased or inhibited; *retroactive* is used because the inhibition seems to work backward to affect previously learned material. Various experimental studies on the topic of retroactive inhibition have given us a considerable understanding of the process of forgetting.

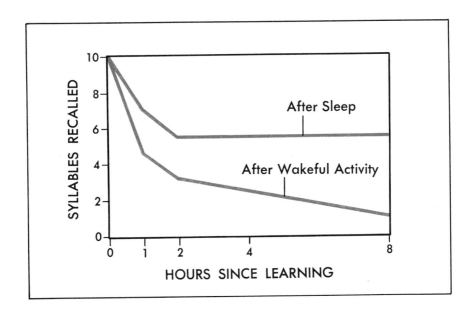

Fig. 4.8 The effect of sleep on retention of learning. (After Jenkins and Dellenbach[10])

Conditions influencing the amount of retroaction

Because a considerable amount of experimental work has been conducted on the problems of retroactive inhibition, we are able to identify many of the conditions influencing the amount of retroactive inhibition that will be generated.[11]

▶ **1. Stimulus and response similarity.** If we are dealing with materials that must be learned in a serial order, as poems or word lists, we find that the more similar the second poem or list is to the first poem or list, the greater will be its inhibiting effect. When, however, we are dealing with materials composed of separate stimulus → response units, as in Morse code or other paired associate tasks, the effect of similarity between the two tasks is somewhat more complicated, for in such instances the degrees of similarity of the stimuli and of the responses of the two tasks may vary independently of each other. *The effects of these variations in similarity seem to parallel for the retention situation those that hold for transfer effects.* If in the two tasks the stimuli are the same or highly similar and the responses are antagonistic to each other, then a very large amount of retroactive inhibition will be generated. That is, the learning of the second task will hinder the retention of the first task very drastically. It will be recalled that

137

this situation also produces strong negative transfer effects. If, however, the responses of the two tasks are the same and the stimuli also are similar, the learning of the second task may actually facilitate the retention of the first.[12] The same condition leads to positive transfer effects. Complete dissimilarity of both stimuli and responses, the zero transfer effect situation, should produce neither facilitation nor inhibition of recall.

► **2. Similarities in the general environment.** The significance of this factor can be illustrated by an experiment.[13] The usual procedure for the study of retroactive inhibition was employed. The subjects first learned one list of ten nonsense syllables, then another list of ten syllables, and finally they were required to recall the first list. Approximately half an hour intervened between the completion of the learning and recall. For one group of subjects the learning of both lists and the recall of the original list took place in the same room. For another group the intervening—or, as it is usually called, interpolated—learning took place in a different room. The characteristics of the two rooms were intentionally made quite different from each other. One was brightly lighted and cluttered with furniture; the other was dimly illuminated and contained only the experimental equipment necessary for conducting the experiment; in one room the experimenter was visually present and in the other he was not; finally the subject stood up while learning in one of the rooms and sat in the other. Necessarily the groups were divided so that any given room was used equally often for the original learning and recall and for the interpolated learning. The results, measured by correct anticipations on the first recall trial and trials to relearn to the same criterion, are shown in Table 4.2. The significance of the results is too obvious to require further discussion.

TABLE 4.2

Original and interpolated learning in:	Correct anticipations	Trials to relearn
Same room	3.47	6.74
Different room	7.12	4.24

► **3. The amount and degree of learning.** The amount of retroactive inhibition will increase with increases either in the amount of interpolated materials or in the thoroughness with which these materials are learned.[14, 15]

► **4. *Time interval between learning the first and learning
the second tasks*.** It might be expected that the time at which the
second task is learned with respect to the time of original learning
or the time of recall would be a significant factor, but consistent
relationships have not been found, and the problem is too complicated to be discussed further in this text.[16]

Proactive inhibition

Retroaction has been defined as the influence of a later
activity upon the retention of an earlier learned activity. Proaction
is just the reverse. *Proactive inhibition* refers to the reductions in
retention arising from the influence of materials learned *prior* to
the learning of the task in which we are interested. Perhaps the
difference between the two may be clarified by the kinds of experimental procedures which would be employed, as shown in the
following plan:

	Step 1	*Step 2*	*Step 3*	*Step 4*
Retroaction:	Learn *A*	Learn *B*	Time passes	Recall *A*
Proaction:	Learn *B*	Learn *A*	Time passes	Recall *A*

Generally speaking, the same kinds and relationships of conditions that lead to high amounts of retroactive inhibition lead
also to high amounts of proactive inhibition.

The detrimental effect of prior learning on the recall of
material that is learned at a later date is demonstrated in the following experiment.[17] The subjects learned a twelve-unit serial list
of adjectives on one day and recalled it on the next, after which
they learned a new list. This procedure was continued for nine
lists. The results of the experiment, plotted in term of percent correct recall of the previous day's list, are shown in Figure 4.9. It is
apparent that the ability to recall the list in question becomes
progressively poorer as the number of previously learned lists increases. It is interesting, incidentally, to contrast this result with
the *learning* of successive lists, as shown in Figure 4.5.

The relative effect of proactive and retroactive inhibition
is illustrated by the retention curves shown in Figure 4.10. It will
be seen that although the proactive condition is much less detrimental for shorter retention intervals, there is little difference
between the two at longer intervals. There are very good theoretical
reasons for expecting this finding, though they are too complex
to be considered in this text.

139

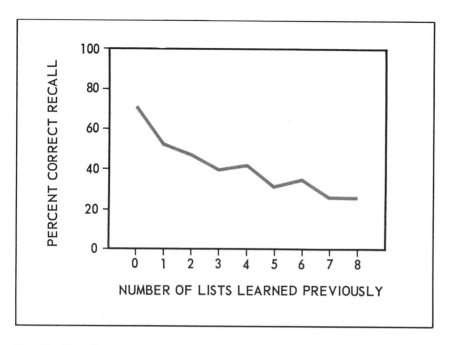

Fig. 4.9 The effect upon recall of previously learning various numbers of similar lists. (After Underwood[17])

Fig. 4.10 The effect upon forgetting of retroactive and proactive inhibition. (From Underwood, *J. exper. Psych.*, 1948, *38*, 29-38)

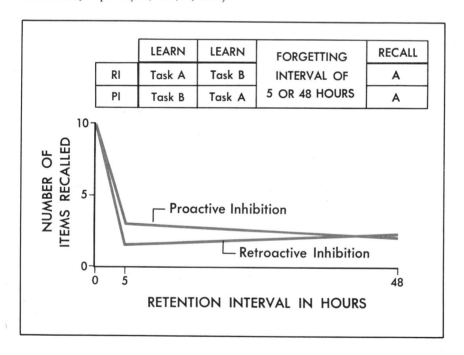

	LEARN	LEARN	FORGETTING	RECALL
RI	Task A	Task B	INTERVAL OF	A
PI	Task B	Task A	5 OR 48 HOURS	A

The original learning

Although forgetting deals with changes in the strength of the habit after the learning has been terminated, certain characteristics of the original learning have an influence on the retention of the material.

Degree of learning

A considerable amount of experimental evidence indicates that materials that are learned to the level of one single perfect recitation are forgotten more rapidly than materials learned to a higher level of mastery. There is a clear implication for study methods in this finding. A student's basic aim in studying a lesson is to be able to utilize this learned material at some later time—let us say on a test on the following morning. If he learns the material only to the extent of a single perfect recitation and then closes his book, he most certainly will forget much of his material by the time the test takes place. Thus, by reaching only a limited level of mastery, he does not achieve the real purpose of his study, for he

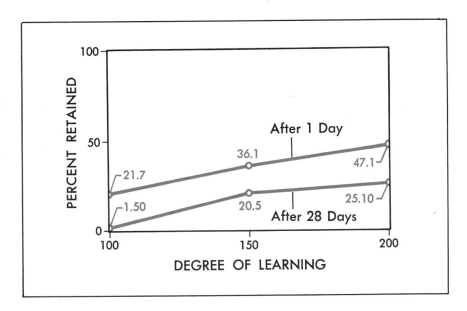

Fig. 4.11 The relationship between degree of learning and retention for two different retention intervals. Two different retention intervals—1 and 28 days—and three different levels of learning—100, 150, and 200 percent—were employed. In all instances retention after 1 day was superior to the corresponding 28-day group. For both retention intervals, the higher the degree of learning, the better the retention.

should aim at performing well at some later period rather than at the immediate moment. He should try to evaluate his level of mastery for the future and not for the present.

The reader may well ask for more specific information than the simple statement that learning should not stop at the level of a single perfect recitation. How many more recitations are required? Technically we say that learning is complete when the learner reaches the criterion of one perfect recitation, and that any practice beyond this point is *overlearning*. If the subject overlearns by as many trials as it took him to reach one perfect recitation, we say that he has overlearned 100 percent. Overlearning by half of the number of trials required to reach one single perfect recitation is called 50-percent overlearning. Retention is considerably better for both 50- and 100-per cent overlearning than for mere learning to the single perfect recitation, but somewhere between these two levels a point of diminishing returns appears. The 50-percent level is considerably better than the zero level, but the 100-percent level is only slightly better than the 50-percent level. Obviously overlearning is desirable, but unless perfect retention is required, the amount of overlearning that is most efficient need not be great.

Motor habits such as swimming or typing are forgotten far more slowly than are verbal habits. It is likely that the primary reason for this lies in the fact that motor habits are usually considerably overlearned, whereas verbal habits are not.

Active vs. passive attitude

In the experiment cited in the preceding chapter, the subjects who read and recited not only learned more in the same amount of time than those who merely read, but they recalled a larger percentage of what they had learned in a later recall test. Here again is a condition in which superiority in learning is associated with superiority in retention.

Kinds of materials learned

Most studies seem to show that meaningful material is retained better than meaningless material learned to the same level. This fact may seem to the student to be worth little, for he may feel that the material he is required to learn is either meaningless or meaningful and that there is nothing he can do about it. Actually this is not true. Often the difference between meaning and meaninglessness in the material lies only in the willingness of the student to look up a word, or perhaps the derivation of a word, in the dictionary or to think about the material and tie it in with his past experience.

Review

Efficiency of recall is greatly enhanced by the process of reviewing subsequent to the original learning. Reviewing after learning follows essentially the sequence of learning, forgetting, relearning, and, finally, recalling at some later date. The sequence of forgetting and relearning—that is, reviewing—may be repeated several times, and each time that it is repeated the amount that is forgotten becomes less and less.

The type of retention test prepared for

Students generally feel put upon if an instructor informs them that he will give a certain type of examination and then administers a different type. They object because they assume that one should study differently for different types of examinations, and that these differences will be reflected in their performance. To a limited degree the objection is justified. Students who study for a multiple-choice, a completion, or a true-false test are at a disadvantage if they are given a type of test other than the one for which they have prepared. Students who have prepared well for an essay test, however, tend to perform well on all types of tests.

The reason for this relationship between test performance and the type of examination for which one has prepared lies in the method of preparation. Students seem to prepare for the so-called objective examinations by such techniques as listing and understanding. When preparing for essay examinations, they use these techniques and in addition tend to organize and structure the material—a method of preparation that probably tends to give more meaning to the materials and may involve more recitation during study.

Massed vs. distributed learning

The relationship of massed and distributed learning to retention was discussed in the previous chapter, and the reader may recall that it is not a simple relationship. In summary, it would appear that if opportunities for proactive (and perhaps also retroactive) inhibition are restricted to a minimum, then retention of materials learned under massed conditions will be equal to, or

143

perhaps superior to, that of materials learned under distributed conditions. If opportunities for proactive (and perhaps also retroactive) inhibition are many, then distributed learning produces superior retention compared to massed learning.

The interpretation of forgetting

Such studies as those cited above, and others as well, suggest that the passage of time *per se* and the mere disuse of a stimulus → response connection are not the important, or perhaps even relevant, conditions of forgetting. What is important is the fact that conflicting responses become attached to the same stimulus and one response blocks the other. This inhibition of the now-desired response can result either from conflicts with responses learned previously (proactive inhibition) or from conflicts with responses learned later (retroactive inhibition). One may disagree and argue that forgetting occurs even though the earlier or later stimulus is different, but actually the principle of stimulus generalization tells us that the stimuli need not be exactly the same. They need only be similar. Time and forgetting may well be related to each other only, or at least primarily, because events occur in time, and the longer the time interval between learning and recall, the greater the number of conflicting response tendencies that will develop.

Data in support of this interpretation are not limited to the studies on retroactive and proactive inhibition. The fact that high degrees of learning result in good retention is consonant with this theory. High degrees of learning will develop S-R connections that are strong, and consequently they are connections which successfully resist competing tendencies.

The explanation of forgetting by reference to the learning of conflicting response tendencies helps us to understand various phenomena that cannot be attributed to the mere passage of time. Some events that happened many years ago we recall with remarkable clarity; others, in the less distant past, we seem to forget completely. If this difference is not due to differences in the original learning, it may be due to the fact that the retention of one event suffered from many interpolated conflicting responses, whereas the other did not. This is one of the reasons why we forget so little of such skills as swimming and bicycling; we are not placed in an environment in which we must learn conflicting responses to the stimuli that arise in these situations. With verbal stimuli, the story is a different one; we are constantly attaching new responses to various words.

A study described earlier found that a procedural task was forgotten to a much greater degree than was a tracking task. The procedural task involved the use of push-button switches and knobs, which had to be operated in a particular order. These kinds of situations are likely to be encountered outside the laboratory but with a different sequence of manipulation required. Encounters with a tracking task of the sort the experimenters used are likely to be infrequent. Hence, competing responses are more likely to have been acquired for the procedural task than for the tracking task, and this could account for the difference in retention of the two tasks.

QUALITATIVE FORGETTING

In our consideration of the process of forgetting we have so far been concerned only with quantitative losses in performance. These quantitative losses have been measured in terms of the number of units of the original material recalled, the amount of loss of speed in performance of the task, or the number of trials required to relearn the material. But these measures do not present the total picture of the changes that occur in the forgetting process; they fail to show that forgetting may also result in changes in the *form* of the material.

Studies of qualitative changes have often used nonsense drawings. A figure is presented to the subject for a brief time; then he is asked to reproduce it. Often the reproduction not only omits details of the drawing but distorts it in some manner or other. Sometimes a specific characteristic is exaggerated or sharpened— for example, an angle is drawn as more acute than the original was. At other times some irregularity is eliminated or leveled. Or there may be marked changes in either direction in the size of the figure.[18]

Distortions do not occur only in the reproduction of visual figures; they occur as well in the reproduction of verbal materials. Here, of course, memory changes have their greatest social significance, for out of such distortions rumor grows. Also, the potential significance of distortion in the psychology of testimony is apparent.

Far less research has been conducted on these qualitative changes occurring with the passage of time than on quantitative changes, but it seems very likely that the principles that operate in quantitative forgetting operate also in qualitative forgetting.

THE RETENTION OF

TRANSFERABLE MATERIAL

We have already considered losses arising from a change in the nature of the stimulus and those associated with the passage of time. It is logical now to consider what will occur when these two interact—to consider, in other words, forgetting in a transfer situation.

An experiment to measure forgetting in a transfer situation was set up in the following manner.[19] Ten groups of subjects learned a paired associate list composed of letters for the stimulus item and numbers for the response item. At 0, 2, 14, 30, or 90 days after the original learning separate groups of subjects either relearned the original list, or learned a list composed of a different set of numbers and letters. The performance of the groups of subjects that relearned the original list will therefore give a measure of retention over the time span studied, while the performance of the groups learning the new list will give a measure of the transfer resulting from the learning of the first list. Their performances are, of course, always compared with those of a group that learned this list without prior experience with this type of laboratory situation.

The results of this experiment are presented in Figure 4.12. A loss in retention of the specific items of the first list is shown by the fact that, in general, the percentage saved in relearning decreases with increase in time since original learning, dropping from slightly more than 90 percent savings at 2 days to slightly more than 50 percent savings after 90 days. In short, a fairly typical forgetting curve was generated by these groups. Groups that learned a new list in the second sessions performed about 40 percent better than did the control group, and approximately this same figure was obtained regardless of the length of the time span since the original learning. In other words, the positive transfer effects which resulted from the learning of the first list persisted without diminution over the 90-day period. In another study similar results were found for the learning of a serial list of nonsense syllables.[20]

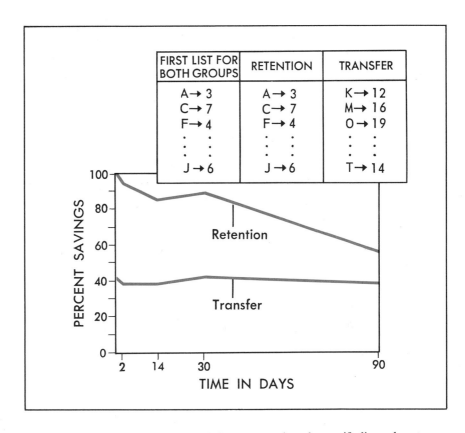

Fig. 4.12 The effects of the passage of time on retention of a specific list and on transfer effects. (After Bunch[19])

These results seem to indicate that although a great deal of specific information may be lost with the passage of time, much is still retained in the form of generalized responses which will aid in the learning of new material. This is an encouraging fact. A college education may thus have a value accruing not only from the specific information learned and retained but also from these general transfer effects which enable us to learn new material more readily.

ORGANISMIC FACTORS, THE BASIS
OF INDIVIDUAL DIFFERENCES

The fact that individuals differ from one another in their ability to learn and to utilize their learning is familiar to all of us.

We have looked with envy and awe at the quick learner, who acquires his lessons with astounding ease, and at other times we have viewed with sympathy the dullard who strives so hard and gains so little. And as we noted these contrasting abilities, we may have speculated on how these persons got that way.

The material in the previous chapter that showed that efficiency of learning is a function of the methods employed in learning clearly implies that some of the difference in learning ability is due to the methods used by different persons. Other things being equal, the individual who uses all the most efficient methods and uses them only, will excel the one who employs inefficient methods. Since the methods we use are a matter of training, part of the individual differences in learning ability must arise from the fact that some of us have acquired efficient learning habits and others have not.

The data presented in the section on transfer of training indicate that environmental influences make for grave differences in our ability to learn specific kinds of material. The individual who has worked much or learned much in a certain field will learn new materials in that field with greater ease than if he had not had this previous experience. Thus, our present learning is likely to make it easier for us to learn similar kinds of material in the future. Two individuals, then, who differ greatly in their ability to learn certain materials may differ only because of their disparate background of experience with the materials.

The fact that the more and the less rapid learners may differ from each other because of differences in learning techniques or in the possession of transferable material must not be interpreted to mean that genetic factors are unimportant. In human society it is extremely difficult to distinguish the effects of the environmental factor from those of the genetic factor; hence, we turn for clarification to a classic study on the maze learning of white rats.[21]

The experimenter began his study by running a group of 142 rats through a long maze and recording the total number of errors made by each animal during 19 trials in the maze. At the end of the maze was the animal's daily food ration, and thus the animal's behavior was motivated by the need for food. The distribution of the ability of this population of rats to learn is shown on the top graph of Figure 4.13. The error frequency is plotted on the horizontal axis, and the percentage of animals having a specific error frequency is indicated on the vertical axis. It is apparent that

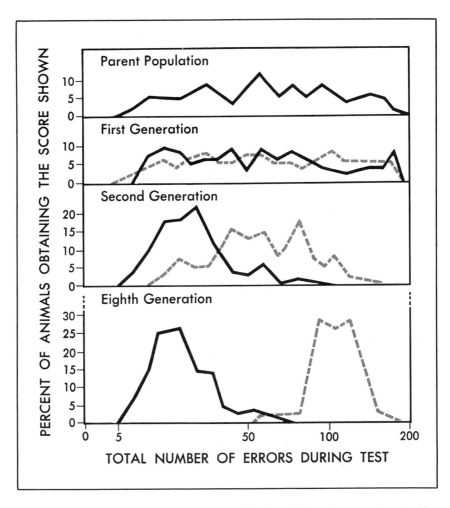

Fig. 4.13 The effect of breeding on the maze-learning ability of two strains of white rats. (After Tryon[21])

a few of the animals learned with extreme rapidity and made fewer than 9 errors, whereas others committed more than 200 errors.

The bright rats were then bred together, and the medium and dull ones were interbred. The performance of the offspring of each of these parental groups is shown in the second graph of Figure 4.13. For this generation no real differences in performance between the groups occurred, but the same assortative mating process was continued and the results of other generations are shown in the same figure. By the second generation the groups have begun to be distinguishable, and they continue doing so until by the eighth generation it may be said that two different races of rats

149

have been isolated—a bright race and a dull one—at least with respect to learning in this type of situation.

The experiment has been continued for more than twenty generations and these differences still persist, showing that a stable difference in learning ability has been achieved by the process of assortative mating. The experiment clearly indicates that genetic constitution is an important factor in producing individual differences in ability to learn this task. There is no reason to believe that this basic conclusion does not apply to human beings as well as to rats.

There is not, however, a single, general kind of learning ability that operates with equal force in all sorts of learning activities. Many studies have been conducted on both human beings and animals in which the rate of learning in one activity has been compared with the rate of learning in another. Even when we compare such similar things as the learning of one kind of maze and the learning of another, the relationship is far from perfect.

In one study the bright and dull groups described above were run on a number of different mazes and on other kinds of learning activities as well. Furthermore, different incentives to perform were used on some of the tasks. That is, instead of running to obtain food, the rats might be required to swim through the maze, the reward being the landing platform at the end of the tank. The experimenter found that the maze-dull rats were not inferior to the maze-bright rats in some types of activities. It was evident from the results that the inferiority of the dull group on the original maze resulted not only from differences in intellectual ability, but also from differences in susceptibility to different kinds of rewards or motivating conditions, and to tendencies to be emotionally disturbed in certain kinds of situations.[22] These statistical and experimental facts corroborate the observation that students who are highly capable in one area of learning may show only moderate skill in another, and that the academically bright may sometimes be socially inept. In such instances as these, motivational or interest factors further complicate the issue.

To summarize what we have been saying in this section, individual differences in the ability to learn are a product of both environmental and genetic factors. There is probably no one alive who could not, if he were to use the most efficient methods of learning, improve his present ability to learn. Yet even if we all used the same methods, differences among us in rates of learning would still persist.

A similar conclusion can be drawn about the utilization of habits. Amount of retention, we know, is not an unalterable constant but can be varied by conditions during the original learning and conditions that operate before and after learning. These, to some degree, we can control, and by so doing we can also determine to some degree our efficiency of retention.

STUDY AND THE PSYCHOLOGY
OF LEARNING

The especial relevance of the psychology of learning to the reader—a student and learner—is obvious. The principles of learning, retention, and transfer can be used to make his task an easier one. It may be useful, therefore, to reconsider these principles in the light of a student's tasks.

First we must note that a student's progress is ordinarily evaluated by an examination which he takes some few hours after he has finished studying. Often the examination requires not an exact repetition of textbook materials but some application (transfer) of a fact or principle learned. This means, then, that studying should be oriented to result not only in the quickest possible learning but also in the maximum *retention* and *transfer*.

Fortunately, it is generally true that the conditions optimal for learning are also optimal for retention. It is of major importance that the student approach his mtaerial with an active, participant attitude rather than with a passive one. This means in part that he should read and recite, rather than merely read in a relaxed fashion. By so doing he not only prepares himself to recite at some later date but he acquires information on how well he has learned the material. Evaluation of performance is important; he does this for himself when he tries to recite to himself the material he has just gone over. The remedy, if he fails to recall certain sections of the materials in this recitation, is obvious.

Usually the student can, if he wishes, find an adequate way of *distributing* his studying. It is often suggested that at the beginning of a term the student should work out a time schedule, budgeting his hours for studying each subject. The periods of study for a specific subject need not be long and may be separated from other periods by dissimilar activities, for these are likely to reduce both proactive and retroactive inhibition. If, for a scheduled study period, there is no new assignment to work upon, the student can use the period for review or *overlearning*, which leads, we know, to an increase in retention.

Meaning can be given to materials in many ways, for in part what is meant by the meaning of something is the degree to which it is related to other materials. Ordinarily any single textbook chapter is made up of a number of concepts, each of which bears a certain relationship to the larger concept defined by the chapter heading. Generally the author has organized these minor concepts in some logical sequence. The student should survey the chapter as a whole by glancing through the topic headings or by reading the summary before beginning the detailed reading of the chapter. This will usually serve to indicate the relationship of these minor concepts to one another and to the major purpose of the chapter. Thus, when the minor concepts are encountered in the reading of the chapter, they will be more meaningful and hence more easily learned and better retained.

But the effort to give meaning to concepts should not stop at this point; the student should attempt to extend these concepts to materials beyond those found in the chapter of the textbook. He might require himself to discover other examples of the concept described in the text, or attempt to apply the concept to new situations. When he does so, he is learning to transfer these materials and preparing himself for the examination, which is likely to measure his textbook knowledge by measuring transferred rather than specific information.

If doing all these things seems to demand a great amount of effort, he may be encouraged by considering the significance of the section on "Learning to Learn." This section should lead him to believe that if he uses techniques that cause him to learn better, he will find it progressively more easy to learn similar materials later.

REFERENCES

[1] Cantor, Joan H. Amount of pretraining as a factor in stimulus predifferentiation and performance set, *J. exper. Psychol.*, 1955, *50*, 180-184.

[2] Bruce, Robert W. Condition for transfer of training. *J. exper. Psychol.*, 1933, *16*, 343-361.

[3] Hall, John F. Learning as a function of word frequency, *Amer. J. Psychol.*, 1954, *67*, 138-140.

[4] Osgood, C. E. The similarity paradox in human learning: A resolution, *Psychol. Review*, 1949, *56*, 132-143.

[5] Harlow, H. F. The formation of learning sets, *Psychol. Review*, 1949, *56*, 51-65.

[6] Harlow, H. F. Analysis of discrimination learning by monkeys, *J. exper. Psychol.*, 1950, *40*, 26-39.

[7] Burtt, H. E. An experimental study of early childhood memory, *J. Genetic Psychol.*, 1932, *40*, 287-295.

[8] Ammons, R. B., Farr, R. G., Block, E. N., Dey, M., Marion, R., and Ammons, C. R. Long-term retention of perceptual motor skills, *J. exper. Psychol.*, 1958, *55*, 318-328.

[9] Weiss, Walter, and Margolius, Garry The effect of context stimuli on learning and retention, *J. exper. Psychol.*, 1954, *48*, 318-322.

[10] Jenkins, J. G., and Dallenbach, K. M. Obliviscence during sleep and waking, *Amer. J. Psychol.*, 1924, *35*, 605-612.

[11] Underwood, J. J. *Experimental Psychology*, Appleton-Century-Crofts, 1949.

[12] Hamilton, R. J. Retroactive facilitation as a function of degree of generalization between tasks, *J. exper. Psychol.*, 1943, *32*, 363-376.

[13] Greenspoon, Joel, and Ranyard, Redge Stimulus conditions and retroactive inhibition, *J. exper. Psychol.*, 1957, *53*, 55-59.

[14] Twining, P. E. The relative importance of intervening activity and lapse of time in the production of forgetting, *J. exper. Psychol.*, 1940, *26*, 483-501.

[15] Underwood, B. J. The effects of successive interpolations on retroactive and proactive inhibition, *Psychol. Monogr.*, 1945, *59*, No. 3.

[16] Newton, John M., and Wickens, Delos D. Retroactive inhibition as a function of the temporal position of the interpolated learning, *J. exper. Psychol.*, 1956, *51*, 149-154.

[17] Underwood, B. J. Interference and forgetting, *Psychol. Rev.*, 1957, *64*, 49-60.

[18] Bartlett, F. C. *Remembering: A Study in Experimental and Social Psychology*, Macmillan, 1932.

[19] Bunch, M. E. The amount of transfer in rational learning as a function of time, *J. comp. Psychol.*, 1936, *22*, 325-337.

[20] Bunch, M. E., and McCraven, V. G. The temporal course of transfer in the learning of memory material, *J. comp. Psychol.*, 1938, *25*, 481-496.

[21] Tryon, R. C. "Individual differences," in F. A. Moss (ed.), *Comparative Psychology*, Prentice-Hall, 1942.

[22] Searle, L. V. The organization of hereditary maze-brightness and maze-dullness, *Genet. Psychol. Monogr.*, 1949, *39*, 279-325.

Chapter Five

MOTIVATION

AS WE HAVE POINTED OUT PREVIOUSLY, the task of the psychologist is to make predictions about behavior—to predict that in a given stimulus situation the organism will respond in a specific way. It is apparent that an understanding of the behavior mechanisms to which we have been introduced in the preceding chapters may help us in prediction. If we know, for example, that a certain type of conditioning episode has occurred in the past history of the organism, and if we understand the principle of stimulus generalization, we may be able to predict the organism's behavior in a new situation. Again, a knowledge of the conditions of forgetting may enable us to predict that some previous learning will not be utilizable in a given situation.

However, even though we may know a great deal about the habits that an individual has developed and about the way in which habits operate, we shall frequently find ourselves in error if we use only this information in making our predictions. Let us look at a simple example. An individual has learned to respond to drinking fountains by bending over, pressing a knob, and drinking. We may say that these responses have been attached to and are elicited by the drinking fountain. If, however, we predicted that, each time the stimulus of the drinking fountain was presented, the individual would respond by drinking, we would make numerous errors. The horse that is led to water does not always drink.

Time and again, in fact, we find that a subject's behavior toward external stimuli is variable. In one instance, the learned reaction will be elicited; in another, the stimuli will be disregarded. The learned behavior is not always called forth on an all-or-none basis; sometimes the response is strong and at other times it is weak. Sometimes an organism will respond persistently to some stimulus complex in the environment, reacting first to one aspect, then to another, and then perhaps again to the first. At other times, the organism responds with no more than a psychological sniff at the stimuli and then moves off to respond to other, quite different ones.

These facts about the variability of response to external stimuli imply clearly that the psychologist cannot predict behavior adequately on the basis of external stimuli alone. He must take account of momentary internal states of the organism which influence its reactions to these stimuli. Thus, in the example cited above, we could make more accurate predictions if we knew something about the subject's physiological need for water at the time he was stimulated by the drinking fountain, as well as about his past habits relating to drinking fountains. To learn about these internal aspects, we must turn our attention to the topic of motivation. Only by considering behavior as arising from an *interaction* between internal conditions and the external environmental situation can we develop an ability to predict and understand behavior.

MOTIVATED BEHAVIOR

Perhaps an example will make clear the basic processes involved in motivated behavior. It is five-thirty in the afternoon, and four-year-old Christopher, who has been playing outside, tramps noisily into the house and toward the kitchen, where his mother is preparing the evening meal. Just as he crosses the threshold, he demands a banana. He is refused, but he counters in a moment with a request for a slice of bread with honey on it. Again the answer is no, but with the added statement, "Supper will be ready in a moment."

Perhaps Christopher reacts with a stamp of his feet or a little dance of anger and with continued verbalization. He moves restlessly about the kitchen and spies some carrot sticks. "Then can I have a carrot?" he asks, as without waiting for an answer he climbs a chair by the table and reaches toward the dish. The answer, "Yes, you may," comes just before his little hand closes on a carrot stick. He munches it noisily; supper is on the table before the last bite is consumed; Christopher eats with a vengeance.

After the meal, Christopher is much quieter. Even while he was spooning up the last bit of dessert, his movements were slow and languid. Once he is down from the table, he makes no more requests for food but plays quietly with his blocks. And so to bed.

Now, if we describe this behavior in more abstract terms, we can see in it a pattern that applies to motivated behavior in general. We find first an organism that is highly active. And for the most part the activity is directed along one specific channel—in this case one that leads to the obtaining of food. The activity does not cease after a single frustration but continues until the goal is achieved. The achievement of the goal is followed by relative quiescence on the part of the organism, and the behavior is no longer directed toward the same goal. In our example, building blocks rather than food occupy the child's attention after his meal.

Perhaps the essential characteristic of motivated behavior is persistence—persistence that is likely to continue until a certain end result is achieved. The same characteristic is found in the more complex states of social motivation. We speak of a *consuming* ambition, a *burning* desire, or a *steadfast* longing, and each of these phrases implies the persistence of a general way of responding. Most of us have known some strongly ambitious person who seeks always to excel his friend or his neighbor. He seems to be driven onward, trying first this, then that, achieving one goal after another. For him a single victory is not enough; success in reaching one goal seems only to open vistas of new worlds to be conquered. He does not show, in other words, the cessation of activity characteristic of the satiation of our biological motives, such as hunger or thirst. There are good theoretical reasons to believe that for some kinds of social motives goal attainment increases rather than decreases the motive state. In general, however, the process of being motivated is a process of directing one's behavior persistently toward some goal and terminating this type of activity when a response is made which achieves the goal.

By now it is apparent that the first steps in our consideration of motivation are the identification of our *most significant behavioral motives* and the discovery of the *processes which initiate and maintain* the goal-directed activity.

We shall begin by stating that, so far as origin is concerned, we may divide motives into two broad classes: the *biological* or unlearned and the *socially learned*. The use of these terms is not completely satisfying, for they may imply that no learning enters into the one and no biological determination into the other. This is not true, and in the next section an attempt will be made to clarify the essential differences and similarities of these two classes of motives.

BIOLOGICAL NEEDS AND THEIR CONSEQUENCES

Like the lower animals, man is an organism. If he and his species is to survive, he must keep his physiological machinery functioning within certain limits. He must supply his body with certain chemicals obtained from the world about him, and he must avoid contact with certain stimuli that can destroy the tissues of his body. The organism does not have at birth some rational foreknowledge of its limits of physiological tolerance. It does not know what to seek and when to seek it, or what to avoid and when. Nevertheless, the organism is provided with certain mechanisms that initiate activity when its condition begins to depart from some physiological optimum, and that sustain activity until the physiological balance begins to return to normal. It is a mechanism of this sort that underlies much of the concept of motivation.

A living organism is then a complex physical structure, and as a physical structure it can be maintained only if it can replenish the many kinds of energy it has used up, can eliminate wastes, can

157

remain at a temperature at which it operates efficiently, and can prevent its parts from being destroyed. We refer to the demands that the tissues of the organism must make upon the environment if it is to survive as the *needs* of the organism. So complex an organism as man has many needs, and the exact identification of these is more the task of the physiologists and biochemists than of the psychologists. We are concerned with the nature of the behavior mechanisms that permit the individual to meet these needs, even though, as our previous sentence implies, we may not know precisely what they are.

The general pattern of biological and psychological processes that make it possible for the organism to meet most of the demands of its physical well-being appears to be as follows:

1. The deprivation of certain necessary chemicals or the occurrence of stimuli which, if continued, will eventually undermine the organism's ability to function successfully (noxious stimulation), gives rise to a very complex series of biochemical and physiological reactions. These widespread reactions give rise to a more localized condition called a drive state: This drive state is not the behavior, but, interacting with the environment, it is responsible for a change in the behavior.

2. Neither the nature of these drive states nor the processes that lead up to them in terms of their physiological properties will concern us now, but will be considered in Chapter 19. In general, the *drive state persists* so long as deprivation or noxious stimulation continues. In addition, *the various drive states associated with different classes of needs are specific,* and thus can be distinguished one from another by the organism. If, for example, you feel thirsty or hungry it is not a momentary feeling, but a continuing one, and the feeling of being hungry is different from the feeling of being thirsty.

3. These drives ordinarily result in increased activity on the part of the organism, and this activity increases the probability that the organism may encounter objects that are capable of eliminating the drive. These responses are called *instrumental responses.* For example, you look for a restaurant or for a drinking fountain.

4. The object that is capable of eliminating the drive is termed the *incentive or goal object.* For example, food or water.

5. If upon contacting the incentive it is utilized, this act is called the *consummatory response.* For example, eating the food or drinking the water.

6. As a consequence of this final act the drive state is lessened, and this class of behavior is terminated. For example, you cease to feel hungry or thirsty after eating or drinking and you turn to other activities, leaving the restaurant or drinking fountain.

On the basis of this analysis it is possible to describe more precisely what the term *biological in origin* means. Motives are classified as being biological in origin if learning is not required for the deprivation (or the stimulus condition) to produce the drive state—although, it should be added, the drive state may not lead directly to the appropriate instrumental or consummatory response. The nature of learned motives and the manner in which they originate will be discussed in a later section of this chapter.

The biological or unlearned sources of motivation

The most obvious of the biological motives that have a significant impact upon behavior are listed in the table below:

Deprivation or stimulus conditions leading to →	Drive state
1. Food	Hunger
2. Water	Thirst
3. Continuous activity	Fatigue
4. Noxious stimulation	Pain
5. Warming and cooling	Temperature
6. Bladder and intestinal distention	Elimination

There is little need to justify this list, since the reader should readily understand how these internal conditions of the organism would eventuate in the kinds of responses that we have described as characteristic of motivated behavior. There are, however, other motive sources that are also significant determinates of behavior but whose inclusion as unlearned drive conditions requires some justification.

Activity

Whether or not an independent drive or a mechanism analogous to a drive to be active exists is uncertain. Frequently, however, one finds organisms simply being active, the behavior not being directed toward any incentive object, such as food or drink. Are they being active just for the sake of activity? And is the goal of this drive sheer movement? Such behavior is particularly noticeable in young organisms. The infant in his crib kicks his legs, babbles, and waves his arms. The older child skips about and lets out piercing, and to the more inhibited adult, senseless shouts. There seems to be no goal other than movement. It is possible, however, that this behavior may be not the result of a drive toward activity but rather a combination of drives that are weakly present. The organism may be a little hungry and a little thirsty, or activated by other drive systems. The combination of these drives plus the exuberant health of the organism may give rise to activity that is not focused upon the satisfaction of any specific drive.

The case for activity as a unique drive analogous to hunger or thirst would be stronger if it could be shown that enforced inactivity would result in increased activity when the opportunity to move freely about became available. One experimenter kept rats in a very small enclosure for varying periods of time up to 24 hours and then placed them in an activity wheel similar to the one illustrated in Figure 5.1.[1] Their activity during a half hour was compared with that of animals who were taken from the normally large living cages. He concluded that deprivation did

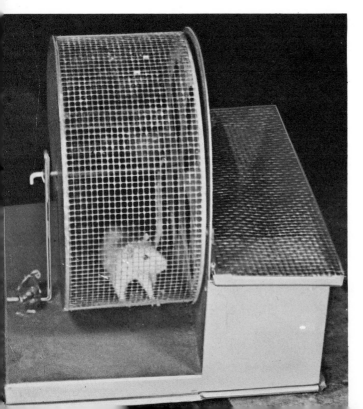

Fig. 5.1 An activity wheel. The animal lives in this apparatus, finding food and water in the small rectangular cage. He may enter the wheel portion of the apparatus at any time. The number of revolutions of the wheel which he produces in his running is recorded by a counter. (Courtesy Laurence Alexander)

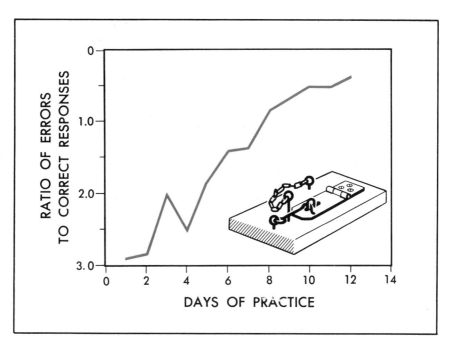

Fig. 5.2 Improvement with practice in solving a puzzle. No reward was given to the subjects (monkeys) for the correct solution. The puzzle was simply reassembled and presented again. (After Harlow[3])

increase activity and that the longer the period of enforced inactivity, the greater the increase. Certainly this experiment offers some support for the notion of an activity drive, although additional research has shown that the relationship between the duration of enforced inactivity and the subsequent behavior is a rather complex one.[2]

Curiosity

Evidence in support of an unlearned source for curiosity comes from a study in which monkeys were presented with puzzles of the sort shown in Figure 5.2. The monkeys quite promptly took the puzzles apart. When the puzzles were reassembled by the experimenter and once again presented to the monkeys, they were again taken apart—and so on in an almost continuous cycle. Certainly the reward for the monkeys' behavior could not be understood by reference to any of the motive states that were included in our basic list.

In another experiment monkeys were placed in a darkened box and periodically were given access to a pair of closed doors.

Pressing one of these caused it to open and the animal could peer outside for a period of seconds before it was closed. Pressing the other produced no such opening, for this door was locked on the outside. The monkeys rapidly established a tendency to press on the door which opened, and they would do so for hours on end.[3]

Behavior analogous to that of the monkeys in the two studies mentioned above is frequent in man. When a famous mountaineer of the early Everest expeditions who subsequently lost his life high on its slope was asked what drove him to attempt the mountain, he replied simply, "Because it is there." A scientist or scholar may spend years in his laboratory or in the quiet of his library, gaining only meager monetary rewards, but happier nevertheless than an affluent businessman. These men, and others like them, may be happy in such a life because it satisfies for them a drive that is as biologically based as those that lead to food and drink.

The need for variety

There is in the experimental literature of psychology a considerable body of data indicating that organisms tend not to repeat a response that has just been made, even though that response may have been reinforced.[4] It has been postulated that this kind of behavior arises from a basic, unlearned drive to avoid response repetition.

The demand for variety seems to be something more than a tendency not to repeat a particular response; it seems also to involve the preference for a varied as opposed to a constant stimulus environment. Several experiments illustrate this fact. In one experiment rats were used as the subjects.[5] They were placed at the choice point of a T-shaped maze. Glass doors permitted them to see into the two arms of the maze, but prevented the rats from entering the arms. One of these arms was painted black and the other white. After they had viewed the two arms of the maze for a short time, they were taken to the starting point of the maze. The experimenter then changed one of the arms, making it the same color as the other arm, and at the same time removed the glass doors. The rat was then permitted to run through the maze and enter the alley of his choice. The animals showed a strong preference for entering the alley that had been changed in color.

The next experiment deals with the reactions of college students who were paid to remain in an environment that had been as nonstimulating as possible.[6] These subjects lay on a comfortable bed, wearing translucent goggles that would not permit pattern vision. Except when they were eating or going to the toilet, they wore gloves and cardboard cuffs from elbow to wrist, so stimulation arising from manipulation was reduced. The room was sound-deadened and ordinary noises arising from outside the experimental cubicles could not be heard. The experimenters and subjects could communicate with each other by means of a small speaker system.

This situation proved to be extremely disturbing to most of the subjects and few of them were willing to continue serving in the experiment for more than two or three days despite the fact that the pay was more than double what they would normally earn.

Most subjects reported that they began to have hallucinations under these conditions of reduced stimulation. All of them reported that they saw changing colors and simple arrangements of geometrical patterns. A good number of them saw more complex scenes with people or animals in them, and some of them heard voices or music. Tests of intellectual functions were given to them

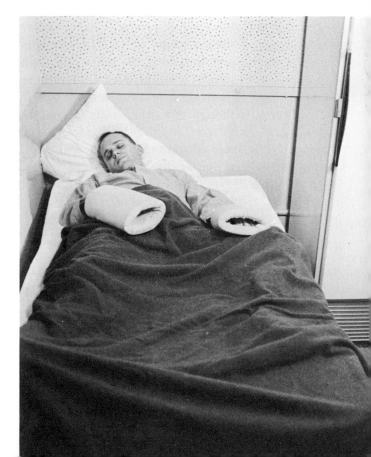

Fig. 5.3 The type of environment employed in stimulus-deprivation studies. The subject is wearing soft pads on his hands to decrease differential external cutaneous stimulation. He may remove them in order to obtain liquid food or water from the refrigerator at his left. During the experiment the room is completely dark. (Courtesy Task ENDORSE, U.S. Army Leadership HRU [Hum RRO], operating under a George Washington University contract to the Department of the Army)

during their period of isolation, and typically their performance became poorer the longer they stayed in the experimental situation. The results offer some support to the view that lack of variation of external stimulation leads to a disturbance condition of motivational significance in humans.

Examples of this tendency to avoid repetition are common. A long-continued topic of conversation becomes boring, and we shift to a different one. Sometimes we do it suddenly, with an awareness that we are bored; at other times the change is slowly and subtly achieved. We tire of eating a certain kind of food; we change husbands or wives in mid-life; and we throw an honest and hard-working politician out of office merely because "we need a change."

One should not fail to note the importance of these three drives—activity, curiosity, and the avoidance of repetition or demand for variety. Their implications are considerable for the entire structure of social living and for the educational system in particular. In our modern educational system there is a basic belief —and it is a sound one—that learning progresses best if it satisfies some strong motivations of the learner. If the sole sources of motivation of mankind are those that were listed earlier plus certain learned and primarily social motives which will be described later, then it would be wise for our educational system to operate in a certain fashion. If, on the other hand, we can count upon a motivation to solve problems for the mere sake of solving problems, a motivation to try something new in order to avoid repetition even though repetition leads to some reinforcement, and a motivation to work or to be active for the reward that activity brings, then our educational system will not have to restrict itself to those activities that are indubitably "practical."

All in all there is a large body of data that points forcefully toward the conclusion that the higher organisms have unlearned tendencies to engage in the kinds of behaviors which result in broadening its contact with the environment.[7] It is difficult to account for these behaviors by the drive states which were listed in the preceding table, and it is equally difficult to account for their origins by the principles of learning, so they are given a separate position in this section. It is not, however, difficult to understand how at least some of these behavioral propensities would be of adoptive value to the organism. Curiosity, exploration and activity cause. the organism to learn more about the

Fig. 5.4 What is the driving force that causes these men to make the effort and take the risks necessary to bring them to the peak of this mountain? (Courtesy Swiss National Travel Agency)

environment in which it dwells. These knowledges may lead him to escape from a predator or to discover rich sources of supply from which his many needs may be met.

Contact comfort

Although one cannot speak of a need for gentle contact in quite the same way one can speak of a need for food or water, there is evidence that young organisms are as strongly motivated to bring themselves into contact with soft and yielding surfaces as they are to obtain food or water. Powerful support for this assertion is found in a program of research on the psychological development of infant monkeys conducted at the University of Wisconsin.[8] In a typical experiment the infants were reared singly, and without their simian mother, in small but adequately sized cages. The infants were, however, supplied with surrogate mothers, as illustrated in Figure 5.5. One mother was made of uncovered wire,

Fig. 5.5 Contact comfort in the human infant and the infant monkey. (Courtesy Vattano and Sponholz)

but was equipped with a nippled milk bottle from which the infant could nurse. The other mother was covered with terry-cloth towelling. A record was then obtained of the time the infants spent clinging to each mother. The infants exhibited a marked preference for the terry-cloth mother and spent a large portion of their days clinging to and climbing over her. In addition, they showed signs of disturbance if the cloth mother was removed and would surmount barriers to reach her.

Human infants show similar tendencies, and at a slightly older age it is expressed in their demands to be held or in their trailing of a treasured pillow or blanket behind them. At present, at least, we cannot readily apply the principles of learning to account for the origin of this tendency to seek soft and yielding surfaces, and so it is classified in the list of motivational conditions that are unlearned.

Sex

At least for the human, and for the higher mammals in general, the sex drive seems to occupy an ambiguous position with respect to its classification as learned or unlearned—as ambiguous as society's attitude toward its acceptability. One difference between the sex drive and those we have already previously mentioned is that sexual behavior is not a necessary condition for the survival of the *individual*. That this is true does not, of course, prevent its being classified as a simple biological drive. What is significant is the fact that we have no definite evidence that deprivation of sexual activity produces a drivelike condition which, in the absence of appropriate external stimulation, is persistent and can be reduced only by engaging in a sexual act. Sexual excitation is highly dependent upon stimulation arising from the presence of or verbalization about members of the opposite sex. In other words, learning plays a large part in sexual arousal. The biological side of the picture is represented by the fact that, especially in the lower animals, sexual activity is greatly influenced by the presence or absence of male or female hormones in the body—that is, by chemicals secreted by the sex gland.[9]

Thus the determination of sexual activity in higher animals seems to be a function of both learned and unlearned processes. So far as the origin of the instigating forces are concerned, it does not belong in the same category as hunger or thirst; but at the same time it differs from the socially learned motive states.

167

DRIVES AND THEIR GOAL RESPONSE

A drive, as we have described it, consists of a persisting condition which can be removed only if the organism obtains the appropriate stimulus object. This object we call the goal, reward, or incentive. It is legitimate to ask: How fixed at the time of birth is the tendency to make the appropriate instrumental and consummatory response to a specific drive? Is the appropriate response given by our biological heritage at birth or must we learn how to satisfy our drive conditions?

We have evidence that indicates that in some of the lower animals the appropriate response to many drive conditions may occur without any dependency upon learning. In such animals as the white rat, patterns of both sexual and maternal behavior occur in the appropriate situation without there ever having been an opportunity for the animal to learn these patterns before they are put into use, although the execution of these responses does improve with practice.

For many drives in the higher species, the evidence seems to indicate that the appropriate responses to most, if not all, of the drive states must be learned. Many newborn children will not suck and swallow when they are first presented with the breast or the bottle, and it is not until they are several months old that they seem to recognize the feeding situation as related to their hunger state. The writer knows of one adult who seldom seemed to realize when she was thirsty. She would become restless and very active until someone who was aware of her quirk would suggest that she get a drink of water. Invariably she would return with a smile, remarking that water was what she had needed and that now she felt fine.

In all probability the relationship between drive and innate tendency to make either the appropriate instrumental or the appropriate consummatory response varies from drive to drive. The response that brings air into our lungs almost certainly does not need to be learned—though for some infants the obstetrician may find it necessary to speed up its initiation with a well-placed slap. The sucking reflex may be elicited more readily if the infant is hungry or thirsty, but well-coordinated sequences of sucking or swallowing do not appear on first contact with the nipple.

It appears that the drive state, in conjunction with stimulation from the external environment, operates in the immature organism to produce activity that is not directed toward specific environmental objects but is general in nature.[10] Within limits, this activity will continue as long as the need that gives rise to the drive stimulus remains unsatisfied. In a sense, then, the naive organism roams about until it makes some response which eliminates the drive. The satisfying of need states is reinforcing and, as we know, responses that are followed by reinforcement become fixated. In this manner appropriate instrumental and consummatory responses both become attached to the drive stimulus.

For very complex reasons, which will be touched upon later, it often happens that an individual does not recognize the exact nature of his motives, and this fact may lead to psychological complications. Sometimes one of the major tasks of the psychiatrist or the clinical psychologist is to guide his disturbed client into the recognition of his motive states.

Some definitions

Because some words—or rather the way in which some words are being used—in this chapter may be unfamiliar to the reader, it is desirable to digress and define them formally.

Need

Organisms, as biological creatures, have certain physical requirements that must be met if the organism is to survive. These requirements are referred to as the organisms' needs.

Drive

When an organism is deprived of certain substances or is stimulated by a class of events that are potentially harmful, a condition arises within it that leads to activity. This condition we refer to as a drive. Obviously we do not see the drive; we infer it from the organism's past history and from its behavior. The tendency for certain drives to occur in response to certain stimuli is not learned but is innate.

Most of the organism's usual needs eventuate in drives, but this is not always the case. Thus, the organism has need for a variety of vitamins, but the deficit of some of these in the diet does not seem to result in a drive state which is continued until the vitamin is supplied. By and large, however, most needs result in drives that eventuate in action and in ultimate satisfaction of the drive.

Drive stimulus

A drive condition results in or could almost be defined as a source of stimulation. The different common drive states produce their own unique conditions—conditions which may be conceived of as drive stimuli, thus making it possible for the organism to react appropriately to its needs.

Incentive

The incentive is the environmental object that is capable of removing the drive state. Thus, food is the incentive for the hunger drive.

Instrumental act

The instrumental act is the behavior that leads the organism to the incentive. It is an action that is instrumental in reaching the incentive.

Consummatory response

The consummatory response is the act that eliminates the drive condition.

Perhaps an example will help to concretize some of these terms. You have been driving your car for some hours now and you have not had a drink—that is, you have been deprived of water —for an even longer period of time. This has resulted in a thirst *drive*. You see a pump in a roadside park; you stop your car; you take a cup you happen to have in the glove compartment; and, holding it under the spigot, you pump it full and lift it to your mouth. These are *instrumental acts*, which have attained water, the *incentive*, for you. You swallow the water gratefully, making the *consummatory response* which relieves the thirst drive.

Motive

The term *motive* will be used in a broader sense than the term *drive*. A drive is simply a state of the organism that arises from certain conditions; it is not learned; and, as we have suggested above, it may not unerringly guide the organism to the appropriate incentive and consummatory response. The term

motive refers to the relationship which is established between
drive and incentive. Thus a motive implies learning and a relationship between the nature of the instigating force and the consummatory response, but a drive does not.

THE SOCIAL MOTIVES

Man does not live by bread alone, and the list of drives that
we have mentioned by no means exhausts all our sources of motivation. Another very powerful group of motives we might, for
want of a better term, classify as *social motives.* They are so designated because their origin seems to depend in one way or another
upon the social past of the individual. Most of them have a goal
that is related to the way in which other individuals react to us.

How many social motives should be listed and what names
should be given to those that are listed are questions for which no
final authoritative agreement is available. At the present time, it
would seem that most of the behavior we must account for can be
handled by four broad motive conditions. Their motives, together
with a general characterization of each of them, are:

1. *Achievement motivation,* resulting in actions directed
toward performing well in various activities.

2. *Affiliation motivation,* resulting in actions that may lead
the individual to be accepted by others.[11]

3. *Self-esteem motivation,* resulting in behavior that enhances the individual's opinion of himself, or prevents him from
losing respect for himself.[12]

4. *Anxiety motivation,* resulting in a wide variety of acts
that tend to remove the individual from certain situations.

The reader may be troubled by the fact that we have listed
but four social motives, while the variety of behaviors which he
may have observed in himself and his acquaintances is almost
infinitely great. People, he knows, may conform to social norms or
aggressively depart from them; they may work almost exclusively
to further their individual gains or submerge themselves for the
good of the group; they may be arrogantly indifferent to the
opinions of others or servile in their concern for these opinions.
He knows, also, that one man may disregard the feelings of others

and ride roughshod over his fellow men to obtain a position of preeminence in which he can exert his power and command respect, while another may quickly give up the striving for power in order to avoid censure. The reader may feel, therefore, that more than four social motives must be operative if we are to account for all of these behaviors.

The problem of accounting for a variety of behavior with a limited number of motives is not so great as it may at first seem to be. The solution comes by recalling that different instrumental acts may be used to obtain the same goal. The child who is rewarded by his parents for cooperating learns that cooperation is a way to gain favorable attention, while the child who has been encouraged to rebel may fixate this way of gaining favorable attention. Thus when we observe one child quietly cooperating and the other kicking over the traces, we are observing two different kinds of instrumental acts directed toward satisfying the same motive state; and not two motives, one to rebel and the other to cooperate.

Origin of nonbiological motives

The motives that are closely tied up with our social behavior are so common and so powerful that years ago psychologists considered them as instinctive in origin. More recently, however, data from various sources have led psychologists to reject this hypothesis and to believe instead that these motives are learned.

One of the chief sources of information that has thrown considerable doubt on these instinct theories is the work of the cultural anthropologists. Their field studies have shown that there may be vast differences among the kinds of social motivation predominating in various cultures. In the Kwakiutl Indian culture, for example, a native spends a very large part of his time in competing with his lifelong rival by acquiring more of his world's goods. Even to the competitively minded American, the Kwakiutl's preoccupation with acquiring more blankets or more valueless copper disks than his rival seems completely disproportionate. In the Zuñi tribe, one finds the reverse of this situation. Competition is looked down upon, and cooperative behavior predominates. It is difficult to believe that if these nonbiological motives were instinctive there could possibly be such vast differences among cultural groups. Rather, it seems more likely that each individual has learned to react in his own fashion partly because of the nature of the culture in which he was raised.[13]

It will be convenient to consider two general classes of learned motive states: (1) those in which the organism's behavior seems to be directed toward *approaching* specific objects or events and (2) those in which the behavior is concerned with *avoiding* or moving away from specific objects or events. The former are termed *positive,* or *approach,* motives and the latter *negative,* or *avoidance,* motives.

The learning of approach motives

A number of laboratory experiments have demonstrated that stimuli that have been associated with the satisfaction of a biological drive acquire the capacity to elicit approach responses and hence to serve as goals or incentives even when they are no longer associated with an incentive that satisfies a biological drive. The process by means of which a previously neutral stimulus may acquire the capacity to serve as an incentive is demonstrated in the following study.[14] A thirsty rat was placed in a Skinner box equipped with an automatic water-delivery mechanism. At irregular intervals of time a buzzer was sounded for two seconds and was immediately followed by the presentation of water. Soon the animal learned to approach the watering mechanism whenever the buzzer sounded. At this point a regime of partial reinforcement was introduced, for the sounding of the buzzer was not followed by water on every trial. Eventually, water was given only one time out of ten presentations of the buzzer. Nevertheless, the response of approaching the water mechanism continued to be elicited by the sound of the buzzer. Next, a lever was introduced into the box and when this lever was depressed by the rat, the buzzer was sounded, but no water was given following the bar press or the noise of the buzzer. Despite this fact, the rats developed the bar-pressing habit and the response became extinguished when it no longer was followed by the sounding of the buzzer. Thus the buzzer had acquired the capacity to reinforce other responses and influence the animal's behavior in the same way that a sip of water following the bar press would have done.

In another classic study in this field it was shown that chimpanzees will work to obtain poker chips which can be cashed in at a later time for food, and that they will work almost as hard to obtain poker chips as to obtain food itself. The chips, in this case, serve the champanzees as money serves the human.[15]

A stimulus that has acquired its motivational value by having been associated with another stimulus is called a *secondary reinforcer*. We have reason to believe that a stimulus may acquire secondary reinforcing values by being associated either with incentives which reduce a biological drive, such as food or water, and are called *primary reinforcers,* or even with another secondary reinforcer. A fairly simple example of this relationship between secondary reinforcements is the relationship between checks and money. Money is a secondary reinforcer, since it in itself does not satisfy a biological drive. Like the poker chips of the chimpanzees we have just mentioned, however, it does lead to the attainment of biologically satisfying incentives. Thus money acquires reinforcement values, and checks do the same because they can usually be converted into money. The example is not perfect since occasionally checks lead directly to some biological incentive.

In recent years a great deal of research with humans and lower animals as subjects has been conducted on the topic of secondary reinforcement and we know that it shows many of the characteristics of conditioned responses.[16] The most significant of these characteristics are:

1. A stimulus will lose its secondary reinforcing properties if it is presented repeatedly without further pairing with the original or primary reinforcement.

2. If partial reinforcement is employed in the original training (the potential secondary reinforcer sometimes being presented without primary reinforcement) then the secondary reinforcer shows more resistance to extinction than would be true if a 100 percent reinforcement schedule had been used.[17]

3. The greater the number of secondary reinforcement training trials that are given the more effective will the stimulus be as a secondary reinforcer.[18]

If we may extend these principles, which have been found to operate in many laboratory experiments, to the more complex environment of man, we can begin to see how social motives develop. The human infant is for many months a helpless creature who has his biological needs satisfied by the tender ministrations of the parent. The parental stimuli are thus associated time and again with biological reinforcement, and they should thereby

acquire secondary reinforcing properties. From our knowledge of
the phenomenon of stimulus generalization, we can readily predict
that this response would not be limited to the parents but would
spread to other individuals as well. Since other stimuli may acquire
incentive value by association with secondary reinforcement, the
way is open for an elaboration of motives.

The similarity between the development of these learned
motive states and the development of conditioned responses was
mentioned above. It is plausible to assume that many of the principles of behavior that determine the characteristics of the conditioned response function in this situation as well. One such
principle is that of extinction, and herein there seems to lie a
contradiction. Why do these learned motives not extinguish as
conditioned responses do? The answer is that they probably would
if they were presented repeatedly without reinforcement. We know
that rats will eventually cease to run to the food box if time after
time they enter it but find no food; chimpanzees will eventually
stop working for poker chips which can no longer be cashed in
for food. But this is no different from our attitude toward money
that cannot be exchanged for the staples of life. Witness the phrase
"not worth a continental," or our indifference toward a Confeder-
ate dollar.

It is probable that in the first place these social motives have
their origin in a partial-reinforcement environment and are therefore from the beginning highly resistant to extinction. We know
also that conditioned responses, once developed, may be maintained by only an occasional reinforcement. Moreover, responses
developed by one kind of reinforcement may be maintained by a
totally different kind of reinforcement. It is not difficult to suppose
that these principles operate for the learned motive states and
serve to keep them strong throughout life.

The learning of avoidance motives

Not all our motivated behavior is directed toward some positive and pleasurable goal; we are often motivated to move away
from some undesirable state of affairs. If we encounter pain, we
strive to escape from its source. Using the terminology of the preceding section, we would say that this behavior is a response to
a primary drive. Yet we also move away from situations in
which there is no actual pain but in which we are activated by

stimuli which in the past were associated with pain—situations in which we react, in other words, to *secondary* rather than to *primary* reinforcement.

This fact was clearly demonstrated in an experiment conducted on white rats.[19] The rat was first placed in a box whose floor consisted of an electrified grid (Figure 5.6). When the current was turned on, producing a shock, the animal quickly learned to escape through a door that led out of the box. Several such reinforcing trials were given, and soon each animal learned to run to the escape door even before the current was turned on. In a later part of the experiment, the animal acquired a new instrumental act as a result of the secondary reinforcer. The door was locked, but it could be opened by the manipulation of a little wheel. During this time no shocks were delivered and the behavior was not motivated directly by a pain stimulus. Nevertheless, the animals acquired the habit of turning the wheel and thereby escaping from the box. Later changes were made so that the wheel would no longer open the door, but it could be opened by pressing a bar. As a result, the wheel-turning response became extinguished and it was replaced by the bar-pressing response. It should be emphasized that no shocks were administered during the period when the animals learned either the wheel-turning or the bar-pressing response.

We may assume that because the stimuli within the box were formerly paired with shock, a state of *anxiety*, or tension, was

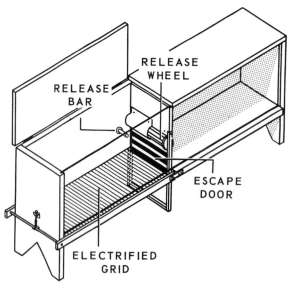

RELEASE WHEEL

RELEASE BAR

ESCAPE DOOR

ELECTRIFIED GRID

Fig. 5.6 Apparatus used to study the acquisition of avoidant motivation. (After Miller, *J. exper. Psychol.*, 1948, *38*, 89-101)

aroused in the rats. It was this tension state that motivated them and resulted in their learning to turn the wheel and thus to escape from the box.

When this instrumental response was no longer effective, that is, when it ceased to result in reinforcement, it was extinguished and the new reinforcing bar-pressing response was acquired.

By escaping, the rat would have removed itself from the stimuli that gave rise to its tensions, and the previous motivation would be reduced.

On the human level, we can all think of instances in which we struggled to remove ourselves from a stimulus situation that we conceived as being potentially painful. Perhaps what we called our conscience was the motivation, and it may have worked somewhat in the following manner. Our ideas of what is right and what is wrong are derived, for the most part, from the training given us by our parents. When as children we transgressed, we suffered punishment in one form or another at their hands. Now, when we, as adults, commit acts which our parents would have forbidden or at least frowned upon, an anxiety state arises. This happens even though our parents may be dead or have no knowledge of our act, and simply because we are placed in the type of situation that once led to punishment. The feeling of guilt or anxiety may continue until we have done something that quiets our conscience or, in psychological terminology, reduces the anxiety state.

BIOLOGICAL VS. SOCIAL MOTIVATION

One is always tempted to ask which is the more important, man's biological or his social motives. This is not an easy question to answer. In our present-day American culture, probably far more of the adult's daily behavior is directed by social than by immediate biological motives. This would seem to imply that our social motives have become more powerful than our biological motives. It must be recalled, however, that most of us live a life in which our biological drives are fairly well satisfied. Few of us have, for example, gone more than twelve working hours without food or water. Thus we can afford to delay dinner a few minutes for a

177

belated guest or to turn the handle of a drinking fountain for our friend to take the first drink.

Yet, if our physiological deprivations were greater, we might well find that some of the social niceties would fall by the wayside. Indeed, murder and cannibalism, perhaps the most abhorrent acts known to our culture, occurred in the Donner Party, a group of California immigrants who started late on their journey and were forced to winter with insufficient rations in the Western mountains. During the depression years many a man in order to obtain bread committed acts that he would have strongly condemned a few years earlier; acts of the same sort have been reported of prisoners on insufficient rations in concentration camps.

Obviously, the question of which motivation is stronger can be answered only within the framework of how well the particular society is satisfying the biological drives. If the biological drives are being well satisfied, we would expect social motives to occupy a position of great importance in daily living. If biological drives are not satisfied, they will be of greater significance.

The social and the biological motives are not, of course, completely independent. For one thing, our social behavior is most certainly influenced by the biological drives that happen to be operating at the moment. Every parent knows that the child's social behavior may deteriorate markedly when he is hungry or tired, or needs to eliminate. Even the adult's social behavior is not freed of this dependence upon his physiological states. How often have we reacted irritably to a companion, or made mountains out of molehills at a time when we are fatigued, hungry, or coming down with a cold? Later, when our physiological state has improved, we may think back to the situation and conclude that we had overreacted considerably.

Our social motives, in turn, largely determine not only when we shall satisfy our biological motives but also how. A food considered a delicacy in one culture may be violently rejected by persons of another culture, even though it is nutritious and quite capable of alleviating hunger pangs. We learn to direct our sexual behavior not toward the opposite sex in general but toward specific individuals. The standards of sexual attractiveness in one culture differ from those of another, and even within the same culture they may change from one decade to the next.

Thus we cannot hold in sharp contrast to each other the biological and the social motives. Although the biological drives may

be responsible for the origin of the social motives, they may later
become subservient to the offspring they have spawned. At the
same time, the social motives seldom gain complete independence
of our biological functioning and may be modified by it.

THE SPECIFICITY OF GOALS

Although our environment affords us a large number of
goal objects that are capable of satisfying a certain drive, we do not
accept all of them with equal readiness. Food that is considered a
delicacy by some may, as we have said, be an object of indifference
or even aversion to others. The demand for specific incentives is
not limited to food or even to drink; it includes our socialized goals
as well. The physical conformations considered beautiful in one
culture may be judged as ugly in another, and the very ways in
which people behave in the daily give and take of life may be most
acceptable to some subcultures and most objectionable to others
within the same culture. Even for the same individuals, preferences
in goal objects shift from time to time. For example, a food which
we scarcely notice today may be a source of great longing tomorrow.

In so far as preferences for foodstuffs is concerned, there
seems to be good evidence that at least some of our preferences are
determined by physiological need. Rats upon whom an operation
had been performed which resulted in a physiological need for
increased salt consumption immediately showed a marked preference for salted water as against unsalted water.[20] Again, rats deficient Vitamin B_1 chose a diet containing this vitamin in preference
to a diet without it. In these experiments, and in others, there was
no evidence that the animals *learned* that salt or Vitamin B_1 was
good for them. Rather, their behavior arose from certain physiological changes that led without the mediation of learning to a
preference for the needed food.[21]

We do not know what the mechanism is which leads to increased consumption of the needed food. A plausible theory which
has been advanced states that the need results in making the sense
organs more sensitive to the flavor of the needed food. Careful
experimentation, however, has indicated that this does not occur
and the ability to detect the flavor of the particular substance is no

179

greater in the animal which has a considerable need for it than in an animal whose immediate requirement for the particular substance is low.[22, 23]

We would be greatly in error to conclude from these experiments that all our specific preferences—we often use the word *appetites*—are solely the products of specific physiological needs. It has been shown time and again, both in experiments and in everyday life, that organisms may prefer foods that are markedly *lacking* in some necessary substances. In the East Indies, death is frequently caused by a Vitamin B_1 deficiency which arises because the sufferers live on a diet consisting primarily of polished rice. The population prefers polished rice, which lacks the vitamin, to unpolished rice, which contains a plentiful supply. There are many other instances of major or minor deficiencies that arise because the individual prefers an inadequate to an adequate diet.

The fact is that the custom of the country, or even of the locality in which we live or in which we have been reared, does much to determine our specific food preferences. In other words, the psychological mechanisms of learning are potent factors in determining our tastes, and it is likely that these mechanisms are more powerful than the physiological ones we have mentioned above.

MOTIVATION AND BEHAVIOR

Thus far we have identified our motives, both the biological and the social, and have given a brief sketch of the manner in which the social motives develop in the individual. We now turn to the problem of how motives operate to influence our behavior, and we will discuss this problem under the following three headings:

1. The influence of different levels of motivation on the adequacy of performance.

2. Motivation as a director of behavior, that is, as a mechanism for selecting the appropriate, and previously learned, instrumental response.

3. The influence of motivation on the acquisition of instrumental responses.

Levels of motivation and performance

Drives and incentives

Before considering the effect of different levels of motivation on performance, it is necessary to distinguish between two different ways in which the motivational level may be changed. One of these is by raising or lowering the level of the drive, that is by making the subject more or less hungry or more or less thirsty. The other is by manipulating the value of the incentive, that is by giving a larger or more desirable reward at the completion of the response as opposed to a smaller or less desirable reward. It is apparent that control of motivation level in adult human society is based primarily upon manipulations of incentive values, and one is promised more money or less money for working; or a higher grade or a lower grade; or much honor and praise or only a modicum of honor and praise. Fortunately, the effects of the level of motivation upon behavior are highly similar, whether the particular level has been achieved by manipulating the drive or the incentive value. For this reason we will not distinguish between these two means of manipulating motive level in the following discussions.

Moderate levels of motivation and performance

Certain baseball players, known as pinch hitters, are consistently able to make hits when teammates are on the bases and when a hit is necessary to win a close game. Often these players do not have exceptionally high batting averages, for they are not so likely to make hits when their team is well ahead and victory does not depend on their next hit. Thus, their batting efficiency is clearly related to the level of motivation. When their motivation is high, they perform exceptionally well; when the motivation is low, their batting performance is only moderate.

This relationship between performance and motivation can be expressed in the following equation:

$$\text{Performance} = \text{Habit level} \times \text{Motivation level.}$$

Now, as we recall from algebra, this equation means that the level of performance will vary as we change *either* the habit level *or* the motivation level. Of the pinch hitters, we can say that their batting habits remain unchanged but that their motivation level changes. And so they perform better at one time than another.

Perhaps we can illustrate this relationship more clearly by means of a formal and carefully controlled conditioning experiment similar to the sort that Pavlov employed.[24] By means of the familiar technique of presenting a tone and then food, dogs were first conditioned to salivate when a tone was sounded. After considerable training, the magnitude of the response remained quite constant from day to day for each animal; the conditioned response, in other words, had reached a stable level. Then came the crucial test—a testing of the conditioned responses under varying degrees of hunger. Tests were run on several days when the animals had been without food for 0, 24, 48, and 72 hours respectively. The magnitude of the conditioned response was determined by measurement of the quantity of saliva that was evoked by the conditioned stimulus alone. The results of the experiment are shown in Figure 5.7.

Since the strength of the habit had reached an essentially constant level before the variation in drive level was introduced, the differences in amount of salivary secretion are not due to differences in habit strength. The difference in the magnitude of the response can thus be due only to the differences in level of motivation at the time of testing.

Fig. 5.7 Relationship between the magnitude of the conditioned response and the drive level after the habit has been firmly established. (After Finch[24])

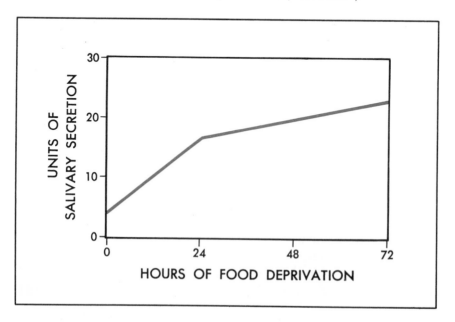

This principle of motivation has frequently been applied in industrial and other situations. The establishment of a bonus system is usually followed by an immediate increase in production. The coach who gives his team a pep talk during the half-time period and then sees them overwhelm the opponents during the last half is supplying the additional motivation which leads to superior performance.

The principle expressed by our equation—that habits and motivation are somewhat independent of each other—is an important one. Efficiency of performance is a function of two variables—the strength of the habit and the strength of the motivation. Often in our daily life we overlook this fact. Strive as we may, we cannot expect to perform well if the proper habits are not in our repertoire or are not well developed. Particularly in dealing with children, who because of their very youth have not had time to develop strong habits, we may falsely expect that if we motivate them properly they will do well. If the habit is inferior, so also will be the performance. Conversely, we may also commit the error of failing to supply sufficient motivation. In these circumstances even individuals who are highly skilled may perform in an inferior manner.

Performance at high levels of motivation

It is fairly obvious from what we have said thus far that some motivation is required to initiate performance and that increased motivation is associated with increased efficiency. Paradoxically, however, very strong motivation may be associated with a deterioration in efficiency. In all probability the relationship between motivation and efficiency on many tasks is a curvilinear one of the sort shown in Figure 5.8. Translated into words, this graph simply indicates that performance will increase in efficiency as we increase motivation *up to a certain level*. Thereafter, increases in motivation produce declines in the efficiency of behavior.

Some examples will show this principle in action. In one laboratory experiment, college students had learned to leave a room by way of one of three doors, one being unlocked, the other two locked. The unlocked door was changed from trial to trial and was never the same for two successive trials. Discovering this principle and remembering which door had been unlocked on the preceding trial constituted what the subjects were to learn. On any one trial this information cut down the number of choices of doors from three to two. After the subjects had become skilled in the

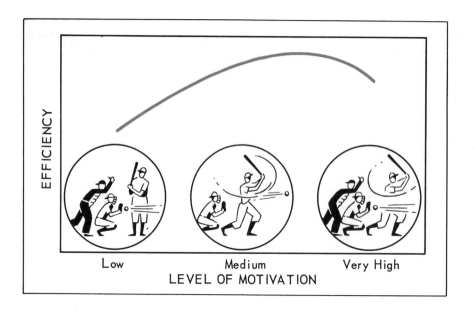

Fig. 5.8 A schematic representation of the relationship between level of motivation and efficiency of behavior. At low and high levels of motivation the result is the same, a strike-out, but the behavior of the batter is quite different.

task, working under the motivation of a small monetary reward, they one day entered the room and found an additional motive for escaping, supplied by an electric shock to their bare feet, for the entire floor of the room consisted of shock grid which could be electrified by the experimenter. For most subjects the performance on this day was not better but much poorer. They would try the door which had been unlocked on the preceding trial, or they would try a locked door, turn from it, then turn back and futilely try it again. Under the heightened motivation supplied by the shock, they were much less efficient in escaping from the room than they had been under the lower level of motivation. The increase in motivation led to an inferior rather than a superior performance.[25]

Another experiment—this time with chimpanzees as subjects and hunger as the motivation—illustrates the same principle. The task for the animals was to obtain food by solving various kinds of problems (Figure 5.9). The food was beyond the bars of the cage, in sight but out of reach, and the chimpanzees could obtain it only if they discovered and used some tool, such as a stick, with which the food could be pulled in. Animals were tested at low,

Fig. 5.9 An experiment to determine the relationship between strength of the hunger drive and efficiency of problem solution. The monkey is restrained from reaching the food directly with its arms by the chain. In the photograph above, the food can be pulled in with the stick the animal holds. In the photograph below, he must first pull in the longer stick with the shorter one and then pull in the food. (Courtesy Harry F. Harlow)

medium, and high levels of hunger, and the ability to solve proved to be inferior at both the low and the high levels.[26]

Examples of deterioration in efficiency under increased motivation are not infrequent in our daily life. The case of stage fright is a common one. A person who can recite his lines well before an empty auditorium may be speechless when he steps onto the stage on opening night. His failure cannot be attributed to a loss in motivation but rather to a motivational level that is too high. Some athletes who are outstanding in their performance on the practice field blow up on the day of the big game. College students frequently state that a poor showing on an examination resulted not from a lack of motivation but from such an excessive amount of motivation during the examination that they could remember nothing. Infants, when they are very hungry, often kick, squirm, and lose coordination of the sucking response. As a result they feed themselves less well than when their hunger is lower.

Performance, task difficulty, and motivation level

In the previous section we have arrived at the conclusion that performance is likely to deteriorate if the level of motivation is very high. The conclusion is an important one, but it would be a far more useful one if we could predict in advance how high the level of motivation could be raised before deterioration in performance occurred. A simple and single answer to this question can be obtained only if the optimal level of motivation is the same for all tasks; but such is not the case, for the motivational level which is optimal is not the same for different tasks, as the following experiments indicate.

▶ *Experiment 1. Drive level in discrimination learning.* The subjects of this experiment were white rats who were required to learn to enter the brighter of two illuminated alleys.[27] The apparatus in which they worked was a Y-shaped tank that was filled with water to a level slightly higher than the wire grating that covered the alleys. The rats moved through the equipment by swimming down the stem of the Y, and were confronted with two alleys with a door at the end of each of them. Each of these two doors could be illuminated independently; one of them was always more brightly lighted than the other, and this door was always unlocked. When the animals pushed it open they entered the goal compartment where they could arise to the surface and obtain a much-needed breath of air. If they approached the other, darker,

Fig. 5.10 A photograph of the type of underwater discrimination box discussed in the text. The animal begins his underwater swim at the bottom of the picture and exits from the situation through one of the two lighted doors shown in the upper center. The wire mesh is just below the surface of the water, thus preventing the animal from escaping except by way of the correct door.

door they found it locked and were forced to turn around and swim to the lighter one. The apparatus is pictured in Figure 5.10.

Tasks of three degrees of difficulty were produced by changing the difference on brightness between the doors. For the easiest task, the ratio of the illumination of one door to the other was 1 to 300; for the medium level task this ratio was 1 to 60; and it was 1 to 15 for the most difficult task. In other words, in the easy problem there was a marked contrast of the brightness of the two doors, while in the difficult problem the contrast was slight. An equal number of animals were trained under each condition.

Different motivational levels were produced in the following manner: A door was closed between the starting compartment and the rest of the maze. The animal was submerged in the starting compartment and was forced to remain there until the experimenter opened the door and admitted him into the discrimination box proper. Different delay periods—0, 2, 4, and 8 seconds—were used for various groups, and it is certainly plausible to assume that the level of motivation increased with the increase in submergence time. The question was, how would different motivational levels influence performance in the three different tasks. The results of

187

this experiment expressed in terms of the number of correct responses made during 100 trials are presented in Figure 5.11. This figure shows three curves, one for each problem: the easy, the moderate, and the difficult. In the case of the easy problem, the performance becomes progressively better through the first three drive levels. This is not true of the difficult task, however, for in this case the best performance is achieved by the 2-second group, and the two groups with the higher drive show rather marked inferiority in their performance. For the moderate group, the nature of the relationship between motivational level and performance seems to be something of a compromise between the relationships for the easy and for the difficult tasks.

Fig. 5.11 The effect of drive level (as produced by length of time of submersion in the starting chamber) on discrimination learning for three levels of difficulty of discrimination. (After Broadhurst[27])

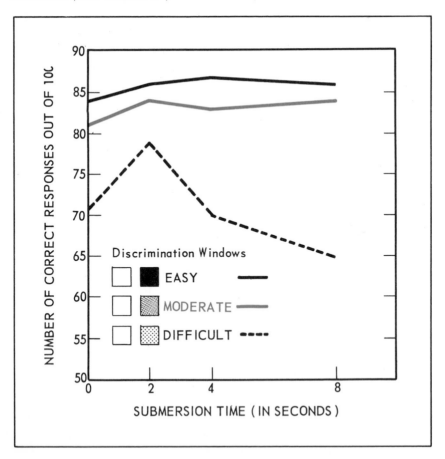

The fact that the highest oxygen-deprivation level did not result in the best performance for the easiest discrimination task might suggest that the motivational level was not so high for this group as it was for the 4-second group. That such is not the case is indicated by the results obtained in an even easier task. In this task the subjects simply swam down a straight alley and were permitted to come to the surface at the end of it. The experimenter measured their speed of swimming and found that it increased consistently up to a delay as long as 20 seconds.

This interaction between the influence of motivation level, performance, and discriminability of stimuli is called the Yerkes-Dodson Law, being named after two psychologists who first demonstrated it in an experiment similar to the one described above.

▶ *Experiment 2.[28] Anxiety and serial learning.* In Chapter 3 it was pointed out that the degree of difficulty involved in learning a list of verbal items is a function of the degree of similarity of items in the list and also of the ease of making associations to the individual items. The next experiment employed the technique of manipulating association value and item similarity in order to obtain lists of three different levels of difficulty. The three lists were learned by two groups of subjects, one high in motivation level, the other lower. If the assumption of an interaction among task difficulty, level of motivation, and efficiency of performance on the task is a correct one, then we would predict that the group with the high motivation level would surpass the low motivation group on the easy list, but be inferior to it on the difficult list.

Before the results of this experiment can be described, it is necessary to consider in some detail how the two different levels of motivation were obtained. First a questionnaire was used which was designed to measure the subjects' level of anxiety. That is, the questionnaire was made up of items which, according to the judgment of a group of clinical psychologists, were indicators of anxiety. If a subject answered many of the items in a certain way he would obtain a high anxiety score; if he answered in the opposite way he would obtain a low anxiety score. When a large group of subjects are given this test, scores are obtained ranging from a high to a low inferred anxiety level. In the present experiment, this test was given to a large group of students in an elementary psychology class and the 60 highest and 60 lowest subjects in anxiety score were selected to serve in the learning experiment proper. Each of the three lists was learned by 20 subjects from the high and the low anxiety groups.

The results of this experiment are presented in graphic form in Figure 5.12 below. The figure shows the learning curves for the most and the least difficult task, as well as the items in the two lists. It is apparent that an interaction among anxiety level, task difficulty, and efficiency does exist, for the anxious subjects— the colored lines—are superior to the nonanxious for the easier list, but inferior to them on the more difficult list. That the two lists actually did differ from each other in difficulty is shown by the fact that the groups in the easy list were making about 11 correct responses after 25 trials, while the groups on the difficult list were making only about 9 correct responses after 45 trials.

Fig. 5.12 Relationship between the level of anxiety as measured by a personality test and the learning of two lists of nonsense syllables, an easy and a difficult one. (After Montague[28])

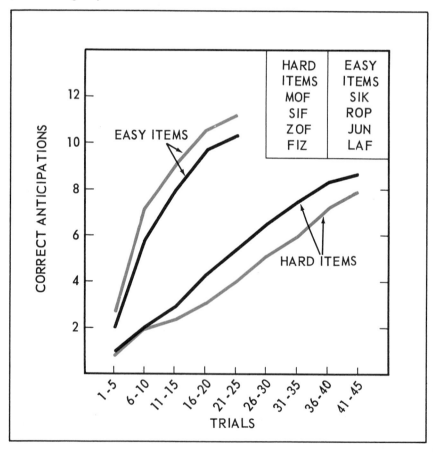

The interpretation which may be placed upon this experiment is that both anxious and nonanxious subjects were motivated to learn the list because they were requested to do so by the experimenter, the normal and pleasing reaction of students participating in psychological experiments. One of these groups, the anxious group, reacts to a variety of challenging situations by becoming strongly motivated, probably the result of a high level of achievement motivation, fear of failure, or both. This characteristic of them as a person is expressed by their responses on the anxiety questionnaire and is also elicited by the stimuli of the learning task. This additional motivation aids them on the simpler task, but proves a handicap to them on the difficult one.

▶ *Summary.* Although, as these two experiments indicate, the psychologist will never be able to identify a particular level of motivation that is optimal for performance on all tasks, he can indicate something about the nature of tasks in which high levels of motivation may be detrimental. These would seem to be tasks which are difficult to learn because they require fine discrimination of the individual stimuli, involve much similarity among the individual responses, and probably those which require fine coordination in the execution of the response. They are, in other words, tasks in which there is a high probability that erroneous responses will compete with the correct one.

The drive stimulus as a cue for instrumental responses

Thus far we have dealt with the motivational stimulus only as if it were something of an energizer of behavior that activated or strengthened responses to various external stimuli. Actually, however, the drive stimulus can guide behavior as well as generally energizing it.

An experiment with rats as subjects illustrates this principle in a very simple manner.[29] A maze like that shown in Figure 5.13 was used. Water was placed in the left-hand goal box and food in the right-hand one. On some days when the animals were placed at the starting point they were hungry but not thirsty; on other days they were thirsty but not hungry. Learning thus consisted of responding to the right when they were hungry and to the left when thirsty. This the animals learned to do.

At first glance the experiment may not seem particularly significant, but let us analyze it. Consider the animal's situation when he is standing at the choice point. Whether he is hungry or

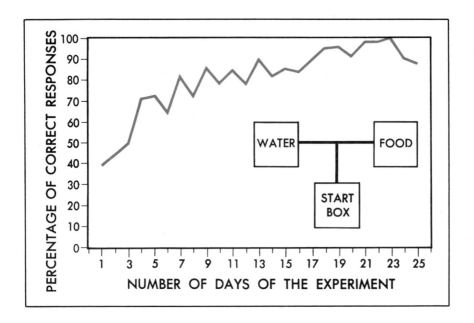

Fig. 5.13 Results of an experiment in which rats were required to make discriminatory responses in an unchanging external environment according to their current motivational status. The type of maze employed is shown below the graph. As the graph indicates, improvement was gradual, but perfection was never achieved during the experiment.

thirsty, the external environment is exactly the same. There is nothing in it to tell him that food is on one side and water is on the other. The rewards were not in sight, and we know from other experiments that no odors from the food could be detected to serve as a clue. The only differential stimulation which could be used to guide him to the correct response consisted of the stimuli within himself—the hunger stimulus or the thirst stimulus. Thus the motivation stimuli were not only energizing the animals but were eliciting the appropriate right- or left-turn response. The response of turning left had become attached to the thirst drive stimulus, and the response of turning right had become attached to the hunger drive stimulus.

In this case the drive stimulus is functioning in the same manner as the typical conditioned stimulus in a conditioning situation. The tone or the light becomes, we recall, a stimulus that evokes a specific response—salivation, movement of the eyelid, or a lifting of the finger. In a similar manner the drive stimulus acquires the power of evoking a specific instrumental response; a turning right for one drive stimulus, a turning left for the other. Its guidance of behavior is a very important characteristic of the drive stimulus, and one that gives us an understanding of the behavior of maladjusted persons who repeat an act again and again. The clinical psychologist has frequently found that successful treatment involves not working on the act itself but rather removing the motivational stimuli that give rise to the act. We shall return to this problem in Chapter 16.

Motivation and the acquisition of instrumental responses

Earlier in this chapter, we presented the simple formula: Performance = Habit level × Motivation level. The formula implies that the two psychological mechanisms, habit and motivation, are independent, that is the level of one may be changed without changing the level of the other. This conclusion is not merely theoretical speculation for there is a considerable body of experimental evidence which indicates that the conclusion is a sound one, and some of this evidence has been presented above. In this chapter we have described ways in which the level of motivation may be varied, as by the length of the deprivation period or the quantity of the incentive; in Chapter 3 we pointed out that the strength of a habit will be a function of the number of times it has been practiced. We now ask the question: What is the relationship between the magnitude of the incentive at the time the habit is being practiced and how strong the habit becomes?

Several studies have been performed in which one group of animals learned to run a maze for a large incentive, while another group learned to run for a small incentive.[30] After a number of practice trials, the large-incentive group now received the small reward and the small-incentive group now received the large reward. The typical finding, which is illustrated in Figure 5.14, is that the performance shifts almost immediately to correspond with the value of the reward being obtained. The rapid shift in performance is dependent upon the organism's ability to discriminate the difference in magnitude of the incentives, and there is evidence that the shift may not occur in certain situations until the organism has had experience with both rewards.[31] After shifting, the previously high reward group seems to perform no better than if

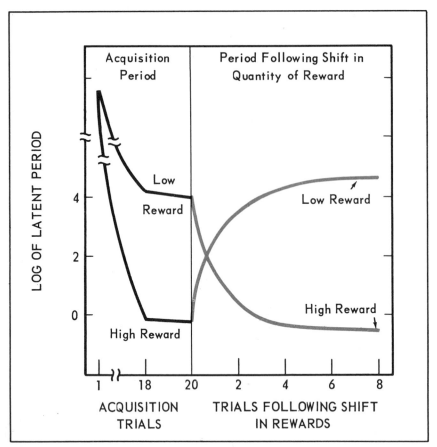

Fig. 5.14 Influence of quantity and a change in quantity of reward on performance as measured by time of leaving the starting box (latency). The left portion of the figure shows the performance during acquisition. The right shows the performance following the shift in reward. Notice the rapid effect of the shift in reward on performance. (Modified from Zeaman)

it had been receiving a small reward throughout the entire training session. Conversely, the group shifted to the larger reward seems not to have suffered from its training with the small reward. Since we consider habits to be permanent acquisitions of the organism we should not expect such dramatic changes in performance of the instrumental response. Therefore we may conclude that the habit strength of the two groups were the same, and that they did not develop at different rates because one group received a large reward and the other a small one. They perform differently from each other, it is true, but this is because the motivation level differed under the two incentive conditions, not because the habit values differed. The relationship between variations in drive level and habit is similar to that described above for variation in incentive value, although there is evidence that shifts from high to low drive levels sometimes do not result in a decline in performance.[32]

These laboratory studies indicate that magnitude of motivation influences only performance and not strength of the habit; but the facts of behavior in the work-a-day world seem to be contradictory. How can the contradictory conclusions be resolved? In the first place it is likely that events in the work-a-day world seldom involve the shifting in incentive value in either direction, and the occurrence of this shift is necessary for testing our conclusion. Thus we may seldom, if ever, have the opportunity of observing the kind of situation that isolates the effect of habit level and motivation level, and we confuse performance level with habit level.

In another, but indirect manner, motivation may determine the habit strength that the individual will develop in his every-day environment. This indirect effect arises from the contrast between the environment of the rat in the maze and a human in his world. A rat maze is usually a simple and austere environment, offering to the subject little to distract him from the main task of running its length and obtaining food in the goal box. Once he is placed in the starting compartment, it is fairly certain that he will practice the response that the experimenter demands of him. In the daily environment of the human, however, there are many, many stimuli that compete for his reactions, and reactions to these stimuli may satisfy various motivational states. As a result, unless the motivation to perform a particular task has at least a moderate strength, this task may not be practiced; instead, other activities may be learned. Thus, in a world of competing stimulation the motivation to engage in a particular activity must be strong enough to guarantee that the task will be practiced. Therefore, learning may be better if the motivation is high simply because this leads to more practice, and it is the frequency of practice which leads to strong habit formation, not some relationship between degree of motivation and amount of habit-strengthening resulting from a single trial. The contradiction between the results of laboratory research and the characteristics of every-day behavior may therefore be more apparent than real.

We have concluded that strength of motivation during learning influences performance and not habit growth. We may push the topic farther and ask if any motivation and reinforcement is necessary for learning. Stated somewhat more specifically, this is asking if S-R connections are formed because the response of the motivated individual is followed by reinforcement, or simply because the response is made in the presence of the stimulus. The question is a very difficult one to answer, and for good reasons different psychologists hold opposing views on the question. Some maintain that fixation will not occur unless reinforcement is given following the response, and the fixation occurs because the reinforcement is given. Others hold that motivation and reinforcement are important only in that they make the organism respond in a particular way, and that it is the frequency of responding in the presence of the stimulus which is responsible for the development of the habit.

From a practical point of view, however, it may not make a great deal of difference which of these views turns out to be the correct one. One position states that reinforcement is of intrinsic importance in habit formation; the other says that reinforcement is not intrinsically important although it is necessary for making the organism perform, and performing is required for habit formation. Therefore, both points of view imply that at least a minimum of motivation and reinforcement is essential. The theoretical issue is indeed an important one, but it is a problem which, because of its complexity, is more appropriately handled in detail in an advanced course.

PUNISHMENT

Punishment as a device for the control of behavior has had a long, though not an honorable, history. Society uses it as a means of preventing its members from violating both its formal and its unwritten laws, although its confidence in the effectiveness of this technique is not great. There is little enough justification for confidence, for time and again the threat of punishment has failed to keep the members of society in line. At numerous times in the history of civilization, the punishments prescribed for various crimes have been most severe. As recently as the nineteenth century, for example, long years of punishment and even death could be—and were—meted out for the theft of nothing more than a loaf of bread. Yet despite such inhuman penalties, transgressions occurred. As a deterrent to another world war we have legally prosecuted the leaders of aggressor nations as criminals and have punished them for their acts. Even so, the capitals of the world's great nations do not sleep easily, for we are not confident that the threat of punishment will deter other men or other nations from waging another war.

Psychologists themselves originally accepted the popular belief in the value of punishments—the belief that is expressed so dogmatically in the adage "Spare the rod and spoil the child." Experimental work of various kinds, however, soon indicated that the effectiveness of punishment is not consistent; sometimes it modifies our reaction to a stimulus and sometimes it does not. This seems to imply that punishment is not a single psychological mechanism which works in a single fashion but rather that its effectiveness will be a function of the various conditions in which it is used. It remains for the psychologists to analyze these in a scientific fashion. For the present we can do no more than consider some of the factors that may generally influence the effectiveness of punishment.

Let us first recall the usual situation in which punishment is brought into play. Generally it is simply one in which the organism has responded to a stimulus in a way which we wish will not recur. In other words, we are dealing with a stimulus→response connection which we hope to destroy by punishment. This connection may be one that has been strongly learned and, because of its strength, is likely to show great resistance to destructive efforts. Thus, one or two punishments may not prevent the response from occurring when the stimulus is again presented. Actually these punishments may decrease the probability that the response will occur, but we do not measure the response with sufficient precision to be aware of this. We wrongly expect Rome to be built in a day; we give up the punishment, thinking it has failed us. Thus, sometimes we may erroneously decide that the psychological mechanism has failed, whereas the failure lies in the fact that we did not apply it long enough.*

One reason for the ineffectiveness of punishment is that it usually takes place long after the response that it punishes. Let us

---

* This does not imply that it is necessarily desirable to use punishment as a technique for training; it simply states that the consistent use of it may serve to block certain stimulus→response connections. While this connection is being blocked, others which are also undesirable may be learned. A sound thrashing may break the child of the response of disturbing his father's workbench, but it may also teach him to hate his father.

take a not unusual case of a child who shortly before dinner opens a cupboard door and takes a piece of candy from a forbidden box which he knows is kept there. He pops the chocolate into his mouth, but tell-tale smudges are left on his lips. His misdemeanor is discovered, and punishment follows. Let us consider now the entire situation. To the stimulus of hunger pangs and the sight of the cupboard door, he made the response of opening the door and the box, and of taking and eating the candy. The candy acts as a reward, and that particular stimulus→response connection is reinforced. Later he may be punished for this same response, which just previously has been reinforced. Note the time relationship: the reward was immediate but the punishment was delayed. We recall that the sooner the consequences follow an act, the greater the learning effect. This fact would serve to give the rewarding effect of the act greater power than the punishing effect. Thus punishment frequently is required to work against the positive reinforcement that is intrinsic in the very commission of the act. Because the punishment almost always comes later in time than the reward, its effectiveness is lessened.

In Chapter 3 we described the manner in which conditioned responses may be eliminated by the withdrawal of reinforcement, an action which results in extinction. It will be noted that in the situation above reinforcement was never withdrawn and no opportunity for extinction occurred. The thief who, in a hold-up, obtains money and spends it has his antisocial actions reinforced. Even if later he should be committed to prison for his behavior—punished, that is—his antisocial actions may have been strengthened by the reinforcement received. If crime truly did not pay, then criminal acts would be extinguished.

Another and unfortunate characteristic of punishment is that often it tells the victim only *what not* to do but does not tell *what* to do. It does not build up by the process of reinforcement a strong positive way of reacting; it builds up only an avoidance of a certain way of acting.

We have mentioned some of the possible reasons why punishment may be ineffective. How, then, may punishment operate when it is effective? As we understand it today, punishment seems to operate in the same manner as the avoidance learning described earlier in this chapter. Behaving in a certain fashion leads to painful consequences and we tend to move away from these painful consequences. At the same time, through a process like conditioning, the stimuli that have been associated with the painful consequences acquire the tendency to produce anxiety reactions.[16] Since we tend to escape from an environment that produces anxiety, we tend to make a difference response than the one which has been associated with the pain of punishment. Thus punishment works not by weakening the original habit, but by substituting a conflicting response to the same stimulus.

The fact that punishment produces avoidance responses and anxiety is the reason that punishment often results in poorer rather than better performance. We have described above an experiment whose results demonstrated that high anxiety may be associated with inferior performance on a difficult task. If, therefore, punishment is involved in a task that is difficult, enough anxiety may be generated to lead to inferior performance. The very fact that the task is difficult to learn may be the reason why the punishment is introduced, the introducer feeling that punishment will have the desired effect of increasing the motivation to learn and thereby improving performance. If the task were a simple one which is quickly mastered, then we would not think it necessary to introduce extra motivation. Ironically, then, the additional anxiety motivation is supplied for the task where it is likely to do the most harm, and not for the one where it might facilitate performance.

REFERENCES

[1] Hill, W. F. Activity as an autonomous drive, *J. Comp. Physiol. Psychol.*, 1956, *49*, 15-19.

[2] Hill, W. F. The effect of long confinement on voluntary wheel running by rats, *J. Comp. Physiol. Psychol.*, 1958, *51*, 770-773.

[3] Harlow, H. F. "Motivation as a factor in new responses," in *Current Theory and Research in Motivation*, Edwards Bros., Ann Arbor: Univ. of Nebraska, 1953.

[4] Lepley, W. M. Variability as a variable, *Journal of Psychology*, 1954, *37*, 19-26.

[5] Dember, W. N. Response by the rat to environmental change, *J. Comp. Physiol. Psychol.*, 1956, *49*, 93-95.

[6] Bexton, W., Heron, W., and Scott, T. H. Effects of decreased variation in the sensory environment, *Canadian Journal of Psychology*, 1954, *8*, 70-76.

[7] Berlyne, D. E. *Conflict Arousal and Curiosity*, McGraw-Hill, 1960.

[8] Harlow, H. F. The nature of love, *Amer. Psychol.*, 1958, *13*, 673-685.

[9] Beach, F. A. "Characteristics of the masculine sex drive," in *Nebraska Symposium on Motivation*, Univ. of Nebraska, 1956.

10 Campbell, B. A., and Sheffield, F. D. Relation of random activity to food deprivation, *J. Comp. Physiol. Psychol.*, 1953, *46*, 320-322.

11 McClelland, D. C., Attkinson, J. W., Clark, R., and Howell, E. L. *The Achievement Motive*, Appleton, 1953.

12 Sears, P. S. "Problems in the investigation of achievement and self-esteem motivation," in *Nebraska Symposium on Motivation*, Univ. of Nebraska, 1957.

13 Mead, M. *Cooperation and Competition among Primitive Peoples*, McGraw-Hill, 1937.

14 Zimmerman, D. W. Durable secondary reinforcement: Method and theory. *Psychol. Rev.*, 1957, *64*, 373-383.

15 Wolfe, J. B. *Effectiveness of Token-Rewards for Chimpanzees*, Comp. Psychol. Mono., Vol. 12, No. 5, 1936.

16 Mowrer, O. H. *Learning Theory and Behavior*, Wiley, 1960.

17 Saltzman, I. J. Maze learning in the absence of primary reinforcement: A study of secondary reinforcement, *J. Comp. Physiol. Psychol.*, 1949, *42*, 161-173.

18 Miles, R. C. The relative effectiveness of secondary reinforcers throughout deprivation and habit strength parameters, *J. Comp. Physiol. Psychol.*, 1956, *49*, 126-130.

19 Miller, N. A. "Learnable drives and rewards," in S. S. Stevens (ed.), *Handbook of Experimental Psychology*, Wiley, 1951.

20 Richter, C. P. Salt thresholds of normal and adrenalectomized rats, *Endocrinology*, 1939, *24*, 367-371.

21 Young, P. T. Appetite, palatability and feeding habit: A critical review, *Psychol. Bull.*, 1948, *45*, 289-320.

22 Pfaffmann, Carl, and Bare, John K. Gustatory nerve discharges in normal and adrenalectomized rats, *J. Comp. Physiol. Psychol.*, 1950, *43*, 320-324.

23 Carr, W. J. The effect of adrenalectomy upon the NaCl taste threshold in rats, *J. Comp. Physiol. Psychol.*, 1952, *45*, 377-380.

24 Finch, G. A. Hunger as a determinant of conditional and unconditional salivary responses, *Am. Journal of Physiol.*, 1938, *123*, 379-382.

25 Patrick, J. R. Studies in rational behavior and emotional excitement: II. The effect of emotional excitement on rational behavior in human subjects, *J. Comp. Psychol.*, 1934, *18*, 153-195.

26 Birch, H. G. The role of motivational factors in insightful problem-solving, *J. Comp. Psychol.*, 1945, *38*, 295-317.

27 Broadhurst, P. L. Emotionality and the Yerkes-Dodson Law, *J. exper. Psychol.*, 1957, *54*, 345-351.

28 Montague, E. K. The role of anxiety in serial rote learning, *J. exper. Psychol.*, 1953, *45*, 91-96.

29 Leeper, R. The role of motivation in learning: A study of the phenomenon of differential motivational control of the utilization of habits, *J. Genetic Psychol.*, 1935, *46*, 3-40.

30 Pubols, B. H., Jr. Incentive magnitude, learning and performance in animals, *Psychol. Bull.*, 1960, *57*, 89-115.

31 Meyer, D. R. The effects of differential rewards on discrimination reversal learning in monkeys, *J. exper. Psychol.*, 1951, *41*, 268-274.

32 Deese, J., and Carpenter, J. A. Drive level and reinforcement, *J. exper. Psychol.*, 1951, *42*, 236-238.

Chapter Six

CONFLICTS

WE LEARNED IN THE PRECEDING CHAP-
ter, that a large variety of motive states demand relief and drive an
organism into action. Along with this great variation in motive
states, there is, not surprisingly, also a variation in the kinds of
activities that lead to a satisfaction of motives. This fact becomes
significant and disturbing for the organism when at one and the
same time two strong motive states are in operation, each demanding satisfaction but each requiring a different type of activity to
reach that satisfaction. An organism cannot perform both types of
activities at the same time and so may become like A. A. Milne's
shipwrecked—

> . . . old sailor my grandfather knew
> Who had so many things which he wanted to do
> That whenever he thought it was time to begin
> He couldn't because of the state he was in.

. . . . . .

201

And so in the end he did nothing at all.
But basked on a shingle wrapped up in a shawl
And I think it is dreadful the way he behaved—
He did nothing but basking until he was saved.*

Fortunately most of us find that our concurrent wants usually are not all so strong and so equal in strength that they imperiously and simultaneously demand appeasement and by their separate and conflicting insistences result in our doing nothing at all. Yet this type of situation does lead to difficulties in personal adjustment, and there are few of us who have not at sometime suffered, to a mild degree at least, from the demands of conflicting motives.

When we are in the old sailor's predicament, our life seems to be vague and jumbled, chaotic and whirling. Nevertheless, though to ourselves our status may seem to defy analysis, it is usually true that our situation can be considerably clarified if we can identify the motives that are operating. More often than not, this identification will lead directly or indirectly to the solution of the difficulty. It is worth while, therefore, to consider the basic types of situations in which motives conflict and the ways in which these conflicts are sometimes resolved.

TYPES OF CONFLICT SITUATIONS

An analysis of conflict situations is best achieved if we classify the various types of motive situations as (1) those in which our behavior is that of *approaching* some goal object or situation, or (2) those in which our behavior is that of *avoiding* or moving away from some goal object or situation.

Before we consider how a combination of approach tendencies and avoidance tendencies may lead to conflict, it is well for us to examine the changes that occur in motive strength as we move toward a positive goal or away from a negative one.

The reader will recall how in childhood his impatience for the arrival of Christmas or a birthday grew as the day approached. Rather than being lessened by increasing proximity, our longing

* From *Now We Are Six*, by A. A. Milne. Copyright, 1927, by E. P. Dutton & Co., Inc.

for the day grew stronger. Or he may remember how, as he approached some desired locale—home after a long sojourn away, or
an oft-visited vacation spot in June—his eagerness to reach the
journey's end mounts with diminishing distance.

A similar phenomenon occurs in negative, or avoidance, situations. We may be full of certainty on our way to the swimming pool that this time we shall dive from the highest board; from a distance the height does not seem fearsome. But as we climb the many, many steps leading to the platform we grow more and more concerned and, after standing for many indecisive moments peering at the hard sheen of the water below, we beat an ignominious retreat. A dental appointment scheduled for a week hence does not trouble us, but we feel quite differently as we sit in the dentist's office nervously fumbling through a magazine.

This tendency for the strength of our motivation to increase as the individual nears a positive incentive or an avoidance stimulus has been measured in the laboratory.[1] In one of the experiments rats were strapped on a saddle on a platform which slid backward and forward on a track. Ten seconds after a light was presented, the platform was moved forward about three inches on its track and this movement gave the hungry rat access to a food tray. The saddle itself could be pushed a short distance forward or backward on the platform by the rat, much as you can move a chair you are sitting on, and the amount of this push was the response that was measured in the experiment. A number of trials were given during which the ten-second light was followed by the forward movement of the platform and the receipt of food. As a result, the animals developed a tendency to push the saddle forward during the time the light was on and prior to the receipt of food. Concurrently with this training an avoidance reaction was also being acquired. Using the same setup, the experimenter sounded a buzzer for ten seconds, and an electric shock was administered after the platform was moved forward. Thus, for the rat the light became a stimulus for making an approach reaction, and the buzzer for making an avoidance reaction. In both instances the response of the rat was recorded during the ten-second interval when either stimulus was presented. The results of this experiment are presented in Figure 6.1. It shows the amount that the saddle was displaced by the rats' pushing toward or away from the end of the track during different times after the onset of the stimulus. It is apparent that one stimulus produced an approach reaction and the other an avoidance reaction;

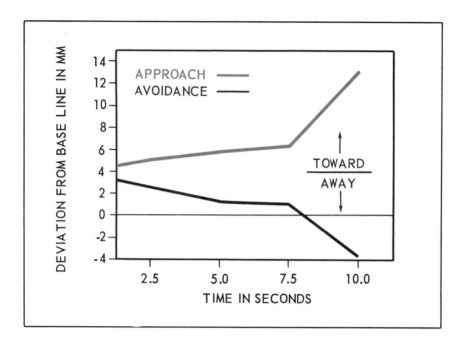

Fig. 6.1 Approach and avoidant gradients in time, as generated by rats in response to a positive and a negative stimulus. (After Rigby[1])

and, further, that the magnitude of both of these reactions increased as the time for the reception of the food or the shock approached. Similar results have been found in a study in which rats ran down a straight alley either to escape a shock or to approach food.[2] These studies, as well as observations in everyday life, permit us to draw the following conclusions:

1. As the individual nears the time or the location of a positive incentive, the level of the motivation toward that incentive increases.

2. As the individual nears the time or the location of a painful or undesirable event, the level of motivation to avoid that event increases.

3. There is evidence that for most avoidance situations the level of motivation rises more steeply as the organism nears the significant event than it does in approach situations.

We shall soon see how this phenomenon of changing strength of approach and avoidance responses as a function of what we will hereafter call psychological distance from the positive or negative stimulus contributes to the complexities of our behavior and leads to disturbing dilemmas.[3]

The approach-approach, or positive-positive, conflict

When we agree to go out on a date for Friday night with one campus personality rather than another, when we choose fried chicken rather than roast beef from the dinner menu, or when we decide to attend one movie rather than another, we are resolving conflicts of the approach-approach variety. The conflict occurs because it is not possible to date the two people, to eat the two dishes, or to attend the two movies simultaneously. By the act of responding to one of the incentives, we at the same time turn our backs on the other. The situation is not of the gravest importance. We may vacillate for a time, leaning first in this direction, then in the other, but after a while we make a choice.

The situation is illustrated graphically in Figure 6.2. There are two goals, Goal 1 and Goal 2, one to the left and one to the right. The individual cannot approach both goals simultaneously, for as he goes toward one he must move away from the other. We

Fig. 6.2 A schematic representation of the approach-approach conflict situation, in which both goals are equally acceptable.

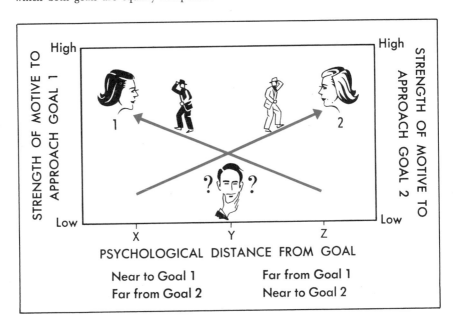

shall assume that we can represent the individual's psychological distance from either goal by the physical distance on the horizontal axis. At point *Y*, he is equidistant from each goal; at *Z* he is closer to Goal 2 than to Goal 1. We shall also assume that the height on the vertical axis indicates the strength of the motive. Let us for the time being disregard Goal 2 and speak only of Goal 1 and the tendency to approach it. The strength of the tendency to approach Goal 1 is indicated by the height of the line with the arrow pointing toward Goal 1. When the organism is at position *Z*, at the right of the graph, he is a considerable psychological distance from Goal 1 and the tendency to approach it is not strong. However, as he moves closer to Goal 1, his motivation to reach that goal increases—the line slopes upward. The same relationship holds for Goal 2 and its appropriate motive state.

So far we have been considering these motive-goal relationships separately. What would happen if both were operating in the organism at the same time? If the subject were located at a position equidistant from the two goals, where the strengths of instigation toward the two are equal, he would be subjected to conflicting tendencies, pulled in opposing directions. He would be in the situation of the jackass in the fable who starved to death while standing equidistant from two bales of hay. Actually, however, the fable is psychologically unsound; conflicts of this sort are quite temporary. Organisms are like sticks balanced on a knife edge; the slightest environmental change will destroy the precarious balance. When this occurs and there is a slight movement toward one goal, the strength of the motivation to reach this goal increases, and the strength of motivation toward the other goal decreases. The organism moves rapidly toward one goal, just as the balanced stick, once thrown out of equilibrium, falls ever more rapidly to one side. In such a situation as this, therefore, there will be a time of indecision, but once the approach to one goal is begun, the behavior is smooth and satisfactory. Thus, we may hesitate over our choice of dates, menus, or movies; but once we have chosen, the conflict situation is terminated.

It will be noted that in all the examples we have cited, either one of the two goals that are responsible for the brief conflict will satisfy the same basic motive state. And we may assume that the subject reacts to either goal as equally capable of satisfying the motive, for, if this were not so, there would be no cause for conflict. Thus, if any definite positive response is made, the conflict is solved in a very real sense, for the response—either response—will serve to decrease the major motive tensions that are driving the organism.

Other conflict situations of this same approach-approach variety may be caused by two *different* motives. The choice may lie between dinner at an expensive restaurant or the purchase of a handsome tie when our budget is too limited to include both. We may be trying to choose between attending summer school next summer and working on a well-paying job. In these situations both of the paired activities may prove equally attractive, but the consequences of choice are quite different from those described in the preceding paragraphs. If the dinner is chosen, the hunger drive is appeased, but the social or esthetic motive behind the demand for the tie is unaffected.

The difference in behavior between these two varieties of approach-approach conflict situations has been clearly illustrated in a laboratory experiment. Some young children were asked to choose between two kinds of candy, or two kinds of toys, with the understanding that they could keep the object chosen. The time required to make these choices was measured. Then, in another part of the experiment, they were asked to choose between candy and a toy. The time required to make a choice in this latter situation was considerably longer than the time taken when both objects satisfied the same motive.

A further difference between these two types of conflict situation will be found in the reactions of the organism after the choice has been made. In one type of conflict, the major motive state is eliminated by the choice—either choice; in the other, one motive remains unrelieved after choice and the organism's total satisfaction is less—so much so that it may lead to regret and to longing backward glances toward the forsaken object. The situation gives rise not only to more moments of conflict but to subsequent unrest and incomplete satisfaction as well.

The approach-avoidance, or positive-negative, conflict

Often a single object combines the tendency to attract us with the tendency to repel; it is both positive and negative in character. Although at one moment we are drawn toward this thing or this person, at the next we flee. The tendency to approach and the tendency to avoid clash with each other.

207

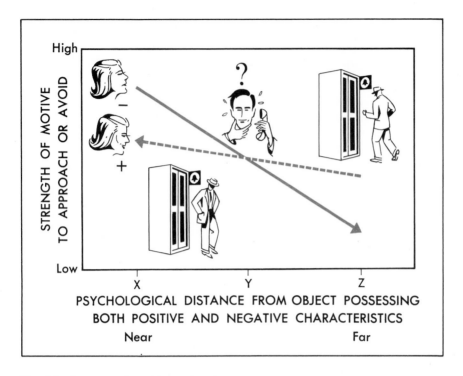

Fig. 6.3 An approach-avoidance situation. Although the strength of the tendency to approach increases as the individual approaches the goal, the avoidance tendency increases even more rapidly. As a result, a conflict arises.

Conflicts of the approach-avoidance variety may be graphically illustrated by the diagram shown in Figure 6.3, which is quite similar to Figure 6.2. Again we represent psychological distance by position along the horizontal axis and strength of motivation by position along the vertical axis. There are two motives represented; one is the tendency to approach the object—the broken line, and one the tendency to avoid it—the solid line.

As we have said, the closer we are to a desired object, the greater its motive strength. A similar principle applies to an avoidance object: the closer we are to it, the more repellent it becomes. There are reasons to believe, however, that as we near the dreaded object, the avoidance tendency builds up more rapidly than the motivation for a desired object. The result is that while we are some psychological distance (as at point Z) from the object which both attracts and repels us, the approach tendency predominates. When we come close to the object, however, the relative strengths of the two opposing tendencies are reversed (point X) and we are forced from the object. One may wonder why we do not stop motionless at point *Y*, where the approach and avoidance tendencies are of equal strength. It would seem that there is some sort of psychological inertia which carries us beyond it, but once beyond it we reverse our direction, and so, unless some change occurs in the relative strength of the two motives, we vacillate back and forth "unable to make up our minds."

An experimental demonstration of the behavioral consequences of a simultaneous approach and avoidance situation is illustrated by the second part of an experiment described earlier in this chapter, in which rats learned to push forward on their saddle when a light flashed on and to push backward when a buzzer sounded. Following this training, the light and the tone were presented simultaneously, thus placing the animals in an approach-avoidance conflict situation. The reactions of four animals to this conflict are illustrated in Figure 6.4. Three of the animals remained nearly motionless throughout the ten-second period, suggesting that the tendencies to approach and to avoid were nearly equal to

Fig. 6.4 The behavior of animals in a conflict situation. In this experiment positive and negative stimuli were presented simultaneously. These curves should be contrasted with those of Figure 6.1, showing the results when the positive and negative stimuli were presented separately. (After Rigby[1])

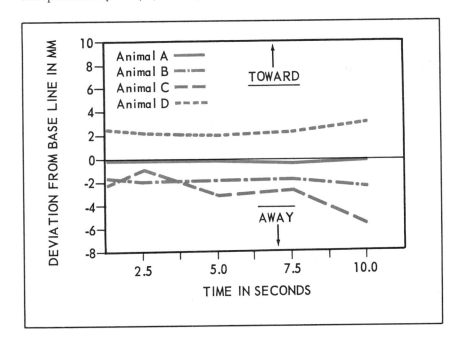

Fig. 6.5 Many of us may enter some novel situation—the first day of school, a new job, or a social event—with combined approach and avoidance tendencies. We hope to succeed in the activity and to be accepted by our associates, but we are haunted by thoughts of potential failure and potential rejection. (Courtesy *Columbus Dispatch*)

each other throughout the period of stimulation. The fourth animal vacillated at first, but showed a predominant avoidance tendency during the latter part of the duration of the stimulus. The responses of the animals during this ten-second period of double stimulation are clearly different from their responses to either stimulus alone. They did not react by avoiding or approaching; they reacted by making a compromise of the two, and the result for most of them was inaction. Vacillation and inaction are the characteristic behaviors associated with the approach-avoidance conflict situation.

The young man is enticed by the thought of dating the girl of the moment, but he fears that she may rebuff his efforts or scorn him for his awkwardness on the dance floor. As he mulls the problem over, he is sure he cannot fail, and with dime in hand he approaches the telephone. But as he comes closer to the goal—a goal which both attracts and repels—the avoidance tendency predominates. He therefore pockets his dime. But this does not close the episode; he mulls over his dilemma further and again decides to telephone her but again thinks better of his resolve. The result, in this situation, is just another of those intended phone calls that never get made.

Planning for one's vocational future often leads to conflicts of this sort. Perhaps a certain profession appeals strongly to us, but to gain it we must take a series of courses that we do not like. Or perhaps conflict occurs when we are invited to perform on some occasion; we are drawn toward accepting by the thought of the acclaim we shall gain, but we resist accepting because of a fear of failure, or because of the preparation involved. Time and again we meet such situations, when we vacillate and do nothing about the problem, until, in ways to be described later, we find some means to solve the conflict, or at least to remove ourselves from it.

The avoidance-avoidance, or negative-negative, conflict

Fortunate is the student who has not been confronted with stiff examinations in a course in which his grades are already so low that failure is imminent. The thought of failure is repellent, but so too is the thought of studying on an early spring evening.

This situation can also be represented graphically. Unlike the two preceding conflict situations, this situation has nothing in it that attracts the individual, and the strong wish of the organism is to escape from the whole unhappy business, to move away from both unpleasant situations. In Figure 6.6 this means to move in the direction of the broken arrows.

Let us see how this operates for our conflicted and unhappy student. The evening meal is now over, and his studying is yet to be done. Yesterday he had promised himself that he would study this afternoon, but somehow it had not worked out that way. There were other things to do. But now there is no further putting it off and he will get right to it—as soon, that is, as he finishes the sports page or just one more rubber of bridge. At last he is in his room at his desk with his textbook before him. But everything is not yet in readiness—a pencil needs sharpening or a pen needs filling. He does this and actually begins to work. Yet, without quite knowing how or why, he discovers that he is not studying but is thinking of something a thousand miles away. The reverie is pleasant, but it is disturbed by thoughts of failure over the examination. Firmly he decides: back to the book. And so through the evening, with work and daydreaming alternating.

One of the notable characteristics of the behavior of our procrastinating student is that he is constantly attempting to escape

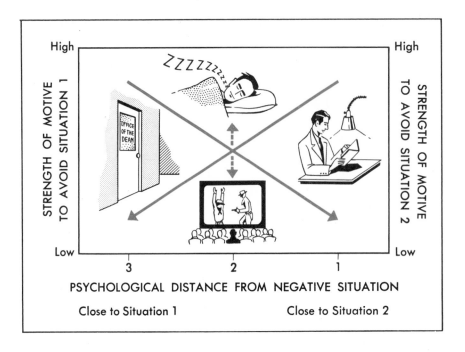

High — STRENGTH OF MOTIVE TO AVOID SITUATION 1 — Low

High — STRENGTH OF MOTIVE TO AVOID SITUATION 2 — Low

3   2   1

PSYCHOLOGICAL DISTANCE FROM NEGATIVE SITUATION

Close to Situation 1   Close to Situation 2

Fig. 6.6 An avoidance-avoidance situation. The student is repelled by both activities: threat of a conference with the dean and studying. His solution may be to escape from thoughts of these into irrelevant activities.

from the situation. He may escape by finding little odd jobs that need doing, by accepting readily some interruption from outside, or by daydreaming. In any case he is moving away from both the Scylla of study and the Charybdis of fear of failure. So it is with conflict situations of this sort: we tend to remove ourselves from the situation because we cannot readily approach either undesirable object or activity.

A simple demonstration of the reaction of organisms to the avoidance-avoidance conflict situation is provided in the following experiment.[4] White rats were trained to escape from an electric shock which was administered at both ends of an alley. Whenever the shock was applied, a buzzer was sounded and a light was flashed on at the particular end of the alley that was being electrified. Thus the buzzer and the light became conditioned avoidance stimuli for the particular locus in which they occurred. In the critical test trials the animal was placed somewhere near the middle of the maze and the signals at *both* ends of the maze were presented simultaneously. If the animals were nearer one end of the maze than the other, they would move away from the nearer end toward the center, and then vacillate back and forth. In addition, many of the animals attempted to climb the walls of the maze and thus escape from the situation.

Complicated approach-approach conflict

At the conclusion of the discussion of approach-approach conflict situation, the statement was made that such conflicts are easily solved, and certainly the theoretical analysis implies that this must be the case. It is likely that this statement did not ring completely true to the reader, for he may have recalled an episode when the decision to choose one of two generally desirable courses of action was arrived at only after a prolonged period of stress and much vacillation.

Perhaps the situation in question is one of choosing which college to attend, and the prospective student has reduced the possibilities to two highly desirable universities. University A appeals in particular because it is close to home, because several high-school friends are going there, and because it offers excellent instruction in an area of work in which the student is quite interested. However, the student does not like the fact that it is so large. University B appeals in particular because it is of moderate size and has an excellent national reputation, and is situated in a very pleasant part of the country. But it too has its drawbacks, for the student has no friends who go there, and it is expensive. What is notable about this conflict situation is the fact that although there is an over-all attractiveness to each institution, there is also at least one characteristic of each place which is undesirable. Since the growth of avoidance motivation as we approach an object endowed with it is usually greater than the growth of the positive motivation, the over-all attractiveness of the goal lessens somewhat as we near such a goal, and the competitor begins to predominate. The consequence is vacillation.

In summary, simple and uncomplicated approach-approach conflict situations are solved with ease; but this is not true if two generally attractive goals have associated with them a small negative characteristic.

Choice and motive strength

Before we consider the methods by which conflicts of motive are resolved, there is one assumption that must be made explicit:

213

when a conflict is resolved, the specific response elicited is made because the motivation to respond in this fashion is, at the moment, stronger than the motivation to respond in any other fashion. The individual does not *will* to do one thing or another; his behavior is determined by the relative strength of the motives that are operating at that instant. When he chooses to do *A* rather than *B*, his action simply indicates that the motivation toward *A* is greater than the motivation toward *B*.

This assumption leads to the conclusion that if we knew a great deal about the strength of the competing motivational tendencies we could predict what behavior will occur in a given situation. In the previous chapter it was pointed out that the strength of an acquired motive increases with increase in practice. We may therefore use our knowledge of the amount of practice given in order to predict the outcome of a conflict situation, as the following experiment demonstrates.[5] Hungry rats were divided into four groups and trained to run down a straight alley and find food in the goal box at its end. The four groups differed only in the number of practice trials given, which were 3, 9, 27, or 81. Thus approach reactions of different strengths were developed. Following this training, each group was subdivided into three small groups, which had different amounts of avoidance training administered to them. The avoidance training consisted of shocking the animals in the goal box, with one, two, or three shocks being delivered. As a result, the goal box acquired an approach-avoidance characteristic, for it had been associated with both a positive and a negative stimulus. The rats were then placed at the start of the runway in order to determine whether or not they would approach and enter the goal box. The results are shown in Figure 6.7. It is apparent that the behavior is a joint function of the strength of the approach tendency (as inferred from the number of training trials given) and the strength of the avoidance tendency (as inferred from the number of shocks given). Although the results of this experiment do not prove that our assumption is correct, it does indicate that the assumption is a useful one in predicting behavior.

The interpretation which we have made of the mechanisms responsible for our actions in conflict situations offers a suggestion of at least one of the methods by means of which conflicts can be solved. The method suggested is to modify the strength of one or the other competing motives so that it will predominate and direct the course of behavior.

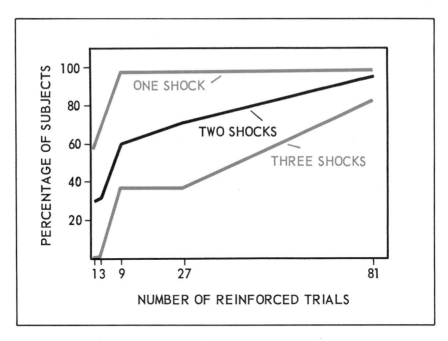

Fig. 6.7 The percentages of animals that reached the goal box after different numbers of trials, as a function of the number of approach-training trials and the number of previous shocks that had been administered to the animals in the goal box.

THE RESOLUTION OF CONFLICTS

The consequences of being placed in conflict situations are not pleasant to any organism. The consequences range from mild unhappiness to the more serious condition that is often, but incorrectly, referred to as a nervous breakdown. Our identification of the cause of such disturbances—whether they be mild or severe—as being a conflict in motives should give us some understanding of how they can be avoided or at least minimized. They can be avoided only by changing the relative strengths of the motives that are present in the situation.

This statement seems altogether apparent—just another of those statements of the obvious, the reader may say, that the psychologist so often makes. Yet in a time of conflict the motive relationships are often not apparent to the sufferer; he feels distraught and nervous, unable to concentrate and perhaps unable to sleep.

215

Failing to identify the causes, but only to well aware of the symptoms, he may think of some former acquaintance who "had a breakdown," or he may be reminded of a mentally disturbed character in some movie or play. And with these thoughts comes the horrible premonition that such is his own destiny, and that he is moving inexorably toward this unhappy fate. The little crotchets, the peculiarities, the odd thoughts that have always been with him—and have always been with all of us—now become sinister forerunners of an inevitable downfall.

These peculiarities are not abnormal—either for him or for us—but his own concern, like a carnival mirror, distorts them into frightening shapes. His twisted interpretations lead to more tension, to more sleeplessness, and to more exhaustion, and these in turn lead to more symptoms and, through fatigue, to less ability to handle the problem. And so a vicious circle is begun, which unless broken may actually lead to the dire consequences he so greatly fears.

In many cases the final break could have been avoided had the patient seen that his problem stemmed not from some inevitably burgeoning seeds of madness within himself but from conflicts of motives that were determined in part by his immediate environment and in part by his past habits. Fortunately for all of us, environments, motives, and habits too may be changed.

Changing the actual environment

Let us note the effects of a change of environment in the case of a very disturbed student whom we shall call Mary. Mary was enrolled in a private college where the emphasis upon academic achievement was far greater than in most universities. A student was respected by fellow students for making good grades, and he lost respect by making poor ones. "Just passing" was not enough, nor was a C; most students were satisfied with nothing less than a B. Furthermore, since only students who had done outstanding work in high school were admitted, the competition was keen.

Mary's problem was simple enough. She was earning C's in most of her courses. By devoting excessively long hours to study she could probably make a larger proportion of A's and B's. But studying would curtail her social life greatly if not completely. To gain the goal of high grades, she would be forced to relinquish the goal of social participation. After some discussion she was advised that this situation was likely to hold for her as long as she remained at this college but that it would not hold in some other colleges. The following fall she enrolled in a near-by state university—one which had a fine academic reputation—and by the following spring she was making good grades and also enjoying her social life. The strain and the conflict of the preceding year had disappeared.

Mary's was a conflict that was solved by no essential change in motivation on her part. The motives of obtaining high academic grades and at the same time of participating in social activities were still present. In one environment both could not be satisfied simultaneously, but in another they could. The solution to the conflict consisted in placing Mary in the environment in which both motives could be satisfied.

Actually the situation was not solved so easily as the description implies. To accept the change, Mary had also to accept the fact that she was not so able as many other students. Most of us have some degree of pride, which makes it difficult for us to see ourselves as inferior in ability. This pride, too, sometimes keeps us working toward goals whose only attainment value is to satisfy this pride. It sometimes takes more courage to admit our own inadequacies to ourselves than to continue struggling in a situation in which success can never be complete. It speaks well for Mary's basically good adjustment and self-honesty that she was able to make the change to a new environment easily.

Changing the perceived environment

As we shall see when we deal with perception (Chap. 9), there is not a perfect and one-to-one relationship between the actual environment and its perception by an observer. And it is to the perceived environment rather than to the physical that we react. Often a change may occur in the observer's perception of his environment without a change in the actual environment. Such a change may resolve a conflict by eliminating or reducing the negative motive or by increasing the positive one. We may perceive a certain facial expression or a casual comment as indicating disapproval and rejection, and our perception of this may prevent us from approaching a perfectly friendly person even though we may wish to do so. Later we may learn from a mutual friend that our perception was wrong. The negative motive is thus eliminated and the conflict between approach and avoidance is removed.

Changing motive strengths

On many occasions it is not possible to eliminate a conflict by some sort of environmental modification. Often it is not possible or desirable to move from one environment to another, and frequently the individual's perception of the environment may correspond perfectly with the actual nature of that environment. In such circumstances the only solution is to change the total level of motivation or to discover other ways of obtaining motive satisfaction.

Often we do not accurately understand the nature of the goals toward which we aspire. We may decide, after seeing a movie or hearing a radio drama, that our vocational ambition is to be a physician. The heroes of these dramas are painted in glamorous colors and their lives seem to move smoothly from one victory to the next, each victory adding to their worldly wealth and social success. The M.D. degree promises, in short, to be the key to great happiness. At the same time we may have other motives which demand a different course of action. Perhaps we are considering marriage, which, with its incumbent economic demands, would make further schooling impossible; perhaps our parents or relatives have long expected us to go into business with them and we do not wish to hurt them. If the appeal of the medical degree is great and that of the other goals is great also, then conflict is inevitable.

It would be wise for us in such a situation to learn something about the life of the average medical practitioner. We are likely to discover that the movie portrayal of his life is anything but an accurate one. In real life, the physician's hours are long; most of the cases examined may be uninteresting; not all operations are brilliant feats of skill viewed with awe by admiring colleagues; patients die and bring heartaches and feelings of doubt; the road to surgery is a long one; and some patients never pay their bills. All these discovered facts, leading as they do to a more accurate appraisal of a medical career, may so devaluate this goal that it can no longer compete with antagonistic ones. In this fashion the conflict is resolved. Incidentally, it is quite characteristic of most of us to evaluate our vocational aims falsely, and one of the techniques of vocational counselors is to help the counselee obtain an accurate picture of the vocation he desires before finally deciding upon it.

This technique usually results in decreasing the value of the positive goal. When this is done, as in the example described above, the other goals become relatively stronger and positive responses may be made to them. A solution may, of course, also be achieved by so increasing the value of one goal that it overrides another. One may find that on further investigation a vocation that at first has only slight appeal turns out to have a number of unforeseen advantages which increase our motivation toward it. The same kind of change often takes place with respect to persons, to courses of study, to books to be read, to places to live, or to cars to drive; with further knowledge, our motivation toward them may either increase or decrease. If this occurs within a conflict situation, the change may serve to resolve that conflict.

Changes in motive strength may, of course, be effective in any of the types of conflict situations that were mentioned above. In the approach-approach situation, they may produce such a disparity in the strength of one as opposed to the other that the solution is made easy. In the approach-avoidance situation, the avoidance tendency may be so decreased that it becomes ineffective or,

Fig. 6.8 Conflict solution achieved by two kinds of change in motive strength. In *A*, the conflict is solved when the positive value of the goal is increased to such an extent that it becomes greater than the negative value. In *B* the negative value is reduced so much that it is less than the positive value. In each figure the black arrow symbolizes the motive that is unchanged and the dotted arrow symbolizes the new value of the changed motive.

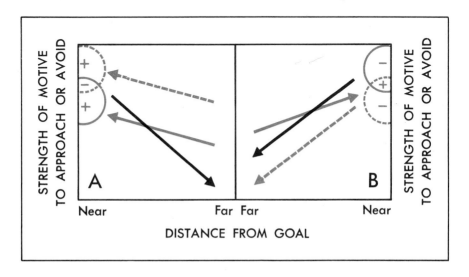

on the other hand, it may become so strong that the approach tendency has little significance.

In the complicated approach-approach situation, a careful evaluation of the significance of each course of action may add to the attractiveness or reduce the undesirable aspects of one of these responses, and so lead to solution.

The same manipulations in the approach strength of the positive goal may solve the problem, for the essential situation producing the conflict is one in which the *relative* strengths of the opposing motives are similar. Avoidance-avoidance conflicts may be solved in the same way. If one of the avoidance stimuli is made considerably subordinate to the other, the individual may be driven to accepting it. At best, however, such a solution would not be readily accepted by the individual and could, in some circumstances, be detrimental to his psychological welfare.

The nature of the goal object

In our discussion of motivation (Chap. 5) we noted that individuals develop preferences for certain types of goal objects rather than others, even though these others are equally capable of satisfying the basic motive. This fact may at times be the cause of, and at times a solution to, a conflict situation.

Suppose, for example, that a coed would like to attend a prom and to be escorted by a certain man. At the moment she is in a state of conflict, for she has obtained an invitation from a less eligible man and her problem is whether to accept or not. As she views it, an invitation from the more favored man is probable but not certain. Whether she accepts the invitation or not and the amount of conflict ensuing before her decision will depend upon the degree to which common motives will be satisfied by either man. If her motivation for going is primarily the pleasure of dancing and the social prestige gained by being seen at the dance, both motives can be satisfied by either date; her conflict will not be great and she will accept the date that is assured. Let us assume, however, that she will gain only slight prestige by attending the prom with the less eligible man and great prestige by attending with the more eligible one. The two men are thus not equivalent in the extent to which they will satisfy the common motives. Each man will satisfy the pleasure-of-dancing motive to the same degree, but they differ in the degree to which they will satisfy the prestige motive.

One act, then, does not serve as a complete substitute for the alternative. Because it is a partial substitute, however, it has some attraction and thus can play a role in producing conflict. Thus the original source of difficulty in the prom situation arose from the fact that the identical act—attending the prom—involved the satisfaction of more than a single motive. One goal object was the act of dancing, and another was to be dated by a certain person. To the extent to which either choice satisfied some common motive, they are equally satisfying but to the extent to which one choice promises an additional kind of fulfillment, it will be preferred.

MOTIVE STRENGTH AND INCENTIVE PROBABILITY

As we have said, the choice between goals is influenced by the comparative values they hold for the individual. But, in addition, his choice is swayed by his estimate of the relative probabilities of attaining these goals. Thus if our coed feels quite certain that the favored man will invite her, she will refuse the less favored man with little hesitation; on the other hand, if she is quite doubtful of the favored man's interest in her, she may accept the first invitation with little or no hesitation.

It is only in recent years that psychologists have become deeply interested in the influence upon choice behavior provided by the individual's estimate of the probability that the desirable or undesirable event will occur. As a consequence, we can at the present time give only a brief and uncertain glimpse of some of the complex relationships between the mathematical probability that the incentive will be obtained, its value to the individual, and choice behavior. We shall describe the findings of some of this research, but before doing so we shall present a formula that could guide choice behavior where both the value of the incentives and the probabilities of obtaining these incentives differ.

The type of formula that is applicable to this situation is based upon an assumption that has been implicit and explicit in much of economic theory. It expresses the notion that man, in his choice behavior, is a highly rational creature who carefully predicts the amount of gain or loss that could be associated with the contrasting courses of action, estimates the probability that these gains or losses will occur, and then chooses the course of action which would be of most benefit or of least harm to him.[6] Our rational man must therefore simultaneously consider both probability and value of the goal in making his choice. It can be demonstrated mathematically that the following type of formula would solve the problem for him: *Value of the Incentive* × *Probability of Obtaining It* = *Desirability of the Act*.[7]

The simplest way of applying this formula is in some sort of gambling situation where the Value of the Incentive (pay-off) is known as well as the Probability (odds). Two such situations and their outcome are given below:

Pay-off	×	*Probability*	=	*Expected Outcome*
100	×	1 in 5 ($\frac{1}{5}$)	=	20
30	×	1 in 2 ($\frac{1}{2}$)	=	15

Thus, mathematically the first choice of action would be the one which *in a long series of trials* would result in the greater expected outcome, and if we assume that the rational and the mathematical are synonymous, the first course of action is the one which should be chosen. Nevertheless, there is no certainty that most people would choose the most rational course.

Much of the research in this field has employed a gambling situation of the sort suggested by the example above.[8] The primary reason for doing so is, of course, because for all persons in our culture 100 dollars has a greater value than 30 dollars. The same could not be said for a seat at the World Series against a seat at an opening of a Broadway musical; or a vacation in Europe against a new car. Thus the experimenter using money as a reward can be certain that a large amount of money has more value for each of his subjects than does a small amount of money.

The experimenter can also present to his subjects the objective odds associated with each choice, and he can be fairly certain in predicting, for example, that the subject feels more certain of winning if the odds are 2:1 against him than if they are 3:1 against him.

Now suppose the subject is presented with the following pairs of choices of dollar bets and told that he must choose one of each pair. (It is assumed in this situation that the subject does not risk any money himself, and he can only win or not win.)

	Pay-off	Odds	Expected Outcome
1. a.	100,000	¾	75,000
b.	900,000	⅓	300,000
2. a.	20	¾	15
b.	180	⅓	60
3. a.	2	¾	1.5
b.	18	⅓	6
4. a.	1,000	¾	750
b.	9,000	⅓	3,000
5. a.	2,000	¾	1,500
b.	18,000	⅓	6,000

The expected gain resulting from each condition is listed in the third column and there is one in each pair which produces a higher figure than the other of the pair. If choices were made on a strictly mathematical (rational) basis, then this is the one out of each pair which would be chosen. The experiments indicate that there is a tendency to pick the alternatives which give promise of yielding the most gain but there is not a perfect correspondence between the human preference and the mathematically largest value.

This lack of correspondence is not haphazard, and there are some rather systematic trends in the way most subjects' preferences depart from the mathematical optimum. If the value of both choices is very large, there is a tendency to pick the one with the higher probability. This would mean that there would be a tendency to choose condition *a* in example 1, even though the mathematics of the equation favor choice *b*. However, when the values are low or moderately high we tend to follow the mathematically optimal choice. In examples 2 and 3 this would result in choice of item *b*, and it is probable that most college student subjects would make this choice, particularly in item 3. Examples 4 and 5 are moving in the direction of large values and it is likely that an increasing preference for the *a* choices would be evidenced.

So far we have dealt only with situations in which the subjects would lose nothing if they did not win. What of the situation where a possible loss is involved? In this instance subjects avoid extremely large risks. That is the situation which would require

223

them to pay out a good deal of money. They also tend to be more conservative about losing even a small amount than winning a small amount. As one experimenter reported, subjects just don't seem to want to lose.

The data of these experiments seem to justify the view that the choice made by an individual in situations where risks are involved may sometimes be predicted by the formula: *Subject's estimate of probability* $\times$ *Value to the subject of the gain or loss* $=$ *Tendency to perform that particular act*. However, the gap between expressing behavior by this general formula and predicting behavior for a particular subject in a particular situation is very wide. It is wide because of the difficulty in assigning numbers to the probability estimate and to the value of the gain or loss to the subject. The individual's estimates of the probabilities may not conform with the actual probabilities, and what may have a particular value for one subject at one time might be quite different for another subject or even for the same subject at another time.

We already have evidence that there are great differences among individuals in the way they react to the same risk-taking situations, with some subjects being quite conservative and others rather extravagant. One experiment has demonstrated that choices in a gambling situation are related to personality characteristics which can be measured by particular personality tests, and are related also to the socio-economic level of the subject, with middle-class subjects being somewhat more conservative in their betting than are lower-class subjects. The broader implication of this study is that, with further research, it may be possible to narrow the gap which at present exists between prediction with the general formula and prediction for a particular individual in a particular situation. Again, as in so many psychological areas, the answer to the question of the adequacy of this approach for predicting behavior will be determined only by extensive research.[9]

This section on the effect of probabilities and incentive values on behavior—a field sometimes referred to as Decision Theory—may at first seem somewhat out of place in a chapter on conflict of motives. If, however, the chapter is viewed more broadly as dealing with the behavior of making choices, then the relevance of this section becomes obvious. It has emphasized the fact that a knowledge of the strength of the motivation alone is not sufficient for making accurate behavior predictions in a choice situation. We must also know the individual's estimate of the probability of success or failure.

Motive conflicts and personal problems

Although our analysis of the psychological mechanisms that lead to personal conflict has been brief, it embodies principles that have wide application. Too often many of us spend our time in fruitless turmoil; we worry and we are troubled; and we do not know how to extricate ourselves from a most unpleasant dilemma. Yet often we can help ourselves if, recognizing that our troubles arise from conflicting motives, we scrutinize and re-evaluate these motives and the goals for which we are striving. When we do so, we may often find that the previously alluring goal is not as compatible with our motive state as we had first thought it to be. We may find also that we had misunderstood our own motivation and what before seemed so desirable, or so necessary to avoid, is no longer of salient importance to us. With the occurrence of these changes in the strengths or the natures of our motives and goals, the conflict may disappear. Sometimes, however, we ourselves cannot achieve a solution and we must seek the help of an expert.

REFERENCES

[1] Rigby, W. K. Approach and avoidance gradients and conflict behavior in a predominantly temporal situation, *J. Comp. Physiol. Psychol.*, 1954, *47*, 83-89.

[2] Brown, Judson S. Gradients of approach and avoidance responses and their relation to level of motivation, *J. Comp. Physiol. Psychol.*, 1948, *41*, 450-465.

[3] Miller, N. E. "Liberalization of basic S-R concepts: Extensions to conflict behavior, motivation, and social learning" in Sigmund Koch (ed.), *Psychology: A Study of a Science*, Vol. III, McGraw-Hill, 1959.

[4] Miller, N. E. "Experimental Studies of Conflict" in J. McV. Hunt (ed.), *Personality and the Behavior Disorders*, Ronald, 1944, Vol. I.

[5] Kaufmann, Edna, and Miller, N. E. Effect of number of reinforcements on strength of approach in an approach avoidance conflict, *J. Comp. Physiol. Psychol.*, 1949, *42*, 65-74.

[6] Edwards, W. The theory of decision making, *Psychol. Bull.*, 1954, *51*, 380-417.

[7] von Neuman, J., and Morgenstern, O. *Theory of Games and Economic Behavior*, Princeton, 1944.

[8] Davidson, D., Scippes, P., and Siegel, S. *Decision Making*, Stanford, 1957.

[9] Scodel, A., Ratoosh, P., and Minas, J. S. Some personality correlates of decision making under conditions of risk, *Behav. Sci.*, 1959, *4*, 19-28.

225

EMOTIONS

IN THE PRECEDING CHAPTER WE DIS-
cussed the conditions that give rise to adjustment problems of the
organism, and we noted how the organism meets the conflicting
demands of its various needs within the structure of the environment. In some but not all of these conflict situations, the individual
reacts in ways that are markedly different from his usual modes
of behavior. He may become violent or excited or elated or depressed; in short, he may be almost transformed into another
person. This kind of behavior we refer to as emotional.

Emotions and emotionality have many aspects, and each of
these aspects has at one time or another been the concern of various
psychologists or schools of psychology. To some, the major problem has been to understand the personal feelings of the individual
under emotional stress and to describe or analyze the feelings that
characterize the emotional state. Other psychologists have been

concerned primarily with the nature of the reactions occurring within our bodies during emotion and have sought to understand and even to classify our emotions as responses of the heart, the stomach, or the lungs.

Still other psychologists have stressed the fact that the overt or observable behavior of the individual who is said to be emotional is often poorly organized and poorly executed.

This concern with what aspects of the behavior of the organism should be studied during periods of emotion is closely related to the problem of defining an emotion. When, in other words, are we justified in saying that a person is behaving emotionally or is experiencing an emotion? It is desirable to attempt to answer this question before the topic is considered in greater detail.

As we have said earlier, modern psychology is primarily concerned with the behavior of individuals rather than with their conscious experiences. This does not mean that modern psychology is uninterested in reports of personal experience but it does mean that the primary criterion for defining a psychological concept shall not be one which depends on obtaining reports of conscious experiences from the subject. For this reason we shall not refer to conscious experience in a definition of emotions. Similarly, it is premature at the present stage of development of both psychology and physiology to attempt to define and identify emotions by reference to particular physiological processes that are associated with this kind of behavior. In a later chapter of this book some of what is now known of the processes that go on within the body during emotional states will be considered, and a deeper understanding of emotional behavior will be made possible, but we will not define emotions by reference to these associated physiological processes.

It is, then, to some characteristic of behavior that we must turn in our search for a definition of emotions. If, for the moment, the reader will recall his own behavior or the behavior of another which he would label as being emotional he will undoubtedly identify one salient characteristic of this behavior. This characteristic is the high degree of psychological reactivity that is shown. In describing the behavior one is likely to use such words as "loud" and "violent" and not such words as "soft" and "calm." It is this aspect of behavior that seems to be the key to the definition of an emotion. The term *activation* has been used to describe this aspect of behavior and it refers to the readiness of the organism to react to the events of his psychological environment.

Behavior may be conceived of as ranging from a low level of activation as in sleep to a high level of vigorous mobility and responsiveness.[1,2] The word "emotion" is to be used to identify behavior at the high-activation end of this range. The definition makes the further requirement that the high level of activation is a consequence of certain kinds of psychological situations. Such a requirement means, therefore, that in order to describe behavior as emotional we must know something about the nature of the psychological situation which preceded the behavior. The psychological situation is not only responsible for the occurrence of the emotional response but it also determines the kind of emotion that will be expressed.

EMOTIONS AND THE SITUATIONS PRODUCING THEM

Our language is rich in the number of words that are available to describe our emotional reactions. One may look into a thesaurus and discover the following nouns listed under "fear": timidity, diffidence, apprehension, solicitude, anxiety, care, misgiving, mistrust, suspicion, alarm, dread, awe, terror, horror—and even so the list is not exhaustive. But if we were writing a theme or a novel we should not be content to choose at random one of these words as a substitute for "fear," for, although each holds something in common with that word, each has a flavor of its own. The size of the list attests to the fact that there are many reactions that are emotional in nature. This is simply another way of stating that the word chosen—or, to get back to the organism itself, the reaction made—will be a function of a number of variables: the intensity of the stimulus, the nature of the stimulus (social or physical, for example), the degree and kind of motivation, the individual's evaluation of possible solutions to the situation, and many others. A slight difference in the structure of the psychological situation will inevitably make for differences in the reaction of the individual and hence will create a unique condition to which we may wish to apply a special name.

Very little progress, however, will be made toward a basic understanding of emotional behavior by attempting to classify and describe the stimulus situation and the characteristics of all the many emotional reactions. It is considerably more efficient to reduce the list of emotions to a few major classes and to determine their general characteristics. Doing this, however, is not the same as stating that there are only three or four emotions. We can produce a large variety of different colors by mixing only three colors, but this does not mean that we can experience only three colors.

The major trend in psychological research has been toward dealing with four broad classes of emotional reactions: fear, anger, a general depressive reaction which might be called grief, and love. We use these names not for the purpose of denying the existence of other emotional states but simply to designate general classes under which these states can be grouped.

Fear

One of the most troublesome of all emotional reactions is fear. From the point of view of the individual experiencing it, fear seems to disable him at a time when he most needs his abilities. From the point of view of a concerned observer, it seems to isolate the individual and encapsulate him in a shell that is impervious to quieting or directing stimuli which, if reacted to, would serve to lessen the emotion. Many a mother has experienced feelings of impotence when she has tried to break into her child's psychological environment to assure him that a nightmare was not true, or that a friendly dog would not harm him.

Many years ago John B. Watson, the father of Behaviorism, advanced the hypothesis that fear is a consequence of two kinds of stimulation, namely, the occurrence of a *loud sound* and also of a *sudden loss of support*. He was able to show that stimulation of this sort produced violent emotional responses in infants. Experiments on adults have indicated that these stimuli are also effective at higher age levels, and one experimenter has produced emotional reactions by causing the back of a chair in which the subject was seated to drop backward suddenly.[3] Other experimenters have devoted considerable attention to the startle reflex, which can be produced by firing a gun behind the subject's back. Despite repeated shots, the stimulus remained effective.[4] There are few of us who have not felt fear in response to situations of this sort.

At the same time, Watson and his co-workers observed the reaction of infants to other stimulus conditions such as the dark, high places, and snakes, conditions which frequently evoke fear responses in adults. Since his infants did not react with fear to these stimuli Watson concluded that fear reactions to them must result from learning, whereas fear reactions to *loud sounds* and to *loss of support* were the consequences of innate or unlearned characteristics of the organism. He felt, in other words, that fear reactions given to any other class of stimuli than these two must arise from some sort of learning experience.

It seems likely, however, that Watson's interpretation of his experimental results placed too much emphasis upon physical characteristics alone. Actually these two stimuli do not inevitably produce fear reactions. One is not frightened by the loss of support resulting from the act of jumping off a footstool, and the noise of a gun is not likely to frighten the person who pulls the trigger.

The essential psychological characteristic of the situation that results in fear seems to be the occurrence of the strange and the unexpected for which no counter or controlling reaction is immediately available to the individual.

There are a number of bits of observational and experimental evidence that point to the importance of the unexpected and strange as determinants of the fear reaction. It is extremely common for infants to react with fear to the sight of a stranger, even though the stranger may be doing nothing more than quietly approaching the child. One experimenter evoked marked fear reactions from chimpanzees who had been raised in a laboratory by presenting them with various novel stimuli.[5] The chimpanzees were first trained to approach a box held by the experimenter and receive food. After this response had been firmly learned, the experimenter, in addition to giving the animal food, would open the box and expose certain stimuli within it. Fear reactions were given to *papier-mâché* models of a chimpanzee or human head; the strangeness of this situation presumably lies in the fact that there is a head without the accustomed body. Other stimuli such as a wax snake or a rubber dog were also effective fear stimuli.

The significance of this research lies in the fact that these laboratory animals had no opportunity to learn to fear these objects before the experimental tests were begun. The fear reaction seems to have been evoked by these essentially inocuous objects because they were strange and unexpected. Even familiar stimuli may evoke fear reactions if they are introduced suddenly and while the subject is reacting to a series of stimuli quite unrelated to the fear-producing stimulus. Almost everyone of us has been startled, when, as we are engrossed in our thoughts and psychologically isolated from our environment, a taxi horn sounded near us, someone called to us, or a bell rang. We were not expecting the horn, the voice, or the bell, and it startled us. We were unable to shift the direction of our responses with the rapidity that the changes in the external environment demanded.

As was stated above, it does not seem to be the strange or the unexpected alone which is responsible, but also the fact that the individual does not have immediately available a means of controlling the situation. He may lack these means because the unexpected occurs with great rapidity. Again, inadequacies in the handling of a situation, and hence fear, may arise because the individual does not possess techniques for dealing successfully with the task at hand. If we have not studied the subject matter of a course diligently, we are very likely to be frightened by an examination; but if we know the material "cold," we find no cause for alarm. Our first public speech may be an emotional ordeal, but it is lessened if the material is well learned and we are confident that we can answer adequately any relevant questions that we may be asked. Another car coming toward him down the road will frighten the novice, but the experienced driver will not give it a second thought. One's fear of social situations decreases as he becomes more adept at handling a teacup, at dancing, or at the give and take of light conversation.

The nature of the situation to be confronted may be such as to make it impossible for the individual to feel that he can cope with it. Probably much of the emotional disturbance that many persons feel on their first dates arises from the fact that they cannot predict how the other one will react. No amount of training or skill on the part of a soldier in a combat situation can completely safeguard him against injury or death and yet he may lessen the psychological danger of the situation by telling himself that the bullet that will get him has not yet been cast. In this manner he removes, for himself, the fear-producing event.

Of course, it is not necessary that the situation itself be uncontrollable; all that is necessary is that the participant believe that it is. Such a belief underlies many of the fears of children.

Learning

The analysis of the fear-producing situations which we have presented implies that, given a certain structuring of the psychological environment, the organism may react emotionally. It is not necessary to assume that the individual has ever before been present in this situation: the reaction may arise spontaneously because of the psycho-biological structure of the individual and the psychological structure of the environment. Fear reactions as a whole, however, are too diverse to be described only in these terms, and there are countless instances in which neither the situation nor the motivation seem sufficient to warrant the intensity of the reaction.

Fears arise also because we have learned to show a specific emotion in a particular type of situation. There are many instances in which the fear of a specific object has been acquired through conditioning. In a famous experiment, Watson and Raynor showed that it was possible, and in fact quite easy, to produce a fear reaction in a small child by the conditioning technique.[6] After first ascertaining that the child had no fear of a white rat (indicated by his interested reaching for the animal when it was introduced into the room), they later presented a fear-producing stimulus—a sharp, loud sound—simultaneously with the entrance of the animal. After a few days of training, the child's positive reactions to the animal were converted to whimpering and to withdrawal responses. The emotional response that had formerly been given to the sound was now elicited by the animal alone when the sound was discontinued and the animal entered the room without its accompaniment. When the child's reaction to other white, furry objects was tested, it was discovered that he responded negatively to them as well. Obviously this is an example of conditioning and stimulus generalization.

This experiment presents in a clear-cut way the entire natural history of the development of a fear reaction. The meaning of the rat for the child, as defined by his responses, changed from an interesting, attractive object to one to be dreaded, and with this change the meaning of other objects for him changed as well. Thus we can see how many objects with which we have never had an unfavorable experience may produce fear reaction because they have some aspect in common with a previously conditioned stimulus. The potential ramifications are many.

It is probable that many phobias—that is, abnormally strong and apparently irrational fears—have their origin in events of this type. An instance of claustrophobia—a fear of enclosed spaces—illustrates this. A psychiatrist was visited by a client who reported that he was experiencing intense fear whenever he entered small enclosures—elevators, the subway, and even his own room. After many sessions with the psychiatrist, the patient was able to recall an incident in his childhood which accounted for the reaction. While rummaging about his yard, he had discovered and collected various old objects, which he decided to sell to a junkman. Actually there was some question as to whether or not all these objects were no longer of use to his parents, and the boy was not certain that they would permit him to dispose of them. Nevertheless, the lure of the anticipated monetary return was strong enough to send him sneaking off to the junkman with his loot—not, however, without some qualms of conscience. He completed his transaction and, while leaving the junkman's house he was forced to pass through a small, dark vestibule. While he was in there, a large dog, which he had not seen, suddenly and unexpectedly leaped upon him. The unexpected event coupled with his own guilt feelings for his dubious conduct produced a violent fear reaction.

This is exactly the type of event that, as we have pointed out earlier, is likely to produce a fear reaction, and of course it did. It served, in other words, as an unconditioned stimulus, and, through stimulus generalization, his own room and any other small place became conditioned stimuli which could elicit the same response.

The reader, with his knowledge of the fact that conditioned responses will extinguish if the conditioned stimulus is presented many times without reinforcement, may doubt that persisting fear could be accounted for by the conditioning process. However, both experimental evidence and logical reasoning justify this interpretation.

A logical analysis suggests that a potent reason why fear reactions do not extinguish is that the situation which leads to extinction is avoided in the essentially unrestricted environment of the everyday world. Extinction, by definition, results only from frequent contact with the nonreinforced conditioned stimulus, but in a relatively free environment the individual tends, by the very nature of the reaction, to avoid contact with the stimulus and he therefore prevents extinction from occurring.

It is also true that conditioned responses can be remarkably resistant to extinction even though the events required for extinction are present. In one experiment dogs were placed in what is called a shuttle box.[7] It was composed of a grid floor with a fence which divided the box in half, but which was low enough to be hurdled by the dog. The conditioning procedure consisted of sounding a buzzer and following it a few seconds later with a very strong shock emanating from the grid floor. The animal could escape the shock by jumping the fence into the other compartment. Later this side also would be electrified following the sounding of the buzzer but the animal could again escape by jumping back to the original side. After a very small number of trials the dogs developed the conditioned avoidance response of jumping the fence to the sound of the buzzer alone and prior to the onset of the shock. The response proved to very difficult to extinguish, and one animal failed to extinguish after 490 trials, even though it had taken it only 11 trials to become conditioned. This was not an exceptional case and most of the animals showed a great resistance to extinction.

If now we combine the known fact that fear responses of this sort may be highly resistant to extinction together with the tendency to avoid the extinction situation itself, it can be readily understood how learned fear reactions may persist over long periods of time.

Simple conditioning is not, however, the only process through which emotional reactions are learned. For the complex and highly intelligent organism that man is, words—though they are merely symbols—acquire great potency and may operate as stimuli for the learning of emotional reactions. Because one has heard many unfavorable comments about a certain race or group, one may learn to hate that race or group even though he has never laid eyes on its members or despite the fact that all his experiences with them have been favorable.

Parents, in their efforts to direct the behavior of their children, often describe in exaggerated and terrifying terms the consequences that may befall the transgressor, and so produce an unnecessary and widely generalized fear. A husband and wife taking a trip through the Southwest knew that sanitary conditions in Mexico were not the best and repeatedly warned their 10-year-old daughter against eating unless they were assured that the source of the food was acceptable. When they crossed the border, they found that she would eat nothing. She had learned through these verbal warnings an emotional avoidance reaction that had generalized too broadly. Her parents had intended that she accept food in certain Mexican restaurants and reject it in others; she had learned to reject all food prepared in Mexico. Thus, from the verbalizations of adults or peers—or indeed, from some story told or read—children may acquire fears of objects or events that they have never directly experienced.

It is likely, also, that the young, impressionable child's imitation of an adult's fear may serve as a source for learned emotional reactions. Social stimuli become very powerful, and the behavior of others can set the pattern for an emotional response which may persist when the situation is met again. It is reported, for example, that various psychological disturbances in young children following the bombing of cities in World War II were more attributable to the overanxious reactions of the mothers than to the bombing itself. It is not surprising, therefore, to find that there is great similarity between the fears of the parents and those of the child.

Fear and anxiety

In our discussion of motivation (Chap. 5), we described the learning of avoidance motives, and we used the term *anxiety* to refer to these learned motive states. The reader may wonder whether there is any distinction between the behavior referred to by this term and the behavior referred to by the term *fear*. Unfortunately the two terms are not defined precisely in modern psychology, but they are nevertheless used with at least implied differences in meaning.

The term *anxiety* seems to refer to the reaction that occurs before the stimulus for the fear or avoidance reaction has taken place. It is an anticipation on the part of the individual of a potentially punishing event. It is a response not to the punishing stimulus itself but rather to stimuli which, the organism has learned, tend to be followed by the punishing stimulus. The term *fear* seems to be broader in nature; it seems to include anxiety reactions and also the reactions that occur after the punishing or disturbing event.

Anxiety is a narrower term than fear; we use the term *anxiety* only when the occurrence of the response to the stimulating situation can be understood on the basis of some prior learning experience. The term *fear*, though it includes anxiety reactions, does not imply that the response to the stimulus must have been learned. Thus the infant's reaction to a sudden loud sound is a fear reaction. If the sound had been repeatedly preceded by some originally ineffective stimulus, and the child later began to react emotionally to this previously ineffective stimulus, this reaction would be called an anxiety reaction, but it would also be called fear.

One further question may be asked: Should all avoidance learning be classified as emotional behavior? It was stated earlier in this chapter that a high level of activation was an essential characteristic of emotional behavior. Obviously not all avoidance behavior can be so characterized for we often rather calmly avoid threatening situations and therefore not all of this behavior would be termed emotional. It is only when the behavior resulting from the stimulus is characterized by a high level of activation that this behavior would be called emotional.

Anger

Restraint of an infant's activity may give rise to crying and anger behavior. In older children many such frustrating circumstances eventuate in temper tantrums: a kiddy-car wheel catches on the leg of a chair; the child is made to sit on the toilet while his outstretched arms are reaching vainly for a jar of cold cream on the window ledge; or a younger sibling stumbles through his carefully arranged layout of sticks, books, and chair cushions which represent a train yard. At adult age levels we react with anger when goals close to our hearts are made unattainable, when we cannot achieve the level of performance that we feel we have a right to expect of ourselves, when our economic or social ambitions are thwarted, and when an aggressor nation disrupts the peacetime structure and goals of our own nation.

In each of these situations there is a basic core of psychological similarity. The organism is moving along a certain path and a stimulus complex arises which blocks this path. If this frustration continues, anger reactions are aroused. Any motive may be frustrated, and any agent may act as a frustrator. Variations in the nature of the motive and of the frustrator make each situation psychologically different, and so we may use different terms to refer to the resulting reactions, even though their basic psychological structures are identical. Hence, if the motive of love is blocked by another individual in attaining the desired object, we label the reaction *jealousy,* but if another individual inconsiderately gets in our way when we are in a hurry to go someplace, we are simply angry at or irritated with him.

Depressive reactions

The situations giving rise to depressive or grief reactions are very similar to those that produce anger. The major difference seems to be that there is more of an element of finality in the depressive than in the anger situation. A frustration has occurred time and again, and the individual sees no manner of overcoming the obstacle: death or insuperable distance may remove a loved one and make reunion impossible; or we may break a valued object beyond repair. When, for one reason or another, hope can no longer spring from our breasts, or the obstacle blocking our motive cannot be removed by the aggressive action that characterizes anger, our reaction is turned to grief.

That situational instigations to anger and to depression hold much in common is indicated by the fact that in response to the same situation we may react at one time with anger and at another time with depression. The daytime reaction of impotent anger is often replaced during the long vigil of a sleepless night with black depression. In an experiment in which subjects reported on their feelings after they had been roundly scolded and berated for apparent failure in an examination, reports of "anger" and "disgust" were made by the same subjects. Although some subjects seemed to react primarily with anger or rage, in others a note of shame and sadness bordering on grief predominated.[8]

This tendency for anger and grief to arise from the same situation was illustrated in another study in which subjects were presented with verbal descriptions of various situations and asked to describe what, if any, emotional response they might make in this situation.[9] Both grief and anger were identified as the reaction that was likely to occur in a situation wherein some strongly desired goal is blocked, the grief resulting from the loss of the goal and the anger directed toward an individual or an event that could be considered responsible for this loss.

Love

The fourth and final major emotional reaction is love, a term which refers to a response that is characterized by a strong

237

approach reaction toward another individual. Although this may be an adequate description of the structure of the psychological situation that gives rise to this emotional response, it does not, of course, indicate how the response develops.

In the case of love of the child for the parent, the development of the motivation that leads to the response can possibly be understood by reference to the concept of secondary reinforcement described in Chapter 5. There it was pointed out that stimuli which are associated with the satisfaction of biological needs acquire reinforcing characteristics and, to go a step farther, presumably become attractive and desirable objects. For the child, the parent is associated with the satisfaction of a wide variety of biological needs. When hungry the child is fed and when thirsty he is given liquid by the parent. It is the parent, too, who cuddles him when he is tired, warms him when he is cold, and supplies him with fascinating objects to explore. With increase in age and experience the child acquires other motives and here too the parents may often be instrumental in his attaining the goal that satisfies these motives. It does not seem strange, therefore, that the considerate parent will become an object of great attraction to the child, and that this strong positive motivation should result in the emotion of love.

In Chapter 5 brief space was devoted to the description of a study of infant monkeys in which it was shown that a contact with a terry-cloth mother is highly reinforcing and the term *contact comfort* was used to identify this motivational tendency. Additional research on these infants has shown that the monkeys develop strong affectional responses toward their terry-cloth mothers.[10] Then when a frightening object is introduced into their cages they scurry to and cling upon her, and they are perturbed, upset, and withdrawn if she is not present; especially so if they are placed in a strange environment without her. In short, their behavior toward this terry-cloth object seems to exemplify affection and love. They do not, however, show this same reaction toward the wire mother even though they had obtained milk from her. Indeed, in the many different studies of this general type that were conducted with these subjects there was no evidence that feeding operated as a secondary reinforcer. A similar study has been conducted on puppies, and they too showed a preference for the soft cloth mother, although they preferred her even more if they obtained their milk from her.[11] The studies do not deny the theory that affectional responses

Fig. 7.1 Reactions to a fear-producing situation with and without a surrogate mother present. (Courtesy of Harry F. Harlow)

to an object—or individual—develop through the association of that object or individual with motive satisfaction, but they do point to the great importance of contact comfort as a reinforcer.

The reverse relationship—that of love of the parents for the child—cannot be so simply accounted for. If for the moment it is assumed that the strong motivation of the parent for the child is based upon the child's being associated with motive satisfactions of the parent, these motives of the parents are not the simple biological ones such as hunger or thirst. Instead they are more likely to be complex social motives. In a society in which a high value is placed upon parenthood, the parents receive some desired recognition from other adults from the fact of being parents. They meet new people who are also parents and find a common topic of conversation. Their own parents are pleased with the prefix "grand" and this is a satisfaction to these now adult children. In many cases the child functions as an extension of the parent's own self and there are few of us who do not have a fondness and a feeling of protectiveness for our own personal selves. Along with all of these socially desired satisfactions, many parents derive a satisfaction from viewing the changing behavior of a small growing organism. All these kinds of motive satisfactions, and many more, may be conceived of as offering possibilities for the parent to learn strong positive motivation toward the child, and this is the basis for the emotion of love.

Lastly, of course, there is the love of adults of the opposite sex for each other. In these instances the strength of various socialized approach responses are reinforced by the biologically powerful sex drive and a strong motive is generated.

In summary, the emotion of love represents a response to a powerful approach motive toward another person, a motive that has become sufficiently strong to result in the characteristically high level of activation of the emotional response. It is this that forms the psychological core of the emotional response of love, and we identify different kinds of love by pointing to the individual toward which the approach response is made.

GENERAL PSYCHOLOGICAL
AND ORGANIC CONDITIONS

In the previous section the psychological nature of the situations that generate—one might almost say compel—emotional reactions were identified. If one were to make value judgments of the organism's behavior in these situations one would be inclined to feel that the reactions, though violent as emotional reactions may be, were justified by the very nature of the situation. Fear reactions are understandable when the welfare of the organism is threatened, and there is a righteousness to the anger that arises when honorable and important goals are blocked. Perhaps such interpretations would be justified if it were true that our reactions were determined only by the essential characteristics of the immediate situation, but there is evidence that our emotional responses may have sources in events which are irrelevant to the actual emotion-producing incident. These sources are of several kinds:

General physical condition

In one study a group of college students kept a diary of their emotional outbursts for a period of a week.[12] Their reports showed that emotional disturbances were most likely to occur before the evening meal and they were next most frequent before breakfast. It is difficult to believe that the environmental situations conducive to emotional responses were most likely to occur at these times of day; it is more likely that the organic state of hunger and fatigue influenced the individuals' reactions to the situations that did occur. A similar relationship between organic states and emotionality was obtained in another study in which parents recorded data on the anger reactions of their young children.[13]

Various studies together with other bits of data indicate that our emotional reactions do not stem solely from the psychological nature of the immediately precipitating situation but stem also from situations which are irrelevant to that situation, such as hunger, illness, and fatigue.

Pre-disposing events

A biasing to react emotionally may also be established by psychological events that have occurred prior to the precipitating situation. Thus, in the dark of the night, after the reading of a detective story, the customary sounds that occur in a house with the descent of the night and inactivity of the occupants—the shifting of coal in the bin, the rattle of a window, or the creak of a timber as it shrinks in the cooling night air—take on sinister meanings. These stimuli, which on other nights or during the day are either ignored or are rightly understood as arising from the operation of natural physical forces, now send a shiver up our spine.

The same phenomenon was found in the behavior of some of the civilian population as a result of the bombings during World War II.[14] After a severe raid, many individuals, though "physically" unharmed, would show a residuum of disturbance that resulted in their overreacting to many ordinary situations for days and even weeks after the raid. They would become irritated by minor events and frightened by innocent causes. After bombing raids, such ordinarily minor stimuli as the sparking of trolley cars or the noises of radios would produce emotional disturbances. It should be emphasized that these reactions were found in people who never broke down sufficiently to be classified as abnormal and who recovered from these tendencies without treatment other than the absence of further bombings.

The term *displacement* has been applied to the circumstance where an emotional reaction, usually one of anger and aggression, is directed toward an "innocent" individual rather than against the appropriate agent. Many examples of this mechanism in operation can be found in individuals. The industrial psychologist is not surprised to learn that the troublemaker on the job is often a man who is having difficulty in his home life. The aggressive child in the schoolroom or the bully on the playground may be a child whose relations with his parents and his siblings are fraught with frustration.

In groups, we find indications of the same mechanism in the fact that lynchings are more likely to occur under adverse, and therefore frustrating, economic conditions than under conditions of prosperity.[15] It is indicated also in the fact that nations under rigid control of a dictator may engage in violent persecution of minority groups.

The phenomenon of displacement has been studied experimentally in the following fashion.[16] Pairs of white rats were placed in a box with an electric grid flooring. Then a relatively mild current, but one strong enough to keep the animals active and agitated, was turned on. In their hustlings about, the animals would occasionally contact each other and adopt fighting postures. When this happened, the experimenter turned off the current, thus reinforcing these aggressive acts. Soon each rat learned to respond to the onset of the shock by attacking the other rat. Later a small doll was placed in the box. If shock was now administered with the other rat in the box, aggressive responses would be made toward the other animal, but if shock occurred in the absence of the other animal, the lone rat would attack the doll. This experimentally developed behavior is an analogy to displacement in humans, for a response that was appropriately made to one stimulus was elicited inappropriately by a different stimulus.

We humans like to think of ourselves as rational and evaluative; as organisms that, for the most part, behave as they do in any given situation because it is this behavior and not another that the situation demands. The material presented in this section, however, indicates that at least some of our emotional reactions in particular situations have their roots in occurrences which are external to the situation itself. It is worthwhile to attempt to analyze why this should be the case.

At first blush one might be tempted to assume that the emotional reaction which is initiated in one situation is bottled up and remains within the individual as a potentially explosive force that is bound to erupt at some time or another. However, from what we know of the physiological processes of the organism, we can find no evidence that the energy of a particular response can be stored up to explode as this interpretation demands. It would appear more likely that this behavior can best be accounted for by the nature of the second situation as well as by any persisting effect that the preceding situation has left in the individual.

In the experimental demonstration of displacement which was mentioned before it is not difficult to account for the aggression against the doll by means of the mechanism of stimulus generalization. The doll was not attacked so long as the more appropriate stimulus object (the other rat) was present. The celluloid doll has some similarity to another rat and hence it can elicit the aggressive response, but this tendency is not as strong as the tendency to respond to the rat itself. If it were only a matter of a bottled-up response ready to be tripped off at any time, the rats would have been just as likely to respond to the walls of the box as to the doll.

When clinical instances are considered, as in the illustration of the disgruntled worker or the problem child in school where the irritation stems from difficulties at home, the explanation is more complicated in that there are probably several different psychological mechanisms at work. For one thing, we must assume that the stimulus events in school or at the shop have some similarity to the stimulus events at home to which the irritable responses have been attached. Again, difficulties at home may have taught these unfortunates to interpret particular words and actions as being indicative of an attack, even though they are not meant in this fashion at the shop and school. Nevertheless, because of their own interpretation of these words they are cause enough for them to react with anger. These suggestions are certainly not complete accounts of all the instigators of the behavior, but they are plausible enough to suggest that there is no pressing need to introduce the notion of bottled-up energy demanding release.

The fright exhibited by civilians at minor events following a severe bombing raid can perhaps be accounted for more readily. The noises and sights that set off the emotional disturbances may be thought of as generalized stimuli which bear a relationship to the actual stimuli that were produced by or occurred during the bombing.

Fatigue and illness may be associated with frequent emotional reactions because they lower the individual's capacity to deal effectively with his environment. It was mentioned earlier that fear is a consequence of an unreadiness to cope with the suddenly changing environment. The individual who is ill or fatigued may, because of his temporary organic state, be unable to deal effectively with situations that otherwise he could handle with no great difficulty, and hence he reacts with fear. Anger is the consequence of frustration, and when we are ill or fatigued we may be less able to overcome the barriers which in normal conditions we could brush aside with relative ease. This interpretation suggests, therefore, that, because of our lowered efficiency, the *psychological situations* leading to emotional reactions occur with more than the normal frequency when we are ill or fatigued. Since this is the case, the frequency of emotional reaction is higher than when we are feeling well and efficient. Therefore, these states result in frequent emotional reactions because of a lowered capacity to make effective instrumental responses rather than because there is some inevitable connection between illness and fatigue and emotionality.

In summary, there is a fair body of evidence which indicates that the occurrence of an inappropriate emotional reaction in a particular situation may be attributed, in part, to conditions external to this situation. One interpretation of this phenomenon holds that a residue of the original emotional reaction remains in the individual's behavior system and is released in the new situation. This interpretation was rejected in favor of one which attempts to account for the behavior primarily by reference to the similarity of the stimuli in the original emotion-provoking situation and in the second situation.

Motivation and emotion

It must be apparent to the reader that the relationship between motivation and emotion is a very close one. Before his meal, a hungry child may break into angry tears if he cannot reach some tidbits, but if he is less hungry he will accept the same frustration and turn with no emotional upsets to more available and desirable goals. The loss of someone dear to us may give rise to grief, whereas the departure of a comparative stranger leaves us untouched. If motivation is not strong, we may turn from a barrier calmly, but when it is great, we continue to respond until our frustrations turn to anger.

Strength of motivation plays its part in fear reactions as well as in anger and grief reactions. If the stimulus is evaluated as being highly significant in its possible effect upon the structure of the individual's life, it is more likely to produce fear than if it were judged unimportant. The final dress rehearsal is a less anxious moment than the first night, and the final examination is ordinarily more disturbing than a ten-minute quiz. The more serious the consequences of a situation, the more likely are we to face it with qualms and trepidation.

A summary

The word *emotion*, as we have used it and as the preceding sections illustrate, refers to a *way* of responding, and not to the *cause* of the responding. We find the cause in the strength of the motives that are operating, in the psychological nature of the situation, and in the previous learning experiences of the individual.

EMOTION AND EFFICIENCY OF BEHAVIOR

For many years it has been noted that behavior during an emotional state departs markedly from the ordinarily well articulated pattern of nonemotional behavior. The driver becomes confused and loses control of his car; we panic and do foolish things

245

in the height of our fright; and the ordinarily stolid parliamentarian loses his temper and, through ill-chosen words, the issue he supports.

This incapacity to respond adequately which is so often associated with emotion-provoking incidents is well illustrated by the behavior of survivors of a violent tornado which struck a portion of the city of Worcester, Massachusetts, late in a summer afternoon in 1953. The following account was given by a doctor who came into the stricken area very shortly after the tornado had passed: ". . . As I would encounter people who were not hurt I would say, 'Help me move some of these wounded people out,' and they couldn't. I would talk with them and explain what I had in mind, and they seemed to react and respond in a normal way, and then just stand there or wander away, and nod their heads and not do anything. I wouldn't say that they were dazed, but they were not functioning; and almost everyone I met was like this . . ."[17]

This frequent association of emotional reaction and incompetence can best be understood by recalling that emotions are a consequence of strong motivational states, and also by recalling that high levels of motivation may result in inferior behavior. This matter was discussed in Chapter 5. In that chapter it was pointed out that strong motivation leads to inefficient behavior in certain kinds of tasks, but not in others. It would be predicted, therefore, that very frequently emotional reactions would be accompanied by inefficiency in performing many instrumental acts, but not in all actions. This seems to be the characteristic of emotional behavior. In conclusion, it means that emotional behavior and inefficiency go together so often because they are both a product of powerful motivational states and in tasks which are generally complex in nature, as our culture so often demands, strong motivation often results in poor performance.

THE EXPRESSION OF EMOTIONS

As a social stimulus, the facial expression of the other person is of prime significance. In our conversations, our courtings, our business transactions, and our poker games, we are ever alert to the facial expression of our *vis-à-vis* for its potential value as a barometer of his feelings. Not infrequently the success or failure of our enterprise can be ascribed to our ability to interpret properly, and to use as cues for future action, the changes in expression on the face of our companion. Because of the significance of facial expressions as social stimuli, there has been considerable psychological investigation of the relationship between facial expression and emotional states.

The customary method employed in most of these studies involves a series of photographs of individuals portraying a variety of emotional states through facial expression. These photographs are shown to a group of subjects who attempt to identify the emotion being expressed. The success of the observer in ascribing to the pose the same emotion as that intended by the performer has not been great; indeed, one is often more impressed by the frequency of errors than by the frequency of correct choices. That failure did not arise solely because of the artificiality of the poses has been indicated by a later experiment making use of candid camera shots.[18] Once again success in matching was slight.

Even though errors have been frequent, the modicum of accuracy has warranted pursuit of the topic. One experimenter attempted to discover which part of the face is most influential in determining an observer's judgment.[19] He cut a series of candid photographs horizontally in two and joined the upper half of the face in one picture with the lower half in another. From the spliced picture, the subject was required to name the single emotion being portrayed when in actuality he was seeing a composite which had been produced by the joining of photographs portraying two different emotions. By comparing the judgments made with the emotions expressed in the upper and in the lower halves of the face, it was possible to determine which half of the face was most influential in determining judgments. The results of the study indicated that the lower half dominated the upper half in determining the observer's judgment. The notion so dear to the pens of many poets—that the eyes are the windows of the soul—seems to be more poetry than truth.

There are a number of factors that seriously limit our ability to judge facial expressions. For one—although this does not enter into most of the experiments above—there is the fact of individual differences in facial reactions to the same emotional situation. Such differences are due to differences in the structure of the face, in the mobility of the facial musculature, and in the extent to which the individual has learned to inhibit or express his emotional responses overtly. Even if we assume that the psychological states of "glee," "happiness," "merriment," "ecstasy," and "joy" clearly differ from one another, it does not follow that an ordinary observer could attach the appropriate label to a facial expression indicating each of these emotions. Some of us call any mixture of blue and red "purple"; others distinguish "orchid," "lavender," and "violet" as gradations of the two basic hues. Some of us are color-sensitive and others are not. Similarly, some of us are highly acute in our perception of the patterns of facial expression, whereas others are rather obtuse. Little wonder, then, that subjects do not show high agreement in the various experiments.

The low degree of success in identifying an emotion through its portrayal in a photograph is consistent with the reasoning we used earlier in this chapter in dealing with the topic of the basic emotions. A few basic emotions were described there, but the reader was warned that between these there are many other shades and patterns of emotional reaction which merge gradually one into the next with no sharp line of demarcation. This should lead us to expect that facial expressions cannot be readily classified into clearly demarcated and separated categories but instead should be regarded as points along a continuous scale, just as hues can be arranged in a sequence from, let us say, those with much red and little blue in them to those with much blue and little red.

In an experiment designed to test this hypothesis, subjects were asked to sort a series of photographic portraits according to the emotion shown.[20] The results were then treated by a mathematical technique that permitted the experimenter to locate each picture at a certain point on a circular scale, which, starting with one emotion, ran through the gamut back to that same emotion. The results of this experiment are illustrated in Figure 7.2, which represents a roughly circular pattern. The photographs showing strongly emotional reactions lie on the periphery of the circle. But, although photograph 41 indicates disgust and photograph 28 indicates surprise, the photographs that lie between them show no clear demarcation between one and the other of these emotions. Instead of a clear-cut distinction, they show a gradual transition.

These experimental results illustrate graphically the continuity of the facial expression of emotions. At the same time they aid in explaining the marked failure of the observers in earlier experiments to matching poses with verbal descriptions of emotional states. Consider, for example, photograph 62, which stands midway between "acute disgust" and "surprise." Suppose that it

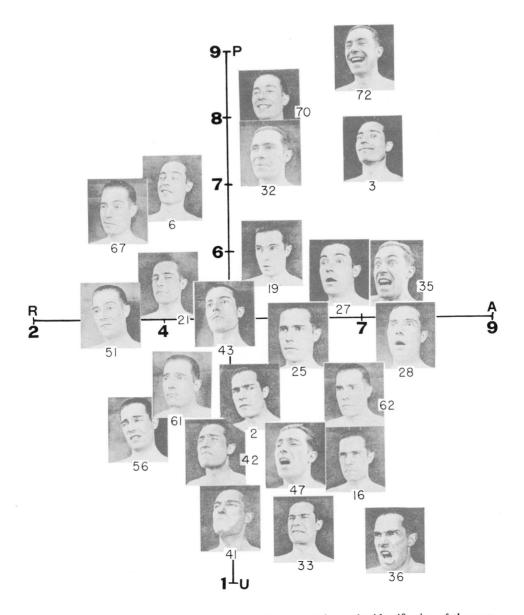

Fig. 7.2 The pictures used in the Schlosberg study on the identification of the emotional state shown by facial expression (see text). (From Schlosberg, *J. exp. Psychol.*, 1952, *44*, 229-237. Courtesy American Psychological Association)

had been intended as "surprise" by the actor who posed it and a group of individuals were required to classify it into either of the two categories, "surprise" or "acute disgust." The subjects would be right only 50 percent of the time, for half the time it would go into one category and half the time into the other. The same would apply to many of the other expressions.

Thus far our interest has been centered on the observer and his ability to identify the reactions of another person. What of this other person? Why do our facial muscles react in a sufficiently standardized way so that at least some success in identification may be attained? The biologist Darwin held that the facial expressions of the human are the vestiges of adaptive responses in the lower animals. Thus, the clenching of the teeth in anger is what is left to us of the fighting response of our evolutionary ancestors, whose defense was achieved not with words or fists but with jaws and fangs. Such a view implies, of course, that the expressive facial movements are not learned but come to us ready made because of the nature of our evolutionary inheritance.

There is evidence of the unlearned nature of these responses from more valid sources than the analogy used by Darwin. Dennis, who brought up some children in an environment free from the encouraging smiles that the fond parent usually lavishes on his off-spring, found that the children began to smile at the usual age and in the usual circumstances.[21] It could not be said that these children learned either the pattern of muscular movements involved in smiling or the appropriate situation in which to smile. Another experimenter observed that normal facial expressions of emotion occurred in a girl who was totally blind and deaf from birth. Here the source of sensory data necessary to learn the response is obviously absent.

Neither of these studies indicates or implies that learning plays no part in the expression of our emotional reactions. Through learning we may acquire the ability to tell a lie with a straight face, or to fill an inside straight without giving our opponent a hint of our luck through a change of facial expression. Convention may teach us to endure pain without a grimace, or at least without the excessive vocalization that characterizes the responses of a child to pain. Thus in the adult, in the expression of emotions, as in everything else, there is a great overlayer of learning, and we cannot conceive of these expressions as simple unlearned responses.

THE DEVELOPMENT OF EMOTIONAL BEHAVIOR

Emotional behavior, like almost every other kind of behavior, shows characteristic changes with the advancement of age.

These changes may be noted in the manner of expressing the emotion, in the frequency of emotional outbursts, in their duration, and in the type of psychological event that gives rise to them.

The differentiation of emotional reactions

The emotional reactions of the infant are frequent, but they are not well defined. In one study, a group of medical students and nurses observed motion pictures of emotional reactions in newborn infants and attempted to identify the stimulus that had provoked the reaction. The number of correct judgments made were little more than would be expected on the basis of chance guessing. Although similar studies with adults have not been, as we have noted above, entirely successful, the percentage of correct responses runs somewhat higher in most studies than in this one with infants.

One reason for the difference in achievement between observers judging adult expressions and those judging infants' expressions is indicated by a study[22] involving intensive observation of a number of children over a period of several months. These observations led to the conclusion that the different kinds of emotional responses are not present at birth but gradually develop with increasing age. This postulated developmental trend is shown in Figure 7.3.

Fig. 7.3 As the infant grows older, his emotional reactions become increasingly differentiated. (After Bridges[22])

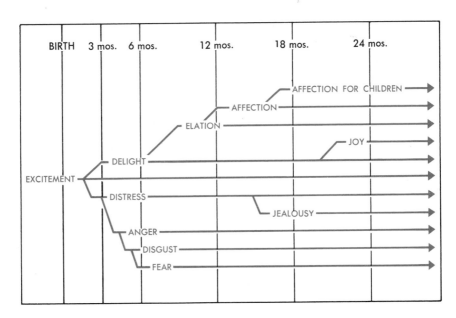

Changes in the stimulating situation

In a study of fears in children, which covered a range from birth to 8 years, marked shifts in the types of situation producing fright were noted.[23] Some of these trends are shown in Figure 7.4. The data may be roughly summarized in the statement that, whereas there is a decline in the tendency for fear reactions to be given to specific stimuli such as noises or other immediate situations, there is an increase in the tendency for them to be evoked by the type of stimuli that symbolize remote and absent situations as, for example, robbery and death. We may interpret these shifts to mean that the child has met and learned how to handle effectively much that goes on in the physical world. He is acquiring the capacity to live in a new world, a world represented by words and symbols, but he is still uneasy in, and unsure of, the nature of this expanding world.

Fig. 7.4 As the infant grows older, there is a change in the relative frequencies with which various types of stimulus situations produce fear responses. (After Jersild and Holmes[23])

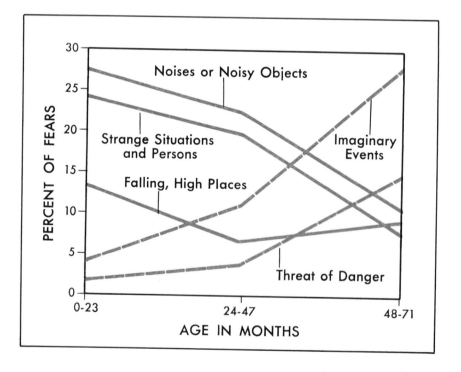

Because motive states are so intimately associated with the occurrence and nature of our emotional reaction, the nature of our concerns and worries will shift as our values and dominant motives change with age. In many cultures, including our own, the period of adolescence and post-adolescence is characterized by rather rapid shifts in values. It is especially true of these periods that the motive of being accepted by one's like-sex peer group expands to include acceptance by the opposite sex. Especially after adolescence, the motives of economic and social self-sufficiency increase in strength. Yet the increases in motive strength may not be paralleled by the development of new modes of behavior which will serve to satisfy these motives. Small wonder, then, that college freshmen report that they worry frequently about social success and their vocational future. With increasing age and the development of adequate and organized ways of handling such situations, most of these worries may be eliminated. But, as in the case of a few of us, if the problems presented by these situations cannot be adequately solved, the fear reactions will persist throughout adult life, and we shall never face these specific situations with equanimity.

Anger reactions show similar modifications with increasing age. In the one-year-old, anger arises most frequently out of conflicts related to the performance of the necessary physical routines, whereas in the four-year-old, who is both more play-directed and more socially directed, conflicts center most frequently about demands for attention and sharing with others.

Nonsocial disturbances of our activities always remain sources of anger reactions. Ink spilled on one's clothes, a broken shoelace at a hurried moment, a bolt that won't screw in, or a window that persistently jams can easily precipitate a hot flush of anger. In contrast with children, however, adults are more prone to find the sources of anger in social situations, and these are likely to occur more frequently than the nonsocial ones. A large number of these situations touch the person directly—a slight, real or fancied; a person pushing into line ahead of him; an unfair grade; or a criticism of his activities. It is characteristic of the adult, in contrast to the child, that such situations do not need to affect him directly in order to arouse his anger. He may become irked when as a passerby he sees someone push ahead of others in a line; the cruel treatment of an animal may anger him; or he may be aroused by social or political injustice in a remote land. By the time we

253

reach adulthood, we have developed so clear and integrated a picture of what the world should be that impersonal violations of our picture become personal and there is no need to ask for whom the bell tolls.

Changes in the form and frequency of emotional reaction

Emotional outbursts change markedly in form, as well as in other respects, with age. With age, the overt expression of these reactions becomes minimized, and a response that an observer cannot miss in a two-year-old may pass unobserved in the adult of twenty-two. With age, moreover, the reaction becomes more verbal, and heated words replace flying fists. The duration of the outburst and its aftermath also changes. The tears of the child may quickly turn to smiles and the outburst may be forgotten shortly after its inception, but the dry eyes of the adult may conceal an emotional smoldering which may persist for a long time, or the outburst itself may leave behind a mood which colors his perception for the entire day.

This age differential in the persistence of the emotional response is not, in all probability, due to increasing stability of the emotional response that is an inevitable consequence of age, but rather to quite other reasons. The adult has learned to meet many trying situations with equanimity, and he has learned also that emotional responses are not usually the most effective means of solving the problem at hand. Or if they do cause him to win through in the immediate situation, they may nevertheless lose him an advantage at a later time because, in our culture at least, his respected contemporaries frown upon and scorn this means of gaining one's end. As a consequence, the average adult reacts emotionally only to those situations which are of great importance to him, and because they are important the instigating situation is not readily forgotten. The result is that the stimulus for the emotional reaction remains, at least in symbolic form, to produce a continuance of the original emotional reaction.

Precise data comparing the frequency of emotional reactions at various age levels are not available, partly because changes in form of the reactions make it difficult for an observer to collect comparable data. One study of a large group of normal preschool children indicates that there are considerable changes in frequency even within this narrow age range, as shown in Figure 7.5. The trends are apparent: a building up in frequency and then a decline, which undoubtedly results from a greater adjustment to and understanding of the realities of the environment.

In a questionnaire study, subjects ranging in age from approximately twelve to twenty-two years showed a progressive decline in frequency of worry from all sources from an average of 50 items at the younger ages to an average of 5 items at the oldest age.[24]

Decline in the frequency of emotional reaction with increasing age may properly be predicted from a knowledge of the nature of the psychological situation in which the emotions have their inception. The emotional reactions of fear or anger occur when we meet situations for which we have no ready and organized response patterns, and when our motivations are strong and the frustrations many. The acquisition of skills of all sorts gives us greater ability to deal with situations as they come our way, and hence we meet fewer stimuli with which we cannot cope. At the same time our motives and goals become more socially acceptable and thus less

Fig. 7.5 As the infant grows older, changes occur in the nature of his emotional reactions. (After Macfarlane, *Child Behavior and Development*)

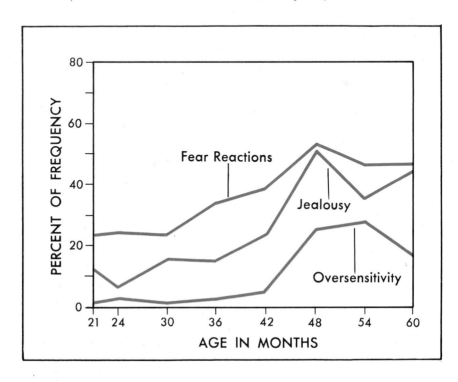

likely to meet resistance. In addition we become more realistic as adults and learn to avoid those situations in which we have little hope of gaining our ends.

THE CONTROL AND ELIMINATION OF
UNDESIRABLE EMOTIONAL BEHAVIOR

The two basic methods involved in the reduction of the total frequency of emotional reactions are (1) the avoidance of situations that may give rise to the emotional reaction and (2) the elimination of the tendency to make an emotional reaction in this particular situation.

Avoidance of situations that evoke emotion

Although avoiding a situation that will evoke an emotional response may seem unrealistic and may seem to imply that the individual should be wrapped in cotton batting, safe from the slings and arrows of outrageous fortune, this is not, in reality, the case. Not infrequently, we become involved in emotional situations which leave behind them aftertastes of unpleasantness and which offer no long-range solution of the problems for any of the participants. Many of the anger responses of children are of this useless sort; an altercation may arise over the possession of a particular toy when a duplicate toy may be within reach of each of the principals; two children may fight to occupy the same square foot of sand in the sandbox when the sitting is just as good in another place. The wise parent learns that certain types of play at certain times of day are bound to end in quarrels or frustration; he therefore terminates the activity before the inevitable. Adults may themselves anticipate that a useless quarrel may be precipitated by an ill-chosen word or action and may inhibit their speech or avoid the situation.

There are reasons other than immediate unhappiness for avoiding the potentially emotional situation, unless, of course, participation in the situation is a necessary part of achieving normal goals. We have mentioned, in our discussion of learning, that, for whatever reason, once a response has been made to a stimulus and it gains some reinforcement that response is likely to recur when the stimulus is again presented. Since emotional reactions often result in reinforcement, the habit of reacting emotionally to a specific situation may develop, and the difficult task of eliminating this reaction may have to be undertaken at some later date. As we have noted, emotional reactions may occur because of rather short-lived organic states or inadequate skills in handling a situation. It is almost certain that at a later time the organic state will be different, or additional skills which will transfer positively will have developed, and that the situation will then be approachable without emotional disturbance. Thus the situation need not be avoided persistently but only when there is reason to believe that it cannot be handled without undue emotional disturbance.

Elimination of the emotional reaction

It is impossible to live a normal life and to meet the many social and physical stimuli that modern living entails without developing specific emotional habits. We cannot always be in the optimal physiological condition, and we cannot look into the future with sufficient discernment to prepare ourselves for all the problems and conflicts that will come our way. Because of this we shall always be saddled with emotional reactions that are maladaptive and unpleasant. These responses need to be eliminated.

One of the first careful studies of the elimination of a fear response in children employed the conditioning technique to alter the fear reaction shown by a small child to a white rabbit.[25] This was accomplished by employing as an unconditioned stimulus the pleasant situation of eating a chocolate bar. The conditioned stimulus was the white rabbit. While the child was eating, the rabbit was introduced into his visual field some distance away, and this procedure was repeated over a number of daily experimental periods, the animal gradually being brought closer and closer to the child. After several days of this procedure, the fear response produced by the animal was eliminated. A new and different conditioned response had been developed.

One may rightfully ask why such a method caused the child to overcome his fear of rabbits instead of developing a fear of eating chocolate. The reason for this seems to lie in the fact that in the early sessions the rabbit was always kept at some distance from the child, and at these long distances the rabbit was only mildly effective in producing the fear reaction. Once it had ceased to produce

257

the reaction at this distance, it could be brought closer until actual contact could be tolerated. Because the potency of a stimulus decreases with distance, we may often eliminate an avoidance response by gradual extinction of the negative stimulus.

A clear demonstration of the effectiveness of the extinction procedure wherein the conditioned stimulus is presented at a very weak intensity in the beginning and with increasing intensity on later trials is shown in the following experiment which used rats as the subjects.[26] The conditioned stimulus consisted of the illumination of a light bulb, and approximately five seconds after its onset a shock was delivered to the animal by way of the grid on the floor of the box in which the animal had been placed. A movable wheel was located at one end of the box and rotation of the wheel by the rat terminated the shock. Each animal was given 60 training trials and they soon learned to turn the wheel after the buzzer sounded, thus avoiding the shock. Following this an extinction series of 30 trials was begun. For one group this extinction series was conducted in the classical manner by presenting the original conditioned stimulus without reinforcement. This group made a total of 14.4 responses during the extinction test. For the experimental group extinction was begun by starting with a very faint light and increasing its intensity on successive trials until, after 7 trials, it had attained the intensity of the original stimulus. Whereupon 30 more stimulations were given. This group gave only 6.5 responses during the complete series of 37 trials.

A nonlaboratory study dealing with fear reactions of children in their day-to-day living and the techniques their parents employed to overcome these fears used as its data the records kept by parents of their children's fears, the methods they used to overcome these fears, and the success of the various methods. The methods employed and the comparative success of each, ranked from most to least effective, are listed in Table 7.1.[27] Because the parents used some methods more than others, no percentage statement of relative success is very meaningful. However, the first three methods were very successful and the last three were generally unsuccessful.

The effectiveness of the first method in Table 7.1 could be readily predicted from our earlier and somewhat theoretical consideration of what the fear response consists of and how it is produced. Fear reactions arise from situations in which we either have no way of adequately handling the event or anticipate that we shall not be able to handle it. This highly effective method is obviously

TABLE 7.1. THE RELATIVE EFFECTIVENESS OF PARENTAL PROCEDURES FOR OVERCOMING FEARS OF CHILDREN

1. Specific attempts to promote skills, to encourage child to develop specific methods of his own in coping with feared stimulus, to bring the child into active experience with or participation in the feared situation.
2. Providing opportunities for child to grow acquainted with feared situation of his own accord by making it accessible to him in his daily environment but without using compulsion or ulterior allurements or promoting specific skills.
3. Graded presentation of fear stimulus; increasing intensity of stimulus by degrees: introduction of part of fear stimulus, then entire stimulus.
4. Positive but passive "conditioning": attempts to associate feared object with pleasant or unfeared familiar stimulus or reward but without calling for active participation by child.
5. Verbal explanation, reassurance, plus demonstration (without involving active participation by child): attempt to demonstrate source of sound, take feared engine apart, "show" there is no bogey, etc.
6. Verbal explanation and reassurance: telling child that there is no danger, attempt to explain nature of noise, assure him there is no bogey, etc.
7. Example of fearlessness in others.
8. Ignoring the fear: taking no notice when child seems afraid, changing subject when he mentions feared situation, etc.
9. Enforced contact with or participation in feared situation; also verbal pressure to participate, including ridicule and invidious comparisons.
10. Removing the cause of fear or introducing palliatives: steering him away from contacts with feared situation, comforting him and helping him when he is afraid.

based upon the development of ways of dealing effectively with the situation.

The second and third methods are probably essentially identical so far as the psychological mechanisms involved are concerned. Both of them seem to involve presentation of the conditioned stimulus without reinforcement of the original fear response. Method 2 almost certainly involves graded presentation of the intensity of the conditioned stimulus, the gradations being determined by the subject himself rather than by the parent as in Method 3. This is illustrated by the manner in which a child will, when presented with a fearsome but attractive object, retreat from it and then gradually move closer and closer to it. One can conceive of each approaching step as constituting an extinction trial with ever-increasing intensity of the stimulus.

The ineffectiveness of the last two methods might also have been predicted by the parents if they had possessed or employed some knowledge of the theoretical principles of the psychology of learning. Method 9 is simply a way of requiring the child to practice the response that is already acquired, and it might have been expected to increase rather than decrease the tendency to make that same response at a later time. Method 10 is based on the expectation that forgetting will occur as a simple function of the lapse of time, but we know that this does not necessarily happen.

It goes without saying that these methods would operate in much the same fashion in older individuals. Social situations, a frequent source of fear for the younger adult, particularly in the adolescent and post-adolescent years, can be encountered with more equanimity if one approaches them with some preparation, even though the preparation be no more than some little system for finding topics to talk about, or a moderately polished dance step. Fear reactions will arise if we are not able for one reason or another to respond adequately to a situation, but it is also true that we may eliminate a previously established fear by acquiring skills with which to deal with the situation.

In a study dealing with anger responses in children, it was found that the most successful method of eventually eliminating the response was to disregard it when it occurred.[28] This finding contrasts markedly with the fact that the technique is ineffective when used with fear reactions; but the situations are totally dissimilar. Temper tantrums are often used as a method of social control, and if the response is disregarded by the parent, it has no goal-achieving value. Therefore it will be eliminated in the same way and for the same reason that a rat ceases to enter the blind alleys of a maze, or that a dog, once conditioned, will cease to respond if the conditioned stimulus is presented repeatedly without accompaniment of the unconditioned stimulus.

Most of the techniques mentioned above have dealt with emotional reactions that are tied to certain rather specific stimulating objects or situations: a neighbor's dog, a motor that makes a frightening noise when it is turned on, or (in the anger response) the requirement that the shoes be put on before play begins. These situations are concrete, and unless the child shows a very large number of such reactions, the existence of a specific stimulus→response connection has no great significance in the larger integration of habits that constitute the personality. They may be treated specifically and, so to speak, as local ailments, for they represent no major cause for alarm.

Frequently in adults and occasionally in children certain emotional reactions, even though they may be very specific, cannot be treated as isolated stimulus→response connections. They are likely to be symptoms of a more general disturbance which the elimination of a specific response may do nothing to correct. Instead, elimination of the underlying disturbance may be achieved only through a long and slow process of psychotherapy—a process which may result in the reorganization of the fundamental personality structure of the individual. Such work can be conducted only by an expert therapist and not by the layman, for it involves the understanding of underlying motives as well as specific fears.

Psychotherapy is achieved through a large number of interviews between client and therapist. During these many interviews the patient talks; he tells of his innermost wishes, his goals, his habits, his likes, and his dislikes, and he recalls fragment after fragment of the long-forgotten experiences of his childhood. Often out of this series of interviews data are obtained which permit the therapist to aid the patient in restructuring his personality and obtaining relief from the abnormal emotional reactions. The process will be described in greater detail in Chapter 16.

INDIVIDUAL DIFFERENCES

IN EMOTIONALITY

Individuals differ among themselves in their degree of emotionality, just as they do in every other psychological characteristic. There are the calm ones and the excitable ones; the hot-tempered and the easy-going; the buoyant enthusiastic soul and the dull phlegmatic clod; the man who is afraid of his shadow and the man who fears no one. And between these extremes lie the vast majority of persons, some closer to one extreme and some to the other.

Genetic background and emotionality

Precise and unequivocal data linking variations in emotional behavior with genetic backgrounds are few. One may find, for example, that there is a close relationship between the number of fears of the child and the number of fears of the mother. But although this is interesting and significant in itself, its implications are not clear. Does the child learn to have many fears through the precepts of a highly emotional mother, or has he inherited a structure that is biased in the direction of emotional responsiveness. The study cannot tell us.

Somewhat more meaningful data are available from a study conducted on rats.[29] The experimenter used as his measure of emotionality the frequency of urination and defecation when the animal was placed in a large, brightly lighted, circular field. He then bred together the animals with high emotionality scores and also those with low emotionality scores. The offspring of the emotional parents, even in the first generation, were more emotional than the offspring of the nonemotional parents, and by the eighth generation there was a very marked difference between the two breeds of rats. The increase in difference was due primarily to increasing emotionality on the part of the emotional animals; the nonemotional animals showed little change from one generation to the next. Unless—and this is not very likely—the offspring in generation after generation learned to become increasingly emotional in the test situation because of the cage behavior of their parents, the results of the study must be accounted for in terms of the inheritance of some structural differences which resulted in a greater readiness to react emotionally in the open field.

It is consistent to expect that the same biological factors operate in humans and could be used to account for some of the individual differences in general emotionality. To speak of a readiness to react emotionally to a certain situation is by no means the same as stating that a fear or love or hate of a specific object has been inherited. There is no acceptable evidence that anything of this sort is true. There is some evidence, as mentioned above, that genetic factors may predispose individuals to react more in one way than in another in particular environments, but this is far different from assuming that specific reactions to specific stimulus conditions are inherited. It is a difficult lesson to learn but it is nevertheless true that what we are in all respects is a product of an interaction of both our genetic background and our environmental experiences.

Environmental factors and emotionality

In an earlier discussion of the learning of emotional reaction, we have pointed out the manner in which specific fear reactions may be learned. Such learning situations are environmental determinants of individual differences. It is reasonable to expect that, in addition to learning to react emotionally to specific situations, one may acquire a general habit of reacting emotionally. Clinical data have shown that the child who lives in a home characterized by parental tensions, who learns to get his own way through outbursts of emotion, or who lives a life of frustration and inhibition, is likely to develop personality difficulties which frequently contain an element of heightened emotionality.

To attempt to make any evaluation of the relative importance of these two factors—genetic and environmental—in the determination of individual differences would be futile at this time, for we know too little. Certainly the nature of the specific objects to which emotional reactions are made would be determined environmentally, and in the determination of general emotionality inheritance and environment would be highly interrelated. They could serve both to supplement and complement each other. This topic will be discussed more fully when the topic of Personality is considered in Chapter 15.

REFERENCES

[1] Lindsley, D. B. "Emotion" in S. S. Stevens (ed.), *Handbook of Experimental Psychology*, Wiley, 1951.

[2] Schlosberg, H. Three dimensions of emotions, *Psychol Rev.*, 1954, *61*, 81-88.

[3] Blatz, W. E. The cardiac, respiratory, and electrical phenomena involved in the emotion of fear, *J. exp. Psychol.*, 1925, *8*, 109-132.

[4] Landis, C., and Hunt, W. A. *The Startle Pattern*, Holt, Rinehart & Winston, 1939.

[5] Hebb, D. O. On the nature of fear, *Psychol. Rev.*, 1946, *53*, 259-276.

[6] Watson, J. B., and Raynor, R. Conditioned emotional reactions, *J. exp. Psychol.*, 1920, *3*, 1-14.

[7] Soloman, R. L., Kamin, L. J., and Wynne, L. C. Traumatic avoidance learning: The outcome of several extinction procedures with dogs, *J. abn. soc. Psychol.*, 1953, *48*, 291-302.

[8] Ruckmick, C. A. *The Psychology of Feeling and Emotion*, McGraw-Hill, 1936.

[9] Hunt, J. McV., Cole, M. W., and Reiss, E. E. S. Situational cues distinguishing anger, fear and sorrow, *Amer. J. Psychol.*, 1958, *61*, 136-151.

[10] Harlow, H. F., and Zimmerman, R. S. Affectional responses in infant monkeys, *Science*, 1959, *130*, 421-432.

[11] Igel, G. J., and Calvin, A. D. The development of affectional responses in infant dogs, *J. comp. physiol. Psychol.*, 1960, *53*, 302-305.

[12] Gates, G. S. An observational study of anger, *J. exp. Psychol.*, 1926, *9*, 325-336.

[13] Goodenough, F. L. *Anger in Young Children*, Univ. of Minnesota, 1931.

[14] Janis, I. L. *Air War and Emotional Stress*, McGraw-Hill, 1951.

[15] Hovland, C. I., and Sears, R. R. Minor studies of aggression: VI. Correlation of lynchings with economic indices, *J. exp. Psychol.*, 1938, *9*, 301-310.

[16] Miller, N. Theory and experiment relating psychoanalytic displacement to stimulus-response generalization, *J. abn. soc. Psychol.*, 1948, *43*, 155-178.

[17] Wallace, A. F. C. *An Exploratory Study of Individual and Community Behavior in an Extreme Situation: "Tornado in Worcester."* Publication 392, National Academy of Sciences. National Research Council, Washington, D. C., 1956.

[18] Landis, C. Studies of emotional reactions, *J. comp. physiol. Psychol.*, 1924, *4*, 447-509.

[19] Dunlap, K. The role of eye-muscles and mouth-muscles in the expression of the emotions, *Gen. Psychol. Mono.*, 1927, *2*, 196-233.

[20] Schlosberg, H. The description of facial expressions in terms of two dimensions, *J. exp. Psychol.*, 1941, *29*, 497-510.

[21] Dennis, W. Infant development under conditions of restricted practice and of minimum social stimulation: A preliminary report. *Gen. Psychol.*, 1938, *53*, 149-158.

[22] Bridges, K. M. B. Emotional development in early infancy, *Child Devel.*, 1932, *3*, 324-334.

[23] Jersild, A. T., and Holmes, F. B. Children's fears, *Child devel. Mono.*, No. 20, 1935.

[24] Pressey, S. L., and Pressey, L. C. Development of the interest attitude test, *J. Applied Psychol.*, 1933, *17*, 1-16.

[25] Jones, M. C. The elimination of children's fears, *J. exp. Psychol.*, 1924, *7*, 383-390.

[26] Kimble, G. A., and Kendall, J. W., Jr. A comparison of two methods of producing experimental extinction, *J. exp. Psychol.*, 1955, *45*, 87-90.

[27] Jersild, A. T. Methods of overcoming children's fears, *J. of Psychol.*, 1935, *1*, 75-104.

[28] Goodenough, F. L., *op. cit.*

[29] Hall, C. S. "The genetics of behavior" in S. S. Stevens (ed.), *Handbook of Experimental Psychology*, Wiley, 1951.

Chapter Eight

STIMULUS SELECTION AND RESPONSE VARIABILITY

IN THE PRECEDING CHAPTERS WE HAVE been concerned mainly with identifying principles of behavior that define certain stable relationships between the environment and the actions of the individual. We have referred to stimuli as though they were single physical events occurring either in the environment or within the individual (as in the case of the drive stimuli), and we have described responses as though they were stable and constant. But in life such is not actually the case; stimuli are neither simple nor single, and responses to identical stimulus situations are variable. One may ask how psychology dares aspire to be a science which predicts behavior if stimulation is complex and responses vary. The answer is, of course, that we must learn more than we know now. We must explore the ways in which an organism reacts to an environment that is complex, and we must discover why its responses are variable. We must seek some principle that will determine to which of the simultaneously impinging stimuli of its complex environment the organism will respond and explain why its behavior will vary even when the environment remains constant.

STIMULUS SELECTION

In our environment even the simplest situation is complex as regards the potential stimuli contained within it. Consider the book you are reading. It stimulates your eyes with patterns of black and white; it can also stimulate your touch sense organs and even your temperature sense organs; if you lift it, it will stimulate the sense organs in the muscles that produce the sensation of lifting; it has a slight odor. Consider more minutely these patterns of black and white—the words. Each word is a stimulus, and to each you have in the past attached many responses. You can react to words as they fit into the context of a sentence or you can react to them as individual and isolated stimuli. When you react to them in context, you are studying your lesson and learning psychology. Yet you could let each word stand alone and remind you of something else. You could react to the word "temperature," used in an earlier sentence, by being reminded that you are chilly or too warm; "white" may make you think of snow. If you behaved in this fashion, you would probably learn very little of a psychology lesson. Yet in terms of the physical stimuli present, there is nothing that prevents such a way of responding. In short, this object, a book, is not a single stimulus; it contains many potential stimuli.

Now let us examine a larger scene—the room in which you are working. Here the potential stimuli are almost innumerable. On your desk there is, perhaps, an ashtray littered with cigarette butts; a pencil and a pen; books of many kinds and with different titles; a photograph or two; a letter in its torn envelope. Around you are pictures or stimuli from the walls, doors, windows, and furniture. This list is far from exhaustive of the objects in the room, let alone of all the potential stimuli. If each object were to be evaluated as a source of stimuli in the manner in which we evaluated the text in the preceding paragraph, this chapter could easily occupy the remainder of this volume.

The enormous richness of our physical environment in potential stimulation sets up an important problem that the psychologist must solve. The reader will undoubtedly define this as a problem of attention, which is another way of saying that the organism reacts selectively to the richness of its environmental stimuli. The term *attention* has become loaded with many implications and for that reason the more neutral phaze *stimulus selection* is being used to describe this behavior. The concept may be identified best by the description of an experiment.[1]

The subjects were presented with a sheet of paper such as that illustrated in Figure 8.1. Through earphones they heard questions such as: "S_1 from G.D.O. Is there a cross in Position 1? Over." To such a question the correct answer would be: "G.D.O. from S_1. No. Over." This simple task was complicated by the fact that at the same time that this inquiry was being made, the subject heard a different voice in his earphones asking a question like the following: "S_3 from Turret. Is there an arrow in Position 5? Over." Since the subject was always designated as S_1, only the first of these two messages was addressed to him, and so in this instance he would answer G.D.O. and disregard the question from Turret. On some trials the question to S_1 would come from Turret and on others

Fig. 8.1 Type of display information given to the subjects in the experiment on listening to two simultaneous voices. The subject, upon request, reports what (if any) figure is found in the numbered rectangle that is referred to on that trial.

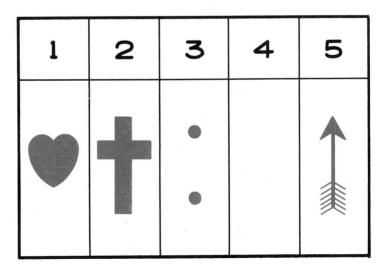

from G.D.O., but on every trial the two voices were heard simultaneously and there was always one question addressed to S_1, and one to S_2, S_3, S_4, or S_5. Throughout the experiment one particular voice always spoke for Turret and the other for G.D.O. Obviously the subject's major task was to select, at command on a given trial, one particular source to respond to, and to disregard the other.

This was the basic procedure for one group in the experiment; for a second group a visual stimulus was presented just before the message and this stimulus informed the subject which voice he was going to be required to answer; for a third group this visual stimulus was presented toward the end of the message.

The performance of both the first and the third group was very poor, their scores being just about what one might expect by chance, whereas the second group did quite well and was correct about 70 percent of the time after only a small amount of training. It is apparent, then, that the human is capable of reacting selectively to the auditory environment supplied by two persons speaking simultaneously, but that slight differences in the character of the situation makes for very marked differences in the efficiency with which this can be done.

These slight differences are worth considering. The results for the third group indicate that the individuals were not capable of listening effectively to both messages simultaneously and then of responding selectively afterwards. Why, however, was performance poor in the first group, for the questioner began by identifying himself and the subject whom he was addressing? The difficulty seems to lie in the fact that the subject has to attend to one voice or the other voice to discover which one wants to speak to him and it is only after he makes this identification that he can respond properly. But since the two voices come on simultaneously he cannot attend to both sufficiently to get this directive information.

The experiment has been described not primarily because it answers many questions about the psychological mechanisms involved in stimulus selection—though it does give us some clues —but because it demonstrates that the organism can react selectively in some instances while in others it cannot. As this experiment has so nicely demonstrated, the number of potential stimuli that are constantly and simultaneously bombarding the individual cannot all be reacted to with effectiveness at one time. Adequate behavior can occur only if the organism simplifies for itself this highly complex environment. This the organism is capable of doing. Our task in the first part of this chapter is to identify the principles that lead to the selection of one stimulus or class of stimulus as causes for responding.

It may ease the understanding of this selecting behavior if we divide its determinants into two major groups: (1) The first are those determinants that are related to the nature of the stimulus with respect to other stimuli and, of course, to the nature of people in general. This group of determinants permits us to predict with fair accuracy what an individual will respond to although we know nothing about him personally. (2) The second group consists of those determinants that are based upon the characteristics of the individual—that is, those that permit accuracy of prediction only if we know something about the individual's history and characteristics. The first type of variable leads to uniformity of stimulus selection for the individuals of a given species; the second produces differences among individuals' reactions to the same stimulus. The first group of variables depends primarily on the nature of the external stimuli; the second group depends upon the internal states of the organism.

Factors based on the nature of the stimulus

The effectiveness of much modern advertising depends to a very great extent on the principles of stimulus selection. The advertiser's efforts will be of no avail if he does not use a stimulus form that is reacted to with great frequency. His advertisement must compete with the many other stimuli that impinge on the potential buyer; hence he must use principles of advertisement construction that lead to a high probability of success in competition with other stimuli. But these principles are general ones and apply to all stimulus situations.[2]

Size

A large stimulus is more likely to be responded to than a small one. Perhaps this is one reason why we often say that a large man has a commanding presence. Experiments evaluating the effectiveness of advertising have demonstrated that more notice is taken of full-page than of half-page advertisements.

Intensity

The more intense a stimulus, the greater the likelihood that it will produce a reaction. There is no simple, straight-line relationship between either size or intensity and psychological effectiveness, for when either of these factors is doubled or tripled or quadrupled, a point of diminishing returns is reached beyond which psychological effectiveness is increased by smaller proportions. If, therefore, the stimulus is already large or intense, little may be gained by increasing its size or intensity.

Motion or change

The potency of movement as a stimulus is illustrated by a study made of responses to a window display. The display was set up motionless on a table, and observers recorded the number of persons who stopped to examine it. The score was 6 percent. On the following day the same display was made to rotate continuously, whereupon the score jumped to 45 percent.

Novelty

Closely akin to motion and change as a factor inducing stimulus selection is the degree of novelty of the stimulus. The effectiveness of this characteristic is illustrated in the following experiment:[3] The subjects were presented with a stimulus panel with four apertures, and under each aperture was a push button. Each of these windows could be lighted by the experimenter and the subject was told to press the key under the appropriate light as quickly as he could. During the first part of the experiment a white light appeared in each of the four apertures and they flashed on in a random order, one at a time. After a series of these trials the subjects were told that in the next session two lights were to come on simultaneously and they were to respond to only one of them, but it did not matter which one. The experimenter now changed *one* of these four white lights, so that occasionally the subject would be presented with a red and a white light. Typically, when a red and a white light appeared simultaneously it was the key under this novel red light that was pressed. To make certain that it was the novelty of the stimulus that was important rather than its color, another group of subjects received the initial training with four red lights and then were tested with three red and one white light. Typically, in this case it was the white light to which the reaction was given. It was not, then, the particular color of the stimulus, but its novelty that determined its effectiveness as a stimulus.

But there is still one other logical explanation of the results. It is that the responses were made because that light is in a minority, since there are three other lights different from it but like each other. To investigate this possibility another pair of groups were trained with three identical lights and one different one being used in the first part of the experiment. These subjects, however, did not show the preference for the unusual light when it was paired with the other lights.

Stated generally it appears that changes in the accustomed stimulus pattern of the environment result, other things being equal, in stimulus conditions that are highly effective in producing responses.

A story is told of a keeper in a lighthouse which emitted a loud blast of its warning horn every five minutes. One night the mechanism failed and the horn fell silent. Immediately the keeper awoke with a start and shouted, "What was that noise I heard?" How many times have all of us reacted to the ticking of a clock only when it stopped abruptly?

Repetition

Stimuli that are intermittent are, other things being equal, more effective than continuous stimuli. This principle is frequently applied in electric display signs that flash on and off. Danger signals also utilize this principle; all of us have seen the flashing warning light at railway crossings.

Duration

In order to be effective, stimuli must have a minimum duration. It is not possible to specify an absolute time value for the minimum duration, for this will depend upon the intensity of the stimulus. Thus, an intense light which is on for $\frac{1}{100}$ second may be effective, whereas a weaker light with a duration of $\frac{1}{10}$ second may not be. The relation between intensity and duration has been expressed in an exact mathematical equation known as the *Bunsen-Roscoe law*.

While on the topic of duration, it should be pointed out that stimuli which have extremely long durations lose their effectiveness. Thus, what has been said concerning characteristics of stimuli which lead stimulus selection pre-supposes that these stimuli will be of a certain minimal duration but not of excessively long duration. It is this fact that was hinted at in the anecdote of the lighthouse keeper.

Contrast

Effective stimuli also must stand out in contrast to their background. The use of this principle in a negative manner is illustrated by military camouflage, the aim of which is to conceal an object by decreasing the contrast between it and its background. The olive drab color used by the armed forces was chosen because it fades unobtrusively into the usual terrain. Even the towels and underclothing used by military personnel are dyed khaki, for white pieces of laundry lying on the ground or hanging from bushes easily reveal the location of a bivouac area to an enemy plane. Man-made objects contrast with nature not only in color but also in linear structure. Seldom does nature present a terrain of straight lines and sharp angles, but the objects that man makes usually have such contours. Effective camouflaging often involves painting so that flat surfaces, regular lines, and sharp angles are obscured. In present-day psychology we refer to the relationship of the object to its background as a *figure-ground relationship*. When we camouflage, we decrease the figure-ground contrast.

An example of the opposite of camouflaging is the marking of planes so that they will have a maximum probability of being located if they are downed in an isolated region and being searched for by rescue planes. Here there is a clear need for marked contrast between figure and ground. One group of psychologists made a study to determine which plane markings would be most effective for planes downed in arctic regions.[4] The problem is complicated by the fact that the visual characteristics of the terrain vary considerably with the time of day, the season of the year, and the contours and elevation. Their experiment indicated that a plane is most easily seen in all kinds of terrain if the back half of the wings and the entire fuselage are painted red or orange and the front half of the wings are the usual aluminum color.

The concept of figure and ground is not restricted to stimulation in the visual field but may be used in any situation in which one aspect of the total environment stands out from the remainder. Thus, in music, a melody or the sound of a specific instrument may emerge sharply from the tonal complex, and the accompaniment may be almost completely disregarded.

Although the ground may not be specifically reacted to, it nevertheless influences the reaction to the total situation, for the same physical figure may be responded to in one manner on one ground but in quite a different manner on a different ground. The same tie does not go well with all suits, or the same scarf with all dresses.

Unstable figure-ground relationships

Figure-ground relationships are not always stable, and in many instances what was figure becomes ground and what was ground becomes figure. This shift from one to another is often instantaneous and, so far as the observer is concerned, often seems to occur for no good reason at all. An illustration of this type of situation is shown in Figure 8.2. Looking at it in one way, we report a black cross in a white field; yet we can also see the drawing as a white cross on a black field. Sometimes these contrasting figure-ground relationships are described as a Maltese cross and a propeller. If the reader will look at this figure for a few moments, he will almost certainly find that the figure-ground relationships shift for him with no effort on his part. From the point of view of stimulus selection, the total pattern is an unstable one, for first one and then another aspect of it is reacted to.

Interaction

All the preceding factors seldom operate in complete isolation from one another—a fact corroborated by a study conducted on night lookouts aboard a ship.[5] The ability of trained lookouts to sight objects during their watch was checked under different weather conditions. On a bright moonlit night, an object with an area of only 60 square feet would be reported at a certain distance, but under a moonless, clear, starlit sky the object needed to have an area of 1000 square feet in order to be reported at the same distance. On an overcast night, a lookout would be unable to spot a small cargo ship at 2500 yards, although he could spot a large one at this same distance. Contrast and size work together to determine these results. If the contrast between object and sky is great, a small object can be spotted; but if the contrast is slight

Fig. 8.2 A reversible figure. As you look at it continuously, you will perceive it alternately as a black Maltese cross and a white propeller.

Fig. 8.3 A complex—and potentially confusing—figure-ground relationship. Both these instruments—artificial-horizon indicators—show the pilot whether his plane is level or banking. In this illustration both instruments indicate that the plane is banking to the left—that is, the left wing is lower than its right. But in the instrument at the left, the horizon (*figure*) moves and the plane (*ground*) does not. In the instrument at the right, the plane (*figure*) moves and the horizon (*ground*) does not. The pilot's ability to determine which is figure and which is ground is, of course, critical to his safety, and a change from one instrument to another is likely to result in negative transfer. (Courtesy Wright Air Development Center)

(as on an overcast night), an object at the same range must be large in order to be spotted.

Factors based on characteristics of the individual

The infinite variety of the world about us is sometimes forcefully brought home when, in passing a familiar scene, we suddenly discover in it a characteristic that we had never noted before. We are amazed, and we may even conclude that the recently noted characteristic had not been there before; but we may learn from others that our conclusion is in error. Although in the past all the stimuli from the scene may have acted on our sense organs many times, we have never before responded to the specific stimulus that now attracts our attention. Why has this happened? Since, in this hypothetical example, the scene has remained constant, it must be that some change has taken place within ourselves. The factors that determine stimulus selection in such instances must be sought for in some changeable characteristic of the organism, not in the nature of the environment. Let us note these factors.

Motivation

The state of our various motives is one of several factors that determine the stimuli to which we will react. The strength of our motives undergoes change with the passage of time. At times a certain motive is strong; at other times, when we are satiated, it is weak. When we are hungry, we tend to respond to stimuli which have to do with food; when thirsty, we select from among the many other competing stimuli those associated with potable liquids. The adolescent of sixteen will observe much about a member of the opposite sex that would be overlooked by the ten-year-old. The new father finds himself responding to infants and to objects of infancy, which in bachelor days had no existence for him.

Capitalizing on motives that touch upon our basic drives is common in advertising. A scantily clad pin-up girl may appear on a calendar advertising stockings, a soft drink, or a coal yard. The illustration need not be appropriate to the commodity advertised; it is used simply because it activates a basic motive. It is a stimulus likely to be responded to, and it is used in the hope that the observer will also read and remember the name of the stockings, the soft drink, or the coal yard.

If our drive or motive is weak, we tend to respond to a large variety of stimuli not relevant to it. If our motive is strong, however, we tend to respond to a more restricted number of stimuli and we are not so likely to notice parts of the environment that are unrelated to our dominant motivation. In one experiment, two groups of college students were asked to memorize a sequence of geometric forms presented on a memory drum.[6] One group was offered a money bonus for quick learning, whereas the other group was given no bonus and was told not to try very hard and to pay no more attention to the task than they would to an uninteresting lecture. Various colors were used in the drawing of the forms, but these colors were not mentioned in the instructions of either group. It turned out that the group working for money learned the sequence of forms more quickly but that later they were unable to identify as many of the colors correctly as the group that had learned under lower motivation. Thus, the students strongly motivated to learn did not respond so much to the color stimuli, which were irrelevant to their motive, as did the less strongly motivated students.

275

Prior experience

That the influence of an individual's prior experience is a factor in determining the stimuli he will select from an environmental array is fairly obvious. The country-bred person's description of a scene is likely to differ from that of the city-bred person; the geologist, in his trip through the country, observes phenomena different from those that the botanist observes.

The selecting tendency resulting from prior experience serves to filter out certain aspects of the environment for that individual; and this may retard his learning if these filtered-out aspects are actually relevant to the guidance of his behavior. On the other hand, his performance in a situation may be greatly improved by such biases if they cause him to neglect irrelevant aspects of the stimulus situation and respond only to the significant ones.

In one experiment, college students were presented with stimulus figures which they were required to learn in order to make certain responses. Four different figures were employed, and each was presented in a different color. Although the students were not told this, the colors of the figures were irrelevant and the problems could be solved only if they reacted to form regardless of the color. The problem was solved, and some days later they were asked to solve another problem similar to the first; but in this instance it could be solved only by reacting to color and disregarding form. It was found that the learning in this second situation was made difficult for them as a result of their prior experience. Negative transfer resulted because the students had previously learned to disregard an aspect of the stimulus which in the new situation was relevant to the guidance of their behavior.[7]

Set

Prior experience, as we have used the term, refers to habits which were developed in the organism many days, weeks, or months earlier. Closely related to prior experience is the phenomenon referred to as *set*.

By the term *set* is meant the tendency to respond to stimuli in a certain general way, this tendency or readiness being established by events immediately preceding the stimulation. Sets are shorter lived in their effects than are the effects of what we have termed prior experience, and they may be established by a single verbal command. The meaning of this term, and its distinction from prior experience, may be clarified by the presentation of several experiments.

In one experiment, stimuli were presented upon a screen to the group of college students by means of a tachistoscope, an instrument used to present a stimulus for a small fraction of time, usually from $\frac{1}{10}$ to $\frac{1}{100}$ second.[8] The stimuli used were cards of the sort shown in Figure 8.4. A series of these cards, with four to eight letters on each card, were flashed on the screen. Before each exposure the subjects were told that they were to report the number of letters on the card, the location of the letters, or the names of the letters. In other words, for each exposure they were given a specific set: to count, to locate, or to name.

Under the control conditions, the subjects were told to find out everything they could about the card. No special sets were established *before* the card was exposed. *After* each exposure they were asked to report upon only one aspect of the card—the number, the location, or the names of letters. The number of correct responses was much higher under the experimental conditions than under the control. In other words, when the subjects were set to respond to a certain aspect of a stimulus pattern, they discovered more about it than when they were instructed to respond to the pattern as a whole. It is significant that the experimental condition was superior to the control on all the three aspects being measured. Depending upon the directions given before each trial, the subjects could shift to counting, to locating, or to naming, and perform better than if no specific set had been established.

Thus, set serves to establish biases to select certain aspects of the stimulus situation. It is a temporary phenomenon in the sense that a new set may be established a moment later which causes new aspects of the stimulus situation to predominate.

Fig. 8.4 Two of the cards used to demonstrate the influence of set on the accuracy of report. Subjects can be asked to report on the specific letters, the number of letters, or their location.

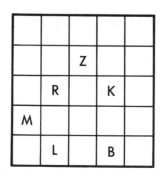
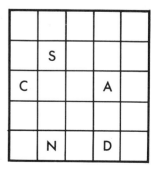

The operations of set do not lead to a generalized increase in the efficiency of behavior. Our increase in efficiency is almost exclusively limited to that aspect of the stimulus situation for which we are set. On the other hand, when we are set for one aspect of the situation, we are less prepared than usual to react to some other aspect of it. The effective magician uses this principle constantly, and one of the major purposes of the line of patter that he employs is to establish sets that will psychologically blind his audience to some aspect of the stimulus situation which, if noticed, would give the trick away. The entire plot of Edgar Allan Poe's story "The Purloined Letter" is based upon this principle. A thorough search of a room fails to reveal an important letter; yet the letter is there. The reason for failure is simple: for the letter is lying in clear view on the table, but the searchers were not set to find so important a document in so exposed a position.

The problem of set is of especial interest to the legal psychologist, because the manner in which set may function to determine what the witness can report on the stand is obvious. Very few citizens are set for correlating events with date of occurrence or time of day. We are not usually set to view people suspiciously, and behavior must be rather grossly atypical before we begin to respond to it as being of especial interest. As a result, we may have witnessed a significant event and yet be able to tell very little of crucial value about it. The psychologically sophisticated often view with incredulity the testimony of witnesses who purport to describe in minute detail events and persons that are in no way outstanding and that occurred weeks or months earlier.

Perhaps it is well to distinguish once again the terms *set* and *prior experience.* It is obvious that the two conditions achieve the same results, and possibly they do so by the same mechanisms, but there still remains a difference between them. Prior experience refers to biasing from events that may have taken many years to establish; set refers to biasing that occurs shortly before the stimulus event and that can readily be shifted by some new demand or direction. Both conditions, however, cause the organism to react selectively to the stimuli of its environment.

The significance of stimulus selection for prediction

The fact that motives, sets, and habits of long standing influence the specific aspect of the total stimulus that is reacted to is of considerable significance. It means that two individuals in the same physical environment may react quite differently because one is reacting to one aspect of the total stimulus and the other is reacting to a different aspect of it. In other words, the stimulus for one is not the same as the stimulus for the other. This fact would seem to contradict our position that behavior is a response to a stimulus, for the same physical environment seems to constitute one stimulus for one person and a different one for another. How can this be?

It is necessary to assume that the actual stimulus that elicits some response is not the physical event in the environment but rather the reaction to this physical event by the individual. This reaction constitutes or defines the stimulus to which the subject responds; his response generates stimuli within himself, and he responds, once again, to these. We might, therefore, elaborate our S → R diagram in the following fashion:

$$S \longrightarrow (r \to s) \longrightarrow R$$
$$\textit{external} \quad \textit{internal} \qquad \textit{observed}$$

In this diagram the external stimulus gives rise to the response represented by r, and this r produces a stimulus condition s within the organism which is the stimulus that gives rise to the observed response, R. The small s is usually referred to as a *response-produced cue*.

In essence what we have said above is that the nature of the response-produced cue will vary as a result of motivation, habits of long standing in dealing with such material, and momentary sets of the individual. It is apparent that if an $r \to s$ of one kind occurs, it is likely to lead to one kind of observed response (R), and an $r \to s$ of another kind is likely to lead to a different response (R). It is likewise apparent that if we are to predict this response (R), we must also predict the nature of the response-produced cue.

The few paragraphs above contain a very important notion and, though the notion is adequately expressed in those paragraphs, its significance is worthy of additional emphasis. From the **first** chapter of this book onward we have made the assumption that behavior can be understood as responses to stimuli, and for the most part we have identified the stimuli as events in the external environment. Now we have added another complication to the S → R event; for we have said that it is not the external stimulus itself, but some personally generated representation of it—the response-produced cue—that becomes the actual stimulus for the

279

observed response. But if the organism is given the responsibility of generating stimuli and reacting selectively to the multiple stimuli of the environment, one may well ask how behavior can be predicted. The question is a legitimate one since the effective stimuli, at least in many instances, are no longer observable to the experimenter. The answer to this is, first, that there are principles (described in the previous section of this chapter) which permit us to predict what stimuli will be selected. Second, we may assume that the relationship between the external stimulus and the personally generated stimulus—between S and $(r \rightarrow s)$—is a lawful one that can be predicted. Some justification for this assumption will be presented in the following chapter on Perception.

Stated simply, it means that, if we are to predict behavior, we must have more than a knowledge of the physical situation—we must also know about the individual's present motives, his present set, and the nature of his experience with this kind of material in the past. If we know these things we may predict the $r \rightarrow s$, or response-produced cue, for the individual, and then we may predict his actual overt behavior.

The number of single stimuli that can be selected

The football spectator who is not thoroughly familiar with the game is likely to observe only the man carrying the ball and to be quite unaware of the simultaneous actions of the other twenty-one players on the field. Such restriction of observation indicates that only a limited number of stimuli in the environment can be reacted to at the same time.

Data bearing upon this fact can be obtained from a reconsideration of a previously described experiment—the one involving the subjects who were trying to identify each letter on the cards as they were exposed for a time interval of less than $\frac{1}{10}$ second. The experiment actually measured the number of separate stimuli that can be reacted to simultaneously in an appropriate manner. Under the optimum condition, that of the pre-established set, the subjects consistently reacted successfully to the four- and possibly five-stimulus-unit cards, but they had virtually no success in identifying the seven- or eight-stimulus-unit cards. Other experiments of this general sort have produced the same pattern of results. The greatest number of separate stimuli that we can react to in a single instant with any high level of consistency is about five or six, although with special training this score can probably be improved by several units.

Our efficiency is greatly enhanced by a tendency to group objects into patterns. If you glance successively at the separate parts of Figure 8.5, you will note how grouping operates. You will probably find that you react to Part *A* and Part *B* at about the same speed, although *A* contains only five units and *B* fifteen. Part *C* with its fifteen units you may have handled even more quickly than you did *A*. You were certainly slowest with Part *D*, although it contained no more units than *B* or *C*.

How do we account for these differences? Actually you do not react separately to each of the small physical units—the dots; you react to each group of them. Because organisms can respond to groups or patterns as units, their efficiency becomes immensely increased. The football coach may acquire the ability to see an entire play as a single moving unit, and all of us can read long words at a glance because the words and not the letters become the psychological units. Psychologically, groups themselves become units, although physically they are composed of separate units.

On monitoring

The individual is frequently given the task of keeping watch for the occurrence of some stimulus event. This may be a particular sign as one drives along the highway, or, during the time of a cold war, the appearance on some electronic detecting device of a signal produced by an enemy attempting to approach in stealth. Such a situation requires of the searcher that he be constantly stimulated by an environment of greater or lesser complexity and then that he respond when some particular stimulus

Fig. 8.5 The number of individual items that can be reported is influenced by the way in which the items are grouped.

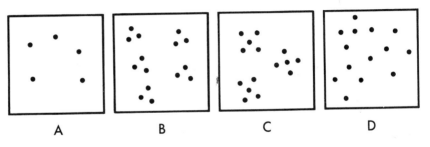

A   B   C   D

emerges. As so described the task is a simple one, but it is pertinent to ask how well we can expect it to be done. The following experiment helps to answer the question.[9]

The experimenter required the subjects to watch the face of an oscilloscope very similar to the radar that is used for the detection of distant aircraft. Their task was to observe the 'scope face continuously and to report any appearance of a small, faint spot of light that remained on for a very short time. The spot, or target as it is usually called, appeared at random intervals and in random locations on the 'scope face. The subjects, in other words, had no forewarning of when or where the spot was to appear. The subjects worked under four conditions, differing in the average rate of occurrence of the target per hour. The rates were 10, 20, 30, and 40. The subjects observed continuously under each condition for three hours and their score for each period consisted of the percentage of targets detected. The results are presented graphically in Figure 8.6.

The figure, it should be noted, indicates the percentage of targets that were detected and not the total number. One is impressed with how poor performance is when the rate of target

Fig. 8.6 Relationship between the average rate of target presentation and the percentage of targets detected. (After Deese and Ormond[9])

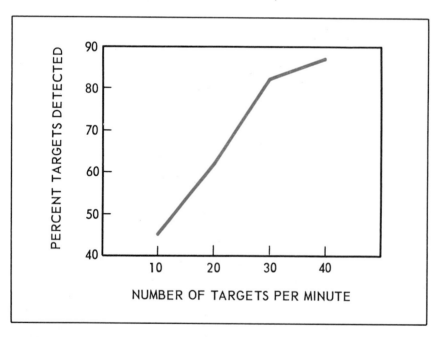

presentation is low, as well as with the progressive improvement in performance as target rate becomes greater. It would appear that monitoring is something that humans do not do well.

The improvement in performance with increased target rate can be predicted from the principles of reinforcement. We need only to assume that target detection is the result of the subject's making an active searching response and that this response will be reinforced if a target is detected. If the rate of target presentation is high then it is very likely that a target will occur while the response is being made. This reinforcement will increase the probability that the searching response will continue to be made and another target detected. If, however, target presentation rate is low, the searching responses will begin to be extinguished, for they will not be reinforced very often.

THE BIOLOGICAL UTILITY OF
STIMULUS SELECTION

The fact that organisms behave selectively toward the stimuli in their environment is of extreme significance so far as survival is concerned. In the first place, our normal environment is very rich in stimulation, so rich that it would be impossible to respond to all of these stimuli simultaneously, for potential responses would compete with each other and none could occur. Only by being selective, by pauperizing the psychological environment, is it possible to deal effectively with even a small part of it, and so with any of it at all.

There is an interesting parallel between this characteristic of organismic behavior and the effectiveness of telephone systems. It has been found that telephone systems which were completely automatic often failed altogether during city-wide emergencies and alarms, but continued to be at least moderately effective if they were manned by human operators. The reason for this is that, as a consequence of the alarm, many people placed calls simultaneously. The automatic system tried to accept them all, and as a consequence it could accept none of them. The human operators were selective, accepting some calls and disregarding others. Not everyone was served, it is true, but complete paralysis did not result. So too in the behavior of the individual; he does not respond to all stimulation, but so long as the important signal stimuli are reacted to, this neglect of the others does not ordinarily hinder his adjustment.

The particular characteristic of the stimulus that leads to its selection is also of significance from the point of view of the organism's capacity to survive in a preditory world. Species have evolved in and, even now, must sometimes live in an environment where attacks from other organisms are an almost constant threat. To survive, the organism must be equipped with a means of detecting and then of avoiding the threat before it can harm him.

Consider the characteristics of stimuli that result in their being selected from the other potential stimuli in the environment. These are also the stimulus characteristics that would be produced by any but the most stealthy of attackers. To have the capacity to select these stimuli from the momentary flux of stimulation is to have the capacity for effective self-protection if detection is followed by flight or successful attack.

VARIABILITY OF RESPONSE

Variability of response, as we mentioned briefly in Chapter 2, is a prerequisite for learning in many situations. An organism that lacked the ability to vary would be hopelessly chained to its past; it could do nothing except repeat one response endlessly. Indeed, if the response that it was making failed to lead to biological satisfaction, it could not long survive. And it is inevitable that some day every organism will encounter a situation which, if it is to be handled successfully, demands a new mode of behavior. It is only through the process of varying its response that an organism is capable of hitting upon a mode of behavior that leads to a solution. There is no organism in the world today, from the single-celled ameba to man, that will not vary its behavior in the face of repetitive stimulation. The tendency to vary the response is, however, so pervasive that it occurs in situations in which it is not essential for adjustment. It may even result in the organism's obtaining less satisfaction or no satisfaction of some obvious biological motive. In this section we shall deal with variability and we shall attempt to identify the factors that lead to it.

The nature of the environment

In the preceding section we noted that the physical environment is rich in the number of stimuli it offers to the organism at
any one time. Any *object* is ambiguous in terms of the *stimuli* it
offers to our receptors; we are capable of reacting to one or another
of the stimuli or to the total pattern of stimuli which emanate
from the object. A book may be reacted to as a thing which is red,
a thing which has weight, a thing with a specific physical form
made up of straight lines and 90-degree angles, or a thing full of
the symbols we call words. This fact makes it possible for us to
react to the object, *book,* in a variable fashion. We may use it to
refer to the color of a new dress; we may use it to weigh down
papers that the wind is blowing from our desk; we may use it as a
straightedge in the absence of a ruler, or we may use it to increase
our knowledge or as a source of conversation in a social situation.

It is not surprising, then, that in a specific environment an
individual may behave in a variable fashion, because at one time
he is reacting to one stimulus or to one aspect of the complex
stimulus, whereas at another time he is reacting to another stimulus
or to a new aspect of the stimulus complex. Knowing that any
organism is confronted with a very complex environment and has
many stimuli impinging upon it, we can, to some extent, understand why behavior will be variable.

The multiplicity of the stimuli in our environment sets the
stage for some of our variability, but it does not explain why the
organism reacts to one aspect of the stimulus object now and to
another aspect of it later. It also fails to account for the fact that
the organism's response to the identical stimulus may vary from
one time to the next.

Factors leading to variability

There are a number of factors that produce variability in
response to the same stimulus by the same individual at different
times. Most of these factors involve principles with which we are
already familiar.

Motivation

The significance of motivation for producing response variability has already been discussed, and at this time we need do no

more than remind the reader of its importance. In the example of the different ways of reacting to a book, just mentioned, it is obvious that the manner in which it will be reacted to at any given moment will be determined by the nature of the individual's motivation at that moment.

Extinction

The phenomenon of extinction leads toward variability of behavior. In the discussion of this phenomenon in Chapter 4, we noted that when the conditioned stimulus was presented repeatedly without reinforcement, the conditioned response would gradually diminish or become extinguished.

This technique of non-reinforcement is often used when we wish to break an undesirable habit. A dog which has been fed scraps of food from the dining table may soon develop the habit of begging each time the family sits down to eat. To break the habit, the family agrees that no one is to feed it when it comes begging. If the perseverance of the family is greater than the strength of the dog's habit, its begging response to the stimulus of the family-at-the-table can be eliminated. Sometimes, if a child bothers a guest with one request after another, the considerate parent may say, "Pay no attention to him and he'll soon stop." To cite another example, if people no longer laugh at our favorite joke, we stop telling it.

In these situations, food for the dog, attention for the child, and laughter for the adult reinforce the response to the stimulus. If these reinforcements are consistently withdrawn, the dog, the child, and the adult will vary their behavior and different responses will appear. Essentially, what has occurred in these situations is that the stimuli have lost their effectiveness: the $S \rightarrow R$ connection has become weakened and the response is lost. Variability occurs, and a new response replaces the old one.

Spontaneous recovery

In a certain respect spontaneous recovery also results in variability. Through the process of extinction, a response may be caused to disappear, but through spontaneous recovery it returns. Thus, spontaneous recovery results in changing the organism's behavior toward the stimulus from that of no response to that of responding.

Avoidance of repetition

In an experiment conducted some years ago, a long list of words was read off to the subjects and they were directed to call out any number between 1 and 10 to each word. They were informed that no particular number was correct for a particular word and all they were required to do was to respond to each word with a number.[10] The condition that was varied in the experiment was the rate at which the words were read out and the five different speeds which were used are indicated in the top line of Table 8.1. The experimenter recorded each response made by the subjects.

The particular question which concerned the experimenter was the frequency with which the subject gave the same numerical response to two successive words. The percent of repetition for each group is shown in the second line of the table.

TABLE 8.1.

Seconds between words	1	2	4	8	16
Percentage of number repetitions	3.12	6.19	7.16	6.25	9.76

The table shows clearly that there is a marked tendency not to repeat a response with the fastest rate of stimulation, and that as the rate of responding required becomes slower, this tendency to avoid repetition decreases.

It should be emphasized that it was just as appropriate for the subject to repeat a response that was just made as it was to give a different number. Nevertheless, the subjects seemed to specifically avoid doing so except in the condition with the longest interval between responses.

This phenomenon is demonstrated even more strikingly in an experiment involving white rats.[11] The animals were trained on a simple maze which was shaped like a T. During the training, one of the arms of the maze would be removed, making a figure like an inverted L, but at the end of the arm the hungry animals always found a food reward. Many trials were run in the L-shaped pattern; the L led off half the time to the right and half the time to the left. As a result of this training, the animals acquired equal habits of turning to the right and to the left to find their food.

Now came the crucial tests. The animals were given ten trials on the L leading, let us say, to the right. Food was always found at the end of the maze. After these ten trials, both arms were placed on the maze and the animal was given one more run. If reactive inhibition does operate, and there is a tendency *not* to repeat responses, then the animals would be expected to turn in the direction opposite to the previous ten turns, even though these ten turns had led to food. Actually, when this test trial was given immediately after the ten reinforced runs, every animal avoided making the response that had just been repeated.

Tests were given to animals not only immediately after the ten trials but also at varying time intervals afterward, and it was found that this tendency to avoid making the same response disappeared with the passage of time; after 24 hours .it no longer operated (Figure 8.7). In summary, this experiment demonstrates that there is a tendency not to repeat responses just made even though these responses have been reinforced. The tendency is not a permanent one and disappears with the passage of time.

There are several kinds of interpretations of the basis for the behavior that has been so clearly demonstrated in the two experiments described above. One of these interpretations is called the *reactive inhibition* interpretation.[12] (Notice that it is called reactive inhibition and not retroactive inhibition.) This interpre-

Fig. 8.7 Relationship between the tendency to avoid repeating a series of responses that have just been reinforced and the time elapsing since the responses. (After Zeaman and House[11])

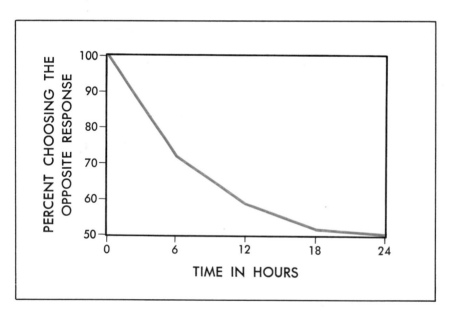

tation assumes that the inhibition against responding is generated in the response system itself. It is a concept that bears some similarity to the familiar term "fatigue," but it is not meant to imply the depletion of energy or the accumulation of waste products in the muscles, as seems to be true of the term fatigue. Reactive inhibition simply states, without making assumptions about underlying physiological processes, that immediately following a response there is generated a tendency against making that response, and that this tendency decreases with the passage of time.

An alternate interpretation of the same behavior emphasizes some change in the degree of sensitivity the individual shows to the stimuli associated with the response. This interpretation, which can be referred to as the *stimulus satiation* or *environmental change* view, holds that the organism tends to avoid making a response that will lead it into an environment or result in a stimulus pattern with which it has recently had much familiarity.[13] It is apparent that this interpretation very readily accounts for the T-maze experiment mentioned above, but it is less obviously applicable to the first experiment. It also provides a plausible explanation for the fact, only too familiar to dormatory dwellers, that the same food repeated weekly palls upon us long before the school term is over.

It is quite possible that both of these interpretations, the one emphasizing the response side and the other the stimulus side, are needed, but this can only be established with further careful analytical research.[14] For the purpose of our discussion it will be sufficient to emphasize the resultant tendency to avoid repetition of a response executed in the immediate past.

Often the effect of this nonrepetitive tendency is overcome by reinforcement, which works in the opposite direction since it tends to cause the organism to repeat the response that was made to the stimulus. If such reinforcement effects are stronger than the inhibition effects, inhibition fails to prevent the response from recurring. Nevertheless, inhibition depresses the response. The difference between spaced and massed learning is probably a case in point. Improvement in performance will occur under either condition, but the spaced curve rises more rapidly because massing permits a greater amount of inhibition to build up. The difference in the rate of gain between the two conditions seems to arise from the inhibitory effects produced by successive presentation of the same stimulus in relatively rapid succession.

The nonrepetitive tendency may, then, produce variability by depressing the strength of a stimulus→response relationship; the response may even drop out and a different response may be given to the same stimulus.

Set and response variability

Earlier in this chapter we described the manner in which set may operate to vary the aspect of a stimulus complex to which the individual will react. Even when identical single stimuli are presented, however, set can cause a variation of response. We can illustrate this by the word-association type of experiment we described in Chapter 1. Suppose you were asked to give the opposites to a list of words, and the word "city" appeared in the list. You would most certainly say "country." Suppose, however, it had appeared in a list of terms for which you were asked to provide specific examples. "City" would have produced a response such as "New York" or "Washington." The stimulus is the same; the response varies according to the set present at the time the stimulus occurs.

In nonlaboratory situations sets are not often intentionally established by some other person. Nevertheless, we may pick up a set from something we have just read, seen, or heard, and since the set may vary from time to time, so also do our responses to the same stimuli on different occasions.

Competition among responses

To understand how extinction may lead toward variability, we must note that often a number of responses can be given to a specific stimulus. An example may add to your understanding of this principle.

Solve the following problem:

$$12$$
$$11$$
$$\overline{}$$

If you give the answer 23, it is wrong. Try again. The answer 1 is also wrong. The arbitrarily correct answer is 132. Let us assume that you went from addition to subtraction to multiplication. You may not have followed this pattern, but if the first two answers were called wrong, and your arithmetic was not faulty, you would have gone on to the third process. The problem, as it was set up, was admittedly arbitrary, but so often is life itself. The important point to note in this demonstration is that the same stimulus was capable of eliciting three responses. When one response was made and that response was called "wrong," you did not repeat it, nor did you do merely nothing. Using the same stimulus, you shifted to a different response. In other words, to the same stimulus more than one response was attached.

Obviously this fact leads to variability of behavior. If reactive inhibition or failure to obtain reinforcement weakens the strength of a stimulus→response connection, then a different response may occur to that same stimulus. If, in turn, this second connection is weakened, a third may be utilized. The pattern of such variable behavior is not simply a haphazard shifting about; it is based in part upon the fact that different, incompatible, or competing responses have been attached to the same stimulus. If, for any reason, the connections between one of these responses and the stimulus becomes sufficiently weakened, the other stimulus→response connection will take over.

Another form of competition among response tendencies arises from the fact that our environment contains many stimuli. If, for any reason, a specific stimulus→response connection is weakened, some other stimulus may be reacted to. Picture a student sitting at his desk prepared for a long session of study. After fifteen minutes of uninterrupted work, some fatigue and reactive inhibition result in his looking up from his book. As he does so, he spies a letter on his desk and he responds to it by taking it from its envelope and rereading it. For a while he pauses to muse about its contents; then he returns to his textbook. A little later he lifts his eyes and is stimulated by the photograph of a very special person. This leads to a recall of some incident of the previous week end, and then of many other week ends. And so the studying progresses haltingly through the long evening. It is because many stimuli may compete with the studying response that the psychologist advises the student to keep his desk or study table bare of materials that are not relevant to the work at hand.

Now it should not be assumed that variability of this sort is always undesirable. On the contrary, the variability produced by this type of situation makes the learning of many new adjustments possible. Do you recall, from our discussion on page 33, the example of a child who learned to open a gate and thus retrieve a toy on the other side of the fence? He succeeded in doing so only because he reacted to one stimulus after another until the key stimulus, the latch, was reacted to in the proper manner. Variability of this sort often leads to discovery of the correct response, the response that surmounts the barrier and achieves the sought-for goal. Its great significance in the solution of problems will be described in later chapters.

General variability

Because some of the factors that lead to response variability have been identified, it is possible to control these factors and thus eliminate much variability. Within certain limits, we may control the kind and strength of motivation, and carefully worded directions may establish some sets and avoid others in the person whose response we are trying to predict. Appropriate reinforcement can prevent extinction from occurring, and appropriate spacing may reduce the nonrepetitive tendency. The application of these stabilizing measures reduces the difference between the behavior we predict and the behavior that occurs. It reduces, in other words, the magnitude of our errors of prediction.

Control of all these conditions does not, however, eliminate all variability; organisms do not seem to be able to do the same thing in the same way each time, even though they may be trying hard to do so. The expert golfer, though he is far less variable than the novice, cannot repeat time after time his best drive; a pitcher's curve may cut the corner of the plate on one throw but be well outside on the next one; the basketball player does not score with every one of his foul shots.

Variability under controlled psychological conditions is well illustrated in what are referred to as reaction-time experiments. Some stimulus—say a light or a tone—is presented and the subject is asked to react by pressing a key as soon as he can. The subject is usually aided in his work by presentation of a warning signal a second or so before the reacting stimulus is presented. Thus, he knows what is coming and approximately when. Even under situations so favorable as these, the speed of reaction varies, as shown in the distribution of responses obtained from such experiments in Figure 8.8. We note that although most of the responses cluster around a certain time interval, they are not all the same; the subject varies.

Fig. 8.8 Distribution of scores in a reaction-time experiment. Although most of the reactions cluster about .175 second, reaction time varies from trial to trial.

Variability within the individual is observable in all the data of psychology and, of course, in our everyday behavior. We recite a poem or a list of nonsense syllables correctly during one trial but stumble during the next one; our signatures are slightly different from one writing to the next. Despite any controls that the psychologist may introduce, there will always remain some variability in response.

The fact that there always seems to be a residuum of variability does not mean that the psychologist's aspiration of predicting behavior is futile. It means only that we must not expect to predict with complete accuracy. The problem of lack of complete precision in prediction is not unique to psychology; in no science are predictions ever completely accurate. But although performance varies, it varies around some central clustering point, as in the curve of Figure 8.8, and this central clustering point may be used to characterize the individual. Despite the fact that our signatures are variable, they have sufficient stability for a handwriting expert to identify a forgery. Certain baseball pitchers and certain golfers are referred to as consistent winners, although they may occasionally lose a game or a tournament to some ordinarily inferior rival.

Undoubtedly one of the causes for this variability lies in minor variations of the stimulus from trial to trial. Thus in a reaction-time experiment the subject may be looking slightly above,

Fig. 8.9 Variations in the pattern of movement made by a subject who is trying to make the identical movement each time. These pictures were made by photographing on a single plate a light attached to the top of a stick that the subject held in his hand.

below, or to the side of the stimulus light at the moment it happens to be illuminated. This would produce a stimulus for his behavior that is slightly different from the one that would be produced if he were looking directly at the light. In an environment that is less controlled than is the typical laboratory experiment even more variability in the qualitative and quantitative aspects of the key stimulus might be expected.

In addition to the variability arising from this source, a variability which could be greatly reduced, there is a certain amount of variability attributed to fluctuations in the organism itself. The living organism is constantly carrying on its metabolic processes. In addition to the fact that it breathes, its heart beats and its blood flows, and there are continual changes in the minute cells of which the body is made. These changes are quite capable of influencing the efficiency of behavior from moment to moment.[15]

We have noted in this chapter that there is no direct linkage between the stimulus and the individual's response. In the next chapter we shall deal with another of the mechanisms that complicates this linkage—the way in which the individual perceives the stimulus.

REFERENCES

[1] Broadbent, D. E. Listening to two simultaneous messages, *J. exp. Psychol.*, 1952, *44*, 51-55.

[2] Burtt, H. E. *Applied Psychology* (abr. ed.), Prentice-Hall, 1952.

[3] Berlyne, D. E. Stimulus intensity and attention in relation to learning theory, *Quart, J. exp. Psychol.*, 1950, *2*, 71-75.

[4] Wilcox, L. R., and Grether, W. F. Color markings for aircraft operating in arctic regions, *U.S.A.F. Air Material Command. A. F. Technical Report* No. 5814, May 1949.

[5] Prentice, W. C. H. A study of the performance of night lookouts aboard ship. *O.S.R.D. Report* 4087 (October 15, 1944). Princeton University, Washington, D. C., Applied Psychology Panel, NDRC.

[6] Bahrick, H. P. Incidental learning under two incentive conditions, *J. exp. Psychol.*, 1954, *47*, 170-172.

[7] Eckstrand, G. A., and Wickens, D. D. Transfer of perceptual set, *J. exp. Psychol.*, 1954, *27*, 274-278.

[8] Chapman, D. W. Relative effects of determinate and interdeterminate aufgaben, *Amer. J. Psychol.*, 1932, *44*, 163-174.

[9] Deese, J., and Ormond, E. Studies of detectability during continuous visual search, *WADC Tech. Report,* WADC-TR-53-8, 1953.

[10] Telford, C. W. The refractory phase of voluntary and associated responding, *J. exp. Psychol.*, 1931, *14*, 1-36.

[11] Zeaman, D., and House, B. J. The growth and decay of reactive inhibition as measured by alternation behavior, *J. exp. Psychol.*, 1951, *4*, 177-186.

[12] Hull, C. L. *Principles of Behavior*, Appleton, 1943.

[13] Dember, W. N., and Fowler, H. Spontaneous alternation behavior, *Psychol. Bull.*, 1958, *55*, 412-428.

[14] Thompson, M. E. A two-factor theory of inhibition, *Psychol. Rev.*, 1960, *67*, 200-206.

[15] Lansing, R. W. Relation of brain and tremor rhythms to visual reaction time, *EEG and Clinical Neurophysiol.*, 1957, *9*, 497-504.

Chapter Nine

PERCEPTION

ALTHOUGH THE TERM PERCEPTION will not be associated in any significant way with consciousness in this text, perhaps an initial approach to an understanding of the term may be achieved by describing how it was used some years ago by one group of psychologists who felt that the major aim of this science was to understand consciousness. They had decided by carefully examining their own experiences that all of our mental life was composed of three elements and that the great variety of experience was but a combination of these three elements. One of these mental elements is *sensation*—the experience we get when our sense organs are stimulated—the experience of a color or a sound or pressure. Sensations, they insisted, are not the experience of something that is colored, the sound of a thing, or the touch of an identified object; they are simply the awareness of a color, a sound or a touch. When, however, the sensation is combined with another mental element, then we have a perception and we see an apple, hear an auto horn, or are aware that someone is tapping us on the shoulder. This other element they called *images;* illustrated by the experience we can obtain by closing our eyes and imagining some object. They felt that these fleeting images usually accompanied sensations and, combining with them, resulted in the psychological process called perception. The presence of these images added something like a meaning to the sensations.

It is important to emphasize again that most modern psychologists are not concerned with a study of consciousness but rather with a study of behavior, and this is certainly true of the approach taken by this text. Nevertheless the above description of the experiential nature of perception may give us some appreciation of the term as it is applied to behavior, for it suggests that perception is a process which gives significance to the stimuli, making it possible for the perceiver to react to the event in an adaptive manner. Let us now consider some examples of perception that emphasize the behavioral definition of the term.

Example one

Suppose that, as we are sitting at our desk studying, we become aware, faintly but unmistakably, of an unpleasant, acrid odor. We sniff a few times. Then hurriedly we arise from our chair and begin trying to locate the source of the odor, using our nose to guide us. The odor becomes more intense by that overstuffed chair near the window. We lift the seat cushion; a thin column of blue-gray smoke curls upward. At once we see a blackened hole, glowing orange about the edge. In a moment, with the aid of several glasses of water, we have squelched the miniature fire. Through our prompt action we have avoided a serious loss.

Now let us consider why it was possible for us to act promptly. Fire is a complex physical stimulus. It produces heat, which can stimulate our temperature receptors and, if it is intense enough, our pain receptors. It also usually produces an odorous gas which can stimulate our olfactory receptors. Because of the latter fact, we did not need to wait until a noticeable change in room temperature made us recognize the danger. On the basis of the smoke alone, we concluded that a fire was present and we acted accordingly.

Example two

You are in your room, feeling a bit at loose ends and wondering what you are going to do on this dull Sunday evening. Suddenly you hear intermittent but regular noises that grow louder, followed by a thud, a metallic jingle, a click, and a squeak. "Good," you think as you start for the door. "Joe's back from his week end. Maybe we'll be able to cook up something after all."

Here your reactions are made possible by the fact that Joe's physical presence in the house produced certain auditory stimuli. You did not need to see Joe, or talk to him, or touch him in order to be assured of his presence. On the basis of audition alone you were able to infer that Joe was climbing the stairs, setting down his bag, reaching for his keys, unlocking his door, and opening it. The human animal produces a complex of physical stimuli; we can use many of these to tell us what he is doing.

Example three

You are engaged in a conversation with an acquaintance and are voicing an opinion of dislike and disrespect for all people who come from a certain part of the country. As you do so you notice a change in his facial expression and something like a faint frown begins to appear on his face. You interpret this as indicating that he disagrees with you and it suddenly occurs to you that he might come from that part of the country and that your sweeping statements may hurt his feelings. You begin to modify your original statement emphasizing that not every one from this part of the country is objectionable.

In each of the foregoing three examples there is an important and—for the organism who is to make an adjustment—a very useful association of physical events. Associated with the physical process of burning is the physical process that results in an odor; ordinarily the approach of another person has associated with it certain physical disturbances that we call noises; in the example cited the acquaintance's total reaction of rejecting the statement is associated with a change in facial expression. These associations are like the shadows that events cast before them. And observation of the shadow made it possible to predict the substance. Were it not for the fact that such an association of stimuli exists, it would be impossible to react to substance until it was present in the form of some stimulus energy to which we are sensitive. If smoke did not excite our olfactory organs, or if we had no such sense organs, we would need to see or feel the fire before we knew it was there. If Joe had come in noiselessly, or if his friend had been deaf, then his presence would not have been discovered until a later time. If the acquaintance maintained a poker face his negative feelings would not have been diagnosed, until, perhaps, he spoke in anger.

In each of these examples a single aspect of the total situation has been used to imply the total situation. This is the process of perception. *Perception occurs when a partial stimulus is used to predict the coming or presence of the total stimulus complex.* In less formal terms it is a prediction of the substance from the shadow.

Perception might have been described in another fashion by saying that perception gives meaning to the stimulus. There is nothing wrong with this statement other than the fact that the term "meaning" needs to be given a psychological definition. If the term implies that the individual associates with the stimulus some further characteristics that are not immediately present or obvious, then the definition of perception as the act of giving meaning to a stimulus is in complete agreement with the somewhat longer definition that was given above.

Throughout our lifetime and in many, many ways we make perceptual reactions. When the car in front of us slows down and veers toward the center of the road as it approaches an intersection, we predict that the driver is planning to make a left turn. When a strong wind blows up and darkening clouds begin to gather, we run to shelter to avoid the coming shower. When we are awakened in the early morning by some noise, we listen to it with puzzled attention and then relax back to sleep as we conclude it is the paper boy.

It must be obvious from a consideration of the examples we have given that perception serves an extremely useful function for the individual. In general, perception decreases our chances of being victimized by unforeseen circumstances or events. It simplifies the process of living and makes our adjustments more rapid and more effective.

PERCEPTION AND LEARNING

Perception is made possible by the complexity of the physical situation, by the fact that most physical events contain many stimuli and one of these may be used to imply the remainder. This complexity is inherent in the physical situation, but it remains for the organism itself to make the psychological association between

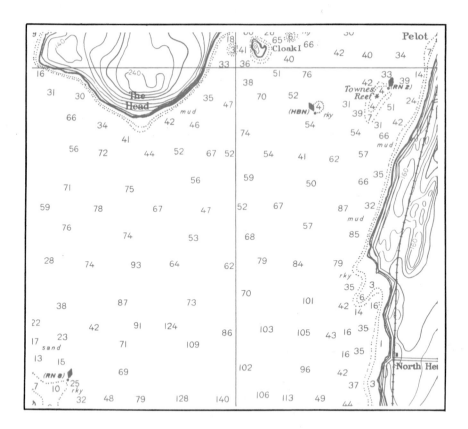

Fig. 9.1 Perception is always influenced by learning—and in some instances extensive and complex learning. All of us would recognize this illustration as "a map of some sort." But to the navigator every symbol has especial significance. The diamond at the lower left, for example, represents a channel-marking buoy of a certain type and color. The *rky* next to it indicates the nature of the lake bottom. The two dotted lines next to the shoreline indicate the 6- and 12-foot depths. The contour lines on the headland at the upper left indicate a steep, high bluff. But complete perception of this situation requires more than a knowledge of chart symbols. The navigator must learn to translate information from this "bird's-eye view" into what he sees horizontally from the bridge of his ship.

the partial stimulus and the characteristics of the whole. The question is how the organism achieves this association.

This problem was one of very active concern for the philosopher-psychologists of the nineteenth century, and in particular they were concerned with the origin of our ability to perceive things in space. The conceptual battle lines were drawn between the Nativists and the Empiricists, those who felt that the ability is directly inherited and those who felt that it is learned. At that time, there was, of course, very few experimental data to support the

position of either side, for there was little knowledge of how our
sense organs function and of the principles of learning. The basic
position taken by the Nativists seemed to rest primarily upon the
facts that everyone was capable of space perception, that one did
not need special training to acquire the skill, and that it is evidenced in very young organisms. The Empiricists presented logical
arguments to show how space perception could be learned, but they
could not support their position by reference to experimental data,
for adequate experimental data did not exist.

As a consequence of the large amount of experimental
knowledge that is available to us today we are in a position to
answer the question with more certainty. There is not time in an
elementary course to consider the problem in detail, but some
appreciation of modern methods employed in attacking this problem may be gained by considering the topic of the spatial perception of sounds.

Typically, when one hears a sound, he recognizes it as the
sound coming from some particular object and also as coming from
some place, that is, he localizes the source of the sound in space. A
physicist could point out that a sound originating from one or
another side of a person—but not directly in front or behind him—
would have slightly different physical characteristics when it arrived at the two ears. He might suggest that because the sound
must travel farther to reach one ear than the other, it would arrive
at one ear before the other; it would be a little less intense at one
ear than the other; and, since the head itself might block out some
of the sound waves, its qualitative pattern might be a little different
at the two ears. He could show also that a sound coming from 10°
to the right would have different characteristics from one originating 30° to the right. But in addition he would also show that
these physical differences would be extremely small, perhaps too
small to be of use to an organism.

Careful psychological experimentation has indicated that
we are sensitive to some of these minor differences and that we undoubtedly use them in perceiving the direction of a sound source
in the plane parallel to the ground. A typical experiment investigating this topic was conducted in the following manner.[1]

The subject wore a pair of earphones through which a
sound of exactly the same physical characteristics could be delivered
independently to each ear. By means of delicate instrumentation
the experimenter controlled the time at which the separate sounds

reached the two ears. When the two sounds came on simultaneously the subjects reported hearing a single sound which they located directly in front of them. However, when one sound came .00016 second before the other, a single sound was heard which was located slightly off center on the side of the leading sound. As the difference in onset time increased the sound moved farther and farther from center, until with a difference of .00276 second it seemed to be located beside the ear of the leading sound. With time differences of greater magnitude two independent sounds were reported. This and other experiments have shown that the human is sensitive to the minor types of physical differences that are associated with sounds originating from different locations.[2]

If now we draw upon the principles of learning discussed earlier in the text we can show how this ability to localize can be acquired. We have the fact that sounds originating in different locations will produce different patterns of stimulation, different in the sense that there will be a disparity in the way the two ears will be stimulated by the same sound. In short, different patterns of stimulation are associated with different locations of sound origin. This is called binaural disparity. These differences are the consequences of the nature of the physical world and they will be the same, or essentially the same, from the day of our birth until the day of our death. This affords the organism a stable basis on which the principles of learning may operate.

The infant lying in his bassinette hears the fond murmurings of the parent coming from one side of him. His almost random head movements will be stopped when he turns in the direction of the sound and the rewarding nipple of his nightly bottle. Thus responding to this pattern of stimulation by a head orientation in a particular direction leads to reinforcement, but a response in another direction does not do so. It is not difficult to conceive of a number of situations of this sort, situations where orientation in the direction of the sound source leads more rapidly to reinforcement than does orientation in any other direction. Since different patterns of sound correspond with different directions of sound sources, the learning of discriminatory responses becomes possible. When one considers the number of times during a day that reinforcing events of this sort can occur, he can readily appreciate how sound localization could be acquired long before the child learns to talk. Small wonder then why none of us remember a time when we could not localize sounds, and why, therefore, we might presume that we were born with this skill. So much for logical argumentation in support of the view that the spatial localization of sound may be learned. We will turn now to a study which indicates that subjects can acquire new ways of localizing sound.[3]

In this experiment subjects wore earphones which were designed so that the sounds coming to the left ear were those which would ordinarily come to the right ear and vice versa. At first, the subjects heard noises that were on one side as coming from the other, and often sounds from in front as though they came from the rear. Such illusions would persist even though they were obviously absurd, as in the case of one subject who heard a radio playing among the branches of a tree, though he knew that it was located in the dormitory on the other side of him. Gradually the subjects learned the new perceptions, and more and more they began to experience the sounds as coming from their correct spatial position. The experiments were terminated, however, before this reversed localization became completely habituated, and success in experiencing the sound as coming from its proper place was usually dependent on visual cues—that is, on seeing the object as well as hearing it.

Similar experiments have been conducted in the field of vision, and lenses have been worn which rotate the visual field 180 degrees so that what is ordinarily seen as above is seen as below, and vice versa; right and left are similarly interchanged.[4] Other experimenters have changed the relationship between visual perception and our motor responses less drastically by having their subjects wear lenses that shift the visual field by a smaller number of degrees. In all these experiments the introduction of the lenses is at first highly confusing, frustrating, and disturbing to the subject. With continued wearing the subject begins to learn this new way of perceiving the visual world and he responds with increasing precision to the location of the objects about him. In nearly all instances where the glasses are worn for prolonged periods of time the subjects reach the point where this new arrangement of the visual world becomes quite natural to them. It is not surprising that prolonged wearing is needed to reach this stage of experiential naturalness, nor that some subjects never do so. They were all adults with many years of experience in reacting in particular ways to visual stimulation, and the experiment demanded that new responses—sometimes even antagonistic to the already learned responses—be made to the visual stimulation. This type of situation produces *negative transfer,* and the amount of transfer must be especially great because the stimulus→ response that was being broken had been reinforced by a lifetime of practice. It should be expected that many many hours of experience with this new arrangement of the visual world would be required if naturalness were to be achieved, and relative to the subjects' previous lifetimes these experiments were of short duration.

It must be admitted, of course, that none of these experiments directly prove that our normal proficiency in perceiving space is learned. They do show that a new way of perceiving can be learned—or at least partially learned—in a relatively short time and this fact makes all the more plausible the belief that our original perceptions of space are learned. The topic of the manner in which we are able to sense and to make discriminations about the physical world about us is one which will be considered in greater detail in later chapters. For the present we are concerned with an analysis of the general characteristics of perception.

As we move to more complicated types of perceptual activities, the significance of the learning process becomes even more obvious. The hungry bottle-fed infant does not, in the beginning, react in any clear-cut way to the sight of the bottle. Its sucking responses begin only when the nipple stimulates its mouth. But after a few months of life the hungry infant will squirm and kick when the bottle is brought into view, and sucking movements will begin long before the bottle reaches its mouth. When this happens, we say of the infant that it now perceives the bottle as a source of food.

The infant's reaction to the adult face follows a similar pattern. In early infancy the child seems no more responsive to the adult face than to any other moving object that stimulates it visually. It will stare blandly at the fond parent as if it were inspecting an object of little more than passing interest. By the second month of age it will, if well fed, smile at the proud parent. It will not, however, react differently to a smiling and to a frowning adult; it is only somewhat later that differential reactions occur.

The reader must certainly have noticed that there is a basic similarity between the conditioning situation and the perceptual situation. In each case we are dealing with stimulus situations that are somewhat complex. In the conditioning situation there is a bell *and* food, tone *and* shock, or light *and* a puff of air. In the examples of perceptual behavior that we have described there is smoke *and* fire, noises *and* the presence of people, or the visual stimulus of the bottle *and* food. In each case there is an association of two or more stimuli, and one of the stimuli can become the symbol or sign for the other. In all likelihood, many of the same basic mechanisms of behavior that operate in the development and maintenance of conditioned responses also operate in perceptual learning. Nothing is gained by simply calling a perception a conditioned response, but our understanding of at least some aspects of perceptual behavior may be enhanced by our knowledge of the mechanisms that operate in the conditioning situation.

PERCEPTION AS A MATTER
OF PROBABILITY

Essentially as we have pointed out above, perception consists in making predictions. We react to the occurrence of event *A* by predicting *B*. Obviously, then, the validity of our perceptual processes can be determined by the extent to which our predictions are fulfilled. But we all know that our perceptions sometimes lead us to behave inappropriately, for in many instances in the actual world about us *A* is not invariably followed by *B*. Consider the example of our prediction that the car ahead of us is about to make a left turn. Sometimes drivers who pull over to the center of the highway are planning a right turn, and the *A* will not be followed by the *B*. If we had acted with the utmost confidence on our perception of an intended left turn by trying to pass the car on its right, a pair of crumpled fenders would likely have been our reward. True, as a general rule this perceptual error is not likely to occur, since usually the driver who veers to the center is not planning a right turn. Nevertheless, some unthinking drivers do this, and there is always the slight possibility that our perception may be wrong. For this reason—because this behavior of the other car does not always eventuate in a left turn—the experienced driver does not completely commit himself. He is primarily prepared to accelerate his car as his predecessor turns leftward off the road, but he is also ready to brake and swerve leftwards if the turn is in the opposite direction.

In both the physical and the social world there are many degrees of probability that event *A* will be associated with event *B*, and so our perceptions have many different degrees of correctness. Here are some examples. We strike up a conversation with a stranger, and on the basis of his grammar we make the assumption that he is or is not a college graduate; on the basis of a phrase, we classify him as a Democrat or as a Republican; by his facial expression we conclude that he is a happy or an unhappy person. If we have learned well in the past, we are more likely to be correct than incorrect in our assumptions about this person; nevertheless, our chances of being correct are not nearly so good as they would be if, seeing smoke, we predicted fire.

Even physical relationships are not always stable. An example of this is our use of the clarity of the atmosphere as a cue for judging distances. Because of atmospheric conditions and the nature of the eye mechanism, distant objects are seen in less detail and with less clarity than are near-by objects. We therefore use the degree of clarity, along with other cues, as a means of judging the distance to some object. Here, too, we may make mistakes. When a person who lives at sea level travels to the mountains, where the atmosphere is clearer, he is likely to estimate distant objects as being much closer to him than they actually are. Even at the same altitude his estimates of distances will be distorted by the immediate atmospheric conditions. Distant objects seem much closer on a dry day than on a humid one.

Within recent years a great deal of research has been done in the area of what is called probability learning. In the typical study the subjects see a panel with two lights, one on the right side and one on the left. In the center and above these two is another light. This is a warning light. When it flashes on the subject knows that the right or left light—but not both—is going to be illuminated within a few seconds and his task is to guess which one of these two lights will come on. The procedure is designed so that it is impossible to discover on any particular trial which light will be illuminated. However, over a large number of trials the flashes can be programmed so that half of them will come from each light, or—and this is of the greatest significance to us now—so that they are divided between the lights in any desired proportion. The studies show that the subjects soon learn to sense the objective probabilities of a particular light flashing and that they begin to predict in accordance with these probabilities. This seems to be achieved without a conscious counting and calculating of the events. The results for one of these experiments is shown in Figure 9.2 and it demonstrates that the subjects show a tendency to predict according to objective probabilities with remarkable accuracy.

In far more subtle ways our perceptions probably follow patterns similar to this. Undoubtedly they do not eventuate in guessing alternates in so clear-cut a fashion as in the type of experiment we have described, but rather they must determine to some extent the degree of confidence we have in the accuracy of our perceptions.

These experiments are very reminiscent of the studies on partial reinforcement in conditioning situations. It will be recalled that conditioned responses can be established when reinforcement occurs less than 100 percent of the time, and that responses so acquired show a considerable resistance to extinction. If we may generalize from conditioning to the development of perceptions, we can readily understand that the consequences of our perceptual

Fig. 9.2 Results of an experiment in which subjects guess which one of two lights will be illuminated. The blue lines indicate the objective frequency with which one of the two lights come on for each of the three groups in the experiment. The black lines show the subjects' performance. Notice that the subjects' guesses closely approximate the objective frequency. (After M. H. Detambel, Master's thesis, Indiana University, 1950)

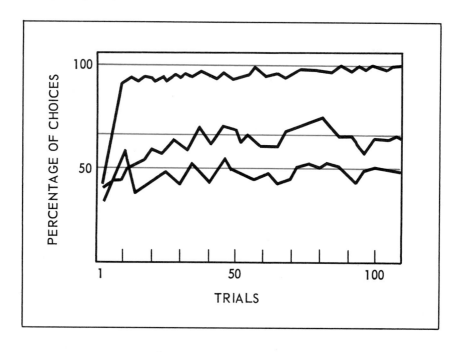

responses need not always be correct for the perception to be established. Partial reinforcement data also predict that a few occurrences wherein our perceptional reactions are shown to be invalid do not necessarily destroy this way of perceiving. We continue to maintain a way of perceiving because it is correct often enough, but probably we are more confident of the validity of our perceptions than is warranted by the facts.

Perceptual responses that are more often incorrect than correct may persist if we never learn that we are in error. As children we may have heard that persons whose eyes are set close together are dishonest and, if we accept this and we meet such a person, we may thereafter avoid him because of our assumption of his untrustworthiness. We do not give him an opportunity to prove otherwise; we do not submit our prediction to a test; we do not enter a situation in which extinction might operate. If we are not quite so naive as to make a prediction of personality on the basis of distance between the eyes, we may use some other slight cue—some gesture, the manner of speaking, the way in which a person shakes hands, or the form of his handwriting. Whatever our conclusion may be, we probably make no further effort to check its validity, for most of us pride ourselves on being "pretty good judges of human nature." Thus, our perceptual biases are insulated from reality, and the possibility of correction is removed.

The awareness of this fact supplies the rationale for much of the experimental methodology of modern psychological research. To the layman it often appears that psychologists frequently devote needless efforts to developing measuring instruments and even in running experiments on what seems to be the obvious. Psychologists do so, however, because they know that what seems to be a fact of behavior may only be the consequence of a persisting perceptual bias, so the rigorous experimental method is introduced to eliminate this bias. Sometimes the experimental results support the preconceived answer and sometimes they do not.

CONFLICTING PERCEPTUAL CUES

Occasionally, the observer is presented with perceptual cues that conflict with one another. When this happens, the observer may discover that his interpretation of an event does not agree with what has actually occurred.

Fig. 9.3 If you turn this picture upside down, the dents in the tank will look like bulges and the rivet heads will look like dents. (Courtesy C. H. Stoelting Co.)

Look at the tank in Figure 9.3. You undoubtedly perceive it as a boiler with rows of rivets and with occasional dents in it. Turn the photograph upside down. Now you discover that what is convex has become concave, and what was concave has become convex —that is, the dents look like bulges and the rivets look like dents. This abrupt shift in your perceptual interpretation occurred because of a reversal of the cues that you use in perceiving convexity and concavity in such an object. Ordinarily, an object is illuminated from above, and you have learned that anything projecting from its surface casts a shadow *below* its center, whereas an indentation has its shadow *above* its center. When the photograph is reversed, you continue with this way of perceiving, but now, since the actual convexity casts its shadow above its center, you see it not as convex but as concave. Your perception of the physical nature of the tank differs from its actual physical nature. The cues that you receive from the inverted photograph conflict with what you have learned in the past; you react by remaining faithful to your previously learned reactions. In this example, there is a complete reversal of the perceptual cue which in the past was used to differentiate bulges from dents.

309

In most instances of perception our responses depend upon several cues working together. Occasionally the cues conflict with one another. This, too, may result in a disturbance of our perceptions, creating what is called an *illusion*.

A simple laboratory demonstration of conflicting cues utilizes two lighted balloons in a darkened room. As the observer watches the balloons, one of them is made to increase in size and at the same time to become darker. In everyday life, increasing size is associated with the approach of an object, whereas decreasing brightness is associated with the moving away of an object. This situation thus brings these two cues into conflict with each other. As a result, some persons will have the illusion that the balloon is approaching (because they respond to the change in size), whereas others will see it as receding (because they respond to decreasing brightness).

An illusion which all of us have noticed at one time or another is that the moon seems larger near the horizon than it does overhead. This is truly illusory, for the area on the retina of your eye stimulated by the moon is the same regardless of the moon's elevation (see Figure 9.4). Often the hypothesis has been advanced that the illusion is created by the fact that, when the moon is low, we compare it with objects on the earth's surface—a silhouetted tree, a house, or a hill, and thus the moon seems larger than it does when it is high in the sky, where no immediate comparison is possible. The illusion persists, however, in controlled situations in which ground objects have been eliminated from the visual field. Careful experimental work has indicated that the occurrence of the illusion is connected with the posture we assume when looking at the moon on the horizon and overhead. When we crane our necks to look upward, a reflex causes the pupils of the eyes to contract, and this contraction permits less light to stimulate the retina of the eye. At the same time other reflexes occur and stimulate the muscles which move our eyeballs inward and outward. The total stimulation, both visual and muscular, is different when we look at the moon in the two different positions. This conflict between the total stimulus conditions in the two positions causes the illusion that the moon is larger in one position than in the other, despite the fact that the size of the retinal image is the same in both cases.

This interpretation implies that our perceptual reactions within a given sense field are not determined solely by data from this field but are influenced by relevant or even irrelevant stimu-

Fig. 9.4 This series of photographs, taken as the moon was rising from the horizon, indicates that the moon does not change in size even though we see it as larger at the horizon and smaller when it is overhead. The dimness of the images in the lower portion of the picture is a result of the greater density of the intervening atmosphere at the smaller angles of inclination.

lation from our other sense fields as well. This fact is nicely demonstrated in an experiment on the perception of the vertical.[5] The subject was seated in a room, completely darkened except for the presence of a luminous rod located several feet from him. The rod was tilted from the vertical and the subject was asked to align it with the vertical. He did this by calling out directions to the experimenter who changed the tilt of the rod until the subject was satisfied that it appeared vertical to him. A number of such trials gave a control score for the subject. Following these control trials another group of tests were run. During these tests the subject either heard a tone in one ear or received a mild electrical stimulation on one side of his neck. Under these conditions the luminous rod was perceived as vertical when it was slanted a few degrees in the direction opposite from the side of the stimulation. In other words, what is presumed to be a purely visual activity is influenced by the simultaneous stimulation of other senses. This experiment simply adds evidence to the view that perceptions usually are the consequence of a number of simultaneous stimulating events. It would not be difficult to list a large number of similar incidents. It must be obvious that, since perceptions are not always accurate,

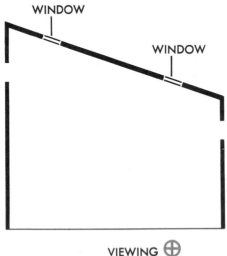

Fig. 9.5 There seems to be a marked difference between the sizes of the men's faces, and both men seem to be at windows of equal size in a wall parallel to the front of the room. The illusion is created by the design of the room (see floor plan at right). The two windows at the right are smaller than those at the left, and the man at the left is farther from the viewer than the man at the right. In the actual situation, the illusion works only if the viewer closes one eye. A photograph produces the same effect (Courtesy Ross Mooney)

the introduction of this extraneous stimulation could serve to make our perceptions more accurate as well as to make them less accurate.

These concrete examples of cue conflict and its resulting distortion of our perceptual behavior seem striking to us. Actually, many such conflicts occur in daily life, but they pass unnoticed, either because they are less dramatic or because we do not pause to determine the exact accuracy of our perceptual process. At times, when we are aware of these discrepancies among cues, we may hold our response in abeyance until further data and careful checks describe the situation more thoroughly for us. When, for example, on a hot day we see "puddles" on the highway ahead of us, we do not immediately conclude that there has been a shower or that we are seeing an illusion that is caused by heat. We delay decision until we can check further—although the outcome is actually of no serious consequence to us.

PERCEPTION AS ORGANIZATION

In Chapter 8 we described the conditions that at a given time cause an organism to react to certain stimuli rather than to others in its complex environment. Stimuli take various shapes and forms: a curve, an angle, a shading of one hue into another; a large or small expanse of pressure; sounds of high and low intensity, sounds that are continuous and sounds that are intermittent. We are stimulated, in short, by a babbling in all the many tongues of our many sensory fields. Nevertheless, our sensory world is not a world of booming and buzzing confusion. On the contrary, it is structured and organized. The angles, the curves, the shadings, are not isolated and independent units; they are parts of a face, a chair, or a passing car.

Thus, out of a welter of stimulation, *organized patterns of things emerge,* and on the basis of such organization we react in an appropriate manner. There is, then, another aspect of the perceptual process that must be considered—the organization of sensory stimuli into a pattern or figure which then may be used as a cue for later response.

At first glance it might appear that the process of organization may be explained if we say simply that because these stimuli form a certain pattern in the physical environment, they must form a certain pattern in our nervous system, and therefore they must have a certain perceptual organization. As long as we can remember, a circle has always looked like a circle, a square has always looked like a square, and a triangle like a triangle. As time went on, we may have learned more about these forms—how to calculate areas, or how to measure an angle—but we feel that from the beginning we reacted to them as different forms.

There is some evidence, however, that suggests that there may have been a time when we did *not* see things in this clear, organized fashion. Studies have been made of people who, blind from birth, were operated upon in adulthood and given sight. As soon as the visual world was opened to them, they were able to perceive total figures against their background, and perhaps even to perceive separate groups of things. Perception of *form* differences, however, was not immediate. A square and a triangle were differentiated from each other only by the process of counting corners, even after more than a week of experience with these forms. An egg and a cube of sugar, both of which had been seen repeatedly and could be identified, were not recognized when illuminated by a colored light. A patient who had learned to identify a square of white cardboard failed to do so when the cardboard was reversed, presenting a yellow color.[6]

In another investigation, two chimpanzees were raised in the dark for the first 21 months of life.[7] Although various visual reflexes were found to function moderately well when they were exposed to light, the animals behaved almost as if they were blind. When an object was pushed rapidly toward their faces, they did not blink their eyes, as normal chimpanzees and humans do. As an object was moved slowly toward their faces, they made no reaction until they were touched and then they reacted with a sudden, violent start. No visual recognition of the feeding bottle was evidenced until the eleventh day, even though it was familiar to their touch.

These two lines of evidence lead us to suspect that many of the perceptual organizations that seem so natural to us and seem always to have been part of our behavior repertoire may not always have been with us but may have come about through a process of learning. Although the small amount of data available pertains only to the visual field, there is no reason to believe that the phenomenon is limited to vision; on the contrary, it seems likely that the same processes operate in the other sensory fields as well.

If prior experience is required for the organization of the simple forms to which we have referred above, its influence must be even stronger in our perception of complex figures. One experiment will illustrate this point.[8] Figure 9.6 may be seen in two ways, either as a profile facing toward the right or as a profile facing toward the left, although while one is being perceived the other is not—that is, the figure and the ground shift. During the first part

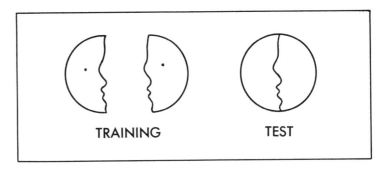

TRAINING   TEST

Fig. 9.6   The ambiguous figure employed in the Schafer and Murphy[8] study (see text).

of the experiment these figures were broken vertically into halves, and when each half was presented, the subjects learned to call out a particular nonsense syllable. The subjects were given a small monetary reward when the forms facing in one direction were presented, but money was taken away from them when the profile faced in the other direction. In a subsequent part of the experiment, in which monetary rewards were not involved, the subjects were presented with the total figure and were simply asked to identify what they saw. It was found that their perceptual structuring conformed with the direction of the profile that had previously been rewarded. Their past experience, in other words, had caused them to organize the ambiguous figure in one way rather than in another.

In some instances the nature of the physical situation seems to force an organization upon us, even though we do not possess the necessary information to say with certainty to what extent, if any, learning has played a part in these perceptual organizations. Because of the fact that these organizations are so insistent and pervasive, most psychologists believe that they are not learned.

315

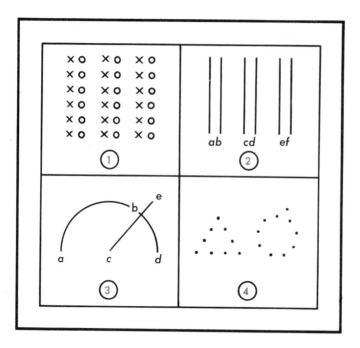

Fig. 9.7 Illustration of the principle of perceptual organization. The separate units are readily organized in definite ways.

Some of these organizations are illustrated in Figure 9.7 and described below:

1. *Similarity*. Columns rather than rows are seen because similar objects are classed together.

2. *Nearness*. We see three pairs of lines, *ab, cd,* and *ef*. We class them together because they are near each other. We do not see *bc* and *de* together.

3. *Continuity*. We see the arc *ad* and the line *ebc,* and not *abc* and *ebd*. We do so because *bd* seems a continuation of *ab,* and *be* seems a continuation of *cb*.

4. *Closure*. We see a triangle or circle, tending to close the gap between the elements to form these figures.

5. *Whole-part*. There is a tendency to see things as total figures rather than as parts. When we read, we see words, not letters strung together. The inexperienced spectator at a football game is likely to see only a mass of movement when the ball is snapped into play. Training is needed to see the individuals carrying out their separate but coordinated assignments. In most of our perceptions we begin by reacting to total objects; then, out of the totals, the individual elements begin to emerge.

A summary

It may be helpful to summarize the chapter up to this point and to relate it to the total process of perceiving. Perception is made possible by the fact that most environmental events are complex and they stimulate several different senses or the same sense in different ways and at different times. As a consequence, a part of this stimulation may be used as an indication of the occurrence of the whole, and the organism is able to respond to the total event on the basis of partial stimulation. This, as our earlier definition stated, is the process of perceiving. Although complete proof is lacking, it seems very likely that the tendency to predict the total from the portion is the product of experience and of the operation of the principles of learning. The accuracy of perception is determined not only by how strong the learning has been, but also by the consistency of the relationship between some part event and the total event. It is an efficient, adjustive way of behaving, for it permits the organism to prepare itself for effective action in the future. But in order for the final perceptive act to be maximally useful, the mass of sensory data must be structured in some meaningful way. This structuring is the process of organizing, which we have described above. The structuring seems to be based upon prior learning, and also perhaps upon basic characteristics of the stimulus field which force a specific type of organization on the perceiver.

PERCEPTUAL CONSTANCY

There is a great inconsistency between the structural stability or constancy of individual objects in the physical world and the way these objects stimulate our sense organs. This fact may be illustrated by the case of an automobile driving away from the observer. When it is close to him its image stimulates a large area of the retina of the eye, but as it moves away the area of retinal stimulation becomes progressively smaller. The physics of the situation is illustrated in Figure 9.8. Since our judgments about the physical world are made on the basis of our sensory impressions it is permissible to assume that the observer would see the car as shrinking in size as it moves away from him. As the reader well

317

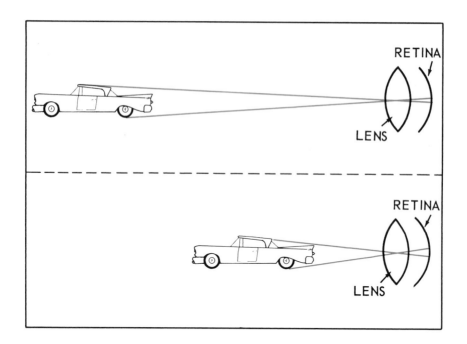

Fig. 9.8 Illustration of the fact that the same object produces different magnitudes of stimulation on the retina of the eye at different distances from the observer. The retina is the sensitive portion of the eye that is activated by the physical stimulus of the light waves. It is comparable to the film in a camera. The lens brings the object into focus on the retina. Notice that the amount of retina stimulated by the far object is less than that stimulated by the near object, as indicated by the red lines of sight drawn from the cars. It is apparent that the area of stimulation would become smaller and smaller as the object moves farther away.

knows, nothing of the sort occurs. The car is perceived as being the same size regardless of its distance from the observer.

The perceived stability of physical objects, despite the fact that the sensory impressions produced by them are variable, is called *perceptual constancy*. The example given above was concerned with the maintenance of the size of the external object and it is specifically referred to as an example of *size constancy*. This, of course, is not the only characteristic of objects wherein the constancy effect is found. It occurs for *shape,* for *brightness,* and for *hue.*

Shape constancy

When we look at a circular object from any angle other than one exactly perpendicular to it, the image produced upon our retina is elliptical, and this is how the artist paints it from certain perspectives. Nevertheless, we do not, when we approach the dinner table, see a table set with elliptical plates which miraculously become round when we lean over to eat our soup.

It might appear that constancy occurs only when we are unthinking and careless and that it would cease if we were directed to pay attention to and report on a specific characteristic of an object. But such does not seem to be the case. In one experiment subjects were shown a circular disk at such an angle that the shape it made upon the retina was elliptical.[9] They were also presented with a series of cardboard cutouts of different ellipses varying in proportions from considerably more to considerably less circular than the actual image of the disk upon the retina. There was also a cutout that was identical with the retinal image, this ellipse being calculated by precise measurement of visual angles. The subjects were asked to select the cutout that was identical with the retinal image of the disk. The results of the experiment are illustrated in Figure 9.9. In their choices, each of the subjects tended to move toward the actual form of the disk, which, it will be remembered, was a perfect circle. This phenomenon the experimenter called *regression to the real object*.

The tendency to regress to the real object is consistently noted by the art teacher, who finds the novice painting not what he sees, in the sense of the pattern of light rays that stimulate his retina, but what he perceives the real world to be like. One might expect, in an experiment such as the one with the ellipses, that persons with some art training would show less regression to the real object than would the artistically untrained. Such actually was the case in the experiment described above. Art teachers were

Fig. 9.9 An illustration of phenomenal regression to the real object. The object at the left illustrates the plate as it actually stimulates the retina. The object at the right illustrates the plate as it looks to us—that is, as we would draw it. In the center the two images are superimposed so that the difference between them may be noted. (Courtesy Conrad Kraft)

most successful in approximating the shape produced by the stimulus on the retina, art students were next, and the general college population was least successful.

Brightness and hue constancy

Suppose that on a bright winter evening you are standing at a window and a psychologist asks you to look out across a snow-covered field and judge its color. You will say it is white. Suppose in the blaze of noon he asks you to judge the color of a piece of coal you hold in your hand. You will call it black. If, now, the psychologist calls in an illuminating engineer and asks him to measure with his light meter the strength of the light coming from the coal and from an equivalent patch of snow, the engineer will report that the intensity is greater for the coal than for the snow. What is paradoxical about this situation is the fact that normally the experience of whiteness is the consequence of high levels of physical energy and the experience of black is associated with lower levels of energy and, if in the same visual field, one object reflects more light than another it is said to be brighter than the other. Coal in this example reflects more physical energy than snow. Once again perceptual constancy is at work to cause the observer to perceive in the manner that is appropriate to the physical object despite its immediate sensory effect. It is an example of *brightness constancy*.

The reader may be reminded of the operation of *hue constancy*, recalling the fact that a neighboring yellow house remains yellow even in the red glow of the setting sun. At this time of day the house is reflecting to his eye a heavy proportion of the light rays that would normally lead to the experience of red. It is quite possible that the red cast will be recognized and appreciated, but it will not be interpreted to mean that the paint of the house has turned to this color. Again, perceptual constancy, this time hue constancy, prevents the physical object from changing.

By now the reader may have felt that this discussion of perceptual constancy has been belaboring the obvious. The fact that perceptual constancy does exist is obvious, but its almost inevitable occurrence does not explain it psychologically. A considerable amount of research has been done on the various forms of perceptual constancy and it turns out to be somewhat more complex than it appeared to be initially. For one thing, constancy is far from complete and what the observer seems to experience is some-

Fig. 9.10 Distortion of perceptual constancy. Your eyes *see* it thus; you *perceive* it differently.

thing of a compromise between the particular characteristic of the physical object itself and the sense impression it produces.

Perceptual constancy is not inevitable; we may train ourselves to adopt an attitude wherein it is minimized. This, of course, is not necessarily desirable. As one psychologist remarked, the artist may find it to his profit, but the mechanic looking along his bench for the proper bolt to fit a nut would be at a loss if size constancy did not function for him. And for most of us, in our daily life, stability of the characteristics of the physical world is to be desired. It is the phenomenon of perceptual constancy that provides this experience of stability for us.

The field of the constancies is more complex than has been implied by our simple identification of the kinds of constancies, and a number of very technical studies—too complex to be considered here—have been conducted on the topic. We are at present primarily interested in the identification of this prominent and important characteristic of perceiving.

TIME AND PERCEPTION

The testimony of our personal experience tells us that most of our usual perceptual responses are made instantaneously. Some moving object comes into our visual field; as we focus upon it we seem to recognize immediately what it is, how far it is from us, what its size is, and in what direction it is moving. True, we seldom stop to catalogue all these perceived aspects of the object, but we could probably do so if we were asked to. All this information seems to be gained in the instant of seeing, and usually without any conscious evaluation and consideration.

Form perception and time

It is not the case, however, that the seeing of something and the perceiving of that something are accomplished in the same instant. This has been established by presenting materials to subjects in a tachistoscope. It is a device which will expose visual stimuli for extremely short durations, durations as low as $\frac{1}{100}$ second. Typically, the experimenter warns the subject that the shutter of the tachistoscope is about to be tripped and the subject looks at the viewing screen. Then the material is shown for a brief predetermined time interval and the subject reports what he has seen. Let us assume that the materials the experimenter is using consist of various geometric figures outlined in black on a white card.[10] If the exposure is extremely brief the subject will report that he saw only a white field—essentially the card with nothing on it. With an increase in exposure time he will report that there is something on the card, but he will not be able to identify it. Only if the exposure time is increased again will he be able to report that it is a triangle or a star or whatever it might be. If we may distinguish between knowing that something is there and being able to perceive the various aspects of this something we may conclude that even in simple situations of this kind the perceptual response is not instantaneous with the cruder response of reporting the mere presence of something in the visual field.

Perceptual constancy and time

In the previous section an experiment on shape constancy was described, and it was found that subjects perceived an elliptical image produced by a circular object as more circular than was true of the sensory stimulation. A more recent experiment measured this effect under two conditions.[11] In one of these the subject was allowed a considerable time to give the circular dish a careful inspection before attempting to match it with the elliptical cutout supplied by the experimenters. Under these conditions the usual shape-constancy results were obtained; the chosen ellipses were rounder than the actual visual image. Under the other condition the subject was permitted to view the disk for only $\frac{1}{10}$ second, though he was permitted to take a number of separate looks. Under this condition the choices were in agreement with the retinal image and the shape-constancy effect was not apparent. Thus it would appear that more stimulation time is required for the occurrence of the perceptual activities which lead to shape constancy than for those leading to the perception of shape itself.

It will, perhaps, help the eventual understanding of the constancy effect to note that restriction in time does not influence size and brightness constancy in the fashion we have described for shape constancy. Size constancy seems to be unaffected by duration of the exposure, while brightness constancy is somewhat enhanced by brief exposure.

This section has constituted a very brief excursion into the topic of time and perceptual activity. These few experiments have been chosen to show that despite what personal experience seems to tell us, we do not perceive even simple events all at once. We are biological organisms composed of living tissue and time is required for the tissues to be activated and for complex responses to occur.

CONSCIOUSNESS AND PERCEPTION

If many words could be read in the time required for the reading of a single word, perhaps our description of the perceiving process would more closely approximate the process itself. A situation is perceived in a split second: the stimulus impinges, the subject responds, and the psychological event is over. But the words necessary to describe this short event may run into the hundreds. This alone would not be disturbing; what causes difficulty is that somehow, in the course of a description of the phenomenon, perceptual activity is made to seem more rational, more deliberate, and more dependent upon conscious evaluations and considerations than it actually is.

In perceiving that his friend Joe was back from a week end, our student in the example cited earlier did not make his perception by means of a careful evaluation of the sensory data. Certainly he would not have gone through a process such as the following: "What is that? It is a noise. Yes, a noise, but what makes it? It is intermittent and each successive noise is louder than the former. Therefore it must come from a moving object, an object that is approaching me. What moves and makes intermittent noise? Aha, it is a person; that is a good hypothesis. But what person? Wait, there is another noise, a thump. Does that mean the person has fallen? If so, he has fallen by the door of Joe's room. Perhaps the person is Joe. That thump could be his suitcase which, if released abruptly, would make just such a heavy hollow sound. I shall act upon this conclusion and assume it is Joe."

No such elaborate conscious activity would have occurred. In all probability our student was getting up from his chair to greet his friend almost before he was aware of this perception.

In Chapter 18 we shall describe in greater detail the cues we make use of in perceiving such environmental relationships as the distance of an object from ourselves and the location of a sound. When we do so we shall, by citing experimental studies, show that responses such as these are made possible by the use of stimulus relationships which come as a surprise to us, despite the fact that we have been using them most of our lives. Although we readily locate a sound as coming from our right or our left, how often are we aware of why we can locate it so accurately? Although we easily perceive an object as being closer or farther away than another, how often are we aware of the many cues we employ in making this judgment? The perceptions are usually made immediately, usually without a conscious evaluation of the specific relationship among "things out there."

Subliminal perception

In addition to the fact that perceptual responses are usually forthcoming at speeds too great to permit conscious and rational evaluation, there is also evidence which indicates that perceptual responses are frequently determined by stimulus cues of which we are not conscious. Perhaps the best example of this is found in our lack of awareness of the cues we use in localizing a sound. It was pointed out earlier in this chapter that careful experimental evidence has indicated that sound localization is based upon the fact that the auditory pattern reaching one ear is slightly different from that which reaches the other. It is doubtful, however, that we are even aware of this fact; we simply hear the sound as coming from a particular place. Certainly in this instance we are not conscious of the nature of the cue that guides our behavior.

This general fact may be demonstrated somewhat more obviously by the description of a formal experiment on subliminal perception.[12] The subjects in this experiment performed two tasks at two different times. In one of these, and following a warning sign, a sound was presented in the earphones which they were wearing. The sound was either the radio signal dot-dash, or the signal dash-dot. The subjects reported which of the two signals they thought occurred subsequent to the warning sign. They also reported how confident they were of the accuracy of the report, using three steps: (1) certain, (2) doubtful, (3) no confidence whatever—a pure guess. The intensity of the sound varied from trial to trial, from being loud enough to be heard clearly to being so soft that the subjects had no conscious awareness that it had occurred. They only knew that they were required to make a report following the warning sign.

At this point the technical word subliminal should be defined. The word is a derivation of the Latin word *limen* which means *threshold* in English. It may be said that a stimulus is below the threshold or limen if it is too weak for the observer to be aware of its occurrence. This is called a subliminal stimulus. It is above the threshold or limen if the observer is conscious of it. In this experiment trials in which the subjects reported that they had no confidence in their judgment and were simply guessing were defined as trials wherein the stimulus was subliminal. It does not follow that because a stimulus is subliminal it cannot have an effect upon the subjects' behavior, and the purpose of the experiment was to discover whether such an effect might actually occur.

In the second part of the experiment the same procedure was employed except that the stimulus to be discriminated was presented visually. It was either the mark $+$ or the mark $\times$.

The brightness of this visual pattern was varied from trial to trial in the same manner as with the sound. At times its intensity was high and the subjects made their judgments with confidence,

325

and at other times the intensity was so low that the subjects felt that their judgments were pure guesses.

The results of this experiment are presented in graphic form in Figure 9.11. The percentage of correct choices is indicated on the Y axis. It ranges from 100 to 50 percent, or the chance score that would be expected in a two-choice situation. The physical value of the stimulus is indicated in a two-choice situation. The physical value of the stimulus is indicated on the X axis. The vertical line at 0 represents the limen, for all judgments at this physical value were reported as pure guesses. Also, all the judgments of the even weaker stimuli to the left of the 0 line were made in response to a subliminal stimulus as defined by the fact that the subjects had no confidence in their reports. Only for the stimuli to the right of the threshold did the subjects report some degree of confidence in their judgments.

Fig. 9.11 The percentage of correct identifications plotted against intensity of the visual or auditory stimulus. The zero mark in the center indicates the highest intensity level at which the subjects reported "no confidence" in their judgments. By chance the expected error level would be 50 percent. It is apparent that the subjects perform better than this even at several intensity levels below the highest "no confidence" level. The black dots represent the actual data points. The blue curve is the approximate best fit of the data. (After data from Baker[12])

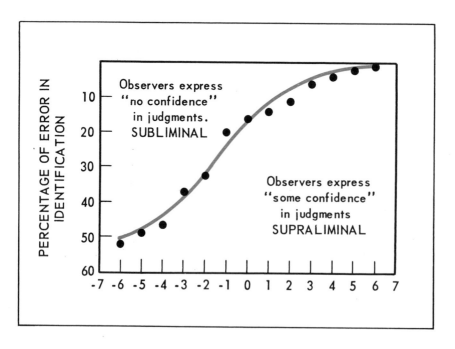

The notable feature of these data is not only the fact that the performance is better than chance for the first completely subliminal stimulus, but that complete loss of effectiveness does not occur until the physical intensity has been reduced by several further steps. The experiment offers very clear support for subliminal perception.

The concept of subliminal perception has recently become a matter of public concern because of the suggestion that stimuli of this type may be employed for advertising purposes. It is physically possible for the advertiser to insert some slogan onto the screen during the showing of a movie or television film for an instant too brief for supraliminal perception. By such means it is thought that the viewer might be lead to desire the commodity, and yet never become aware of the source of physical stimulation which gave rise to this desire.

A careful evaluation by disinterested psychological researchers of the effectiveness of subliminal advertising is not available, but on theoretical grounds there is reason to believe that this form of advertising is not likely to be very effective. The experiment described above has shown that some subliminal stimuli may guide behavior, but it should be noted that supraliminal stimuli are considerably more effective. Furthermore, the weaker the stimuli the less effective they become. Experimental work has shown that the perception of a stimulus can be blocked or inhibited if it is followed immediately by a moderately strong positive stimulation. Presumably the slogan would be inserted between frames of interesting material, and would be subject to this sort of inhibition. Furthermore, evidence presented in the previous chapter indicates that if an individual is reacting positively and strongly to one class of material he is not very receptive to material of another sort. Presumably he would be reacting in this manner to the supraliminal stimulation. So for a variety of reasons it does not appear that subliminal advertising would be effective sources of motivation despite the fact that our behavior can be guided by stimuli of whose presence we are unaware.

FACTORS PRODUCING VARIATIONS

IN PERCEPTION

Whenever eyewitnesses report the events of a complex situation, a great diversity is found. Although more often than not witnesses will agree on the nature of some single, central event, they will almost certainly disagree upon details, and some witnesses may even give a completely discrepant account of the central event. The two broad, basic mechanisms responsible for this diversity of report are *perception* and *forgetting*. Some of the changes that occur in the forgetting process have already been described. For the present we are concerned with why perceptual activity should so often go astray. As an example, let us consider some of the contradictions in the following testimony given by witnesses who have observed the same event. Except for the substitution of fictitious names, this is an exact transcription of a court record.

IN THE COURT OF COMMON PLEAS OF FRANKLIN COUNTY, OHIO

Alexander Snide,
Plaintiff,
The Starling Hall Trucking Co.
Defendants

Case N. 178481

*The witnesses disagree on the location of
the truck following the accident*

Q. [Mr. Digman, the lawyer] This is East Woodruff, now, will you place the cars as they were when you came to the scene?

A. [Mr. Platt, the witness, does as requested.]

Q. Now, aren't you mistaken again there, the truck involved never was east—the truck, let me ask you this, for the purpose of the record, the truck and trailer were never east of the travel line, were they?

A. The tractor and trailer?

Q. At the time he saw them.

A. At the time I saw them, the truck was over the center line, was astraddle the center line, is what I want to say, and the back end of this car has to come over into this lane, and this vehicle here, No. 3, is astraddle of this lane [indicating].

Another witness testifies

Q. Where did you say the truck stopped, Mr. Fitzwater?

A. You mean my truck now, or the tractor?

Q. No, the tractor truck.

A. It stopped on the right-hand side, heading south.

Q. Which lane was he in when he stopped?

A. On the outside lane.

Q. Over towards the curb?

*The witnesses disagree on the number of cars
involved in the accident*

Q. Calling your attention to June 29th, 1949, at approximately 2:30 p.m., will you state whether or not on that date and time you witnessed an accident at the intersection of Woodruff and South High Street?

A. I did.

Q. Can you state where you were at the time, approximately at the time the accident occurred?

A. I was in the filling station on the northeast corner of Woodruff and High, facing west.

Q. Now, would you state what automobiles were involved in the accident?

A. A 1937 Chevrolet, a tractor-trailer, and a maroon Chrysler, I don't know the year, I would say about a 1940.

Another witness testifies

Q. The truck hadn't been moved until Officer Riley arrived at the scene?

A. That is correct.

Q. And the automobiles were all in the same position when he arrived, as they were immediately after the accident?

A. All except Model A Ford that ran into Mr. Snide's right front pulled around us and took off down the street, I don't know whether—

Q. A Model A Ford?

A. Yes.

Q. Is that another car, were there four cars involved in this accident?

*The witnesses disagree on the make and
color of the truck*

Q. Do you recall what kind of a truck this was?

A. It was a Chevvy.

Q. The truck?

A. The tractor?

Q. The tractor.

A. I won't be positive, I know it was red, I wouldn't swear as to the make.

Another witness testifies

Q. What kind of an outfit did you have?

A. '49 GMC tractor and Fruehauf trailer, flat bed.

Q. Flat bed in back of a tractor?

A. That is right.

329

Q. The tractor is a GMC tractor?

A. That is right.

Q. What color?

A. It is a two-tone, it was green and black, the cab was green and the fenders was black.

Q. It wasn't red at all?

A. No, it wasn't red, it was setting on the lot down there.

Of course, some of these contradictions may have arisen because the several witnesses viewed the accident from different vantage points and some of the witnesses may have had keener vision or hearing than others. Often, however, discrepancies in testimony are far greater than can be accounted for by differences in sensory data alone; they must therefore arise from some factors that influence the perceptual process itself and thus cause us to perceive a given physical situation in one way now and in another way later.

Motivation as a determiner of perception

To determine whether an object is perceived differently when we are hungry and when we are not, two experimenters presented subjects with pictures whose interpretation was unclear and asked them to write a story about the events they imagined might be occurring in each picture.[13] The subjects in one group were presented with pictures and wrote their stories an hour after they had eaten a good meal. A second group was tested four hours, and a third group sixteen hours, after eating. Eight pictures were presented, and each subject wrote a story about each picture. One of the subjects in the sixteen-hour group wrote the following story.

The persons are a man from the black market and an honest citizen of a small Southern town. The citizen hasn't had any meat for a couple of weeks and the man from the black market knows it. The man from the black market thinks he can sell the meat for twice what it's worth. The citizen doesn't want to buy from the black market but he is wanting the meat. The citizen doesn't buy the meat and reports it to the police.

The story not only contains references to food but also has a theme of frustration and deprivation.

For all the stories the experimenters tabulated the frequencies with which references to food were made; whether or not the goal of eating was attained (as it was not in the story above); whether references to deprivation of food were made; whether means were employed to overcome the lack of food; and several other characteristics. Some of these results are plotted in Figure 9.12.

The data in Figure 9.12 indicate that the pictures are reacted to or perceived differently by the three groups. Under conditions of high hunger motivation, the pictures are more often seen as portraying events which deal with food deprivation and the frustration of goal-seeking behavior. There was, then, a relationship between level of hunger motivation and what was perceived in these pictures.

Physiological needs, as we noted in Chapter 5, are only one source of motivation. We are activated also by socially determined motives, and one such motive is that of doing well in some socially valued activity, such as an intelligence test. In an experiment which parallels the one described above, two groups of subjects

Fig. 9.12 Changes in story content as a function of the strength of hunger motivation. Food *imagery* is defined as any mention of food or eating; *instrumental activity* as action directed at obtaining food; *goal activity* as mention of having finished eating; and *deprivation theme* as mention of food scarcity. (After Atkinson and McClelland[13])

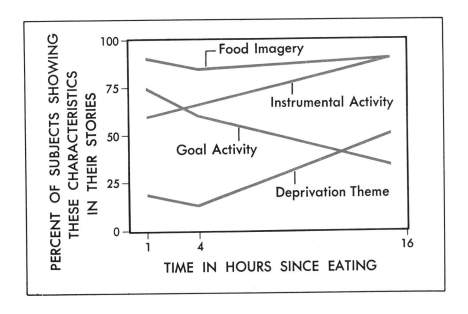

were given intelligence tests.[14] One group was led to believe that it had done very well and the other very poorly on the test—although the actual performance of the two groups was equal. We could say that for one of these groups its need to achieve, which had been aroused by the testing situation, had been satisfied; for the other, this same need had been frustrated. Both groups were then presented with pictures, which they were asked to interpret. The results were similar to those found in the hunger-deprivation experiment. The group that had just "failed" the intelligence test —and as a result had, we assume, a high need to achieve—saw in these pictures more instances of barriers and frustrations which blocked the achievement of the characters than did the group that had "done well" on the intelligence test.

Many examples of the influence of motivation upon perception occur in daily life. In a close play, the home team is always right, though a "half-blind" referee may call the play wrongly. When a quarrel breaks out between two toddlers in the sandbox and the sand begins to fly to the accompaniment of heartrending wails, each mother—though both have observed the event—is likely to perceive that the other child is to blame. The grass is greener and the air is clearer in a locale where we have had many pleasant experiences. The beloved one becomes more beautiful as love grows stronger. In other ways, and in more subtle ones, our motives enter in to determine our perceptions. We shall see, in Chapter 15, how the psychologist uses this phenomenon in developing personality tests. The tests require the client to interpret ambiguous figures, such as ink blots or certain kinds of pictures, and the psychologist tries to identify the underlying motives that influence the client's perceptions.

Set as a determiner of perception

In the preceding chapter, we noted that the phenomenon of set can determine the stimuli to which we react and the character of the response we make. Set serves also to determine how a complex situation may be structured perceptually; thus it can determine our perceptual reactions.

The set may be established in several ways. It may arise from stimuli that are external to the object to be perceived—from directions that are given—or from an initial reaction to the stimulus itself. In this latter case a hasty or indistinct view of the stimulus may lead to a false interpretation which will persist when later and clearer presentations of the stimulus are made. These two conditions may be more clearly understood by reference to experiments.

Set established by external stimuli

In one experiment children were presented with photographs of strangers cut from a magazine and asked to rate these individuals on the degree of maliciousness they seemed to show. Later the children played a game of murder and were told hair-raising stories. Shortly afterward, they again rated the photographs, and this time the entire group of photographs was rated as somewhat more malicious than on the first rating.[15]

In another experiment subjects were instructed to look for an animal in a series of six ink blots and then to draw it.[16] Later they were shown a second series of ink blots and asked to identify and reproduce mountain scenery. One of the blots was the same in both series, but 64 percent of the subjects failed to recognize it as the one seen before. In a control group which was directed to look for either mountain scenery or animals, only 10 percent failed to recognize the blot on the second seeing of it.

Name-calling is one of the most common means by which perceptions are distorted or modified in our social world. For example, one politician calls another a labor-hater, a Red, or a wild-eyed visionary, and the voter—given this set—may see these characteristics exhibited in the positions the man takes on various issues. Another politician not so labeled may take a similar position, but his views are interpreted in a more favorable light.

This has been demonstrated experimentally in the following manner.[17] Subjects divided into two groups were presented a series of twelve nonsense figures for a few seconds each in a memory drum. After all twelve figures were shown, the subjects tried to draw all of them. The list was shown repeatedly until all the figures were drawn. Before showing each nonsense drawing, the experimenter would name an object that was similar to it. The first group was told that it looked like one thing, and the second that it looked like something else: a broom *vs.* a gun, a bottle *vs.* stirrups, and so on for each of the twelve figures. The drawings were then judged on their degree of similarity to the words given. The two groups were found to have produced different figures,

333

each group tending to distort in the direction of the key word. Apparently the words produced a set that determined the manner of perceiving. The nonsense figures, together with some of the biased reproductions, are shown in Figure 9.13.

Fig. 9.13 The stimulus figures used in measuring the effect of verbalization upon perception, and some typical distortions for each of the groups. (After Carmichael, Hogan, and Walters[17])

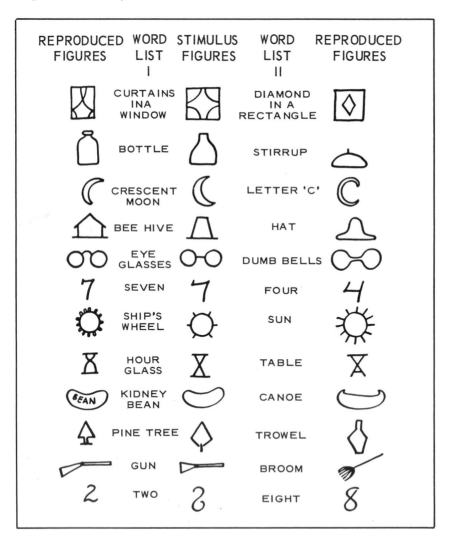

Set established by an imperfect initial reaction

Often our first impressions of a certain situation are hazy. We catch a glimpse of something out of the corner of our eye, we overhear a fragmentary sentence, or we briefly observe the behavior of someone in a special situation. Nevertheless, we may make a judgment about the characteristics of the scene, the topic of conversation, or the person in question. The judgment that we make may constitute a set which determines the way in which we shall perceive this same situation when an opportunity for more detailed and comprehensive observation occurs.

This kind of set has been demonstrated experimentally. An experimenter presented a series of slides to subjects and asked them what they saw in the pictures. At first the pictures were purposely projected badly out of focus; nevertheless the subjects were instructed to guess the contents. On subsequent presentations the focus became sharper and sharper. It was found that observation of the slide out of focus interfered with correct perception later. This was confirmed by a control group in which the subjects first saw the slides in sharper though not perfect focus. These subjects were more accurate in their judgments about the true nature of the slides.[18] It would seem, then, that a set was established by the initial viewing of the slides in poor focus, and that this set interfered with the subsequent attainment of a correct perception.

In brief, set establishes bias; and when sensory stimuli subsequently play upon the organism, they are perceived in a specific fashion because the set is operative. Were the identical physical situation to occur at a time when a different set had been established, it would be perceived quite differently.

Sets, as we have pointed out, may be established in a number of ways. They may arise as a result of previous contact with apparently unrelated material, as a result of some premature and inappropriate reaction to the materials themselves, or as a result of verbal directions. Sets produce a bias for perceiving in a particular way and they may facilitate an accurate interpretation of the stimulus or they may lead to error in interpretation, depending upon the nature of the set and the stimulating situation.

READING AS PERCEPTION

Reading is a perceptual activity. The pattern of letters that makes up a word forms a stimulus which serves as a cue for some actual event or object. The ten letters arranged in the sequence R E S T A U R A N T appearing on the window of a building in a strange town permit us to predict that here we may satisfy our hunger. A dog could not make this prediction until he had received some olfactory stimulation; an illiterate would need to wait for some similar type of cue—an odor or the sight of food or other paraphernalia of a restaurant. To one who reads, the letter pattern will serve as a predictive cue that informs him of some further state of affairs. When we read, we engage in a perceptual activity in which we react to a group of stimuli which by convention have become symbols representing some object or process.

One way of studying the process of reading is to observe the eyes of someone while he is reading. The method employed in making records of eye movements during reading is relatively simple. A small beam of light is directed at the eyeball and is reflected by the eye to a moving strip of film located in an otherwise lightproof camera. Just as a mirror we hold in our hand will reflect the sun's rays and this reflection will move as the mirror is moved, so the movements of the eyes move the beam of light on the film. The subject is asked to read a passage of material, and a permanent film record of the activity of the eyes is thus obtained.

Studies of these records have disclosed several interesting facts. As we read a line of type, our eyes do not move continuously across the page. They fixate a certain point on the line, remain fixated at this point for a few tenths of a second, then jump to another point along the line, fixate, and so on until the end of the line is reached. From here they swing smoothly back to somewhere near the beginning of the next line, and the process begins anew. Occasionally *regressions* occur—that is, after advancing to a new point of fixation, the eyes may swing back to fixate some earlier point in the line—and the ground that has been gained is lost.

It is of the utmost significance that the fixations per line are considerably fewer than the number of words per line. Readers do not look at every word on the page, and ordinarily a single fixation spans several words. Logically, then, it would appear that we could increase reading speed by increasing either the span or the speed of the eye movements. Since normally we do not look at each word, it might be possible to increase the span of words covered by a single fixation so that fewer fixations would be required per line. Or we might reduce time per fixation and also perhaps eliminate regressions, which are costly of time.

For a period of years after the first careful measurements of eye movements during reading were made, it was hoped that reading speed could be improved by eye-movement training. A variety of studies touching upon this approach have indicated, however, that poor eye movements are the symptoms of poor reading rather than the cause. We cannot improve reading to any great degree by using some sort of mechanical eye-movement trainer; however, eye movements will improve automatically if the individual's skill is increased.

The perceptual factors that operate in the rather highly complex process that constitutes reading may be better appreciated if we observe them in a simpler process—one in which we measure the speed of perceiving a single word or unit.

If words are exposed for extremely short periods and the subject is asked to report the word he sees, words that are in common usage will be perceived more rapidly than words in less common usage.[19] The more familiar the word is, the more rapidly we perceive it. The significance of this fact for reading speed is obvious. The individual who reads a great deal and becomes familiar with many words will read more rapidly than the occasional reader. The process of reading, through increasing our familiarity with words, improves itself.

Many studies have shown that letters of meaningful words are perceived as groups and therefore are read with greater rapidity than are series of disconnected letters of the same length. Meaning, then, is significantly related to perceptual speed. This fact suggests that the reader who increases his vocabulary and who acquires a precise knowledge of the meaning of words will thereby improve his reading speed.

Another important factor in perceptual speed is the influence of set or context. Let us suppose the word "whale" is flashed

337

on the screen before the subject. If the presentation of the word had been preceded by another group of words such as "mammal" and "ocean," it would be perceived with greater rapidity than if it had been preceded by unrelated words or no words at all. Any given word, then, does not have some absolute rate at which it can be perceived; the rate will vary with the extent to which the context has prepared the subject for the word. Too often readers attempt to stumble along from word to word, paying little attention to the significance of what they are reading and thus failing to supply the context that will facilitate perception of later words.

The use of context in reading is important in another way, and that is in defining the word itself. A brief examination of a dictionary will illustrate the fact that most words in our language have a number of meanings, sometimes highly similar but at other times quite different from one another. Hence it is frequently true that we must know the context in which the word is being used in order to know which of its many meanings it is conveying.

The principles governing the perception of single words clearly suggest that the nature of our eye movements during reading will vary with our perceptual competence for the kinds of materials to which we are being exposed. This fact is nowhere so clearly verified as in a study of the eye movements of good and poor readers as they read materials that were quite easy, moderately difficult, and quite difficult.[20] For the poor readers the number of fixations and regressive movements for the three kinds of material remained the same. For good readers, on the other hand, the frequency of fixations and regressions increased as the material became more difficult. Their eye movements seemed to mirror the changes in the perceptual difficulty of the task, whereas the eye movements for the poor reader were mechanical and unrelated to the nature of the work.

REFERENCES

[1] Trimble, O. C. Some temporal aspects of sound localization, *Psychol. Monographs*, 1928, *28*, 172-231.

[2] Christman, R. J. "The perception of direction as a function of binaural temporal and amplitude disparity," in Glen Finch and Frank Cameron (ed.), *Air Force Human Engineering, Personnel and Training Research*, ARDC Tech. Report 56-8, Baltimore, 1956.

[3] Willey, C. F., Ingles, E., and Pearce, C. H. Reversal of auditory localization, *J. exp. Psychol.*, 1937,

20, 114-130.

[4] Taylor, J. G., and Papert, S. A theory of perceptual constancy. *Brit. J. Psychol.*, 1956, *47*, 216-224.

[5] Wapner, S., Werner, H., and Chandler, K. A. Experiments on sensory-tonic field theory of perception: I. Effects of extraneous stimulation on the visual perception of verticality, *J. exp. Psychol.*, 1951, *42*, 351-357.

[6] Senden, M. V. *Raum-und Gestaltauffassung bei operierten Blindgeborenen vorund nach der operation,* Leipzig: Barth, 1932.

[7] Riesen, A. H. The development of visual perception in man and chimpanzee, *Science,* 1947, *106*, 107-108.

[8] Schafer, R., and Murphy, G. The role of autism in a visual figureground relationship, *J. exp. Psychol.*, 1943, *32*, 335-343.

[9] Thouless, R. H. Phenomenal regression to the real object, *Brit. J. Psychol.*, 1931, *21*, 339-359.

[10] Wever, G. E. Figure and ground in the visual perception of form, *Amer. J. Psychol.*, 1927, *38*, 194-226.

[11] Liebowitz, H., Chinetti, P., and Sidowski, J. Exposure duration as a variable in perceptual constancy, *Science,* 1946, *126*, 668-669.

[12] Baker, Lynn E. The influence of subliminal stimuli upon verbal behavior, *J. exp. Psychol.,* 1937, *20*, 84-100.

[13] Atkinson, J. W., and McClelland, D. C. The projective expression of needs: II. The effect of different intensities of the hunger drive on thematic apperception, *J. exp. Psychol.*, 1947, *38*, 643-658.

[14] McClelland, D. C., Atkinson, J. W., and Clark, R. A. The projective expression of needs: III. The effect of ego-involvement success and failure on perception, *J. Psychol.*, 1949, *27*, 311-330.

[15] Murray, H. A. The effect of fear upon estimates of maliciousness of other personalities, *J. Soc. Psychol.*, 1933, *4*, 310-339.

[16] Zangwill, O. L. A study of the significance of attitude in recognition, *Brit. J. Psychol.*, 1937, *28*, 12-17.

[17] Carmichael, L., Hogan, H. P., and Walters, A. A. An experimental study of the effect of language on the reproduction of visually perceived form, *J. exp. Psychol.*, 1932, *51*, 73-86.

[18] Wyatt, D. F., and Campbell, D. T. On the reliability of stereotype or hypotheses, *J. Abn. and Soc. Psychol.*, 1951, *46*, 496-500.

[19] Solomon, R. L., and Postman, L. Frequency of usage as a determinant of recognition thresholds for words, *J. exp. Psychol.*, 1952, *43*, 195-201.

[20] Anderson, I. H. "Studies in the eye-movements of good and poor readers," in *Studies in Psychology of Reading*, I, University of Iowa Studies in Psychology, No. 21, 1-35.

Chapter Ten

PROBLEM SOLVING AND CONCEPT FORMATION

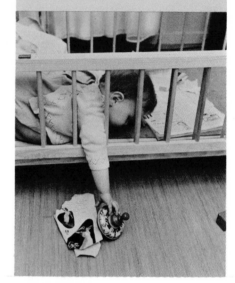

THE PAST FEW DECADES HAVE witnessed a tremendous expansion in man's knowledge about the physical world and his control over it. It is an expansion that has been made possible by man's ability to present problems to himself and to solve these problems in original and creative ways. This success has led in this country, at least, to a greatly increased awareness of man's capacity to be creative and also of the rewards that are the fruits of this creativeness. Psychologists have responded to this general concern by greatly enlarging their research activities in this area during the past ten years. Essentially the research has been directed toward discovering more about the problem-solving process itself, learning how individuals differ in their ability to

340

solve problems, and investigating how people may be trained to THE PROBLEM
become more skillful in this activity.[1] SOLVING
SITUATION

THE PROBLEM-SOLVING SITUATION

Before an attempt can be made to understand the psychological processes involved in problem solving the nature of the situation that leads to problem-solving behavior must be described and examined. Such an analysis can lead to at least a tentative identification of the kinds of responses that are required of the problem solver and will enable us to set the stage for understanding the process itself.

The situation that will be analyzed was devised many years ago and since has become something of a standard situation for laboratory work on this topic. The subjects—who might very well be college students—are brought singly into a large room containing many objects, such as poles, ringstands, clamps, pliers, extension cords, tables, and chairs. Two cords are hung from the ceiling, and are of such a length that they reach the floor. One is hung near a wall, the other from the center of the room. The subject is told, "Your problem is to tie the ends of those two cords together." He soon learns that if he holds either cord in his hand he cannot reach the other. He is then told he can use or do anything he wishes.

Four solutions to this problem are possible: (1) One of the cords is anchored to some large object such as the chair and the free cord is grasped by one hand and brought over to the anchored cord. (2) One cord is lengthened by attaching the extension cord to it. (3) While one cord is held in the hand, the other is brought over to it by use of a pole. (4) The pair of pliers is attached to one string to make a pendulum and this cord is set to swinging while the subject grasps the other cord and waits until the pendulum swings to him. It is usually the last solution—the most imaginative of all of them—that is studied, and the subjects are required to continue from one solution to another until the pendulum solution occurs or the experimental session is terminated.[2]

Using this experiment as an example of the problem-solving situation in general, it can be seen that the emphasis is placed upon the discovery of the particular response or responses which lead to the goal. The actual manipulations that are required of the subject in achieving the pendulum solution are not difficult. He has long ago fixated the skill of attaching objects to cords by means of knots, and he has long known how to push swings, to grasp cords, and to walk. These are about all the manipulative responses that are required of him. Undoubtedly the subjects also know how a weight on the end of a dangling rope will affect the way the rope swings. In short, the subject has come to the task with all the necessary responses to solve it in his behavior repertoire, and all that is demanded is that these particular responses be selected.

This, in general, seems to be the characteristic of problem-solving situations. Usually—but not always—the solution can be achieved without need for the development of new skills, and the emphasis is placed upon discovering which of the already present skills are appropriate to the situation. Perhaps this is the reason why, after a subject has failed to solve some problem and has the solution described to him, he is disgusted with himself for his failure and is convinced that he really should have been able to solve the problem himself.

In Chapter 2 we described a general type of situation that confronts the organism hour after hour, day after day, and year after year—the situation in which some barrier, physical, social, or conceptual, stands between the organism and its immediate goal. In Chapter 3 we considered the factors that determine the effectiveness and the speed with which the organism can fixate the pathway to the goal once this pathway has been discovered. The problem-solving situation causes us to be concerned with the conditions that lead to variability of behavior in the presolution period; variability that permits the organism to react to different aspects of the environment and to discover the response that can surmount the barrier. Analyzed in this fashion, problem-solving behavior is not fundamentally different from other forms of adjustive behavior, for many of them demand a certain amount of variability. In the problem-solving situation, however, this is the characteristic which is emphasized.[3]

Essentially this analysis assumes that the individual who is trying to solve a problem has the correct response in his repertoire of behavior (or at least could acquire it without much effort) and that his primary task is to select the appropriate response or responses. If such is the case, a fruitful method for understanding the problem-solving process will be to identify the conditions which facilitate or inhibit the variability that is a prerequisite to the discovery of the correct response.

FACTORS INFLUENCING DISCOVERY

Definition of the problem

Ordinarily we solve a problem by varying our responses to a situation until we hit upon one response that circumvents the barrier. Often, however, little progress can be made toward the goal until the problem is defined and localized.

Let us assume that the engine of your car will not start and that there is no mechanic near by to aid you. You would remain immobile indefinitely if you were content with defining your problem in such broad terms as "starting the engine." You must define the problem in more specific terms. Perhaps you will first look at the gasoline gauge and, mistrusting it, you will poke a stick into the tank itself to determine the quantity of fuel remaining. The gauge is correct; there is gasoline in the tank. Then, because it is a humid day, you may unscrew and wipe off all the spark plugs. This, too, is of no avail. It may occur to you then that even though the tank is nearly full, gasoline may not be coming into the carburetor. You therefore disconnect the line leading into the carburetor, and when you press on the starter no gasoline flows from the line. Now the problem is better defined; somewhere between tank and carburetor there is a stoppage. You therefore disconnect the fuel line at the fuel pump and find that, at a touch of the starter, gasoline flows from the pump opening. Now your problem is completely defined. The stoppage is in the small piece of tubing you hold in your hand. Now you need only to find a way to remove the obstruction—perhaps by blowing, perhaps by pushing a small wire through the bore. After you replace the unobstructed tubing, your car starts; the engine runs smoothly. Your success was made possible first because you specifically defined your problem and then because you overcame this more localized problem.

Essentially, the defining of any problem consists simply in identifying the factor that is producing the difficulty. Let us look at an example. An industrial engineer is consulted on the problem of increasing production in a factory. He may find that a department that produces an item essential to the finished product constitutes a bottleneck, and his problem now becomes that of increasing the rate of production in this department. There may be several

343

possible solutions: changing the work layout, instituting more efficient production methods, purchasing better machinery, inventing or developing new machinery, or changing the interpersonal structure of the group. Any one of these solutions may pose a subproblem within the larger one of total production.

Here is an example from another area. A grade-school pupil who is about to fail is sent to a psychologist for help in bettering his class work. The psychologist now has a problem to solve. By means of various diagnostic tests he may learn that the boy's general failure is due to a specific deficiency in reading rather than to low general ability. This reading difficulty may in turn be a reflection of an emotional problem stemming from jealousy of a younger brother or sister. Now the psychologist's task is no longer one of improving reading but of improving the boy's relations with his parents and his younger sibling.

Many other examples can be cited to point to the fact that the first step in solving a problem is to discover exactly what the problem is. This conclusion may seem so completely obvious that the reader may well wonder why so much space is devoted to it. It is stressed because persons in problem situations often neglect this obvious fact. They may work at cross purposes with themselves and even give up their striving and accept defeat because they are seeking a solution without having clearly defined the problem that they are trying to solve. What is so obvious in principle is not always so obvious in a concrete situation. It is not always easy to discover just what the problem is, and it sometimes requires complex equipment and methods to do so. Witness the elaborate instruments that the physician employs in making a diagnosis, the tests that psychologists have developed, or the many devices in an automobile repair shop.

It sometimes happens that problems are difficult to solve—difficult, that is, in the sense of requiring much time and effort—solely because the would-be problem solver defines the problem incorrectly. His error may result from ambiguity of directions, as is illustrated in the following problem. Some wag comes up to you and confronts you with *what seems to be* the following problem: "I'll bet you ten cents that you can't completely cover the four legs of the camel on this pack of Camels with this dime." After several futile attempts, you concede defeat, whereupon your friend takes the dime and the pack from you and covers the two front legs of the camel. When you protest, he replies, "All I said was to cover the *fōr* legs of the camel; I meant *f-o-r-e,* not *f-o-u-r.* You lose." The directions were ambiguous; the auditory stimulus *fōr* has both a numerical and an anatomical meaning. In the context of the sentence neither of these meanings was specified, and you chose the one that was inappropriate. The problem becomes immediately soluble once it is properly interpreted; its difficulty arose solely from the fact that the would-be solver did not define it correctly.

If one fails to define the problem correctly it is likely to mean that the potentially correct response is not included in the group of responses that the hopeful problem solver considers to be appropriate to the solution. So long as this is true, no amount of trying can produce the correct answer; the problem must be redefined. Many of the trick parlor game problems are of this sort—there is very little to them once the problem is correctly defined. The nine dot problem presented below tends to be poorly defined and so does the following problem: Make four equilateral triangles using only six matches. The matches may not be broken.

Fig. 10.1 Problem: connect all the dots in this figure with four continuous lines. You may not retrace any line.

The match problem is solved by forming a pyramid and using three rather than two dimensions. The directions do not imply that only two dimensions may be used but many people define the problem in that manner. In the nine dot problem it is not necessary to keep the lines within a square formed by the dots, but most people try to solve it thusly.

The use of sub-goals

It occasionally happens that the solution to a problem is possible only if a certain sequence of responses is made. If any one of the responses in the sequence is incorrect, then we will be unable to solve the problem. But we may fail to recognize this until very late in the day and very late in the sequence. Sometimes we can avoid failure by working backwards from the end state that we wish to attain, and thus discover some intermediate station, or sub-goal, which, if reached, will lead inevitably to the final goal. Such a technique may be employed in the following problem:

You are standing by the side of a river with two cans, one of which has an 11-quart and the other a 6-quart capacity. You are asked to measure out exactly 4 quarts of water. The cans, incidentally, are not graduated in any way, and hence you cannot determine when, for example, the 6-quart can is two thirds full. You may pour water back and forth from one can to another, you may pour water from a can back into the river, and you may refill the cans as many times as you wish.

Now, if we start working backwards from the goal, we may decide that if the 11-quart can had a capacity of only 10 quarts, the solution would be simple, since $10 - 6 = 4$. We may then set up a goal of producing exactly 10 quarts in the 11-quart container. We therefore solve the problem in the following steps:

Step 1. Fill the 11-quart container and pour its contents into the 6-quart can until the latter is filled. This leaves 5 quarts in the 11-quart can.

Step 2. Empty the 6-quart can and pour the 5 quarts left in the 11-quart can into the 6-quart can. It now takes one more quart to fill it.

Step 3. Fill the 11-quart can and pour from it into the 6-quart can until the latter is filled. Since it had 5 quarts in it, it will hold only one more. This leaves 10 quarts in the 11-quart can, and this was our sub-goal. Now the solution is in sight.

Step 4. Empty 6 and pour from 11 into 6 until the latter is filled. This leaves the desired quantity of 4 quarts remaining in the 11-quart container.

Other problems may be approached in the same fashion. A chess player may see that if several of his pieces are located in certain positions, he can checkmate his opponent in two or three more moves. He works to obtain this advantage, knowing that success will be inevitable from that point on. Sometimes in social situations we see that problem solutions will almost be assured if a certain first step is taken; we therefore direct our efforts toward achieving that first step. An algebra problem may be very simple to solve once we attach the correct symbols to the unknown quantities. Once this is done, the remainder of the task may consist only in using routine algebraic operations.

The awareness of the fact that a sub-goal may lead to solution, and the identification of that sub-goal, often aid in the solution of problems which otherwise may be nearly insoluble or soluble only at high cost in time and effort. It is obvious that the sub-goal may be at any level. The important point is that its identification may simplify an otherwise difficult problem. And it has been shown that if the problem is a difficult and lengthy one, the better problem solvers are inclined to structure it in such a manner that it becomes possible to work toward sub-goals.[4]

Part of the reason for progress in science is that scientists have learned to ask better questions, questions which are specific and precise enough for their answers to be found by the methods of problem solving. Essentially, this asking of better questions—questions that represent sub-goals on the way to larger goals—leads to specific hypotheses that can be tested by research.

The availability of the response

If it is true that problem solving consists—at least to a large degree—of selecting the appropriate response, then one would assume that the more available the response is to the subject, the easier it would be for him to solve the problem. This hypothesis has been tested by asking the subjects to list possible uses for the materials that are available to solve the problem and noting whether there is a relationship between the ease of solving the problem and the uses listed for the critical material. Thus, in the two-cord problem one might expect that subjects who stated that a pair of pliers could be used as a weight would solve the actual problem more easily than subjects who did not mention such a use for pliers. The assumption is that the listing gives some indication of the degree of availability of the response. The results do suggest a slight relationship between use in solving the problem and the listing of this type of use for the material. They imply, therefore, that general availability of the response is a factor which is related to problem solution.[5, 6]

In another study the experimenters tried to increase the availability of the pertinent response by having the subjects learn lists of words several days before they were asked to solve the two-string problem.[7] For the experimental group one of the lists contained the following items in this order: "rope, swing, pendulum, clock, time." Another group had a list containing all these words but in a different order and mixed in with other words, while a third group learned "rope, hemp, twine, tie package." It is apparent that the order of the words in the first list is appropriate to the actions that must be taken to produce the pendulum solution, and the prior verbal learning could make these responses more available during the problem-solving period. This was found to be true for the male but not the female subjects, but just why there is this sex difference is unexplained.

All in all these experiments suggest that the efficiency of problem solving will be determined by the ease with which the appropriate response becomes available for use in the problem situation. Any condition that decreases the availability of this response should retard solution, and any increase in availability should facilitate solution. It will be seen that the variables to be considered operate in this fashion.

The nature and arrangement of materials

If one recalls instances when he has worked upon some problem, he is not likely to recognize the extent to which his success or failure may have been influenced by conditions that were apparently irrelevant to the problem's solution. Nevertheless, there is a fair amount of experimental data which indicate that these "irrelevant" aspects may help or hinder solution. This fact is rather nicely shown in the solution of what is called the disk-transfer task. Three disks are stacked in a particular order in one of three squares. The subject is asked to transfer this stack to the same order in another square, using the smallest number of moves possible and operating under the following rules: only one disk may be moved at one time and only the one at the top of a pile or in an otherwise empty square, and a disk may not be placed under any other disk that was originally above it. The experiment under consideration used small boxes rather than disks, the boxes differing not only in size but also in weight and in color.[8] It was found that if the "natural" order in one dimension disagreed with the size order, then the problem was made more difficult than if they agreed. For example, if the smallest box was the heaviest and the largest the lightest more errors were made than if the smallest was the lightest and the largest the heaviest. Weight is not truly relevant to the problem, but nevertheless it influenced the behavior.

Order of presentation of the materials is another essentially irrelevant variable that can influence the way we solve a problem.

A simple demonstration of this fact is to be found in an experiment in which the subjects were asked to identify the dissimilar word of a group of four words. An example is *prayer, church, cathedral, skyscraper*. The word *prayer* is dissimilar to the other three if they are interpreted as kinds of buildings, and *skyscraper* is dissimilar if the others are interpreted as being related to religion. When a series of problems of this sort was given, it was found that the subjects tended to accept the first of the unambiguous words rather than the later one.[9] Thus, the way the subject solved the problem, the way he interpreted the meaning of the ambiguous words, was to a certain degree influenced by the simple matter of order of presentation.

These studies and other similar ones are significant in relation to problem solving in general because they indicate that the problem solver tends to be sensitive to and guided by aspects of the situation which are not at all essential to the problem's solution. If these irrelevant aspects point in a certain way then they may facilitate solution, but they could just as readily inhibit solution if they chanced to point in another direction.

The influence of set

We have described earlier (see p. 276) how a set established by some preceding group of stimuli may predispose the organism

TABLE 10.1. THE SERIES OF PROBLEMS USED TO DEMONSTRATE THE INFLUENCE OF SET ON PROBLEM SOLVING

Problem	Given empty water containers of the following capacities in gallons			Obtain exactly the following quantity of water in gallons
	A	B	C	
1	21	127	3	100
2	14	163	25	99
3	18	43	10	5
4	9	42	6	21
5	20	59	4	31
6	23	49	3	20
7	15	39	3	18
8	28	76	3	25

to respond in certain ways rather than in others. It is obvious, then, that set may operate to reduce variability in problem solving. If the set predisposes the subject toward the class of response needed for surmounting the barrier, it will facilitate his problem solution; if it predisposes him in another direction, however, it may retard his solution. An illustration of the inhibiting influence of set can be noted in the series of problems in Table 10.1, all of which are variations of the water-container problem explained on page 346. The reader may wish to try to solve these problems before continuing with the text.

Set influences the solution of this group of problems in the following manner. The first five problems are solved by the formula $B - A - 2C$, where the first container is called A, the second B, and the third C. The sixth and seventh problems, however, can be solved more easily and directly, and the last problem cannot be solved by this formula at all. The first series of problems, which are all solved by one method, tends to establish a set to solve other problems by the same method.

Actually the subjects in this experiment continued to use in Problems 6 through 8 the method that was effective for the first five problems and thus solved Problems 6 and 7 inefficiently and failed to solve Problem 8.[10] Thus, set leads to inefficiency when the subject is faced with problems that cannot be solved by this method or that can be solved more readily by another method.

In Chapter 8 it was pointed out that sets which influence stimulus selection may be established in a number of ways, and, of course, the same thing is true of sets as they influence problem solving. In the example cited above, the set was established because this general way of responding had been reinforced—it had been effective in solving previous problems. One would expect that the strength of the set would be a function of the number of times this way of responding had proved successful and if the set is consonant with the next problem to be solved it would facilitate performance, but if the set is antagonistic it would hinder solution. This has been found true in the water jar situation.[11]

Sets can be established by telling the subject that a certain way of responding will be more effective than others. This has been done with anagrams, the subjects being told that the letters can be rearranged to produce the name of a fruit, for example. This results in better problem solution than if no such restricting directions are given.[12]

Sets may also be established because an object has been used in a particular way—to serve a particular function—and, as a consequence, the subject finds it difficult to use it in some other fashion. The term *functional fixedness* has been employed to refer to this kind of situation, and its meaning can be clarified by describing an experiment.

The subjects were given the task of mounting three candles on a vertical screen at a height of about five feet from the floor.[13] There were a number of objects available on the table before them, but the only ones that made possible the solution were three pasteboard boxes, matches, and thumbtacks. The subjects were told that they could use any or all of the objects on the table. The solution consisted in attaching the candles to the boxes and affixing the boxes to the screen with thumbtacks. Thus, in a sense, the boxes are converted into shelves which support the candles. A subject in the act of solving the problem is shown in Figure 10.2.

Fig. 10.2 The solution to the candle problem used in the investigation of functional fixedness. (Courtesy Conrad Kraft)

For the control group the boxes lay among the other materials on the table; but for the experimental group the candles, matches and thumbtacks were placed in the boxes. In the 20 minutes allowed for the test, 86 percent of the control subjects solved the problem as compared with only 41 percent of the experimentals. Solution required that the boxes be conceptualized as things-that-can-support-candles, and the subjects' ability to do this was obviously interfered with by the immediately preceding experience of seeing boxes as things-that-can-contain-objects.

Several studies have investigated different characteristics of functional fixedness, and they have used the familiar two-string problem in the investigation. In these investigations the critical object to be used as the pendulum bob is either a switch or an electrical relay, and ordinarily subjects show no preference for one over the other. Functional fixedness is demonstrated by having the subject wire a simple electrical circuit before he is presented with the two-string problem. Half the subjects use the relay in wiring the circuit and half use the switch. Functional fixedness is demonstrated by the fact that the groups tend to choose as the pendulum bob the object which was *not* employed in the circuit wiring. This preference is marked if the two-string problem is given immediately after the circuit has been completed but is not so evident if the problem is given a week after the circuit wiring.[14]

Functional fixedness also will be reduced if, following the circuit wiring, the object is used for some other purpose, for example, as a prop for a card or as a straightedge. In other words, it is susceptible to a retroactive inhibition-like condition.[15] In short, the functionally fixed response can be forgotten, and the factors responsible for forgetting it are those which were described in Chapter 4.

The present analysis of the activities involved in problem solving would lead to a prediction that an individual's skill in solving problems will be influenced by the ease with which previously established sets can be eliminated if they lead to responses which are ineffective or needlessly cumbersome in solving a problem. Experimental work has demonstrated that individuals who score well on reasoning tests also tend to eliminate unprofitable sets with relative ease.[16]

In the present section and, to a certain extent, in the previous one we have stressed, by the citation of numerous experiments, the fact that events which appear to be irrelevant to the problem at hand often interfere with its solution. The opposite should also be true, and a fortuitous series of circumstances may lead to an important discovery, insight, or invention. It is strange and almost degrading to think that highly creative acts may be influenced by small events which seem to be extraneous to the central task, but it is a conclusion which is inescapable. Yet, if it can be said that a kingdom and a battle were lost for want of a shoe, and the shoe for want of a nail, it can also be said—with the authority gained from careful experimentation—that problems are solved or left unsolved for equally minor causes.

Past experience

Many years ago a series of experiments was conducted which suggested that the nature of previous experience was *not* an important determinant of certain types of inventive problem solutions. Shortly before World War I, Wolfgang Köhler, a German-educated psychologist, organized a program of research aimed at an understanding of the psychological processes that operate in the solution of problems. His subjects were chimpanzees, and he tested them on a variety of problems whose solutions depended on their discovery of the correct response. The behavior of one of the animals in solving one of these many problems is described by Köhler as follows:

Neuva [a chimpanzee] was tested three days after her arrival. . . . A little stick is introduced into her cage; she scrapes the ground with it, pushes the banana skins together into a heap, and then carelessly drops the stick at a distance of about three-quarters of a meter from the bars. Ten minutes later, fruit is placed outside the cage beyond her reach. She grasps at it, vainly of course, and then begins the characteristic complaint of the chimpanzee; she thrusts both lips—especially the lower—forward, for a couple of inches, gazes imploringly at the observer, utters whimpering sounds, and finally flings herself onto the ground on her back . . . about seven minutes after the fruit had been exhibited to her—she suddenly casts a look at the stick, ceases her moaning, seizes the stick, stretches it out of the cage, and succeeds, though somewhat clumsily, in drawing the bananas within arm's reach. Moreover, Neuva at once puts the end of her stick behind and beyond the objective, holding it in this test, as in later experiments, in her left hand by preference. The test is repeated after an hour's interval; on this second occasion, the animal has recourse to the stick much sooner, and uses it with more skill; and, at a third repetition, the stick is used immediately. . . .[17]

353

A basic question that arose from this experiment was that of the importance of past experience in attaining problem solution. The chimpanzees had never before in their laboratory existence been faced with this sort of problem, and it seems unlikely that they would have been forced to cope with such a situation in the jungle prior to their capture. Many psychologists were inclined, therefore, to interpret this experiment as indicating that past experience is of no great importance for solving such problem situations as these. Instead, the solution seemed to them to arise immediately out of the structure of the environment and would seem to consist of a new way of perceiving the relationships among food, stick, arm, and the barrier of the cage.

However, this interpretation cannot be accepted unless we are certain that the chimpanzees had had no previous experience with certain elements involved in the solution of this problem. One such element is the stick used for the purpose of extending the reach of the arm. This element is, of course, the key to solution. It may well be that past experience in handling sticks and using them to extend the reach of the arm was essential for the solution of the problem. Certainly this was the basic principle employed by Köhler's chimpanzees.

The question of the importance of previous stick handling was specifically attacked in an experiment with six chimpanzees who had been separated from their mothers since their second week of life and raised in a controlled laboratory environment.[18] Of the six chimpanzees, who at the time of the experiment were between four and five years of age, only one, Jojo, regularly used a stick as a tool. She would, for example, reach through the screening of her indoor cage and flick a light switch off and on with a stick.

The six chimpanzees were given the problem illustrated in Figure 10.3. The task seems simple enough; it consisted only in raking in the food, which was out of direct reach, with the hoe. A thirty-minute test was given to each of the subjects singly, and four of the six animals failed to solve it. Of the two who did solve it, one was Jojo, who had previously used sticks, and the other was Bard. Jojo reached the solution in twelve seconds and behaved from the outset as if she perceived the potential fundamental value of the hoe. Bard required about five minutes to obtain the food, and his solution seems to have been based upon the fact that he accidentally hit the hoe and caused it to move the food. (It is worth noting that he had previously served in an experiment in which food was

Fig. 10.3 The type of problem employed by Birch in his investigation of the influence of past experience on problem-solving behavior. The subject in this illustration, however, is a monkey rather than a chimpanzee. (Courtesy Harry F. Harlow)

drawn in by a string, and he reacted to the hoe handle very much as if it were a string.)

During the next three days, the animals were given no more tests on the hoe problem but instead were given sticks to play with in their home enclosures. From the outset the animals reacted positively to the sticks. They carried them about in their hands, and by the third day they were using them as extensions of their arms—that is, for activities such as poking at one another or at the experimenter. When, on the fourth day, the animals were once more tested on the hoe problem, all solved it and the slowest animal took only twenty seconds to do so.

There is something gratifying about the notion of the brilliant young scientist, inventor, artist, or businessman who looks briefly into a problem and almost in an instant surmounts the difficulty that has been baffling older hands for years. One is tempted, on hearing such stories, to assume that previous experience is of little or no significance for the creative worker, and that his inspiration is the simple product of a brilliant and insightful process out of the blue. That the creative worker himself is not aware, at the time, of items of previous experience that were necessary for his successful solution is entirely likely. Indeed, many of the habits that we have acquired in the past become so well developed, so

355

much a part of our whole reaction system, that when we use them we feel that they were always with us and are therefore essentially unimportant. This is probably not the case at all; on the contrary, these old and well-developed habits may well be a part of the necessary groundwork which, if lacking, would prevent us from solving some problem.

One is reminded here of the performance of the monkeys who had received much practice on discrimination problems and as a result were able to solve new problems in a single trial (see p. 128). We know from the behavior of these animals how important this past experience is.

Motivation

Motivation of some sort must be present in order to direct the organism to the problem to be solved, but it does not follow that stronger motivation leads inevitably to more rapid and more efficient problem solving. This fact is demonstrated by an experiment, already described (see pp. 184-185), in which chimpanzees were found to solve problems more rapidly at a medium level of motivation than at higher or lower levels.

Although the strongly and the poorly motivated groups were very similar in over-all efficiency—that is, they did not solve many problems—they were unlike each other in the manner of their failure. Whereas the poorly motivated group wandered off from the problem situation, the strongly motivated animals were so oriented toward the food alone that they did not seem to observe the nonfood objects which could be used to pull in the food.

The diagram of the motivated organism meeting a barrier on its way to the goal (see p. 33) makes clear one reason for this relationship between levels of motivation and problem-solving efficiency. Motivation must be high enough to keep the organism directed toward surmounting the barrier and to prevent it from moving away from the problem altogether. Motivation that is too high, however, cuts down the all-important pre-solution variability that leads to the discovery of the correct pathway to the goal, and this is one reason why high motivation may result in inferior problem-solving behavior.

In both this section and the preceding one, the experiments cited were performed with lower animals as subjects. Our choice was dictated by the nature of the problems investigated. If as experimenters we wish to control rigorously the past experience of our subjects, the task is not a difficult one when we work with lower animals, for they can be raised in the laboratory under controlled conditions. Similar control is not, of course, possible with humans. Obviously this does not mean that previous experience operates in the behavior of lower animals and not in that of humans; it means only that the experimenter cannot introduce and control these experiences to the same degree and for the same period of time for humans as he can for animals. Similarly, motivation, especially if we wish to introduce long periods of deprivation, can be better controlled with lower animals than with humans.

There is evidence that the motivational variable of "anxiety" has an influence upon problem solving. In Chapter 5 a study was presented which indicated that persons who made high scores on an anxiety scale did less well on certain kinds of learning tasks than did subjects who made low scores in the scale. Groups of this sort have been used on the water-jar problem described above, and the high-anxiety subjects did less well on the final problems than did the low-anxiety subjects. In this instance the set established in the early problem interferes with the solution of the later problem and the high anxiety motivation aids in maintaining this detrimental set. When, using anagram problems, a set was established which was consonant with the final problem, the high-anxiety group performed better than did the low-anxiety group.[19]

Motivation, then, would seem to be related to problem solving in the following manners. Obviously a certain level of motivation must be present to initiate the problem-solving activity. This level of motivation must be strong enough to resist sources of competing activities, and persistent enough to maintain the activity until solution occurs. Very high levels of motivation may produce a loss in variability of response and this restriction in behavior may result in inadequacy of problem solution. High motivation may also retard the elimination of strong erroneous response tendencies which in turn prevent the correct response from occurring.

Personal biases

It is a very frustrating experience to present coldly and logically a series of arguments, all of which lead inevitably—if one follows the laws of logic—to a certain conclusion, only to find that one's listener has reached a quite different conclusion. One may point out that the laws of logic require him to conclude that, if such and such is the case, then *this* rather than *that* must follow. Nevertheless he may insist that *that* and not *this* follows. Such a discussion soon reaches an impasse because the listener cannot, or will not, be guided by the laws of logic.

In such instances one is inclined to wonder what causes an opponent to behave so stupidly or pig-headedly. Is he simply ignorant of logic? Do his biases make it impossible for him to follow the laws of logic? Is he intentionally misusing the laws of logic in an effort to win his point? Any of these possibilities may be true, and none is flattering to our opponent.

It is perhaps difficult to believe that a person can be fully acquainted with the steps of logic and yet fail to follow them unless he is intentionally dishonest. But that this can be the case is illustrated in an experiment in which some logical arguments were presented to college students.[20] They were asked to choose the correct conclusion to each argument on the basis of its logical justification. Parallel arguments were presented, one in an abstract form and the other in a concrete form, as the following examples show:

Abstract. Some X's deserve K; Z is X; therefore:
  1. Z deserves K.
  2. Z may deserve K.
  3. Z does not deserve K.
  4. None of these conclusions logically follows.

Concrete. Some ruthless men deserve a violent death. Since one of the most ruthless men was Heydrich, the Nazi hangman, therefore:
  1. Heydrich, the Nazi hangman, deserved a violent death.
  2. Heydrich may have deserved a violent death.
  3. Heydrich did not deserve a violent death.
  4. None of these conclusions logically follows.

It is apparent that the two arguments are identical in logical structure, but one argument deals with a neutral situation whereas the other deals with a situation in which feeling runs high. In the neutral situation, 75 percent of the subjects chose Item 2 and only 1 percent chose Item 1. In the non-neutral form, Item 2 was chosen by 56 percent and Item 1 by 37 percent—this despite the fact that the students were asked to judge the arguments on the basis of their logical merit and not on the basis of their own feelings.

In this and in other types of problem solving, our personal biases may intrude themselves, and if these biases point in the incorrect direction, they may interfere with our ability to solve the problem at hand.

Atmosphere effects

Closely related to the influence of inherent personal bias is the influence of the atmosphere created by the problem itself. When we state a problem in a negative fashion, we create a "negative atmosphere"; a negative conclusion is then more likely to be accepted than if the problem had been stated positively.[21]

In true-false examinations, certain words, such as *never, always,* and *all,* will generally produce a "false" response, regardless of the nature of the question. The student has learned that statements containing these words are usually false. Of course, such statements are not always false, and thus, the manner in which a problem is stated may serve as a barrier to its correct solution.

Time elapsing between "cause" and "effect"

In Chapter 3, we noted that for adequate learning the reinforcement had to follow closely upon the instrumental response. The same relationship is also important in the area of problem solution. It took many years for medical science to discover the significant connection between the bite of the mosquito and the occurrence of malaria. One of the reasons for this must have lain in the fact that the occurrence of the bite and the onset of the disease are separated by a considerable interval of time. Our understanding of the relationship between certain physical symptoms must also have been retarded by a similar delay between cause and effect. Vitamins and their influences, for example, are relatively recent discoveries, whereas the quick-acting poisons were identified centuries ago. Such problems—problems in which cause and effect are widely separated in time—can be solved only after a systematic collection of all the data on many cases. A systematic analysis of all the data may then serve to locate the responsible factor. We may be deceived by some irrelevant condition that is frequently present along with the responsible one, and we may confuse this irrelevant condition with the true cause. At one time, for example, damp

359

night air was thought to be the cause of malaria. We know now that the only importance of the dampness lies in its relationship to the breeding of mosquitoes.

Even in simple problems a similar effect may operate. Often the solution to a problem is dependent upon executing a sequence of steps, ordered in such a way that the opportunity to make a particular step occurs only if the previous step is correct. Since one may not know that he is making the correct steps until the goal is achieved, he is not likely to know which step was incorrect until sometime later when he realizes that the goal is unobtainable. It is obvious that problems differ tremendously in the extent to which they inform the would-be solver at the successive stages in his activity as to whether the last response is leading him toward the goal or not.

Induction and deduction

From the point of view of formal logic, our solution of problems often falls into one of two classes of operation: induction and deduction.[22] In *induction* we are presented with a number of separate and unique events or instances and we discover some characteristics that are common to all these otherwise different instances and that permit us to classify them together. In other words, we *induce* some principle that is common to many situations. In *deduction* we proceed in the opposite direction. We begin with some principle and apply it to some specific situation. Thus a Sherlock Holmes might reason in the following fashion: "A certain clay and sand mixture is found only in area Y. Mr. X has this clay and sand mixture on the heel of his boot. Therefore Mr. X has come from area Y."

It would be wrong to assume that all problems can be solved only through an inductive or a deductive process. In dealing with problems—problems of science, problems of society, and problems of personal relationships—we often shift from one type of logical solution to another. By the process of induction we may arrive at a principle that seems generally valid; then we test our principle in some deductive situation. The results of our test may be ambiguous, neither clearly proving nor clearly disproving our inductively discovered principle. We may then slightly modify the principle, or we may decide that some other deductive test is necessary. Thus, through constant interplay between induction and deduction, we work toward the solution of our problem. The history of

science is filled with examples of this process: theories are developed (induction) and put to test (deduction), and this alternation
continues until more refined, more useful theories are developed
that predict with increasing precision what will occur in some concrete situation.

Once again, however, we must remind the reader that these
activities are not inevitably accompanied by conscious awareness
of each rational, logical step—nor, for most of us, are the processes
themselves channeled by the rules of logic. On the contrary; more
often than not, we blunder almost blindly in the correct direction
or we attain the solution with a leaping speed that outpaces the
stolid rules of the logician.

These terms, induction and deduction, describe processes
we may and frequently do follow in our solution to problems, but
they do not serve as psychological explanations of our problem-
solving behavior. In a sense they map out a route that our problem-solving behavior can take, but they do not explain why we take
the route at all or why we turn off into a short cut or into blind
alleys.

The human organism is constantly engaged in the processes
that are suggested by the terms induction and deduction. Perhaps
it is better to say that we tend to place specific events and objects
in broad categories of "kinds of happenings" and "kinds of things."
Furthermore, once something has been identified as belonging to a
particular category, we assume that this something will have the
characteristics of that category. For example, certain four-legged
animals are referred to as *cats* and others as *dogs*. Furthermore,
there are certain defining characteristics which can be perceived
visually that make it possible for us to place an animal in one or
another of these categories simply by looking at it. Once it is categorized as cat or dog we make inferences about how this particular
animal will behave. If it is called a cat we expect that this particular
animal will scratch rather than bite, that it might run up a tree if
we chased it, that it would purr if petted rather than wiggle its
hind end, and so on. We may describe this behavior as conceptual
and one speaks of the concept of *cats* or *dogs* or of some other systematic event in nature. When we develop or attain concepts we
acquire the capacity to identify the stimulus characteristics that
permit these variously different objects to be identified in a category. In addition, we have knowledge that the various objects or
events so categorized have many characteristics in common.

361

The development of concepts

Because concepts develop through the process of learning, their development is studied by methods similar to those we use in studying the development of simpler habits. A description of one experiment illustrates how this process is studied in the laboratory.[23] The subjects were presented with the pictures shown in Figure 10.4. The pictures were presented singly and they were followed by the response word that the experimenter had assigned to the stimuli. The subjects' task was to learn to make the assigned response to each stimulus. The situation is obviously very like the typical paired associates learning described in Chapter 3, but it differs in that a number of stimulus objects were connected with the same response word and in that there is an underlying reason why each response is given to each stimulus. The task for the subject involves not simply giving the appropriate response to each stimulus but also discovering the principle that determines this response. To do so, the subject must cease to react to each figure as a unique stimulus. He must begin to perceive that the

Fig. 10.4 Types of stimuli used by Heidbreder[23] in her study of the development of concepts. Note that although each of the stimuli differs from the others, the four stimuli that are given a common name have a basis of similarity.

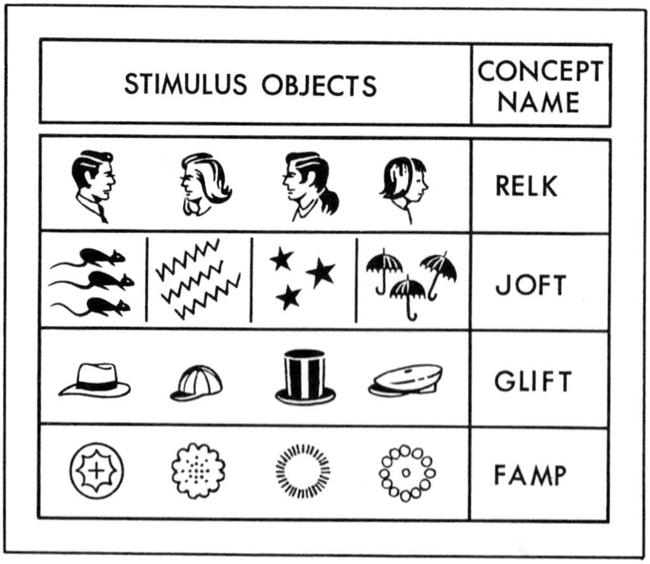

STIMULUS OBJECTS	CONCEPT NAME
	RELK
	JOFT
	GLIFT
	FAMP

TABLE 10.2. EXAMPLES OF VERBAL CONCEPT MATERIALS

Concept A	Milk	Bone	Baseball
	Chalk	Collar	Fang
	Snow	Frost	Paste
	Teeth	Lint	Sugar
Concept B	Bed	Bread	Custard
	Chamois	Flannel	Lips
	Fur	Jellyfish	Moss
	Pillow	Moccasin	Sheep
Concept C	Moon	Bracelet	Snail
	Doughnut	Derby	Cherry
	Knob	Platter	Grapefruit
	Balloon	Pill	Skull

figures may be classified by the possession of certain psychological dimensions or characteristics, and that it is a specific dimension or characteristic that determines the appropriate response to the stimulus. Thus, the four figures in the example called *Joft* must be reacted to along the dimension of *number* and within this dimension to the *specific number* of three. Similarly the four figures called *Glift* are classed together because they are *hats*.

Another type of material used in concept studies is shown in Table 10.2. All the twelve items listed beside *Concept A* share a certain characteristic in common, and the same is true of the items listed beside *Concept B*. The reader, by this time, has probably discovered the characteristic shared by each item in the three concept groups. The sense impression associated with all the *A* items is whiteness, while the impression associated with the *B* items is softness and with *C* is roundness. Similarly, other groups of words would produce a sense impression of small or smelly or heavy or nearly any other arbitrarily selected characteristic. Words from several of these groups may serve as the stimuli, and the subjects may be required to discover the common response for each group.[24]

An examination of these experimental situations may lead to a better understanding of the nature of concepts and how they developed. Each item within a concept class, whether picture or word, is different from every other item. Each item, however, shares a certain common characteristic with all the rest. In the concept *Relk* for example, the matter of sex is irrelevant, as is age, how the hair is worn, and any characteristic other than the sheer fact of being a human. Similarly, in the verbal examples, there are all kinds of characteristics implied by each word, but only one is relevant to the concept in question—whiteness or softness. In these experimental situations the subject learns to identify the significant characteristic of the various stimuli and to give the appropriate concept name when these stimuli are exposed because the responses to the appropriate characteristics are reinforced. Responses to the irrelevant characteristics are reinforced if they happen to be associated with the correct stimulus, but no reinforcement occurs to them if in another occasion they are not associated with the concept's defining characteristic. For example if the response "A" were given to the stimuli "milk" and "sugar" they would be reinforced, so the characteristics of being white and being edible are both being reinforced. However, if the response "A" is given to "custard" and to "bread" reinforcement will not be forthcoming. The tendency to respond to the irrelevant aspects of the stimuli should, therefore, become extinguished and the tendency to respond to the correct aspects should increase since this response is always reinforced. This analysis implies that the learning of the significant characteristic which defines a concept is similar to the kind of paired-associate learning described in Chapter 3. Concept learning is made difficult because irrelevant aspects of the stimulus may sometimes be reinforced and because the relevant or defining characteristic may not be perceptually obvious. Concept learning is, then, a problem-solving situation in the sense that there is a certain characteristic of a number of stimuli which permit them to be classified together, but this characteristic is not immediately obvious. It is often hidden in irrelevancies and the concept learner must discover which is the wheat and which is the chaff. This is the problem to be solved, and if it can be done, a large group of stimuli may be subsumed by a single response.

The fundamental economy of being able to group together classes of objects that have a common characteristic is fairly obvious. The subject is not required to remember a specific name for each object; instead, a single name may be applied correctly to several objects. Furthermore, if a new stimulus is introduced, it may be referred to by its concept name; it is not necessary for the subject to learn a new name for it.

A number of research studies have been conducted in an effort to discover and evaluate the conditions which determine the

ease or difficulty with which concepts are acquired. As a consequence it has been suggested that the following conditions are of
basic importance for concept attainment.[25]

The definition of the task

The formulation of a concept is greatly hastened if in his
dealings with his environment the subject expects to discern the
operation of some underlying principle. In an experiment similar
to the one just described, one group of subjects were informed
that they were to seek and should be able to find an underlying
principle that would guide their response; another group was not
given such instruction.[26] Although the materials were the same
and were presented in the same sequence, the group that was set
to find a unifying principle did so in fewer trials than the un-
instructed group. It is not at all unlikely that one reason why a
Galileo or a Newton makes an important discovery from the same
materials that many other men have seen is that he believes that
some unifying principle can be found within what seems to another
to be a heterogeneous and disorganized mass of data.

The nature of the objects encountered

The reader has probably already noted that the sense impressions of whiteness or of softness, in the examples above, are
not so readily evoked by the words in column 3 as by the words in
column 1. An experiment was conducted in which different groups
of subjects learned these concepts and other similar ones.[27] One
group learned with its whiteness concepts drawn from the column
3 class, its softness concepts from column 2, and its roundness
concepts from column 1. Other groups learned the same concepts
but with the examples coming from different columns. It was
found that the concept learning progressed most rapidly for the
column 1 type of material, next for column 2, and most slowly
for column 3. Speaking more generally, we can say that the ease
of learning a concept will be influenced by how perceptually dominant the critical characteristic is for the learner. Obviously, this
dominance will be determined not only by the physical characteristics of the cue, but also by the particular biases of the individual.

Other conditions in this category deal with such matters
as how frequently or systematically the concept instances are encountered, or whether several similar concepts are learned at the
same time.

The nature of the validation

In our daily living we are required to develop concepts under conditions that are not always so favorable for learning as were the conditions enjoyed by the subjects in the foregoing experiment. Whereas these subjects were informed as to the correctness or the incorrectness of responses almost immediately after making the responses, no such omniscient creature as a pre-set memory drum is always available to us for this kind of learning in everyday life. Parents, teachers, and friends serve this function, but they may not always be available; textbooks, encyclopedias, and dictionaries may be consulted, but we do not always make use of them. Then, too, there may be occasions when the essential characteristic has not yet been set forth in some textbook and is, indeed, not yet known to anyone. Then the discovery of a concept may be very slow indeed. Today we have no difficulty in conceiving of disease as a reaction to microorganisms in our systems; yet less than a century ago Pasteur was roundly criticized by many important and powerful medical practitioners for advancing such a concept. Some of the concepts introduced in this course may at first seem objectionable and strange to you.

The consequences of correct or incorrect conceptualizing

In developing concepts in real life a decision that a given object or event is or is not a member of a concept group may be a costly one. The oil geologist, for example, may encounter a rock formation which he cannot definitely classify as one with which oil is associated, or as one with which oil is not likely to be associated. The crucial test of how it should be classified is an expensive one—the sinking of a well. If his company is a wealthy one it might conclude that it can afford such a test; a company with lesser resources might decide to reserve its funds. In one instance information about this particular rock formation will be obtained and in the other it will not. Again, a scientist in his laboratory may be forced to make a decision whether to follow a lead or to disregard it. It could mean either waste of time or further insight into some important problem. Inevitably, the consequences of being right or wrong in classifying a given instance as an example of the concept in question will have an effect upon the acquisition of the concept because these consequences may determine whether the hypothesis will be tested or not.

The nature of the imposed working conditions

The concept material may be presented at a fast or slow rate, just as is the case with the paired associate material described in Chapter 3. And here, too, concept mastery is achieved in fewer trials with the slower rate of presentation.[28] Again, the subject may be permitted to keep a written record of his responses, and review them when he undergoes another trial, or he may be required to recall the previous events without such aids. Certainly the former method would be more efficient. In a fashion analogous to the laboratory experiments we may impose such restrictions on our concept learning in everyday life by being systematic, casual, or utterly neglectful of note taking and record keeping.[29]

The utilization of concepts

While the authors and some colleagues were on an automobile trip, a rear tire blew out. When they prepared to change the tire, it was discovered that the base plate for the bumper jack was missing. The absence of this piece of equipment constituted a barrier to the attainment of the goal of raising the rear wheel from the ground. Although it did not seem to be a practical solution to their problem, they tried to jack up the car by simply resting the jack on the ground without a supporting plate. This did not work; the vertical bar of the jack was simply pushed deeper and deeper into the ground without lifting the car.

They then searched the roadside for a piece of flat metal that could act as a plate, but all they could find were a few rusty tin cans. Then someone suggested that a moderately flat stone would serve as a base if it could be kept from slipping sideways. This, he thought, could be done if it were placed in a small hole so that the earth around it would prevent it from moving. A stone was found, a hole was dug just large enough to hold it, the stone was fitted into the hole, and the end of the jack was set on the stone. Gingerly they began working the jack handle up and down. The stone did not slip and the jack did not dig into the ground. The car rose; the tire was changed; and the trip was resumed.

Consider the substitution of the stone for the base plate of the bumper jack. What are the characteristics of base plates that enable them to be used for their proper purpose? They have enough strength to support the jack when the weight of the car is placed upon it. Their flatness prevents them from slipping laterally. A stone might serve the purpose if it were broad, strong, and flat. But if no stone sufficiently flat and broad is available, is there another way to achieve the non-slipping-laterally characteristic? When the stone was set into a hole in the ground, the surrounding earth buttressed it and prevented the lateral slipping. Thus the problem was solved because it was possible to conceptualize the essential characteristics of the complex stimulus (base plate) and find these characteristics in other objects. The strength characteristic of the base plate was found in the stone; the resistance-to-lateral-slippage characteristic was found in the buttressing support of the surrounding earth. The dual characteristics found in the base plate alone were obtained by using two objects—stone and supporting earth. This is an example of how previously learned concepts—the concept of strength of materials and the concept of stability—were utilized to solve a problem.

This way of reacting—recognizing a particular characteristic in some object and using this object to supply this characteristic in some situation—occurs in many problem-solving situations. In the two-string problem, the pendulum solution becomes possible because the solver sees in the pliers the characteristic of having a fairly dense weight. In the functional-fixedness studies, the prior use of an object in its normal fashion inhibits the subject's ability to conceptualize it in another manner.

THINKING AND PROBLEM SOLVING

It is obvious that in ordinary speech one would be inclined to use the word *thinking* to refer to a great deal of the activity that we have discussed in this chapter on problem solving. Perhaps many persons would be inclined to say that we solve problems because we think about them. We have not said this, and our reasons for not equating thinking and problem solving need some amplification.

Actually it appears that *thinking* refers to a *way of responding* rather than to any single and continuous psychological process, such as problem solving. You could be asked to think about what you did yesterday between eleven o'clock and noon. This thinking would constitute a recall of your activities of the preceding day. The accuracy of the thinking would be determined by the various conditions that influence recall—conditions we have discussed in Chapter 4. Again, you could be asked to think about what you would like to do tomorrow. The nature and the content of your thinking in this situation would be determined mainly by the nature of your motives. In either of these cases, the word *thinking* is used just as appropriately as it is when used to refer to activities in a problem-solving situation. Furthermore, instead of asking you to *think* about yesterday or tomorrow, we might have asked you to *talk* about it. The events enumerated in either case—in thinking and in talking—would undoubtedly have been much the same; thinking and talking would have resulted in the same or nearly the same products. In one instance, however, the nature of your products could readily have been observed by another person, whereas in the other they could not. The word *thinking* seems to refer to a class of responses that are abbreviated and, in a sense, private. But the private thoughts that occur at any time are determined by the same psychological mechanisms that determine the public, or overt, responses.

Thinking responses usually consist of words, and words are symbols for objects and actions. This means that, given a problem to solve, we can begin to move toward the solution by manipulating the symbols rather than by manipulating the object or performing the action. Thus, when our car does not start, we may first think, "Well, perhaps I'm out of gas—no, that couldn't be—I bought 10 gallons yesterday and I've driven it only a little since then." By means of language we have made one tentative response to overcome our problem and have, again by means of language, found that the response was ineffective. Thus, through the use of symbols, we can respond to one or another aspect of the problem, and by means of symbols again we can test out this way of responding. Our process of symbolizing permits us to explore and test without actually dealing with the object itself, to make trials and discover errors without having to go to the length of putting our trials to test.

Although in general symbolizing leads to greater efficiency and economy, such a procedure is not foolproof. The actual object may have some characteristic which our symbol does not imply, or the consequence of actually doing something may be different from the presumed consequences arrived at by our symbolizing. All this is implied in the oft-made statement "It looks good on paper, but . . ."

In summary, the word "thinking" is used to refer to a type of response, a response whose nature is not readily observed by another person. This type of responding can occur in a number of situations and it is very likely to occur in the problem-solving situation, but the two terms are not synonymous. Thinking is a broader, more inclusive term than is problem solving.

PROBLEM SOLVING, INVENTION, AND CREATIVITY

In the first paragraph of this chapter reference was made to the great technical advances of modern times, and it was at least implied that such activities as these were to be the subject matter of this chapter. Our space has been devoted to rather mundane activities, to solving anagrams and tying strings together, or to learning to call all headwear by the nonsense name *Glift*. This is a far cry indeed from the development of a theory of relativity, the creation of a symphony, and the invention of an internal combustion engine, but most psychologists would feel that the basic psychological processes are the same in both.

The great creations are usually made by individuals who have prepared themselves for work in the field and who have established goals toward which they are working. Their achievements are usually attained only after many ineffectual responses have been made, either by the achiever or by others, responses which obviously fail to solve the problem. This would imply that the correct response was not readily available, perhaps because the set was wrong, or perhaps because the correct response had not yet been acquired. Invention and creation also require far more judgmental skills on the part of the worker than is demanded for these laboratory problems. The artist and the author must make something like taste judgments, concluding that a particular word or a particular color is needed in order to impart something special to the entire product. The creative scientist may be especially able to make some judgment that activity in a particular direction is the most promising one, and this hunch—a judgment based upon very little evidence—pays off for him. The important discoveries and creations are far more complex and require a far greater degree of sustained activity and systematic analysis of the situation than does solving anagrams or tying two strings together, but in a small way these laboratory problems seem to involve the same psychological processes as do discovery and creation, and they lead to a better understanding of this socially important activity.

A REVIEW

In Chapter 2 we presented a schematic picture of how the motivated organism, confronted with a barrier to its ongoing behavior, varies its responses and, if the selection of responses is broad enough, discovers a way of reacting that leads it around the barrier to motive satisfaction. The topic of problem solving is concerned primarily with the psychological conditions that determine how our behavior will vary. The extent and the nature of this variability determines whether or not the problem will be solved. By way of summary, then, it is worth our while to consider the conditions that determine the variability of response.

First, it is important that we shall have acquired in the past a wide variety of reactions; the more we know, the more likely we are to find a way around the difficulty. Few of us have not had the experience of being baffled by some difficulty. Referring our problem to an expert, who solved it in a trice, we have been either awed by his apparent brilliance or disgusted with our own stupidity. The well-educated twelve-year-old of today can solve with relative ease many problems that would, and probably did, puzzle for long periods the brilliant scientist of yesteryear. He can do so only because his heritage of knowledge opens pathways to him that did not exist for earlier generations. Reasoning or problem solving does not consist in creating something out of nothing; it is to a great extent a process of using in different ways the materials of a prior learning. Hence, the broader the prior learning, the more likely are we to reason effectively. One of the first steps along the road to adequate problem solving, then, is to learn broadly and well.

The very essence of the problem-solving situation is that the correct responses are not immediately available. If they were, we would have no problem to solve but would simply be engaging in a routine kind of behavior. The solution to the problem comes when, in our casting about, we discover the appropriate response. Thus, efficient problem solving demands of us that we vary our responses, that we do not persist in repeating again and again the very method or type of approach which has failed us. We must in these situations be prepared to discard the approaches that produce no results and try something new, occasionally something that is radically different from our original approach to the problem. This means that we must tread a fine line between prematurely giving up an approach that may lead to solution and doggedly persisting in a method that leads nowhere or, at the most, to only partial solution.

REFERENCES

[1] Duncan, C. P. Recent research on human problem solving, *Psychol. Bull.*, 1959, *56*, 397-429.

[2] Maier, N. R. F. Reasoning in humans: II. The solution of a problem and its appearance in consciousness, *J. comp. Psychol.*, 1931, *12*, 181-194.

[3] Maltzman, I. Thinking from a behavioristic point of view, *Psychol. Rev.*, 1955, *62*, 275-286.

[4] Rhine, R. The relationship of achievement in problem solving to rate and kind of hypotheses produced, *J. exp. Psychol.*, 1959, *57*, 253-256.

[5] Saugstad, P. Problem solving as dependent upon availability of functions, *Brit. J. Psychol.*, 1955, *46*, 191-198.

[6] Statts, A. W. Verbal and instrumental response hierarchies and their relationship to problem-solving, *Amer. J. Psychol.*, 1957, *70*, 442-446.

[7] Judsen, A. J., Cofer, C. N., and Gelfand, S. Reasoning as an associative process: II. "Direction" in problem solving as a function of prior reinforcement of relevant responses, *Psychol. Rep.*, 1956, *2*, 501-507.

[8] Solley, C. M. Problem solving difficulty as a function of deviation of "meaning" of physical cues from expected "meaning," *J. gen. Psychol.*, 1957, *57*, 165-171.

[9] Judsen, A. J., and Cofer, C. N. Reasoning as an associative process: I. "Direction" in a simple verbal problem, *Psychol. Rep.*, 1956, *2*, 469-476.

[10] Luchins, A. S. Mechanization in problem solving: The effect of einstellung, *Psychol. Monogrphs.*, 1942, *54* pp.

[11] Gardner, R. A., and Runquist, W. N. Acquisition and extinction of problem-solving set, *J. exp. Psychol.*, 1958, *55*, 274-277.

[12] Hunter, I. M. L. The influence of mental set on problem solving, *Brit. J. Psychol.*, 1956, *47*, 63-64.

[13] Adamson, R. E. Functional fixedness as related to problem solving: A repetition of three experiments, *J. exp. Psychol.*, 1946, *36*, 71-87.

[14] Adamson, R. E., and Taylor, D. W. Functional fixedness as related to elapsed time and to set, *J. exp. Psychol.*, 1954, *47*, 122-126.

[15] Flavel, John H., Cooper, A., and Loiselle, R. H. Effect of the number of pre-utilizations functions on func-

tional fixedness in problem solving. *Psych. Reports,* 1958, *4,* 343-350.

16 McNemar, O. W. An attempt to differentiate between individuals of high and low reasoning ability, *Amer. J. Psychol.,* 1955, *68,* 20-36.

17 Köhler, W. *The Mentality of Apes,* Harcourt, 1925.

18 Birch, H. G. The relation of previous experience to insightful problem solving, *J. comp. Psychol.,* 1945, *38,* 367-383.

19 Maltzman, I., Fox, J., and Morrisett, L. Some effects of manifest anxiety on mental set, *J. exp. Psychol.,* 1953, *46,* 50-54.

20 Morgan, J. J. B., and Morton, J. The distortion of syllogistic reasoning produced by personal convictions, *J. soc. Psychol.,* 1944, *30,* 39-59.

21 Sells, S. B., and Koob, H. F. A classroom demonstration of atmosphere effect in reasoning, *J. Ed. Psychol.,* 1937, *28,* 514-518.

22 Leeper, R. "Cognitive process," in S. S. Stevens (ed.), *Handbook of Experimental Psychology,* Wiley, 1951, 367-383.

23 Heidbreder, E. The attainment of concepts: III. The process, *J. Psychol.,* 1947, *21,* 93-138.

24 Underwood, B. J., and Richardson, J. Some verbal materials for the study of concept formation, *Psychol. Bull.,* 1956, *53,* 84-93.

25 Bruner, J. S., Goodnow, J. J., and Austin, G. A. *A Study of Thinking,* Wiley, 1956.

26 Reed, H. B. Factors influencing the learning and retention of concepts: I. The influence of set, *J. exp. Psychol.,* 1946, *36,* 71-87.

27 Underwood, B. J., and Richardson, J. Verbal concepts learning as a function of instructions and dominance level, *J. exp. Psychol.,* 1956, *51,* 229-238.

28 Richardson, J., and Bergrem, B. O. Distributed practice and rate learning in concept formation, *J. exp. Psychol.,* 1954, *47,* 442-446.

29 Lorge, I., Tuckman, J., Aikman, L., Speigal J., and Moss, G. The adequacy of written reports in problem solving by teams and by individuals, *J. soc. Psychol.,* 1956, *43,* 65-74.

Chapter Eleven

MATURATION

THROUGHOUT THIS BOOK WE HAVE been concerned with identifying various psychological principles that we can employ in predicting how the individual will behave in a certain situation. For the most part, the principles we have discussed thus far have their roots in the environmental history of the organism. Because Tom and Dick have different environmental backgrounds, they have different habits, they perceive differently, and the goals that attract one repel the other. In this chapter we turn to the consideration of another principle—one that points to the significance of biologically determined characteristics as influencing how and when we shall behave. This principle will be introduced—or perhaps we should say defined—through descriptions of some experiments on lower animals. Then we shall see how it applies to the complex human organism.

During their normal course of development, young salamanders progress from a condition in which they are unable to move in response to a stimulus to one in which they swim rapidly about the tank. The transition between these two stages is not a sudden one, but rather it passes through the two clearly identifiable stages. The sequence of this development is illustrated in Figure 11.1. In stage 2 the animal is capable of bending the anterior part of the body slightly, while in stage 3 the response to the same stimulus—a touch—is the vigorous bending of the entire body. Neither of these responses result in actual locomotion, the S-shaped response of stage 4. The question with which we are concerned is: What factors are responsible for the emergence of

Fig. 11.1 The development of locomotion in the salamander. In stage 1 (nonmotile), the animal will not move in response to external stimulation; in stage 2, it bends slightly near the head end; in stage 3, the bending is more vigorous and involves muscles along the entire length of the body; in stage 4, muscles on both sides of the body coordinate to produce swimming. These changes in behavior are the result of structural changes in the nervous system, not of practice. The tendency for the development to progress from head to tail is called cephalocaudal progression and is a characteristic of nearly all organisms, including man. (After Coghill[2])

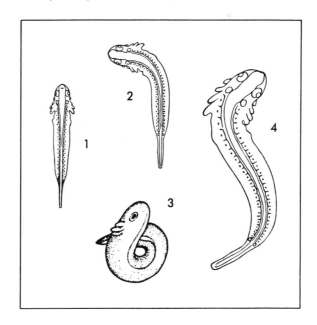

the swimming response? Is it a consequence of inevitable and biologically determined growth factors, or does exercise obtainable in stages 2 and 3 permit the young salamander to learn this act?

This question was approached experimentally some years ago.[1] Salamanders still too young to move in response to stimulation were placed in a water solution of chlorotone, a drug that paralyzes the animals, making them incapable of movement, although it does not interfere otherwise with the normal processes of growth. These salamanders remained in the chlorotone solution until they reached the age at which normally raised salamanders can swim, and then they too were placed in pure water. Within a few moments, just long enough for the immediate effects of the drugs to wear off, the experimental animals were swimming briskly about, and seemed to be indistinguishable from the normally raised control animals. The experimental results imply that the development of the salamander's ability to swim is dependent not upon practice but upon some process of growth that occurs in the absence of specific environmental stimulation.

This conclusion was supported by the findings of an anatomist.[2] He undertook the painstaking and tediously detailed task of examining the nervous and muscular systems of salamanders at these various stages of behavioral development. He came to the conclusion that the behavior changes could be accounted for by structural changes which were occurring in the nervous system during this period of time, and it was the current status of the nervous system which determined what behavior would occur. Thus, in the pre-motile stage certain connections between parts of the nervous system had not been established: in stages 2 and 3 some but not all the connections had been made; and the behavior of stage 4 could occur only because the necessary growth had been completed.

The implication of these two studies—the behavioral and the anatomical—seem clear. One experiment gives evidence that certain structural changes occur within the organism during the process of growing older, and that these structural changes are correlated with behavioral changes. This finding, together with our general knowledge of how the nervous system functions, implies that the behavior could not happen unless the structural changes had already taken place. Since the behavioral experiment seemed to indicate that exercise or practice was unnecessary for the emergence of locomotion, it has generally been concluded that the structural changes which made the behavior possible did not result from practice but rather were the consequence of the biological laws of growth that are characteristic of the species.

Later the behavioral experiment was repeated in a somewhat modified form.[3] In the original experiment the locomotion of the animals was simply observed visually and was not measured in any precise way. In the later experiment the animals were placed in a runway where the extent of the locomotion could be accurately measured. This experiment demonstrated that the previously immobilized animals were actually somewhat inferior to the control animals when they were given an opportunity to swim at the same age as the controls. It demonstrated further that this inferiority occurred only if the animals were placed in the drug during stages 2 and 3. That is, if they were raised in the normal environment until the time that stage 2 would occur and then immersed in the drug during the stage 2 and 3 growth periods, in stage 4 they showed some inferiority to the controls. However, if they were raised in the drugged solution up to the age when stage 2 was expected and then placed in a normal environment they were not inferior to the controls.

These experiments have been described in order to introduce the student to a new concept which must be employed in order to obtain a full understanding of the mechanisms that are responsible for the individual's behavior at any given moment. This concept is termed *maturation*. The concept states that there are changes in the organism which are paced primarily by its biological and genetic make-up and which are relatively independent of the psychological environment. Furthermore, the concept implies that the behavior in question will not occur *until* the necessary structural changes have developed.

MATURATION IN HUMAN BEHAVIOR

The salamander is many levels below man in the evolutionary scale, and one may rightfully ask whether a concept derived from experiments on such an animal is applicable to the human level. There are several experiments that indicate that a principle of this sort does operate at the human level.

377

One such experiment investigated the development of a form of locomotion in children, that of climbing stairs.[4] The subjects were identical twins. At the age of 46 weeks, one twin was given training in climbing stairs, but the other twin was given no such opportunity until she was 53 weeks of age. In her first test at 53 weeks, the deprived twin climbed the stairs much better than the trained twin had climbed in her first test at 46 weeks. After two weeks of training, the previously deprived twin performed far better than the earlier-trained twin had performed after five weeks of training. Since the twins were genetically identical, the differences in acquisition of the habit could be accounted for not by

Fig. 11.2 Maturation and language development. The subjects were identical twins. For one twin, training in vocabulary was begun when he was 84 weeks old and continued for 5 weeks; for the other, the same training was begun at the age of 89 weeks. Training consisted in showing the child a common object and pronouncing its name. In testing, the object was shown and the child was asked to name it. The study shows the importance of both maturation and training in the development of language. The importance of maturation is shown by the fact that, except for the first training period, the later-trained twin has a higher vocabulary on each day of training. On the eighth day of training, for example, he knows 8 words, whereas the other knows only 2. The importance of training can be seen by comparing the two children at the same age but after different amounts of training. For convenience in making this comparison, the ages in weeks of the children on their eighth, twentieth, and twenty-eighth days of training are shown on the graph. Note that when the early-trained twin is 87 weeks old he does as well as the later-trained twin at 90 weeks. (After Strayer[5])

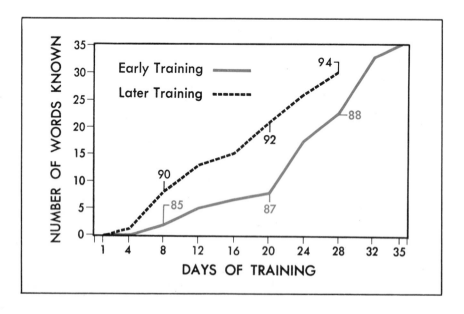

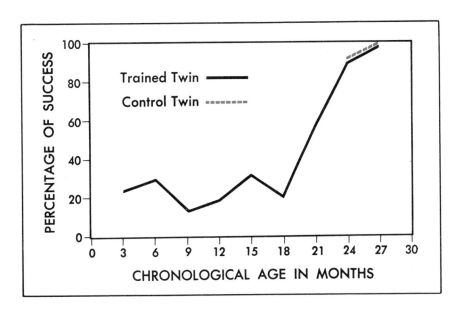

Fig. 11.3 The influence of maturation on the development of bladder control. The subjects of this experiment were identical twins. Training for one was begun before he was 3 months old; the other received no training until he was 24 months old. Early training does not seem to facilitate the attainment of bladder control, and it is acquired rapidly once the appropriate maturational level is reached. The rapid gain in control after the age of 18 months is undoubtedly influenced by increasing language skill as well as by structural changes. Since maturational rates vary from one child to another, the age at which these twins attained a high degree of control should not be interpreted as normal for all children. Because the control twin was not subjected to training until the beginning of the twenty-fourth month, data on his performance are not reported for the first two years. One may assume that his performance curve during the early months would be essentially the same as that of the control. The essential point of the experiment is that without prior training he performed as well from the twenty-fourth to the twenty-seventh month as did his trained twin. (After McGraw[6])

differences in genetically determined ability but rather by differences in the levels of maturity at the time at which training began.

A similar study investigated the development of language. Special language training was begun for one twin at the age of 84 weeks and continued through her 88th week. Beginning at the 89th week, the other twin received the same training. The results are similar to those of the preceding experiment: the later-trained twin learned more rapidly than did the twin whose training had begun at an earlier age.[5]

Several other experiments might be cited—one dealing with the development of bladder control[6] and another with tasks involving fine finger coordination[7]—but it would be repetitious to do so, for the findings are essentially the same. The child whose training begins at the later age learns the response more rapidly than the child whose training begins at the earlier age.

These experiments seem to justify the conclusion that in each case the difference in speed of learning is a function of the difference in the level of maturation. In addition, the experiments suggest that the structural changes which were responsible for the differences in behavior resulted primarily from biologically determined growth factors rather than from effects of the psychological environment.

Some experiments

Although we have briefly described a few experiments that can be interpreted as demonstrating the operation of maturational effects in human behavior, more definitive evidence has been found in the study of lower animals. An important reason for this statement is a humanitarian one: A careful study of the potential effects of maturation demands that a control group be employed and that this control group be deprived of the opportunities to learn the critical activity for some period of time. During this period the experimental group is given practice, and, later, practice is supplied to both groups. If a certain maturational level is required before the results of this practice can be utilized successfully, then the control group has not been handicapped, but if such is not the case, the experimenter has been responsible for preventing his control subjects from reaching a level of attainment in this activity which is truly within their grasp. It is primarily for this sort of reason that the most thorough studies on maturational effects employ lower animals as subjects, but there is every reason to believe that these findings have an equal significance for the human animal. So we now turn to a series of studies on the monkey, a lower animal that is relatively close to man on the evolutionary scale.

This series of studies has been conducted in the Primate Laboratory at the University of Wisconsin, where facilities and techniques have been developed for raising monkeys from birth.[8] This fact means that the experimenters are able to control the learning experiences of their subjects and to introduce groups of monkeys to different kinds of learning tasks at various ages. By so doing they can assess the importance of maturation for the learning of various activities.

Maze learning

The young monkeys were placed one at a time in a Y-shaped maze and the home cage, which is a powerful incentive for monkeys at this age, was located at one of the arms of the maze. If the monkey entered the wrong arm he was started again at the beginning, so the score on a trial consisted of the number of errors made before the home cage was entered. Two groups of monkeys were employed in this experiment, one group of 15 days of age and the other of 45. After the task was learned, the cage was located at the other arm of the maze and the subjects were required to learn this modified task. The results for the experiment are shown in Figure 11.4. It is apparent that there is little difference in the performance of the two groups, and the most plausible interpretation of these results is that, for this task, maturational factors have made their contribution by the fifteenth day of life.

Discrimination learning

In this experiment the monkeys were presented with two compartments, one black and one white, in one of which the mon-

Fig. 11.4 The percentage of correct responses by baby monkeys in learning a maze. The two groups started the learning on the fifteenth and the forty-fifth days of life. (After Harlow[8])

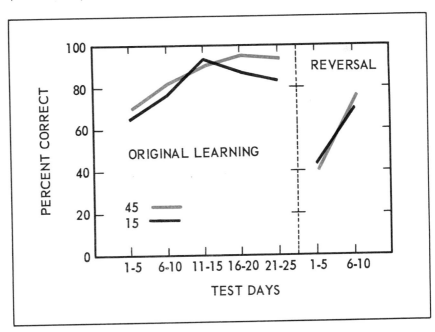

key could find a nursing bottle filled with milk. The food was always associated with the same color, but, of course, the compartment with the bottle was sometimes to the right and sometimes to the left of the starting position. Thus, correct responses required the animals to disregard position and respond to the color of the box. One group began the experiment when they were one day of age and the other began at eleven days and for each group 9 trials were given per day. The average number of trials required to reach a criterion of 80 percent correct on two consecutive days was 75.5 for the one-day group and 12.5 for the eleven-day group. We shall not dwell on the surprising fact that monkeys are capable of learning a problem as difficult as this at so young an age; for our present considerations it is significant that there is a clear differ-

Fig. 11.5 Performances of groups of monkeys of different ages on the parallel string problem. (After Harlow[8])

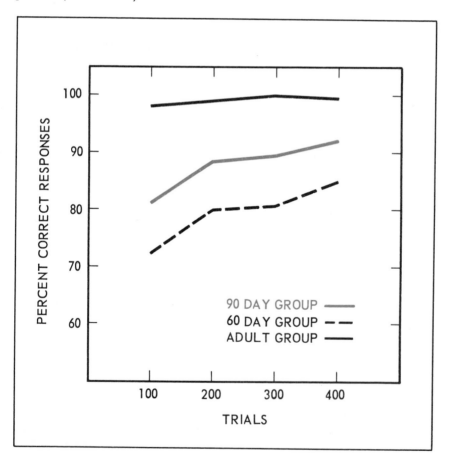

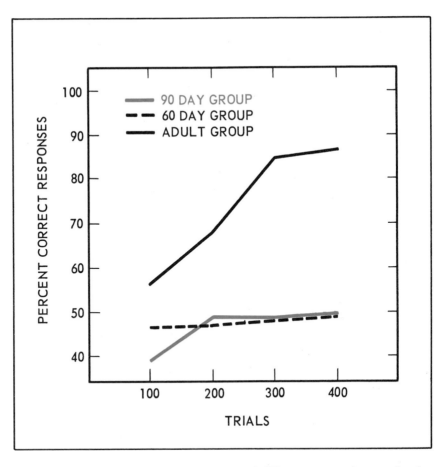

Fig. 11.6 Performances of groups of monkeys of different ages on the crossed string pattern. (After Harlow[8])

ence in learning ability between the one-day and the eleven-day groups.

String pulling

In this task the animal was presented with two strings and at the distant end of one of them a piece of food was attached. The complete length of both strings was visible to the subject, who simply grasped one of the strings and wound it in. An error was scored if the wrong string was chosen. Two arrangements of the strings were employed. For one they were laid out parallel to each other and for the other they crossed, producing an X pattern. The performances of groups of sixty-day, ninety-day and adult animals on the two problems are shown in Figures 11.5 and 11.6. Although the younger animals are inferior to the older ones in the parallel-string task, they improve consistently throughout the training period. In the crossed-string task, however, neither of the younger groups scored much above a chance level during the 400 trials.

Significance of these studies

These studies illustrate something of the complexity of the maturational variable in its influence upon behavior. They show that the mechanisms necessary for the establishment of some habits —such as positional learning—are present at birth, whereas animals of four months of age are incapable of mastering what must appear to the adult reader to be a relatively simple activity, the crossed-string problem.

The reader should not assume that there is some particular psychological mechanism for maze learning, discrimination learning, or string pulling and that these mechanisms mature at different ages. There are undoubtedly a number of psychological mechanisms that operate in the learning of any one of these tasks, some facilitating and others inhibiting the performance. The simple but important finding that level of maturity effects rate of learning does not at the same time indicate what psychological mechanisms are instrumental in producing any particular effect.

Furthermore, it cannot be assumed that the mechanisms that are instrumental in the achievement of an adequate performance have developed only as a consequence of some biological growth factor. Even though the groups of monkeys had no experience with a particular task until they were presented with it, they had been experiencing some contact with their physical environment. In the chapter on Perception it was pointed out that even relatively simple perceptual responses seem to depend upon environmental stimulation for their development, and the environment required for this development does not need to be very complex. Thus, for example, performance on the two-string problem is very likely to be influenced by what the animal has learned about the spacial arrangement of things as he moves about his home cage. We are once again confronted with the fact that environmental and maturational factors constantly interact and it is naive to consider that a particular behavior is the exclusive consequence of one and only one of these variables.

MATURATION AND THE ENVIRONMENT

The observant reader may have noticed that there is a subtle difference in the concept of maturation between its definition in the experiments on the salamander and its demonstration in the studies on twins and on monkeys. In the salamander experiments, the concept seems to refer to the occurrence of behavior at a certain age as soon as the environmental occasion that can elicit and support this behavior is presented (the animals swim within a few minutes of being placed in pure water). In the primate studies, however, maturation was viewed as influencing the rate at which learning will occur when the proper training sessions are begun. The implication of the concept in the studies on the higher animals is not that a response will emerge simply because a given stage of maturation has been attained but rather that the stage of maturation determines the profit obtainable from proper environmental stimulation.

It is only in this modified form that the concept of maturation will be useful in understanding the complex behavior of the higher organisms. We have every reason to believe that any behavior that is at all complex does not develop through maturation alone but is influenced in one fashion or another and to a greater or less degree by the environmental history of the organism. In Chapter 4 we discussed transfer, and we pointed out that what is learned in one situation may transfer either positively or negatively to a new situation. We must always grow up in some sort of environment, and the nature of this environment is likely to have some transfer effect in a later situation. Thus, although we may never practice a specific task, we may be learning something about how to perform this task through the medium of transfer of training. It is usually extremely difficult to determine which transfer effects are operating and whence they come, and to decide how much is attributable to transfer effects and how much to maturation. In the stair-climbing experiment described above, for example, how much of the improvement of the delayed twin could be attributed to practice in crawling about on level surfaces? This we do not know. Indeed, our knowledge of the general interrelationship between transfer effects and maturational trends is at present extremely inadequate. There are, however, a few experiments that indicate that the nature of the environment in which the organism is growing up may have considerable influence on the maturational trend.

One such experiment had to do with the maturation of the fear response in rats.[9] The animals were raised in the somewhat austere quarters that constitute the typical environment of the rat in the psychological laboratory—a wire cage with sawdust on the floor, a water bottle, and a source of food. When the various animals had reached certain predetermined ages, the experimenter placed in one end of the cage a card on which a striped pattern was painted. The younger animals accepted this novelty calmly and with some apparent curiosity, but the older animals seemed to react to it with fear* Since none of the animals had had any prior experience with the striped pattern, we would hardly be justified in saying that they had *learned* to fear the striped card. Rather, the reaction seems to be the result of some maturational process.

This behavior is clearly reminiscent of that of young humans, who will, at certain ages, cry at the approach of a stranger. The infants' behavior, too, cannot be accounted for by direct learning experiences, for how often are children less than a year old given due cause for dreading strangers? Nevertheless this pattern of behavior, which was discussed in the chapter on Emotions, is a fairly common one.

The same tests were performed on another group of animals that had been brought up somewhat differently. These animals were raised in the same kinds of cages, but from their early infancy onward the experimenter had inserted various objects, such as light bulbs or inkwells, into the cages, and permitted the animals to investigate them. The striped pattern, however, was not introduced at these times. When, as adults, these animals were first presented with the striped pattern that had been so effective in producing fear responses in the other animals, no fear reactions were forthcoming. Thus, for these animals there is no evidence of the maturation of the fear reaction to the striped pattern. We must conclude that the maturational process will result in the development of a

---

* By *younger* we mean in this instance animals approximately 75 days old, and by *older* we mean animals of 100 days or more. The age of 75 days in a rat would be comparable to the middle teens in man.

certain kind of response if the animals are raised in a certain type of environment but not if they are raised in another type of environment.

The importance of environmental factors is illustrated in still another experiment.[10] When newborn chicks emerge from their eggs, they will immediately begin to peck at grains of corn that are scattered about the floor. In the beginning, their accuracy is far from perfect, but after a few days it reaches a level of near perfection. Is this improvement due to maturation or to learning? The question may be tested by the simple expedient of keeping the newborn chicks in complete darkness. This prevents them from seeing the grains of corn and therefore from practicing the visual-motor pecking response. If, when they are several days of age, they are brought into the light and their performance is compared with that of animals who had been in the light since they were hatched, the usual findings suggest that both processes operate in the development of pecking. The delayed chicks characteristically perform better on their first test than do the chicks tested immediately upon hatching. Although they do not do quite so well as chicks of the same age that have been raised in the light, they improve with considerable rapidity and within a few practice trials reach the level of the normally raised animals. Such seems to be the relationship for approximately the first week of life; but when animals were maintained in the dark for their first fourteen days, their performance was inferior to that of newly hatched chicks, and indeed some of these animals never acquired this coordination.*

Modern educational theory employs a concept called *readiness,* which is highly similar to the maturation concept. It refers to the fact that children may profit very little from exposure to certain kinds of materials at a younger age, whereas they may master the same activity with relative ease at a later period. This concept, however, should not be interpreted to mean that environmental factors play no part in producing this readiness, or even that the readiness is a consequence of some single psychological variable. A child who has reached the stage of readiness considered appropriate for the teaching of reading has reached this stage not only

* A recent experiment in which chimpanzees were raised in the dark indicates that the retina of the eye does not develop normally in such an environment. The chicks who failed to learn to peck at all may have suffered from some visual defect, but this cannot be ascertained from the description of the experiment. Regardless of the locus of the disability, however, it still remains true that the total visual-motor coordination was lost.

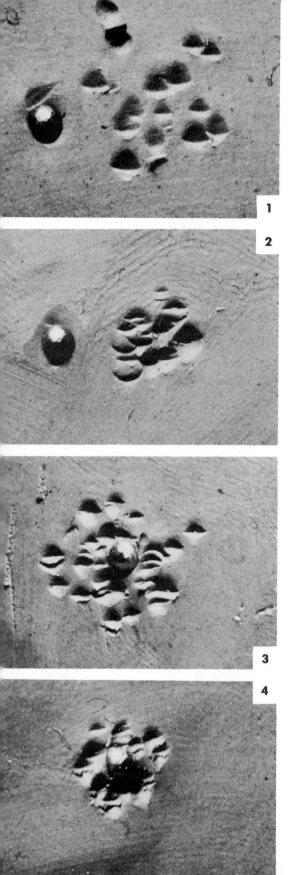

Fig. 11.7 Maturation of the pecking response in the chick. One group of chicks was equipped at birth with prismatic goggles (*see above*) which refracted objects in such a way that the chick always pecked to one side of them. Figures 1 and 2 indicate the improvement of the pecking response in the goggled chicks as they grew older. The peck pattern becomes tighter and more constant with time, even though the chick never manages to get the kernel of corn. Figures 3 and 4 show the same kind of tightening of the pattern in an ungoggled chick. On the basis of the performance of the ungoggled chick, one might reason that the improvement in pecking efficiency is learned, since the correct response is reinforced (the chick gains the kernel of corn), whereas incorrect responses are not reinforced. But the same increase in efficiency is apparent in the performance of the goggled chick, even though none of his responses is reinforced; even when the pattern tightens, he does not gain the kernel. This experiment stresses the importance of maturational factors in the development of this response, but, by the very nature of the experiment, it does not indicate that practice is of no significance. (Courtesy LIFE Magazine, © Time, Inc., and Prof. Eckhard E. Hess)

because of biologically determined changes, but also because he has learned the words of his spoken language, because he has acquired certain visual skills, because he has some rude notion about written symbols, and because he is motivated to acquire this activity. Even this is probably not a complete list of the psychological factors that are the foundations of "reading readiness." The status of any one of the psychological characteristics is obviously the consequence of an interaction between environmental stimulations and biological structure and not solely a function of some "readiness" factor which develops independently of the environment.

The chick study cited above implies another warning. It is altogether possible that we could delay too long before the training is instituted, and the achievement of proficiency in the skill may become more instead of less difficult. An example of this waxing and waning of the capacity to profit from experience may be found in the acquisition of socially acceptable table manners in nursery-school children.[11] Careful observations were made of the adequacy with which children manipulated their eating utensils and developed the motor skills which prevented them from spilling and slopping and eating in a generally messy manner, and information was obtained from the parents as to when and how they had initiated training in table manners. The experimenters concluded that there was an optimal developmental level at which to begin training in table manners. The psychological explanation for this conclusion was that children who had not reached this level did not have the proper motor development when they began learning and so they developed rather crude ways of eating; the children who had passed this level had the appropriate motor basis for performing well but they were not interested in learning the task, primarily because they were more interested in other concurrent activities. At the intermediate age, however, the children not only possessed the motor capacity to perform adequately, but were at an age at which they were intrigued by practicing such simple motor skills. Thus, the psychological variables of motivation and recently developed coordination combined to produce an optimal time for the learning of this activity.

That a skill which depends largely upon maturation may also depend to some extent upon exercise is illustrated by the development of walking in humans. A study of Hopi Indian babies, who are attached to a cradle board for approximately the first nine months of life and are thus somewhat restricted in the amount of

Fig. 11.8 A cradle board of the type used by several tribes of American Indians. Apparently the board does not restrict the child severely enough to retard his development in walking. (Courtesy American Museum of Natural History)

practice they can obtain, indicated that they are not retarded in the age at which they begin to walk.[12] Later the same experimenter brought up two children and severely restricted their movements by swaddling them tightly in blankets for the greater part of each day until they reached seven months of age. These two children were considerably retarded compared to the average child in their acquisition of the skill of walking, presumably because of the degree of restriction rather than its duration. Apparently, then, a certain minimum of exercise is necessary for the maturation of this response.[13]

MATURATION AND COMPLEXITY
OF BEHAVIOR

Although maturation may affect in some measure almost any kinds of behavior, the magnitude of its effect varies considerably from one kind to another. The extent to which various behaviors were dependent upon maturational trends was the subject of an extensive investigation using twins as subjects.[14] One of a pair of twins was given systematic training on a number of activities, whereas the other was given only an occasional test to determine how he was progressing despite his lack of special training. Some responses were found to be almost completely uninfluenced by training. These responses were the reflex patterns of behavior, which are fairly stable from individual to individual and from culture to culture. They include changes in the grasping reflex, which is present in the newborn infant but wanes with increasing age; and development of the postural response which eventuates in walking. These kinds of responses did not, as we have said, profit from special training, but other kinds of behavior were markedly influenced by it. These were the activities which are more culturally determined: riding a tricycle, roller skating, or climbing up to and jumping from heights. These activities—in addition to depending for their occurrence upon the individual's environment—are complex in nature.

If we may generalize from the findings of this study, we have evidence that there are limits to the importance of maturation in the development of behavior in humans. From early childhood, the world demands of the individual more rather than less complex kinds of behavior, and such behavior is less and less dependent upon maturation and more and more dependent upon learning. If the behavior in which we are interested is complex and is a special product of our culture—as is reading a certain language, or doing problems in arithmetic—we would be unwise to hope that time alone will produce these skills in the growing organisms. Maturational changes may cause the skills to be learned somewhat more rapidly at a later rather than an earlier age, but special environmental supports will be necessary if the skills are to develop.

The term *maturation* implies that the underlying structural changes have been produced by biologically determined forces which are relatively independent of the psychological environment. We have seen, that even in the case of locomotion in the amphibian, however, environmental factors ordinarily contribute to the development of this behavior. This is even more true of the complex behavior of the complex organism—man. For practical purposes it is desirable to employ a term that refers to the current status of the individual without reference to how this level was attained. The term *developmental level* is used in this sense. The term simply implies that a certain level of competence has been reached as a consequence of the interaction of maturational and environmental conditions, and it does not imply anything about the relative importance of these interacting variables.

THE PREDICTION OF DEVELOPMENTAL READINESS

The concept of maturation implies structural changes in the organism; and it implies further that, within limits, learning is more efficient when structural growth is more advanced than it is when growth is less advanced. If we are to take advantage of maturational influences, then, we must have some way of determining the maturational status of the individual. Some structural changes, such as growth of the bones, can be identified readily, either through external changes or by X-ray plates. However, we have no way of identifying directly in the intact organism many of the more minute changes in the brain and other parts of the nervous system. And it is these changes that are of utmost importance for psychological processes. We are thus placed in a position of attempting to utilize levels of structural change to facilitate learning without being able to measure directly the most important of these structural changes. There are, however, ways of estimating the developmental level without a knowledge of—or, indeed, any concern for—the underlying structural changes themselves.

Chronological age and developmental level

The most obvious and the simplest way of estimating the developmental level of an individual involves nothing more than a knowledge of his chronological age and of the levels of competency typical of that age. The existence of a relationship between chronological age and the development of specific skills was, of course, recognized long before the psychologist came upon the scene. The psychologist has, however, made a contribution to this general area by his willingness to engage in the tedious work of collecting the data that make it possible to plot age norms for various activities. These data tell us the age at which most children can sit alone, walk, speak a word, or perform any other specific act.

This general method for predicting the individual's readiness to engage in certain activities is used in a variety of ways in our society. The school systems use it when they require that the child be six years of age before he can enter the first grade; and it is recognized by the state governments when they establish a minimum voting age. Useful though this method may be, however, it is a very crude one, and it disregards the developmental characteristics of the *individual* in favor of the *average*. The rate of development varies considerably from individual to individual and, although at a specific chronological age one child may be just ready to engage in some activity, another may have passed well beyond this stage, and still another may have yet to reach it. A technique that can provide some estimate of the developmental level of the individual regardless of chronological age would obviously be desirable.

Sequential characteristics in development

There have been a number of studies in which the development of some specific form of behavior has been carefully observed. One may take as an example the development of the skill of picking up a small pellet.[15] Such an act may seem quite simple, but actually, when we view it developmentally, it is an activity that is fairly complex and slowly developed. As in many other responses, there are wide differences among individuals in the age at which they accomplish the act. But this to-be-expected finding is not the

393

significant aspect of the study. Long before the act can be accomplished even passably well, it is foreshadowed by other and cruder ways of reacting to the object. Some of the typical stages of grasping that precede the development of the thumb-and-forefinger pincer movement are illustrated in Figure 11.9.

We are interested at present not in the exact form of these movements but rather in the fact that they represent a sequence in time, and that this sequence is relatively constant from one child to another. Although children may differ from one another in the age at which they first exhibit one of these movement forms, they tend to progress regularly from one form to another. It is therefore generally true that if a child is accelerated or retarded in the age at which he attains one level of grasping, he will be accelerated or retarded in achieving the subsequent levels. This means that, if we know the present stage of development for an *individual*, we may predict with a fair degree of accuracy the time of occurrence of some future stage for that same individual. It is no longer necessary to disregard his individual characteristics and to use average score for predicting his performance; we may predict the individual's future performance by use of our knowledge of his present performance, provided we know the developmental sequence.

In a sense, then, we infer the level of maturation of an individual by the observation of his behavior. Then, using the fact of the regularity of the developmental sequence, we may predict the time at which the child will enter some new developmental stage.

Fig. 11.9 Stages in the development of grasping. At 20 weeks of age the object is contacted (2) but not picked up. At 28 weeks it is picked up (3–5) by being grasped in the hand without use of the thumb in opposition to the fingers, as is the case of 52 weeks (6–10). (After Halverson[15])

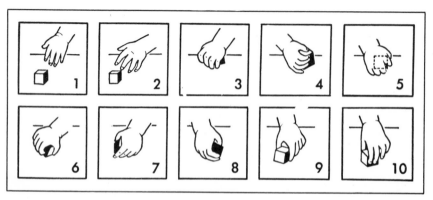

THE VALUES OF KNOWING
DEVELOPMENTAL STAGES

In any society, the primary task of the growing child is the accumulation of knowledge and skills. Most parents provide their infants and children with many opportunities to learn; they show concern if the rate of accomplishment is low; and they beam with pride when some activity is mastered. Later the child attends school, where a systematic learning environment is provided by society. Infancy, childhood, and early adulthood are thus viewed by parents and society alike as a time of learning and preparation for adult life. It therefore behooves society to provide conditions that not only make learning efficient but develop attitudes favorable to more learning.

Our knowledge of the principles of development can be of considerable aid both in making learning efficient and in producing a favorable attitude. The principles indicate to us that it may be very inefficient to begin certain kinds of training at certain levels of development, because much more practice may be required at this time to attain a desired level of skill than would be required at a later stage of maturation. It would be more efficient to devote time to some other useful activity that is more appropriate to the developmental level.

But inefficiency as defined by requiring more learning trials is only one of the less serious disadvantages that may accrue from practicing at too early a developmental level. There are other even more serious consequences which may be associated with premature training.

Persistence of inferior methods of performing

Lacking the necessary development, the child may achieve some success by using an inferior method. The success, by definition, serves as a reinforcement and this way of performing will be strengthened. Even if it is not *always* successful the habit can be strongly developed through partial reinforcement. Later, when the developmental stage that can support more proficient performance has been attained, the child may be prevented from doing so because the older and inferior method has become a stable part of his habit system.

The avoidance of frustration and failure

If training has begun at a time when success is unlikely or infrequent the child will inevitably meet with frustrations and the situation is likely to become unpleasant to him—a thing to be avoided, not sought. If such frustrations are frequent, any pleasure of anticipated mastery is likely to be destroyed and with it the motivation to participate not only in this activity but in others that are similar to it.

The entire situation may be doubly painful to the child if the overseer of the learning—or, more accurately, the failure to learn—reacts critically or with obvious concern over the failure. The child, perceiving the adult reactions, is likely to become emotional in response to this real or imagined rejection; and as he does so success in the task at hand becomes increasingly unlikely. If events of this sort occur frequently, they may affect his attitudes not only toward the learning of many things but toward people as well.

The principles of maturation do not, however, imply that we should continually postpone training with the expectation that learning will be easier the longer we wait. We know that training can be delayed for too long a period of time. We know also that the complex responses of complex organisms do not emerge full blown at a specific stage of development. Rather, they result from the interaction between maturational and environmental factors. There is reason to believe that mastery of some activity can be achieved by proper environmental stimulation long before mastery can be expected through sheer maturation—provided that the stimulation is appropriate to the maturational level and does not introduce concern and repeated frustration.

Of course, if we knew enough about the developmental process and cared enough to make our training as efficient as possible, we could present the growing organism with materials that were always at or slightly above his constantly rising developmental level. On theoretical grounds we might expect that this stimulating interaction between what the organism's momentary capabilities and the environmental demand would lead to competencies which are almost unimaginable to us now. This is the yet unattained aim of a good educational system.

SUMMARY

In the first pages of this chapter the concept of maturation was introduced by the description of a pair of studies—one behavioral and the other anatomical. These studies implied that the development of the behavior of locomotion was the consequence of structural changes which were biologically paced and independent of the effects of the psychological environment. To a certain extent it was in this way that the concept of maturation was interpreted for some years. Additional research over a long span of time has indicated the impossibility of attributing the behavioral and the inferred structural changes to one or other of these two conditions —biological predetermination or effects of stimulation—alone. We know now that we must always think in terms of interactions between these variables. An organism has the biological characteristics of its species and its parentage, but it must always grow up in an environment. The two cannot be completely isolated experimentally or in their behavioral effects.

This more complex interpretation of the forces acting on the growing organism does not, however, destroy the very important fact that there is an orderliness to the organism's growth, and the concept of development has been introduced to describe this fact without making any commitment as to the relative importance of the biologically paced and the environmentally determined in producing a particular level of development.

The concept of development implies the existence of prerequisites to learning—prerequisites that are met by interaction between the current structural level and the acquired accomplishments of the moment. If we could know which prerequisites have been met, we could define the most appropriate step to be taken next. To expect adequate learning before these prerequisites have been fulfilled not only is unrealistic but also may inflict suffering upon the ill-prepared learner. At best, it may try the patience of the teacher; worse, it may prove to be of lasting harm to the learner himself. He may develop inferior habits which cannot readily be abolished, or, because of frequent frustrations, he may acquire a negative reaction toward learning this kind of material or toward learning in general, toward his teacher or toward teachers in general.

To utilize the concept of development fully in the guidance of human performance, we must know a good deal more than we now do about the sequential steps in many specific behaviors. To return to our earlier analogy, we must know which prerequisites are required for which kinds of later learning. Thus, once again we find the ever-present need to extend our knowledge, a need that can be satisfied only by continued research.

REFERENCES

[1] Carmichael, L. The development of behavior in vertebrates experimentally removed from the influence of external stimulation, *Psychol. Rev.*, 1926, *33*, 51-58.

[2] Coghill, G. E. *Anatomy and the Problem of Behavior*, Cambridge, 1929.

[3] Fromme, A. An experimental study of the factors of maturation and practice in the behavioral development of the frog *Rana pipiens*, *Genetic Psychol. Monogr.*, 1941, *24*, 219-256.

[4] Gesell, A., and Thompson, H. Learning and growth in identical infant twins, *Gen. Psychol. Monogr.*, 1929, *6*, 1-124.

[5] Strayer, L. C. Language and growth: The relative efficiency of early and deferred vocabulary training studied by the method of co-twin control, *Gen. Psychol. Monogr.*, 1930, *8*, 209-319.

[6] McGraw, M. B. Neural maturation as exemplified in achievement of bladder control, *J. Pediatrics*, 1940, *16*, 580-590.

[7] Hilgard, J. R. The effect of early and delayed practice on memory and motor performances studied by the method of co-twin control, *Gen. Psychol. Monogr.*, 1933, *14*, 493-567.

[8] Harlow, H. F. The development of learning in the rhesus monkey, *Amer. Scientist*, 1959, *47*, 459-479.

[9] Hudson, B. B. Extinction of the avoidance behavior of rats to strange objects, *Psychol. Bull.*, 1940, *37*, 591 (abstract of paper presented at A.P.A. meeting).

[10] Padilla, S. G. Further studies on the delayed pecking of chicks, *J. Comp. Psychol.*, 1935, *20*, 413-443.

[11] Blatz, W. E. "The physiological appetites." In Murchison, C. (ed.), *A Handbook of Child Psychology*, Clark Univ. Press, 1933.

[12] Dennis, W. Does culture appreciably affect patterns of infant behavior? *J. Soc. Psychol.*, 1940, *12*, 305-317.

[13] Dennis, W. Infant development under conditions of restricted practice and minimum social stimulation: A preliminary report, *J. Gen. Psychol.*, 1938, *53*, 149-158.

[14] McGraw, M. B. *Growth: A Study of Johnny and Jimmy*, Appleton, 1935.

[15] Halverson, H. M. An experimental study of prehension in infants by means of systematic cinema records, *Gen. Psychol. Monogr.*, 1931, *10*, 107-286.

Chapter Twelve

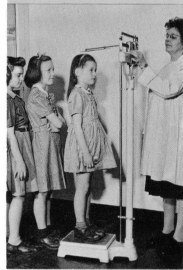

SOME
STATISTICAL
CONCEPTS

ALTHOUGH STATISTICS IS THE INDIS-
pensable tool of psychological research it has been possible in the
preceding chapters to describe most of the fundamental psychological processes without reference to statistical concepts. When,
however, we become concerned with abilities and their interrelationships, and with differences among individuals, it becomes especially helpful to use statistical terminology and somewhat awkward
to avoid them. The fields of intelligence and of personality are
particularly concerned with concepts of this nature and the student's understanding of these fields will be enhanced by the acquisition of a small background of knowledge in statistics. The present
chapter constitutes a brief digression from the subject matter of

399

psychology itself to a presentation of a few elementary concepts of this important tool of psychological research.

A great number of students become unduly perturbed when the word statistics is mentioned and they approach the study of it with the self-defeating conviction that it is a hopelessly complex and confusing field. Perhaps the hesitant student will be at least a little reassured if he realizes that statistics are means of simplifying data, and their use permits the discovery of relationships and the characterizing of large masses of data—represented by numbers —in a manner which would be impossible for the average individual without their use. The material in the present chapter will be restricted to a discussion of only a few methods of representing or characterizing data and to only two methods for showing relationships between sets of data.

THE REPRESENTATION OF

NUMERICAL DISTRIBUTIONS

The problem of representing or characterizing data may be illustrated by using the two groups of scores obtained on an intelligence test and presented in Table 12.1.

TABLE 12.1. SAMPLE GROUPS OF SCORES

Group A	Group B
108	102
98	87
89	95
91	90
100	99
86	107
107	76
99	117
102	106
94	92
92	97
73	120
98	108
70	66
84	81
96	114

Group A	Group B
111	111
68	77
104	104
117	93
91	103
79	76
107	94
80	121
83	98
121	109
114	80
81	117
95	101
76	114
106	98
88	104
94	112
86	72
100	100
97	116
99	86
101	87
85	103
110	96
103	107

By glancing over each column of figures, or even by a careful inspection of each individual figure, it is impossible to make an evaluation of the relative performance of each group as a whole. It would be even more difficult if there were hundreds or thousands of cases in each group. The material is as meaningless as the conversation of the highly verbose individual who is unable to omit any details relevant or irrelevant from his report. Just as that individual needs to learn some way of cutting to the heart of the report and giving the essential facts clearly and concisely, so also we need some way of representing and describing our data in short, comprehensible, but accurate figures.

Basically, it is for this purpose that descriptive statistics are employed by the scientist. A large amount of data is collected, and it is impossible to comprehend the many units of the data without converting them into figures that can be retained in our limited memory span. Statistics, then, are not ways of complicating data as we frequently are wont to believe, they are ways of simplifying the data. Essentially they serve the purpose of characterizing the data simply and briefly. Each statistic is something of a thumbnail sketch of the mass of the material; a sketch that points up simply and briefly a certain aspect of the collection of individual results. Just as the sketches may be made from various vantage points and may emphasize different aspects of the whole, so also the different kinds of statistics used will serve to emphasize different characteristics of the data.

Graphic description

These two sets of data may be arranged systematically and presented graphically to produce what is called a column diagram or *histogram;* this type of figure has been employed earlier in the text, but a more detailed description of how it is constructed can be given at this time. It is made in the following fashion: The scores on the test ranged from a high of 121 to a low of 66, and the total range of scores may be marked off in units of 5 along the X, or horizontal, axis. The Y, or vertical, axis of the graph is used to represent the number of individuals who made a score falling within any particular score unit. It is somewhat as if we had a block to represent each individual, with the score made by that individual on his block. Then all the blocks having a score between 90 through 94 inclusive were assembled and piled on top of each other. Next, all the blocks in the 95 through 99 interval were assembled, piled up, and placed next to the 90 through 94 tower. This process would be repeated for all the scores.

The end result is a structure which would have a block for every individual who took the test, and the structure would be so systematized that we could tell in a glance how many individuals scored within a particular interval. A histogram constructed from the data of Table 12.1 is shown in Figure 12.1. The continuous red curve which connects the midpoint of each interval is another common type of graphical representation of data and it is called a *frequency polygon.*

It is obvious that we have taken a definite step forward in the treatment of our data, and it is possible to make some comparison between two different groups by the general shape of the two curves. Actually, this is a frequent first step in the treatment

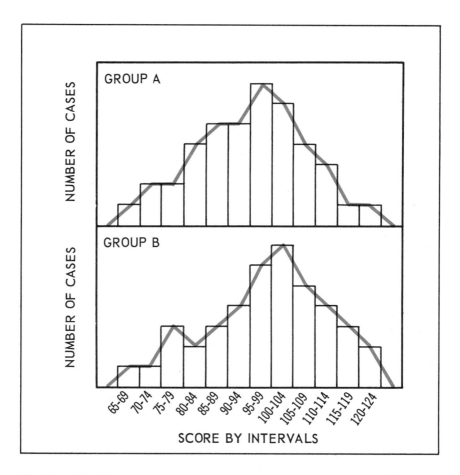

Fig. 12.1 The histograms and frequency polygrams for the data of Table 12.1.

of results, and the use of this method is sometimes enough for one's purposes. It still does not give us a very simple way of describing groups. We could not indicate the difference or the similarity of two groups in a word, and we certainly would be at a loss to evaluate the performance of the groups if we did not have the graph with us. There is a need to pick out some general characteristics of each curve which can be expressed in a simple verbal form.

Numerical description

Even a rapid examination of the curves convinces one that they have a basic similarity to each other in their forms. The most obvious similarity is the hump that rises somewhere near the

403

middle of each distribution; a tendency for the group of scores to cluster about some central numerical value. This is a characteristic that is common to most data, and the location of this identifying piling-up point provides a numerical expression by means of which one group of data can be compared to another.

Measures of central tendency

There are three commonly used statistics, each of which describes in its own way the location of the intermediate point around which the scores have a tendency to cluster. These three measures are called the *mean,* the *median,* and the *mode.*

The statistic that is called the *mean* is very familiar to most of us, although in everyday speech it is often referred to as the *average.* (In technical statistics the term average covers all the measures of central tendency that have been mentioned.) It is the measure typically used for a batting average or the average number of miles per gallon. To obtain this figure all that needs to be done is to sum all the scores and divide by the number of cases. The resulting figure is the mean. The mathematical expression for this process is $M = \dfrac{\Sigma X}{N}$, where M stands for mean, Σ stands for the words "sum of," X stands for the individual score (any symbol can be used here and where we have two distributions, we usually call one X and the other Y), and N stands for the total number of cases in the group. It is a short way of saying: Add up all the scores for this group, divide by the number of scores, and the numerical result of these operations will be the mean of the group. The means for the two distributions listed in Table 12.1 and shown in Figure 12.1 are 94.71 and 98.44 for curves A and B respectively.

The *median* is obtained even more simply. First of all the scores are arranged in ascending order from the lowest to the highest score. Then by counting up this scale, the point is found 'where there are an equal number of cases above that point and an equal number of cases below that point. The value of this point is the median. There is no summing at all to do. We obtain the median by counting *individuals,* or *cases* and not the arithmetic value of the score. Once the entire group is arranged in ascending order, we are not concerned with the value of the scores until we locate the middle score and this is the Median. An easy way to find out when to stop counting is to use the formula $Md = \dfrac{N+1}{2}$ where

Md stands for median, and *N* stands for the number of cases. Thus if we had 99 cases, the score of the fiftieth individual would be the median score. If we had 100 cases the score of the fiftieth-and-a-half individual would be the median score. Of course there is no such thing as a fiftieth-and-a-half individual, so the median score would be midway in value between the score of the fiftieth and the fifty-first individuals. Note, however, that for both the odd numbers and the even numbers the median is the value of the score such that there are an equal number of cases above and below that score. When we had 99 cases, there were 49 above and 49 below; and when we had 100 cases there were 50 above and 50 below. Medians in the example are 96 and 100 respectively for *A* and *B*.

The *mode* is a statistic that is ordinarily easy to identify, for it is the score value which occurs with the greatest frequency. It is not, however, always easy to find the mode. In distributions containing a relatively small number of cases there may, as a result of chance, be several scores with the same frequency. Because of this fact the mode is ordinarily not computed unless there is a fairly large number of cases in the distribution.

There are other cases, however, where the fact that there are two modes or points of piling up on the curve is of considerable interest and significance. If one were to measure the height of all the adults in a certain city and count the frequency of the various scores, he would be likely to find that the resulting figure shows two modes separated by a few inches of height from each other, with, for example, one at 5′ 3″ and the other at 5′ 8″. He would have what is called a bimodal distribution—two modes. If we would examine the nature of the population from which the data were drawn, the reason for this trend in the data would become clear. In a city population we would expect to draw about the same number of males as females; and the two sexes would have different modes. The bimodal distribution arose from the fact that we were combining two essentially different populations. The frequency polygon for the distribution of weights in a mixed population is shown in Figure 12.2.

The inquiring student is likely to ask why three different measures of central tendency should be considered, for if they all measure the central tendency should not one of them be enough? Or, if they each give different answers, is not one of them better than another? The fact of the matter is that they may or may not

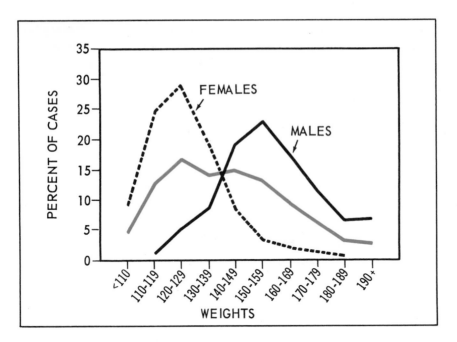

Fig. 12.2 Distributions of weight for a male and female population of average height and 20 to 24 years of age. Notice that the combined data of the red curve produce a bimodal distribution. (After data from Hathaway and Ford, Home Economic Research Report No. 10. Dept. of Agriculture)

give the same answer, because each measure is influenced by slightly different aspects of the data, and each measure may tell something that the others do not. Before this question can be answered, an additional statistical concept must be introduced.

Measures of variability

If one collection of data differed from other collections of data only in its measure of central tendency, there would be no need for additional statistics to characterize the distribution adequately. However, just as individuals differ in more characteristics than hair color, and we find ourselves required to describe other physical details in order to identify any one individual, so also do distributions of data differ from one another in more ways than in their points of clustering, and it is similarly necessary to go beyond the description of measures of central tendency in order to obtain precision of description.

An example of the yardage gained by two hypothetical football players will serve to illustrate the value of our next statistic.

The yards gained on every trial together with the mean and median gain (there are too few to make the mode desirable) for each of the players is presented in Table 12.2. The measures of central tendency for the two players are identical or nearly so, and if only these measures were known, the conclusion might be reached that these

TABLE 12.2. THE STEPS EMPLOYED IN COMPUTING
THE STANDARD DEVIATION

PLAYER A

Trials	Yardage gained (X)	Deviation $x = (X\text{-}M)$	x^2
1	3	-2	4
2	6	1	1
3	4	-1	1
4	5	0	0
5	2	-3	9
6	4	-1	1
7	5	0	0
8	8	3	9
9	6	1	1
10	7	2	4
	$\Sigma = 50$		$\Sigma = 30$

$$M = \frac{\Sigma X}{N} = \frac{50}{10} = 5 \qquad \sigma = \sqrt{\frac{\Sigma x^2}{N}} = \sqrt{\frac{30}{10}} = \sqrt{3}$$

$$\text{Mdn} = 5 \qquad\qquad \sigma = 1.73$$

PLAYER B

Trials	Yardage gained (X)	Deviation $x = (X\text{-}M)$	x^2
1	-6	-11	121
2	12	7	49
3	0	-5	25
4	15	10	100
5	-8	-13	169
6	12	7	49
7	5	0	0
8	0	-5	25
9	14	9	81
10	6	1	1
	$\Sigma = 50$		$\Sigma = 620$

$$M = \frac{\Sigma X}{N} = \frac{50}{10} = 5 \qquad \sigma = \sqrt{\frac{\Sigma x^2}{N}} = \sqrt{\frac{620}{10}} = \sqrt{62}$$

$$\text{Mdn} = 5.5 \qquad\qquad \sigma = 7.87$$

two players are practically identical in their manner of play. An examination of the individual gains made by each player indicates that such a conclusion is at considerable variance with the facts of the case. The means and the medians are not incorrect or inaccurate; they simply do not tell the whole story, and it is necessary to find a statistic that will amplify the meager description contained in these two measures of central tendency.

Player A is remarkably regular in the gain he made each time he carried the ball; no individual gain is much above or below his mean gain. Player B, on the other hand, is somewhat erratic in his performance, with sensational runs intermixed with losses of considerable magnitude. The difference between the two—which stands out clearly in the inspection of the individual trials, but which is completely disregarded by the mean and the median—is the difference in the degree of consistency of the two players. The inadequacy of these measures of central tendency indicates the need for a statistic that will be a measure of the variability of the performance, a statistic that will serve to indicate the degree of departure from the central clustering.

The simplest and the most obvious indicator of variability is called the *range*. It merely is the value of the difference between the highest score and the lowest score. For player A it is $(8 - 2)$ or 6; for player B it is $[15 - (- 8)]$ or 23. Although this measure is easy to understand and simple to compute it is not as widely used as another measure called the *standard deviation*. This measure has certain very important characteristics that cause it to be the most desirable, and therefore the most commonly used, measure of variability.

The mathematical expression for the standard deviation is $\sigma = \sqrt{\dfrac{\Sigma x^2}{N}}$ where σ—the small Greek letter pronounced "sigma" —is the symbol denoting the words Standard Deviation, and the small x denotes, not the value of any one score, which is denoted by a large X, but the amount by which any particular individual score deviates from the mean. The reader is already familiar with the fact that Σ means "the sum of," that N means the number of cases, and he will recognize the symbol for squaring a number as well as for extracting the square root. If for the moment we will disregard the process of squaring and extracting the square root, it will be seen that the standard deviation is a figure showing the mean amount that scores depart from the mean score.

The steps employed in the computation of the standard deviation are shown in Table 12.2. The first step is to obtain the mean of the scores, next the difference between each score and the mean is obtained (column x), and then each of these differences is squared (column x^2). These values are then summed and divided by the number of cases in the group and the process is completed by extracting the square root of this figure.

The reader may wonder why one should go to all of the trouble of squaring each score, and then end up by extracting a square root. It can be shown mathematically that this measure is a better one than would be obtained if the deviation scores were merely summed, but we will not burden the student with this proof.

The advantage of using the standard deviation together with a measure of central tendency as a way of describing the performance of the two hypothetical football players is fairly obvious.

Whereas both the means and the medians would indicate that the two players are essentially alike, the standard deviations differentiate one from the other. We have, in other words, moved a step further in characterizing the two players, and we have synthesized and expressed in quantitative terms the impression of a difference in variability or consistency which we had obtained from an inspection of the raw data. The above example should serve to indicate the great value of this statistic and is an almost invariable concomitant of the mean in the presentation of psychological data.

In psychological investigations it is not uncommon to discover that groups may resemble each other closely when measures of central tendency alone are considered, but may differ in their degrees of variability. An example of this comes from the field of intelligence testing, where differences between the sexes in total test performances are negligible, but where it is not uncommon to find that the males are more variable than the females.

The normal probability curve

Very often the frequency polygon that is obtained from psychological data approximates the symmetrical bell-shaped curve illustrated in Figure 12.3. This figure is called the *normal probability curve,* and the standard deviation for curves of this general shape has the following important characteristic. If one finds the score that is one standard deviation above the mean and the score

409

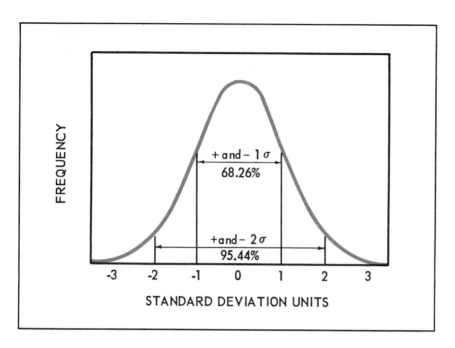

Fig. 12.3 The normal distribution curve. The mean, median, and mode of the curve are identical. The two red arrows show the span of one and two standard deviations above and below the mean.

one standard deviation below the mean, and then tabulates the number of cases bounded by these two scores he will find that about 68 percent of all the scores will be included in this area. If the bounds are set two standard deviations above and below the mean, 95 percent of the scores will be included, and three standard deviations in either direction includes nearly 100 percent of the scores. These facts are true regardless of what is being measured and what the numerical value of mean or standard deviation is, providing, of course, the distribution of scores approximates the bell-shaped normal probability curve. This fact means that the standard deviation can serve as a sort of universal language, or reference term, because it has the same meaning regardless of the raw score values.

These facts may be looked at in another way. In a symmetrical distribution of the sort shown in Figure 12.3, the mean and the median coincide and 50 percent of the scores are below the mean; the other half above. Since one standard deviation on either side of the mean includes 68 percent of the cases, a single standard deviation above or below the mean bounds 34 percent of the cases; two standard deviations in one or the other direction bounds 47.5 percent of the cases. A score in terms of the standard deviation may, therefore, be used to rank an individual with respect to the other individuals in the group. Thus, if someone receives a score which is one standard deviation above the mean he has scored better than 84 percent of the group (50 + 34); a score of two standard deviations above the mean is better than 97.5 percent of the total group (50 + 47.5). Tables are available so that scores of fractions of a standard deviation, such as 1.7, can be interpreted in these terms. It is often convenient to convert the raw scores to standard deviation units because these units have the same meaning from distribution to distribution, regardless of the absolute value of the scores in the distributions.

Parenthetically, we should add that students who have taken national college entrance examinations might be interested to note that the scores on these tests are linked to the standard deviation concept. Two large-scale programs are the College Entrance Examination Board (CEEB) and the American College Testing Program (ACT). In the CEEB the mean for each test is set at 500 and the standard deviation is 100. A score of 600 is, therefore, one sigma or standard deviation unit above the mean and a score of 800 is the maximum while 200 is the minimum—three standard deviations above and below the mean respectively. In the ACT the mean is approximately 18 and the standard deviation is 6. The maximum and minimum of this test is then 36 and zero. A score of 600 on one program would be comparable to a score of 24 in the other.

A comparison of measures of central tendency

Previously the question was raised as to why more than one measure of central tendency is employed and the discussion of the question was deferred. It was deferred because a knowledge of the concept of variability is a prerequisite for answering the question.

We will begin by reminding the reader that measures of central tendency and variability are employed for the purpose of describing a large mass of numbers; they are used, in other words, to characterize the total distribution. A distribution, however, is composed of many numbers and only a few of them will be the same as the number which is associated with any particular measure of central tendency. If, then, we use the central tendency number to guess the score of any individual case in the distribution we will err often, and err by the amount that the score differs from

411

the value of the measure of central tendency which we are using. There are various ways of measuring the error, however, and the three measures of central tendency differ from each other in the kind of error they keep at a minimum.

The mode

If one takes a position that "a miss is as good as a mile," and wishes to keep the number of misses at a minimum, then the use of the mode will result in the fewest number of errors. Since the mode has the same number as the most frequently occurring case, it will be exactly right for each of these cases and wrong for all the others, whereas it is quite possible that the mean or median could have a value which does not correspond to any single case in the distribution, and they could be in error in every instance.

The mode also has other advantages. It will be recalled that there are some instances when a bimodal distribution is obtained, as in the example of heights of a mixed population of males and females. In such a distribution the mean and the median (assuming there is an approximately equal number of each sex in the population) would fall somewhere between the two modes. Neither of these measures would represent the central tendency of the male population or the female population; they would fall in the valley between the two peaks. The total or combined populations would in actuality have two central tendencies, and the mean and the median would falsely represent the situation in terms of one central tendency which would be purely mathematical in nature and would not be very intelligible in terms of the biological facts. The use of the mode would clearly represent the biological facts, since two modes would be presented, each of which could be identified with the central tendency of one of the two groups composing the total population.

The mean and the median

If one is concerned not only about whether an error has or has not occurred but also the magnitude of the error, then both the mean and median are superior to the mode. The error in this case may be evaluated in the following way. Obtain the difference between the actual score and the value of the particular central tendency measure which is being used and add up all of these differences *without regard to whether they are positive or negative in direction*. A specific example of this would be to add the scores in the Deviation column in Table 12.2, acting as if all the scores were positive. The sum obtained in this fashion is called the absolute error. The value of this sum will be smallest if the median is the central tendency measure which has been employed. The median, in other words, results in the smallest error, when error is evaluated in this manner.

An objection that has been levied against this method of measuring error is that it disregards the sign before the number, and mathematicians do not like to disregard plus and minus signs. There is, however, a legitimate way in which these magnitudes may all be made positive, and this is to multiply each number by itself, for the square of a number is always positive. This was the step that is illustrated in the last column of Table 12.2. It can be shown that the sum of these scores will be smallest if the mean is employed as the central tendency from which the errors are measured.

Some other characteristics of the mean and median

It will be recalled that the mean was obtained by summing all the scores and then dividing by the number of cases. In other words, the value of every single score plays an important part in the determination of the mean. A single very high score would pull the mean up, and a single very low score would pull the mean down. This is a fact that any student is sadly aware of if he has dropped far down on one examination, and then received a final grade based upon the mean of all his examination grades. The mean is really the center of gravity of the distribution, and if we were to draw our distribution on cardboard, cut it out, and then find the point where we could balance the cardboard silhouette, that point would be the mean; the same point that we would find if we added all the scores and divided by the total number of cases. We all know from our experiences with see-saws or teeter-totters how a heavy weight close to the fulcrum can easily be overbalanced by a lighter weight placed a greater distance from the fulcrum, and how the neighborhood shrimp could, because of that fact, play on even terms with the big boys.

Such is not at all true of the median. It is quite insensitive to these extreme scores. In its computation one is concerned with the score of the middle individual. The value of the scores of any-one above or below the middle score is of no significance. An

413

example may serve to illustrate the difference between those two measures. Suppose we had only three scores—19, 20, and 21—in our distribution. The mean of this distribution would be 20, and the median or middle score would also be 20. Now suppose that the third score were 51 rather than 21. The median would remain unchanged, for the score of the middle man would remain 20. The mean, however, would rise to 30. Thus, one of the measures is greatly influenced by the extreme score, and the other is completely uneffected.

It is apparent from this analysis that neither of the measures may be considered more correct than the other. Both of them have their uses, though they do not have identical meanings. If for any reason we wish to minimize the effect of one or two highly divergent scores, then the median would be the choice; but if we wished to take into consideration the score made by every member of the group, then the mean should be employed. One other characteristic of the mean should be mentioned in passing: A great number of the more complicated statistical measures are, for one reason or another, based on the use of the mean, and this probably accounts for the fact that it is the most commonly used of all the measures of central tendency.

MEASURING RELATIONSHIPS

The layman as well as the psychologist frequently asks questions about the relationships of two or more conditions. Is a person who is good in his English courses good in French and in Mathematics? Is a good football player also a good basketball player? Are very bright persons physical weaklings or poorly adjusted socially? There are many more such questions. All too often the layman tries to answer these questions by singling out particular individuals and remarking that they do well in one and poorly in the other task or well in both. Yet always we can find an exception and in some instances there are many, while in others there are only a few. Thus such a technique is very crude and it fails to indicate the *degree* of relationship between our two conditions or, to use a better term, variables. There may be more of a tendency for skill in badminton and tennis to go together than skill in badminton and football, or in English and French rather than in English and

Mathematics; but the difference will not become apparent by these simple comparisons.

To meet the problem, it is well to rephrase the question to read: How well, knowing the performance or score in one variable (English, football, intelligence test) can we predict the score on the other variable (French, basketball, height)? If we can predict correctly from one to the other, the relationship is high, if we cannot do so, the relationship is low.

Graphic representation of relationship

The simplest way to determine how accurately the prediction can be made is to resort to a graphical representation of the data. We may start with the data that are presented in Table 12.3, which are the scores for the first two hourly examinations of a class

TABLE 12.3.   SCORES MADE BY THE SAME INDIVIDUALS
ON TWO PSYCHOLOGY EXAMINATIONS

Individual	Exam. I	Exam. II
A	36	41
B	35	29
C	32	35
D	38	39
E	27	27
F	27	30
G	37	31
H	18	18
I	28	32
J	42	46
K	40	36
L	20	18
M	22	27
N	22	25
O	37	30
P	41	38
Q	20	18
R	46	43
S	33	33
T	36	25
U	39	39
V	13	37
W	29	41
X	23	34
Y	34	34

415

in psychology. The individuals in question are represented by letters and the scores for each individual by the numbers after his name. It can be seen that there is a definite tendency for high scores on one exam to go with high scores on another.

These data can be ordered by a graphical technique similar to that used in making a frequency distribution. In this case, however, we must plot two variables, the score on the first examination and the score on the second. This can be done by letting the values on the Y (or vertical axis) represent the scores on the first exam and the values on the X (or horizontal axis) the scores on the second exam. Such a distribution is called a *scattergram*.

A scattergram for this distribution of scores has been constructed in Figure 12.4. The method which was used to locate each

Fig. 12.4 A scattergram for the data presented in Table 12.3.

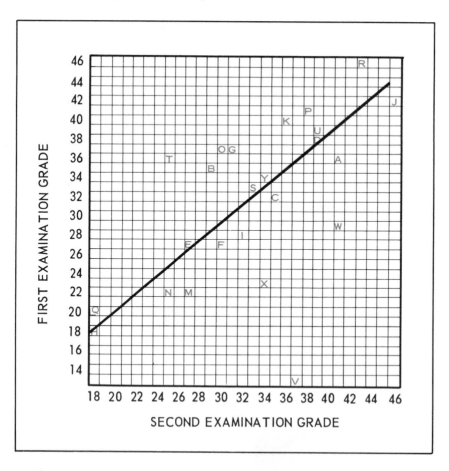

person on the graph can be illustrated by locating a few cases. Student A obtained a score of 36 on the first exam and is therefore located on the vertical level opposite 36. He obtained a score of 41 on the second examination and is placed on the line extending upward from 41 on the horizontal axis. He is located at the intersection of 36 on Examination I and 41 on Examination II. Individual B is located at the intersection of 35 on Examination I and 29 on Examination II. The same method applies to all the other persons in the group.

After the scores of all the members of the class are located, one can look at the scattergram and obtain a general impression of the degree of relationship between the two variables. It is apparent that if the relationship were a perfect one, all the scores would fall on a straight line which slants across the page as does the solid line in the scattergram. If this were true and we knew the score on one of the tests, we could predict the exact score on the other. If, on the other hand, there were no relationship between the two variables, the dots would be scattered more or less at random on the page, and if we looked at it with half-closed eyes, it would form a pattern much like a circle. As the relationship grows closer, this circle changes into an ellipse which becomes narrower and narrower until, if the relationship is perfect, it becomes a straight line.

For the present data, an elliptical configuration is obtained showing a fairly good relationship between the first and second examinations. It is not perfect, for the score of 36 on the first exam was obtained by both A and T, yet A obtained a 41 on the second and T scored 25. Other divergencies can be found in the data, though most of them are smaller than this example.

Numerical representation of relationship

Graphical representation is not sufficient for precise work so a mathematical method of expressing the degree of relationship in numerical terms has been developed. This measure is called the *Coefficient of Correlation* and is usually abbreviated by the letter r. The formula for r is: $\dfrac{\Sigma(xy)}{N\sigma_x\sigma_y}$, where x is the deviation of an X score from the mean of the X's, y is the deviation of a Y score from the mean of the Y distribution, N is the number of cases (which will be equal for both distributions), and σ_x and σ_y are the standard deviations of the X and Y distributions respectively.

A value of zero for this coefficient indicates that there is no relationship between the two variables (the scattergram would be circular); and the value 1.00 indicates a perfect relationship (the scattergram would be a straight line). Values between zero and 1.00 indicate differing degrees of relationship depending upon how high or low the coefficient of correlation is. In the example of the psychology examinations, r is equal to .63, which indicates a fairly high relationship.

We said that r can vary from zero to 1.00, but actually it can vary from 1.00 through zero to -1.00. Coefficients of correlation with negative signs have the same predictive value as coefficients of the same magnitude with positive signs. They differ in that for negative r's, a high score on one variable is associated with a low score on the other variable. This can be illustrated by an example. Let us assume that there is a general athletic ability which determines our bowling scores, our batting average, and our golf scores. A high batting average and a high bowling score would be associated with superior performance. But what about the golf scores? In this case, low scores are associated with superior performance. If a coefficient of correlation were computed between bowling scores and golf scores, a negative correlation would be obtained if there was a general ability. This would occur because high scores on one variable would go with low scores on the other. So far as the scattergram is concerned, the negative correlation would be shown by a line sloping in the opposite direction from that shown in Figure 12.4.

The reader must not interpret a coefficient of correlation to be a percentage. It is simply a number expressing the degree of relationship between two variables. A coefficient of 1.00 or -1.00 indicates that a perfect relationship between them exists and a coefficient of zero indicates that there is no relationship between the two sets of data, and the higher the absolute value of the correlation, the greater the degree of relationship.

There is one more warning to be observed about a coefficient of correlation. One should not interpret a correlation to mean that one of the variables causes the other. There are times when a causal relationship might exist; but two variables could be highly correlated in the absence of any such relationship. They may, for example, both be a reflection of a common condition which determines both of them.

And now this very brief excursion into the topic of statistics can be brought to a close. These few concepts have been presented because they will be of particular use in the following chapters. Perhaps their use in a more meaningful context for the student will produce not only a greater appreciation of their value for the research scientist, but will also clarify the meaning of the statistical concepts themselves.

Chapter Thirteen

INTELLIGENCE

THERE IS PERHAPS NO OTHER ACTIVITY in psychology for which the professional psychologist is better known by the lay public than intelligence testing. Testing, which was originated by Alfred Binet and Thomas Simon shortly after the turn of the century in the Paris school system as a means of distinguishing the dull student from the normal but unmotivated one, is now widely used not only in our school systems but in industry, in the armed forces, and in courts of law. This infiltration of intelligence testing into so many widely divergent areas attests not only the extreme social significance of intelligence in human achievement but also the signal success the psychologist has achieved in measuring this characteristic of the individual.

Despite the fact that the psychologist can construct an intelligence test that is highly useful in making predictions about the future achievement of an individual, it is extremely difficult to formulate a completely adequate definition of intelligence. A variety of definitions have been offered at one time or another, and, although almost every one of them has differed from the others in minor ways, they have all generally stressed the significance of the ability to adjust to, or deal effectively with, the environment. This is usually conceived of as an over-all ability which includes such skills as perceiving relationships, dealing with abstract material, verbal facility, and learning and retaining concepts. The reader will probably find that such a broad definition and analysis agrees fairly well with his own concept of intelligence, but he will probably wish for an exact statement. Later in this chapter, after more groundwork has been laid, the concept of intelligence will be reconsidered, but the definition above must do for the present.

We shall approach the subject of intelligence with no preconceived notion as to whether it is inherited or mainly inherited or mainly due to education. Intelligence is a characteristic of behavior, a characteristic that can be isolated and measured. After the reader understands what behaviors are measured—and to understand this he will have to know how the measuring instruments are constructed—he will be in a position to understand the studies that probe into the reasons for individual differences in intelligence-test performance.

Perhaps the reader is inclined to separate intelligence from intelligence-test performance and to question whether the test score represents the subject's true intelligence. Such a question leads to no satisfactory answer. All that can be obtained on an intelligence test is a score, and we can accept the score as indicating the level of functioning of that individual on that test. We can then ask further questions and try to decide why he obtained this score and not a higher or a lower one, and what this score means in relationship to behavior in other situations. So without too specific a preconception of what an intelligence test measures, we will turn now to a description of how an intelligence test is constructed.

TECHNIQUES FOR MEASURING

INTELLIGENCE

The most commonly used intelligence tests—or at least the most widely known—are those which provide scores that are convertible into *mental age* and *intelligence quotient,* or I.Q. These terms are familiar to anyone who has listened to the radio and read current periodicals, but their meaning can be understood accurately only if one knows how intelligence tests are constructed.

An assumption

In constructing such a test it is assumed that intelligence increases continuously with age from birth to at least 15 years of age. The use of the growth assumption permits the test constructor to validate, or prove the worth of, his test items by the simple process of demanding that each item be completed successfully by an increasingly large percentage of individuals as he progresses up the age scale. If a larger percentage of 12-year-olds fail an item than 8-year-olds—an unusual but not impossible situation—such an item would be considered an unacceptible measure of intelligence, since we assume that the average 12-year-old is brighter than the average 8-year-old. Few persons would quarrel with this assumption; most of us believe that intelligence increases from birth to maturity. Without this assumption or at least that of some systematic change in ability with age, it would be impossible to develop a mental-age type of intelligence test.

The selection of items

The first step in the building of a test is the selection of items that will sample the intellectual ability of the individual. In selecting these items, the test constructor explicitly or implicitly refers to our generalized definition of intelligence and chooses or constructs items that will sample perceptual discrimination, learning, memory, manipulation of numbers, vocabulary, reasoning, and other elements included in the definition.

The test constructor tries to avoid items that include content that will be familiar to certain subcultures of our population but unfamiliar to others. It would not be fair, for example, to ask a San Francisco child to tell what a cable car is used for and to ask a child from the plains of Illinois the same thing. It would be fairer to ask both what a bus is used for. As we shall see later, it is no easy matter to select items that are equally familiar to all of the subcultures and socioeconomic levels that make up our society. There is probably no test in existence that does not handicap the members of some cultures and give advantage to the members of others.

Fig. 13.1 Some types of material used in measuring the intelligence of children. The boy at the left is fitting missing parts into a puzzle picture. Here he is inserting a broken window, although the tray at his right also contains a number of unbroken ones. His choice of a broken window constitutes a correct response, because the picture includes an angry man, broken glass, and a boy kicking a football. The much younger child above is being asked to identify such features as the eyes or the nose in the picture before her. The girl at the left is using the painted blocks to reproduce the design that is on the table to the left of her. Her score will be determined by her speed as well as her accuracy. Tasks such as these are interesting to children and motivate them to perform well.

Another principle that applies in the selection of items is that of interest. A test which can supply its own motivation through the intrinsic attractiveness of its items goes a long way toward enlisting the cooperation of the subject. Thus it becomes a more accurate measure of what the individual can do. Particularly at the younger ages, the items should be so interesting that the child will consider the test a game and even demand that certain items be repeated several times because they are fun to do.

The standardization group

Once the items have been chosen, the next step in constructing the test is to select the subjects for what is known as the *standardization group* or *standard population*. The purpose of assembling this group is to derive from it a "normal" or "average" score for each age level against which individual scores can be compared. The aim of the test constructor is to choose a representative sample of every age level within the range he is studying. For example, if he intends to cover in his test an age range from 4 to 14, he will obtain a group of 4-year-olds, 5-year-olds, 6-year-olds, and so on through 14. Each of these age groups must be comparable to the total age-group population of the country in which the test is to be used. Thus, the test constructor will make his selection from a wide geographical area: he will have the same proportion of rural or urban children in his group as are represented in the population at large; the sexes will be proportionately represented, and so too will the various socioeconomic levels. Assembling such a group is a tremendous undertaking, fraught with difficulties. Since it is not always possible to obtain these ideal conditions, some tests are intentionally limited in scope and are truly applicable to only certain segments of the population. For example, a test may be constructed to be used only with college students.

After the test items have been administered to the standardization group, the percentage of children who pass each item at each age level is determined. The final test is constructed by locating each item at the earliest age level in which from 50 to 75 percent of the group pass the item.

A test then consists of a group of questions, the correct answers to which reflect intellectual activity, and which have been answered correctly by particular percentages of the standardization group at particular age levels. In other words, the test contains a standard group of questions, and the probability of any item

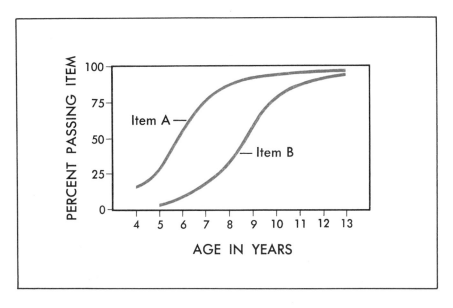

Fig. 13.2 The relationship between chronological age and the percentage of individuals passing two hypothetical test items. Since item *A* is passed by about 55 percent of the 6-year-old group and item *B* by 58 percent of the 9-year-old group, item *A* would be placed at the 6-year mental-age level and item *B* at the 9-year mental-age level.

being "solved" by an individual of a given age is known; the performance of any child may therefore be measured by this yardstick provided by the standard population.

The concept of mental age

The use of tests constructed in this fashion has led to the formulation of the concept of *mental age*. To obtain the mental age the test is administered to an individual and a record is made of the number of questions that he answers correctly. This score that he has achieved can then be compared to the performance of the standardization group, to find the mean age of the group that performed equally well. In other words, the mental age of an individual—regardless of his chronological age—is defined as the mean chronological age of the standard population which has the same score on the test as he has. Although this is the essential meaning of the mental age concept, in practice the steps employed in obtaining it are different from those we have just described, and some of these methods will be discussed later.

Mental age is to a certain extent independent of chronological age, and we may find children of the same chronological age all of whom have different mental ages. The layman, in referring to these children, is likely to say that Kenny is retarded for his age, Terry is advanced for his age, and Johnny is just about average. When he does this, the layman is thinking in terms of some ratio of mental development to chronological age. The intelligence quotient, or I.Q., is a precise expression of this relationship, which we would otherwise perceive vaguely and express loosely. The I.Q. is calculated as follows:

$$\text{I.Q.} = \frac{\text{MA}}{\text{CA}} \times 100$$

where MA is the mental age in months as determined by a certain intelligence test and CA is the chronological age in calendar months. The multiplication by 100 serves the purpose of eliminating the decimal point so that the I.Q. will be a whole number—for example, 95 rather than .95. It is apparent that if the MA is greater than the CA, the I.Q. will be above 100, whereas if it is less than the CA, the I.Q. will be below 100. Apparent also is the fact that bright individuals will obtain high I.Q. figures and dull individuals low figures.

Obtaining an I.Q.

At the close of the section on the mental age it was mentioned that the actual procedure employed in obtaining it differed from the generalized process that had been described. In this section we will present an example of how it might be obtained on the *Stanford-Binet* test, the best known of the age-scale tests. This test has six subtests at each age from year five through year fourteen; six subtests on four adult levels called Average Adult and Superior Adult I, II, and III; and six subtests at half-year levels from age two to five.

Let us suppose that the child to be tested has a chronological age of six years and two months (or 74 months) and that there is no indication that he is either dull or exceptionally bright. The psychologist begins by trying to establish a friendly, cooperative relationship between himself and the child, and at the same time attempts to make an estimate of the child's ability level. The purpose of making such an estimate is in order to decide at what age level to begin the testing. It is undesirable to start with difficult items which the child fails, because this may discourage him at the outset. On the other hand, if testing is begun at a very low level the situation may be prolonged and the child may become bored. Either of these two conditions may result in obtaining a score that is not representative of the child's optimal level of performance. On the basis of what he has been told about the child and his evaluation of him from their conversation, the psychologist decides that it would be appropriate to begin at the five-year level, and so he administers the six subtests at this level, each of which is passed. Without any obvious break he moves on to the subtests on the six-year level, where the child passes five and fails one; with no interruption the seven-year level subtests are presented and three out of the six are passed; but all the subtests on the eight-year level are failed.

The manner in which credit is given so that the I.Q. can be computed is presented in Table 13.1 below. The subject is

TABLE 13.1. ILLUSTRATION OF HOW TESTS PASSED ARE CONVERTED TO MONTHS CREDIT TO OBTAIN THE MENTAL AGE

Year level	Tests passed	Months credit
5 (basal level)	6	60
6	5	10
7	3	6
8 (ceiling age)	0	0
		76

$$\text{I.Q.} = \frac{MA}{CA} \times 100 : \frac{76}{74} \times 100 = 103$$

credited for all the subtests in the test below the age at which every test is passed. This age is called the *basal level*. Since all tests at the five-year level were passed, he is given credit for 5×12 or 60 months. Thereafter a credit of two months is given for each subtest passed because there are six subtests per year and twelve months in a year. It does not matter at what mental-age year the test is located, whether above or below the subject's chronological age, he still receives two months' credit for it. If this subject had passed only two tests at the seven-year level, one at the eight, and then failed all at the ninth, his mental age score would be the same as that which is shown in the table. In the example chosen the result of dividing 76 by 74 and multiplying by 100 is not quite 103, but it is between 102 and 103 so the number is rounded to 103.[1]

Verbal tests and performance tests

Intellectual performance may be manifested in two ways: in dealing with material that is highly verbal or in dealing with concrete materials in which the verbal element is minimal. A test composed of the former type of items is called a *verbal test;* one composed of the latter type is called a *performance test.*

Performance tests have been developed for those persons who would be handicapped on verbal tests either because of extreme youth or because they come from homes in which English is not the native language. The test items are of many types. Young children may be asked to draw a picture of a man, which is scored not on its artistic merits but on the amount of appropriate detail included; they may be required to fit geometrical forms into the

Fig. 13.3 Children's original drawings are frequently used in the measurement of intelligence. The children who produced the drawings above were instructed to draw "a man." The drawing at the left indicates a mental age of not more than 3 years. It is not recognizable as a man, and the child, when questioned, could not identify specific parts. It is more than aimless scribbling, however, and can therefore serve as a measure of mental age. The center drawing reflects a mental age of almost 5 years. Legs, arms, trunk, eye, and nose are identifiable, and the trunk and legs are in correct proportion. The drawing at the right shows a mental age of almost 9 years. Not only are the basic parts shown but there is careful detail in the eyes. Hands and fingers are shown with numerical though not anatomical correctness. There is a representation of clothing, and the juncture of trunk and legs is indicated correctly. The feet, however, are still crude; clothing is rudimentary; most joints are not shown; and much detail is lacking. Obviously the scoring is not based upon the artistic merits of the drawing.

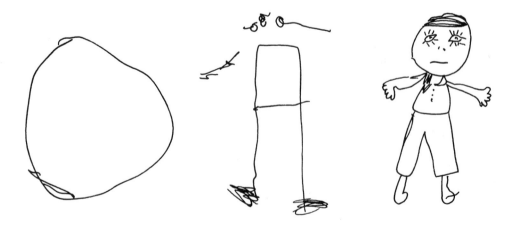

proper cut-outs or to complete a jigsaw puzzle by selecting the appropriate missing piece from a collection of pieces. For older age levels there are mazes to be traced or designs to be made out of multi-colored blocks.

In modern test construction there is a tendency to combine verbal and performance items in a single test, making it possible to obtain a verbal, performance, or total score, for the individual.[2] Ordinarily the relationship between the I.Q. obtained from a verbal and that obtained from a performance test is high. Although in individual cases there may be a difference of as much as 20 points between the two I.Q.'s, differences of this magnitude are exceptional, and the correlation between the performance and the verbal sections of an important modern test—the Wechsler—is about .65 for the age group of 7 to 15 years and about .78 for older groups.[2] Correlations of this order are fairly high and they indicate that in most instances there are small differences in the ranks people obtain on verbal and on performance measures of intelligence.

Group tests

To achieve economy of time, tests have been developed which can be administered to large groups of individuals at one time. Such is the Army Alpha test of World War I and the Army General Classification Test of World War II. Many other tests of this type have been constructed, most of them highly verbal in nature, though it is not absolutely essential that they be so. Their advantage lies in the fact that one tester can administer a test to many subjects at one time. Their major disadvantage is that one cannot be as certain of obtaining cooperation and maintaining motivation as with the use of individual tests. A sample of the type of items used in group tests is presented in Table 13.2.

TABLE 13.2.   SOME TYPES OF GROUP-INTELLIGENCE-TEST QUESTIONS

_____ In the space provided on the left, write the number of the word that is different from the other words.

1. apple 2. orange 3. cup 4. banana 5. peach

In the blanks below write two words opposite in meaning to cold. One should begin with *h*; the other should begin with *w*.

h_____

w_____

Make as many different words as you can using only the letters found in the word C-O-M-B-I-N-A-T-I-O-N-S. You may use long or short words and may include the names of persons, places, or foreign words. In any one word do not use a letter more times than it appears in C-O-M-B-I-N-A-T-I-O-N-S.

_____	_____	_____
_____	_____	_____
_____	_____	_____
_____	_____	_____
_____	_____	_____
_____	_____	_____

The numbers in this row follow one another according to some rule. You are to find the rule and fill in the blanks to fit the rule.

2   4   8   ___   32   64   ___

If the following argument is good reasoning, mark it plus (+). If the argument is faulty reasoning, mark it minus (—).

_____ All people who vote are twenty-one years old.
John Smith did not vote.
Therefore, John Smith is not twenty-one years old.

_____ John has twice as much money as Sam. Jim has three times as much money as Sam. In the blank at the left, write the name of the man who has the most money.

THE DISTRIBUTION OF INTELLIGENCE

The result of administering the Stanford-Binet to a large and representative American population is illustrated in Figure 13.4. The mean of this distribution is slightly over 100 and the standard deviation is 16. The distribution is very similar to the normal curve described in the previous chapter and we may therefore use the standard deviation to enrich our understanding of these results. One standard deviation above and below the mean spans the range from 84 to 116 and this includes about 68 percent of the total population. Within a two-standard-deviation range—from 68 to 132—about 95 percent of the population will be found, leaving only about 2.5 percent who obtain I.Q.'s below or above these values. The fact that such a large percentage of the population falls within the relatively narrow range of 84 to 116 means that most people do not differ greatly from one another in their level of intelligence.

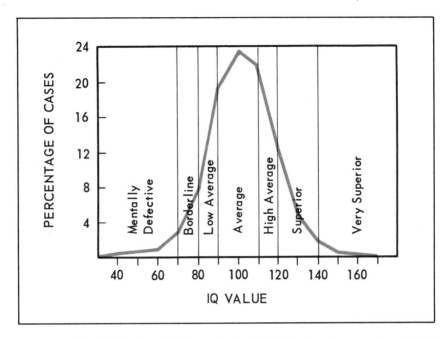

Fig. 13.4 The distribution of I.Q.'s on the Stanford Binet for the approximately 3000 subjects who were members of the standardization group.

It thus becomes possible to use the same educational system and teaching techniques for many persons, to make a movie for the many average men and women, and to publish periodicals that appeal to and are understood by most of us.

To simplify classification of subjects, the total range of intelligence-test scores is often broken down into a limited number of groups. To do this it is necessary to make arbitrary decisions as to where the lines of separation are to be drawn, just as we do, and with about as much validity, when we classify people as short, medium, and tall. A classification that is often used accompanies the distribution of I.Q.'s in Figure 13.4. These classifications are arbitrary and are based solely upon performance on intelligence tests. They have little significance by themselves unless they are related to adjustment in the social, economic, and intellectual spheres of everyday life.

A reconsideration of the I.Q.

The data showing the distribution of the Stanford-Binet scores offer an opportunity to consider a measure of intellectual status different from the I.Q. The I.Q. was introduced many years

431

ago as a short hand expression of the degree to which an individual's level of performance was below or above that typical of his age group. It was an expression that had great appeal to the professional psychologist and layman alike and it quickly gained acceptance. Careful scientific examination over the years has proven it to be less than satisfactory as the following example illustrates.

It is not always possible to develop age scales that have the same standard deviation at all age levels. Thus, the standard deviation at age level A might be 12 I.Q. points and 16 at age level B. This fact would mean that an individual with an I.Q. of 112 at age level A would be superior to 84 percent of his age group; while at age level B one would need an I.Q. of 116 to stand in the same rank. Certainly a subject's relative position with respect to others of the same age is a more significant and revealing statement than is the number that expresses the ratio of his chronological age to his mental age.

For this, and for other reasons, the psychologists in recent years have begun to prefer to base their measures of intellectual status on standard deviation units rather than on the I.Q. The term I.Q., however, has a wide currency and is at least crudely understood by so many people that psychologists have been reluctant to discard it. The I.Q. was introduced with the development of the original Stanford-Binet in 1916, and this test or its revision has been in constant use in this country since that time. As such it has become something of a standard, and the I.Q. interpretations of other tests have generally been keyed to it. In essence, it is a test with the characteristics of a mean of 100 and a standard deviation of 16 points. Through the standard deviation unit, scores from other tests can always be translated into I.Q. units, but it would perhaps have been better—at least for scientific purposes —to have formed the convention of basing scores on standard deviation units.

The reader has now reached a stage of relative sophistication about the meaning of an I.Q. He should try to think of an I.Q. score in standard deviation terminology, with one standard deviation equalling 16 points. In other words when he is told that he has an I.Q. of 130 he should translate this to mean that he is nearly two standard deviations above the mean and has performed better than about 97 percent of the population (and he'd better get A's in most of his courses). Other scores should be interpreted in a similar manner, and the reader can obtain a general idea of the relative standing of a particular I.Q. score by reference to Figure 13.4, though for a precise translation into standard deviations he should consult tables that have been constructed for this purpose.

The relationship of I.Q. to other behavior

It is apparent that the I.Q. is simply a number that the subject receives to indicate what his performance has been in answering the series of items that compose something which is called an "intelligence test." If the I.Q. measures have any significance beyond an academic or purely scientific one it must be shown that I.Q. scores are related to adjustment in the social, economic, and intellectual spheres of everyday life. We begin to answer this question by examining two extreme groups in intelligence test performance, the Very Superior and the Mentally Defective.

▶ *The Very Superior.* In 1922, Louis Terman selected a group of children with I.Q.'s of 140 or above—individuals falling within the Very Superior category—and subjected them to an extensive program of study. The study has continued through the years, and now, several decades later, we can evaluate the achievements of these adults who, as children, promised so much. But first let us consider some of their characteristics as children.[3]

They came, these very superior ones, from parents of many ethnic groups, from parents who were engaged in nearly every sort of work, from the professions to unskilled labor. But they were likely to be the offspring of parents in the higher socioeconomic levels, and the majority came from the professional classes.

There is a widespread belief that, as the result of some principle of compensation, those endowed with some outstanding ability inevitably are lacking in some other trait. Many persons believe, for example, that intellectually gifted persons are socially maladroit and physically awkward or weak. Terman specifically investigated this hypothesis by obtaining measures of physical development and ratings of health, sociability, and personal adjustment. His findings offered no support for this belief and indicated, indeed, that the contrary was true. As a group they tended to be stronger and healthier than the average of the population, though their superiority in this respect was nowhere near so great as in intellectual ability. Much the same was true of their adequacy in social and personal adjustment.

433

The most recent thorough survey of this genius group was conducted in 1945, at which time they were given an intelligence test and data on their economic and social adjustments were evaluated. The mean I.Q. for the group as children was 151. As adults they were given a type of test which did not permit a completely accurate determination of the I.Q. but which provided a rough estimate of it. The estimated mean I.Q. score for the group was 140. This represents some decline from the 1922 level of performance, but it is not great and the group still averages in the very superior class. The decline could be due in part to the lack of comparability of the early and late tests. The educational attainment of this group was high; 48 percent of the men and 27 percent of the women had obtained college degrees higher than the bachelor's. These figures are about double what might be expected of college graduates as a whole. Their economic activities centered, for the most part, in the professional and managerial classes.

Such is the picture of the very superior group to date, the picture of superior children who, on the whole, remained superior as adults. To be sure, there were exceptions—a few were drifters economically, and others held menial jobs—but as a group they fulfilled the promise of their childhood. The not uncommon picture—drawn perhaps in envy—of the genius whose intellectual candle burns at both ends only to flicker out in early manhood or womanhood is not justified.

▶ *The Mentally Deficient.* At the other end of the intelligence scale are those persons whose I.Q.'s are below 70 and who are termed mentally deficient. Although the term mentally deficient has been assigned to this group, they are by no means a homogeneous lot. The range from the lowest to the highest could be as much as 60 points, as great a difference in I.Q. points as that which separates the superior from the mentally deficient.

Of the persons in the group falling below 50 very little can be expected in the form of adequate and independent adjustment to the social and economic world. Many, perhaps most, of them are institutionalized, although there is a trend, at present, to keep them in their homes. Some of them must be waited upon hand and foot, but those of higher levels can learn to perform simple routine tasks and thus contribute in some small measure to their own maintenance. One may gain some rough appreciation of the abilities of these groups when they are adults by thinking in terms of mental age rather than I.Q. The highest mental age for them would approximate nine years—that is, such a mentally deficient adult would have the capabilities of the normal child of nine.

Of considerable interest for the evaluation of the adjustmental capacities of the upper levels (about 50 to 70) of the mentally deficient group is a study which compared the socioeconomic adjustment of a group of 206 adults who as school children tested below 70 with a group which had been classified as normal.[4] As would be expected, there were gross differences between the groups in educational achievement, with the subnormal group averaging 4½ grades completed as against 12 grades for the normals. Delinquency and criminality were approximately three to four times more frequent in the subnormal than in the normal population. These data were collected during the difficult days of the Depression, and some members of each group had appeared on the relief rolls, but the percentage was about twice as high for the subnormal population as for the normal. Although the study indicated inferior adjustment of the subnormal as a group, it also indicated that many individuals in the low group were more capable of making their way in the world than some normal individuals.

Just as a person who is very superior, as we have defined the term, may not be successful in life, so, conversely, the one who is deficient by the same definition—a score on a test—need not be a failure. This is another way of saying that intelligence tests are not perfectly valid as predictors of socioeconomic adjustment. And this fact inevitably leads the psychologist to seek more data than simple intelligence-test scores as a basis for predicting the future adjustment of an individual. And yet, although a prediction based upon test scores may not be accurate in certain individual cases, one should not lose sight of the fact that the very superior *as a group* make an adjustment superior to that of the normal, whereas the feebleminded make an inferior adjustment. That the tests do not predict social, economic, and even academic success perfectly is not surprising. Success in any of these fields is not dependent solely upon intelligence; there are many other factors that contribute to worldly success.

Statistical relationships

The general utility of intelligence test scores as predictors of success in various fields of work can be demonstrated by the correlation between the test and degree of success in various daily activities. Between school grades and I.Q., the correlation ranges from .50 to .70. For other types of activities the correlations usually do not run so high, but they are more often than not positive. A few samples may be given of the correlation between job success and I.Q. for various types of work: skilled labor .55, salesmen .33, clerical workers .35, semiskilled workers .20, and unskilled workers .08.[5]

The values of these correlations indicate that intelligence test scores have a fairly high degree of predictiveness for certain types of activities, but the fact that they are no higher than they are clearly indicates that other psychological variables make important contribution to success in all of these jobs.

The stability of the I.Q.

In the previous section we have presented a small amount of the plentiful data which indicate that I.Q. scores are positively correlated with success in many different walks of life. The studies dealing with the very superior and with the mentally deficient have indicated that scores obtained early in life have some value for predicting general success in adult life. The fact that scores obtained in childhood are positively correlated with adult behavior suggests that there may be at least a moderate degree of constancy to the I.Q. over the span of a number of years, and it is this topic that we wish to consider at this time. Specifically, the question which is asked is: To what degree does an I.Q. measurement taken at one time predict the score a month, a year, or several years later?

The first fact that must be taken into consideration is the often demonstrated but often neglected principle that nothing can be measured with complete precision. Trained workers measuring the same piece of metal several times with good micrometers do not obtain the same result for each measurement.[6] Inexactness in measurement is so common a phenomenon that the psychologist always thinks of an I.Q. as merely an approximation. The magnitude of the expected error is not very great, being in the neighborhood of 5 points in either direction. This means that when we are told that an individual obtained an I.Q. of 112 we should think of his score as being somewhere between 107 and 117 rather than exactly 112.

At this stage in his psychological knowledge the reader should not be surprised to learn that variations of this sort do occur and are, in fact, to be expected. These variations should not be ascribed solely to inadequacies in the test. Differences in level of motivation from one testing to another will result in differences in performance; but even if this is controlled, some variable in performance is the rule rather than the exception, a fact which was stressed in Chapter 8.

An indication of the degree of stability of the I.Q. over the span of a number of years can be obtained by considering the results of a study of 140 individuals who were given intelligence tests each year from the time they were 3 years of age until they were 12.[7] With data of this sort, correlations can be computed between the scores obtained at one time and the scores in other years. A presentation of these correlations is given in Table 13.3,

TABLE 13.3.   INTERCORRELATIONS OF I.Q.'S AT VARIOUS AGES

Age of reference test	Age at time of later test								
	4	5	6	7	8	9	10	11	12
3	.83	.72	.73	.64	.60	.63	.54	.51	.46
4		.80	.85	.70	.65	.66	.55	.50	.43
5			.87	.83	.79	.80	.70	.63	.62
6				.83	.79	.81	.72	.67	.67
7					.91	.83	.82	.76	.73
8						.92	.90	.84	.83
9							.90	.82	.81
10								.90	.88
11									

and a careful study of this table can give much information concerning the stability of the I.Q. at various age levels. The table is read in this fashion: The age at which the "reference" test was given is indicated along the left side of the table, and the ages with which this reference test is being correlated is listed along the top of the table. Some specific examples may help to clarify its use. The test scores which were obtained when the children were three years old correlated with their four-year scores at a value of .83. This is the entry in the upper left hand corner of the table. The correlation of the three-year test with tests on later years being found by moving across the top row. Thus, the three-year test correlates with the performance at age seven at a value of .64 and with the test taken during the twelfth year at .46. If the test at six years is taken as the reference, it correlates .83 with the performance in the seventh year and .67 with the test taken during the twelfth year. A number of interesting characteristics of intelligence-test performance can be identified in this table. In the first place it can be seen that the relationship between performance one year and the following year is rather high, but there is a trend for the relationship to decrease as the number of years between tests increases. This trend is especially strong if the reference test is administered at the youngest age. This is demonstrated by the red diagonal in the table; a diagonal which shows the correlations between reference tests and tests taken four years later, at progressively increasing ages for the reference tests. A similar finding is reported in another study of slightly more than 100 individuals who were tested first in 1931 when their ages ranged from two and a half to five, then in 1941, and finally in 1956. The correlations between the 1931 and 1941 tests was .65; between 1931 and 1956 it was only .59.[8] However, the correlation between 1941 and 1956—a period of fifteen years—reached the level of .85. There was, in other words, a greater amount of instability over the ten-year span from 1931 to 1941 than over the fifteen-year span of 1941 to 1956.

These two studies suggest that, for the population at large, there is a fair degree of stability of the I.Q., but this does not imply that changes of rather considerable magnitude may not occur for particular individuals. The three curves in Figure 13.5 show the I.Q. trends for three individuals in the previously mentioned study in which tests were given each year from the third to the twelfth. The curve labeled A is for the child who showed the greatest gain, while C is the curve for the child who showed the greatest loss. The individual letters by the curves give the actual test scores at each age, while the curves themselves represent efforts to estimate the I.Q. trends for the three individuals.

During the nine-year period the personality characteristics of each child also had been carefully observed and recorded, and the authors compared the personality characteristics of those who gained with those who lost in their I.Q. scores. The two groups seemed to differ from each other in the previously described social-ized motive—need of achievement. The gainers tended to have a high need to achieve, a need which presumably led them to work energetically, to learn well and broadly, and to achieve a good level of knowledge in many areas. One could assume that the learnings that were instigated by this motive produced a positive transfer

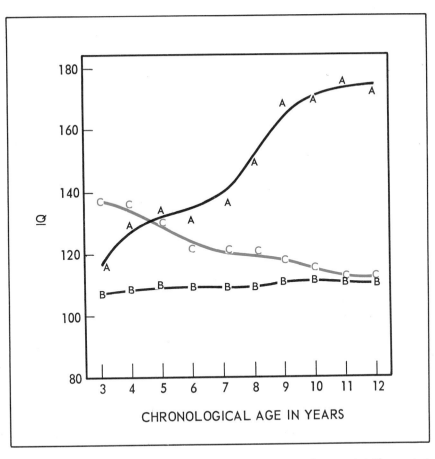

Fig. 13.5 Intelligence quotients for individuals who were given an intelligence test each year from age 3 through 12. The letters indicate the actual value of the I.Q., and the continuous lines suggest the over-all trend of that individual's I.Q. during this time span. These curves were selected to illustrate extremes of increment and decrement in I.Q. as well as one that was very constant. (After Sontag, Baker, and Nelson[7])

effect in the testing situation, and led to their continual improvement in I.Q. scores. The reverse effect would be true for those who were low in need for achievement.

This section may be summarized by pointing out that there is, for the population at large, a moderately high degree of stability of the I.Q. over time. The stability is most in evidence from six or seven years of age onward, a fact which hints at the importance of schooling as a condition for maintaining the I.Q. level. Yet, despite the fact of the moderate constancy of the I.Q., one should not overlook the equally important fact that rather large changes in I.Q. do occur for a number of individuals. These changes may be consistently upward or downward, or they may consist of temporary gains or losses. That such changes do occur should serve as a warning against placing undue weight on a single I.Q. score obtained at a particular time.

FACTORS PRODUCING INDIVIDUAL DIFFERENCES

The data cited in the preceding sections, and other similar findings, indicate that intelligence tests *do* measure something that is significantly related primarily to scholastic adjustment but also to adjustment to living in our complex culture. These data do not, however, provide information as to *why* individuals differ so widely in their performance on intelligence tests, *why* one will obtain an I.Q. of 60 and another of 160.

Thus far we have avoided discussing this question, but it will be faced in the present section. It is hoped that the reader will not draw a hasty conclusion and will instead withhold his judgment until he has read this section; indeed, until the entire chapter is read. This hope is expressed because the question of the causes of intellectual differences is of major significance to opposing political and social ideologies, and it would be unfortunate if the reader's own social biases prevented him from obtaining a scientifically sound understanding of the problem as it is viewed by psychologists today.

By now the reader has a certain degree of sophistication, not only about those instruments of measurement called intelligence tests, but also about the psychological mechanisms that determine one's behavior. We will use this knowledge in our initial effort to answer the question at hand.

The intelligence measure

It is clear that an I.Q. is simply a way of describing an individual's performance on a certain group of items that have been devised or collected and then standardized by the test constructor. Furthermore, the items employed seem to demand, by their very nature, the employment of intellectual skill for their solution; a conclusion which is supported by the fact that only those items which elicit better performance with increasing age are retained by the test constructors. It is, therefore, pertinent to ask what kinds of psychological mechanisms could influence performances on such a task.

Transfer effects and intelligence tests

Since the test constructor makes a special effort to devise materials of his own, and since the exact contents of intelligence tests seldom appear in the various media of mass communication, the usual test-taking subject is confronted with material which may be similar to, but is not likely to be *identical* with, anything that he has previously encountered. Whatever contributions his past experiences may make to his performance must therefore come through the operations of the mechanisms of transfer of training, and we know that the contribution of transfer effects to any current performance may be considerable. The beneficial influence of transfer was spectacularly illustrated by the monkeys who became increasingly adept at learning new discriminations as a result of previous training on discrimination problems; it was illustrated also by the increased proficiency shown in a problem-solving situation by chimpanzees when they had been given an opportunity to handle sticks. Examples of transfer effects are legion and they may be either positive or negative in character. Since in any culture individuals will differ in the nature and the richness of their intellectual experiences, individuals will always differ from each other in intelligence-test performance because of the persisting effects of environmental differences.

Motivation and test performance

In Chapters 2 and 5 we stressed the intimacy of the relationship between learning and motivation. We found that the direction of motivation will determine the kinds of problems that will be met. In addition, the level of motivation will determine in part whether or not the problems will be solved. Thus the nature and strength of motives will influence the amount and kinds of learnings available for transfer. The fact that groups of subjects who contrast with each other in the directional trend of their I.Q.'s over the years also differ in the strengths of their needs of achievement points to the significance of motivation as a determinant of the I.Q. level.

441

Many motives are learned, acquired from the values of the parents and from the values of the social class with which the parents identify themselves. Once again environment steps in to influence intelligence-test performance. It does so not merely by its immediate effect in the testing situation, but also by determining what knowledges and what depths of knowledge the subject will bring to the test situation.

In the light of our present knowledge and sophistication it should be apparent that it is ridiculous to assume that performances on intelligence tests are not influenced by environmental forces, forces which operate at the time of the testing and which have been operating since early infancy to lay the groundwork for the day's performance. Nevertheless, in the early years of intelligence testing in this country, there was a general feeling among psychologists that these tests were somehow probing unerringly into the very genetic structure of the individual, and that differences in test scores between two individuals reflected differences in their respective genetic structures. Psychologists supported this interpretation by showing that both feeblemindedness and genius "run in families" and that parents and children tend to be like one another.

Soon, however, studies began to be published which threw doubt upon the validity of this extreme hereditarian point of view. Somewhat typical of these studies was one conducted on children whose parents operated the canal boats in England.[9] The only homes these children had were the canal boats, and since they were continually shuttling back and forth between the midland industrial cities and the seaports, they had little opportunity to attend school. When these children were tested by a standard intelligence test and the mean I.Q. for each age computed, it was found that the mean became progressively lower with increase in age. This tendency, coupled with an environment that lacked the intellectual stimulation afforded by school, obviously suggested a strong environmental influence on test performance. Similar studies in this country on mountain children in parts of the South corroborated this study.

The intelligence-test data obtained from World War I draftees demonstrated that the mean I.Q. of the citizens of the various states was closely related to the quality of the educational facilities that the state provided for its citizens. No psychologist was surprised to learn that the same relationship was rediscovered in World War II.[10]

Hereditary influences

There is so great an abundance of evidence, both theoretical and empirical, of the great importance of environmental factors as a determinant of intelligence-test performance that it seems unnecessary to belabor the point any longer. We will, therefore, turn now to some studies which demonstrate that heredity, too, plays a part. These are studies in which an effort has been made to vary the degree of genetic, and/or environmental, similarity of the subjects and to measure how intelligence-test performances correlate with these variations.

Usually, these measurements have been obtained by comparing the correlations arrived at between the paired groups of subjects (a) who vary in the degree of genetic similarity, but are raised in the same general environment and (b) who have the same genetic make-up, but are raised in different environments. Table 13.4 presents the correlations for various combinations of genetic

TABLE 13.4. CORRELATIONS ON INTELLECTUAL TASKS OF
INDIVIDUALS OF DIFFERENT DEGREES OF GENETIC SIMILARITY

Nature of the test	Identicals reared together	Identicals reared apart	Non-identicals reared together	Sib-lings reared together	Sib-lings reared apart	Foster chil-dren
Group intelligence	.94	.77	.54	.51	.44	.28
Individual intelligence	.92	.84	.53	.49	.46	.25
Reading and spelling	.94	.65	.91	.85	.49	.55
Arithmetic	.86	.72	.75	.77	.56	.48

and environmental similarities on two kinds of intelligence tests, and on tests of specific skills.[11]

Identical twins, it will be recalled, develop from the same sperm and ovum and are, therefore, genetically identical to each other. If intelligence-test performance were a function of genetic forces only then the values of the correlations in columns 1 and 2 should be essentially the same. The fact that the correlations in column 2 are consistently lower than those in column 1 attests to the influence of environment on intelligence-test performance. The genetic effects can be inferred from contrasting column 2 with

443

column 5. Siblings, meaning brother and brother, sister and sister, or brother and sister, bear only a moderate degree of genetic similarity to each other. For the columns under consideration these siblings have also been reared apart and so comparison between columns 2 and 5 gives some measure of the influence of genetic factors. It is quite apparent that identical twins raised in different environments resemble each other more than do siblings raised in different environments.

One other column should be discussed, column 6. Here we are dealing with children who are unrelated to each other genetically, but who are raised in the same physical environment. They resemble each other in their test performances, but not so closely as do siblings who are brought up together.

There is, of course, much more information that can be obtained from this table, and the interested student is urged to examine it further. It is, for example, intriguing to compare the correlations for the intelligence tests with those for the tests measuring accomplishment in reading and in arithmetic. The comparisons suggest that intelligence-test performance is somewhat more free of specific environmental effects than are these scholastic skills.

A word of warning concerning the data of this table is in order. On the surface they seem to represent the results of rather pure ways of measuring the separate effects of environment and heredity upon intelligence-test performance; but upon more careful consideration it should become apparent that this is not likely to be the case. Children of the same parents who are reared apart are likely to be placed in their separate homes by social workers or to find their ways into them through the mediation of their relatives or friends of their parents. These facts make it most likely that the children will be placed in homes of a similar social class, even if they are widely separated geographically. Thus, differences in homes do not of necessity—indeed are not likely—to mean contrasting or even unrelated environments so far as degree of intellectual stimulation is concerned. On the other hand, being brought up in the same home, does not, by any manner or means, imply having the same psychological environment. This environment is supplied by the parents, real or foster. Perhaps real parents, believing in at least some genetic determination of behavior, tend to have the same expectations of all of their children. The same beliefs might lead foster parents to treat each foster child in a somewhat different fashion; they expect different things of each child because they know they come of different genetic stock. These studies, then, must be interpreted as offering evidence that both environmental and genetic factors contribute to intelligence-test performance, but they cannot be used to obtain a precise estimate of the contribution which either of these variables make to test performance.

Actually we have learned from a wide variety of studies that we cannot discover how much of a person's I.Q. is due to his heredity and how much is due to his environment. All that we can determine even approximately is the proportion of the differences in I.Q. *among a specific group of people* that may be accounted for by differences in environmental opportunity. The phrase "specific group of people" should be noted carefully, for the answer will not necessarily be the same in one group as in another. If all the subjects of our group came from a single upper-middle-class suburb, all attended the same school system, all belonged to similar informal groups or clubs, and all had parents whose work, interests, and goals were similar to those of the other parents, the environments of these children would be so similar that genetic constitution would play a heavy role in producing differences in I.Q. among them. Now suppose that the environmental base were broader and the group included children from good and poor school systems, children whose usual play group was the corner gang as well as those playing in community or parent-sponsored groups, and children from families in which parental education and aspiration for the children were low as well as families in which they were high. The relative contributions of heredity and environment to the differences in I.Q. among the members of such a group as this would undoubtedly differ from those for the first group.

The structure of intelligence

In the opening paragraphs of this chapter a very general definition of intelligence was given, and it was stated that the concept referred to a variety of skills, such as perceiving relationships, dealing with abstract material, verbal fluency, skill with numbers, and the learning and manipulation of concepts. These activities obviously have different psychological foundations and it is pertinent to ask whether the concept of intelligence implies that they are perfectly correlated with each other or whether there is some degree of independence among them. If they were perfectly correlated with each other, one would find that an individual who obtained a high score in one of these activities would be equally high in all the others, and the same relationship would hold for individuals with moderate or poor levels of performance. If they were independent abilities, however, an individual who scored high in one activity might score high, medium, or low in any of the others.[12]

This question is one upon which American and British workers have in the past disagreed. The British have been inclined towards the view of a general ability and the Americans have favored the view of independence among the abilities or factors that contribute to over-all test performance. The means by which these divergent interpretations have been tested involved the use of statistical procedures that are far too complex to be presented in this text, and only a general summary of the findings will be presented. The truth seems to be somewhere between the two extreme positions of a broadly inclusive general ability and a relatively small group of completely independent abilities. There is no doubt that perfect correlations between performances in different intellectual areas are lacking and this disproves the extreme general-ability position. On the other hand, it can be demonstrated that though individuals differ in relative standings in the different areas of intellectual function, there does tend to be a consistent positive correlation between the various areas. This fact is best interpreted as implying that there is a certain amount of common general ability which underlies the performance in each of the partially independent intellectual areas. The problem is more complex than this brief discussion implies, and yet, through the use of certain advanced statistical techniques, it can be tackled with a fairly high degree of precision.

VARIATION IN INTELLIGENCE

Intelligence can be shown to be related to a number of physical and cultural factors. Although these relationships are fairly stable, no one of them alone nor any combination of them is sufficiently precise to permit accurate estimate of the intelligence of an individual. Moreover, although these relationships are clear, they are not necessarily causal. Above-average physical status, for example, tends to accompany above-average intelligence, but neither one is necessarily the cause of the other.

Socioeconomic status

Many studies have discovered a marked relationship between socioeconomic status and intelligence-test performance.
Members of the professions will average highest in intelligence;
next come business managers and executives; and so on down to
semi-skilled laborers and finally unskilled laborers. In one study in
which a number of different intelligence tests were administered
to children coming from various socioeconomic classes the experimenters found correlations ranging from .20 to .43 (depending
upon the test employed) between the socioeconomic level of the
parents and the test performance of the child.[13]

Although it has been fairly well established that the higher
socioeconomic levels *as a group* are superior to the lower levels *as
a group,* one must never lose sight of the fact that there is a great
amount of overlap between the groups in level of test performance. This means that many *individuals* in the lower socioeconomic
levels are superior to many *individuals* in the higher socioeconomic
levels. In short, one cannot predict with much confidence what the
intelligence of an individual is by knowing the socioeconomic level
of the parents.

Differences between socioeconomic levels are found with
consistency, but it is most difficult to determine the extent to which
these differences should be attributed to environmental rather than
to hereditary factors. In the preceding section of this chapter some
of the many and subtle ways in which environmental forces contribute to intelligence-test performance were spelled out, and there
is little doubt that these forces work against the lower socioeconomic levels and in favor of the higher levels. In contrast with
children raised in homes of lower socioeconomic levels, the children who come from the higher levels are more amply supplied
with the material goods that stimulate them intellectually, and
their better-educated parents are more prone to express and instill
in the children a value system that favors doing the things that
transfer positively to the intelligence-test situation. There is an
abundance of experimental evidence which suggests that a very
large proportion of these differences should be attributed to the
environmental characteristics which are associated with different
economic levels in our culture, but space does not permit their
presentation.[14] It seems not at all unlikely that genetic factors may

also be involved, but it is quite probable that they do not contribute as much to the production of these oft-discovered differences as do environmental forces.

Physical status

Physical status is, of course, closely related to the adequacy of nutrition, and this, in turn, to the socioeconomic level. And the relationship between I.Q. and socioeconomic level may cause some studies to show a closer relationship between I.Q. and physical status than is truly the case. However, in a study conducted on school children with a relatively homogeneous socioeconomic background, a slight positive relationship was found between test performance and such physical variables as height, weight, and bone development.[15] Those who were advanced intellectually tended to be accelerated in physical development. The relationship shown in this study was so slight, however, that one is not justified in judging the intelligence of any individual on the basis of his physique.

Sex

Of the many existing studies that compare one sex with the other in intelligence-test performance, none shows a consistent tendency for one sex to excel the other in total test performance. When *total* test performance is disregarded and the sexes are compared on individual subtests, differences do appear. The nature of these differences is rather constant: it indicates superiority of the female on subtests that depend largely upon the verbal element, and superiority of the male on tests involving mathematics. These results can be accounted for almost completely in environmental terms; males are expected to excel in mechanical and mathematical activities and females are expected to become adept at the social skills—which involve conversation.[16]

The astute reader will recognize how the facts presented above could be used to produce an intelligence test that favored one sex or the other. A test heavily loaded with quantitative or mathematical concepts would favor the males, whereas a test lacking these and emphasizing the verbal would favor the females. This poses the knotty question of what the proper proportion of these different kinds of items should be. Most test constructors have discarded subtests which strongly favor one sex and so it is not surprising that the two sexes score about equally on total test performance. It follows that the fact that they do so cannot be cited as unequivocable support for the belief that the two sexes are equal in their intellectual abilities. The justification for such a belief—and it is certainly the predominant one among psychologists—is the fact that on most subtests the two sexes perform about equally. It is this finding that has persuaded the test constructors to discard subtests that heavily favor one or the other sex.

Race

A great social urgency is attached to the question of whether or not races differ from one another in intellectual ability, and psychologists have conducted many investigations of this question. On the surface, the problem appears clear cut; in reality, it is extremely complex and full of pitfalls for the unwary investigator.

There is, first, the need to define *race* itself, and this, the anthropologist tells us, cannot usually be done, for seldom if ever in modern society are "racial groups" composed of individuals whose genetic make-up is unmixed with that of another "racial group." Then there is the problem of how to interpret test differences after they are obtained, for "racial groups" ordinarily will differ from one another in their cultural background as well as in head shape or skin color. The solution of this problem is the crux of the racial issue, because, if racial differences arise from cultural and not from genetic differences, then society has no problem other than that of making cultural opportunities equal for all groups. Solving this problem is, however, no easy task.

During the first period of enthusiasm that followed the successful introduction of large-scale intelligence testing during World War I it was not unusual for studies to be conducted in which racial groups chosen from the far corners of the world—The Bushmen of Australia, the tribes of Africa, national groups in Europe, and many others—were administered intelligence tests which had usually been standardized upon the American populations. In an effort to overcome the language barrier the tests for the most part employed performance rather than verbal items. The purpose of this research was, of course, to compare the intelligences of the different races. Differences among the "racial groups" in intelligence-test performance were found in most instances, and more often than not the performances of these racial groups were inferior to that of the standardization group.

At that time it was quite common to assume that these differences were attributable primarily, if not completely, to basic biological differences between the groups, for it was assumed that by using performance rather than verbal items the effects of cultural difference were eliminated. Since then we have learned a great deal, not only about the psychological basis of intelligence-test performance, but also about cultural differences. This knowledge leads inevitably and forcefully to the conclusion that there is no meaningful intelligence test which is free of cultural influences and that certainly for the present—and perhaps forever—there is no device by which genetic differences in intelligence can be compared for people who live in different cultures.

The factors that make the development of a culture-free intelligence test virtually impossible are many. Obviously one of them is the difference in the degree of intellectual stimulation that is inherent in the various cultures, but there are other even subtler differences; these are differences which are functions of the divergent motivational and attitudinal patterns of the various cultures. A few examples are in order. A typical and valid type of test in our culture is one that requires the work to be completed—the correct answer to be given—within a specific time. If a longer time is taken it is counted as a failure, even though the response is correct. In some cultures, less clock-bound than our own, the requirement of completing the activity within some arbitrary time is without meaning; indeed, it might even be considered appropriate to prolong the activity if it is an interesting one. Such an indulgence leads to failure by the standards of another culture. Browning spoke accurately of one of the attitudes of our culture when he wrote: "Ah, but a man's reach should exceed his grasp"; less poetically, we can say that we strive to succeed even though we risk failure. In other cultures no such attitude prevails, and the test-taker refuses to try unless he is fairly convinced that success is insured. Since one is almost certain to pass some of the tests that border upon the limits of ones ability, the refusal to attempt them leads to a lower score. In certain cultures there is a religious prohibition against representing the human form. Often performance tests contain some elements of this sort, and however innocently introduced, they must inevitably militate against a high level of performance for members of such cultures, or of cultures where such a taboo has existed in the recent past.

These few examples suggest that it is impossible to administer the same test to members of different cultures and expect the results to be comparable. We therefore cannot assume that the numerical scores obtained from members of different cultures are true reflections of the biologically determined intellectual abilities of the "racial groups" involved.

In the United States the question of racial differences in intelligence has been centered on a comparison of the Negroes and the whites. When the data obtained from the mass intelligence testing of the draftees in World War I showed the American white to be superior to the American Negro there were many who concluded that the scores reflected a basic biological difference between the two naively defined "races"—the Caucasian and the Negroid. We have said before, however, that the problem is twofold; first to determine whether or not differences do occur and, second, to uncover the factors which make for those differences.

The data on intelligence collected during World War I (and World War II as well) indicated that the average I.Q. of the Negro population as a whole was lower than that of the white population.[17] But when Negroes living in some of the Northern states were compared with whites living in some of the Southern states, the Negroes were found to be superior. How can we account for this difference? We can assume either that the Northern Negro enjoyed an intellectual environment superior to that of the Southern white or that selective migration occurred in which the superior Negroes moved from the South to the North, where opportunities for self-development were better.

Fortunately we can fall back on research which has given us the correct answer.[18] The problem of selective migration has been carefully investigated by Klineberg, who determined the educational status (average school grades received) of some Southern Negro children who subsequently migrated North. He discovered that their grade average (obtained in the South) was not superior to that of the average of the Southern Negro population, whereupon he concluded that it is not the superior school performers who leave the South. Another aspect of Klineberg's data is pertinent. He administered the Stanford-Binet test to Negro children in the New York City school system and determined the relationship between length of residence in New York and intelligence as shown by their test performance. These data, shown in Figure

451

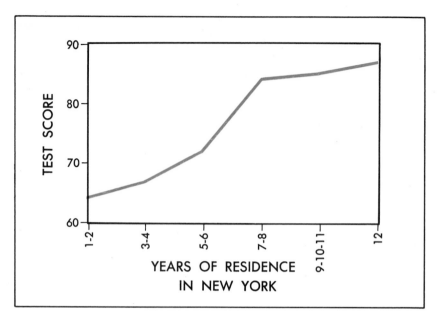

Fig. 13.6 The relationship between scores on an intelligence test and years of residence in New York City of a group of 12-year-old Negro boys. The scores represent not I.Q.'s but simply the number of correct responses on the test used. The significant fact shown here is that test performance improves markedly with length of residence in the city. (From Klineberg[18])

13.6, indicate the stimulating effect of schooling on intelligence-test performance.

A recent repetition of this study in the city of Philadelphia has obtained essentially the same results.[19] On the basis of data of these sorts, as well as the recognized fact that environmental factors contribute heavily to intelligence-test performance, most modern psychologists are inclined to account for the difference between the American white and the American Negro in intelligence-test performance by environmental rather than genetic factors.

It must be remembered that these environmental differences are extremely subtle. As we have found in comparing "racial groups" in various parts of the world, they include differences not only in intellectual stimulation but also in personality pattern. For example, how easily can rapport and cooperation be established between a tester who is of one race and a subject who is of another? And when a race is forced to occupy an inferior position, it is almost inevitable that many individual members will take important matters lightly and not strive to do their best, for what does it avail them to perform at their highest level? These variables and many

others that the reader will be able to bring to mind may serve to
explain differences in test performance among the various racial
groups in this country.

*INTELLIGENCE
FROM BIRTH
TO MATURITY*

INTELLIGENCE FROM BIRTH

TO MATURITY

As we have stated earlier, we assume, in the making of intelligence tests, that intelligence increases with age to, at least, the
age of fifteen. It is not possible, however, to make any definite
statements as to the exact form of the curve that plots intelligence
against chronological age. The form obtained will depend upon
both the kind of intelligence test used and the statistical devices
used in computation. Even with the same test and the same statistical device, the growth curve differs from individual to individual. This fact is illustrated in the data of Figure 13.5.

Although we cannot describe with certainty the exact form
of the curve, we do know that for the population at large the greatest gains are made during the early years of life, that the curve
begins to flatten out at some time during the late teens or early
twenties, and at some time thereafter—perhaps in the thirties or
forties—intelligence-test performance begins to decline.

The measurement of intelligence in infants

When used to test children of school age, intelligence tests
have been extraordinarily successful in predicting the level of intellectual performance at later ages. Success breeds optimism, and
so a number of psychologists have constructed tests for infants,
hoping to be able to make predictions about the infant's future performance as early as his first year of life. These efforts have not met
with conspicuous success. The data presented earlier in this chapter have shown that tests given in the fourth or fifth year of life
correlate with those for the twelfth year at a value of only a little
over .40. Tests given during the first year or two of life are even
less efficient in predicting the performance several years later. At
best these infant tests provide only a very crude estimate of later
intelligence test performance.

Just why such tests are no more accurate than they are is an extremely interesting question, and there are many possible answers to it. At these early ages we may not be measuring the same abilities that we measure later—the abilities that make up the concept of more adult intelligence. Environmental factors, too, may differ more at these earlier ages than at later ages, when compulsory schooling helps to produce a leveling effect. The younger child is not so susceptible to social control as the older child, and there may be more variation in the amount of effort put forth in the examination in the younger years than in the older ones. Perhaps also the younger child is more affected by physiologically produced distraction—slight illnesses, or hunger, for example—and thus produces a less reliable sample of his ability. There may, moreover, be some basic difference in rate of growth of the intellectual abilities of one child as compared with that of another. These are possible reasons for our meager success with very young children, and they offer a stimulating challenge to the research-minded psychologist.[20]

Intelligence-test performance from maturity to old age

The task of making accurate comparisons between the levels of performance of older persons and younger ones is not a simple one. If our comparisons are to be meaningful, we must be certain that the individuals at the older age levels are essentially of the same type as those who comprise the younger age group. The young age groups can be reached with relative ease in the public schools with their large numbers of children coming from widely assorted socioeconomic levels. But adults of such widely varying socioeconomic levels—the rich man and the poor, the lawyer and the ditch-digger—do not congregate in a single social institution where they can be tested. Even if they were, they might not, when approached by the psychologist, care to take part in his testing program. The results of a study which selects its older cases from a single institution, perhaps a county poor farm or a society of professional people, are obviously going to exhibit a bias which makes them difficult to evaluate.

In an investigation which avoided the selection pitfall, the same intelligence test was administered to everyone between 10 and 60 years of age in a New England community.[21] The results of

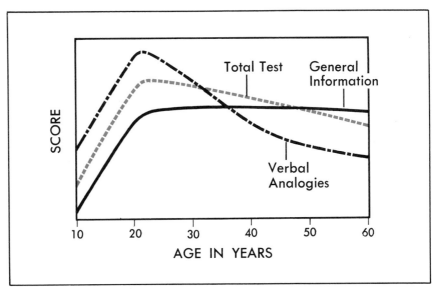

Fig. 13.7 Scores on an intelligence test and on subtests plotted against age. (From Jones and Conrad[21])

the study are presented in Figure 13.7, in which total test performance is plotted against chronological age by the red curve. Similar results have been obtained by other investigators, and it is safe to conclude that if the mean scores on the total test is used, and the data are collected in this fashion, then performance is shown to increase to a maximum sometime during the twenties and decline gradually, but consistently, thereafter.[22]

There are, however, certain important characteristics which are obscured by the use of the total test score and this particular statistic—the mean, and at least some of these have been identified.

The nature of the test materials

When the various subject-matter scores are considered separately, the trend changes. The curves for two different subtests are also shown in Figure 13.7, and we can see that one kind of material, general information, shows little or no decline with age, whereas the loss for verbal analogies is greater than for the total test score. The results usually show vocabulary and general information remaining at a high level, whereas tasks requiring the learning of unfamiliar or meaningless responses show considerable loss. In a similar vein, the decline on performance items is greater than the decline on the verbal portion.[23]

Speed vs. power

When no time limits are set for the completion of a test, it is referred to as a power test. Most intelligence tests, particularly group tests, are not of this sort; instead they place a certain premium on speed of performance and require the individual to work fairly rapidly if he is to pass the item or complete the test. In one study, subjects up to the age of ninety were given two forms of one of the standard group intelligence tests. One form was taken as a power test, and for the other form a time limit for completion was required. Under the power conditions, the decline in performance was smaller up to the sixties, but thereafter the older groups declined as much under the power as under the speed conditions.[24] The conclusion which is usually drawn from this and similar studies is that a certain amount of the decline in performance associated with age is because of a reduction of speed of working rather than of sheer intellectual power.

Characteristics of the individual

There is a fair amount of evidence that the decline in test performance with age is smaller among those who were initially high in intelligence than it is for those who initially were low. In one study the same intelligence test was retaken 31 years after its original administration in the freshman year of college. An inspection of Figure 13.7 indicates that one would expect a drop from age 19 to 50—the approximate age of those tested in this study. Actually, there was a slight improvement over the span of 31 years for the college educated population—a group which initially scored higher than does the population at large.[25] Continued studies of the group identified as very superior in childhood (p. 433) has obtained no evidence of a loss for the group as a whole up to the age of 50. Indeed, there is once again the suggestion of a gain in test performance over the age span.[20] These and other studies suggest that the declining curve for the population at large may not describe the trend for each member of the population with equal precision, and, in particular, such a trend may not be at all true for the originally superior members of the population.

The reasons for the tendency for intelligence-test performance to decline with age among the population at large are probably of many sorts. It is certainly true that there are changes in the structure of the central nervous system with advancing age, but we

know too little about the way the microstructure of the brain contributes to behavior to account for behavioral changes by reference
to particular physiological changes.[26] Perhaps some of the decline
in intellectual proficiency results from these changes, but certainly
not all. Environmental factors are also involved. The younger subjects, much closer to the testing situations of the classroom, are
better prepared to make a good showing on the tests than are older
persons. Also, the general motivational level of the older person is
perhaps not so high as that of the younger. Education aims at a
broadening of our intellectual outlook, but the rigors of economic
life may force on many of us a specialization and a narrowing of
interests after we leave the classroom. The child lives in a world of
relatively general intellectual stimulation, whereas a great many
adults, perhaps the majority, live in a world that is intellectually
restricted. In this connection it is pertinent to note that members
of the professions show less decline in I.Q. with age than do others.
This may be due, in part, to the nature of their work; the professional man must continue to keep alive the same reading, writing,
and problem-solving skills that enter into the make-up of intelligence tests. From these considerations we may conclude that great
declines in intellectual growth are not inevitable, and that the
older person who lives an intellectually active life and develops
habits of approaching new tasks and ideas with open-mindedness
and confidence may maintain a high intelligence-test status for
many years.

THE SIGNIFICANCE OF
INTELLIGENCE TESTS

It may be profitable now to take a backward look over the
materials of this chapter and, in the light of our added information,
attempt to answer two questions that have probably occurred to us
as we learned about intelligence testing: Is the I.Q. inherited or is
it learned? What does an I.Q. imply for social and economic adjustment? Neither question can be answered by a simple statement;
indeed, the first involves so many intangibles that it becomes almost
meaningless in a scientific sense.

The I.Q., as we have seen, is a measure of the performance
of the individual in comparison with the performance of a standard

population. It has that precise meaning and no more. It does not tell us *why* a person obtained this score and no other. The score is a product of two factors—his genetic characteristics and his environmental background—and these two can never be separated. The intellectual environment will be reacted to differently by those of different genetic constitutions. Always the I.Q. will be the result of the interaction of nature and nurture; both are always influential.

Let us consider another characteristic of intelligence tests. The performance that we measure on a test will always be drawn from a certain culture, and strictly speaking the test will be applicable only to those who come from the same culture. We cannot criticize a test because members of one culture will perform on it differently from members of another, but we can say that the psychologist who applied the test to two different cultures was in error if he assumed that the test scores for each would have the same meaning. The psychologist in using his test keeps a sharp eye open to cultural differences among those taking the test. If these differences are great, he will be inclined to take them into account in his interpretation of the significance of the score.

Studies on the very superior and on the mentally deficient have helped us to answer our question concerning the relationship between intelligence-test scores and social and economic adjustment. As a group, the superior ones achieved superior adjustment. But success is not guaranteed by the possession of an I.Q. of 140 or above, for some of the superior group failed both economically and socially. Conversely, many persons in the deficient groups progressed satisfactorily in the work-a-day world, though collectively their adjustment was inferior to that of normal individuals. Knowing these facts, the psychologist is unwilling to make exact predictions about the success of an individual about whom he knows nothing more than his I.Q.* Whatever it is that an intelligence test measures comprises only one factor in satisfactory adjustment, the attainment of which is always determined by many factors. Even in the school situation, where tasks are presumably highly intellectualized, intelligence tests do not predict grade averages perfectly. Grades are not simply a measure of I.Q., as any

* This assumes an I.Q. range of perhaps from 50 to 200. If the test is carefully administered by a skilled clinician, one may be fairly certain that a person testing below 50 cannot be expected to make an independent adjustment to the complexities and responsibilities of modern life.

student who has dated or gone to the movies in preference to study- ing knows, and the score on a course examination will be a function of many variables other than sheer brightness.

APTITUDES

The first age-scale intelligence test, constructed by Alfred Binet in the first decade of this century, was designed to differentiate those pupils who were failing in school because of a lack of intellectual ability from those who were failing because of low motivation or some other reason. From the very beginning, then, this type of test was directed toward making predictions in the area of academic performance. Either directly or indirectly, those test items that failed to predict academic ability were dropped out of the Binet test and other tests of this type. Thus in a way these tests —which are called intelligence tests—are tests of *scholastic aptitude*. It happens that some of the same kinds of abilities required for adequate school work are also required in many other spheres of life. As a result, these tests also predict success or failure in some of these other walks of life. As a rule, however, they do not predict so successfully in these other areas as they do in the academic area.

There are many skills required for success in one occupation or another that are not measured in any way by our typical intelligence test. One job may call for an ability to make fine sensory discrimination, another to coordinate finger movements smoothly and rapidly, and a third to run with great speed. These abilities will not be measured in the typical intelligence test. As a result, we cannot predict success in some of these other fields by a knowledge of the person's I.Q.

Now the social value of an intelligence test arises from the fact that it can predict—that it can tell in advance—how well an individual is likely to do in certain spheres of activity. A score on an intelligence test may indicate, with a reasonable degree of precision, how well a child will succeed in the scholastic world before he has even entered the first grade. We do not need to wait until after he has spent some time in the schools before making a prediction of his degree of success. The intelligence test measures scholastic aptitude, and from this score we may predict school performance with some success.

But what of the types of work that require other sorts of ability? Here, too, society needs to make predictions. Some occupations require months or even years of training before a worker can be expected to perform with any degree of success. And a worker who lacks a certain type of ability may never succeed at all. If he does not discover this until he has completed the training period, or even if he discovers his ineptitude during the training period itself, his failure constitutes a social waste; he has spent his own time fruitlessly and he has been a financial loss to his employer.

In order to avoid such waste as this, tests of specific abilities, or aptitude tests, have been developed. They are designed to make predictions of success or failure in jobs for which intelligence tests alone do not have adequate predictive value.

The usual aptitude test is, as we have implied above, constructed to predict degree of success in a specific job. Specific tests

Fig. 13.8 The two aptitude tests illustrated below test the subject's rate of manipulation and his fine finger coordination. The test at which he is working requires him to turn over and replace each disc as rapidly as he can. The test on the table at the left requires him to insert the metal pegs in the holes on the board. (Courtesy Conrad Kraft)

have been designed to determine whether a certain individual has the abilities to succeed as a meat cutter, a clerk, a bus driver, a mechanic, or an airplane pilot. The nature of the job for which an aptitude test is to be constructed therefore determines the content and form of the test.[27]

Job analysis

The first step in constructing an aptitude test is an analysis of the psychological and physical abilities required in the job. This is made by studying the performance of the trained workers. At this first stage one cannot conclude with finality that a specific ability is either highly important or unimportant. For this reason the psychologist will, when in doubt, assume that some specific psychological function should be included in the job. At this stage, it is better to include too much than too little, for the superfluous can be eliminated later.

Test development and selection

Once the psychological and physical abilities that may play a part in proficiency on the job are determined, it becomes necessary to find or construct tests that measure these abilities. It is quite possible that some other psychologist has already constructed a test that measures one of the abilities considered important. Such a test may be used with no modification. If, however, no satisfactory test exists, the psychologist must build one himself. This stage of work is ended when he has gathered together or constructed tests that measure the various abilities which the job analysis has suggested are necessary. Now the psychologist has what is called a *test battery,* a large test composed of a number of subtests. The battery may include an intelligence test, a test of motor coordination, a test of visual discrimination, and a test of the ability to perceive things in three dimensions. What has gone into the total battery has been determined by the job analysis.

Occasionally, the aptitude test consists of a miniature sample of the job itself rather than of individual subtests that measure the psychological components of the task. Thus, skill in learning radio code may be measured by the ease with which the subject learns a few representative code letters, or success as a bus driver may be predicted by performance in a laboratory duplication of the controls of the bus.

The criterion

The next step that must be taken is to obtain some measurement of proficiency on the job itself. At first glance this appears to be a simple problem, but it is not. Production records are often unreliable, workers may not operate up to their level of ability, and the foreman's judgment of who is proficient and who is not may be biased by personal feelings. Nevertheless, if an aptitude test is to be developed, some measure of proficiency on the job itself—a measure called the *criterion*—must be obtained. Sometimes it is possible to make corrections in the way that production records are kept and thus make them an acceptable measure of each man's proficiency on the job; sometimes a sample of the man's work can be judged for excellence by experts. If foremen's ratings of the workers are used, scales are constructed in such a way that personal biases are minimized.

Correlation of test and criterion

With this task completed, it is possible to make a comparison between performance on the test battery and performance on the job itself. The tentative aptitude test is administered to a group of workers for each of whom a criterion score is obtainable. Then a comparison is made between the criterion and each of the subtest scores in the battery. If any subtest fails to correlate well with its criterion, the subtest is discarded. The end result of this work is to produce a test battery in which each of the subtests predicts to some degree success on the job itself. The score on the total battery predicts with greater accuracy than does the score on any of the single subtests. The whole test measures the individual's aptitude for the type of work for which it was designed, and each subtest adds something to the predictive value of the whole.

Ordinarily a second step is then required: the administration of the same test to another population for whom criterial scores are available. This repetition is referred to as a *cross-validation* procedure. It is done because we have learned that some subtests or items in the original test may show a high correlation with the criterion by chance alone. It is most unlikely that this will happen twice, so if the correlations between subtest and criterion are essentially the same in the first and second situation they are retained in the final test. Items or subtests that fail to maintain their correlational value on the second testing are eliminated. Cross validation has become an essential step in modern test-development procedures.

Factors determining aptitudes

The inquiring reader may wonder why individuals differ in their aptitudes. Investigations of the determining factors for aptitudes other than those measured by our formal intelligence tests have been few. There is little reason to believe, however, that the determining factors would differ from those for intelligence. Some of the differences among persons must arise from environmental opportunities and some from the genetic make-up.

VALIDITY AND RELIABILITY

In the foregoing discussion of aptitude and intelligence tests, we have introduced two important concepts in the field of testing—*validity* and *reliability*. Because of the significance of these concepts for test construction and the fact that these concepts are involved whenever psychologists evaluate a test, a discussion of them is desirable.

Validity

When we say that a test is valid, we mean that the test measures what it is supposed to measure. More precisely, validity means that there is a good relationship between scores on the test and scores on the criterion measure. Thus we estimate the validity of an intelligence test by measuring the degree of relationship between scores on the test and some other performance, such as school grades. We assume that level of intelligence is an important determiner of school grades and hence we may use school grades for our criterion. If we develop an aptitude test to predict success as a life-insurance salesman, we would determine its validity by comparing scores on the test with sales records. If we found that those persons with high scores on the test achieved high sales records and those with low scores achieved low sales records, we could call the test valid.

Obviously tests vary in their degree of validity. Some do a very good job of predicting the criterion score; others predict it with moderate success; and still others have been discarded when it was discovered that scores on the test were almost completely unrelated to scores on the criterion. It can be readily imagined that a large amount of work in psychology is directed toward improving the validity of tests already in existence.

Reliability

The concept of reliability refers to the consistency with which the test measures the same thing each time it is administered. A test is considered reliable if, when it is given to the same persons a second time, they each obtain approximately the same scores that they did on the first administration. A test that indicated one score for a person on one day and quite a different score for him on the next would be an unreliable test. Just as in the case of validity, the degree of reliability varies from test to test.

The reliability of a test is a function of a number of conditions but one of the most obvious of them is the number of items in the test. Almost every student has had the experience of taking a quiz composed of a single item. If the item dealt with one of the few sections of the material which he had not studied, he probably failed the quiz. The quiz score, in this case, was an unreliable measure of his knowledge of the subject matter of the course. If it happened to be the only section of the course that he did study, it would still be an unreliable measure of his knowledge of the course. By increasing the number of items on an examination, accidents of this sort tend to be eliminated. We obtain a more reliable measure of the student's performance, and the student is less likely to obtain a failing grade on one examination and a high grade on another.

The relationship between validity and reliability

The fact that a test is reliable is no guarantee that it is valid. We may measure something with complete reliability even though there may be no relationship between the score on the test and the score on the criterion. The test, in such a case, is not valid because it does not predict the criterion. On the other hand, no test can have high validity unless it also has high reliability. Suppose that a test gives a high score for the individual on the first day and a low score for him on the next. Which of these scores should we use to predict the criterion score? Which is the real measure of his ability? This we cannot tell, and this is another way of saying that we cannot have validity without reliability.

REFERENCES

[1] Terman, L. M., and Merrill, M. A. *Stanford-Binet Intelligence Scale,* Houghton, 1960.

[2] Wechsler, D. *Manual for the Wechsler Adult Intelligence Scale,* Psychological Corporation, 1955; and *Wechsler Intelligence Scale for Children,* Psychological Corporation, 1949.

[3] Terman, L. M. *The Gifted Child Grows Up,* Stanford, 1947.

[4] Baller, W. R. A study of the present social status of a group of adults, who, when they were in elementary schools, were classified as mentally deficient, *Genet. Psychol. Monogr.,* 1936, *38,* 80.

[5] Thorndike, R. L., and Hogen, Elizabeth *Measurement and Evaluation in Psychology and Education,* Wiley, 1955.

[6] Lawshe, C. H., Jr., and Tiffin, J. The accuracy of precision instrument measurement in industrial inspection, *J. Applied Psychol.,* 1945, *29,* 413-419.

[7] Sontag, L. W., Baker, C. T., and Nelson, V. L. Mental growth and personality development: A longitudinal study, *Society for Research in Child Development Monographs,* 1958, *23.*

[8] Bradway, K. P., Thompson, C. W., and Cravens, R. B. Pre-school I.Q.s after twenty-five years, *J. Ed. Psychol.,* 1958, *49,* 278-281.

[9] Gordon, H. *Mental and Scholastic Tests among Retarded Children,* London Board of Education, Education Pamphlet No. 44, 1923.

[10] Ginzberg, E., and Bray, D. W. *The Uneducated.* Columbia, 1953.

[11] Burt, C. A. The inheritance of mental ability, *Am. Psychol.,* 1958, *13,* 1-15.

[12] Vernon, P. *The Structure of Human Abilities,* Wiley, 1950.

[13] Eells, K., Davis, A., Hovighurst, R. J., Herrick, V. E., and Tyler, R. *Intelligence and Cultural Differences,* Chicago, 1951.

[14] Sarason, S. B., and Gladwin, T. Psychological and cultural problems in mental subnormality: A review of research, *Genet. Psychol. Monogr.,* 1958, *57.*

[15] Abernethy, E. M. Relationships between mental and physical growth, *Society for Research in Child Development Monographs,* 1936, *7,* 80.

[16] Anastasi, A. *Differential Psychology,* Macmillan, 1958.

[17] *Ibid.*

[18] Klineberg, O. *Negro Intelligence and Selective Migration,* Columbia, 1935.

[19] Lee, E. S. Negro intelligence and selective migration: A Philadel-

phia test of the Kleinberg hypothesis. *Amer. Sociol. Rev.,* 1951, *16,* 227-233.

[20] Bailey, Nancy   On the growth of intelligence, *Amer. Psychol.,* 1955, *10,* 805-818.

[21] Jones, H. E., and Conrad, H. S. The growth and decline of intelligence: A study of a homogeneous group between the ages of ten and sixty, *Genet. Psychol. Monogr.,* 1933, *13,* No. 3.

[22] Jones, H. E.   "Intelligence and problem solving." In J. E. Beren (ed.), *Handbook of Aging and the Individual,* Chicago, 1959.

[23] Wechsler, D.   *The measurement of Adult Intelligence,* Williams & Wilkins, 1944.

[24] Miles, C. C.   Influence of speed and age on intelligence scores of adults, *J. Gen. Psychol.,* 1934, *10,* 208-210.

[25] Owens, W. A., Jr.   Age and mental abilities: A longitudinal study, *Genet. Psychol. Monogr.,* 1953, *48,* 3-54.

[26] Himwich, W. A., and Himwich, H. E.   "Neurochemistry of aging," In J. E. Beiren (ed.), *Handbook of Aging and the Individual,* Chicago, 1959.

[27] Cronbach, L. J.   *Essentials of Psychological Testing,* Harper, 1949.

Chapter Fourteen

SOCIAL INFLUENCES ON THE INDIVIDUAL

THE EARLIEST CHAPTERS OF THIS BOOK described how the behavior of the organism is molded by its environment. Through the action of the environment, the organism's originally limited number of motive states increases, and various kinds of behavior that lead to reinforcement or that avoid punishment become fixated. We were not, in those early chapters, concerned with describing and specifying the environment itself; rather, we were interested in identifying some general principles of behavior—principles that operate regardless of the exact nature of the environment. In the present chapter we shall consider how behavior is determined by a certain kind of environment—the environment supplied by other organisms themselves—the social environment.

467

If an environment is to mold our responses, it must be fairly stable, consistently reinforcing some responses and failing to reinforce others. The action of gravity possess such consistency all over the world; as a result, children all over the world learn certain motions, certain ways of handling their bodies so that they can walk upright. And the manner in which they walk does not differ much from latitude to latitude or longitude to longitude. Social forces, however, are much less pervasive, and the behaviors that are acceptable—reinforced for the learning organism—may be quite different in various parts of the world. Nonetheless, within certain areas, the social environment is sufficiently stable and pervasive to lead to similar patterns of behavior among those individuals who are brought up in it. By knowing something about the major social forces that operate upon individuals, we may, in the case of a given individual, further our aim of predicting his behavior. We may do so if we know the social groups with which he identifies himself and the behavior that these groups tend to reward or punish.

We can make this abstract discussion somewhat clearer by noting the various kinds of social environment that we may consider pertinent to the learning of the individual. This environment is, of course, very complex and may be analyzed in a number of ways, but for our purpose we shall consider only three conventional, but somewhat arbitrarily drawn classifications of the social environment—*culture*, *class*, and *groups*. Although these three words must have been used many times by the reader, he will perceive as he continues with the chapter that they will be used in a manner that probably differs from his former usage of them. The terms will take on something of the technical flavor that the sociologist endows them with, and they will signify the kinds of social environment, large (culture) and small (groups), which constitute past as well as present determinants of an individual's behavior.

Culture

Every individual is born and reared in a certain geographical area that is inhabited by other persons. For various reasons, these persons have developed common goals and common ways of obtaining these goals, which differ to a greater or less degree from those of other large groupings of persons in other areas. This fact will be of considerable significance for the child as he grows up. To a great extent the adults control the child's reinforcements. If his

Fig. 14.1 Two strikingly different cultures meet as these Chinese peasants experience their first encounter with an American sewing machine. This encounter is clearly a pleasant one, but very often the introduction of one cultural product into another culture can produce serious social and psychological conflict and tension. (Courtesy Singer Sewing Machine Co.)

ways of working for goals are the ways of which they approve, they will permit reinforcements to occur. Reinforcement, as we know from our discussion of fixation, will strengthen the reinforced way of behaving. Conversely, ways of behaving which are not socially acceptable will not lead to reinforcement and will therefore be extinguished. The members of one society will therefore learn that they may achieve goals by particular kinds of instrumental acts, while in some other society these same acts may be unacceptable. In this country, for example, it is not uncommon to indicate one's objection to another's action by signs of irritation or even anger: and it is even more common to demonstrate one's pleasure publicly by expressions of joy. Among the Ojibwa Indians of Canada expressions of anger and irritation are seldom shown. Even though these people are fond of jokes and laugh wholeheartedly at them, they do not express other feelings of sadness or joy openly—as we would if, for example, loved ones were leaving or returning after a long absence.[1]

Just as instrumental acts are learned through the selective operations of reinforcement, nonreinforcement, and punishment, so also are the secondary motives. Thus the adults in a given society perpetuate their own behavioral characteristics because to a very great extent they are the ones who administer the events—reinforcement, nonreinforcement, and punishment—that are essential for the learning of both instrumental acts and motives. The culture of a group of people may be regarded as the common shared ways of behaving that tend to be transmitted to succeeding generations. Culture, by this definition, is not a concrete object but rather a way of behaving within a population.[2] It is an environment which is created by man, and in the sense that tools and homes and other materials are reflections of behavior, these things too are a part of the culture.

As psychologists we are not concerned with how a particular culture developed, but we are concerned with the facts that the culture contributes to the ways of behaving of an individual and that we can predict something about what he will do if we know the characteristics of his culture.

Most of us experience directly only a single culture throughout our lifetime and, knowing no more than this, we may regard the major characteristics of our culture as representing the biological and hereditary common behavioral denominators of all mankind. This view is effectively repudiated by the work of the cultural anthropologists, whose detailed studies of many cultures prove that the behavior of man, as seen in his motives and his instrumental acts, is not uniform. The range of behavioral differences associated with different cultures throughout the world is tremendous, and there is every reason to believe that these differences stem primarily from the great capacity of the human organism to learn different things in different environments rather than from a difference in biological origins.

We in the United States, for example, are predominantly competitive. Competition seems to us not merely a necessary way of obtaining the rewards and worldly goods that satisfy other motives but a basic, unlearned motive in and of itself. There are other cultures in which it is considered to be even more important. The Kwakiutl, who inhabit the North Pacific Coast, seem even according to our standards overly competitive.[3] A tribesman spends inordinate amounts of time and effort in competing with a chosen rival for blankets and for metal disks that represent blankets. He does not need all these blankets for warmth. Their value for him lies in the fact that he defeats his rival by owning more of them.

But in another culture, that of the Pueblo Indians, the pattern is almost reversed.[4] The competitive acts which our culture approves and even cultivates are regarded as acts of bad taste. There are, indeed, few patterns of behavior typical of our own culture that are not almost completely reversed in some other culture or cultures.

Social class

Within most cultures there are smaller social environments which are referred to as *classes*. In some cultures, classes are rigidly prescribed by the culture itself; in others, such as our own, class groupings can be identified even though there is no clear-cut cultural dictum that requires them. Both of these statements seem to follow from the results of a study conducted in 1956 in which a representative sample of adult white males in this country was asked questions concerning class.[5] Nearly 40 percent of this group reported that they did not think of themselves as being members of a particular class. If class structure were a dictum of our culture, one would not expect to find such a large percentage who reported that they were unaware of these social categories. However, the fact that class groupings do exist in our culture is suggested not only by the fact that 60 percent of the sample reported an awareness of class distinction, but also by the fact that most of the unaware group felt able and willing to assign themselves to either the middle or working class when asked by the interviewers to do so. So even though the individual may have no constant awareness of membership in a class he can recognize class structuring as a fact of his environment. Even more significantly, he is prepared to identify himself with membership in one or another class.

The concept of class refers to the fact that within a culture large groups of people may have easy social access to each other but do not readily have access to other persons for such social occasions as family visits, dances, and various informal affairs. A person is considered a member of the social class within which most of his intimate social contacts occur.[6] Although this definition is abstract, most readers can probably translate them into specific experiences of their own past. They may have found that some groups and some kinds of invitations were inaccessible to them despite the fact that they themselves possess the skills and competencies to participate in the activities of the groups if only they were given the chance to do so. Or conversely, they themselves may have excluded others, not because of feelings of contempt or spite, but only because it never occurred to them that these others would fit into or have common interests with the group. Such actions as these may also be a consequence of specific personal idiosyncrasies but often they are a consequence and expression of class differences.

The mechanisms by which class behavior and values are learned must be essentially the same as those of cultural learning. The parent through his own childhood experiences has learned a set of standards and ways of behaving and tends to choose as his friends, neighbors, and associates those who have standards and ways of behaving that are similar to his. Unless the parent has made a complete shift in his own social class since childhood, his children will be reared in these or similar social environments and will acquire the same standards because reinforcement results from behaving according to these standards. A child behaves as he does not only because his parents reinforce according to these standards but because the parents have chosen as their associates others who do the same, and so the values of the child's friends are similar.

Fig. 14.2 The architecture on this street is strikingly homogeneous. How homogeneous are the values and attitudes of the homeowners? The children reared in these homes differ in their genetic backgrounds and in many aspects of their environments. But some similarities in the values and attitudes of their parents are likely to stamp each child with the same class patterns. (Courtesy Carl Silver)

Thus does the class perpetuate itself by molding the individual, who, in turn a class member, strengthens the class structure by his influence upon others. For a given individual, then, knowledge of his class will give us some indication of how he will behave.

That children of different classes are subjected to different environmental demands is demonstrated by a number of studies which have compared the child-rearing practices of middle- and lower-class parents over several decades.[7] On the basis of such items as occupation, education, income, and property ownership and similar data, investigators have classified groups of parents as members of either the middle or lower class. Then they have questioned the mothers on the methods of child rearing they employed. These studies seem to indicate that differences in child training between the middle and working classes do exist, but that the direction of these differences have changed in this country over the past quarter of a century. During the thirties and until the end of World War II the working-class parents seemed to have been more permissive or less demanding than the middle-class parents in such matters as toilet training, feeding on demand rather than by clock, and weaning from bottle or breast. Since World War II there seems to have been a reversal of this trend and the middle-class parents have become more permissive about these matters than the working-class parents. The studies indicate that the parents of one class provide somewhat different environments for their children from that provided by parents of another class. Even though the directions of these differences do not remain stable and the exact psychological impacts of these parental requirements have not as yet been clearly established, it is inevitable that children of the same generation will show behavioral differences which are a consequence of these class differences in child-rearing practices of their parents.

Within the framework of the culture, the classes are arranged in a hierarchy of desirability or *status levels*. As a result, individuals are motivated to change their class membership from one that is lower in the hierarchy of desirability to one that is higher. The term *vertical mobility* is used to refer to these shifts in membership from one class to another. In the American culture, vertical mobility is common; the opportunity "to better oneself" is a part of the American dream, and the right to do so seems almost to be guaranteed by the Declaration of Independence and the Bill of Rights. The individual who strives for higher class status does not, however, always find his path an easy one, for he must modify

473

his earlier habits and acquire the habits of the class he wishes to enter. This shift in habits is difficult, because the habits are truly pervasive; they involve not merely his speech and his spending but such basic matters as his diet and such trivial ones as his choice of a lampshade.

The hierarchy of classes and vertical social mobility are sociological concepts. Their importance for psychology lies in their influence upon the behavior of individuals. To a greater or less degree, most of us in this country would like to attain, and feel that it is possible to attain, membership in a higher status group or, at the very least, to maintain our present social status. As individuals we perform acts which are directed toward the achievement of these goals. It is possible, therefore, to further our aim of predicting the behavior of an individual by discovering not only the characteristics of the class with which he is identified but also the extent to which he is motivated to achieve a higher status level.[8]

The group

Our discussion of the sociological influences on individual behavior began with what is numerically the largest unit—the culture—and moved on to a numerically smaller unit—the class. We shall now be concerned with an even smaller unit—the group. Because the group is numerically smaller than the culture and the class, it has been possible to conduct some experimental studies that throw light upon the extent to which groups influence individual behavior. These studies, which we shall now consider, also indicate the difficulties we encounter when we attempt to define the concept *group*.

If several American college students are brought together in a group and are individually given a series of arithmetical problems to do, each student will complete more problems within a given period of time than he will when working in isolation. This is true even though the students are not directed to compete with one another. One is tempted to account for this behavior by referring to the stimuli arising from the sight of others working and the sounds of their pencils hurriedly scrawling out their answers. But another experiment shows that the reason lies elsewhere. Students were asked to report to the laboratory as a group, but there they were assigned to separate rooms and at a common signal began to work on the problems. Such subjects did more work than subjects who came to the laboratory one at a time.[9]

In another experiment grade-school children were asked to work individually on arithmetic problems in competition with other groups of children.[10] Several types of groups were formed. In one type, the experimenter arbitrarily divided the class into halves; in another type, the children elected two captains, who chose their teams; and in a third, the boys were pitted against the girls. The groups differed in their effectiveness; the most effective were the all-boy and all-girl groups; the least effective were the arbitrarily divided groups.

A study in attitude change in a girls' college during the 1930's has introduced the terms *membership* group and *reference* group.[11] The experimenter found that the students as a whole tended to change progressively from less liberal attitudes as freshmen to more liberal attitudes as seniors. In addition to recording these changes for the group as a whole the experimenter interviewed individual students in an effort to find out why the changes occurred. He discovered, as one might expect, that not all individuals shifted their attitudes. Those who did not change tended to be socially somewhat isolated from the group as a whole. Even though they were *members* of the group their point of *reference* for evaluating their own attitudes was outside the college. Usually the reference points were their families but this was not necessarily the case.

The term *membership group* refers to the group to which one is somewhat formally attached, such as a church, college, club, or fraternity. The term *reference group* refers to the group that serves as a source of motivation for the individual, whether positively or negatively. Thus one may be a member of a group but indifferent to its values and standards, and so this is only a membership group for the individual. If, however, he accepts the group's standards and his behavior is obviously influenced by these standards, then this group is a positive *reference* group as well as a *membership* group. One may also have negative reference groups, groups which influence one's behavior but in a direction opposite from that of the group's standards. As a result one might take a position in opposition to this group's position, though knowing little more about the issue than that the negative reference group favored it.

Together these studies give us some indications of how we must conceive of a group. Group influences can, it appears, operate

475

Fig. 14.3 A laboratory for the study of group behavior. The experimenters, the dim figures in the foreground, sit behind a one-way-vision screen that permits them to observe the subjects but makes them invisible to the subjects. The subjects wear coats of different colors and are identified by—and refer to one another by—these colors. Their conversation is relayed to the experimenters through the microphone suspended over the table. (Courtesy Department of Photography. The Ohio State University)

even though the group members are not physically together. Moreover, a constant degree of group influence on the behaviors of its members is not guaranteed by the mere fact that the individuals are physically together or identified as a single group by some formal criterion or symbol. One may be a member of a group in a formal sense, but his reference group may be totally different.

During his lifetime an individual will be a member of many groups. His membership in some of them will be short-lived and may have relatively little influence upon his behavior; his membership in others may last throughout his adult life and may have a considerable influence upon his behavior not only when he is in the presence of the group members but when he is alone. Thus, we can be helped to predict the behavior of the individual by learning something about the reference groups with which he is affiliated.

Groups as units

In the foregoing discussion, our interest has been centered upon the individual. Because we were concerned with how the group influences the individual, we viewed the group solely as a source of stimulation to which the individual reacts in certain ways. But in modern society there are many activities that involve the cooperative efforts of a number of individuals who are so organized and so interdependent that the activity can be best conceived of in terms of the group as a unit rather than as an aggregate of separate individuals. The passenger thinks of the *crew* of his plane—pilot, co-pilot, engineer, and hostess—and not of a number of individuals flying in the same plane; in many industrial situations production is a group rather than an individual activity; and the reports of a committee are usually the product of the interactions of its members.

Viewed in this way, the group becomes the unit and one can study its operation and its productivity. The words *systems research* is used to describe the study of a unit as a whole, whose productivity is the consequence of the complex interactions of the members of the unit. Extensive research in this field is relatively recent, having been stimulated by problems of efficiency arising in both military and industrial organizations during World War II.

One approach to the study of groups has been the identification of the important characteristics or dimensions in which groups differ from each other, such as, to mention only a few, the size, the intimacy among the members, and its flexibility, which is a measure of the extent to which the group's procedures are formal or informal.[12] Another line of study is concerned with the nature of the communications within a group and the effect of different types of communication networks on its efficiency of operation.[13] Some different communication networks are illustrated in Figure 14.4. Since the concern of this text is primarily with the behavior of the individual, we will not elaborate upon the findings in this area of systems research. It must be obvious to the reader that efforts to construct a more efficient and happy society must involve study not only of the individual as an individual, but also of groups as groups.

477

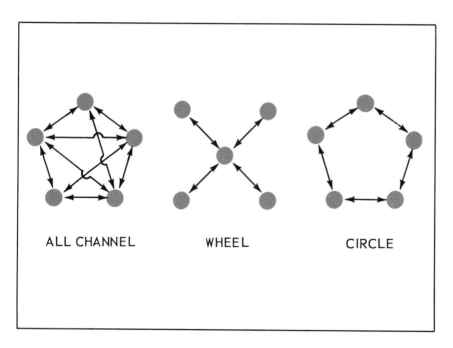

Fig. 14.4 Some different types of communication networks.

Role

One meaning of social environment to the individual is that it defines for him patterns of behavior that are acceptable and unacceptable, appropriate and inappropriate. In this way the environment contributes to the nature of the habits he will learn and, to a certain degree, to the kinds of behaviors he will show in the social environment. The term *role* sums up those behaviors that the individual shows in response to the standards of the group.[14]

The nature of the behaviors that are appropriate to a particular role is defined by relevant social units through the acts of reinforcing certain behaviors and failing to reinforce or even punishing those behaviors that are unacceptable to that role. Examples of this may be found in the typical parental reaction to a son or daughter. Briefly and generally these may be summarized by the usual strong negative attitude toward a "sissy," and the milder negative attitude toward the "tomboy." Such attitudes, and an active reinforcing of masculine acts for the boy and feminine acts for the girl, serve to teach the appropriate sex role to the growing child.

Fig. 14.5 All of us are required to play many roles—not only throughout our lives but often within a single day. Here are a few of the roles that your instructor must play. Although he may wear his academic robes rather seldom, he must play an academic role whenever he is in an academic situation. Certain kinds of behavior toward his colleagues and his students are appropriate; other kinds are not. His behavior is governed by his role. As a parent, his role is quite different; here it governs his behavior toward his wife, his child, his child's peers and teachers, and others who affect him as a parent. As a host at a party, he is cast in quite another role, one that requires behavior radically different from that of his academic role. Although the individual may have to play all three roles (and perhaps others) within the span of a few hours, it is usually possible to shift from one to another without difficulty or conflict. If several roles are demanded of us simultaneously, however, and if these roles conflict, deep personal disturbance and unhappiness may result. (Courtesy Conrad Kraft)

All of us are simultaneously members of several groups that may have different role demands. We are either male or female, and we are expected to behave in a masculine or feminine fashion— that is, to assume male or female roles. We are sons or daughters, and certain ways of behaving toward our parents are expected of us. The college student is a member of another group which is differentiated from the population at large, and within the college he may be a member of several groups, each with slightly different role demands.

The fact that the several role demands may differ from one another means that it is very likely that at certain times the demands of one group will be antagonistic to the demands of another group and that a *role conflict* will arise. One sort of role conflict can occur between our loyalty demands to friends and loyalty demands to social principles or institutions. In one study, subjects were presented with hypothetical situations involving conflicts of this sort to determine whether or not there was a consistency in the role that ultimately prevailed in the conflict.[15] First they were asked what they would do in the following kinds of situations:

A friend with whom you were driving is involved in an accident in which he was driving 35 miles an hour in a 20-mile zone. If you testify that he was going only 20 miles an hour, he will be freed of the charge against him. What would you do?

As a member of a board of directors of a corporation you obtain some confidential information which would make it possible for you to advise a friend to sell some holdings and thus avoid a large financial loss. Should you do so?

Four questions of this sort were asked, and it was found that some subjects answered consistently in terms of loyalty to the friend, and others in terms of loyalty to the principle or institution.

Then the subjects were asked further questions. One dealt with what they would do if they were proctors in an examination and found a friend cheating; another assumed that the subject was an assistant grading examinations and could help a friend by giving him a better grade than he deserved; a third supposed that the reader was working at the desk in the library and could help a friend by hiding a much-wanted book until he came for it. In each case the reader was asked to choose between one role and another— between loyalty to the friend or loyalty to the institution.

The study revealed a tendency for the individual who chose the personal-loyalty role in the first four situations to do so in the academic role-conflict situations and for the individual who chose the institution-loyalty role to show similar consistency. The study suggests that individuals differ in a consistent fashion in the role they will choose in a role-conflict situation, and that the relative dominance of one role over another is a personality characteristic. The implication is that we can predict something about the behavior of the individual if we know the roles that he plays generally and the roles that will dominate when he is in a role-conflict situation.

Leadership and role

Although it may not be obvious, there is a definite relationship between the concept of role and the concept of leadership. The leadership situation is one which by definition involves not only an individual but also a group. Groups differ from one another in many ways: in their goals, in the degree of formality of their structuring, in the degree of cohesiveness, in the manner in which they select their members, and in many other respects. These differences inevitably result in differences in the nature of the role behaviors that constitute leadership for the group in question.

Since the nature of the role expected of the leader will vary from group to group, we shall expect to find no specific pattern of behavior which may be referred to as typical leadership behavior,[16] and no single personality trait of leadership or any other personality characteristics which are inevitably associated with leadership in a variety of groups. Such actually have been the findings of the studies that have concerned themselves with discovering a relationship between leadership and measurable personality characteristics.[17]

These statements do not imply that there are not some characteristics which are more often associated with leadership than others, but only that there is no single pattern for a leader, which is appropriate in all groups. Experimental studies of the behavior of individuals in small groups demonstrate that there are some personality characteristics which are more often associated with leadership than are others. Intelligence has the highest correlation with leadership; personal adjustment seems to be next, followed by what is called extroversion or freedom in making social contacts.[18] Even though these general relationships can be found, this does not mean that the most intelligent or best adjusted or most extroverted individual will become the group leader.

Psychologists are only beginning to investigate the phenomenon of leadership, and they are learning how complex it is. They have learned enough to know that one cannot speak of a born leader, as though leadership were a unitary personality characteristic of which some persons possess much and others little. They have learned that the nature of leadership is inevitably linked to the nature and aims of the group. As these change, so also do the psychological demands upon the leader and the characteristics of the group member who will assume the role.

THE INDIVIDUAL IN SOCIAL SITUATIONS

In the previous section the various aspects of the social environment were described. It was pointed out that each of these aspects—culture, class, and groups—has certain characteristics and that these characteristics partially determine the behavior of the individual because they define for the individual what is appropriate and what is inappropriate. The following section will be concerned with the behavior of the individual in social situations and with the nature of the personal psychological mechanisms that govern his behavior.

Conformity

A series of experiments that dealt with the influence of group opinion on the judgments of an individual involved a simple task.[19] The eight subjects were seated along the side of a table and were required to indicate by calling out one at a time which of three rather obviously unequal lines was equal in length to a fourth line. In the first of this series of experiments all members of the group save one (the critical subject) were accomplices of the experimenter and on certain trials these accomplices, by pre-arrangement with the experimenter, would all make the same obviously wrong choice. The critical subject was one of the last to be called upon to make his judgment, and so, on these twelve rigged trials, he faced a situation in which the majority had responded in a manner which must have been contrary to the evidence of his senses. As a control for nonsocial errors in perception, other subjects were presented with the same problems but they made their answers privately in writing. Differences in performance between the two groups would therefore be a measure of how these publicly announced wrong choices of the majority influenced the critical subject. For the experimental group the mean number of errors in the direction of the majority's false statement was 3.84, whereas the mean number of errors committed by the control group on these same twelve trials was .08. Very clearly some of the subjects, though not all of them, shifted their reports to agree with the inaccurate statements of the other members of the group. In subsequent studies the experimenter employed the same procedure with groups of various sizes and the results of all of the experiments are presented in Figure 14.6. It is apparent that a group will exercise a high degree of conforming force when it consists of only four members, and no increased effectiveness is found by increasing the number of individuals in the group. Further studies of this

Fig. 14.6 The effect of the number of judges on the frequency with which subjects made judgments in agreement with those of the judges, all of whom made the same objectively wrong judgment. (After Asch[19])

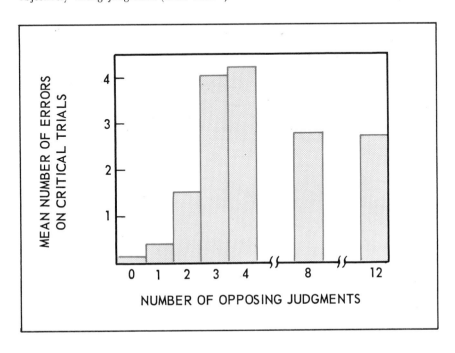

situation have shown that the conforming force is almost completely eliminated if there is another subject who agrees with the critical subject.

In these experiments some of the subjects never conformed to the majority's false statements, others conformed most of the time, and still others occupied an intermediate position. Interviews with the subjects after the experiment revealed that resisting the majority trend was neither easy nor pleasant, and that the resisting subjects often experienced fleeting feelings of doubt and some longing to be with the majority. Some of the subjects who erred frequently in the direction of the majority reported that they saw the lines as the majority announced them to be; the experimenter considered that their errors were due to *distortion of judgment*. A final few seemed to feel that it was more desirable to agree with the group than to make an accurate perception of line length. The experimenter called this a case of *distortion of action*. This analysis of the interview data clearly indicates that conformity behavior is not the consequence of some single psychological mechanism but of several, and these might be considered further.

Distortion in judgment

It is very likely that this conformity-producing mechanism is what is implied when one uses the term *suggestible*. It means only that the individual's perceptions have been biased in a certain direction.

A typical pattern to be found in suggestibility experiments is the following: Subjects are presented with a statement and asked to evaluate it or to express their agreement or disagreement with it. These statements are prefaced with the suggestibility-producing comment that the majority of people agree (or disagree) with the statement or that it was made by Thomas Jefferson or Lenin. Usually it is found that the subject's reaction will be biased by these leading comments—that is, suggestion operates.

In our discussion of perception we pointed out that a single word has multiple meanings and that its meaning in any specific situation is determined by its context. The same may be said of phrases. Thomas Jefferson stands for a certain kind of political philosophy; Lenin stands for a completely different one. Thus the statement attributed to Jefferson stands in a context utterly different from that of the same statement attributed to Lenin. It is not that we agree with a specific statement because Jefferson said it and reject the identical statement because Lenin said it. In the two contexts, these are two different statements. Thus one of the mechanisms determining suggestibility is the difference in the meaning of statements produced by different contexts.

This interpretation of some of the effects of suggestion is supported by the findings of an experiment in which college students were presented with passages attributed to such men as Jefferson or Stalin and were asked to tell what they thought the authors meant by the statements. Quite different interpretations of the meanings of statements were given depending upon the supposed author. The interpretations of the statement varied not because the subjects accepted or rejected the authors but because the meaning attributed to the statement depended upon the identity of the author.[20]

In some situations in which perceptions are modified to agree with those of a majority or an expert, the determining psychological mechanisms may be different from those cited above. In the experiments involving perception of the length of the lines, for example, there were no clear-cut contextual cues. The force of the social situation alone seemed responsible. Yet it is not strange that our perceptual responses should be influenced by others. From infancy, we have frequently depended upon others to check our own perceptions, and more often than not we have found that these others are reliable agents. "Did you hear a noise?" we ask a friend, and we accept or reject our own dubious impression on the basis of his answer. If a traffic light is between us and the setting sun, so that we are blinded in looking at it, we may use the driver traveling in the opposite direction as a cue to tell us when the light changes. During childhood, we frequently turned to our parents to ask them to explain to us—indeed, to tell us—what we saw.

Even as adults our perceptions involve choices not between black and white but between nearly indiscriminable shades of gray, and so we may depend upon others to help us in this discrimination. Thus we acquire strong habits of learning about the physical world around us from others. When, therefore, there is a conflict between our immediate sensory impression and reports on the same physical situation by many others, it is not strange that we should sometimes reject the physical stimuli and accept the social ones.

Distortion of action

A small number of the subjects perceived differently from the majority's false reports, believed their own perceptions, but nevertheless gave verbal reports that conformed with the majority's false statements. These subjects were obviously more strongly motivated to be seen as agreeing with the members of the group than they were motivated to give accurate reports of their own perceptions. The degree of generality of this characteristic—the preference to respond publicly in the same fashion as the majority, instead of stating one's own perception accurately—cannot be determined from the experiments described above. However, in another experiment of a similar nature, the subjects were also administered a personality test that gave some indication of the extent to which an individual was oriented toward doing a task well for its own sake as opposed to doing things in order to please others.[21] There was some tendency for the task-oriented subjects to be less conforming in the experimental situation than were the socially oriented subjects.

Although some relationship between conformity in the experimental task and social orientation was found in this study, one is not justified in concluding that this is necessarily a general personality characteristic which pervades an individual's behavior in all situations to the same degree. The behavior of the subject in any situation such as this is a function of differences of motive strength; one motive is to agree with the group and the other is to make an accurate statement about his perception. The strength of each of these motives will be independent of the strength of the other, and the strength of each of them may vary. As a result an individual may conform in one situation and not in another. Our ability to predict what will occur will depend upon the accuracy with which the strength of these two motives can be estimated.

This brief analysis of the psychological mechanisms which seem to operate when we are suggestible or resist suggestion, when we conform or when we rebel, implies that we are not dealing with an *instinct* to lead or to follow, to go along with the crowd or to be an individualist. We conform because we have learned to perceive in certain ways, and again because in the past we have learned that it is rewarding to do as others do. Yet in any given instance we may buck the crowd, for we may have other goals, other ideals, which have been so deeply instilled in us that it means more to be true to them than to gain some temporary accolade.

ATTITUDES

There is probably no one alive who can view the behavior of persons of another culture or class with complete detachment—without, in other words, being biased in his interpretations by the fact that he himself is a member of a different culture or class. In the process of growing up in our own cultural milieus, both large and small, we learn certain values, certain ways of attaining our goals, and certain ways of perceiving the behavior of others. These ways of behaving, because they have been reinforced by our peers, our parents, and the various figures of authority in our life, become the "right" way of doing things—and for some of us the only way. Inevitably, then, this learning serves as a background against which we evaluate the behavior of others. The concept of the biasing of responses by the influence of context upon our interpretation of stimuli is certainly not new to the reader, for we have discussed the phenomenon earlier, especially in Chapters 8 and 9. At present we are concerned with its application to social events. The term *attitude* is ordinarily used to refer to biases as they affect our relationships with other persons and groups.

The origin of attitudes

If attitudes ranged only from indifference to degrees of liking or acceptance, the problem of their origin would perhaps be of only academic concern to the sociologist and the psychologist. But such is not the case. Attitudes can be negative—sometimes violently negative—and such attitudes often lead to social strife and disharmony. An understanding, then, of the origin of attitudes, particularly of attitudes against other cultures and groups, is a matter of especial concern in a democratic society.

From our knowledge of conditioned avoidance reactions, we might set up the plausible hypothesis that negative reactions against cultures and groups are learned because some member of the disliked group has harmed or frustrated the holder of the attitude, and through stimulus generalization this learned negative reaction has become attached to other members of the group. Perhaps this does occur, but certainly with no great degree of frequency, and unquestionably the vast majority of our attitudes develop in the absence of these specific situational conditionings.

There are a number of arguments against the validity of the hypothesis that attitudes usually develop from direct experience with the group in question. First, persons with strong prejudices are seldom able to cite personal experiences that point to this type of psychological origin of their biases. Second, it is common to find strong prejudices shown against groups with which the individual has had no direct experience and about which he may know no more than that a group by such a name exists in some part of the world.[22]

Probably the origins of attitudes are largely indirect; they arise from the attitudes of those who are close to us. For this reason they are often quite irrational, for they often stem not from the real behavior of the group in question but from the frequently invalid reference statements made by others. We have stated earlier that reactions become fixated as a result of reinforcement, and we have stated also that a word or gesture of approval from another will serve as a reinforcement. The child learns to express the opinions and hold the beliefs of those who are close to him, for when he does so his own expressions meet with approval; they are, in other words, reinforced. It is not at all necessary for him to possess any real data bearing upon the behavior of the group to which the attitude refers; his close associates will reinforce or will not reinforce depending upon the extent to which his expressed attitudes coincide with their own. Whether their attitudes are sound or unsound is immaterial to his learning. If this hypothesis is correct, we should expect to find, among other things, a similarity in attitude of parent and child, and this is typically the case.[23]

This hypothesis alone does not readily account for the fact that negative attitudes are frequently directed against the strange and unfamiliar—a fact dramatically illustrated by a study in which attitudes toward various national groups were measured and a purely fictitious group was included. The fictitious group received a low rating. It is obvious that in this instance the rating is not based upon previous unfortunate experiences with the group or even upon experiences of disapproval of the group by the subject's peers. The only known characteristic of the group is that it is unknown.

In the chapter on emotions we pointed out that one element that produces fear reactions is the strange or the unfamiliar. In the chapter on maturation we described a study in which rats exhibited avoidance reactions to a strange object introduced into their cage. The older rats were more prone than the younger ones to make avoidance reactions. Some mechanism of this sort may be operating in the social realm and may be held partly accountable for the fact that there is a fairly general tendency to reject unfamiliar peoples, cultures, and customs for no reason other than that they are unfamiliar. In summary, this assumption would imply that negative attitudes may arise not because the group in question has harmed the attitude holder or because he has frequently heard ill spoken of them but, paradoxically, because he has not heard of them at all.

Taken quite literally, this statement would mean that everything unfamiliar would be rejected. But on this point it is well to recall that this same fear reaction did not occur among the rats who from infancy onward had found various objects placed in their cages. This would lead us to believe that cultures or subcultures which are isolated from others and whose knowledge of the behaviors of others is minimized would tend to be suspicious, intolerant, and rejecting of other cultures. And, conversely, a more cosmopolitan environment should decrease the tendency to reject others for insufficient reasons.

Influencing the individual, and either supporting or working against the attitudinal direction that this innate mechanism will produce, is the attitude of other individuals about him. As a group they may be characteristically tolerant or intolerant of the new and the unfamiliar, and the group's predominating attitude will inevitably influence the attitude of the individual who grows up and lives within it.

The maintenance of attitudes

Once an attitude has been developed, it may be very resistant to elimination, even in the face of rather considerable evidence against it. Several psychological mechanisms may operate in producing such attitude stability.

The influence of occasional reinforcement

We know, in the case of the conditioned response, that once a habit has developed, only an occasional reinforced trial among a large number of nonreinforced trials is required to keep it at a high level. There is no reason to believe that this same mechanism would not be operative for attitudes. A statement expressing an attitude toward a group may be untrue for the group as a whole, but it may be true of certain members of that group. This is just another way of saying that we should expect to find individual differences within any group. Suppose, then, that the attitude implies that dishonesty is characteristic of a particular group. Almost certainly this will be true of some members of that group, although no more characteristic of that group than of any other group. The attitude holder who hears of or sees an occasional dishonest act will thereby obtain the necessary reinforcement to keep his attitude toward the whole group intact.

It is worth noting, incidentally, that antisocial acts are the ones most likely to be brought to the attention of the attitude holder. He may have little to do with the group in question and may learn of them only through hearsay and newspaper accounts. Newspapers are highly selective in what they print, for they are not intended to be complete accounts of a society but rather to be the records of the unusual and outstanding events of that society. An account of any crime will almost certainly find its way into the columns of the newspaper, but of the many acts of good will that occur each day only a very few will be publicized. Thus, of all the acts committed by a given group, the attitude holder is in a position to hear of a high proportion of the undesirable ones and a low proportion of the desirable ones.

Perceptual biases

Our perceptual responses are not always, as we know, accurate evaluations of the objective stimulus events. They are influenced by our motive states, our sets, and our past habits of various sorts. These characteristics of perceptual activity make it not only possible but altogether likely that we would report quite differently the same event if it were performed by a group toward whom we are favorable and by a group toward whom we are antagonistic. This perceptual biasing almost guarantees that we shall find additional data to justify our attitude.

Such biasing is clearly illustrated by an experiment in which the best-liked and the least-liked children in a class performed exercises before the rest of the class.[24] Before the demonstration was given, and without the class knowing, the least popular students were given special drill on the exercises and the most popular were trained to make errors. In the class demonstration, and as a result of the prearrangements, the objective performance of the best-liked students was inferior to that of the least-liked students. Despite this fact, the audience of pupils judged the performance of the popular children to be superior to that of the unpopular ones.

The same experimenter found that teachers, in their grading, picked up a smaller *proportion* of the errors made by those whom they considered the good students than by those whom they considered the poor students. And thus, in a way, our attitudes guarantee that to those who have, more shall be given.

Errors in logic

In many cases an attitude extends beyond mere objection to behavior exhibited by a group to include an explanation of the behavior in terms of psychological causes. Such an explanation is not readily refuted. Thus, the individual with an anti-Negro attitude may maintain that Negroes are lazy and less intelligent than whites and that these characteristics are due to some inherited genetic characteristic that is correlated with skin color. He could amass considerable data to show that the Negro in America has achieved less than the white. It is not often that Negroes are directors of large corporations, eminent scientists, or important statesmen, or that they hold other positions which require considerable ability and strong motivation. He could then go a step further and account for the data by the assumption of a genetic difference between white and Negro. The conclusion is invalid both logically and scientifically, but very few people are trained in the application of the scientific method to social problems and hence the error is not likely to be discovered.

As we have pointed out earlier in this text, investigating such a problem as this requires careful, and usually costly, experimentation. The casual attitude holder does not ordinarily have the time, money, or inclination to make the sort of study that could test the validity of his hypothesis. Thus, because the error is found not in his statement of the *behavior* of the group but in his interpretation of the *causes* of the behavior, it is very likely to persist. He can point to the actual occurrence of behavior which would be found if his hypothesis were correct; he does not realize that there are other hypotheses that would predict as well or better.

Since attitudes are learned, they can also be unlearned or modified, despite the existence of various psychological mecha-

491

nisms that tend to maintain them. The ways in which attitudes can be unlearned are obviously similar to the ways in which they can be learned—or specifically, (1) by contact with the object itself, (2) through verbal reinforcements and non-reinforcements by reference group members, and (3) through formal communications that are specifically aimed at influencing the listener.

1. The effect of contact with the object

In the previously mentioned study of attitude change in the girls' college, the changes are attributable less to direct experiences that disprove the validity of the attitude than to social influences that are, in a sense, irrelevant to the content of the attitude.[11] That direct experience with the object or person toward whom the attitude is expressed will also change that attitude is illustrated by a wartime study.[25] The problem, which was of both military and social importance, concerned the effectiveness with which Negroes as individuals could be integrated into the predominantly white military units. At the time the study was conducted, there were already in existence predominantly white units containing some Negroes, and the specific information sought was the extent of the Negroes' acceptability to the white members of the unit. The answer to the question is best found by comparing attitudes of the whites in units that had had such experience with those in units that had not, and these data are presented in the Table 14.1.

TABLE 14.1. THE ATTITUDE OF WHITES TOWARD ACCEPTING NEGROES IN THEIR MILITARY COMPANY AS RELATED TO DEGREE OF PREVIOUS MILITARY EXPERIENCE WITH THEM

| | *Attitude* | | |
Degree of experience	*Would dislike it very much*	*Generally indifferent*	*Would like it*
Infantrymen in a company with a Negro platoon	7	61	32
Infantrymen in other companies in the same regiment	20	62	18
Field Artillery, Anti-tank, and HQ units in the same division	24	67	9
Other units which do not have Negro platoons	62	36	2

The favorable attitude toward the Negroes is directly related to the closeness of contact with them. There are probably two basic learning mechanisms that may account for attitude differences in this situation. First, we may assume that there are few if any instances of behavior among the Negro troops that would reinforce the negative attitude. Because contact occurs with little or no reinforcement of the negative attitude, the negative attitude tends to be extinguished. Second, we may assume that there were times when contact between the Negroes and whites occurred in which the Negroes' actions were associated with satisfactions for the whites. The frequency of Negro-white contacts would, of course, be greatest for whites in companies that contained a Negro platoon, and this is the group that shows the least rejection. It is also significant that rejection increases directly with decrease in opportunity for contact. The study indicates that contact modifies attitudes, but we must assume that it will do so only if it results in the appropriate kind of reinforcement.

2. The support of group members

In the previous section, while discussing membership and reference groups, a study of attitude changes in a girls' college was mentioned. The study showed that if the group served as a reference group for an individual, that individual's political attitude changed in the direction of the group's attitude. Those persons whose attitudes did not change were the ones with other reference groups that held different political attitudes, or ones for whom the student body represented a negative reference group. The means by which reference groups modify attitudes are undoubtedly multiple and complex. Included in these means are the various effects described in the previous section on conformity, while others arise from the reinforcement value of the group's reaction. It is safe to conclude, therefore, that one's attitudes are almost constantly undergoing some kind of change in the direction of the norms of our reference groups. This does not imply that all group members have the same attitudes to the same degree, but only that the individuals will shift toward the group norm as a function of the reinforcements and non-reinforcements that are the consequences of the characteristic group feeling.

3. Formal communication

A number of studies have been conducted measuring the degree of attitude change produced by motion pictures, special lectures, or even college courses.[26] In the usual design of these studies measurement of attitude are made before and after the experimental influence was introduced, and the frequency and amount of attitude change is determined. As a result of these studies we are able to specify to some degree the extent to which various kinds of formal communications will produce opinion changes.

▶ *The nature of the source.* As a general rule the studies have shown that an audience is influenced by communications for or against some topic, and usually their attitudes will shift in the direction of the message. The extent of the shift, as measured shortly after the communication, will be determined by the communicator's reputation and acceptability to the listener. In one experiment students were given information concerning the feasibility of developing an atomic submarine which purportedly came from the Russian newspaper *Pravda* or from the American atomic physicist, Robert Oppenheimer.[27] The subjects who thought the information came from *Pravda* were essentially unaffected by the report while those who felt it came from Oppenheimer showed a rather considerable shift in opinion.

In general, sources of low acceptability or creditability have little affect in shifting attitudes in the direction of their message when the attitudes are measured shortly after message delivery. Sources of high creditability are generally effective. However, when opinions were measured several weeks after the experimental session the subjects who had listened to the untrustworthy source had shifted in the direction of the communication; while the subjects who obtained their information from the trustworthy source had moved back toward their original positions. The attitudes of the two groups were now very similar to each other and both had been changed in the direction of the communication. This type of delayed attitude change is called the *sleeper effect.*

▶ *Types of presentations.* A message which is intended to produce a certain point of view or attitude in the listener may be strongly one-sided, mentioning only the arguments in favor of its position, or it may also present arguments on the other side and then counter these arguments. An experiment was conducted to evaluate the effectiveness of these two approaches, using as a topic the subject of when the Russians might be expected to develop an atomic bomb.[28] Groups of high school students were presented either with the one-sided or the two-sided discussion and, when their opinions were measured, there was little difference between the two groups in their attitudes. So far it seems to make little difference which method was employed. Later a largely one- sided discussion presenting the opposite point of view was delivered, and again the students' opinions were measured. At this time marked differences were found between the groups that had originally been presented with the two different kinds of messages. The group that had been exposed to the two-sided presentation maintained its position, whereas the group that had originally heard the one-sided presentation shifted back in the direction suggested by the most recent propaganda.

Another contrast in type of presentation is to be found in the emotional as opposed to the rational appeal. A rather large number of studies have been conducted on this topic and the over-all results of them are inconclusive. A few studies have found the emotional appeal to be more effective than the rational message, but other studies have failed to show a difference between these methods. We must conclude that the problem is more complex than are the comparisons of "rational" and "emotional" appeals and that other psychological factors must play a heavy part in determining the results.[26]

THE MEASUREMENT OF ATTITUDE
AND OPINION

The two major problems facing the investigator who wishes to measure attitudes or opinions concern the kind and number of individuals who should be questioned—the problem of sampling— and the phrasing of the questions to be asked. These problems, which on the surface seem to have simple solutions, are actually knotty ones and have been the subject of many investigations.

Sampling

Often we are interested in measuring the attitude or opinion of a large population which is heterogeneous in nature—as, for example, the student body of a large university, with its fraternity and nonfraternity groups; its coeds and male students; its playboys and its grinds; its students from wealthy and from poorer homes; and its freshmen, sophomores, juniors, and seniors. Perhaps on the attitude to be measured, the fraternity groups are biased in one direction and the nonfraternity groups biased in another; perhaps also the upper and lower classmen have opposite biases. Our task is to discover the attitude of the student body as a whole; but, because the university is large, it is not practical to plan to ask each student his opinion. If we ask the question only of upper classmen or of fraternity groups, our prediction of the attitude of the university as a whole will certainly differ from what it would be if we had asked the question only of lower classmen and non-fraternity groups. Even if both groups were included in our sample of responses but there were proportionally more of one group in the sample than in the actual university population, our answer would err to the extent of the disproportion. We are confronted with the task of representing in our sample all major groups of the total population and representing them in the same proportion as in the total university population: this is the problem of *sampling*.

One method of achieving this end is known as *random sampling*, a technique which assumes that each individual in the group to be questioned has an equal likelihood of being asked. Perhaps the best way to obtain a random sample would be to select at random from a list of all the students in the university those students who are to be interviewed. If our sample is moderately large, we can obtain a fairly accurate measurement of the opinion of the university as a whole.

Such a method as this would almost certainly give us a random and unbiased sample of the total population, but there are other methods which seem to lead to random selection but may not actually do so. Suppose that a ballot were printed in the college newspaper and the readers were asked to return it to boxes located about the campus. It is very likely that only those who felt strongly about the issue would take the trouble to fill out and deposit the ballot, and biasing would almost certainly result. Suppose that interviewers are posted in front of several of the campus buildings or on walks leading across the campus and are instructed to stop and question every tenth or twentieth person who passes by. Here again biases can operate. The walks on which the interviewers are posted may be the most direct route to Fraternity Row and thus may be used more often by fraternity than nonfraternity men.

Or the buildings may be ones used more frequently by upper-classmen than by underclassmen. Lastly, the interviewers are likely to find times when, after their count has reached eight, three or four persons walk by together in a group. Which of these is the tenth individual, the one to be interviewed? Even though he attempts to be objective, the interviewer may unwittingly let his own bias determine which of the group will be selected for the interview.

Often it is difficult or uneconomical to obtain a random sample, and the method of *stratified sampling* is used. In this method the researcher first identifies the important classes or groups in the population, and in addition, determines the proportion that each group represents in the total population. Thus, in our example he would determine how many freshmen, sophomores, juniors, and seniors there are and what proportion of them are members of fraternities. Then, in selecting the sample of students to be interviewed, he would specifically seek out persons in each of these groups and would have each group represented in his sample in the same proportion that they have in the total population. Thus, if in the total student population 30 percent of the students were fraternity members, the researcher would permit only 30 percent of his sample to be fraternity members. The same principle would apply to upper and lower classmen, and to any other significant grouping of the student population.

In the example we have chosen to illustrate these two methods of sampling—the random and the stratified—the researcher's task would not be very difficult. Consider, however, the task that confronts the poll taker who attempts to predict a presidential election. He has no nationwide list of voters from which to select his random sample. Even so, he may use a modified form of random sampling. He may, on some basis other than a random one, decide that he wishes to poll 100 persons in a given city. Then he may choose from the city directory 100 houses at random. The interviewers are then required to ask the question of the voter in these 100 houses. Several trips back to some of the houses may be required before the interviewers find all 100 voters at home.

Using the census data on such group characteristics as occupation, age, and income, the poll taker is in a position to construct a stratified sample, but even the census data are not likely to be so precise as the data he could obtain for a university population from the Dean of Students' office. Some years may have elapsed since

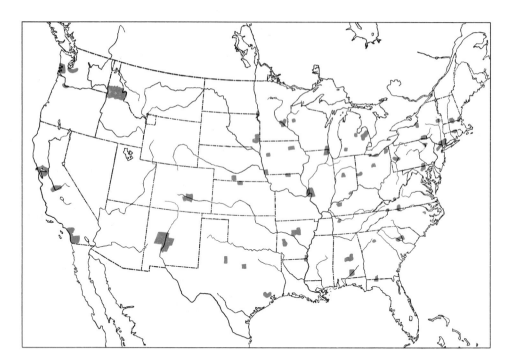

Fig. 14.7 This map shows the areas sampled by the Survey Research Center for the 1952 election. Certain large metropolitan areas are regularly chosen for interviewing by the center, but the selection of the other areas of the country is made by random sampling methods. The method used essentially involves choosing states at random, then counties in these states, then towns or townships, then city blocks or township areas, and lastly a particular residence. The poll-taker then interviews the individual in that residence. In all cases the choices are made at random. (Courtesy *Scientific Monthly*)

the last census, and the reports given to the census takers on income and age may not have been highly accurate in the first place.

Another source of difficulty which the researcher encounters on the national scale but which is likely to be minimized in a university poll is the relationship between the interviewer and the respondent. Assuming, as we did in our example, that students are conducting the college poll, there are some definite common bonds between interviewer and respondent. Both belong, at least, to the same institution and to the same educational group. Between the national interviewer and certain of his respondents, however, a considerable gulf in interest and in social class will exist. The interviewer is likely to come from the middle class, and, in order to hold his position, he must, of course, have a certain minimal level of education. Yet his respondents, if the sample is to be representative of the total population, will vary widely in their socioeconomic and educational levels. The gulf between the two may make for some constraint in the interview and may cause the respondent to answer the questions less frankly than would be the case if the gap did not exist.

Phrasing the questions

Some years ago a questionnaire was sent out through the mail which presumably was designed to measure the public's preferences toward models of automobiles. One of the questions in the survey read somewhat as follows: "Do you prefer a smooth, silent eight or a noisy, jerky six?" We do not know the outcome of the questionnaire, but we have little doubt that when the returned ballots were tabulated, a marked preference was found for the eight-cylinder automobile. The phrasing of this question is such that the respondents would not be reacting by stating a preference for a six- or eight-cylinder automobile but for the riding characteristics of an automobile that is jerky as opposed to one that is smooth. This means that the conclusion which the survey might reach upon the preferences for eight- and six-cylinder automobiles would almost certainly be false; because the number of cylinders probably had little to do with determining the response. Our example is extreme, but the influence of the wording of the question can be considerable even when the biasing is not obvious. A few examples of the way in which wordings influence responses are presented in Table 14.2.[29]

TABLE 14.2. HOW THE WORDING OF THE QUESTIONS INFLUENCES RESULTS

EXAMPLE A. THE CONTEXT OF THE QUESTION.

Form 1. So far as you, personally, are concerned, do you think the United States has gone too far in helping Britain, or not far enough?

Form 2. The same question except that the words "President Roosevelt" were substituted for "the United States."

Results:

	Form 1	Form 2
Too far	15	20
Not far enough	32	17
About right	46	87
No opinion	7	6
(Given in June 1941)		

499

EXAMPLE B. THE ORDER OF ASKING QUESTIONS.

Order 1. "Should the United States permit its citizens to join the French and British Armies?"
"Should the United States permit its citizens to join the German Army?"

Order 2. The identical questions but in reverse order.

		May join British and French army		May join German army	
Results:		Order 1	Order 2	Order 1	Order 2
	Yes	45	40	31	22
	No	46	54	61	74
	Don't know	9	6	8	4

(Given in October 1939)

EXAMPLE C. THE ALTERNATIVE AVAILABLE.

Form 1. If you were asked to vote today on the question of the United States entering the war against Germany and Italy, how would you vote—to go into war or to stay out of war?

Results:

Go in: 29%. Stay out: 66%. No opinion: 5%.

Form 2. Please tell me which of these policies you think the United States should follow at the present time.
A. Go to war at once against Germany and Italy—6%.
B. Supply Britain with all the war materials we can and also use our navy to convoy ships carrying these materials to Britain—36%.
C. Supply Britain with all war materials we can, but do *not* use our navy to convoy these materials—46%.
D. Stop all further aid to Britain—7%.
E. No opinion—4%.
(Given in May 1941)

To the reader who is already familiar with the significance of context as a determiner of the meaning of a stimulus and with the operation of motive states and sets on our perceptual activities, the influence of variations in phrasing upon response should come as no surprise. What may puzzle him as he examines Table 14.2 is the problem of which form of the question to accept as the one he will use in his research. Assuming that the question has been carefully phrased so as to eliminate ambiguity and obvious biasing, one could not conclude that one form is better than another. The answers are meaningful only within the context in which they were given, and the conclusions should make the context explicit. The attitudes researcher can do this by presenting in his conclusion

the completely worded question itself rather than a general statement of what the question meant. If he is able to, he may go a
step further and attempt to estimate how whatever contextual
factors appear in the question may have influenced the results.

We have intentionally steered clear of the topic of the validity of a questionnaire. That is, what do these responses mean with reference to some other kinds of behavior? Do they, for example, predict how the population would vote if tomorrow the issue were opened to voting. This is really the question that we are hinting at when we ask which form of the question is the most desirable. We shall consider the problem of validity in greater detail in the next section of this chapter.

THE VALIDITY OF ATTITUDE

MEASUREMENTS

An attitude questionnaire consists, ordinarily, of a sheet of paper on which the respondent checks whether or not he accepts certain statements about the topic or social phenomenon in question. Assuming that the answers have been given honestly, can we predict that a person who has one score will behave differently toward the social phenomenon in question from one who has another score? How valid, in other words, is our attitude questionnaire?

The primary method for studying validity of an attitude questionnaire has been to administer it to two groups of subjects, one of these being a group readily identified as favorable to the social phenomenon, and the other as unfavorable. Thus a questionnaire measuring attitude toward war could be administered to the members of a pacifist organization and to a military group. The mean scores of the two groups are then compared, and sizable differences are usually noted between the pro and anti scores. Or, again, one may compare the predictions of a public-opinion poll dealing with the next election with the actual election results. More often than not, the polls predict the election results, although, as in 1948, they may be in error. Yet even in that instance the failure may be more attributable to carelessness on the part of the researchers than to any basic inadequacy of public-opinion polling itself.

One study is of especial interest because it indicates that changes in scores on attitude questionnaires are associated with changes in other kinds of behavior.[30] The study dealt with attitudes toward Negroes among a group of children attending an interracial camp. The camp members were given an attitude questionnaire toward Negroes at the beginning and at the end of the camping period. Comparison of the before and after scores indicated that some of the white children had become more favorable toward the Negroes during the camping period and some less favorable. In addition to filling out the attitude questionnaire, each child was asked by his counselor both at the beginning and the end of the period to name five boys in the camp with whom he would like to live. The question that the experimenter wished to answer was whether or not a change in score was associated with a change in the number of Negroes that would be named by the campers. The answer to the question was in the affirmative. The boys who became more favorable toward the Negroes as measured by the attitude questionnaire selected more Negro boys to live with at the end of the camp term than they had done at the beginning. The reverse was true of the boys whose score was less favorable at the end of the period. The experiment, then, offers evidence of the validity of the attitude questionnaire.

It is probable, however, that we cannot speak of the validity of attitude measurements in general, for undoubtedly the degree of validity varies with the attitude in question. In the case of some attitudes, the respondents may readily give sincere and accurate answers; but in the case of others, for a variety of reasons, their responses may be some distance from the truth. This occurs not merely because they wish to put their best foot forward in the presence of the investigator but because they are fooling themselves—an all-too-human tendency.

Even when the attitude score truly reflects the feelings of the individual, it does not follow that he will necessarily behave in accordance with the score, for he may possess other attitudes which work in the opposite direction. Thus, someone may have an attitude of strong antagonism against some "racial" group, an attitude so strong that it may, by itself, lead to physical violence against members of the group. However, the person may also have feelings against the use of physical violence which are even stronger than his attitude against the racial group. Because of this, his attitude against the group never becomes expressed in the form that might be expected. This does not mean that the attitude scale is invalid; it does mean that in order to predict behavior stemming from an attitude we must know more about that person than the single attitude score.

REFERENCES

[1] Hallowell, A. I. *Culture and Experience,* Univ. of Pennsylvania, 1955.

[2] Linton, R. *The Cultural Background of Personality,* Routledge and Kegan Paul, 1947.

[3] Goldman, I. "The Kwakiutl Indians of Vancouver Island." In Margaret Mead (ed.), *Cooperation and Competition among Primitive Peoples,* McGraw-Hill, 1937.

[4] Goldman, I. "The Zuni of New Mexico," *op. cit.*

[5] Converse, P. E. "The shifting role of class in political attitudes and behavior." In E. E. Maccoby, T. M. Newcomb, E. L. Hartley (ed.), *Readings in Social Psychology,* Holt Rinehart and Winston, 1958.

[6] Davis, A., Gardner, B. B., and Gardner, M. A. *Deep South, A Social Anthropological Study of Caste and Class,* Chicago, 1941.

[7] Bronfenbrenner, U. "Socialization and social class through time and space." In E. E. Maccoby, T. M. Newcomb, and E. L. Hartley (ed.), *Readings in Social Psychology,* Holt, Rinehart and Winston, 1958.

[8] Queener, E. L. *Introduction to Social Psychology,* Holt, Rinehart and Winston, 1951.

[9] Dashiell, J. F. "Experimental studies of the influence of social situations on the behavior of individual human adults." In C. Murchison (ed.), *Handbook of Soc. Psychol.,* Clark Univ. Press, 1935.

[10] Moller, J. B. Cooperation and competition: An experimental study of motivation, *Teachers College Contributions to Education,* 1929, No. 384.

[11] Newcomb, T. M. *Personality and Social Change,* Holt, Rinehart and Winston, 1943.

[12] Hemphill, J. K. Group dimensions: A manual for their measurement, *Bureau of Business Research Monographs,* Ohio State University, 1956.

[13] Guetzkow, H., and Simon, H. A. The impact of certain communication nets upon organization and performance in task-oriented groups, *Management Science,* 1955, *1,* 233-250.

[14] Linton, R. *Op. cit.*

[15] Stouffer, S. A., and Toby, J. Role conflict and personality, *Amer. J. Soc.,* 1951, *56,* 395-406.

[16] Hemphill, J. K. Situational factors in leadership, *Bureau of Educational Research Monograph,* The Ohio State University, 1950.

[17] Stogdill, R. M. Personal factors associated with leadership: A survey of the literature, *J. Psychol.,* 1948, *25,* 35-71.

[18] Mann, R. A review of the relationships between personality and performance in small groups, *Psychol. Bull.,* 1959, *56,* 241-270.

[19] Ash, S. E. "Effects of group pressure upon the modification and distortion of judgment." In E. E. Maccoby, T. M. Newcomb, and E. L. Hartley (ed.), *Readings in Social Psychology,* Holt, Rinehart and Winston, 1958.

[20] Asch, S. E. *Social Psychology*, Prentice-Hall, 1952, Chapter 16.

[21] McDavid, John, Jr. Personality and situational determinants of conformity, *J. Soc. Psychol.*, 1959, *58*, 241-246.

[22] Bogardus, E. S. A social distance scale, *Sociology and Social Research*, 1933, *17*, 265-271.

[23] Hartley, E. *Problems in Prejudice*, Crown, 1946.

[24] Zillig, M. Einstellung und Aussage, *Zeitschrift fur Psychologie und Physiologie*, 1928, *106*, 58, 106.

[25] Stouffer, S. A., *et al.* "Studies in social psychology in World War II." In *The American Soldier: Adjustment during Army Life*, Princeton, 1949, Vol. 1.

[26] Hovland, C. I. "Effects of mass medea of communication." In G. Lindzey (ed.), *Handbook of Social Psychology*, Addison-Wesley, 1954, Vol. II.

[27] Hovland, C. I., and Weiss, W. The influence of source credibility on communication effectiveness, *Publ. Opin. Quart.*, 1951, *15*, 635-650.

[28] Lumsdaine, A. A., and Janis, I. L. Resistance to "counter-propaganda" produced by one-sided and two-sided "propaganda" presentations, *Public Opin. Quart.*, 1953, *17*, 311-318.

[29] Cantril, H. *Gauging Public Opinion*, Princeton, 1947.

[30] Mussen, P. H. The reliability and validity of the Horowitz Faces Test, *J. Abn. Soc. Psychol.*, 1950, *45*, 504-506.

Chapter Fifteen

PERSONALITY

FROM THE FIRST CHAPTER ONWARD, this text has repeatedly defined the aim of the science of psychology as the prediction of behavior. The pursuit of this end led, in the early chapters of the text, to identifying and describing the operating characteristics of certain basic mechanisms of behavior, such as habits and motives. In the previous chapter an attempt was made to show briefly how broad divisions within the social environment produce their impacts upon the individuals who dwell within their confines. Culture, class, and group identifications as we described them in the preceding chapter are relevant to psychology because they operate to make the many individuals who are members of a specific culture, class, or group resemble one another in certain ways. But in addition to these common environmental forces, there are other forces, both environmental and

505

genetic, that create behavioral characteristics peculiar to the individual. The study of personality is a study of the factors that determine the total behavior of the individual but it is especially concerned with those factors that make the behavior of the individual unique; the behaviors which cause him to stand out from his fellow humans instead of being a faceless member of a vast body of faceless companions.

The extent to which the concept of personality emphasizes the uniqueness of the behavior of the individual is illustrated in the usual evaluation of plays and novels. If the characters embody nothing more than the typical goals and manners of their major social groupings, they seem lifeless and unreal. We may accept the work as an excellent commentary upon some social phenomenon but not as a commentary on individual human life. When the social phenomenon is no longer of vital interest, the work is dead—dead because its characters were never alive. Thus the concept of personality is used in discriminating and differentiating individuals, in dealing with this person and that person, and not in describing the common characteristics of groups of people.

But it is not enough to say that one person differs from another; we must indicate *how* he differs and we must describe these differences in terms of specific aspects of behavior and relate them to meaningful psychological concepts. For example, if we describe a person physically, we do so by identifying his status along several dimensions—weight, height, complexion, and color of eyes. The same general method can be employed in describing personality. In this description, however, our statements refer to behavioral rather than physical characteristics. A person can be thought of as exhibiting varying kinds and amounts of certain behavioral characteristics, and an identification of his status in relation to these characteristics will describe his personality in the same way that the identification of his status in relation to physical characteristics will describe him physically.

Precisely which behavioral aspects are necessary for personality description is by no means certain. In fact, even now, a large amount of research in the area of personality is focused on determining the most useful way of describing the aspects—or, as they are commonly called, dimensions—of personality. But descriptions of behavior are not sufficient; one must seek further and identify the underlying psychological mechanisms and the way these interact with each other to produce the particular behavior of the individual at a particular moment in time. Most of these mechanisms have been discussed earlier in the text. They are habits, motives, emotional reactions, stimulus selection tendencies, perceptual processes, and intellectual functionings. The task of personality theory is to understand how they develop in a particular way in individuals and how they interact to suppress or facilitate each other. Thus, in its ideal but unrealized aim, personality theory is a theory for predicting the unique behavior of an individual.

HEREDITY AND ENVIRONMENT IN

PERSONALITY DEVELOPMENT

As is true of certain other psychological concepts, an effort to account for personality variations by reference to either environment or heredity alone is fruitless. Personality is not a single and unitary concept; it is comprised of the status of the individual on many aspects of his behavior. And one aspect of his behavior may be very unlike another aspect in cause as well as in characteristic.

Personality characteristics are always manifestations of an interaction between the individual and his environment, primarily his social environment. It is inconceivable that behaviors which are manifested only in the individual's interactions with his environment are not either developed through or modified by learning. One might question this statement by pointing out that personality characteristics need not be defined in terms of environmental and social interactions; we could choose characteristics that are non-social in nature. As an example, we might choose such a characteristic as the sheer tendency to be active. We might measure this by placing the subject in a room with no furnishings and measure the amount of his movement and activity. We could repeat our tests frequently enough to obtain a reliable estimate of his behavior, and, after testing a number of people in the same fashion, we could assign a score to each of them. Yet, having done so, would we be satisfied that what we have measured is a meaningful aspect of personality? Almost certainly not. We would wish to know the relationship between the individual's test score and the amount of ambition he has, the degree of effort he exerts to overcome frustrations, the amount of restlessness he shows in his seat in church or at a lecture, his degree of participation at an open-forum meeting, his behavior at a party, and many other matters. What we wish to know about a person usually concerns his behavior in the everyday environment. And such behavior characteristics as these must in part be influenced by learning.

It is not unlikely that an individual's general level of activity is to a great extent determined by genetic factors, but it does not follow that environmental events may not greatly modify the manner in which these behavior tendencies are expressed. Consider two hypothetical subjects both born with high activity levels. One is reared in a home in which the child "should be seen and not heard," and in which adventurous rovings of any kind are punished. The other is reared in a home that encourages explorations of all sorts and rewards the child for doing new things. It is inconceivable that the two children would not grow up to be two quite different adults, even with respect to the general level of activity they would exhibit in a wide variety of situations. On the other hand, we should expect that a child born with a low activity level and reared in either of these homes would not be like either of the active children.

All this discussion returns us to the statement made at the beginning of this section. Personality characteristics do not arise exclusively from the operation of environmental or genetic factors; they are a product of the interaction of both.

This statement is by no means peculiar to the concept of personality, for geneticists have often demonstrated the importance of interaction in the determination of the presence or absence of some physical characteristic. Thus in the *Drosophila,* the fruit fly used so frequently in genetic experiments, a certain race differs from the normal by the fact it will develop black bands on its abdomen when it is raised on a limited supply of dry food. When raised on a diet of rich moist food these unusual bands are almost completely absent. This characteristic is therefore determined neither by environmental forces alone nor by genetic forces alone, but by an interaction of the two. The queen bee becomes the queen because as a larva it was fed a food—the so-called "royal jelly"—that was different from that which was fed to the larvae which will develop into the worker bees.[1] If genetic-environmental interactions are important in determining the physical characteristics of lower organisms, they are even more important for the complex behavior of the human.

But to return to the problem of psychology, and in particular to the problem of personality development. It is not possible to conceive of meaningful personality characteristics that are not in some way influenced by the principles of learning. But the principles of learning act upon an organism whose structure is determined largely by its genetic make-up.

Because interactions are too complex for simple explanations, we shall, for the next few pages, describe separately the evidence that both environmental factors and genetic factors operate in determining personality. We shall not burden each sentence with some qualifying phrase that emphasizes interaction, but the reader should bear in mind that interaction is always implied.

GENETIC DETERMINATION

The task of demonstrating a relationship between human personality characteristics and genetic variation is an extremely difficult one. A major reason for the difficulty lies in the fact that one cannot, in this field, perform the ideal experiment in which one variable is held constant while the other is systematically altered. Specifically, this would be an experiment in which all the subjects are provided with the identical environment but wherein the various individuals—or better yet, groups of individuals—bear different but known genetic relationships to each other. Experiments of this sort are, however, possible with subhuman species. Since there is every reason to believe that mechanisms of heredity function in the same manner in man and the subhuman mammals, the results of these studies are highly relevant to questions of the origin of personality characteristics in man. For this reason several such experiments will be described.

Earlier in this chapter we described a hypothetical example of the effects of different environments upon children with different activity levels. We implied that the basic level of activity for each child was determined by the parentage and not by differences in environment. This particular characteristic of behavior was chosen for the example because it has been demonstrated that activity level in the white rat is a function of parentage.[2] The experiment began by placing white rats in an activity cage similar to the one which is briefly described in Chapter 5: a cage with an attached wheel in which the rat could run as in a treadmill, but in which the running task took the rat nowhere, so that it might be called a measure of purposeless activity. Some rats revolved the wheel many times during a day and some a very few times; in other words some were active and others were inactive. The rats of the parent population, called P_1, were chosen at random from the total population of the laboratory's animal colony. In each succeeding generation the most active rats were interbred, and the least active were also interbred. The results of this experiment are presented in graphic form in Figure 15.1. It is apparent that the strains grow apart in successive generations, one becoming consistently more active and the other more inactive. These differences developed even though the animals from both strains were living in essentially the same environment, the activity cages themselves and the typical and rather unexciting living quarters of a laboratory colony of white rats. At the human level it is interesting to note that consistent individual differences in level of activity are found in infants as early as the first ten days of life.[3]

The next experiment deals with the inheritance of fearfulness in white rats.[4] The stimulus condition which evoked the fear-

Fig. 15.1 The effect of selective breeding on the generalized activity of rats. Activity was measured by the number of turns of the wheel made by the rat in a given period of time. The most active and the most inactive rats of each generation were then bred to produce separate populations of active and inactive animals. (After Rundquist[2])

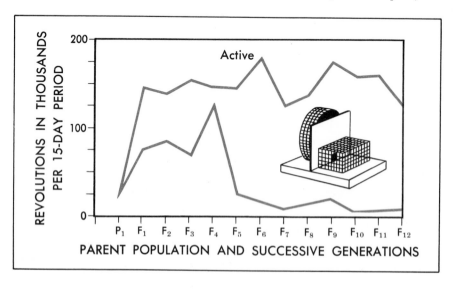

ful response was a large, circular, brightly lighted, open area into which the mice were placed by the experimenter. Most animals when first placed in such an environment react to it with hesistant, tense movements and with urination and defecation. With frequent placement in this test situation their movements become freer and defecation and urination cease. The frequency of these latter responses on successive placings in the test situation is used as a measure of the degree of the individual's fear reaction to this strange environment. When rats were taken at random from the laboratory colony, some adapted quickly while others required many days to adjust to their placement in these surroundings. The same procedure was followed in this experiment as in the previous one: the most fearful rats were interbred, as were the least fearful, and this was continued for a number of generations. The results are presented in Fig. 15.2, which plots the mean number of days before defecation and urination ceased in this open-field situation for the successive generations of the two groups of animals.

The results of this experiment became of even greater significance because of a subsequent experiment, in which the "fearful" and the "fearless" strains were tested in a different situation.[5] Single animals of each of these strains were placed in the home cage of a single animal from the other strain and the frequency with which fighting was initiated by the members of either strain was recorded. The "fearless" animals initiated a quarrel 326 times, in contrast to 68 such challenges on the part of the animals of the "fearful" strain.

This experiment has demonstrated that the behavior characteristics which appear in one situation, and which are susceptible to selective breeding, are correlated with similar behavior in a different situation. For this reason the experiment is of special significance, and it supports the view that the contribution to personality of genetic forces is not the production of some specific behavior pattern, but rather the supplying of a general predisposition which may manifest itself in a variety of situations. The word *temperament* is frequently used to refer to the biasing of behavior that is supplied by the individual's genetic background.

It should be emphasized that these statements concerning the genetic determination of temperament do not imply that particular kinds of personality reactions are inherited and will make themselves apparent regardless of the environment in which the individual develops. They imply only that these broad tendencies

511

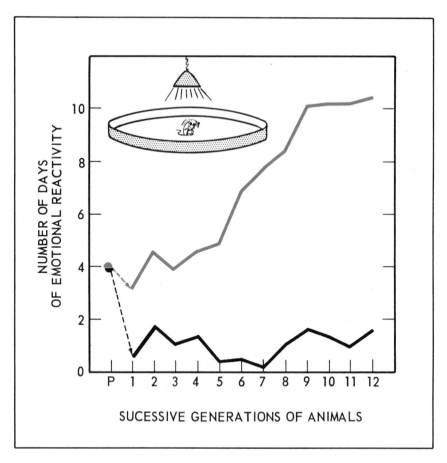

Fig. 15.2 The effect of selective breeding on emotionality in rats, as measured by number of days of defecation or urination when placed in a brightly lighted open field. The first point in the graph shows the mean of the parent population. (After data from Hall[4])

of the individual will interact with the environmental forces to form his personality characteristics. It is a far cry from these general characteristics of behavior to the more specific behavior patterns that have sometimes—though incorrectly—been attributed to heredity. There is no acceptable evidence that criminality, a distaste for mathematics, or any similar specific way of reacting is genetically determined

The final experiment demonstrates an interaction effect between the genetic background and the environment in which the organisms were raised.[6] The behavior characteristic under investigation was one which the experimenters termed "dominance." It was measured by placing two hungry rats into a test box where a

512

In the figure, the y-axis is labeled "NUMBER OF DAYS OF EMOTIONAL REACTIVITY" and the x-axis is labeled "SUCESSIVE GENERATIONS OF ANIMALS" with markings P, 1, 2, 3, 4, 5, 6, 7, 8, 9, 10, 11, 12.

food can was available behind so narrow an opening that only one animal could eat from it at a time. The experimenter recorded the amount of time that each animal had its head in the food can during the five-minute test period, and the animal with the greatest time was given a "win." Tests were conducted on nineteen different days; and it was found that some animals won consistently and were called dominant, while others lost consistently and were called submissive. Next the submissive males and females were bred together, while the dominant males and females were interbred. The experiment is concerned with the offspring of these matings. All of them were raised by foster mothers, with half of each group being raised by dominant and half by submissive mothers. The various combinations of parentage and rearing conditions are presented in the first two columns of Table 15.1, and the last column gives the scores that the offspring obtained on a dominance test of the kind which had been given to the parents.

TABLE 15.1. DOMINANCE SCORE OF OFFSPRING OF
DOMINANT AND SUBMISSIVE PARENTS REARED
IN DIFFERENT ENVIRONMENTS

Type of parentage	Foster mother	Dominance score
Dominant	Dominant	10.7
Dominant	Submissive	16.7
Submissive	Dominant	4.8
Submissive	Submissive	4.3

The higher values are associated with dominance and the lower values with submission. An inspection of the table shows that the offspring of submissive parents are equally submissive regardless of the characteristic of the foster parent. For the offspring of the dominant parents, however, the environment supplied by the foster parent operates to make the offspring markedly less dominant if they are raised by dominant mothers than if they are raised by submissive mothers. Thus dominant behavior in this situation is clearly shown to be a result of an interaction between environmental and genetic factors.

It should be mentioned that the studies on animals do not constitute a direct proof that general personality characteristics in the human are a consequence of genetic forces, but they are consistent with such a hypothesis and they offer indirect support for such a view. Studies dealing with this problem in humans are considerably more indirect and complicated, and require rather complicated statistical operations. Essentially, such studies consist of correlating the behavior of individuals in a number of situations and identifying some common characteristic that permeates many of these situations. This statistically identified psychological characteristic is similar to a temperament in its breadth of influence. For various reasons it has been suggested that genetic factors may be at least partially responsible for these broad behavior tendencies.

In conclusion, it would appear that genetic make-up may determine certain general temperamental factors but that environmental influences will play the major role in determining how these will be expressed.

LEARNING AND PERSONALITY CHARACTERISTICS

Chapter 3 was devoted to an identification of the principles that result in the acquisition of new responses and the elimination of old ones. In the present section we shall attempt to show how these principles of acquisition and elimination contribute to the nature of the major psychological mechanisms of which personality is composed.

Instrumental responses

The term *instrumental responses,* it will be recalled, refers to the responses that are employed by the individual in achieving his goals. These responses form the individual's style of life but not its direction; they do not refer to what he wants, but how he goes about attaining—or even failing to attain—those things to which he is attracted. Instrumental responses are of many types; they include simple and complicated motor skills; but they also include intellectual competencies, for these too are means of gaining goals. Finally, even certain kinds of emotional reactions can be included within this category, for fits of anger, affectionate responses, and even fear reactions may often be means to an end.

Instrumental responses that result in motive satisfaction or reinforcement become fixated. Under similar motivational and environmental conditions, the responses that in the past have led to reinforcement will tend to recur. It would seem, then, that that aspect of personality which involves an individual's behavior in satisfying his motives can be accounted for in great part by the operation of the mechanism of reinforcement.

Some hypothetical examples can show how the principle of *reinforcement* may operate in personality learning. Suppose that the home environment of a child is one in which the parents frequently and needlessly refuse the child's requests. The child persists in his demands and the parents persist in their refusals. Eventually, in response to motive frustration, the child begins to rage and cry. The noise becomes unbearable, and the neighbors can overhear it; consequently the parents somewhat bitterly give in and the child obtains the goal object. The goal object is reinforcing; the response that led to its attainment was one of emotional violence. If this type of situation were repeated frequently in many motive states—with the parents rather consistently refusing at first and then giving way to the onslaught of violence and noise—the many reinforcements that this pattern of behavior achieved could well result in its fixation. The child may then tend to meet any barrier by violent temper reactions.

Undoubtedly the extreme response would not persist, for the parents, too, would learn; they would tend to give way when the first storm clouds began to gather, so that a response of persistent demanding now would become sufficient to obtain the goal object. Such responses are likely to be effective with other persons as well, and so it continues as this individual's way of satisfying his current motivational needs. Such responses need not, of course, prove successful *every* time in order to become fixated. We know that *partial reinforcement* is an effective method of habit formation. Indeed, habits developed under such a regime are more resistant to extinction than those which in the past have received 100-percent reinforcement.

In another family, refusals of the child's demands may be less frequent. His initial demands for an object are likely to be peaceful and pleasant, and he obtains the goal object by this response. Thus, this way of behaving is reinforced and becomes fixated. When, as must sometimes be the case, the parents feel that a refusal is necessary, they may be prepared to hold to their position despite angry behavior on the child's part. Even if occasionally they do succumb in the face of tempestuous actions, the frequency with which pleasant behavior has been reinforced is so much greater that it, rather than irritable responses, will be the child's mode of behavior.

There are an almost infinite number of ways in which a growing organism may react, but if one way leads to reinforcement more often than any of the others, that way will begin to dominate, and it will eventually become the individual's characteristic manner of meeting a variety of situations.

If the training situation is one involving a relationship between parent and child primarily in the home environment, how do these types of responses come to operate in a variety of situations? This broadening of the response tendencies can be predicted from the operation of the mechanisms of *stimulus generalization*. Just as the conditioned dog reacts not only to the tone to which it was conditioned but to other tones as well, so the child reacts to other adults in the manner in which he has learned to react to the specific adults called "mother" and "father." The responses he has learned to make to a brother or sister or neighborhood playmates will be evoked in work and play with other age mates.

Extinction and *differentiation* also play important parts in personality learning. A response in a given situation that is not followed by reinforcement with some consistency will become extinguished. If, however, the same response remains effective in some other situation, it will continue to occur in repetitions of this situation. The fact that differentiations of this sort may be learned leads us to suspect that we shall seldom find a single mode of behavior that runs through all the actions of an individual in all environments. It is more probable than not that a single way of behaving will not prove successful in all environments and that the individual will learn to make discriminations. One way of behaving may predominate, but in a limited number of specific situations quite contrary modes of behavior may occur. There is nothing warped or false about such a personality; if the organism can make discriminations among classes of stimuli, it can also make quite different responses to the classes of stimuli. Thus do we have honor among thieves, and the paradox of the ruthless businessman who is kindly and warm-hearted in his home life.

Motivation

The nature of an individual's motives and values determines the goals toward which he works; by so doing they give direction to his behavior. They lead the individual to seek the company of others above all else or to follow lonely pursuits; to go to college or to a job after high school; to patronize operas or football games; and to follow a multitude of particular activities rather than other ones. But an identification of motives solely in terms of direction is not adequate, for motives also differ in strength. It is to this aspect of motivation that we refer when we speak of someone as being ambitious or without ambition, and certainly this is one aspect of behavior which often enters into our description of an individual's personality. The interrelationship between motive direction and motive strength is of profound importance; for it is out of such interaction that conflicts of motives arise, and, as we have mentioned earlier, such conflicts lead to obstructions in the smooth flow of behavior.

In our discussion of *secondary reinforcement,* we noted that stimuli can acquire incentive value by being associated with active motive states. The motive conditions that are learned may be either of an approach or of an avoidance variety, resulting in the behavior of seeking out or running from certain kinds of environmental conditions. Although organisms of a given species may appear quite similar in the basic motivational states they possess at birth, their postnatal environments will differ, and consequently divergences in motive states will soon develop, leading toward the unique pattern of motivation characteristic of the individual personality. There are reasons to believe—and the experimental support for these reasons have been cited in Chapter 5—that motives develop, generalize, and are eliminated by the same kind of operations that effect the organism's instrumental responses.

Stimulus selection

The environment is rich in stimuli and yet at any moment in time the organism is capable of reacting to only a limited number of them. What he selects from the richness that is available will inevitably determine the nature of his behavior, because different stimuli usually lead to different responses. As we have pointed out

517

in Chapter 8, there are certain characteristics of stimuli that make them capable of dominating the total stimulus environment and of demanding the attention of all people. This aspect of stimulus selection is not important in personality structure since it forces uniformity in behavior while the concept of personality emphasizes its uniqueness. But it was also shown in the same chapter that an individual's motives, his sets, and his past experiences produce a biasing in his stimulus-selection tendencies, and because individuals differ from each other in these determining factors they will differ in the stimuli that they select. Since motives and sets are learned and since past experience is the very stuff of which learning is made, then the mechanisms of learning inevitably influence an individual's stimulus-selection tendencies and consequent behavior.

Perhaps an example of stimulus selection drawn from literature will be of some interest. It is quoted from Smollett's novel, *Humphrey Clinker,* and it contrasts what is seen from the windows of the Pump House at a famous watering resort in eighteenth-century England by Matthew Bramble and his niece Lydia Melford.

[THE UNCLE] My uncle was complaining of the stink, occasioned by the vast quantity of mud and slime, which the river leaves at low ebb under the windows of the Pump House. He observed that the exhalations arising from such a nuisance could not but be prejudicial to the weak lungs . . . of many who come to drink the water.

[THE NIECE] The prospect so amusing; and the ships and boats going up and down the river, close under the windows of the Pump-room, offered such an enchanting variety of moving pictures, as require a much abler pen than mine to describe.

Perceptual tendencies

Perception was defined as the use of a partial aspect of the total situation to predict its further characteristics. If two persons perceive the same objective event differently, their consequent overt behavior is likely to be different. Thus, in some interpersonal situation, a facial gesture or an ambiguous phrase may be perceived by one person as a symbol of rejection and by another as a symbol of acceptance; so one person may withdraw or attack while the other may make further friendly overtures. In ways such as this the perceptual process contributes to the production of individual differences in behavior, and differential behavior is the essence of the concept of personality. In the chapter on perception a considerable space was devoted to spelling out the ways in which the principles of learning mold the perceptual process, so it is not necessary to repeat these points in detail.

A series of experiments has demonstrated that consistent individual differences in perceptual responses can be obtained in a relatively simple situation.[7] In one situation, called the Rod-and-Frame Test, the subjects are placed in a darkened room, and they see before them a luminous outlined square with a single luminous rod pivoted at its center. The orientation of the square with respect to the true vertical can be manipulated by the experimenter and the subject's task is to adjust the rod so that it is vertical to the earth, regardless of the tilt of the square. The situation is further complicated by the fact that the chair on which the subjects sit may be tilted in the plane parallel to the square and independently of it. Thus the subject is asked to indicate the "true vertical" despite chair tilt or the tilting of the dominant figure in the visual field—the square. Examples of the results are presented in Figure 15.3. In these sketches the black line shows how the rod was set by the experimenter and the red line the setting of the rod by the subject at what he thought was the true vertical. The figure demonstrates three classes of results; alignment at or close to the true vertical, alignment by reference to the square, and finally an alignment with reference to the square, but where the subject has subjectively tilted the square 90 degrees so that one of its sides is seen as the top. The subjects were, of course, tested with a number of different initial settings of square, stick, and chair, and the error scores for the different settings were correlated to determine whether or not there was a consistency in magnitude and direction of error from setting to setting. The correlations were slightly greater than .50, indicating that the individuals behaved in a fairly consistent fashion from one trial to the next. In other words, the test is a moderately reliable one.

The same subjects were then tested in a different situation called the Tilting-Room-Tilting-Chair Test. In this test the subjects were seated on a chair in a miniature room which itself was supported by a frame resting upon the floor of the laboratory. Both the miniature room and the chair could be tilted independently of each other. Each trial was begun by tilting both chair and room a different number of degrees, sometimes in the same and sometimes in the opposite direction, and by asking the subject to ma-

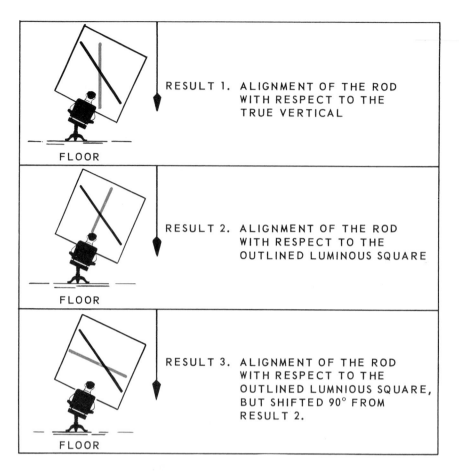

RESULT 1.   ALIGNMENT OF THE ROD
            WITH RESPECT TO THE
            TRUE VERTICAL

FLOOR

RESULT 2.   ALIGNMENT OF THE ROD
            WITH RESPECT TO THE
            OUTLINED LUMINOUS SQUARE

FLOOR

RESULT 3.   ALIGNMENT OF THE ROD
            WITH RESPECT TO THE
            OUTLINED LUMNIOUS SQUARE,
            BUT SHIFTED 90° FROM
            RESULT 2.

FLOOR

Fig. 15.3 Schematization of some results of a study of the relationship between visual perception and personality. The subject is asked to align perpendicular to the true vertical a luminous rod framed within a luminous square in a darkened room as he sits in a tilted chair. The black line shows the tilt of the rod at the start of the trial; the red line indicates the subject's adjustment. (After Witkin *et al.*[7])

nipulate controls which would move either the room or the chair. He was, of course, asked to bring one or the other of these to what seemed to him to be the true vertical. Once again correlations between one test situation and the other were run and again some consistency in behavior was found. The correlations in this case were in the neighborhood of .30. The next step was to correlate the errors in the Rod-and-Frame Test with the errors in the Tilting-Room-Tilting-Chair Test, for only by this means could the experimenters determine whether or not there was some generality in the direction and the nature of the errors in this general type of

520

situation. The median correlation for a number of different tests was about .25, which is sufficiently high to indicate that there is a relationship between the ways an individual errs in the two situations.

It is certainly time to pause and ask how this study is related to our concept of personality, as well as what it implies about the perceptual activities of the subjects in this situation. It is related to the concept of personality because it demonstrates that individuals behave in ways which are personally consistent but which differ from the ways others behave in the two situations. Just why these differences in ways of perceiving have developed the experiment does not explain, but it is apparent that some of the subjects judge the vertical primarily by the cues from the visual world (the stick is aligned with the sides of the square), while others respond primarily to the sense organs which are stimulated by gravitational differences, such as differential pressures on the body. These subjects are like some of the old-time pilots who claimed that they flew by the seats of their pants. If perceptual differences can be found in a situation as simple as this, they must be even more marked, more significant to individual behavior, in social interpersonal situations.

Summary

In this section we have considered the various psychological mechanisms that conjointly are responsible for behavior. Personality grows from the behavior that is a consequence of the way these mechanisms have developed in the individual, and of the nature of their interactions in concrete situations. The account of how the principles of learning may operate in the development of personality characteristics is exceedingly oversimplified—for several reasons. The necessarily limited scope of a text at this level permits little more than an appreciation of the potential significance of some of the learning mechanisms for personality development. Moreover, there are great gaps in our knowledge of the exact details of both the operation of learning mechanisms and the growth of personality. Nevertheless, it is hoped that even this brief survey will lead the reader to view personality not as some static entity, of which individuals possess more or less, but rather as the characteristic ways of behaving that result from an interaction of general hereditary dispositions and the mechanisms of learning.

SOURCES OF ENVIRONMENTAL STIMULI

Since environmental conditions play a large part in the development of personality characteristics, let us consider some of the major classes of environmental stimuli that may function as personality determinants.

Prenatal conditions

It is not uncommon to encounter the belief that the experiences of the pregnant mother may directly influence the eventual motives, interests, and behavior patterns of the child she is carrying. Some aspiring mothers read the classics in the hope of instilling in the growing fetus a love of literature; other mothers, frightened by some event, may expect this same fear to be transmitted to the unborn child. No scientific evidence, however, has been produced in support of the notion that fetal learning results from the psychological experiences of the mother. The child of the literary-minded parent may himself exhibit literary interests beyond the ordinary, but these interests will be due to the postnatal rather than the prenatal environment. The mother whose ambition for the unborn child is clearly expressed by her study of the classics during pregnancy will undoubtedly provide the growing child with books and will reinforce any of his activities that are literary in nature; the frightened mother will surely express her fears in the presence of the child and thus provide him with the opportunity to learn them.

This denial of the influence of psychological experiences of the mother on the fetus does not imply that the growing organism is impervious to environmental changes before birth. The fetus obtains nourishment and oxygen by way of the mother's blood stream, and its growth can be influenced by the nature of the blood supply. We do not, however, have any evidence which permits us to relate such changes in the intra-uterine environment to the occurrence of personality variations within the normal range, although some extreme and infrequent variations seem to be related to intra-uterine conditions.

Experiences during early infancy

The Freudian school of psychoanalysis maintains that the experiences of early infancy are of the utmost importance in shaping adult personality. According to this theory, how the child is fed—whether by the breast or by the bottle—how often it is fed, when it is weaned, and when and how it is toilet-trained are all matters of serious concern—not primarily because of their influence upon the immediate physical health or because they may make a child a poor eater or a bed-wetter but because the theory predicts that these events will have a profound effect upon other kinds of behavior—in short, upon the total personality.

The influence of Freudian theory in the American culture has been profound, and it has served to center the attention of parents, pediatricians, and nursery-school teachers on the handling of the young infant. Some of the modern practices in child rearing and in the education of pre-school children are directly traceable to Freudian theory.

Freud was first led to postulate the importance of infantile experiences upon personality development when his disturbed adult patients, probing into their own pasts, recalled events of early childhood which seemed to him to be clearly related to the present symptoms of maladjustment. Out of the observations he developed his theory of personality, and the theory either drew or implied certain conclusions about how such matters as age of weaning or toilet training could influence adult personality characteristics. Later researchers sought to bulwark these theoretical predictions through the medium of more formalized studies of such specific factors as the influence of the kind of infant feeding or the age of weaning or toilet training on the personality of children. A typical study might, for example, obtain personality measures of a group of early- and late-weaned children while they were in the elementary grades and determine whether one group was better adjusted than the other. Occasionally differences between such groups have been demonstrated. Unfortunately, however, there is a basic ambiguity in such studies, for the whole pattern of environment supplied by parents who wean their child at an early age is almost certainly different from that provided by late-weaning parents.

523

A study cited in the previous chapter has indicated that differences in child-rearing practices, including age of weaning and toilet training, do exist among various social classes. But practices such as these are not the only ways in which classes or parents differ from each other. These other differences must also have their influence upon the growing child. Consequently, age of weaning and toilet training are just two of a number of potentially significant variables that may be correlated with each other in parental practices. It is a violation of experimental logic to attribute personality development to a single one of these factors.

The fact that the parents' method of treatment of the child in one behavioral area is correlated with methods of treatment in other areas is illustrated by a study in which the child-rearing practices of a number of American parents were carefully identified.[8] In one part of the experiment the researchers studied toilet training and found, as would be expected, that the behaviors of the mothers varied from severity (training began at an early age and the child was punished for "accidents") to leniency, both with regard to the age at which training began and the mothers' reactions to failures of control. The degree of severity of the various parents was rated by the interviewers and this score was correlated with other aspects of child treatment. The correlation between severity of toilet training and demands to conform to adult standards on such matters as table manners, neatness, and being quiet was about .20; between severity and the use of physical punishment the correlation was .29; between severity and permissiveness in aggression against the parent —.27; and between estimated warmth of the mother toward the child and severity the correlation was —.30. Clearly the method employed by the parents in toilet training is only one part of a large constellation of attitudes and consequential methods of training in other areas of behavior. Hence, as we have said, the discovery that some personality characteristic is correlated with *one particular* method or technique of child rearing would not offer any really satisfactory evidence that this method of training contributed to the development of that personality characteristic.

In general, research has failed to find important relationships between personality characteristics and certain *specific parental practices* during infancy, and there is no reason to believe that the events of extremely early infancy are as telling for personality development as psychoanalytic theory holds.[9]

In recent years a number of studies with white rats as subjects have demonstrated that various kinds of fairly vigorous forms of stimulation, such as handling or even shocking them while they are very young, do indeed effect their behavior in adulthood.[10] The results in general are to make the animals more capable of adapting to stressful situations at later ages. It is difficult, however, to draw specific conclusions from these studies as to the effects of various sorts of early environmental influences on the personality development of the human animal. It is difficult because the treatments introduced in these experiments probably represent a fairly drastic departure from the normal environment of the animals and it is not easy to find the parallel between these environmental manipulations with the kinds of variations in child-raising which occur in the different homes of our culture. On the basis of these studies as well as psychological theory in general we may assume that the nature of the treatment in early infancy will have some effect upon adult personality, but, since the human infant lacks the capacity to make fine discriminatory judgments about its environment, early infancy is not a period that is rich in stimuli that are effective for personality development.

Family relations

Childhood relationships with parents and other members of the family in the wide variety of situations that arise in the give and take of daily living are of the utmost importance in shaping personality. It is in the home that the child spends most of his day until the time he ventures out to school. His parents and his siblings are the major persons of his little word. This is the environment that encompasses him almost completely during the very early years, and that continues in a diminishing degree into adulthood. Homes vary greatly in their over-all flavor. The parents may be autocratic and willful or democratic and considerate of their children's wishes. The atmosphere of the home may be pervaded with a feeling of warmth and acceptance of the noisy, romping, growing organism, or it may be overhung with a chilling pall of rejection—despite efforts of the parents to hide this feeling from the child and even from themselves. In some homes the child is indulged, and his merest wish is the parents' command; in others there is neglect and indifference.[11] Parents willy-nilly tend to provide for their children fairly definite environmental patterns structured loosely along the lines we have mentioned above.

The significance of all this for personality development lies in the fact that reinforcements will occur for some kinds of activities in certain homes but not in others; that punishments will be meted out harshly and frequently by some parents while the rod is spared by others; that some parents will be consistent about the acts which they reward or punish while others will be consistently inconsistent; and that goal attainment will be frequent for certain children and infrequent for others. It is apparent that these are the kinds of environmental events which produce learning.

That such a relationship between child personality and atmosphere of the home does exist is indicated by a study in which the personality characteristics of a group of problem children were compared with the general nature of their home environment. The experimenters classified the personalities of the children into three basic categories: (1) *unsocialized aggression*—indicated by cruelty, defiance of authority, and the like; (2) *socialized delinquency*—indicated by gang activities, truancy, and the like; and (3) *over-inhibited behavior*—that is, shyness, worrying, secretiveness. Three characteristics of the home atmosphere tended to be associated with the personality patterns in the following way: (1) parental rejection with unsocialized aggression, (2) parental neglect with socialized delinquency, and (3) parental repression with over-inhibited behavior.[12]

Peer relationships

At some time or another the child must meet and interact with other young, growing organisms—his peers. Perhaps one should include in this group his siblings—that is, his brothers and sisters. He plays affectionately with them, he competes with them, and he quarrels with them. They are highly important components of his little world.

Whether the child is the oldest or the youngest of his family group has been thought to have bearing upon his personality development, but, in general, studies have failed to uncover consistent relationships between personality-test scores and order of birth in the family. This failure is probably due in part to the inadequacy of the tests used, and in part to the fact that, in the various subgroups of our culture, children in the same ordinal position are probably treated quite differently. In some groups, the first-born male is designated by parents and by custom as the important child of the family, the one to whom the others must defer. In other subgroups, no formal value is laid upon any particular ordinal position; in still others, the eldest child, instead of being given special privileges, may be expected to become a substitute parent, caring for and protecting the younger ones. If, from all these divergent subcultures with their varied treatment of ordinal position, individuals are simply lumped together in the tests, then it is not surprising that consistent relationships between test scores and ordinal position are not uncovered.

The statements in the previous paragraph do not imply that for a given child ordinal position fails to contribute to personality make-up. Ordinal position influences development by effecting the child's environment, but the manner in which the environment will be effected is partially determined by such cultural and class variables as we have mentioned above, as well as by the specific training techniques and attitudes of the parent. Since these important conditions vary from home to home regardless of the child's ordinal position, they would tend to obscure the effects of position, and this may be the reason that the findings of the various studies have not been consistent.

In addition to siblings, there are the children next door or down the street and—later—his schoolmates. These are the child's real peers. As best he can, he learns to cooperate and cope with them. His ways of cooperating and coping may be the beginnings of habits that will generalize to other peer situations in childhood and later. He may discover not only ways of doing things with others but also the fact that being with age mates is either generally gratifying or generally frustrating. These latter discoveries may begin to shape his motives and lay the foundation for later social attitudes. He may find some age mates with whom his relations are generally successful and others with whom they are generally unsuccessful, and so he learns a discriminatory response of approaching some kinds of people and of avoiding others, of liking some kinds of activities and disliking others.

Competence in work and play

It seems probable that an important interaction exists between skills in work and play and behavior in a social situation.

Fig. 15.4 These two photographs and the one on the facing page illustrate increasing levels of cooperative activity. The three children in the sandbox at left are playing almost entirely independently, although they may interact with one another once in a while. This is known as parallel play. In the photograph below, the boy is "cooperating" with the girl to the extent of holding down the board she is sawing, but he is obviously interested in his own activity, which has nothing to do with hers. The activity shown on the facing page obviously requires the very highest degree of cooperation among each of the individuals involved, for a lapse on the part of one will spoil the work of all. (Courtesy the University School and the Department of Photography of The Ohio State University)

Especially during the early years, play activity is directed more toward the materials on hand and in hand than toward the playmate. The tendency is so marked that psychologists have coined a phrase—*parallel activity*—to refer to this primitive kind of social activity.[13] Such play is common among two-year-olds, who frequently join another child in play by sitting near him and manipulating the same kinds of materials. The play requires no cooperation from the other child, merely that he be in the vicinity. The play is social, but it is even more strongly activity-directed. Later a true social interaction occurs and the other child is asked to assist in the work, to hold up an end of the board, to stack the blocks in a certain way. And later he may be asked to cover second base or to work on a classroom committee.

Thus the other child becomes a participant in an activity whose end is directed toward the accomplishment of some work. If he is clumsy and awkward, his incompetence may prove frustrating to the aims of the first child. If this happens often, the incompetent may be excluded, or at least not enthusiastically

accepted, as a playmate. He may then learn to behave toward his peers differently from the child who performs his work skillfully. And these ways of reacting to others may persist even after he has achieved competence.

Experimental evidence of this interaction between social attitudes and play skills is illustrated by some studies in the nursery school.[14] Children who were judged to be the least dominant members of the group were given special training on such activities as telling a story or assembling a picture puzzle. After training, they were placed individually with a child who had been rated as dominant, and the social behavior of the two was recorded. Supported by their competence with the puzzle materials, many of the ordinarily submissive children became dominant. The study suggests that our social acceptability may often be determined at least to some extent by the competence with which we handle nonsocial materials.

It should be noted that it is not the level of competence itself that determines the personality characteristics but rather the manner in which the child's peers—and the adults as well—react to his level of competence. If the goals set by the others are unreasonably beyond the ability of the child, however high his competence, the child is likely to meet with failure and censure. And if events of this sort occur with any considerable frequency we should expect that he would learn to lack confidence in himself, to become anxious and tense in such situations, and perhaps to become wary and withdrawing in his social relations.

SOME EXPERIMENTAL STUDIES

The previous section has been devoted primarily to the general identification of aspects of the environment that would be expected on theoretical grounds to exert powerful effects upon personality development. In the present section we shall first describe an experiment which will tell us something about the variations in home environment that are to be found in the American culture and then we will describe some experiments with lower animals which conclusively demonstrate that treatment in early life has psychological effects that can be identified in later life.

Child-rearing practices

During the years 1951 and 1952 approximately 400 mothers living in the suburbs of a New England metropolitan area were questioned by trained interviewers about the methods and guiding principles they used in rearing their children.[8] The interviews, which were standardized but not rigidly so, were recorded so that they could be played back in the laboratory to experts who rated the mothers on various aspects of their reported behavior. The five aspects upon which the ratings were made were chosen by the experimenters because they could be considered, on theoretical grounds, to have an important effect upon personality development. These dimensions, with some examples of the behavior composing them as well as of the range of family differences, are presented below:

1. Disciplinary techniques

This dimension, as must be obvious, refers to the particular method a mother employs in the hope that it will prevent the re-occurrence of some action of which she disapproves.

▶ *Physical punishment.* The mothers answer the interviewer's question; "How often have you spanked _____?"

One mother: "Pretty often—it might be every time I turn around. Over the weekend he's the worst. . . . Seems like every week he's got to get a good hard whaling."

At the other end of the scale is this reply.

Another mother: "A spanking is for when she does something really terribly wrong—one Sunday she did kick up quite badly and she did get a spanking from her father . . . that was the only spanking she ever received."

The experimenters found that it was a rare child who was never spanked, but there was, nevertheless, a wide variation in the frequency of its use.

▶ *Deprivation of privileges.* To the question, "Do you deprive him of something as a way of disciplining him?"

One mother: "No I don't think I have ever done that."

Another mother: "Yes, we always do. If there has been some disobedience or a fresh remark . . . we will take something away from her."

531

▶ *Withdrawal of love.* To various questions about the use of techniques of control, some mothers indicate that they employ words which imply to the child that his action has caused the mother to lose some of her affection for him; others carefully avoid implying anything of the sort.

One mother: "You are a bad boy when you do something like that, and Mommy doesn't like bad boys. I'll say, 'I love you, but I don't like you.' "

Another mother: "I definitely disapprove of 'You can't be my child' or 'I will have to send you away!' That is absolutely horrible . . ."

2. Severity of punishment

This dimension of parental behavior refers to the vigor of the punishment. It varied from mild slaps to sound spankings and from deprivation of highly valued activities to deprivation of ones of minor worth in the child's esteem.

3. Permissiveness

Society prescribes certain ways of satisfying such major drives as hunger, elimination, and sex and certain forms of expressing reactions to the thwarting of other motives. The child must learn to conform to the specifications of his culture. The parent not only interprets society's informal laws, but trains the child to behave according to them. Degree of permissiveness refers to the tolerance, or lack of it, shown by the mother both in her interpretation of society's expectations and in her reactions to the transgressions of the faltering learner.

▶ *On toilet training.* A few mothers began training the child before he was five months of age and another few did not begin until after he was two years old. This difference is indicative of the considerable range in the mothers' interpretations of the importance of the age at which the child achieves the control that is characteristic of the adult.

▶ *On modesty.*

One mother: "My little boy is wearing night shirts, and one of the primary reasons they are wearing nightshirts is that they can put their nightshirts on, and they are covered before they take their underpants off."

Another mother: "I don't think it spoils them. In fact, I think they should see each other with their clothes off. . . . They see parents or brothers and they just accept it that you're a boy and I'm a girl."

► **On aggression toward the parents.**

One mother: "They (the parents) never should allow him to hit them back. If he hits them, they should hit him right back. If you let him get away with it once he will always want to get away with it."

Another mother: "I think there's a certain amount that should be allowed. I think that its something they have to get out of their systems."

► **On doing things that might damage the household furnishings.**

One mother: "It was hard for me to get things, and I want them to appreciate them. . . . I don't see the necessity of destruction. . . . If she did (such things) I think I'd give her a good licking."

Another mother: "I think they will do it no matter how much you do . . . but I think that you can just explain to them what is wrong."

4. Temperamental qualities

For this dimension the experimenters attempted to estimate the degree of warmth and affection or coolness and rejection that the mother displayed in her dealings with the child. They found this to be a general and persistent characteristic of the parent which pervaded many areas of behavior. A warm mother might state, "I love little babies. I love to do with little babies. I love to teach them things . . . but at the same time, I think they are interesting when they grow up, too." And a cold mother might say, "Well if I had been well and a little younger, I might have enjoyed him, but I will say frankly that it was just a hard job for me."

Perhaps the significance of this characteristic can best be illustrated by listing the various kinds of behavior that are correlated with the experimenter's estimates of the mothers' position on the scale of warmth and coldness. The warm mothers tended to interact affectionately with the child; to find the time to play with him; to accept his dependent demands pleasantly; to praise him when he showed good table manners; and to use reasoning as a method of training. The cold mother tended to behave in the opposite manner in these same situations.

5. *Positive inculcation of mature behavior*

This rather forbidding phrase is used to describe the kinds of values the mother holds for her child, the heights of the goals she sets for him, and the degree to which she limits or expands his freedom of action.

▶ *On freedom of action.*

One mother: "I always have my eyes on my children. Even when they're outside, I'm looking out the window . . . when they're in the house I'll say: "Sally, where are you and what are you doing?"

Another mother: "I don't worry until it gets around five o'clock. I think if she were into any trouble, someone would call me. She . . . is perfectly capable of taking care of herself."

▶ *On aggressiveness toward other children.*

One mother: "Well, I believe a child has to fight and to stick up for his own rights . . . we have always taught Bill to hit them right back and give them right back and give them one better than what he got."

Another mother: "I go out and ask other mothers what happened and when I find out, I say 'All right come in the house now.' . . . [I] talk it over with her and tell her where she's wrong or where the other child is wrong."

6. Summary

This very brief report of an ambitious study has been presented to give the reader some appreciation of the variations in the psychological environment that is supplied to the growing child in the American home. The researchers were able to show that some of these variations in environment were related to certain characteristics of the children as reported by the mothers. For example, the occurrence of feeding problems was positively related to extent of use of physical punishment and negatively related to the degree of warmth shown by the mother; or, at the kindergarten age, the more dependent children tended to be the ones whose parents punished severely for aggression against themselves, used withdrawal of love as a technique for punishment, and tended to reject them. The study, however, was not primarily concerned with relating child personality characteristics to variations in the environment; its purpose was accomplished by identifying the wide variations in parental behavior—the child's environment itself.

Early experience and pain avoidance

In recent years a number of studies have been reported which have demonstrated that animals differ in their adult behavior as a consequence of the type of environment they lived in during infancy. Only one of these studies will be described here: a study that deals with the effect of early environment on reaction to pain in adulthood.[15]

The subjects and the early environment

The subjects came from six litters of Scottish terriers and the animals from each litter were randomly assigned to the control or experimental groups. The control animals were raised normally as pets in private homes or in the laboratory. The experimental animals were reared in visual isolation from other animals and from humans in cages with a large air vent at the top which also served to illuminate the cage's interior. The cage was divided into two compartments, with a door between them. This door was opened once a day permitting the dog to enter the freshly cleaned compartment where it remained until the following day. The experimental animals lived in this deprived environment from the time of weaning until they were about eight months old, and from this time onward they lived in the normal laboratory surroundings.

Avoidance learning

The experimental test situation consisted of an enclosure six feet long by three feet wide, which was divided lengthwise into two halves by a three-inch-high barrier. The animals were placed into the apparatus a number of times and the experimenters noted the side each animal seemed to prefer. The floor of both compartments was an electric grid, and after these preference tests were conducted, the grid on the preferred side was electrified. At first a weak shock was employed, and it was increased until the dog reacted to it by jumping. The voltage required to produce this reaction in each dog was called his threshold, and the mean threshold level was the same for the control and experimental dogs. For the experiment proper a shock well above threshold level was used. The dogs could escape the shock by jumping over the barrier into the other compartment. The animal was then picked up

535

by the experimenter and placed in the original compartment, and one minute later the shock was again turned on. If the animal jumped into the neutral compartment before the minute elapsed the shock was avoided. Training was discontinued when the animals learned to avoid the shock consistently, and the performance of the two groups was evaluated by comparing the number of trials required to learn this avoidence reaction. The mean number of trials required by the control animals was 5; it was 20.3 for the experimentals.

Avoiding pin pricks and flame

This testing consisted of two separate experiments, but they are so similar in both procedure and results that they may be described together. The experiments took place in a large room and the experimenter stood in the center of a circle that he had marked out with chalk upon the floor. The dog was given the freedom of the room and was permitted to nose about here and there, but the experimenter recorded the length of time that it remained in the chalk-lined area. After this measurement was taken the experimenter called the dog to his side and, striking a match, attempted to hold it up to the animal's nose. With the normally raised animals the attempts met with failure and the dogs twisted their noses from the flame and squirmed from the experimenter's restraining grasp. This was not true of the animals who had been reared in the environment of the boxes. Few of them would dodge the flame, and some of them actually moved their noses into it; then, after jerking away, they once more approached it cautiously only to be burned again. Following this experience the controls spent much less time in the circle than they had prior to it, but the experimentals spent just as much time close to the experimenter as they had previously. A similar procedure was employed later with the painful stimulus consisting of a pin prick on the animals flank. Prompt escape and avoidance once again characterized the behavior of the normally raised animals, while the experimental animals showed the same ineptness in escaping and the same failure to avoid the circle in which the experimenter stood.

Summary

This is only one of a number of studies that have demonstrated that the nature of the early environment can have a profound and surprising effect upon the characteristics of behavior in adult life. It was chosen for discussion not simply because of the dramatic differences in behavior of the two groups of animals, but because the reaction to pain is likely to be conceived of as being completely biological in origin. There is no question that the response to pain falls under the classification of a biological drive and it will be recalled that the thresholds were the same for both groups of animals, but the two groups differed markedly in their use of the environmental cues associated with the pain stimulus as means of protecting themselves from harm.

It is difficult to draw specific recommendations from these animal studies as to the best ways of raising the human infant. They do not answer such recurrent questions as what to do about thumb sucking, bed wetting, and poor eating behavior; whether to breast feed or bottle feed; and when or whether to punish. The answers to these and other important questions can be obtained, obviously, only from research with children themselves. The animal studies do, however, contribute in other ways. In the first place they have shown that the early environment has effects which have, thus far, been unsuspected, and in this way they have increased our appreciation of the tremendous significance of these environmental forces in the development of personality characteristics. From these studies it is also possible to draw a very general conclusion. The conclusion is that a rich and stimulating early environment equips the organism to cope, in many different ways, with the environments of his adult life; conversely, a sterile and limited environment leaves the organism bereft of, or at least handicapped, in acquiring the skills which quickly lead to adjustment.

THE STABILITY OF PERSONALITY

More than a century ago, William Wordsworth wrote, "The child is father of the man." It is difficult to state more strikingly the thesis that patterns of personality are laid down in early childhood and remain essentially unchanged throughout one's life. Echoes of this sentiment persist, and it is dominant in the theory of personality development associated with the psychoanalytic

537

schools, which would almost be prepared to substitute the word "infant" for "child."

In one way or another most of the theories of personality have recognized the almost overpowering effect of early life upon the form and the nature of adult behavior. Few students of personality would question the tremendous importance of the early years in shaping the mature personality, but to state that there is no modification of personality after some specific age is quite another matter. There is no question but that individuals at any age can learn something new; they can even extinguish some existing habit and substitute a different one for it. If, therefore, we accept the hypothesis that personality is not exclusively hereditary—and no other hypothesis seems justifiable—we must also accept the hypothesis that personality characteristics are not static. They can and do change during the entire lifetime of the individual, and yet they do not change altogether. Perhaps the report of an experiment will be useful.[16]

During the years 1935 to 1938 the experimenter had administered a number of personality tests to 300 couples who were engaged to be married; and some 17 to 18 years later the couples were asked to answer many of the same questions. Of course, all 300 couples did not answer the follow-up request, for some of the couples had not married each other, some had died, some had divorced, and still others merely failed to return the questionnaires. However, 227 of the original couples answered, and the data from these subjects can be used to give some empirical information on the stability of personality—as measured by a particular group of tests—over a span of nearly 20 years.

Five different types of test were used:

1. A rating by the subjects of themselves and their marriage partners on the dimensions of physical energy, intelligence, neatness, breadth of interests, conventionality, quietness, temper, modesty, and dependability.

2. Attitude scales toward marriage, church, child rearing, housekeeping, entertaining, and gardening.

3. An interest test, a test which measures one's interest in a wide variety of activities.

4. "Personality" tests, which were designed to measure characteristics such as self-confidence and sociability.

5. A value scale, an instrument designed to ascertain the comparative strengths of broad motivational systems toward theoretical, economic, aesthetic, social-political, and religious matters.

The consistency of personality was then determined by correlating the scores on the earlier tests with the scores on the same tests given nearly twenty years later. The results are presented in Table 15.2, but it is a table that needs some explanation.

TABLE 15.2.   CORRELATIONS BETWEEN VARIOUS
PERSONALITY MEASURES AFTER 20 YEARS

	Reliability	After 20 years
Values	.72	.51
Attitudes	.74	.30
Interests	.89	.61
Personality	.85	.48
Subject ratings	.65	.38

Scores on several different characteristics were obtained in each of the test areas, as the description in the above listing indicates, so several correlations for each test area were obtained. For purposes of simplification, the correlational figure which is presented is the median value of all of the correlations obtained for the test area in question. If this figure were presented alone it could be somewhat misleading, for it is probable that the obtained correlation value would be contrasted with a perfect correlation of 1.00. To do so would be to disregard the important concept of the reliability of a test. For a variety of reasons tests do not have a reliability of 1.00, so the proper way of evaluating the degree of stability of these personality characteristics over the twenty-year period is to compare this figure with an estimate of its reliability. This estimate is simply the correlation between two administrations of the test a short time apart. Unfortunately, the time between the first and second testing for these short intervals is not the same for all tests. In most instances they were about a week apart, but they were a year apart for the value scales. The table includes for each test the reliability estimate and the correlation over the twenty-year span.

The results of this study neither imply a personality structure which is frozen into an unchangeable mold by the mid-twenties nor one that is fleeting and ever-shifting. Furthermore, the degree of stability differs from one aspect of the total personality to another, with attitudes exhibiting a rather large degree of inconstancy, while patterns of interest and broad value systems are fairly stable. This finding has probably come as no surprise to the reader, but it might be well to discuss briefly how we could use our previously identified psychological mechanisms to predict just such a result.

Social motives are learned and so also are the perceptual activities that often initiate the motives and guide the instrumental acts employed to satisfy these motives. An adult is what he is with respect to these aspects of behavior because he has been molded by his environment, and what one environment has produced another can destroy. An organism possesses throughout its entire life the capacity to learn, a capacity which is not restricted to the acquisition of skill, instrumental acts, and perceptions alone, but which operates upon motive states as well. This fact means that a possibility for change always exists and can and will occur if the proper environmental supports come into being.

Constancy of personality is insured in part by a constancy of environment and the fact is that most of us spend our adult life in an environment which maintains the same general flavor year in and year out. Our parents and our friends develop certain expectations of how we are going to react, and these very expectations tend to prevent us from behaving differently. If the demands of the environment remain essentially the same, as is probably the case, then the responses that have been learned in the past as ways of meeting these demands will remain effective and changes in behavior will be unlikely.

There are also certain basic characteristics of behavior itself that cause the organism to resist change. One of these arises from the effectiveness of partial reinforcement in maintaining habits. For personality this means that, even though the environment changes, the individual may obtain enough occasional reinforcement to prevent the extinction of his older personality habits. Even habits that are extinguished through persistent nonreinforcement may show a spontaneous recovery.

Another behavioral characteristic that militates against changes in personal characteristics as the years pass is the development, early in life, of a pattern of interests expressed in the form of likes and dislikes.[17] These likes and dislikes cause us to choose certain kinds of environments and to reject others. As a gyroscope guides a plane on automatic pilot, so do these interests dictate a course for the individual. Because of them his sampling of the nearly infinite variety of his environment is limited and is almost continuously restricted to the same class or classes of stimuli. This self-imposed restriction strengthens itself by preventing contacts with other types of environmental events that could be reinforced and eventually acquire their own motivating value. Apropos this statement, we should note that, in the above-mentioned study, both the males and females were rated after twenty years as being more limited in their interests than they were earlier.

These two facts—that the environment ordinarily remains fairly constant and that certain behavior mechanisms retard the rate of new learning—serve to produce a stability of personality characteristics that has led many to conclude that personality patterns are established in early childhood and cannot thereafter be modified. But, as we have said above, this is not the case; although ordinarily the early years are the most influential, learning of new traits of personality can occur throughout life.

THE ORGANIZATION OF PERSONALITY

Many psychologists insist that the mere listing of the psychological characteristics of an individual is insufficient; they require that a personality description be expressed in a single phrase that sums up all the separate characteristics. Many of us tend to describe an individual's physical characteristics in this manner. We sum up his separate characteristics such as weight, height, and facial conformations in a phrase such as "bearlike" or "sleek as a cat." This same type of summation has been attempted for psychological characteristics.

The assumption which underlies this aim is that there is some style of life—or, better, some essence to the individual—which identifies him and which controls his actions·in his varied contacts with the world of things and people.

Even though so complex a behavior pattern as personality seems likely to defy a one-word description, many attempts have been made to provide general descriptive labels that would identify some underlying organization of the innumerable discrete acts that personality attempts to explain. Behind these efforts is not just a wish to simplify, but a belief in the existence of some single

541

integrating force. To this kind of approach the word *type theory* is given.

Type theory

The *type theory* of personality organization is altogether different from the learning theory. Type theory has the appeal of simplicity, for it holds that all persons may be classified into one of a limited number of categories, each describing the organization and the direction of the individual's many response tendencies. It implies that there is at least a moderate degree of relationship among all the behavioral acts of the individual, and that, knowing what he does in one situation, one could predict what he would do in another. Even further, it implies that, knowing the type name, one can predict an individual's behavior in a variety of situations. Strictly speaking, it implies also that all persons of a given type are alike and should behave alike. Strictly speaking, it permits no inconsistencies in behavior.

The inadequacy of such a theory, at least in so simplified a form as we have described above, is perfectly apparent. Our daily experiences with our fellow men clearly indicate that they cannot be divided into a few categories of behavior; on the contrary, there seem to be as many ways of behaving as there are people. To a lesser degree, our experiences indicate that we and our fellow men are somewhat inconsistent in our behavior. We are pleasant at one time and cross at another, honest and dishonest, gay and depressed, shy and bold, and we assume one role in one group and a different one in another. Perhaps there is predominance in one direction or another, but there is never complete consistency. No single word—the name of a type—is sufficient to describe the diversity of our behavior in a multitude of situations.

Some clear-cut evidence against a simplified type theory of personality is found in researches in which groups of people are given a series of personality tests each of which has been constructed to measure one or another personality type. If persons could be classified into types, one might expect to find the scores clustering at several distinct points on the scale, with each point representing a type. Actually the usual research finding is that most persons score midway between scores representing pure types. A theoretical distribution of what might be expected if there were two types of persons—the introvert and the extrovert—and a distribution actually obtained on a test of introversion-extroversion are shown in Figure 15.5.

Type theorists have not, however, been so naive, so blinded by their theories that they deny the empirically demonstrated inconsistencies of the individual, and they have modified their theories in order to seek a better fit to behavioral reality. They can do this in several ways: (1) they can increase the number of types in their particular system or (2) they can increase the number of categories in their type class. Thus in the example cited above, instead of having two categories—introvert and extrovert—they might have 3 or more degrees of introversion-extroversion. (3) Finally, they can postulate mixed types, individuals who combine different values or degrees of characteristics of the different types. The end results of these elaborations is to eliminate the simplicity that this approach had promised, and to make implausible the assumption that there is a single controlling principle behind the multiple acts of an individual. All in all, type theory does not seem to have met with sufficient success to concern us any longer, and we will turn to another somewhat more complicated effort.

Fig. 15.5 The theoretical distribution of introversion-extroversion scores that would be obtained if there were two distinct types of people—introverts and extroverts—and the actual distribution that was obtained on an introversion-extroversion test. (After data in Heidbreder, *J. Abn. Soc. Psych.*, 1926, *21*, 120-134)

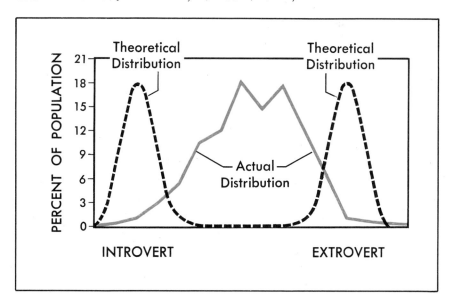

Trait theory

Another approach to personality organization is known as *trait theory*. This theory holds that there are a limited number of basic characteristics of behavior, and that we may describe an individual's personality by his status on each of these characteristic or personality dimensions. These traits or dimensions are independent of one another in the sense that there is little or no correlation between an individual's status on one trait and his status on the others. In its purest form, the theory could hold that knowing how an individual stands on one trait tells us nothing about how he stands on another. As an example, we might consider that some of the traits making up personality are *shyness, emotional stability,* and *intelligence.* Trait theory would assume that one person might be socially ascendant, excitable, and intelligent; another socially submissive, excitable, and intelligent; a third socially ascendant, calm, and dull. In other words, knowing the individual's score on the shyness trait, we could predict nothing about his score on the traits of emotional stability or intelligence. There would, however, be a basic consistency to behavior within these smaller areas. The level of intelligence characterizing the person would make itself shown in a variety of situations, and so too would the levels of shyness and emotional stability.

Within recent years a considerable amount of research has been conducted evaluating the trait approach to personality. The techniques employed in these researches involve statistical procedures that are too complex to be discussed in this text, but the results suggest a traitlike organization of personality. That is, they point toward some consistency, some common flavor, to the individual's actions within limited areas of behavior. This consistency constitutes the trait. They find also that behavior in one of these limited areas is, to a great extent, unrelated to behavior in another area—that is, that one trait is independent of the other.

There is always a danger in listing trait names, for we are inclined, once we have learned these names, to explain behavior by saying that it is due to the operation of a certain trait. There is a danger of assuming, in other words, that the trait is the *cause* of the behavior rather than a convenient label describing an area of consistency in behavior. And perhaps also there is a tendency to assume that the trait is an unlearned characteristic existing

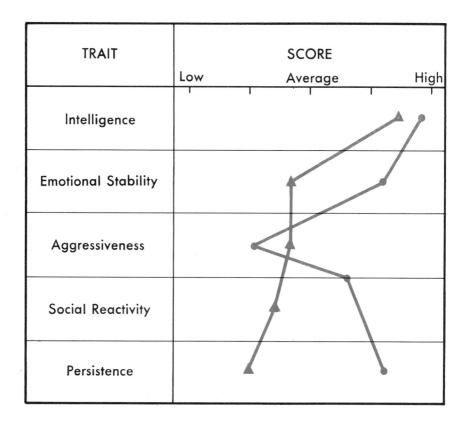

Fig. 15.6 A trait profile for two individuals. The results of personality tests measuring different traits for the same individual are often plotted in this fashion. The method of presentation permits the reader to note readily the interrelationships among the traits in the individual or to compare the interrelationships among individuals.

within the individual rather than merely an arbitrary device for describing behavior economically through the use of a word or two. The identification or the name of a trait implies nothing about how the trait, this consistent way of behaving, has developed. To answer this question a quite different kind of research program would be required. But all the foregoing discussion has implied that we would expect a trait to arise as a result of the interaction of hereditary factors and environmental experience. With this somewhat lengthy warning as a preamble, a partial list of traits that one experimenter has identified by means of a complex statistical analysis can be presented.[18] In describing these traits, we shall not attempt to apply a single name to them; rather, we shall list the characteristics of the extreme ends of the traits.

TRAIT 1. *Easy-going, adaptable, warm-hearted, expressive,* and *trustful* as opposed to *cantankerous, inflexible, indifferent, reserved,* and *suspicious.*

TRAIT 2. *Intelligent, thoughtful,* and *persevering* as opposed to *unintelligent, unreflective,* and *quitting.*

TRAIT 3. *Emotionally stable, realistic, calm,* and *thorough* as opposed to *emotionally unstable, unrealistic, excitable,* and *careless.*

TRAIT 4. *Self-assertive, aggressive,* and *adventurous* as opposed to *submissive, compliant,* and *timid.*

TRAIT 5. *Cheerful, sociable, energetic,* and *witty* as opposed to *pessimistic, retiring, languid,* and *dull.*

TRAIT 6. *Persevering, responsible,* and *ordered* as opposed to *fickle, frivolous,* and *relaxed.*

Once again the reader should be warned against assuming that these traits are fixed and immutable; that they are the final and definitive way of categorizing personality. At present they are useful ways of ordering the data collected on a number of personality tests; how well they will hold up under the scrutiny of future research we cannot say with certainty.

In a sense, trait theory is a modest form of type theory. Type theory assumes that there is a significant relationship among all the responses of the individual—that he will behave in a fashion true to his type. Trait theory holds that there is a significant relationship only among those responses related to the trait in question, but not between them and the responses related to some other trait within the same individual. Type theory implies that we need to know only one thing to predict the individual's behavior—the name of his type. Trait theory implies that we must know his standing on all the traits that are assumed to make up personality.

As we have pointed out, type theory is a considerable over-simplification of behavior; people do not run true to type. We cannot effectively predict the behavior of an individual by knowing only his type name. Trait theory, too, is far from perfect. Few individuals are, for example, shy in all situations, or emotionally stable or unstable in all situations. Trait theory can undoubtedly predict behavior of the individual more accurately than type theory, because it has more dimensions in which to describe behavior, but it will nevertheless be in error, for it, too, over-simplifies.

The position of this text

The organization of personality that is consistent with the approach of this text bears a fair degree of similarity to trait theory. Trait theory relates the total behavior to a number of different behavioral dimensions that are, to a certain extent, independent or unrelated to each other. These traits are usually defined by administering questionnaires covering a number of different topics, to which the subjects respond by checking what they think they would do or like in a wide variety of situations. The responses are then correlated with each other and the values of these correlations indicate which responses may be grouped together. The trait is the name for the inferred psychological mechanism (or mechanisms) that is assumed to be responsible for this cluster of responses. Usually several different clusters of these responses are found and this is taken to be evidence for several different traits. In summary, the trait is inferred from the cluster of responses, and, if the trait is named, the name describes the characteristic which the experimenter judges to be common to these responses.

In an early section of this chapter a group of psychological mechanisms were identified as being responsible for the behavior of the individual. They are mechanisms that have been identified as a consequence of experimentation and seem to be useful in predicting the behavior of man in the abstract. We assume that they have the same degree of validity for predicting the behavior of the individual. These psychological mechanisms are analogous to traits; they determine the behavior of the moment and to a certain extent they function independently of each other in the sense that the same instrumental act may be used to obtain satisfaction for two quite different motive states and in the sense that different instrumental acts may be used at two different times to obtain satisfaction of the same motive state. They are not, however, completely independent of each other. Examples of this fact have been discussed in earlier chapters of the text where it was shown that motive states can influence other psychological mechanisms, such as stimulus selection tendencies or perception.

The use of these psychological mechanisms to predict the behavior of an individual results in a picture of behavior that is similar to what we know is the case. The phenomenon of stimulus generalization would lead us to expect that there would be a similarity of responses in a number of situations provided that these

547

situations bear some similarity to one another. Because of the process of differentiation, we would be led to expect that quite a different kind of behavior could occur in a different situation. Only if the structure of the environment were highly consistent, reinforcing or non-reinforcing the same general way of behaving in one situation after another, could we expect complete consistency of behavior. But such consistency of environment is not to be expected, and if we are correct in our guesses as to how personality develops, we should not expect total consistency of behavior.

In addition to predicting some inconsistency in behavior, this environmental emphasis in personality development makes another prediction: since no two people are likely to have the identical environments, no two would be alike in personality.

Actually inconsistencies may not always be as real as they appear, for the operation of a broad and inclusive motive may provide an underlying unity to behavior which is not apparent on the surface. Consider this hypothetical example. Among his equals, Mr. X is the champion of the underdog. In his conversation especially, and often even in his actions, he attacks the stuffed shirt and the Old Guard. He criticizes their conservatism and rails at their laziness and lack of standards. He accuses them of setting rules and regulations the sole function of which is to keep themselves in power and to block the achievements and recognition of vigorous and able younger men while they reward their mediocre and nonthreatening favorites. Because this role is most pleasing to his peers, he becomes something of a trusted leader and through their support he himself climbs into a position of power.

But his assumption of power does not result in any reforms. He becomes something of a stickler for rules; he finds faults in the younger men; and he, too, erects barriers around his position. Superficially, at least, Mr. X is a changed man. Once a radical, he is now somewhat conservative; no longer does he identify himself with the younger men; instead of sponsoring change, he strives to maintain the *status quo*. If, however, we view his behavior as arising from the motive to gain and exert power over others, then there is consistency in his behavior both as underdog and top dog. His actions among the younger group are consistent with the role behavior expected of their leader, and leadership in this group becomes a steppingstone to a position of power in the older group. If he is to continue in power and to gain more, a new form of role is now demanded of him. Essentially, this is an example of using a different instrumental response to achieve the same motivational purpose. Since the motivation is the same in each case the behavior could not be called inconsistent, even though the effects of the instrumental acts have a quite different impact upon other individuals at one time or another.

Other inconsistencies in overt behavior may arise from a competition among motives. In one situation a particular motive may be the most powerful one and result in a certain kind of behavior. In another situation it may be present, but be dominated by some different motive which was absent in the first situation, and which leads to behavior which not only is different in kind, but directed toward a different end.

These examples suggest that some of the apparent inconsistencies in behavior are inconsistencies only because we have failed to recognize the motive structures of the individual. It is clear, therefore, that broad and inclusive motives are one of the organizing forces of personality.

THE FREUDIAN THEORY OF PERSONALITY

This section represents a departure from the basic organization of this text, for thus far it has attempted to present a description of those theories and those ways of analyzing the data of behavior which at the present time seem to be rooted most soundly in the scientific method and which seem to show the greatest promise of eventual fruitfulness. In this attempt we have avoided the description of theories and methods that do not meet these criteria. For reasons which will be presented at the close of this section, the Freudian theory of personality falls in the category of being less than satisfactory on both counts, and, for the sake of consistency, a discussion of it might well be omitted. However, unlike most, but not all, psychological theories the Freudian theory of personality has gained wide public recognition. Its terms and its concepts appear again and again in literature; in discussions of how to raise children; in interpretations of social events; in college bull sessions; and in a variety of other contexts. Sometimes the user of these Freudian concepts does not know from whence they came and all too often they are used inaccurately. It seems advisable that a student who has taken an elementary course in psychology should have at least a passing acquaintance with so pervasive a theory.[19]

The source of Freudian theory

Sigmund Freud began his professional career as a neurologist practicing in Vienna in the last decade of the nineteenth century. His patients came to him because they were mentally disturbed and sought to cure themselves, with his help, of the disabling fears, anxieties, and foibles which dominated their lives. At first he used hypnosis as a means of treating his patients but this technique caused them to form strong attachments to him. In collaboration with another neurologist, Joseph Breuer, he discovered a different method which achieved the same results, but which minimized the establishment of the undesired and undesirable attachments. The patient simply reclined on a couch in Freud's office and talked; he told of the past; he talked about his current problem and his feelings toward it; he even described his dreams. Freud listened, but he listened with a discerning ear and was sensitive not only to what the patients said, but to what they did not seem to want to utter. At night he made notes upon his cases and thought about the potential significance of what he had heard. These are the ingredients out of which the psychoanalytic theory of personality grew—the many words of these disturbed individuals and the fertile and persistent mind of Sigmund Freud.

The structure of personality

Freud concluded that the personality was comprised of three major systems. These he called the *id,* the *ego,* and the *superego.*

The purpose of the *id* is to provide a means for discharging the tension that arises in the organism as a consequence of its many biological needs. It is guided by the *pleasure principle,* seeking always the release of tensions and the avoidance of pain. It is irrational and amoral and because of its irrationality it must work through some other medium to find in the complexities of the real world the objects or events that can satisfy its current demands.

This other medium is the *ego,* a system which is governed by the *reality principle*. It is in contact with the real world and is knowledgeable about this world. Through its motor, perceptual, and intellectual activities it is able to guide the organism and to attain for it those things which will relieve the tension that has stemmed from the *id*.

The third system is the *superego;* it is the moral branch of the three systems of the personality. It strives for the ideal rather than for the expedient, and it contains two smaller systems, the *ego ideal* and the *conscience.* The ego-ideal represents the standards and values which have been instilled in the child by the parents as they reward his good deeds, while the conscience is the product of their punishments.

The dynamics and development of personality

The id, ego, and superego are the basic structures of the personality; we turn now to the manner in which they interact with each other and develop throughout the life of the individual.

Life is, of course, dynamic and active, and for systems to perform work, be they mechanical, electrical or biological, they need energy. Freud assumed that the physical energy obtained by the organism from the chemicals of the world in which he lived was transformed into *psychic energy* to maintain the activity of the three mechanisms of personality. The id serves as the source of this psychic energy and all of the energy required to maintain the other two systems is derived from the id. The id uses its energy to satisfy the basic organic instincts, and when an instinct is unfulfilled, energy is released toward the end of obtaining the object or performing the action that will satisfy the instinct.

Since the environment is complex and those things which appease the instinct are not always and simply available, the id must work through the mechanism which knows about the real world, the ego. The id supplies energy to the ego, thus making it able to perform the transactions between the real world and the demands arising from the id. The id responds immediately and insistently to any instinctual requirements while the ego must determine when and how gratification is to be obtained. As a consequence the ego is often put into great strain for it must withstand the forces of tension from the id if the environment forbids the action which is needed to satisfy the currently active instinct.

The superego, it will be recalled, develops essentially as an internalization of the prohibitions and ideals that were imposed by the parents, and it too receives its energy supply from the id. The views which are held by the superego of the appropriate ways of behaving and thinking are highly idealized and often unrealistic. This state of affairs means that at times the superego is an ally of the ego in the struggle to withstand the insistent, and sometimes socially unacceptable, demands of the id. At other times it wars against the ego, for the ego is often governed by expediency and sometimes what is expedient is contrary to the ideals and conscience of the superego.

Alliances and struggles among the various structures of the personality are, therefore, an essential characteristic of the Freudian point of view. For this reason various strategies and devices are employed by the different structures in order to gain their individual or occasionally cooperative ends, and a considerable amount of the theory is devoted to identifying these strategies and devices. Some of these adjustment mechanisms will be discussed in the following chapter.

Before leaving the theory, however, something should be said about the relations of these structures to the conscious and the unconscious. In the early days of his theory-building Freud placed a great emphasis upon these two concepts, but they became of less importance in his later theorizing. Essentially, however, the activities of the id are unconscious, while that of the ego and superego are conscious. Since the id contains a vast body of the motivating forces of the individual this statement implies that a large amount of our behavior is instigated by demands of which we are unaware.

A criticism of Freudian theory

Just as it has been impossible, in this elementary text, to present a full picture of Freudian theory, so it will also be impossible to present a complete criticism of that theory. To do so would lead us into the realm of the philosophy of science and into the rather subtle questions about the meaning and significance of theories in general. We will content ourselves with a brief expostulation of only a few of the more obvious criticisms.

1. Freud, it will be recalled, did not take notes during his sessions with his clients, for he thought that to do so would disturb the therapeutic relationship. His notes were made some

hours later, usually in the evening. This means that the raw data upon which his theory stands have been subjected to the omissions and the elaborations of the forgetting process as it operated in Freud from the time of the client's analytic session to the time of the note taking. The modern concepts of proactive and retroactive inhibition would suggest that the extent of forgetting could be rather considerable for so active a man as Freud. To what extent forgetting may have distorted Freud's data we can never know, but we do know that the use of this technique for collecting the raw data violates a basic requirement of scientific investigation.

Another criticism that has been levied against Freud's data is that it consists of reports from clients of what they said they did and what they said had happened to them. Freud made no effort to check up on the validity of these statements and one cannot readily determine how much is fact and how much is fancy in the psychoanalytically obtained autobiographies of these disturbed subjects.

2. The next criticism arises from the very nature of the theory itself. The id and the ego or superego are often in conflict with each other, one demanding one kind of action and the other an action which is the opposite in nature, and tied up with all of this are the concepts of consciousness and unconsciousness. For reasons too complicated to be analyzed in the space available, the theory predicts that a given psychological energy may lead to one kind of behavior or just the opposite behavior. Thus one may express, and believe he holds, a great fondness for someone because he hates him; or he may be pious, and believe in his piety, because he is at heart an unbeliever. The theory, in other words, permits the prediction of one kind of behavior, the opposite, or even behavior that is different from either of these extremes. This aspect of the theory makes it invulnerable to experimental disproof. Typically we demand of a theory that it will be vulnerable in the sense that it can be shown to be wrong if indeed it is. The very nature of Freudian theory rules out the possibility of making the crucial test.

Closely allied to this criticism is another one. Freudian theory is one of *postdiction* rather than *prediction*. It can postdict accurately, that is, tell why something has happened after the event, but it does not predict accurately. Postdiction is of little practical value, for to be maximally useful a theory should tell what will happen before it has happened.

3. The theory as it was originally advanced and modified by Freud puts a heavier emphasis upon instincts as determinants of behavior than seems to be justified, but modern proponents of the theory have changed it to decrease its emphasis upon these instinctual forces and thus have caused it to conform more closely to the reality of experimentation. Obviously it is to the credit of the theory that it can accept these modifications, but it may not be able to accept the more sophisticated and complicated relationships between heredity and environment that are likely to be the conceptual outcomes of further research in this field.

In summary, it may be said of Freud's work in particular and of Freud's theory in part, that they have given modern psychologists a deep understanding of the complexities of behavior. Without Freud, or his like, we would know and understand much less than we do today. But just as any older theory in any science is replaced by newer and better ones as the frontiers of knowledge are extended, so also this has happened to the theory that Freud developed.

THE MEASUREMENT OF PERSONALITY

A fairly complete discussion of how aptitude tests are developed was presented in the chapter on Intelligence, and essentially the same techniques can be employed in the creation of a personality test. However, instead of validating the tests by classifying the population according to their efficiency as measured by production records or the opinions of foremen, personality tests are classified along personality dimensions by close acquaintances, by teachers, by psychiatrists, or any other group of individuals who know the subjects well enough to make competent judgments. In other words, these experts serve to establish the criterion groups. The experimenter then administers his test and afterwards discovers by his tabulation which items were answered differently by the two groups. These and only these items he includes in his new test, which, if he is a careful investigator, he will administer to two new groups for purposes of *cross validation*.

Although there is an essential similarity between test development in the aptitude field and test development in the field of personality theory, special problems arise for the research worker in the latter field. These special problems place the developer of personality tests at a disadvantage, and it will be well to consider some of these difficulties before we discuss the tests themselves.[20]

The behavior dimension to be measured

The aptitude-test developer is usually given a fairly specific aim, which is defined rather concretely by a social institution. Thus, he may be striving to build a test that will predict success as a lathe operator, as an airplane pilot, as an insurance salesman, or as a college student. Because the task is a part of an ongoing, socially defined activity it can be subjected to a job analysis, an extremely helpful step for the experimenter. It should be noted, however, that a job analysis would be easier to perform and could be more complete for the lathe operator than for the college student. The job analysis is useful to the experimenter because it informs him of the behavioral components of the job, and so it gives rather accurate information of the behaviors that should be measured in the test.

The worker in the field of personality theory is, however, ordinarily concerned with measuring the behavior that he believes is determined by one of the psychological mechanisms of his theory. Thus a Freudian might wish to measure *ego strength;* another theorist, *the need for achievement;* and a third, *feelings of anxiety and inferiority*. There is no social agency that deals directly in ego strength, need achievement, or feelings of anxiety or inferiority; no institution from whence a job analysis of the behaviors stemming from these mechanisms can be found. The descriptions of the expected behaviors are derived from the theories themselves. If the theorist meets with poor success in creating his test it is difficult to determine whether the failure should be attributed to technical flaws in his test-development procedure, to errors in his estimates of what behaviors are to be expected, or to a more basic flaw—the lack of validity of the theoretical construct, the psychological mechanism itself.

Difficulties of this sort are not insurmountable, and in part the excitement of scientific research is a consequence of these challenging intellectual barriers, but they do retard progress of test construction in the field of personality theory.

It should be mentioned in passing that there are instances in the field of personality testing where situations similar to those

555

found in the aptitude field may arise. One might, for example, construct a test to detect military personnel who are most likely to have mental disturbances. The test items can be administered to two groups of soldiers who have undergone similar experiences, one group having developed disturbances and the other group having come through unscathed. Subsequent tabulation would probably disclose many items on which the two groups responded differently and these could be combined to form a test which could be used for screening future soldiers. Although this test may be useful, it does not in this form throw much light upon the basic personality mechanisms that were responsible for the stability of one group and the instability of the other. It is not, in other words, an investigation of personality theory.

The nature of the behavior sampled

Intelligence tests and tests of personality may be contrasted with respect to the materials they contain. As we noted in our discussion of intelligence, the materials contained in the intelligence test itself are directly related to the concept being measured. Since intelligence includes the ability to solve problems, some of the items on the tests are problems to be solved; since it involves verbal facility, a vocabulary test is included; so also the other materials reflect other aspects of intelligent behavior. Such a test is said to have *face validity,* for the behavior sampled on the test itself seems to be the same as the behavior that we are trying to measure. Because of the very nature of the behavior we are trying to predict, it is often very difficult to achieve face validity for personality tests. Although a lack of face validity does not invalidate a test, its presence certainly increases the test's general validity. As we shall soon see, types of personality tests vary greatly in the extent to which they have face validity.

The criterion groups

Suppose we wish to develop a test of some aspect of personality. Before we can be satisfied that a test does evaluate this characteristic, we must have some *independent* measure against which to check our test scores. We must, in other words, obtain a criterion in constructing such a personality test—just as a criterion is needed in the construction of an intelligence or aptitude test. In the case of intelligence we could obtain wide agreement that a fairly satisfactory criterion is performance on subject-matter materials in a school situation. This is by no means a perfect criterion of intelligence, for there are factors other than intellectual competence that determine one's school performance. But most of us would agree that the two are undoubtedly related.

In addition to the fact that school grades are acceptable as a fairly adequate measure of intellectual level, there is the important element that they exist *in a precise form*. The grades are based upon tests and recitations that have been evaluated by the teacher with at least a moderate amount of care. These various measures have then been summarized in the form of a single grade, and all the single grades in all the single courses can be converted into a single average. This average is not without error, for it includes grades in subjects which interested the student and in those which bored him, grades assigned by lenient teachers and by severe ones, but all in all it is not a bad measure of intellectual ability.

Although a considerable emphasis in modern education has been placed upon training the general personality characteristics of the student, it is doubtful that the usual teacher possesses as much data for evaluating the student's personality characteristics as his intellectual performance. The student is not put in *special test* situations designed to measure various aspects of personality, and the teacher's judgments are probably by-products of observations in situations that were not intended primarily to compare students in their personality traits. Hence, although he may know how one or two students will react in a specific situation, he may never have seen many of the other children in the same situation.

This same difficulty would be encountered, perhaps to an even greater degree, if we were to design a personality test at an adult level. There are not many sources from which a psychologist can draw personality estimates on a large number of persons, and yet he needs these estimates to validate his test. This difficulty in obtaining an adequate criterion is not insurmountable, but it requires a considerable amount of time and effort.

Differences among personality tests

In an effort to measure various aspects of personality, psychologists and psychiatrists have developed a large number of tests.

Those tests differ from one another in many respects, and it may aid our understanding of the tests themselves if we consider first some of the ways in which they differ.

1. Tests differ in *what they attempt to measure*. Some tests attempt to measure personality as a whole; other, less ambitious ones are designed to measure one or another aspect of the individual's personality.

2. Tests differ in their *face validity*. The Rorschach Test, for example, consists of a series of ink blots as stimulus figures, and the subject being tested is required to tell what these figures remind him of. The test situation is a far cry from the actual situation. Other tests, on the other hand, consist of systematic observations of the subject in situations very similar to those for which predictions are being made.

3. Tests differ in the *degree of restriction placed upon the subject's response*. Tests composed of a series of questions to each of which the subject must answer "Yes," "Sometimes," or "No" obviously place a heavy restriction on the freedom of the subject's response. On the other hand a subject shown a Rorschach ink blot is free to make any response he wishes. The data obtained from tests of this kind are obviously richer in nature but, just as obviously, they are more difficult to evaluate and interpret.

4. Tests differ in the *extent to which they conceal their purposes*. Let us suppose that you are taking a personality test and the statement "I prefer being by myself to meeting new people" appears as one of the items to which you must respond. You need not be a psychologist to guess what the psychological significance of a "Yes" or "No" to this question may be. On the other hand, a particular ink blot may be described as a "hat blowing wildly in the March wind" or a "brightly painted pot of Indian workmanship." It is very unlikely that the untrained individual would find any great significance in either statement, but to the trained tester these statements have meaning within the framework of the theory of that test.

5. Tests differ in the degree of *objectivity with which they can be scored*. In general, tests in which the subject's responses are restricted can be scored altogether objectively. One need merely tally all the "Yes," "No" and "Sometimes" responses to obtain the subject's score. Of course, an error in counting can be made, but it is easily checked and there is no question that a check mark in one column means "Yes" and a check mark in

another column means "No." On the other hand, the responses obtained from some other tests may be ambiguous, and, as a result, one scorer may assign one kind of meaning to a certain response whereas another may ascribe quite a different meaning to it and thus a different score. Rescoring may not help to eliminate the disparity, for each scorer may have strong convictions that his way of scoring was the correct one. It is unlikely, of course, that tests on which no two scorers could agree would come into general use, and actually scorer disagreements are neither frequent nor wide. But the fact remains that some tests can be scored with high objectivity—and the task of scoring can be readily turned over to a machine—whereas others must be scored by an expert. Interpretation even by experts always leaves some room for disagreement.

6. Tests differ in the *source of the response they require.* In most tests, data describing the individual under consideration are obtained from that individual himself. He himself takes the test and answers its questions. But in some types of personality measurement the data consist of responses from another person, or from several of them, about the individual in question. The person in question is evaluated by the way others react to him.

SOME TYPES OF PERSONALITY
MEASURES

A large variety of techniques and approaches has been applied to the measurement of personality. The basis for the particular content of the test has ranged from unsubstantiated hunches about personality to predictions from reasonably well formulated personality theories. In their form the techniques range from highly structural multiple-choice forms to free interview situations. Hundreds of these tests have been developed, and many hundreds of articles contain attempts to evaluate them. For this reason the presentation below will be concerned primarily with identifying the major types of approach to personality measurement rather than with consideration of particular tests. The discussion of the general validity of these techniques will be postponed to a later section.

Personality and physical characteristics

If it were possible to predict how a person would think, or feel, or act merely on the basis of the shape of his nose or the height of his brow, measurement of personality would present no obstacles. One's physical features can be measured with a high degree of precision, and if a sizable correlation existed between physical and psychological characteristics, the psychologist could borrow the measurement tools and techniques of the physical anthropologist and thus predict personality. Perhaps one of the reasons for the recurrence of theories that postulate close relationships between personality and physique is the very simplicity of the position and its extreme workableness—if only it worked!

Theories of this kind demand a fixed relationship between some feature of the body and some aspect of behavior. They assume that the physical characteristic is completely or almost completely determined by hereditary factors. Since the relationship between physical and psychological characteristics must be fixed if we are to use the one to predict the other, the theories also imply a parallel genetic determination of personality. We have already presented our reasons for objecting to a theory of personality which attributes all or most of personality determination to genetic factors, and we might expect that efforts to measure personality by use of such an assumption would not be fruitful.

Actually experimental studies have not supported a relationship between physical and psychological characteristics.[21] Studies of the results of tests predicting that certain psychological and physical characteristics are interrelated indicate that, as a rule, the correlations are extremely low.

In individuals suffering from certain glandular disturbances, relationships between general personality characteristics and physical conformation do occur with some consistency. Within the normal range of physical variations, however, there is little satisfactory evidence that any even moderate relationships exist between the physical and the psychological.

Research in this area is fraught with many obstacles which becloud interpretations and which in the past have led to positive findings that are more apparent than real in their support of the theory. An example of this is found in the research of Lombroso, a nineteenth-century Italian criminologist, who reported that there was a high tendency for criminals to have bodily defects of various sorts. He felt this was due to an inherited throwback to prehistoric man, who, he believed, was physically and morally inferior to modern man. Statistics supported Lombroso, for his criminal population did have more physical defects than the population at large, but his interpretation of the cause was wrong. In general, criminals come from a lower socioeconomic level, where diet and medical care are inferior. Small wonder that as adults they show physical blights. Both the criminality, which we shall loosely call the psychological characteristic, and the physical defects arose from the social and the economic environment in which the criminals were reared. The two conditions were tied together by environmental rather than genetic conditions. The fault in Lombroso's hypothesis lay not in his facts but in his interpretation of them.

If relationships between physique and personality are occasionally found, this does not mean that a genetic factor is necessarily responsible for the correlation, which could be accounted for in other ways:

1. The beliefs of society itself may produce certain relationships between physical and psychological characteristics. A common belief is that redheads have hot tempers. If parents and friends hold this to be true, the temper tantrums thrown by the redhead may be condoned and considered inevitable. It is likely, then, that the redheaded child will obtain some goal by his tantrums, and this behavior is reinforced. The little blue-eyed blonde who reacts to frustration in the same way may be sent to her room to cool off; she does not obtain her goal by the same behavioral technique, and this technique therefore drops out. But for the redhead it persists. Here environment once again shapes relationships—this time because society believes them to be inevitable. The belief, in other words, produces support for itself.

2. Certain kinds of physiques may, in a particular culture, be more appropriate for some kinds of activities than for others. If particular kinds of values, attitudes, or patterns of interests are associated with these activities this fact could lead to similarities of psychological characteristics among the participants. Consequently, an association between psychological traits and physical traits may be evidenced, but it has occurred only because it is mediated by the reinforcements supplied by the culture. A high school junior who is six feet three inches tall is very likely to be a member of

the basketball team, and as a successful athlete he is likely to acquire certain interests and attitudes. The example is oversimplified, but it illustrates the view that certain "jobs" favor some body builds over others and could lead to associated psychological characteristics.

3. Perceptual biases entering into measurement may lead to, or at least inflate the apparent relationship between the physical and psychological traits. One's interpretation of the psychological characteristics of another is a complex perceptual process, and perceptual responses are determined by a large number of cues, which are often subtle and even ambiguous. Included in our perception of an individual's behavior is our perception of his physical characteristics. If we hold to a particular theory of the relationship between certain physical and psychological characteristics, then our perception of the behavior of an individual can be biased by the presence or absence of these physical characteristics.

It seems likely that this error entered into the research of one of the recent efforts to relate physique to body type. The experimenter reported correlations in the neighborhood of .80 between body build and behavioral traits among a college population, and correlations of this magnitude are unusually high for almost any measure of behavior. Unfortunately the experimenter himself made the personality judgments and, since he was well aware of the subjects' physical characteristics and knew what the theory would predict, his judgments of the personality characteristics could readily have been distorted.[22]

We close this section with the general conclusion that there is very little satisfactory evidence supporting the theory that physique and personality characteristics have sufficient correlation to use one as an effective means of predicting the other.

Direct observation of behavior

Tests with the greatest face validity are those involving systematic observation and recording of the behavior of the individual in certain more or less standard situations. Perhaps the best example of this type of approach comes from studies conducted with nursery-school children.[23] Such studies are more difficult to conduct than they appear to be. The observer must be trained; he should record not all the behavior of the child but certain aspects only—social contacts or aggressiveness, for example—and he should record short samples of the child's behavior at different times of the day, and over a period of several days. Clearly such work as this is time-consuming, but the data obtained are true samples of the child's behavior in real-life situations.

Since the nursery-school situation is somewhat standardized, one feels justified in comparing one child's behavior with that of another. To follow the same procedure with adults is certainly more difficult. Indeed, it would not be feasible to follow the adult about in his daily routine. He would be more self-conscious than the child in the presence of an observer, and the situations that one adult encounters throughout the day are likely to differ considerably from those encountered by another.

In an effort to establish situations that are standard for adults, a technique has been developed in which the subject is required to perform in certain situations and his performance is observed. This technique is called *role playing*. Obviously the term as it is used here has a meaning somewhat different from its earlier use in our discussion of social influences.

A program of testing conducted during World War II for the evaluation of men assigned to the Office of Strategic Services illustrated this type of testing situation.[24] The men being observed lived together for three days at an estate outside Washington, D.C. During this stay they were required to perform in certain standard situations under the careful observation of psychologists and psychiatrists. In one of the situations the candidates—under constant observation—were required to find a way of getting a dummy rocket launcher over a "canyon" consisting of two high wooden walls. In another situation the men were to construct some equipment with the aid of two helpers. These helpers, however, were "stooges" who were instructed to hinder and obstruct and not to help. Still another situation put a man through a grilling third degree while he attempted to maintain a falsified story.

You will note that these situations are not real ones—the rocket launcher was a dummy, the canyon walls were wooden fences, and the grilling was directed by friendly fellow-Americans and not by members of a hostile army. Nevertheless, the situations had some face validity to them. The subjects met real problems to be solved and real people with whom they were forced to deal. This kind of testing situation has somewhat less face validity than

563

the one exemplified by nursery-school studies; other role-playing situations may be somewhat more removed from real-life ones but in general all of them have the degree of face validity involved in dealing with real people, even though the situation is a "pretend" one. This type of test can be, and has been, adopted to a variety of situations, such as the behavior of the business executive.

A basic assumption involved in the use of such tests is that some of the individual's true characteristics come through via his performance even though the situation is a make-believe one. Obviously this assumption must be tested against a criterion even though the test seems to have face validity.

Questionnaires and inventories

One of the most common types of personality-measurement instrument is a paper-and-pencil questionnaire or inventory in which the subject is required to answer questions about himself. The questions may deal with what he likes, how he feels or has felt, and what he would do in certain situations. Some sample items are shown in Figure 15.7.

In the sense that words can describe actual situations and that the subject understands this, tests like these may be said to have face validity. However, there may be a great difference between what the subject *reports* he might do in a situation and what he might do in practice. There are several reasons for this. The subject may wish to deceive the tester or, because of the operation of certain mechanisms of personality that will be described later, he may not be able to estimate correctly what he might do or even what he has done.

Rating scales

A measuring device that suffers from the same difficulty of biasing influences as the questionnaire is the rating scale. Generally, however, the rating scale is used for the evaluation of a given individual by someone else, more often than not his immediate superior—a foreman, a supervisor, or a superior officer. This type of instrument can readily be understood by an examination of the typical items shown in Figure 15.8.

MOTIVATION QUESTIONNAIRE

Answer each question by placing a check after the answer which most closely describes your feelings.

1. Do you feel that it is all right to turn down friends who want favors, even if they act annoyed about being turned down?	Yes_____	No_____
2. Do you plan to become one of the top men in your chosen profession?	Yes_____	No_____
3. Do you sometimes get homesick for your family and old buddies?	Yes_____	No_____
4. Do you feel it is worth your effort to earn straight A's, even if you have a hard time doing it?	Yes_____	No_____
5. Do you find that you get along better if you do not get too involved with the people around you?	Yes_____	No_____
6. Do you feel that you must do everything as close to perfect as you can?	Yes_____	No_____
7. Would you, on some occasions, rather go to a movie by yourself than go on a double date?	Yes_____	No_____
8. If you knew you would get more out of the course would you be willing to read a 50-page assignment every day?	Yes_____	No_____
9. Is it very upsetting to you if any unfriendly remarks are exchanged with your friends?	Yes_____	No_____
10. Are you planning to go to summer school in order to get through college more rapidly?	Yes_____	No_____

Fig. 15.7 This questionnaire is intended to measure two motivated characteristics of individuals—the need for achievement and the need for affiliation. The reader should have little difficulty in identifying which items are relevant to which motive. (Courtesy John K. Hemphill)

Forced choice

The forced-choice test was developed specifically to prevent a respondent from intentionally biasing the results of a test.[25] The demand for such a test grew out of the fitness reports that Army and Navy officers are periodically required to fill out on their subordinates. Sometimes, and for a variety of reasons, the reports were intentionally biased either for or against a subordinate.

```
┌─────────────────────────────────────────────────────────────────┐
│                INSTRUCTOR EVALUATION RATING FORM                  │
│   For each question place an X in the box before the item which most │
│ accurately describes your feelings about the instructor of this course. │
│                                                                   │
│  1.  In his availability for consultation this instructor         │
│          □ goes out of his way to be available for help.          │
│          □ is frequently available for help.                      │
│          □ is usually available for help.                         │
│          □ is seldom available for help.                          │
│          □ is scarcely ever available for help.                   │
│                                                                   │
│  2.  The instructor of this course                                │
│          □ welcomes differences of opinion.                       │
│          □ is almost always tolerant of differences of opinion.   │
│          □ is usually tolerant of differences of opinion.         │
│          □ is occasionally intolerant of differences of opinion.  │
│          □ is often intolerant of differences of opinion.         │
│                                                                   │
│  3.  In his attitude toward students this instructor is           │
│          □ exceptionally friendly.                                │
│          □ friendly.                                              │
│          □ fairly friendly.                                       │
│          □ variable in his friendliness.                          │
│          □ cold and indifferent.                                  │
│                                                                   │
│  4.  In respect to his enthusiasm this instructor                 │
│          □ shows a lively interest.                               │
│          □ is a "self-starter" or essentially interested.         │
│          □ is moderately interested.                              │
│          □ is quite dead and indifferent.                         │
│          □ has no enthusiasm at all—a "wet blanket."              │
│                                                                   │
│  5.  The content of the classroom presentation is                 │
│          □ always interesting.                                    │
│          □ more often interesting than dull.                      │
│          □ half interesting and half dull.                        │
│          □ more often dull than interesting.                      │
│          □ regularly dull.                                        │
└─────────────────────────────────────────────────────────────────┘
```

Fig. 15.8 An example of a rating form. To obtain a score from such a scale the experimenter might assign a numerical value ranging from 1 to 5 to each of the choices under each item, a value of 1 being given to the most favorable choice and 5 to the least favorable. The values for all items could then be averaged to provide a single score for the instructor.

The forced-choice technique attempts to forestall intentional biasing by presenting the respondent with four statements. Two of these refer to socially desirable characteristics; two to socially undesirable characteristics. The respondent is required to check the one of each pair which best describes the individual who

Fig. 15.9 A forced-choice rating scale. In Part I one item of each pair is more frequently associated with good instruction than is the other; in Part II one item is more frequently associated with poor instruction than is the other. The determination of which item in a pair is the significant one must be accomplished by empirical research. Some preliminary research has been conducted on this scale, and the manner in which it would be marked to produce the most favorable score for the instructor is presented at the end of the chapter.

FORCED-CHOICE INSTRUCTOR RATING SCALE

Part I   Place a cross (X) in front of the one item of each pair which is most like your instructor.

A. ( ) 1. Defined all new, difficult, or ambiguous terms.
   ( ) 2. Used humor and imagination to enliven class.

B. ( ) 1. Always came to class well prepared.
   ( ) 2. Had a tremendous store of information and knowledge.

C. ( ) 1. Always had time to help students who had difficulty.
   ( ) 2. Knew how to put material across to the student.

D. ( ) 1. Had complete control of the class at all times.
   ( ) 2. Showed important implications and significance of points covered.

E. ( ) 1. Got points across without a lot of senseless verbiage.
   ( ) 2. Used visual aids to supplement what was said.

Part II Place a cross (X) in front of the one item of each pair which is least like your instructor.

A. ( ) 1. Answers on tests had to be word for word from the book.
   ( ) 2. Could not command respect of the class.

B. ( ) 1. Never answered a question directly but talked all around it.
   ( ) 2. Prone to go off on tangents irrelevant to the topic.

C. ( ) 1. Blackboard illustrations were jumbled and difficult to follow.
   ( ) 2. Tended to get sidetracked into insignificant details.

D. ( ) 1. Did not care whether students understood or not.
   ( ) 2. Spent time of class in aimless discussions.

E. ( ) 1. Left classroom as soon as bell rang to avoid students.
   ( ) 2. Used ridicule and sarcasm with the students.

is being rated. Only one of each of the two pairs of statements is related to performance on the task. The existence of this relationship must, of course, be established by previous experimentation in which a group of good and a group of poor workers have been compared. The rater is now forced to choose one of each pair, but it is very unlikely that he will be able to guess which one is actually important for performance on the job. Thus, it is difficult for him to bias his ratings. An example is shown in Figure 15.9.

Sociometric evaluation

Like the two immediately preceding types of test, sociometric evaluations usually involve ratings by others.

This technique can be employed only when a moderately cohesive social grouping is in existence, the members of which will be able to answer questions such as the following:

1. Who are your three best friends in the group?
2. If you were choosing group members to play on a baseball team, what three members would you choose first?
3. If you could choose three people to sit nearest you, who would they be?
4. Which three people would you choose to represent the group at an intergroup meeting?

By this method of evaluation one can obtain a picture of how an individual is regarded by other members of his group, and how he himself reacts to them. Figure 15.10 shows a sociogram— that is, a graphic presentation of the data obtained through this method.

Projective techniques

Perhaps the most imaginatively intriguing of all of the types of personality tests are the projective techniques. In a projective test, the subject is presented with materials which do not have any unique and clear-cut meaning. One test, the Rorschach, consists of a series of standard ink blots and the subject tells what he sees in them; another, the Thematic Apperception Test (usually abbreviated T.A.T.), consists of a series of pictures about which the subject tells a story. These two are perhaps the best

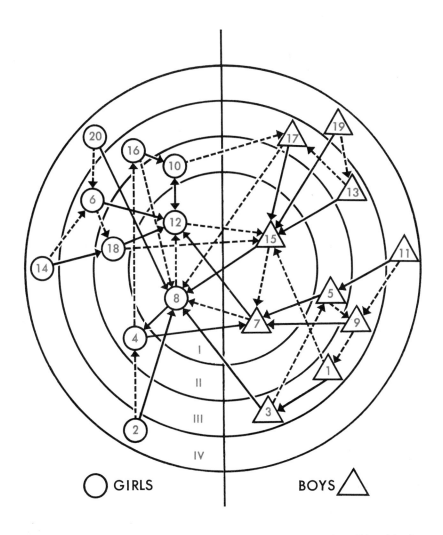

Fig. 15.10 This sociogram shows the first and second choices (the solid and broken arrows, respectively) of a group of students who were asked to select the classmates with whom they would prefer to work on a class project. Girls are represented by circles; boys by triangles. The numbers identify the individuals; names are not generally used because information is confidential. The four individuals closest to the center were those most frequently chosen by their classmates. The individuals farther from the center were chosen less frequently, and those in the outermost circle are the "isolates"—those who were not chosen at all by their classmates.

known of all of the projective tests, but the same principle may be applied to many kinds of materials. Stems of sentences such as "I hate . . . ," "People are . . ." may be the stimulus material to which the subject adds a completion; a series of cartoons may depict some incident, but in the final panel the "balloon" of one of the

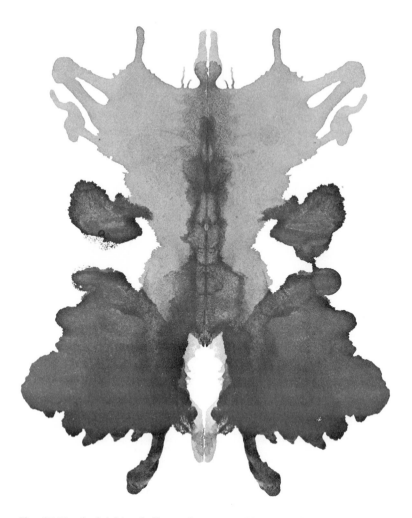

Fig. 15.11 An ink blot similar to the type used in the well-known Rorschach Test. What the subject "sees" in this configuration and reports to the trained tester is used to infer certain personality characteristics.

speakers is blank and the subject fills in the appropriate response; or children may be given dolls accompanied by doll-house furnishings and told to play with them while the tester records what is said and how the dolls are made to act.

The essential nature of these tests is that they are *unstructured;* they initiate activity, but they do not limit the responses to a single category in the way questionnaires and rating scales do. They are called projective tests because the subject must *project* his own perceptions and motivations into the material. He does so as he gives meaning to these essentially ambiguous materials.

The essential theoretical justification for the use of these kinds of materials is that the nature of an individual's perceptual responses is a function, not only of the materials, but also of his current motives. Some support for this position has been presented in the chapter on Perception. This relationship implies, therefore, that something about the individual's motives can be inferred from the way he responds to these unstructured materials.

The method of scoring projective tests tends to be different from that used for the structured tests. In the latter the scores can be obtained by counting—a task that a machine can perform. One cannot make out a simple scoring key for a projective test because the answers do not fall into one of several predetermined categories. The rich and diverse materials obtained from these tests must be interpreted by the test administrator, who himself must decide how particular responses should be classified. The administrator does not interpret these in a purely individual fashion since there are manuals for the tests which he uses as guides. The fact

Fig. 15.12 A picture from the Thematic Apperception Test. As the subject tells the tester "what this picture is about," he reveals certain personality characteristics. Like the Rorschach Test, the TAT can be administered only by a highly trained specialist. (Courtesy J. B. Rotter)

remains, however, that the administrator's own biases can enter into the final scoring, and this possible source of biasing error introduces special problems in designing the validation studies of projective tests.

Validation of tests

If we are to accept the results of personality tests, it must be shown empirically that the tests measure what they purport to measure. It is not sufficient that they be based upon the application of some general theoretical principle, however sound that principle may be, or that they have face validity. Experimental validation is therefore necessary so that we may determine how well the test achieves its purpose.

There are, in the technical literature of psychology, many studies that have validated, or have failed to validate, one or another of these personality tests. The experiments differ from each other in a number of minor ways, but in essence the methods for validation can be reduced to two major types.

▶ **1. Validation by contrasting groups.** The main method employed in validation studies consists of the administration of the test to two groups of subjects who differ widely in the trait or characteristic presumably measured by the test. A group of subjects considered by psychiatrists or clinical psychologists to show neurotic tendencies may be compared on a test with a group considered normal. A group of Army officers who are rated by their peers as "very superior" may be compared with a group who are rated as "inferior." Patients who have suffered injuries of the brain may be compared with individuals of similar age, socio-economic level, and education who have had no history of brain injury. The purpose is to find out whether or not the mean score of one group differs significantly from that of the other. A significant difference between mean scores of the two groups may be considered as some evidence of the test's validity.

In practice the psychologist is likely to be working with a test composed of a number of items. He compares the scores of the two groups on each item and then selects for use in his final test only those items on which the two groups react differently. After this is done, he is likely to give his new test to two new groups of subjects. This procedure is known as cross validating and has been discussed in the chapter on intelligence.

► **2. Validation by manipulation of motive strength.**
This method is somewhat more theory-oriented than is the previous one. It starts with the assumption that a given motive is activated by some particular environmental event. This event is then introduced for one group of subjects but withheld for another: the two groups are then given the test and their performances are compared by the same procedures that are used in the previous method. For example, a test to measure the need for achievement may be validated in the following way: One group of subjects is given a test which obviously measures intellectual ability. When it is completed and scored on the spot the experimenter informs them that they have done exceptionally well. Another group, given the same test, is led to believe that they have done very poorly. If the acting of the experimenter has been good enough the two groups will now differ from each other in their need for achievement, for one group has just failed and the other has just succeeded. The personality test is then given to each group and the differences, if any, in their ways of responding are assumed to be the results of the differences in motivational conditions aroused by their reported success or failure on the test of intellectual abilities. Obviously the validity of the test is supported only if a number of differences are found in the personality-test responses of the two groups. Obviously, also, the experimenter is careful to inform both groups—after the personality tests are completed—of the exact nature of the procedure and the reasons for it.

► **3. Some special precautions.** In any test where the individual's final score must be interpreted by the test administrator—and where the results may therefore be biased—special safeguards must be introduced into the validation procedure. Perhaps an example will make the reason for the precautions more obvious. Suppose the experimenter is validating a test by comparing a group of individuals classified as neurotic with a group of individuals classified as normal. It is very likely that he will know, through one means or another, the group from which the particular subject he is testing has come. If he knows this much about the subject, he may unintentionally tend to score ambiguous items in the direction indicated by his knowledge, with a resulting spurious increase in the validity of the test.

One technique that has been devised to eliminate this type of experimental bias is called *blind matching*. An expert will be given the test responses of the two groups of individuals with nothing more than a coded identification on each test form. He may then be informed that some of the subjects have been classified as normal and others classified as neurotic. His task is to interpret the test results and then sort them into two piles, one for the neurotic and one for the normal. The degree of validity of the test is measured by the extent to which the various experts employed in the blind matching procedure are able to match the outside criterion. There are, of course, many variations of the blind matching procedure, growing from the kind of problem being investigated and the ingenuity of the experimenter; but the purpose of all of them is to prevent any contamination of the results by the tester's unintentional biases.

There are some who object to this procedure as being needlessly secretive and as depriving the clinician of the full knowledge as he would have if he were working with a real client. One can only answer by pointing out that the purpose of the research is to validate the test and not elicit other sources of information. Like so many other apparently cumbersome methods that have been devised by psychologists, it testifies to our deep appreciation of the fallibility of perceptual and judgmental processes among even the best intentioned experts. The use of this technique in experimental studies does not imply that the clinical psychologist should disregard all information other than the test score in dealing with a specific client; it simply means that when we are engaged in the scientific operation of validating a test we should not permit extraneous knowledge to influence the results.

▶ **4. The validity of personality tests.** The reason for conducting validation studies is, of course, to determine how useful the various tests are in measuring what they are intended to measure. Personality tests are designed to tell us something important about an individual or some aspect of the individual. At the present time we can make only modest claims for the effectiveness of personality tests in general. The use of tests by the trained clinician ordinarily gives him insights into the client's psychological structure which would be difficult to obtain in any other way. Some of them can also be used as crude screening devices to identify a group of persons who would have an unusually high percentage of failure or success rates in some activity because of personality inadequacies. However, the usual personality test does not achieve the predictive value of standardized intelligence tests, and even these are far from perfect. Obviously the obstacles in the way of constructing personality tests have not been completely overcome, or probably fully understood. Yet it does not follow that this will always be true. Undoubtedly future research will overcome many of these obstacles, and gradually—as is almost always true of any science—our measuring devices will be refined and improved.

A VERY GENERAL SUMMARY

This has been a long chapter, and perhaps for the readers who hoped to find in it the formula for removing their own uncomfortable psychological quirks it has also been a disappointing one. Apologies may perhaps be in order for its length, but not for its lack of therapeutic value, for it is asking too much of a chapter in a textbook that it succeed in modifying the behaviors you have taken a lifetime to learn.

We have attempted in this chapter to identify the concept of personality, a concept which is widely but vaguely used. As we have employed the term, it refers to the total behavior of the individual, but especially to the behavior that is unique to him and that differentiates him from his brothers and sisters and parents and neighbors—from all the millions of other people who live on the earth. Because this has been our aim, the chapter has been directed toward a discussion of the forces that lead to individuality in behavior. Those forces were found in the individual's genetic background and—to an overriding and predominating degree—in his environment. Very briefly we attempted to identify some of the aspects of the environment that are of potential importance for personality development, and—primarily by reference to animal experimentation—to show that environmental events do indeed determine personality characteristics. Thence we turned to the problem of the relationships of various dimensions of behavior within the individual and spoke of type and trait theory, the former being rejected and the latter being described as one that is partly, but not completely, consonant with the approach of this text. Finally, we turned to more technical matters, to consideration of the tests the psychologists have developed to measure various aspects of individual behavior. This topic is continued in the next chapter and there we shall be concerned with the somewhat dramatic characteristics of individual behavior: the quirks of the normal in solving his problems and the behavior of those who depart from normality.

SCORING OF FIG. 15.9

To give an instructor the most favorable rating for the forced-choice rating scale in Figure 15.9, the following ratings would be made: Part I. *A* (2) , *B* (1) , *C* (2) , *D* (2) , *E* (1) . Part II. *A* (1) , *B* (2) , *C* (2) , *D* (2) , *E* (1) . In other words, these choices represent either the most favorable statement of the pair in Part I or the least unfavorable statement of the pair in Part II.

REFERENCES

[1] Guthrie, M. J., and Anderson, J. M. *General Zoology*, Wiley, 1957.

[2] Rundquist, E. S. The inheritance of spontaneous activity in rats, *J. comp. Psychol.*, 1933, *16*, 415-438.

[3] Senderling, E. W. Individual differences in the behavior of new born infants in relation to emotionality of parents. Unpublished dissertation, Ohio State University, 1939.

[4] Hall, C. S. "The genetics of behavior." In S. Steven (ed.), *Handbook of Experimental Psychology*, Wiley, 1951.

[5] Hall, C. S., and Klein, S. J. Individual differences in aggressiveness in rats, *J. comp. Psychol.*, 1942, *33*, 371-383.

[6] Uyeno, E. T. Hereditary and environmental aspects of dominant behavior in the albino rat, *J. comp. physiol. Psychol.*, 1960, *53*, 138-141.

[7] Witkin, H. A., Lewis, H. B., Hertzman, M., Machover, K., Meissner, P. B., and Wapner, S. *Personality Through Perception*, Harper, 1954.

[8] Sears, R. R., Maccoby, E. E., and Levin, H. *Patterns of Child Rearing*, Row, Patterson, 1957.

[9] Orlansky, H. Infant care and personality, *Psychol. Bull.*, 1949, *46*, 1-48.

[10] King, J. A. Parameters relevant to determining the effects of early experience upon the adult behavior of animals, *Psychol. Bull.*, 1958, *55*, 46-58.

[11] Baldwin, A. L., Kalhorn, J., and Breese, H. F. The appraisal of parent behavior, *Psychol. Monogr.*, 1949, *63*, 4.

[12] Hewitt, L. E., and Jenkins, R. C. *Fundamental Patterns of Maladjustment: The Dynamics of Their Origin*, Green, 1946.

[13] Parten, Mildred B. Social participation among preschool children, *J. Abn. Soc. Psychol.*, 1932, *27*, 243-269.

[14] Jack, L. M. An experimental study of ascendant behavior in preschool children, *Behavior of the Preschool Child*, 1934, *9*, 7-65.

[15] Melzack, R., and Scott, T. H. The effects of early experience on response to pain, *J. comp. physiol. Psychol.*, 1957, *50*, 155-161.

[16] Kelly, E. L. Consistency of

adult personality, *Amer. Psychol.*, 1955, *10*, 659-681.

17 Tyler, Leona S. Toward a workable psychology of individuality, *Amer. Psychol.*, 1959, *14*, 75-81.

18 Cattell, R. B. *Personality*, McGraw-Hill, 1950.

19 Hall, C. S. *A Primer of Freudian Psychology*, World, 1954.

20 Rotter, J. B. *Social Learning and Clinical Psychology*, Prentice-Hall, 1954.

21 McClelland, D. C. *Personality*, Holt, Rinehart and Winston, 1951.

22 Humphreys, L. G. Characteristics of type concepts with special reference to Sheldon's typology, *Psychol. Bull.*, 1957, *54*, 218-228.

23 Thompson, G. G. *Child Psychology*, Houghton, 1952, Chapter I.

24 U.S. Office of Strategic Services, Assessment Staff, *Assessment of Men*, Holt, Rinehart and Winston, 1948.

25 Sisson, D. E. Forced choice: The new army rating, *Personnel Psychology*, 1948, *1*, 365-381.

Chapter Sixteen

PATTERNS

OF

PERSONALITY

IN THE PRECEDING CHAPTER WE POINTED
out that we err in the direction of disregarding individuality when
we classify persons in a limited number of categories. With this as
a warning, we shall, in this chapter, describe some rather common
patterns of behavior that appear in a great many individuals. We
do not wish to imply that individuals showing similar patterns are
identical to one another in other respects, or even that the common pattern is precisely the same. We wish only to identify certain basic patterns of behavior that occur frequently enough to be
given special names.

The patterns that we shall consider in this chapter vary in
their frequency and in their general significance for over-all adjust-

ment. Almost any person who is classified as normal or well adjusted is likely to exhibit some of these behavior patterns; other patterns are of the extreme sort which lead their exhibitors to be classified as abnormal. These latter patterns are known as *neuroses, psychoses,* and *personality disorders.*

SOME TYPICAL NORMAL REACTIONS

The kinds of behavior with which we are now concerned are almost exclusively devices that the individual acquires in satisfying his motive conditions. Essentially they involve a devious rather than a direct approach to motive satisfaction. The reason for this lies in the fact that these mechanisms or patterns of behavior are mobilized into action at times when there is a conflict of motives and when the demand of one motive is antagonistic to the demand of another. The very devious and subtle character of the mechanisms often makes it possible for both motives to be satisfied, even though on the surface they are incompatible. They permit us, in other words, to eat our cake and have it too.

There is one sort of motive condition which is almost always present in the situations in which these mechanisms operate. It is a complex condition, and it is difficult to name, but we shall identify it here as a *tendency to maintain self-respect.*

From childhood on, we learn to perceive and evaluate our own acts in much the same way that we perceive and evaluate the acts of others. We develop a concept of ourselves as a behaving organism, an organism that suffers when punishments are administered to it and that is elated by the receipt of rewards. We learn, in other words, that when this organism—ourselves—is attacked it suffers, and so we attempt to make protective responses.

Our parents, our peers, and other figures of authority teach us that some acts are right and some acts are wrong, and we learn that these wrong acts often lead to punishment. All of us, then, long before adulthood find that fences of custom, erected both by our family and by society as a whole, bar us from certain areas of behavior. To trespass into these areas is to risk punishment. At the same time these figures have also identified for us those areas of behavior that are considered admirable and that often eventuate in rewards.

579

Through the process of motivation learning, of the sort described in Chapter 5, we come to avoid these banned areas, even though when we are adults the hickory stick of an external prohibiting authority no longer threatens us. Essentially this is what we mean when we say that our conscience would bother us if we committed some act. In the same way we also learn of the good, the true, and the beautiful and that actions so classified lead to strong rewards and commendations—that is, to reinforcement. In short we carry with us the ability to reward or punish our own actions just as those external forces once did.

Unfortunately, most of us are activated at some time or another by powerful motives which can be satisfied only by the very acts which we would condemn in others and in ourselves. But not to perform the act is to leave this motive unsatisfied. So it is that we develop devious mechanisms which satisfy this motive but by a trick of psychological magic do not cause us to see ourselves as misbehaving, of being less than angels. These mechanisms thus prevent us from losing our self-respect.

Rationalization

"Politics," we say, "makes strange bedfellows." By this we mean that we often find persons with highly divergent points of view banding together for common action, or at least voting the same way on the same issue. The fact is, however—and this we often forget in the heat of a political battle—that identical voting on one issue does not mean that the voting groups are essentially alike either in their stand on other issues or in the basic motives that have led to that vote. One man may vote against a bill because he considers it too liberal, and another because it is not liberal enough. In this case two highly antagonistic motives produce the same response.

Now let us look at a politician who is eager to be re-elected and who is not entirely scrupulous. When talking before a liberal audience, he may claim that he voted "no" on a certain bill because it was "not sufficiently liberal," and he is hoping for a better one; to a conservative audience he may say he voted "no" because he is opposed to "such liberal falderal." If there is no communication between these groups, he may win the support of both. He has his cake and he eats it, too. Just as our politician fools one or both of these groups as to what his true motivation was, so likewise may we dupe ourselves.

We are very frequently confronted with situations in which the same response would be appropriate for two different motives; the act, in other words, could be interpreted as arising from either motive. This fact lays the groundwork for the mechanism of rationalization. Our actual instigation to perform some act may originate from a motive that is not acceptable to us—that is, one that would cause us to lose respect for ourselves. However, we might perform the act under the instigation of a second motive—one that is not only acceptable to us but may even be generally commendable. If we can convince ourselves that it is the second motive that determines our behavior and not the first, we can perform the act without losing face.

An example may make this clearer. A businessman has a chance to close a deal that will gain him a considerable profit. The deal involves a few ethically questionable maneuvers and, in addition, will result in a severe, though not complete, financial loss for a younger man. Because of his previous training, our businessman would not care to see himself as the sort of person who would either seriously harm a fellow man or who would engage in even slightly unethical business deals. Nevertheless, the sum of money that would be gained by the transaction is most attractive.

The businessman's conflict is of the approach-avoidance type. He is drawn toward the act by the promise of financial gain, but he is repelled by the knowledge that he would lose some self-respect if he were to harm another seriously in order to profit personally. Soon we find him telling himself that if he were to close the deal, the younger man would learn a valuable lesson. After all, it would not result in complete ruin for him; he could recover and he would never allow himself to get into such a position again. In fact, the young man might be protected from a subsequent loss, the consequences of which might be more serious. To wish to teach the young man a lesson so that he will be better able to cope with the future is a motive that is approved by society and by our businessman alike.

By reasoning in this manner, the predominantly negative motive—the threat of blame arising from the act of harming a younger person—becomes a predominantly positive one. Perhaps the situation is seen as being analogous to putting iodine on a child's cut; it inflicts pain now, but it prevents a greater pain in the future. As a consequence of this reasoning, two motives point to the same act, financial gain can be achieved and a younger man can be taught a lesson that will be "good" for him. Both lead to the same act. The deal is closed, and our businessman is convinced that he acted not for profit but to teach the younger man a lesson.

When rationalizing behaviors such as the one above are described in textbooks, the reader is inclined to conclude that the rationalizer is a mealy-mouthed hypocrite who really knows why he performed a certain act. In true rationalization this is not the case, for the success of the gambit depends entirely upon his fooling himself. If our politician failed to convince one of the groups that his motivation was what he claimed it to be, he would lose their respect; so too the rationalizer loses his self-respect if he fails to convince himself that his behavior was instigated by the acceptable motive.

How, one might ask, could he—or we, since most of us rationalize—be so naive, so stupid, as to accept this conclusion? There are many reasons why such self-deceit is possible. Who is to gainsay in any one incident that the motive named is the incorrect one? Since almost always at least two or three motives lead to the same act, how can we prove that it is one rather than another that dominates the individual? The performer is, in a sense, placed in the position of trying to make a judgment as to which of several psychological forces is the greatest. It is a difficult judgment to make unless there is a great disparity in their strengths, and this is not the case in the rationalization situation.

In Chapter 9 we noted that interpretations of ambiguous situations are influenced by motivation. This mechanism operates for the interpretation of visual forms, the behavior of others, or the behavior of oneself. The individual is motivated to see his own behavior in the best light, and, since the situation *is* ambiguous, it is easy for him to perceive his acts as stemming from the acceptable rather than the unacceptable motive.

In circumstances such as these, it is not difficult to fool oneself as to the source of one's motivation. In fact, we may wonder how some other person dares to state that our motivation is different from what we ourselves claim it to be. We cannot logically prove a person's motivation in such a situation. We can, however, tabulate other behavior in his past, and if his behavior in one situation after another is consistently in the direction of one motive, then we can assume that it is highly probable that the same motive dominated in this particular situation.

Compensation

The process of rationalizing is made possible when several motives converge upon the same goal object; compensation is made possible when two quite different instrumental acts may satisfy the same motive. Let us see how this may work.

By a very early age most of us have learned to seek the approval of our peers, and we do so by performing the acts that have high value for our age mates. The exact nature of these acts changes with the age group in question, and the process of growing up is in part a process of changing one's own values and competences to agree with those of our age group. Adolescence is a time of hardship for many because it is a period during which a rather marked shift in values occurs. One of the major ways—though there are others—of gaining respect with one's own sex is to be popular with the opposite sex. Gone are the days when it is achieved by owning a prettier doll or riding a bicycle no-handed.

For a variety of reasons, many individuals find great difficulty in making the transition, for although they may have had the competences to succeed with their same-sex peers at age ten, they lack the new set of competences—perhaps the proper dance step, a captivating line, or a mature build—to succeed at age sixteen. One of these reasons arises from differences in the age of occurrence of pubescence—that is, in the age of acquiring the primary and secondary physical changes of sexual maturity. Maturing late is especially troublesome for the male, since as a group males mature more slowly than females. A boy of sixteen who is still prepubescent is not likely to be considered an acceptable date by a postpubescent girl of his own age; he stands less chance of gaining the respect of his same-sexed peers because he is not successful with girls. There are, however, other things that his peers admire. As a group they admire daring behavior and may stand somewhat in awe of any of their members who successfully defy authority.[1] Perhaps, then, a sequence of minor delinquencies will lead to this admiration. So he may let it be known that he dares to drink or smoke; he may pilfer from the local hangouts and generously pass out the booty; he may drive a car recklessly; or he may engage in even more serious crimes. If he stays within the limit of what is acceptable to his peer group, he may achieve some dubious respect

583

from them—respect that he could not obtain through the process of dating, for this avenue is not open to him.

Of course, compensation need not take the form of antisocial activities; he may instead turn to some constructive hobby, or to his studies and become recognized as the genius of his class or at least as a specialist in some area. If any of these activities, the antisocial or the socially acceptable ones, lead to some restoration of prestige, they are moderately adequate substitutes for the activity of dating.

Compensation, then, is characterized by the substitution of *one instrumental act* for another; it is not, it should be emphasized, the substitution of one *motive* for another. In the example cited above, the dominant motivation is not stealing but rather obtaining prestige with his peers. The activity of stealing is simply a pathway to the social goal. This fact is of considerable significance if we wish to change the behavior, for if we can give an individual some other means of satisfying the basic motivations, the undesirable actions may quickly drop out. They drop out because they were never wanted for their own sake.

Compensatory behavior is, of course, helpful to the individual at the time he is using it, for it permits him to adjust to an otherwise difficult situation. In the long run, it may be harmful or helpful, depending on its nature. In one example cited above, it could lead to further delinquencies and eventually to clashes with the law and tragic consequences for the individual. On the other hand, extra work on hobbies or school subjects can give the individual valuable skills which may help him in later life.

There is another form of behavior that is often referred to as compensation but that is psychologically quite different from the behavior we have described above. It is exemplified in the lives of Theodore Roosevelt and the Greek orator Demosthenes. As a child Roosevelt was sickly and weak, but to overcome this he exercised systematically and became as an adult hardy, vigorous, and very much attracted to the rough outdoor life. It is said of Demosthenes that as a youth his voice was soft and that he spoke with a stutter. To overcome these deficiencies he went to the seashore and shouted above the roar of waves. He became a great orator in a city and in a time of great orators. The type of behavior represented by these two men is quite different from that which we have previously referred to as compensation. Instead of seeking other instrumental

acts, these men attacked directly the obstacle—their own incapacity
—that blocked them from goal attainment.

Projection

It is not difficult to describe the phenomenon of projection,
but it is difficult to understand why under certain conditions it is
an effective adjustment device. Projection is a tendency to see in
others the motives that dominate our own behavior. Data would
seem to indicate that this holds true for both our acceptable and
our unacceptable motives, and this fact suggests that the phenomenon may in part be accounted for by the influence of motivation
upon perception,[2] a phenomenon discussed in Chapter 9. Projection considered in this light alone would not, however, seem to
serve any important motivational purpose for the individual, and
yet there are times when it does seem to do so.

One manner in which projection functions to fulfill individual needs is in conjunction with the mechanism of rationalization. Let us couch our example in terms of university politics. A
new departmental chairman arrives on the scene, an ambitious man
bent upon expanding his department. He would like to add some
courses to his departmental offerings, but these courses are perhaps
a little more appropriately given by Department X, and he cannot
picture himself as one who willfully steals from another. Yet suppose he were to observe in Department X signs of greed and aggression which threaten the very existence of his own department. If
this were true, then who could blame him for following the laws
of self-preservation? The new courses could serve as a sort of no-
man's land—a buffer state—between the aggressive Department X
and the group of courses that constitute the proper territory of his
own department. Surely in this instance projection serves a motivational need; it permits aggression under the guise of self-protection. To the historian familiar with the rise of ambitious expan-
sionist states, this is an old story.

There is another form of behavior classified under the name
projection for which it is more difficult to determine how the behavior leads to motive satisfaction. There is reason to believe that
some of the people who are most ardent and belligerent in observing and condemning particular actions in others are strongly activated by the very motives that they so fiercely condemn. One who

585

did so would, of course, obtain some satisfaction from the real or anticipated acclaim he would receive from others for exposing this evil, and it might absolve him of the guilt he may feel for possessing this motive. His own strong motives in this area could account for his readiness to perceive actions related to this motive condition in others. None of these conditions, however, would be expected to result in reduction of the strength of the instigating motive itself. It is perhaps pertinent to note that subjects who are undergoing extreme food deprivation have a tendency to collect food-related objects such as menus or even tea cups.[3] It would appear that these symbols, which are related to the instrumental acts of satisfying the motives, have themselves some motive-satisfying quality. This fact suggests that the individual who is projecting and attacking the real or apparent activities of another may gain from satisfaction from talking about, from using the verbal symbols which are intimately related to this personally forbidden activity.

A word of warning is in order, for there is a danger of over-generalizing and of assuming that all reformers are projecting and that basically they seek the very thing they condemn. This rather cynical interpretation of behavior is not justified, for there is no reason to believe that in most cases the apparent motive is not also the real motive for the behavior.

Hysterical reactions

The following episode, told by a psychologist, illustrates an hysterical reaction—that is, the solving of a psychological problem by the development of a physical disturbance.

During my graduate-student days I occasionally dated a girl who worked in one of the university offices. I had known her for several years and our relations at this time were friendly but not romantic. I had several times invited her to attend one of the very informal dances which were given at the Graduate Club nearly every month but she had always refused, saying she couldn't dance. I think I had told her that if she ever changed her mind I would be glad to take her, and it was more or less tacitly understood that she had a standing invitation to the dances, assuming, of course, I hadn't dated someone else in the meantime. As a result she called me one evening and said she would like to go to the next dance, and so it was arranged. How or why she ever managed to gather up enough courage to commit herself to this bold step I don't know.

When I stopped by her apartment to pick her up Saturday evening she was ready to go, but from the expression on her face it was apparent that something was wrong.

I didn't inquire about it but as we prepared to leave she handed me, along with the inevitable lipstick and compact, a box of aspirin.

"Will you put these in your pocket, too?" she asked. "I have a terrible headache—migraine—and the aspirin may help me through the evening. I'm afraid I'll be terrible company and won't be able to dance worth a darn."

I suggested, none too positively, that we skip the dance, but she refused, though she emphasized again the prediction that she would be poor company and too ill to dance well.

The dance turned out to be one of those in which the proportion of unattached males to females was unusually high. Even though she did not dance very well, she was constantly cut in on and so, of course, were all the other girls who were there. She was obviously enjoying herself. When, a short time after we had arrived, I cut in on her, I inquired about the headache and found that it was gone and she was now feeling fine. Her recovery was so fast (she had said she was feeling worse just before we stepped onto the floor) that I feel quite certain it was more related to the stags who had immediately begun to cut in on her than to the aspirins. Headaches usually don't disappear that fast. Her headache never returned that evening.

The behavior of this young lady sounds suspiciously like a hysterical reaction. She had apparently attended few, if any, dances up to this time, and apparently she did not dance well. Since she lacked this skill, which is a major prerequisite for success on the dance floor, she had reason to believe that her evening would be a social failure. It is always difficult to accept failure; it would be especially difficult for her to attribute the failure to the lack of a skill which most young women of her age and cultural group possess. But, on the other hand, failure to perform well on a given occasion because of an illness is understandable and excusable. The fact of having a violent headache on this occasion could serve as a sort of insurance against the loss of face that might result from social failure, or at least social inadequacy. In the present instance the failure did not materialize and the headache was no longer needed; the abundance of stags did what the aspirins had failed to do.

It would be most incorrect to assume that the illness is faked in the sense that the person states to others that he is ill while actually he feels in good health. It would also be a mistake to assume that the illness is produced by some sort of conscious calculation. The hysterical reaction is, after all, a sort of personal alibi that permits the individual to accept failure without loss of self-respect; it would not serve this purpose if the person knew how and why it came about. It must therefore be as painful or incapacitating as any similar illness arising from orthodox causes.

We do not know in detail what the underlying physiological mechanisms are that can produce symptoms or feelings so similar to those produced by obvious organic changes or the presence of disease-producing organisms in the body, but the reaction becomes somewhat less mysterious if it is considered from another point of view. The young lady described above was probably excited and worried during the hours preceding the dance. As we shall point out in detail in Chapter 19, emotional reactions produce profound changes in the general bodily processes. These changes could lead to an incipient headache which becomes greatly magnified. Probably most of us most of the time could, if we introspected long and thoroughly enough, identify aches and pains, irregularities of heart beat, or spots before our eyes as we work hard. These common seedlings could, if fertilized and watered by the promise of psychological utility, become full-grown plants of self-deception. If in the past there had been many instances when we were released from some disagreeable task because of illness, then through such reinforcements, this reaction may be the response that we learn to make to the stimuli that characterize an unpleasant task. These symptoms—a feeling of nausea, perhaps—may be produced by the anticipation of facing the situation or by an actual concomitant illness; yet if they serve as a source of reinforcement by removing us from the situation, the responses may become attached to these types of stimuli. In Chapter 3 it was pointed out that any response can become conditioned provided that the appropriate unconditioned stimulus is associated in the proper way with the conditioned stimulus. This type of learning situation may very likely form the basis for the development of hysterical reactions.

Hysterical reactions are of many varieties, but their common characteristic is that they develop in the face of a conflict situation and serve as a means of removing the individual from this situation. Many writers, when faced with a difficult problem in their manuscript, develop a "writer's cramp" that incapacitates them, even though in other situations they have written for much longer periods with no signs of strain. Combat soldiers have developed paralysis of the hand or leg, or a blindness in the eye used in sighting. It appears, then, that hysterical reactions may take on almost any form, from the pattern of symptoms associated with some illness or disease to a loss of a motor or sensory function.

Since hysterical reactions—or *functional disorders,* as they are often called—are highly similar to disorders produced by orthodox *organic disturbances,* how does one differentiate between the two? Sometimes it is most difficult, and at other times it is fairly simple. A person with a functional paralysis of the arm may move it quite normally while asleep. This could not happen if there were an actual lesion of the motor nerve leading to the muscles. A person suffering from functional blindness may show normal light reflexes—such as the pupillary response to changes in illumination—and this, too, would not occur if the sensory nerves were not functioning. Where reliable tests for the measurement of organic involvements have been developed, these can be applied, and a differential diagnosis of organic and functional disorder can be made with some confidence. In the case of reported aches and pains, the task is more difficult. If, however, these aches and pains seem to serve some psychological purpose, if their comings and goings are associated with classes of psychological events, and if they are not alleviated by the usual kinds of medical treatment, there is reason to suspect that they are hysterical reactions.

Repression

Hysterical reactions do not alter a conflict situation but they do incapacitate the individual so that he may escape from the situation without losing his self-respect. Repression, on the other hand, "removes" the conflict situation itself, as the following example indicates.

A young woman of good heredity developed during her childhood a severe phobia of running water. She was unable to give any explanation of her disorder, which persisted without noticeable improvement from approximately her seventh to her twentieth year. Her fear of splashing sounds was especially intense. For instance, it was necessary for her to be in a distant part of the house when the bathtub was being filled for her bath, and during the early years it often required the combined efforts of three members of the family to secure a satisfactory washing. She always struggled violently and screamed. During one school session a drinking-fountain was in the hall outside her classroom. If the children of the school made much noise drinking, she became very frightened, actually fainting on one occasion. When she rode on trains, if was necessary to keep the window curtain down so that she might not see the streams over which the train passed. These are some of the more typical features of her reaction to running water. It can be imagined that her life was very seriously interfered with by the disorder.

During the young woman's twentieth year, an aunt came to visit at her home. This lady had not seen her niece during the whole period of thirteen years through which the phobia had persisted. She was met at the station by the mother of the girl, who gave a brief account of her daughter's condition. On arrival at the home, the aunt met the girl at the front steps and said immediately, "I have never told." This statement served to provoke a recall of the condition under which the fear of running water had been established. The fact is doubly interesting because such determined efforts to stimulate her memory had previously been made by her parents and by various physicians.

The mother, the aunt, and the little girl—she was seven years old at the time—had gone on a picnic. Late in the afternoon, the mother decided to return home but the child insisted on being permitted to stay for a while longer with her aunt. This was promptly arranged on the child's promise to be strictly obedient and the two friends went into the woods for a walk. A short time later the little girl, neglecting her agreement, ran off alone. When she was finally found she was lying wedged among the rocks of a small stream with a waterfall pouring down over her head. She was screaming with terror. They proceeded immediately to a farmhouse, where the wet clothes were dried, but, even after this, the child continued to express great alarm lest her mother should learn of her disobedience. However, her aunt reassured her with the promise, "I will never tell." So at last they returned home and to bed. As the older woman left the next morning for a distant city, the girl had no one in whom she could confide. On the contrary she repressed all thought of her accident and presently she was unable to recall the facts even when a serious effort was made to have her do so. This is the most distinguishing feature of a phobia, its ostensible lack of explanation.[4]

If the event by the waterfall was so important to the individual that it was responsible for a psychological disability, why should it not be recalled? Surely an event so traumatic, so psychologically significant, should not be casually forgotten. It seems far more plausible to assume that it has been, shall we say, *actively* forgotten, that it has been *pushed* into the realm of unremembered things. The term *repression* is used to refer to such convenient forgetting of the things that are troublesome to our self-esteem.

The literature of clinical psychology abounds with cases that involved repression—cases in which the patient seems to be unable to recall an event in which he has behaved in an unacceptable fashion. The knowledge of having behaved unacceptably threatens one's self-respect, but if this knowledge can be wiped out, the threat is removed. Hence repression serves for the individual a useful function by eliminating this threatening knowledge.

The situation need not be a dramatic one, and the reaction is by no means abnormal, for it is characteristic of a large number of persons and can be demonstrated experimentally. The essential procedure in these experiments is to give two groups of subjects identical tasks to perform. One group is led to believe that the materials of the task are part of an intelligence test and that poor performance is an indication of low intellectual capacity. The other group is informed that the experimenter is merely trying out some problems to discover whether or not they are useful.

Both groups are permitted to finish some of the problems but are interrupted before finishing the rest. One group is led to believe that interruption was a sign of failure and hence low intelligence; the other group is led to believe that the interruption occurred because the problem was not worth spending more time on. Later the two groups are asked to recall as many of the problems as possible. Usually the interrupted tasks are recalled less well by the group that interprets interruption as failure than by the other group.

There are, of course, great individual differences, some persons recalling proportionally more interrupted tasks and others proportionally more completed tasks. The significant fact is, however, that the whole group that interprets interruption as failure is biased toward an inability to recall the interrupted tasks. Since the groups are usually composed of college students taking elementary courses in psychology, it is hardly sensible to consider that a large proportion of such a group is abnormal. Hence the phenomenon is neither unusual nor indicative of a warped personality.

The behavior seems to be explicable in the following fashion. The individual tends to avoid situations that are punishing or unpleasant, and a situation that produces feelings of guilt or failure is such a situation. Words, whether spoken by oneself or by others, can symbolically recreate a situation. Words spoken by oneself that describe the situation constitute recalling or remembering the event. But the very act of doing this produces a consequence—say unhappiness—which tends to be avoided. Thus the individual learns to substitute some other response to the stimuli that might evoke recall. The responses that are substituted are those that lead to positive reinforcement, or at least not to punishment. The stimulus→response connection which constitutes the recall is still present in his habit structure, but another, antagonistic response is attached to the stimulus, and, being stronger, it blocks the recall. The situation is analogous to retroactive inhibition (see p. 136).

Recall of a "repressed" situation becomes possible under several conditions. One of these involves the presentation of more numerous or more potent stimuli for recall. In the case of the young lady described above, recall seems to have occurred as soon as the aunt came upon the scene. The aunt, because of her association with the event, would serve as a stimulus for the recall—a stimulus that had been absent during all the time that the event had been "repressed." Previous failure in recall may be in part due to lack of adequate stimuli for recall.

Recall also occurs in the quiet of a psychiatric interview. Here there is no dramatic introduction of some more adequate stimuli, and one must search for other behavior mechanisms to explain these events. The recalls can probably be attributed to the operation of extinction upon the conflicting response. Repression, as we have noted, occurs because a competing response has been affixed to the stimulus that might otherwise produce recall of the emotional, or, as it is usually termed, *traumatic* event. In the psychiatric interview, the patient is invited to talk about the things that bother him, but in the beginning he responds to the "dangerous" stimuli by describing events that are obviously of no great significance. The psychiatrist, however, brings him back time and again to the topic. Doing so is like calling the first response wrong, like not reinforcing it. Eventually this response tendency becomes weakened. The other and crucial response, which had never been lost, eventually reaches the point at which it is stronger than the more acceptable competing response, and it is recalled. The repression has been eliminated.

Hypnosis is another means of producing a recall of repressed material and an example of its use is illustrated in the following case report:[5]

The patient, after seeing a movie in which hypnosis had been used, came to the therapist with the request that she wished to overcome a life-long fear of dogs. Since she appeared to be an intelligent, sensitive, and flexible person, the therapist agreed to her request to attempt to eliminate this phobia by the use of hypnosis. After several sessions in which she was trained to become hypnotized and to return to the normal state readily she was given the post-hypnotic instruction that the meaning of her fear of dogs should come to her. A word about post-hypnotic suggestions is in order. A subject in the hypnotic trance can be told that he will do or remember something after he has been brought out of the trance, hence the word post-hypnotic suggestion. As a general rule they seemed to be strongly impelled to do what has been requested of them, even though they are unaware of the fact that such a request has been made.

Shortly after this she reported a dream, a dream which was horrible and disturbing to her. She dreamed of two little girls, one of whom was her own, and this girl played with the other one as if she were a doll, when actually she was dead. Then there was an undertaker who was dressing the dead child and some notion that a dress had been torn and that she sat at a sewing machine trying to mend it. Finally there was only one child, the dead one, but it was her own child.

After telling of this dream she said, "Oddly enough when I woke from that horrible dream, I recalled my little sister's death. . . . It was so long ago I just never think about that . . . about 41 years ago, I was four."

For ten minutes she sat in silence, and then she spoke of the death of her little sister, an event which had occurred when the patient was four. She and her sister had been playing in the backyard when their dog had knocked the girl down and caused a splinter to be driven into her cheek. Infection had set in and the little sister died, the mother blaming the patient for the accident. She recalled also the day of the funeral and being with her dead sister when the dog tore her dress; and again her mother was exasperated with her.

When she came out of the hypnotic trance she said that she vaguely remembered the episode, but she did not recall that her mother had blamed her for her sister's death. Later she wrote to members of her family and was able to obtain sufficient confirmation of her story to the therapist to believe that her recall—stimulated by the hypnotic session—was an accurate one. Most important of all, her strange fear of dogs was eliminated so that she was able to say of them, "All of my life the touch of one gave me a feeling of something horrible. I am still surprised that I feel so differently now."

Daydreaming, or fantasy

Words, as we have said before, are symbols which represent things and events, and they may do so in the absence of the thing or the event itself. Since words can be manipulated freely and need not be tied to reality, we may use them to construct an environment that never was but that is more pleasing than the real world about us. This we do when we daydream or fantasy; we make a new world for ourselves—one in which we gain the goals that are unobtainable and satisfy the motives that are unsatisfiable in the real world.

Thus it is apparent that daydreaming is a device which may lead to satisfaction while the daydreamer is in a frustrating situation. It permits him to close his eyes to the frustrations of the real environment and to gain happiness in a make-believe world. Unlike some of the other mechanisms of adjustment, daydreaming does little or nothing to solve the actual problems that confront the individual; it permits only a temporary escape from them.

If it is employed to an extreme degree, and the user becomes content to gain his glory through dreams and not through overt action, daydreaming becomes a psychological opiate that deprives one of objective achievement. This is probably true in some cases, but it is also probable that daydreaming is a normal and harmless device that all of us use at some time or another.

Daydreaming as it is used to avoid a frustrating situation should not be confused with the kind of fantasy that is based in reality and may lead to constructive action. All of us engage in certain kinds of planning and imagining that in many respects resemble daydreaming but involve attainable goals and formulate directions for reaching them.

The functions of normal adjustment mechanisms

When the behavior mechanisms we have described are analyzed and are clearly seen as devices for fooling ourselves or for avoiding the harsh realities of the everyday world, they appear so obviously deceitful that the reader is inclined to feel that they must be symptoms of abnormality. It is true that these devices do distort reality and permit the individual to see himself as he is not, but their occasional use is not a symptom of an inevitable psychological break-up. They occur very commonly, and there are few of us who have not used them at one time or another. Actually it is not at all unlikely that these mechanisms may protect us from more serious psychological stress and in this sense preserve normality rather than lead to abnormality.

ABNORMAL BEHAVIOR PATTERNS

The behavior disorders that are classified as abnormal are ordinarily divided into three major groups: the *neuroses*, the *psychoses*, and the *personality disorders*.[6] It is very difficult to convey in words the behavioral characteristics—or *symptoms*, as they are called—of the neurotic and the psychotic without implying that neurotics and psychotics always differ more sharply from one another than is sometimes the case. Although a certain way of behaving may be typical of the psychotic, there may be an occasional disturbed individual who behaves in this manner even though he is definitely classified as a neurotic. There is, in other words, no single symptom which, if present, clearly indicates a psychosis and not a neurosis or, conversely, a neurosis and not a psychosis. As we shall see later, the personality disorder presents a somewhat different problem.

Perhaps the major general difference between the neurotic and the psychotic is the degree to which they maintain contact with the world about them. Except for his specific area of difficulty, the neurotic seems to perceive the world very much as the normal person does, whereas the psychotic is more inclined to live in a world of his own, a world that may differ in many respects from that which the majority of us perceive. Thus, many psychotics may experience hallucinations and report that they hear sounds or see visions when there is in the world about them no physical source of energy that can account for their experiences. In addition to suffering distortions of this kind, psychotics may also in their thinking do violence to the more abstract physical laws. They may, for example, become convinced that they can walk through a stone wall, or that they can obtain a well-balanced diet by writing out a menu on a slip of paper and then eating the paper. The psychotic perceives the world and its physical and biological laws radically different from the way in which the normal person of the same educational level would perceive them. We express this by saying that he loses contact with, or distorts, reality. This distortion of reality is not typical of the neurotic. He will have his own particular trouble spot, and he may be quite irrational with respect to it, but he is not likely to exhibit the broad and patently absurd interpretations of the world that the psychotic does.

Because the psychotic distorts reality to a considerable degree and the neurotic to a lesser degree and then usually in only a limited area, the neurotic is far more likely to be gainfully employed and the psychotic far more likely to be institutionalized. The neurotic may not be a pleasant person to live or work with, and he is likely to be a troublemaker, but even so he may carry on his job with an acceptable degree of efficiency. There are, as we have noted, exceptions, and some psychotics can make a better adjustment to the demands of the work-a-day world than some neurotics.

In general the neurotic differs from the psychotic in that he faces the world with an overdriven, overstriving behavior pattern. The neurotic may show an inordinate desire to succeed and an equally exaggerated fear of failure which he often unsuccessfully tries to hide behind a mask of indifference. Combined with these symptoms, and probably caused by them, is a large and persisting measure of anxiety.[7]

Another general difference between the two classes of disorders lies in their amenability to treatment. The institutionalized neurotic is, with proper treatment, somewhat more likely to recover from his difficulty than is the psychotic. Furthermore, once he has been released from the institution, he is less likely to be returned to the institution than is the recovered psychotic. Again, of course, there are exceptions.

Perhaps the meaning of these very broad differences between these two classifications of abnormal behavior will become clearer if we examine some of the specific behaviors exhibited by members of each class.

The neuroses

There are a number of forms of behavior that lead to the classification of neurosis. Conversion reactions of a far greater degree of severity than that described earlier constitute one of these. The patient may be paralyzed, may exhibit apparent loss of functioning of some sense organ or unusual sensitivity to pain stimuli, or may complain of heart disorders. Physical examination, however, fails to show any organic or physical disorder that can account for the difficulties.

Similar to hysterical disorders, but nevertheless differentiated from them, are the *psychophysiological* or *psychosomatic disorders*. These are organically real and measurable disorders in physiological functions that stem from psychological causes. Frequent among these psychophysiological disorders are peptic ulcers, high blood pressure, and asthma.

Some neurotics seem to be in a constant state of exhaustion. Their sleep is fitful and does not refresh them. They complain of feeling run down and are greatly preoccupied with their health; they lack confidence and do not seem able to face the responsibilities imposed upon them by their jobs, their families, or society in general.

The behavior of other neurotics is characterized by an almost constant feeling of anxiety. The patient may be unable to report any reason for the anxiety or depression; it simply seems to come upon him without cause. Actually the clinician or psychiatrist may find the cause with relative ease; the patient simply fails—refuses, one almost feels—to identify it. In other cases the client may have impulses to commit some crime or social *faux pas*. These behaviors are inhibited, but anxiety arises for fear that someday these acts will be carried out and the consequences will be dire.

Fears of other sorts also characterize some neurotics—intense compelling fears that are termed *phobias*. The neurotic does not know why, but he may be irrationally afraid of falling, of dirt, of small places or large places, or of almost anything under the sun. Just as fears may be compelling, so also may thoughts be compelling. An idea occurs and recurs repeatedly and cannot be suppressed, although evidence that the idea is absurd may be plentiful. A neurotic woman may feel that hair is growing on her chin, though her mirror and her associates may offer abundant proof to the contrary.

These are some of the many behavioral patterns of the neurotic. Perhaps by this time the reader has decided that he is neurotic, for he will almost inevitably have discovered some neurotic behavior that he himself has engaged in. He may rest assured that nearly all of his fellow men have felt the same way at some time or other, and that such experiences are normal. The characteristic of the neurotic is the extreme degree to which these behaviors are carried and the fact that they are often an overreaction to the immediate situation or, indeed, are unrelated to it. The normal reader may have felt tired or worried, but usually with good environmental reason, and so this fact is no cause for alarm. In the neurotic, however, these worries and fears, these feelings of inertia and indecision, these compulsive tendencies reach a stage at which they usually incapacitate him in his daily behavior.

The psychoses

The psychoses are divided into two major groupings, one of which is called *organic* and the other *functional*. The groupings are based not so much upon the characteristic behaviors shown by the two classes of patients as upon the apparent cause. In the organic psychoses, there is good evidence that the disorder is associated with some condition that leads to actual destruction of part of the nervous system, especially the brain itself. The functional psychoses are disorders in which no satisfactory evidence of neural degeneration or neural abnormality has been discovered.

The organic psychoses

There are a number of toxic substances—such as opiates, alcohol or industrial poisons—and also various diseases that are capable of destroying parts of the nervous system. Such destruction may be associated with deterioration of behavior sufficiently severe to lead to the classification of psychotic. Sometimes these behavioral disturbances are temporary and sometimes permanent. We have space to consider only a few of them.

The disease of syphilis, if not arrested at an early stage, is very likely to result in destruction of the nervous system—a disease known as *paresis*. As a result abnormal behavior may gradually develop. The patient, who perhaps up to this time has been economically and vocationally successful, may become slipshod in his work. He may make elaborate plans for expanding his business—plans that are far from sound and that involve a reckless expenditure of his savings. He may, in fact, spend money he does not possess, if a trusting creditor can be found. Not infrequently he develops feelings of grandeur and hints that a president, a prime minister, a king, or a business baron is interested in his financial welfare and is ready to back him in some new venture. Sometimes he evidences *paranoid* feelings—that is, feelings that he is being persecuted by some identified or unidentified person. Sometimes, too, he has *hallucinations* and hears voices or sees visions when no stimuli are present to produce them.

For some persons, old age may lead to a psychosis known as *senile dementia*. The term "second childhood," which usually refers to this condition, is often appropriate, for the patient frequently seems to be out of touch with his present environment and talks as though the scenes of his early life were actually present.

The functional psychoses

The functional psychoses are themselves broken down into several different smaller groupings: *affective psychoses, schizophrenia,* and *paranoia.*

The *affective psychoses* are characterized by extremes of mood. A patient may be almost constantly in a state of exaltation or of depression, or he may vary from the extreme of one mood to the extreme of the other. In the *manic,* or exalted, state, the patient is likely to be highly overactive, highly talkative, speaking rapidly, and laughing a great deal. The *depressive* condition is in marked contrast to this. The patient looks sad; he is so absorbed in his misery that he cannot attend to what goes on around him; he moves about slowly with head bowed. The weight of the world seems to be on his shoulders, and he may constantly reproach himself for some fancied misdeed.

In *schizophrenia,* a lack of contact with the normal world is especially marked. In a sense the schizophrenic seems to behave according to a set of rules of his own and seems quite indifferent to the fact that his rules are at variance with those of others about him. Intellectually he may seem to be well aware of things that are happening in the real world, but they seem of little or no significance to him. Thus, if he is told of a tragedy that befell someone who had been near and dear to him, or of a threat to himself, he seems to understand the event or the threat but he may react to the information with complete indifference. Actually there are a number of subclasses of schizophrenia, each showing slightly different behavior characteristics.

Schizophrenia may make itself evident abruptly or gradually. The individual, a hard and conscientious worker, may cease to work well and may shift from job to job, often blaming others for his deficiencies. He may withdraw from communication with others, or his speech may become elaborate and vague. He may show paranoid reactions and have delusions—that he is being persecuted, that he is controlled by radar, or that his stomach is made of concrete. Some schizophrenics will remain in one posture for long periods of time, almost as if they were statues; if their arms or legs are placed in some peculiar position, they remain that way for a long period or until they are placed in a new position: this characteristic is referred to as *catatonia.* Schizophrenic disorders frequently occur at younger age levels, and the psychosis was once

599

called *dementia praecox* which means a psychosis that occurs at an early age. Actually, however, it can develop at any age.

As we have mentioned, paranoid reactions are often associated with some of the types of psychosis described above. When such reactions occur in a patient who has been classified as schizophrenic or paretic, the delusion is often patently absurd. The patient may say that he is being persecuted because he is the son of an emperor or that he is Napoleon himself. Even though his delusion may be a somewhat plausible one, his behavior in other respects is so abnormal that there is little chance that others will believe his story. In *paranoia* itself, the delusions of persecution tend to be convincing and systematic. The paranoiac's behavior in other respects may seem quite normal, and his delusions may be built upon some objective half-truth to which he can point. His stories of being persecuted are, in other words, plausible even though in the final analysis they are untrue. This type of disturbance is extremely rare. Some authorities believe that it should not be considered as a special class of psychosis.

Personality disorders

There are a variety of other abnormal patterns of personality reactions that cannot be readily fitted into the categories of neurosis or psychosis. The general term *personality disorders* has been used to refer to them. The term includes drug addiction, alcoholism, and a broad grouping of disturbances often described by the term *psychopathic* (or more recently *sociopathic*) *personality*.

Sociopathic personalities do not generally feel that they have problems, but society sees them as being deviant. The behavior in these instances departs from the norms of society—as does that of the neurotic and the psychotic—but the individuals exhibit neither the high degree of anxiety characteristic of the neurotic nor the bizarreness of action and thought found in the psychotics. They may show many of the specific characteristics of the psychotic, but they are not out of contact with reality. Often they are antisocial and amoral in their actions; they have little concern for the rights and wrongs of society or for the feelings of those who are close to them.

The sociopaths may be charming people who attract others to them by gaining their sympathies or by an almost elfin and care-free romantic appeal that stems in fact only from a lack of responsibility. Yet they themselves may show no deep concern for these others, for they take much and give little. As husbands or wives they may commit countless infidelities, and they may have married several persons in different localities without bothering to divorce the last before marrying the next. They may set out on a trip with a companion only to leave him at some midway point with no word or reason to explain their departure. In short, they show no consideration, no concern, no affection for others. They are neither inhibited by threat of punishment nor spurred on by normal rewards; they seem to have no loyalties, no allegiance to any of their fellow men.

The sociopaths' sense of indifference to the code of behavior that a society expects of its members almost inevitably leads them to clashes with the law. Wanting money, they will forge a check or pilfer and pawn some small article; drinking to excess, they may precipitate and become the central figure of a brawl that is stopped only by the arrival of the police. Once they are in custody they may become contrite and apparently sincerely perturbed by their own behavior, freely giving plausible promises of reformation which gain them freedom without punishment. But the promises are not fulfilled and in no time at all they become involved in some new incident.

The sociopath does not, then, present a picture of a person who is unhappy with himself, as the neurotic tends to be, or of a person who sees the world in a distorted manner, as does the psychotic. On the contrary, he seems to know what others consider right and wrong, appropriate and inappropriate, but he acts as if these rules did not apply to him. His own immediate personal whims take precedence over anything else, and he is indifferent to the pain and the trouble his actions produce for others.[8]

The significance of classification

The question has often been raised as to the utility of classifying abnormal behavior into categories. Is treatment of the disorder facilitated in some way because the individual is classifiable as one or another of the psychosis types? This question is especially pertinent when we know that classification is not a simple, clear-cut process. A specific patient may be first placed in one category and then, upon reconsideration by the doctor, in another. The doctors may disagree among themselves on a patient's classification. In certain hospitals a high proportion of one class of disorder may be reported with a considerably smaller proportion of another disorder. In another hospital, drawing from a similar total population, the proportions may be reversed. The disparities are so marked, but the parent populations from which these cases come are so similar, that there is good reason to believe that the differences in relative frequencies do not reflect differences in patient behavior so much as differences in the biases of those doing the diagnosis. Finally, clear-cut, typical patterns of behavior illustrating one or another type of disorder are not so common in actual life as textbook descriptions may imply.

The model upon which classification of abnormal behavior is based is undoubtedly that which the physician employs when he diagnoses a physical illness. With physical illnesses, if a specific diagnosis is made, a specific kind of treatment is indicated and some information on the probability of recovery is available. The diagnosis clearly aids the physician in his treatment of the case, for it gives him information on the locus of the infection or disorder or the types of microorganism producing the disease. Unfortunately, this is not the case with psychological disturbances. We do not know with much certainty the circumstances that lead to one pattern of behavior disorder as opposed to another, and we have no specific remedy for the various functional psychoses or neuroses.

It would seem that one purpose served in classifying a disturbed individual is economy of description. Knowing that a person is placed in one category of behavior disorder as opposed to another, and knowing the general behavior characteristics of the categories, we may predict something about his behavior. Perhaps the situation is similar to classifying a person as a Republican or a Democrat. Knowing which party button to pin upon him, we can make better-than-chance predictions as to how he will stand on certain issues and as to the candidates he will vote for. We do not, however, know from his party designation alone how he got that way or what we can do to change his party affiliation. Furthermore, we are not even positive as to how he will behave at the polls on a variety of specific issues and candidates. Nevertheless, we are better off knowing his party affiliation than not knowing it.

There is another very real advantage to classification. If we are to conduct research that will increase our knowledge of the causes of these abnormal reactions, it is necessary that we separate as clearly as possible the various specific behavior patterns instead of dealing with abnormal reactions in general. It is very unlikely that the identical factors are responsible for all of the many forms of behavior that fall within the broad classification of abnormality.

CAUSATION AND THE FUNCTIONAL

DISORDERS

The statements made about the difficulties of diagnosing the particular types of functional psychoses implies that we know relatively little about the origin of these disorders, and indeed this is the case. The three major classes of causal factors which have been suggested are toxics, genetic predispositions, and environmental forces. No single one of these explanations is so convincing to the various workers in the field that it has been uniformly accepted, while at the same time no one of them has been completely discredited. There is space for only a brief consideration of each of these proposed causal factors.

The *chemogenic theory* assumes that some kind of chemical imbalance or a toxic effects the nervous system in such a way as to produce abnormalities in functioning. The theory need not, however, specify how the toxic condition arose in the individual. The proponents of this view can point out that certain drugs—notably mescaline and lysergic acid—produce symptoms in normal subjects which are similar to some of the behaviors of the schizophrenic. But this fact, of course, by no means proves their case. The case would be proven if it were shown that some kind of chemical was present in the abnormal patient which when injected in the normal individual in essentially the same concentration would produce similar behavioral abnormalities. They would also need to show that this chemical had not been produced because the patient was hospitalized, had been fed an institutional diet, or had been inactive for a number of years, as is true of most institutionalized individuals. The proponents of the chemogenic theory have not been able to demonstrate the existence of such a toxic, and so the direct positive evidence for their theory is lacking.[9]

The *genetic theory* is supported primarily by the type of research that shows a greater frequency of these disorders in certain families than in the population at large, and a greater similarity in symptoms among identical twins than among ordinary siblings. Such relationships have been demonstrated, but their interpretation is not simple and unequivocally supportive of the hereditary interpretation.[10] In the first place, the environment of identical twins is undoubtedly more similar than that of ordinary siblings, and certainly there is more similarity in the way children of the same family are treated than are children of different families. Hence these kinds of data do not effectively rule out the possibility that environmental similarities may be responsible for the behavioral similarities. Another criticism of these findings stems from the problem of diagnosis. If one member of a family is diagnosed as showing a certain type of functional disorder the behaviors of other members of the family are likely to be scrutinized with more care than usual, and they might be institutionalized whereas a similarly disturbed individual from another family may continue to make his way, though somewhat ineffectively, in the work-a-day world. Thus one becomes a statistic in the study because he is noticed and the other does not.

There is one fairly serious criticism applicable to both of these theories. Both of them seem to imply that the pattern of the abnormal behavior would be relatively fixed and constant from one patient to another. They also imply that the genes or chemicals responsible for the affective psychoses would be different from those producing schizophrenia. As was pointed out above, however, the behavior patterns are not clear cut and precise, and a single patient may be diagnosed differently by different experts, or even in one way at one time and in another way later, each diagnosis being based upon essentially the same behavioral data.

The *environmental theory* finds its major direct support in the fact that research has demonstrated relationships between personality characteristics and environmental variables. It finds some support, too, in the fact that the onsets of the disorders are often associated with environmental changes such as a transfer from civilian to military life. Since the pattern of environmental treatment is likely to vary from individual to individual, the pattern of symptoms would be expected to vary, and this is the case. Actually the environmental theory would have a greater difficulty in accounting for the similarities among the symptom patterns than their differences. As must be apparent from the materials presented in the previous chapter, we cannot describe with confidence the kinds of environmental treatments that convincingly account for the development of particular disorders.

Despite this particular inadequacy, it seems most likely that environment forces are the major determinants of the development of the functional behavioral disorders. Recent years have seen the accumulation of a vast amount of evidence of the importance of the environment in shaping our motives, our perceptions, our intellectual functions, and our emotional reactions. Since these are the psychological mechanisms of the abnormal, as well as of the normal individual, there is excellent reason to believe in the overwhelming significance of the environment in producing even extreme psychological disorders. But, as with the normal personality reactions, these disorders are most wisely viewed as the results of interactions between environmental and genetic factors.

METHODS OF TREATING

BEHAVIOR DISORDERS

The *therapy,* or treatment, employed in attempting to effect recoveries from these behavior disorders is of two fundamentally different kinds. One method employs *somatic procedures*—that is, it employs drugs or some other agents to produce a physical or physiological change in the individual which, it is hoped, will in turn eliminate the behavior disorder. The other method, *psychotherapy,* approaches the problem by applying what, for want of better words, we may call purely psychological stimuli and psychological principles.

Somatic procedures

It is fairly obvious that, in the case of the organic psychoses, specific kinds of physical treatment may be effective in eliminating the toxic organism responsible for the disorder. Such treatment can arrest the progressive deterioration, although it may not produce complete return to the previously normal state. It is, for example, a common practice to administer penicillin to the paretic in order to destroy the syphilitic spirochete which has been producing neural degeneration. The destroyed nervous tissue will not regenerate, but further destruction by this agent will have been stopped.

Although the functional psychoses and some neuroses offer no such specific target for attack as do the organic, certain kinds of physical treatments are frequently employed. *Shock treatment,* one

605

of the most common of these, is effective in some cases even though the basis for its therapy is not known. Strong electrical currents are passed briefly through the brain, producing violent convulsions in the patient. The procedure may be repeated a number of times over a period of months. Similar convulsive reactions may be produced by the use of certain drugs. A very drastic method of treatment is *psychosurgery*. In this method, surgery is used to destroy the neural tracts connecting certain areas of the brain. The nature of this work is discussed in more detail in Chapter 20.

Recently a rather heavy emphasis has been placed upon the use of drugs—in particular, upon a group of drugs termed the *ataratics* and more popularly called tranquilizers. This class of drugs are not general sedatives or general depressants, but act somewhat more specifically to reduce emotional and anxiety reactions. These drugs are often used, not with the expectation that they will directly alleviate the condition, but with the expectation that they will make the patient more receptive to treatment by psychotherapy by reducing the patient's immediate overwhelming perturbations and calming them sufficiently so that he can participate in the therapeutic relationship.

Psychotherapy

Various methods of psychotherapy differ from one another in certain characteristics, depending upon the specific personality theory that the therapist accepts. Despite these variations, however, there is a technique that seems to be common to all methods— namely, the establishment of a strong interpersonal relationship between therapist and client. The client finds in the therapist someone to whom he can talk freely of the matters that trouble him. He can tell of his misdemeanors, real or fancied, without fear of punishment or reprisal; he can speak of his fears or ambitions free from the threat of scorn; his likes and dislikes can be expressed without fear of ridicule. There is a technical word, *permissive,* that is often used to describe the therapy situation. In a permissive atmosphere, the client feels that he may speak freely of any and all his foibles without apprehension. He learns that although he exposes his psychological Achilles' heel, he does so without danger of having it wounded.

It does not follow, of course, that the therapist will approve of all that the client says; he may point out misinterpretations of facts or suggest alternate ways of acting, but he does so without making the client feel ridiculed or disapproved of, for his attitude is one of objective—almost detached—friendliness and warmth. By means of this permissiveness, the therapist opens and keeps open channels of communication between the client and himself. This general type of situation prevails in almost all therapy.[11] Even in *group therapy*, in which small groups of people describe and discuss their troubles together under the guidance of a therapist, the same spirit of permissiveness predominates.

The permissive environment probably serves to help the client in more ways than one. It makes him able to express motives, anxieties, doubts, and feelings of guilt which he may have been concealing for years. As he describes them, he may realize that they are unsound and without adequate foundation. The fact that through words he may relive some situation in which he feels he has failed or done wrong and find that the therapist does not criticize or punish him may do something to eliminate his response of shame or anxiety. The response occurs but, because it is not reinforced by dire social consequences, it begins to be extinguished. Thus, even if the therapist does or says relatively little in the interview, the client may gain aid.

A major difference between types of psychotherapy lies in the extent to which the therapist reacts to and acts upon the client's words. In *nondirective* therapy a minimum of therapist participation—the nondirective therapist would almost say interference—is the rule. Nondirective therapists believe that the client begins to perceive himself in a new way as a result of his own verbalizings. This changing perception of himself, they feel, cannot be forced upon him by arguments, however logical, from the therapist; it must come from the client himself. Therefore the therapist does not direct the course of the interview; he supplies a permissive and warm but neutral environment in which the client by his own verbalizations may grow to perceive himself in a healthier fashion.

The role of the nondirective therapist in the interview situation is an outgrowth of the theory of personality the group accepts. They view behavior as arising from the manner in which the individual perceives himself in relationship to the world. By perceiving himself as being one kind of person or another, as having one set of values or another, the individual determines his possible courses of action. The function of therapy is to modify the client's self-perception from one leading to unsuccessful action toward goals that are unattainable to ones that are in line with the individual's capacity in his particular environment. These changes in self-perception, they say, can be achieved only by the client himself; they cannot be forced upon him by others. Hence the nondirective technique keeps therapist intrusion at a minimum.

In the Freudian technique of psychoanalysis, the therapist is unobtrusive in the initial but not the later stages of the therapy. The personality theory upon which psychoanalysis is based assumes that all individuals are activated by a limited number of instincts, or unlearned motives. In the normal course of the individual's development, the object that leads to satisfaction of the motives changes. Primarily these changes are forced on the growing individual by the demands of society with its laws, its taboos, and what it calls sins. For some persons—and this leads to maladjustment—this normal shifting of goal objects during the course of maturing does not occur. The satisfying object or action that was appropriate or usual for some earlier stage of development remains unchanged for the adult. This fact places an individual in a state of conflict; society accepts one set of goal objects as appropriate for satisfying his adult needs, but the individual has fixated some goal object which society deems appropriate only at an earlier level. To scorn the demands of society is punishing, but to accept the restriction of society is to fail to satisfy the needs of the individual.

It is apparent that the conflict could be removed if the individual's goal objects could be changed from those that are unacceptable to society to those that are acceptable. It is this that the psychoanalyst attempts to do. But doing so is not an easy, straightforward procedure. The things that trouble the patient are unacceptable to society, and as a consequence he cannot verbalize them freely. They may even be unacceptable to the individual's interpretation of himself, and he may therefore resist admitting them even to himself. According to the psychoanalyst, this means that they have been pushed into the client's unconsciousness.

Before progress can be made, the client must become able to verbalize these materials and to begin to recall many of the events of the past that in some way or another may be related to his present difficulties. Thus once again we find the therapist playing the role of willing and permissive listener before whom the client can speak freely and without fear of condemnation. Later in the analytic situation the therapist begins to interpret and explain and, according to Freudian theory, changes the goal objects to which the motive has become prematurely fixated.

Other types of personality theory emphasize the importance of *learning*—not only of the ways of satisfying motives but also, unlike the Freudians, of motives themselves. These groups tend to interpret the therapy situation as a learning situation, one in which the client may, with the guidance and reinforcement supplied by the therapist, learn new ways of satisfying his current motives and perhaps new sets of values or motives themselves. This is essentially the interpretation of personality that has been made earlier in this text. Such an interpretation of personality is likely to involve more participation by the therapist from the beginning, for the therapist views himself as a teacher, and teaching is an active process. Nevertheless, the same general permissive atmosphere prevails in such therapy situations, for this view demands that responses must be made by the client in order that learning may occur.

Psychotherapy and personality theory

One occasionally hears the statement that a certain theory of personality must be correct because a therapist who adheres to it produces many cures. The preceding discussion of some of the essential characteristics of the therapy situation would suggest that the similarity of method employed by different therapists is so great that one cannot at present use the results of therapy to evaluate a personality theory. This fact has been illustrated by an experimental study.[12] The performances of expert and novice therapists representing the three types of therapy that we have described above were carefully observed by judges, who characterized the actions of each therapist. The judges' descriptions of the behavior of the therapists were then treated statistically, and it was found that the experts of all schools were more like one another than they were like the novices of their same school. If these findings have generality, they imply that, for the present, success or failure in therapy may be more attributed to the therapist himself than to the theory of personality he espouses. This statement must, of course, be limited to the three types of therapy, and it does not imply that any kind of therapy based upon any kind of personality theory would be successful or desirable. It would appear that as long as therapists of different schools of personality behave in so similar a fashion in the therapy situation, we must look to other sources of data to evaluate theories of personality.

BEHAVIOR DURING THERAPY

Freud noted early in his career that, although the symptoms and the immediate problems of his patients differed, most of them tended to exhibit a similar pattern of behavior during the long series of therapy sessions. These patterns of behavior were so marked and so regular that Freud gave names to them.[13] Essentially psychoanalytic theory was developed by Freud in an effort to account for the nature of the sequence of behavior which evolved in this situation where the patient, lying on his couch, was asked to speak out his thoughts to the unseen listener. Actually the theory, and hence the technique, of the therapist will influence the degree to which particular behavior characteristics are manifest, but the trends are sufficiently common to be considered fairly typical of the behavior of patients during therapy.

In the sections following a brief description of these behaviors will be given. They are the behaviors which are likely to occur during long-term therapy, that is, during sessions of approximately an hour in length given several times a week over a minimum period of nearly a year.[14] Typically also it is therapy with a patient who is not psychotic and who continues in his lifework during the course of the therapy.

The therapy setting

In the very beginning the therapist and patient arrive at a firm agreement about the schedules of the therapy sessions and the payment for them. These matters are considered to be for more than mere bookkeeping purposes, and are, rather, a very essential part of the total therapy situation. At a certain stage of therapy the patient will actively seek to avoid meeting with the therapist, and hence the requirement of a firm schedule in the beginning, and one that requires him to pay for a session whether he attends or not. The financial aspect of the situation is considered of importance because it clearly establishes for the patient his rights upon the time and attention of his therapist and because the successive outlay of funds serves as an incentive to improve. Typically the patient begins by describing his current problems and difficulties, but he is encouraged to speak of other things, no matter how trivial; no matter how embarrassing.

Regression

Gradually he begins to speak more freely and to describe events or express opinions and wishes which normally he would not utter. The content of the patient's verbalizing begins to include proportionally more material dealing with the events of his early life and his feelings about these events. In addition his behavior changes generally and he becomes more emotionally dependent upon his therapist and more childlike in his attitudes. Freud called this behavior *regression,* and he interpreted it as a reliving of his early life in the analytic situation. To the psychoanalyst *regression* is an essential stage in the cure. The patient relives his inadequate past in the present, and it is only by doing so that he can be reborn. The very nature of the psychoanalytic method—the couch and the unseen listener—fosters the return of childlike behavior and the term regression has a special meaning in psychoanalytic theory. Nevertheless, something of this kind of behavior is likely to occur to some degree in other kinds of therapy situations.

Transference

The phenomenon of *transference* is inevitably associated psychologically, as well as in time of development, with regression. It refers to the fact that the patient begins to demonstrate toward the therapist those motivational attachments which had characterized his reactions to the dominant figures of his childhood. It is a reaction which is somewhat ambivalent in nature; a strong attachment, even love, for the therapist may have associated with it reactions of antagonism.

Resistance

The phenomenon of transference is usually followed by *resistance.* Actually the patient, from the very beginning, will exhibit a tendency to skirt around certain topics and will show an understandable reluctance to describe events that are embarrassing to him and put him in a bad light. The term *resistance* refers, however, to a much stronger revolt by the patient and one which occurs relatively late in therapy. He finds excuses to skip the scheduled therapy sessions; he may be silent for long periods of time; he may aggress verbally against the therapist and have strong feelings of

611

dislike toward him. Freud felt that the occurrence of the resistance was the sign that the therapy was approaching the core of the difficulty and that the resistance arose because the individual was fighting to maintain the difficulty which had been his style of life for so many years.

The termination of therapy

As the resistance is overcome—and indeed throughout the entire therapy sessions—the individual becomes better able to see himself as he is and as he has been. It is not just that he understands the things which have happened to him; he also accepts himself and he begins to develop new goals and new ways of thinking and looking at things. If this is the case (it is not always so), he is reaching the time when therapy can be terminated and when he will be able to face the daily environment with its challenges and its chores without support from the therapist. Usually it is the patient who recognizes that the time has come and he suggests termination to the therapist, but often it is the consequence of the subtle prodding of the therapist.

This account of the behavior of the client in a therapy session has been, of necessity, brief, and because of its brevity it may cause the process to appear less dynamic and less continuous—and more successful—than is actually the case. Although various stages in the total series of therapy sessions have been listed and identified, they do not in actual fact suddenly emerge; they are rather characteristics which dominate at certain times, but which are present to a greater or lesser degree throughout. And another fact should be reiterated; the degree of magnitude of any of these stages is to a certain degree a function of the therapeutic technique which is used. Finally, of course, many psychotherapeutic courses never come to a successful termination.

THE EVALUATION OF

THERAPEUTIC TECHNIQUES

The task of evaluating the degree of the effectiveness of any of the therapeutic techniques is immensely difficult, and it is very hazardous for even the highly skilled investigator. The first of these hazards—a beneficent effect for the disturbed individuals—is created by the frequent occurrence of what is called *remission*. The term refers to the well-established fact that patients will quite unaccountably revert to their normal behavior. They will do so even if they have been receiving no treatment beyond the most routine custodial care. Their recovery is more than sufficient to return them to their preinstitutional environment, and their behavior there may be identical to that before the episode had occurred. More often than not the condition recurs several years later and their psychotic or neurotic behavior is resumed, but for some the remission remains for many years, even for the duration of their lives. The problem which the fact of remission poses for the investigator is that he cannot be certain that a recovery during the course of therapy might not have occurred in its absence. The therapy, in short, might just happen to coincide in time with the remission. The task of evaluating is further complicated by the fact that any change in treatment may precipitate a remission. Since a reversion to the disturbed state some months or years later is characteristic of remissions, one obviously cannot determine how effective a therapeutic method is by counting the number of "cures" that immediately follow its administration. Not even a moderately adequate notion of its effectiveness can be obtained until several years after its use.

At the present stage in the science of human behavior it is quite impossible to make any quantitative statement about the permanent value of the various kinds of therapy, and it would be somewhat misleading to do so in an elementary text. Certain of the somatic techniques have been of moderate value, but there is no wonder drug or wonder technique, and it is often thought that their major value is to bring the patient into closer contact with his environment and thus make him more accessible to psychotherapy. That psychotherapy can and has produced cures is beyond doubt, but even the most experienced practitioners have on occasion failed to aid their patients in any substantial manner, so this method too is far from perfect. Continued, extensive, and costly research, not merely on techniques of therapy but also on the basic principles of behavior is needed to solve the riddle of how to improve the adjustment of the disturbed individual.

REFERENCES

[1] Tryon, C. M. Evaluations of adolescent personality by adolescents, *Monographs of the Society for Research in Child Development*, 1939, *4*.

[2] Sears, R. R. Experimental studies of projection: I. Attribution of traits *J. Soc. Psychol.*, 1936, *7*, 151-163.

[3] Keys, A., Brozek, J., Henschel, A., Mickelsen, O., and Taylor, H. C. *The Biology of Human Starvation*, Univ. of Minnesota, 1950.

[4] Bagby, E. *The Psychology of Personality*, Holt, Rinehart & Winston, 1928.

[5] Moss, C. S. Brief successful psychotherapy of a chronic phobic reaction, *J. Soc. Psychol.*, 1960, *60*, 266-270.

[6] Committee on Nomenclature and Statistics, American Psychiatric Association *Diagnostic and Statistical Manual of Mental Disorders*, American Psychiatric Association, 1952.

[7] White, R. S. *The Abnormal Personality*, Ronald, 1956.

[8] Cleckley, H. M. *The Mask of Sanity*, Mosby, 1950.

[9] Bradley, P. B., Deniker, P., and Rodovico, T. (ed.) *Neuro-psychopharmacology*, Van Nostrand, 1959.

[10] Kallman, F. J. Psychogenetic studies of twins. In Sigmund Koch (ed.), *Psychology: A Study of a Science*, McGraw-Hill, 1959, Vol. 3.

[11] Fiedler, F. E. Factor analysis of psychoanalytic, nondirective and adlerian therapeutic relationships, *J. Consult. Psychol.*, 1951, *15*, 32-38.

[12] Fiedler, F. E. A comparison of therapeutic relationships in psychoanalytic, nondirective and adlerian therapy, *J. Consult. Psychol.*, 1950, *14*, 436-445.

[13] Menninger, K. *Theory of Psychoanalytic Technique*, Basic, 1958.

[14] Dollard, J., Auld, F., Jr., and White, Alice M., *Steps in Psychotherapy*, Macmillan, 1953.

Chapter Seventeen

THE BIOLOGICAL FOUNDATIONS OF BEHAVIOR

WE HAVE BEEN CONCERNED, IN THE chapters just completed, with the task of finding laws that govern our behavior as integrated organisms. As psychologists we need to go no further, for it is our business to describe the principles that deal with individual human beings. The laws of learning, motivation, and perception serve to illustrate these principles, and together represent unique contributions of psychology to human knowledge.

Psychology, however, is but one of many different sciences of life. A deeper understanding of ourselves as living things, and of the societies we build, can be achieved only through the perspective we obtain by sampling from many disciplines. Science has no bounds except the ones created for convenience, and this is just as true for the science of behavior as it is for any other science. The individual can indeed be studied as a whole, but he nonetheless has parts, and the parts differ in the roles they play in synthesizing patterns of action.

A problem in the biology of vision

The study of a part will very often give us the kind of information that we need in order to progress beyond the mere description of behavior.[1] As an illustration of this fundamental fact, consider our ability to see under near-dark conditions. "Seeing" is something that an individual does, and is something that we measure by observing behaviors in response to light. Psychologists have done many such experiments with people, and have observed that wavelength of the light is crucially important. Lights of certain wavelengths are not seen at all, while others can be readily detected, and it is possible to state the differences in quantitative terms. If we get a measure, then, of the intensities required for seeing lights of different wavelengths, we can plot a curve which shows that human beings are most sensitive to "blue-green" wavelengths.

When we ask ourselves why this is so, we find that we are left without an answer so long as we insist that people should be studied as people. To find it, we must study people's eyes instead, and then we are dealing with an organ, and in doing so we enter upon the province of the physiologist. Here we learn that eyes of many animals contain a pigment sensitive to light; it is called rhodopsin, and normally is deep red in color. However, rhodopsin bleaches rapidly in sunshine, and the bleaching process can be shown to take place more rapidly with certain wavelengths of light than with others. Hence, if we vary wavelength systematically, we find that we can work out a curve that summarizes the pigment's different rates of bleaching.

The latter relationship, although we have obtained it from measurements of bleaching in a bottle, turns out to have about the same maximum as the curve for human seeing. It thus looks as though we have identified a part that controls the responses of the whole, a substance whose properties alone account for differences in low-level seeing. However, although the curves are almost alike, they are separated very slightly; further, the difference is reliable, and thus must be accounted for.

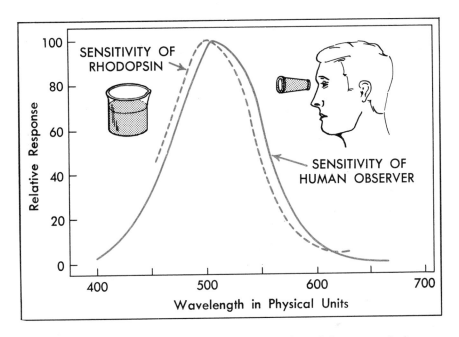

Fig. 17.1 Sensitivity curves for the chemical rhodopsin and for a normal observer. Wave lengths with values around 500 units are the most effective in activating both mechanisms.

To do this, we remember that the stimuli employed for working out the curve for human seeing are defined in terms of what the lights are like as they enter into the eye. Nonetheless, the bleaching of rhodopsin is by light that finally strikes the retina, the sensitive structure at the rear of the eye in which the photochemical is found. But, in passing through the eye itself, the light is partially absorbed, and measurements have shown it to be modified enough to cause the difference between the curves.

The fact that the properties of rhodopsin control our vision under dim illumination enables us to make some further predictions with respect to how we see. Rhodopsin can be studied in a test tube, and its other properties can thus be assessed by purely biochemical procedures. One such result is that rhodopsin is related to the compound vitamin A, and this is interesting because the vitamin is not manufactured in the body. From this, we suspect that a person on a diet which is lacking in this vitamin will gradually become unable to see well at night.

Since the last hypothesis concerns behavior, the methods for testing it are those of the psychologist. Such experiments have been performed, and the prediction is fulfilled. Thus a combination of psychology, physiology, and biochemistry has led us to an understanding of behavior which no one discipline alone could have given us. Cooperative ventures of this kind remind us that the divisions within biology are more those of labor than of outlook. They are representative of many that contribute to a way of looking at behavior, and it is with this approach that we will be concerned in the closing chapters of this book.

THE INTERNAL ENVIRONMENT[2]

The first thing we need to know, in following this plan, is how the human body is built. Since anatomists have worked upon this basic question for many centuries, it obviously has no simple answer. But there are a number of useful principles with which we can begin to sketch the outlines. The first of these is that the body can be thought of as a leaky container that is filled with fluids similar in composition to ordinary sea water. Packed into this portable and private ocean are cells numbering in trillions, and the living elements maintain themselves by exchanges with the fluids. So long as this internal environment contains supplies and is cleared of poisonous wastes, the individual cells of the human body prosper. However, should the fluids become contaminated, or should they undergo depletion, the cells are in peril of destruction. Most of them are permanently anchored into place, and lack characteristics that would be required for them to lead an independent life.

There are of course such things as one-celled organisms—the ameba is a common example—that exist by making exchanges with their fluid surroundings. Their solution to the problem of existence is largely one of locomotion, of movement from contaminated, food-free zones to other more favorable locales. Human cells, in contrast, maintain their positions, and it is the fluids that move. Furthermore, instead of leaving fluid compositions to the vagaries of chance, all the cells cooperate in the manufacture of the fluids. Thus the human body is a complex factory that synthesizes body fluids, that makes the medium by which we have been freed from our watery beginnings. That, as individuals, we live on land and range from the valleys to the mountains is a most direct consequence of these provisions for cellular survival.

The specialization and interdependence of organs

The body is composed of organs, each of which is specially fitted by the cells within it to carry out some step in the production or distribution of the body fluids. Organs are grouped together into systems for the performance of broad functions, and the systems form the body as a whole. Each organ system depends upon the rest for operations other than its own, and this delegation of functions is unusually complete. Thus, for example, the respiratory system gets its own oxygen supply by the self-same means—the blood—by which all the other systems are supplied with this commodity.

The circulation of the blood provides a pathway for the movement of materials, including the removal of waste products to organs specialized for their disposal. These materials enter and exit from the blood as it passes through the capillaries, and these can be regarded as a boundary between the blood and the fluids that surround the cells. Essentially, the blood provides the same service to the other body fluids that these fluids give to the individual cells. Transfers of materials to and from the blood are at the expense of the blood, and the changes that result are then corrected by exchanges between the blood and organs through which the blood stream passes.

Hormonal integration and homeostasis[3]

Many such reactions involve the exchange of materials with storage organs, for we live largely on supplies built up through past exchanges with our outside surroundings. These exchanges are regulated by a group of circulating chemicals, and among the latter are the compounds called the hormones. Hormones are produced by a special set of organs which secrete their products directly into the moving blood stream, and these secretory organs are the endocrine glands. In a sense, the endocrines are meters. They are more sensitive to changes in the blood than are the organs at large, and we can think of the secretion of a hormone as a chemical alarm.

A hormone, when liberated by its gland, is carried to all parts of the body, but its effect is limited to certain organs. These are termed its target organs. A target organ, in the presence of the hormone, operates to counteract the changes in the blood which

619

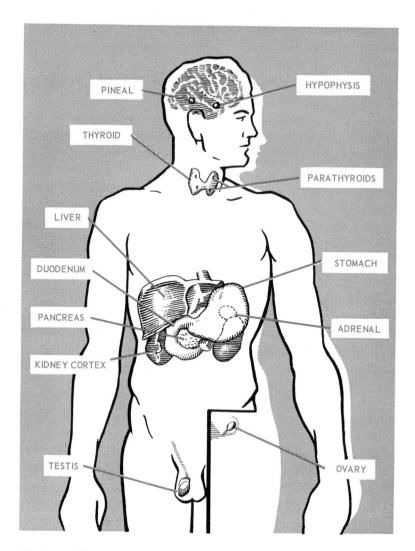

Fig. 17.2 The endocrine system. (After Turner[3])

initially had led to the secretion of the hormone. Thus the hormones integrate, or tie together, the actions of different organ systems. With the restoration of the balance of the blood, hormones are no longer secreted, for it was the change in composition that had served to stimulate the gland in question. Through such mechanisms, the blood is kept remarkably stable, tending always to a state of equilibrium that is known as homeostasis.

The vast majority of changes of this kind do not affect our momentary actions, but they all contribute something to the ultimate control of our behavior. If, for example, we are carrying reserves of compounds that supply energy, transformation of the compounds can go on for a period of time before the depletion of these compounds produces any sort of stimulus. Hence internal regulations free us from demands which, in simple organisms, are always clear and present dangers to their very lives.

BEHAVIOR MECHANISMS

No living system, however complicated, can operate continually without exchanges between it and its outside world. Like all other mechanisms, we human beings run down and run out of gas. Replacement, refueling, disposal of wastes, defense, and reproduction all involve reactions of a person as an individual. These reactions, furthermore, usually take place to changes in the two environments, for stimuli within and stimuli without both determine how we will behave. And, as other functions have been delegated to specific groups of organs, so behavior can be thought of as the product of certain specific organ systems. Behavior mechanisms are, in turn, composed of organs with specialized subfunctions, and this fact is best appreciated through comparisons of organisms.

Evolution of behavior mechanisms[4]

The sponge, to take a first example, is an animal composed of cells whose functions are all very much alike. As an organism, it exhibits only one important pattern of response. This consists of a simple pumping action which moves sea water through the sponge, and in doing so continually renews the fluid medium of the cells. In this action of the cells, some work better than the rest, and these cells are thus considered to be a primitive variety of muscle. Such groups of cells are representative of organs which we broadly term effectors, devices that perform the mechanical and chemical actions that produce behavior patterns.

A second evolutionary specialization is found in animals with cells that differ in their sensitivity. Some of the cells in such organisms respond to small environmental changes, while the rest are activated only by comparatively large ones. The former cells are primitive receptors, and typically develop in the vicinity of specialized effector cells. Receptors, when stimulated, activate effectors, and do so when environmental changes are unable to do so by themselves. Hence, in this arrangement, we have a simple form of

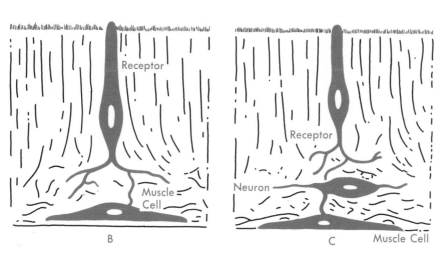

Fig. 17.3 The early stages in the evolution of the behavior mechanism. In *A*, only a specialized muscle cell (an effector) is present. In *B*, a receptor has been added. In *C*, receptor and effector are linked by a neuron. (After G. H. Parker, *The Elementary Nervous System*)

S-R behavior mechanism, and the cells that form it are exclusively concerned with fashioning appropriate responses.

There are limitations to the patterns of behavior produced by simple S-R mechanisms. In the main, responses are sharply localized, for processes induced in a receptor can affect only the neighboring effectors. Such coordination as there is between responses arises rather indirectly, as by the action of a common stimulus upon a group of S-R mechanisms. The form of the body also contributes to the process of coordination, for some combinations are mechanically impossible in any given kind of organism. Individuality, as thus endowed, is very primitive indeed; the animals in question, behaviorally speaking, are barely more than aggregates of pieces.

Human beings are not like this, and the reason is that we are so constructed that each of our effectors is under the control of every one of our receptors. This in turn is possible because, in evolution, nervous systems have arisen. These provide the linkages by which the separate actions of huge groups of cells are put together. Some nervous systems are relatively simple, but man's is

enormously complex; its complexity compares, in fact, with the
entire telephonic system of North America. To our nervous systems we owe our unity as behaving individuals, and their operations are the key to our outstanding psychological abilities. Responses can be flexible only if responses have multiple determinants, and it is exactly this that multiple connections between receptors and effectors give us. Behavior is plastic, and this plasticity
arises in neural processes: processes that sort, sum, select, and shape
events that lead to visible reactions.

Receptors, effectors, and the nervous system, the mechanisms of behavior, are therefore the most interesting components of
the body to the student of behavior. We will look upon them as

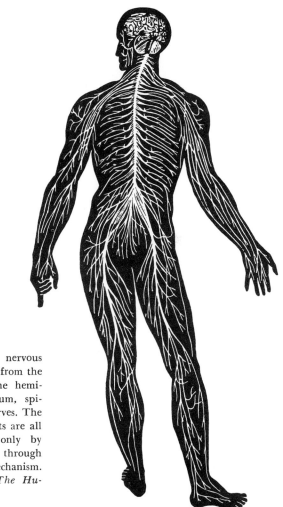

Fig. 17.4 The nervous
system as viewed from the
rear, showing the hemi-
spheres, cerebellum, spi-
nal cord, and nerves. The
various body parts are all
connected, but only by
routes that pass through
the central mechanism.
(From Martin, *The Hu-
man Body*)

something separable from other organs in the organism, just as we could similarly separate the systems concerned with other organismic functions. In this discussion, the remainder of the body is considered from the same standpoint as is the world that is external to the organism as a whole. It is a part of the environment and hence a source of stimulation, a source that together with external events constitute behavior's beginnings.

CHARACTERISTICS OF SENSE ORGANS[5]

Since we think of stimuli as the instigators of all patterns of behavior, first consideration must be given to devices specialized for their reception. These devices more or less define the class of changes that will serve as stimuli, for organisms actually do not respond to more than a small fraction of environmental fluctuations. A striking example of this fundamental fact is given by our sensitivities to the different kinds of electromagnetic radiation. The lights we see are only one small portion of the spectrum,

Fig. 17.5 The electromagnetic radiation spectrum, showing the comparatively narrow bands perceptible as heat or light. Note that the scale is logarithmic.

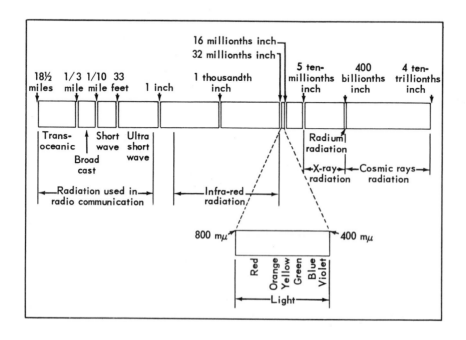

as are the waves detectable as heat; by far the largest fraction is without direct effect upon the human senses. Cosmic, radio, and X-radiations do undoubtedly exist, but to detect them we must use an instrument whose output does affect receptors. Much of the world is therefore a construction that we know by inference alone, and what we sense directly is but one small segment of events within the cosmos.

What we do detect, we detect extremely well so far as sensitivity goes. With our eyes we see a burning match at fifteen miles, given appropriate conditions, and a sound that we can hear can be an air movement that is small enough to fit into the bounds of hydrogen atoms. Our fingertips, with training, can detect a film of oil a mere molecule in thickness, and our tongues and noses, as chemical detectors, are as good as anything we make. Clearly, then, receptors are delicate devices and, comparatively speaking, the other body cells have no sensitivity whatever. Receptors exhibit a hairspring quality that is lacking in most cells, and this sharply limits the instigative channels of behavioral control.

Properties of conductive apparatus

Receptors typically are found in sense organs, of which by far the most familiar are the ones that are specialized for the detection of external environmental stimuli. Receptors occupy the best-protected portions of these organs, and usually are at some distance from the surface of the body. Stimuli, accordingly, do not in general act directly upon receptor cells. Rather, they affect conductive mechanisms which, in turn, stimulate receptors. These mechanisms frequently transform the patterns they conduct to the receptors, and a good example is the focusing of light as it travels inside the eye. Some conductive mechanisms also have provisions for attenuating overloads and will work efficiently only when a stimulus is mild.

The structure of the conductive apparatus in the ear serves to illustrate these general features. Receptor cells for hearing are buried in the wall of the skull, and hence are at a distance from the air that carries the changing pressure patterns of a sound wave. The resulting gap is bridged by a system starting with the outer ear, a funnel-like device that transmits sound waves to a membrane stretched across its tip. Beyond the membrane is the middle ear, and within this cavity are three tiny bones. Movements

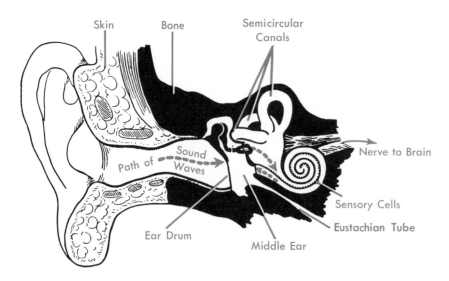

Fig. 17.6   The structure of the ear. (After H. Davis, ed., *Hearing and Deafness*)

induced by sound waves as they strike the membrane set the bones into vibration, and these in turn initiate pressure waves within a chamber that contains receptor cells. Two tiny muscles are attached to the system, and, when sounds become intense, one of the muscles contracts and tightens up the drum membrane of the outer ear. The other, which is joined to the innermost member of the chain of middle ear bones, contracts and pulls this bone away from the inner chamber of the ear. Finally, when sounds reach intensities so great that the load cannot be counteracted, the bones of the middle ear are thrown out of joint and become extremely poor transmitters.

Analogous arrangements are found within most major sense organs. The visual receptors are deep within the eye and served by a system of lenses, and the pupil and the eyelid shut out light that has grown to be too bright. Receptors of the skin are in its lower layer, protected by the tough epidermis, and its response to long-continued stimulation is formation of a callus. Receptors for taste and smell are on the body surface, but in well-protected nooks: those for smell are deep within our nostrils, and those for taste occur in pits that surround the bumps which we term the taste buds of the tongue. These provisions for protection are important, for by virtue of them the receptors themselves need not be ruggedly constructed.

Detection of internal changes

Generally, arrangements for internal reception are simpler than those for the external, but the body nonetheless is well equipped with such receptors. One important group is concerned with the detection of the characteristics of the blood, and these are most appropriately found within enlargements of sinuses of large arteries. One such group of cells is known to be responsive to the carbon dioxide content of the blood, and is important in the regulation of breathing. Another group detects and helps to regulate the pressure of arterial blood, which requires the action of muscles over which the nervous system has control. There are certain places in the neck where such receptors can be fired by pressure from a finger; this, by making blood pressure drop very quickly, can readily induce unconsciousness.

For some kinds of stimuli, behavior mechanisms have no specialized receptors. Rather, the stimuli operate directly upon the cells within the nervous system. Thus, for example, the majority of organs are pain-sensitive, and yet the nerves responsible for such effects are not connected to receptors. Bare nerve endings with a pain-sensing function can also be found within the skin, and actually the so-called receptors for smell belong to the nervous system proper. Finally, at least some components of the brain demonstrate receptor properties, for these cells are selectively responsive to certain blood-borne chemicals. We will see that each of these provisions for control has its implications for behavior, and that different aspects of behavior are related to these different methods of reception.

THE NERVOUS SYSTEM[6]

Receptors are connected to the brain and spinal cord by way of the peripheral nerves. The central nervous system is itself enclosed within the skull and spinal column, and its bony armor is further supplemented by a series of protective membranes. Two enormous masses, the cerebral hemispheres, dominate the head end of the system. These are each connected to the brain stem, and the latter to the spinal cord. The cerebellum, another brain

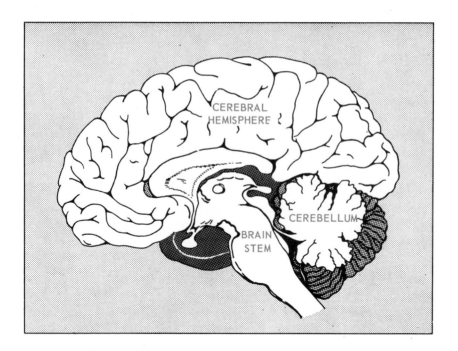

Fig. 17.7 The brain as it would look if split lengthwise, showing the three major divisions. This drawing shows the right side of the brain.

Fig. 17.8 The cerebral hemispheres as they would appear if the brain were cut crosswise. Note especially the cortex, or layer of gray matter, covering each hemisphere and the masses buried in the white matter.

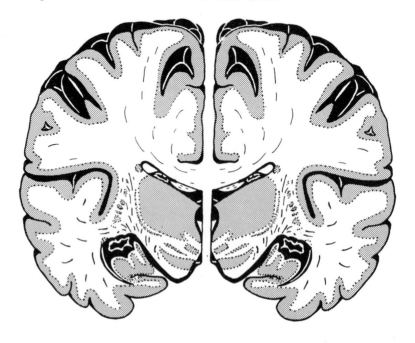

component, is connected to the brain stem and is tucked beneath the two great hemispheres. Almost universally, the nerves of the body connect with the spinal cord and brain stem, and the hemispheres and the cerebellum thus are isolated from direct peripheral control.

Two broadly different kinds of tissue can be found in different portions of the nervous system. One type of tissue is pinkish gray in color and the other creamy white. The gray matter forms a cortex or covering upon the hemispheres and cerebellum, and is also found as buried masses within both the brain and spinal cord. The white matter makes up nerves, the coverings of spinal cord and brain stem, and also the bulk of the interiors of the hemispheres and cerebellum.

The neuron and signal transmission

Microscopic study of the nervous system has shown that it consists of many individual cells or neurons. These cells generally comprise a cell body and a group of fiber processes. The neurons themselves are gray in color, but their longer fibers are often covered with a sheath of fatty material known as myelin. Gray matter, then, consists principally of cell bodies and the shorter, unsheathed fibers, and the white matter consists of fiber bundles that travel for long distances.

We are led by this result to ask what kinds of signals the neural fiber bundles carry. The experimental answer to this question has been based upon the fact that all cells of the body can be shown to behave as batteries. Between the outside and the inside of their membranes, we can measure differences in voltage and sensitive electrical equipment thus reveals what happens when a nerve is stimulated.

Such experiments have shown that a neuron is something like a firecracker fuse. The signal it transmits is indicated by a sharp change in voltage that travels by utilizing energy that is stored within the fiber. Hence neural signals never weaken or die, regardless of the distance that they travel, and the signals always are the same regardless of the strength of the stimulus that led the neuron to conduct in the first place. This is termed the principle of all-or-none, and is reminiscent of the fact that a fuse burns with a characteristic brightness no matter how many matches might be used to ignite it. Finally, and also in keeping with the

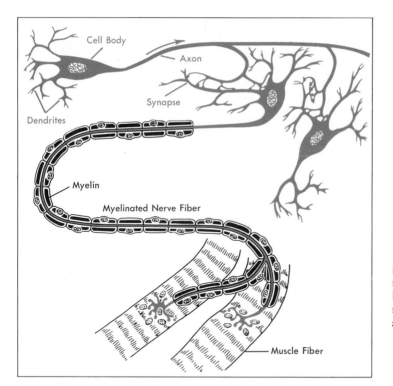

Fig. 17.9 Some typical neurons, the connections between them, and a connection between a neuron and an effector.

Fig. 17.10 The similarities between signal conduction in a neuron and the functioning of a firecracker fuse.

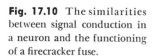

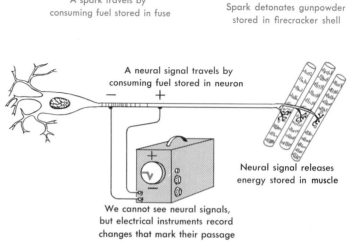

A spark travels by consuming fuel stored in fuse

Spark detonates gunpowder stored in firecracker shell

A neural signal travels by consuming fuel stored in neuron

Neural signal releases energy stored in muscle

We cannot see neural signals, but electrical instruments record changes that mark their passage picture, neural signals are discrete events; time elapses between them while the neuron is readied to fire once again.

Most nerves are made up of fibers of two kinds of neurons. These groups differ mainly in that they conduct their signals in opposite directions. Those that connect receptors to the central nervous system are the sensory neurons, and those connecting the central mechanism to effectors are the motor neurons. The signals carried by the two types of neurons, sensory and motor, seem so far as present methods tell us to be basically the same. This is our first indication of the fact that there are many simplifying rules that govern the operations of the nervous system.

Synapses and central integration

Neural signals entering the central nervous system eventually arrive at gray matter. In doing so, they set up stimuli for neurons that begin within the gray matter. So far as we can tell, such stimulation is effective only if several neurons are involved.

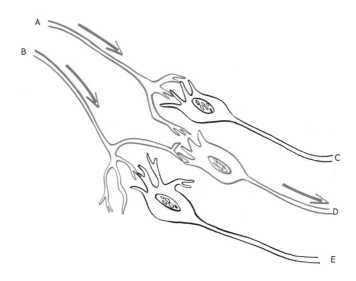

Fig. 17.11 An illustration of the "voting" principle in integrative processes. Note that neuron *D* is synaptically connected with both neurons *A* and *B*, but that *C* and *E* are connected with only one neuron each—*A* or *B* respectively. If we assume that synaptic excitation takes at least two incoming signals or "votes," then *D*, but not *C* or *E*, will conduct when signals arrive over neurons *A* and *B*. For either *C* or *E* to be excited, a signal in *A* or *B* would have to be combined with signals in some neuron not shown.

631

In other words, a single signal into gray matter does not, itself, produce a stimulus. It merely has a "vote" as to whether the neurons with which it is connected will be fired. Polling of this kind in the central nervous system seems to have a chemical basis. Arriving neural signals release tiny drops of chemicals, and these combine to act as stimuli for neurons in the neighborhood. Just what neurons will be activated thus depends upon the signal pattern, and from this we see that the number of different kinds of action is potentially enormous.

Central interruptions, or synapses, are important features of the nervous system. They impose directionality upon conduction of all neural signals and, without them, there could be but little flexibility in stimulus-response relations. Synapses can best be looked upon as switches that are sensitive to neural signals from many different places. Thus the gray matter of the central nervous system is primarily concerned with signal integration and actually comparatively little integration can be said to go on elsewhere.

CHARACTERISTICS OF EFFECTORS[7]

The muscles form the largest group of organs of response, and are most diverse in form and function. We recognize at least three major groups of muscles, and each has a characteristic cellular arrangement which reflects the work it does. The muscles that we feel just beneath our skin are made up of long, thin fibers. Since these fibers have prominent striations, the organs formed are called the striate muscles. Each of the fibers is a single cell and hence is independent of the others, and this means that the striate muscles lend themselves to changing modes or patterns of action.

The significance of this is most apparent if we contrast the striate muscle with the muscle of the heart. Heart muscle proves to be constructed of cells which form an interlocking network, and the heart, accordingly, contracts as a unit in one efficient pumping pattern.

The third kind of muscle is termed smooth because its cells lack the cross-striations of the heart and striate muscles. Smooth muscle fills the walls of many blood vessels, and we find it also in such hollow organs as the stomach, the intestines, and

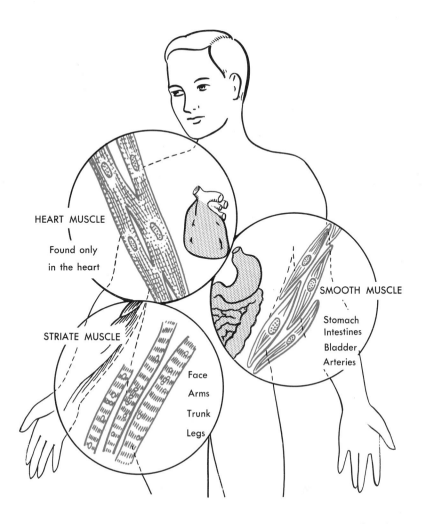

Fig. 17.12 The three major types of muscle and some organs in which they are found. Note that each striated muscle fiber is separate, in contrast with heart muscle. Also note the absence of cross-striations in smooth-muscle fibers.

HEART MUSCLE

Found only
in the heart

STRIATE MUSCLE

Face

Arms

Trunk

Legs

SMOOTH MUSCLE

Stomach
Intestines
Bladder
Arteries

the bladder. Smooth muscle is lethargic, but it is resistant to fatigue, and hence is well-suited for taking the continuous pounding of the blood with every pulse. Smooth muscle also has a certain degree of plastic length-adaptation and is well suited by this property to the changing loads of materials in the hollow organs.

Some smooth muscles are apparently constructed in the manner of the heart, that is, all the cells are linked together by protoplasmic bridges. This variety, the visceral, gets its name from its occurrence in big, soft organs of the body cavities. Other smooth muscles are like the striate, seemingly built of separate cells; this type is found in the blood vessels and is known as vascular muscle.

Properties of glandular effectors

The muscular effectors may be contrasted with the glandular effectors. The latter consist of cells whose products are secretions, rather than varied kinds of movements, and these effectors deliver their secretions to some external body surface. Because of the latter fact, we call them exocrine in order to distinguish them from the internally secreting endocrine glands. Exocrine products reach the body surface by way of small tubes or ducts, and the tear duct of the lower eyelid serves as a familiar example. In structure, the glands producing exocrine secretions range from single isolated cells to groups of cells that best can be conceived of as deeply folded body surfaces.

The ducts of many exocrines terminate in places that are hidden from our view, and prime examples are the ducts that deliver digestive juices to the stomach and intestines. Nonetheless, in keeping with the definition, such secretions are external, for however deep within us swallowed food may seem, it is still outside us until it is absorbed. The exocrines, accordingly, always modify the world external to the organism, and generally do it in ways that help promote internal and external exchanges.

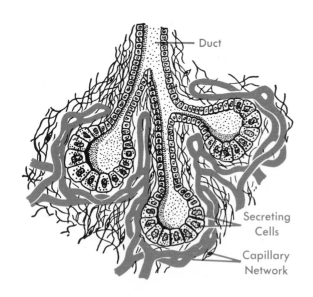

Duct

Secreting
Cells

Capillary
Network

Fig. 17.13 Structure of a typical exocrine gland, showing the secreting cells and their relation to the duct. (After T. Hough, W. T. Sedgwick, and J. A. Waddell, *The Human Mechanism*)

Most behavior patterns are syntheses involving all the varied types of effectors. Consider, for example, our ways of keeping cool in the middle of a summer's day. One general method is to cut down heat uptake, which we might accomplish by putting on a hat or walking to a nearby shady spot. This is done, of course, with skeletal muscular effectors. A second general method is to increase rate of heat loss, and in this adjustment the cardiac, vascular, and exocrine effectors are involved. The heart beats faster, and the blood is shunted to the surface of the body; sweat glands secrete, and evaporating sweat makes the skin a more effective radiator of heat. These alternatives are interchangeable despite the basic differences between them, and hence our different types of effectors endow us with important flexibilities.

A MODEL MECHANISM OF BEHAVIOR[8]

To illustrate and summarize the ways in which receptors, effectors, and the nervous system work together in fashioning patterns of behavior, let us next consider a mechanism for control of a particular performance. Breathing is an ideal beginning, for most of the principles of psychophysiology are represented in its synthesis. Breathing, as we all know, accomplishes a transfer of oxygen and carbon dioxide; we think of it, accordingly, as one of the simplest of conceivable behaviors. However, in supplying the power of our voices, breathing is also a component of extremely complicated human skills. We can think of breathing, and the methods we will use, as models of the problems and procedures that we will encounter in the analysis of many different patterns of behavior.

It is most convenient to begin with the effectors that produce the breathing responses. In its simplest form, breathing is a sequence of inspirations and expirations, and these responses involve the expansion and contraction of the lung cavities. During inspiration, the rib case is raised and the diaphragm is flattened, and this action is accomplished by appropriately placed striate muscles. In expiration, the rib case falls and the diaphragm relaxes. During quiet breathing, expiration is a largely passive process; only during vigorous breathing are the muscles of expiration called into play. Our first important problem is thus to find the

635

reasons for contractions during inspiration, contractions which in working with the framework of the chest yield the inspiratory movements.

The steps in definition of a center

If we cut the nerves leading to these muscles, all respiratory movements cease. Further, the muscles that produce these movements tend to lose their normal firmness. From this we conclude that the muscles operate only during neural bombardment, and that the breathing pattern is superimposed upon a resting action of the muscles.

Proceeding inward, then, our next important question is one of where the neural signals come from. One way of finding out is to see how much of the central nervous system can be destroyed before breathing ceases. Such experiments have shown that huge amounts of neural tissue can be sacrificed, and that all that one must spare for breathing to occur is the lower brain stem and its pathways to the muscles. This result does not, of course, imply that other structures have no role in breathing regulation, but it does define an indispensable region for any kind of breathing that we do. The lower brain stem is thus a bottleneck, and such bottlenecks are centers.

Control of the respiratory center

Having thus defined a respiratory center, we next consider its control, and the basic problem is one of understanding rhythmicity in breathing. We know that inspiratory signals to the muscles are emitted by the center, but we have yet to learn what triggers off the center itself. There are two important possibilities, and the first of these is that the center's operations are paced by the respiratory movements. That is, we might suppose that lung receptors relay signals to the center, and that these signals are the pacemakers of the inspiration-expiration cycle. To test this hypothesis, we isolate the center from all other central nervous structures, and then cut all the nerves that relay information inward from the lungs and chest. But when this is done breathing still goes on, and the proper answer is the second alternative: the rhythmicity of breathing is intrinsic to the respiratory center.

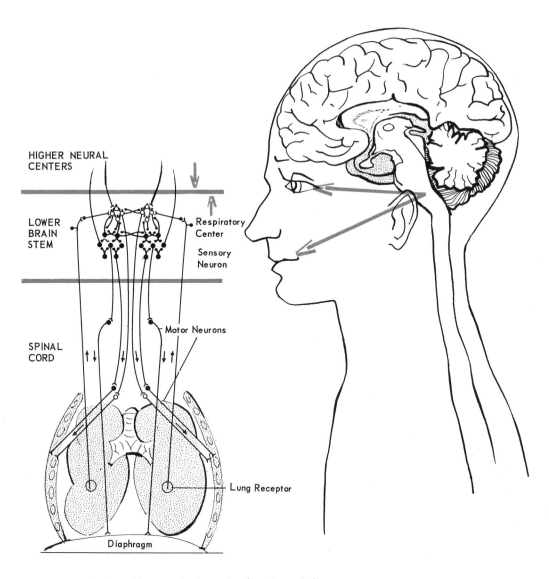

Fig. 17.14 The breathing mechanism, showing the relations among receptors, effectors, and neurons of the sensory, motor, and internuncial types. (After Pitts, *Physiol. Rev. 26,* 1946)

External and internal environmental changes modify the pattern of intrinsic rhythmicity, and the stimuli that now are best understood are those within the organism. First, we know that neurons in the lower brain stem are sensitive to carbon dioxide, and that its effect when present in the blood is to increase lung ventilation. The neurally isolated center thus responds, and responds appropriately, regardless of whether its peripheral receptors are functioning or not. We have here an instance of central

637

neural cells themselves behaving as receptors; this, of course, can happen only when the stimuli in question are present in blood.

Conventional receptors do play a role, and here other compounds are effective; as we might suspect, the receptors occupy the walls of arteries. To show that this is so, we isolate a piece of blood vessel holding such receptors, and run solutions through it whose properties are known and variable. If these solutions are high in CO_2 and the nerves from the blood vessel to the center are intact, we observe an increase in breathing similar to that obtained by central stimulation. These receptors are also sensitive to changes in blood oxygen, and make their measurements of changes of this kind just beyond the left side of the heart.

Other determinants of respiratory control

For breathing to be modified in other ways than the ones discussed already, connections between the lower brain stem and the other centers of the brain must be intact. As larger and larger segments of the brain are included, other receptors become contributors to the control of breathing patterns. In some such preparations, for example, the cutting of a nerve which normally sends signals to receptors from the lung results in a pattern in which the breath is drawn and held for a period of time. Such a breathing action is, of course, a part of voice communication, and we gain the notion that such performances suppress the basic alternation pattern by in some way blocking the signals from the lung receptors.

In speaking, singing, whistling, and the like, drawing in a breath is not the end; we breathe out as well, and form different sounds as we do so. These coordinations are of the highest order, requiring an interplay between the lips, the larynx, and the tongue in addition to the breath. In most of them, external stimuli are crucial factors in control, and their central mechanisms are of a complexity appropriate to their elevated status. Hence it is no accident that they involve massive portions of the brain, for in such actions breathing is but one of many critical components.

PROSPECTUS

A basic assumption of the general biological approach to problems of behavior is that such analyses as these can be applied to any behavior that we please. Of any action pattern by an individual, we can ask the same sort of questions: how is it accomplished, how is it controlled, and how has it been integrated? The methods we have cited are but several of many that are used to solve such problems, and others will be outlined in succeeding chapters as we need them in the study of further action patterns or behavior. All such methods are nonetheless alike in their derivation from the view that one can study people both as people and as complicated systems in which we can find, identify, and measure the interacting mechanisms. This, as we have seen, is not a task for the psychologist alone; it is rather the business of all varieties of science.

REFERENCES

[1] Le Grand, Y. *Light, Colour and Vision,* Wiley, 1957, Chapter 17.

[2] Bernard, C. In Hall, T. S. *A Source Book in Animal Biology,* Mc-Graw-Hill, 1951, pp. 241-248.

[3] Turner, C. D. *General Endocrinology,* Saunders, 1960, Chapter 1.

[4] Ranson, S. W., and Clark, S. L. *The Anatomy of the Nervous System,* Saunders, 1959, Chapter 1.

[5] Geldard, F. *The Human Senses,* Wiley, 1953.

[6] Gardner, E. *Fundamentals of Neurology,* Saunders, 1958, Chapter 2.

[7] Gardner, E. *Fundamentals of Neurology,* Saunders, 1958, Chapter 9.

[8] Hoff, H. E., and Breckenridge, C. G. In Fulton, J. F., *Textbook of Physiology,* Saunders, 1955, Chapter 42.

Chapter Eighteen

MECHANISMS
OF
RECEPTION
AND
RESPONSE

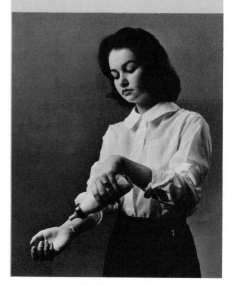

SINCE THE NEURAL INTEGRATIVE MECH-
anisms share the body's receptors and effectors, a closer look at
what is going on within our bodies necessarily begins with a further
study of the properties of these important organs. First we need to
know how the world is represented in the form of neural signals,
and then we must consider how a neural signal pattern ultimately
leads to a behavior. In this chapter, then, we will be concerned with
problems of reception and response, and we will consider first the
questions posed by the facts of human sensing.

Every discriminable feature of events, be these internal or
external, has some implication for our thinking with regard to the
workings of receptive mechanisms. But the simplest questions, the

ones best understood, are the ones that ask how receptors register and relay variations in the quality, intensity, and place of stimulation. To illustrate, consider that we have a rose, an object of many qualities: It may be a pink or perhaps a yellow rose; what are "pink" and "yellow" neural signals? The rose has an odor, a comparatively strong one; what then is a "strong" neural signal? We see and feel it, finally, as being in a given place in space; how then do receptors and the sensory nerves signal "where" to central mechanisms?

QUALITATIVE SENSORY ENCODING[1]

The simplest qualitative question is the basis of the distinctions we can draw between such uniquely different sensory events as sounds, lights, touches, and tastes. These are known as modal differences, and we can relate them to the fact that each of the major sense organs has a private set of sensory nerves connecting it with central mechanisms. But the problems posed by the differences within each broad form of sensing are complex. We can find no separate nerves for "blue" or "red," or for "sweet," or "bitter," or "sour." Somehow, then, a single nerve manages to keep several kinds of information sorted, and the mechanisms of the sorting thus become our first important analytic problem.

Specialization of receptors

The necessary sorting presumably begins before the fibers in a nerve are active, and the usual view is that this is done by specialized receptors. But the question, then, is how many kinds are required to do the sorting task, for it seems unlikely that we have special organs for every itch and tickle and ache. If there were, most of our receptors would be idle the greater part of the time, and this could hardly be considered good design in a body otherwise well built.

In consequence, we think that any given sense organ has receptors that are differentiated into just a few specific types. These types are then presumed to work either singly or in combination with each other to encode or represent all qualitative facets of a given class of stimuli. Of the lines of evidence supporting such a theory, several have been most influential, and the first of these are demonstrations that some qualities do in fact arise from combinations.

The evidence from syntheses of sensing

As an illustration of this first kind of data, let us take the skin as an example. A common presumption is that there are no more than four types of cutaneous receptors, and that these are specialized respectively for warm, cold, pain, and touch or light pressure. Obviously such a group of sensing categories leaves us with a great many gaps, and hence we have to ask if these can be filled in by having receptors work together.

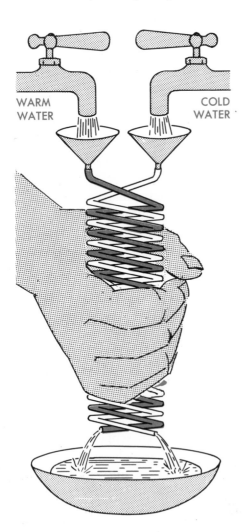

WARM
WATER

COLD
WATER

Fig. 18.1 An experiment designed to demonstrate the synthesis of a sensation of heat from warm and cold stimuli. Warm and cold water is passed through the interlaced tubes. When the subject touches warm and cold tubes at the same time, he experiences the sensation of heat, even though the warm water by itself does not produce the effect. (After Miner, "Basic odor research correlation," *Ann. N.Y. Acad. Sci.,* 1954, *164*)

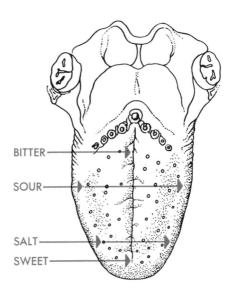

Fig. 18.2 The regions of the tongue that are most sensitive to different taste solutions. (Courtesy Scientific American)

BITTER

SOUR

SALT

SWEET

A simple instance of such a combination underlies perception of "hot," and to show that this is so we first construct a pair of fine, intertwining water pipes. Then, individually, we raise or lower their temperatures by passing water through them, and note the consequences when we touch our hands to the pipes. When their temperatures are such that the pipes, by themselves, are either warm or cool, touching both pipes at the same time resembles touching a red hot stove. This illusion is complete. It has a burning, sticking quality, and occurs because we have arranged a situation in which the effects of hot objects on receptors specialized for cold have been replaced with the normal stimuli for such receptors.

The evidence from distribution of sensitivity

The second line of evidence comes from studies of the distributions of sensitivity in sense organs. Here the tongue, and taste, provide a good example of the facts and arguments. With our tongues, we recognize taste differences that we describe as salty, sour, bitter or sweet. However, different areas upon the tongue are not alike in their capacities for such distinctions. Thus a sweet substance is more readily detected if placed upon the tip of the tongue than if it is placed upon the sides or back of the tongue. The latter areas, respectively, are most sensitive to salty or to sour and bitter substances. Now, if there were just one type of taste receptor, we would not expect these differences; that they do exist suggests not only that the taste receptors are of several different kinds, but also

643

that each type has a different concentration in the varied regions of the sense organ.

Similar experiments have also been conducted with the skin. First, a small region is marked off with a grid that serves as a spatial reference, and then stimulators with extremely fine points are applied within this region. Such experiments have shown, first of all, that the sensitivity of skin varies markedly from one place to another. More than this, however, sensitivities to different kinds of stimuli are different, for a point that proves to be quite sensitive to touch may not be responsive to cooling. Like the distribution of

Fig. 18.3 Procedures in the study of skin sensitivity. The experimenter has marked the region that is to be explored and is searching it with a fine, stiff bristle. (Courtesy LIFE *Magazine*, © TIME, Inc.)

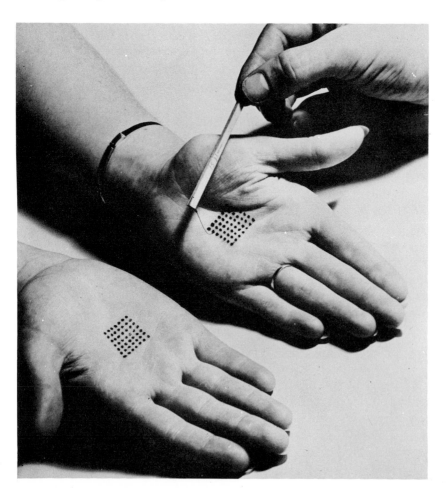

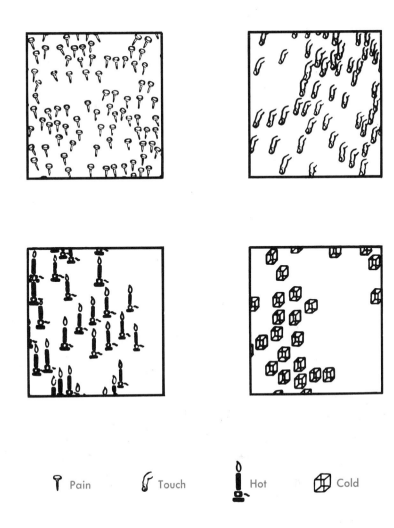

| ᵀ Pain | ᶠ Touch | 🕯 Hot | ⬚ Cold |

Fig. 18.4 Spatial distribution of sensitive spots within a small skin area. Notice that both touch and pain may be encountered in a region insensitive to cold, and that cold spots may be present in regions that are relatively insensitive to hot stimuli. (From Gerard, *The Body Functions*)

taste upon the tongue, these results suggest that there are different populations of receptors in the skin.

The evidence from structural research

All such experiments as those just discussed are inferential in their approach. If indeed we do have specialized receptors, why do we not simply cut up the skin and look for evidence of differentiation in the structure of receptors? This is the third line of evidence, but it is at present very weak: when we have looked for such

645

variations, we have found too many or too few. This is not to say that the approach has not been tried. A great many workers have actually studied regions of their own skin surface, and then have sliced it off to see if they could draw conclusions as to what goes with what. Seemingly, our methods are not yet good enough to tell us what we need to know, and all that we can do at present is to make the grossest kinds of differentiations.

ANALYSIS OF COLOR VISION[2]

By far the most developed of attempts to understand the bases of qualitative sensing are those that have been directed toward the problems posed for us by human color vision. This special case can fruitfully be taken as a representative example of approaches to the problem of sensory quality in all sense organs. First, we have the question as to what receptors are involved in human color vision, and then we have the problem as to how many different types of hue receptors there are.

We take, as a beginning, the important fact that colors are visible only so long as there is good illumination. The hues of objects fade quite markedly at dusk, and along with fading there are changes in the relative brightnesses of hues. Objects that are red under high illumination then become extremely dull, and those that are blue become comparatively bright. This change, known as the Purkinje shift, is due to a transfer of the operations of the eye from a daylight mechanism to a twilight system that is incapable of making hue discriminations. We would thus expect to find that retinas contain at least two groups of receptors, and the question then is whether we can find them by opening and studying the eye.

If we next remove a section of the retina for microscopic study of its structure, we note that the receptors can in fact be separated into two general types or classes. Some of them are short and squat, and are known as cones; others, long and slim, are termed the rods. Of these groups, according to a viewpoint that is called the duplex theory, the second has to do with twilight vision and the first with vision in the daylight.

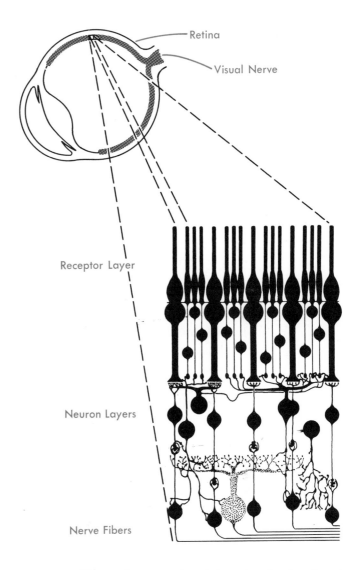

Fig. 18.5 Microscopic cross section of the retina, showing the rods and cones. (After Walls, *The Vertebrate Eye*)

The evidence for cone differentiation

It would be convenient if the cones themselves could next be separated into classes, but there is no obvious criterion by which such a separation can be made. Structurally, except for certain differences that we must ignore for the moment, cones in the retina

647

resemble one another very closely. Thus, if we wish to make a separation, we must use some other methods, and we can begin with certain facts of color vision that suggest some numbers to us.

First, we know that white light is a combination of many different wavelengths of light. We can break it up into its rainbow of components by having it travel through a prism. The resulting band or spectrum is of interest in that certain colors stand out. Red, green, blue, and yellow each do not appear to be a mixture of the other colors. We can think of orange as a reddish yellow and of chartreuse as a yellow-green, but the four salient colors cannot be so described. These observations suggest that there may be four different types of hue receptors, and that other colors are encoded by combined operations of these groups.

Certain other laws suggest that three types of hue receptors might be quite enough. Studies have revealed that the hue of any wavelength can be matched so closely by a mixture of red, green, and blue light that an observer is unable to distinguish the pure light from the combination. Thus, although a yellow is not a "reddish green," the effects of mixed beams of red and green light cannot be distinguished from those produced by beams of pure yellow light. Thus we see that visual observations alone cannot wholly settle the issue; we have to turn to other disciplines to help us to decide upon the number.

Some properties of color blindness[3]

First, we need to know some facts of color blindness so that we can do experiments with people who have simpler-than-normal mechanisms for discrimination of hue. Many people—one in twenty men and one in one hundred women—are to some extent color blind. A majority of these are able to distinguish many hues, but have trouble with the reds and greens. Furthermore, we are all color-blind for blues and yellows in a portion of our visual fields, and this region corresponds to a zone within the retina that apparently has only cones within it.

Fig. 18.6 Producing the solar spectrum. When a narrow beam of light is passed through a prism, light of short wave length is bent to a greater degree than light of a longer wave length.

Fig. 18.7 Laws of color mixture as illustrated by the effects of combining beams of light from three projectors. (Figs. 18.6 and 18.7 courtesy LIFE *Magazine,* © TIME, Inc.)

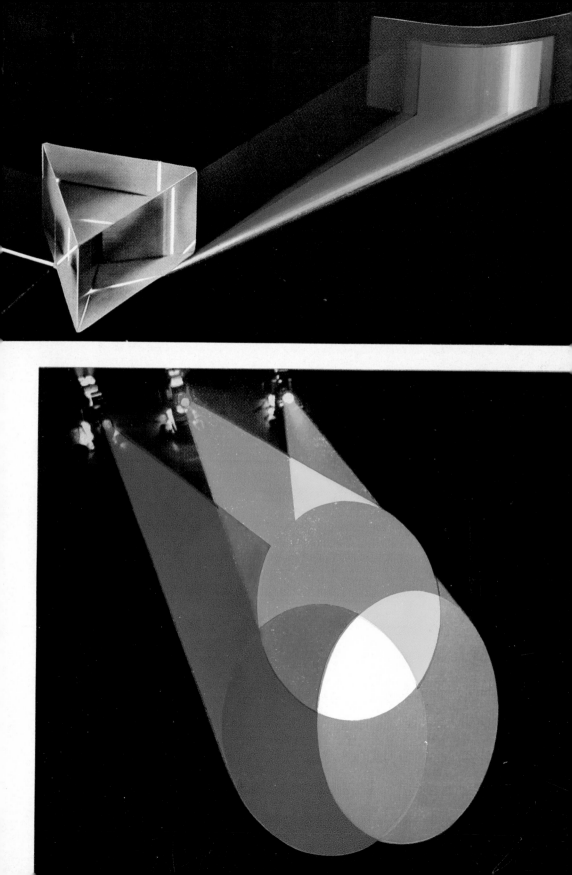

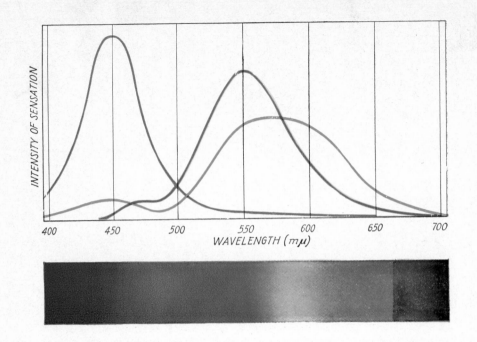

Let us now suppose that there are forms of color blindness of the red-green sort that arise because the "red" cones of the retina are missing. Such people, if we argue for the three receptors, just have "green" and "blue" mechanisms. But if this is so, and if the universal yellow-blue blindness of central vision means that none of us have "blue" receptors in our central retinas, then a red-green-blind individual of this type must have only one variety of hue receptor in the central zone.

If we next consider that light must be absorbed if it is to stimulate, visual receptors must contain something that absorbs the light. Materials that absorb light are pigments, and different pigments are selectively absorptive of the different wavelengths of light. Such selective responsivity is what would be required of a receptor if it is, in fact, to be effective as a hue discriminator. This all reduces to the supposition that, if we could measure human pigments, we could find but one such pigment in the central retinas of persons who lack "red" receptors. What we need, accordingly, is some sort of method for assessing this conclusion, and preferably a method that will not commit mayhem on our rather precious eyeballs.

The physical measurement of human cone pigments[4]

Relatively recently, a method has been found for making just this kind of measurement, and moreover of the pigments as we find them in the eyes of living human beings. What we do is shine a light of known composition into the pupil of the eye, and measure the small amount of light that is reflected outward from the pupil. The returning light will be of changed composition if it is selectively absorbed, and hence by comparing light that enters and exits, we can measure what the pigment takes. Such comparisons have shown that there is but one pigment in the central cones

---

Fig. 18.8 Curves to show the hypothetical sensitivity of each receptor for hue to the pure lights of the solar spectrum reproduced below the graph. (By permission from *College Physics*, 2d ed., by Weber, White and Manning. Copyright 1952 McGraw-Hill Book Co., Inc.)

Fig. 18.9 The parrot at the left was colored by a man with normal color vision. The remainder were colored by men who saw the same bird but were color blind. Note the confusion in the tail feathers and the accuracy with which blues were reproduced. (By permission from *The Handbook of Physiology and Biochemistry*, by R. J. S. McDowall. London: John Murray)

of our red-green-blind individuals. Similar measurements with normal people have detected two such pigments there, and these are presumed to be contained in types of cones that we can describe as "red" and "green."

What is still missing from the picture is the third or "blue" receptor. By some workers it is thought that rods, or perhaps a special type of rod, serves this function in addition to subserving twilight visual processes. This conclusion is in keeping with the fact that the central retina is rodless; to see a faint star, for example, we must look to one side of it so that its image falls outside the central rod-free area. It is still too early to know if this is so, but that there are different types of cone pigments now cannot be reasonably doubted.

Neural events in color vision[5]

The differentiation of receptive mechanisms leads us to suspect that the nerves themselves are mixtures of different types of sensory neurons. The question is one that we can readily approach with experimental methods, and these methods are derived from the fact that conduction in a nerve is signaled by electrical

Fig. 18.10 Arrangement for the measurement of neural signals in individual visual nerve fibers. (After Granit[7])

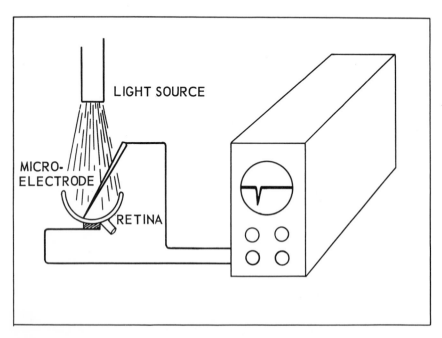

changes. With small enough electrodes, or pick-up wires, it is even possible to measure the changes that occur within a single neuron of a nerve. If this neuron is in the visual nerve, we can stimulate it very simply. We merely flood the eye with light of known composition and this will stimulate receptors; these receptors then evoke a measurable conduction of signals in related visual neurons.

We can substantially refine such a study by using light of but a single wavelength, and by changing the intensity of light determine the sensitivity of any given neuron to this wavelength. Then, by changing wavelengths, it is easy to determine how such sensitivity varies, and hence to obtain a curve for the sensitivity of an individual unit. The frog is a convenient subject for this work, and such experiments have shown the visual nerves of frogs indeed contain fibers that respond selectively to different wavelengths of light. Fibers have also been discovered that have curves corresponding quite closely to human twilight sensitivity, and these presumably are neurons related to the rods in frog retinas.

General conclusions on qualitative sensory encoding

In summary, we know a lot about the processes that underly perception of color. These are of interest not only in themselves, but also because of their suggestions with regard to processes in other kinds of qualitative sensing. Differentiation of receptors in the eye makes it seem a bit more probable that there is a differentiation of receptors in the skin, the nose, and the tongue. Furthermore, the fact that differentiation of the hue receptors is more relative than absolute has within it a suggestion that this circumstance obtains in other sense organs too. And the fact that there is corresponding segregation of the fibers in the visual nerve leads us to suspect that all the nerves are put together in this general manner. We would not, at least, be surprised if it were shown that there are several types of nose receptors, and that the fibers of the olfactory nerve respond differentially to odors.

Where these speculations have been matched with data, they have found a general confirmation. Possibly the best example of all of them is given by experiments in taste.[6] Although taste receptors have not been, as yet, segregated into groups, there is an undoubted segregation of the fibers of the nerves for taste. These can be made to fire differentially when substances are placed upon the tongue, and yet, as visual data lead us to suspect, the segregation is not absolute. Such results are possibly the greatest of rewards to students of processes in sensing, for they show that most important regularities exist within a complex domain. This domain is neither seeing, hearing, or feeling, but rather is all of them; nature seems to play by a book in which the rules are sometimes common to all sense organs.

ENCODING OF STIMULUS INTENSITY AND LOCUS[7]

Experiments involving the recording of events within the fibers forming a nerve are the main source of our present understanding of the signaling of stimulus intensity. An experiment with the frog's eye and light will serve to illustrate the basic laws. If the light we use is made somewhat brighter than it has to be to barely trigger off conduction, an individual neuron in the visual nerve responds by conducting several signals. If the light is made still brighter, the rate of firing goes up again, and continues to increase until a final limit has been reached for its frequency of firing.

When several neurons operate together, the frequency of firing in a nerve proves to be a function both of the rates of individual fibers and of the number of those fibers. The number of fibers that are active depends upon the strength of stimulation, for some stimuli are so weak that they fire only the most sensitive receptors. When stimuli are stronger, somewhat less sensitive receptors and their neurons operate, and their rates of firing are added to the rates of firing in the more responsive units. These simple principles seem to work for every kind of sensing, and illustrate the way in which the same neural signals can convey both qualitative and quantitative information.

A recent experiment devoted to this topic is of most unusual interest, for it illustrates that what is true for frogs' eyes can also be true for human skins.[8] In this study, college students first were asked to judge the strength of a "thud" that was brought about by stimulation of their arms with brief electrical pulses. Next, these same stimuli were once again presented, but instead of asking for a judgment, the experimenter measured the events that took place in the subjects' nerves. This was done by picking up, directly

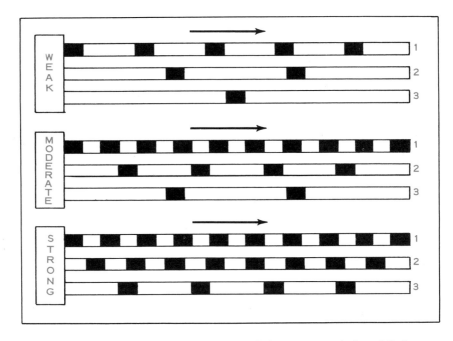

Fig. 18.11 These sketches represent a group of three neurons, 1, 2, and 3, that are of progressively lower sensitivity. Note that the weak stimulus excites them all, but that the impulses carried by 1 are much more frequent than those in 2 or 3. All three rates of firing go up as the strength of the stimulus applied is increased, but the increase is relatively greater in the less-sensitive elements.

through the skin, a signal generated by the nerve that amounted to the sum of all the different signals carried by a certain group of fibers. The outcome of the study was that the subjective and the neural measures of response were, as expected from the laws just stated, very highly correlated. It was also shown that, so long as the pulses were spaced so as to give a single "thud," their time relations did not matter so far as either the subjective or the neural response was concerned.

Mechanisms for encoding locus

The question next arises as to how these same signals preserve information as to locus. This is not of equal importance for all modalities. The nose, for example, is unable to detect the source of an odor except by taking several samples at a number of positions. In touch and vision, on the other hand, sense of locus is precise; accordingly, the skin and the eyes and their nerves preserve this most important datum.

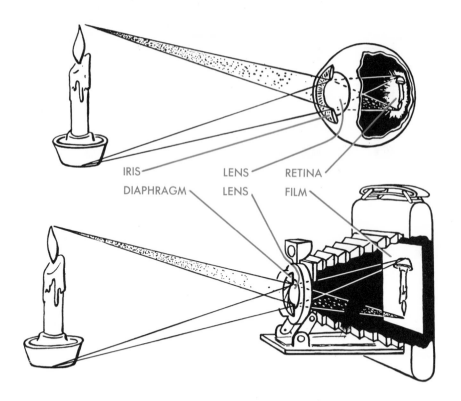

IRIS LENS RETINA
DIAPHRAGM LENS FILM

Fig. 18.12 A comparison indicating similarities between the eye and the camera. (From *Psychology and Life,* ed. 3, by Floyd L. Ruch. Copyright, 1948 by Scott, Foresman and Company, and used with their permission)

All such judgments seemingly depend upon an orderly arrangement of receptors in the sensitive surface of the sense organ in question. This is illustrated particularly well by the structure of the eye, which in more than one respect resembles a camera in construction. Both the camera and the eye can be regarded as boxes lined with black, into which light enters through a system of lenses and is brought to focus on a screen. In both systems, the "receptor surface" samples several places at once, and hence as a group the retinal receptors can encode a pattern that would be beyond the capacities of any one of them. A similar arrangement is to be observed in the skin, for its receptors are spread out in a surface as are receptors in the eye.

The problem of pitch in hearing[9]

In the hearing mechanism, signals that relate to locus in both touch and vision are appropriated for an entirely different function. The qualities of simple sounds are what we term their pitches, that is, whether they are high or low, and quantity appears in the phenomenon of loudness, which is like the brightness of a light. Now, although the loudness of a sound is represented by rates of firing in the nerves for hearing, different pitches do not have their bases in receptor differentiation. Rather, pitch perception is analogous to that of spatial locus of a light, or to perception of the place upon our skin where we have been touched at the moment.

The "skin" of the inner ear is a strip of cells found inside a tubular, snail-shelled organ called the cochlea. It is a portion of the inner ear, which lies inward from the bones of the conductive apparatus. The cochlea is filled with fluid, and its receptors are stimulated by pressure changes set up within the fluid by the movements of the chain of middle-ear bones. If a sound stimulus is high

Fig. 18.13 The inner ear. The cochlea is shown at the right, the vestibular apparatus at the left. The internal structure of the cochlea is diagrammed in the inset. (After Hardy, *Anat. Rec.,* 1934, *59,* and Munn, *Psychology*)

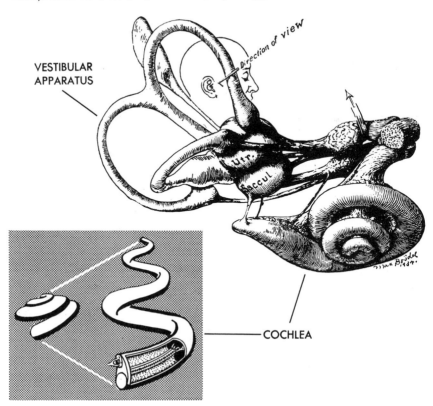

in frequency, receptors at the base of the coil are more strongly activated than are the receptors at the apex. A tone of low frequency, on the other hand, has its principal effect upon the receptors in the upper turns of the coil. Pitch thus varies with the point upon the strip that is stimulated the most, and loudness with the total rate of firing that is being carried by the nerve as a whole.

Much of the evidence for this conclusion is a little indirect. For example, studies have been made of the ears of dead persons who had hearing losses when they were alive. These, in general, have not been completely conclusive because selective hearing losses for low frequencies are rare. Somewhat more convincing data have, however, been produced by animal studies. In these, selective low-tone hearing losses have occurred following the surgical destruction of the upper cochlear turns.[10] But the final evidence, and the most complete, comes from experiments in which the ears of dead human beings have been taken out and studied. In these, a device which served to substitute for all of the hearing apparatus besides the inner ear was coupled to the cochlea, and the movements of the cochlear strip were measured with a microscope. It was found that when the cochlea was driven at low stimulating frequencies, the upper turns responded relatively more than did the middle or the lower turns. Exactly the opposite relation was observed with high stimulating frequencies, and middle frequencies had their maximal effects upon the middle cochlear turns.

SOME BASES OF PERCEPTION OF SPACE[11]

Assignment of the spatial arrangement of cochlear receptors to a pitch-encoding function leaves the single ear without a mechanism for assessing sources of sounds. Even so, we do make some such judgments, and our capacity to do so stems from the fact that we have two ears each. A sound coming from the right or left is more intense at one of our ears, and also reaches it before it arrives at the other. The differences in power and time of arrival typically are not very large, but careful listening experiments have shown them to be quite enough. These cues, however, disappear whenever the source is equidistant from the ears, and so we are unable to distinguish a sound as coming from the front or rear.

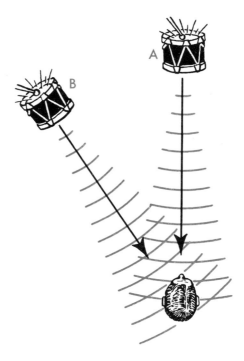

Fig. 18.14 Generation of the cues related to sound localization. The sound source at *A* furnishes no cues for localization, for the two ears are stimulated alike and simultaneously. If the source is at *B*, however, the head shields the right ear from part of the sound and is farther away so that successive waves reach the right ear at a later time than the left. (From Boring, Langfeld, and Weld, *Foundations of Psychology*)

These facts have recently been put to widespread use, for they are the basis of the depth effect obtained from stereophonic records. What these records have that others do not have is a double needle track, and the two tracks are recorded with microphones that correspond to each of the ears. In a proper system, signals from the tracks are fed to two separate speakers, and these, if listened to from the right position, duplicate the sound that would have been delivered to the listener's ears had he been in the recording studio. Since the only basis that we have for judging depth are the differences between the signals received by the ears, this effect, if properly produced, cannot be told from actual depth in sources of music.

Just as the two ears cooperate in judgments of auditory depth or space, so our two eyes cooperate to give us information as to visual space. Just as we hear the world from slightly different angles with the ears on each side of our heads, so we see it differently with our left and right retinas. Here again, the differences are not large at all, and are not perceived as such; rather, we see a single image with a marked third dimension. This phenomenon is called the stereoscopic effect, and it is the basis for devices that convert a pair of flat pictures into one scene with three dimensions.

659

Examples of the latter are the stereoscope, now in very streamlined versions, and the short-lived stereo movies of a few years ago.

Space and the vestibular system[12]

A final group of organs supplement the cues provided by our skin, ears, and eyes as to our position in space at any moment, and to some extent what we are doing. Most of us, at one time or another, have thought ourselves in motion while sitting in a railroad train—only to find that a neighboring train has pulled out from alongside our own. This confusion is natural enough, for rarely do we see everything about us moving simultaneously unless we, and not our environment, are doing the moving. Rarely do we judge that we are at rest unless our surroundings are largely stationary as well. Such perceptual problems seldom arise when we are walking down the street, for cues from other senses are consonant and not conflicting.

But there are other cues apart from those discussed, and these further cues arise from sense organs whose specific function is detection of the position and motion of the body. In the inner ear, adjacent to the cochlea, is one set of such sense organs. This is the vestibular mechanism, and it includes the saccule, utricle, and three semicircular canals.

Fig. 18.15 Internal structure of the vestibular apparatus. The stimulating cap in the utricle is shown in side view; it would look like the comparable structure in the saccule if viewed from above. (After Camis, *The Physiology of the Vestibular Apparatus*)

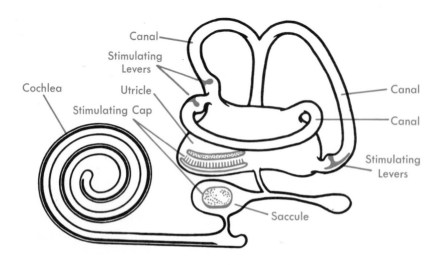

The function of the saccule remains in doubt, but the utricle is known to be concerned with indicating tilt of the head. It contains a massive membrane that rests upon a group of specialized receptors, and the membrane is attached to the receptors by a set of interlacing hairs. The membrane or cap slides to some extent whenever the head position changes, and also moves from its resting place in response to such accelerations as we encounter in driving a car in city traffic. The three canals, on the other hand, respond to twisting movements of the head. When the head rotates, fluids in these tubes tend to lag behind the tubes themselves, and thus are thrust against levers that are found within enlargements at the end of each tube. The three tubes together form a set of a spatial coordinates for movements of this kind, for the receptors in each respond to the extent to which the plane of head rotation matches the plane of the canal.

Vestibular receptors operate whenever their component parts are not all moving in the same direction and at the same speed. It makes no difference to the inner ear how a movement comes about: the utricle will signal an acceleration if we break from walking to running, but it will operate in much the same way when we pull away from traffic lights. The basis for perception of the difference between an active and a passive movement is certain receptors in effectors which together form what we term the kinesthetic group. Receptors in the joints appear to be the most important kinesthetic receptors, with receptors found in tendons supplementing them. There are, finally, receptors in the muscles, but these are not important in perception; rather, they are parts of mechanisms for the maintenance of posture.

SKELETAL RESPONSE MECHANISMS[13]

With this consideration of the way we detect the fact that we have made a response, we can turn from problems of sensory reception to those of response execution. The simplest of peripheral response mechanisms are those for skeletal movements, and the basic principles can be summarized by way of a familiar example. Bending of the elbow is accomplished by contraction of the well-known biceps muscle; straightening the elbow is accomplished largely by the triceps muscle. In both of these events, the action is

661

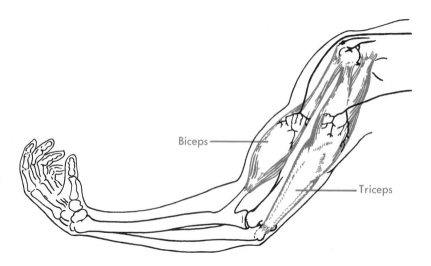

Fig. 18.16 The biceps and triceps, a typical pair of antagonistic skeletal muscles. (After Dashiell, *Fundamentals of General Psychology*)

achieved by contractions working in conjunction with a set of levers made of bone.

Wherever there are joints within the skeleton, pairs of striate muscles operate them. When one member of the pair is operating, the other is usually relaxing. These reciprocal relations are important, for, if things were otherwise, a great deal of work by muscles would be wasted in overcoming other muscles. Such reciprocity, however, is not a built-in feature, but rather is a kind of elementary integration that depends upon the neural centers.

Regulation of the strength and pattern of striate muscular movement

Muscular activity of this general kind always quite directly reflects the patterns of neural signals that are being carried outward over motor nerves. We can very readily record these signals with electrical equipment, and, as we have said, they seem to be similar to sensory signals carried to the nervous system. Every motor nerve contains many fibers, and each fiber terminates in a group of muscle fibers of a given muscle. Thus the selection of a skeletal movement depends upon the neurons activated, and this is the motor analog of problems of spatial sensory encoding.

There are certain very striking parallels between the sensory and motor nerves with regard to mechanisms by which quantitative variation is achieved. We have seen that stimulus intensity affects sensory neurons in two ways. Strong stimuli affect a greater number of such neurons than do weak ones, and the neurons individually fire more rapidly. Basically the same situation, in reverse, governs strength of muscular contraction. The stronger contractions involve more muscle fibers, and each fiber shortens more. More muscle fibers are called into play because more motor neurons are active, and each muscle fiber shortens in accordance with the rate at which its motor neuron is conducting neural signals.

The most marked differences between the striate muscles from one body part to another are found in the extent to which a given muscle is supplied with motor neurons. The most favored groups are the muscles of the eyes, the face, the tongue and the fingers, and these quite obviously are the body parts in which the greatest numbers of different kinds of movements are observed. In such movements, furthermore, a few muscle fibers make a difference: the difference in the accent of a spoken word serves as an excellent example. Such control can only be achieved if not too many fibers share a motor neuron, for the motor neurons in themselves cannot select single fibers from their group. For some kinds of movements, for instance, of the back, such fine detail is not required, and in this region a single motor neuron will control a large amount of muscle.

Apart from such differences as these, the organization of the skeletal response mechanism is simple and straightforward. The fashioning of patterns of skeletal movement is largely a central affair, with the motor neurons and the muscles contributing comparatively little to the process. This is altogether proper, as these mechanisms must reflect a host of subtleties. For moment to moment, single muscle fibers contribute to very different patterns.

VISCERAL RESPONSE MECHANISMS[14]

Response mechanisms for visceral effectors:—the heart, the hollow organs and the exocrine glands—exhibit a peripheral complexity which stands in greatest possible contrast to that of the skeletal muscular effectors. Typically, the visceral organs have a dual supply of motor neurons, one from each division of what is

663

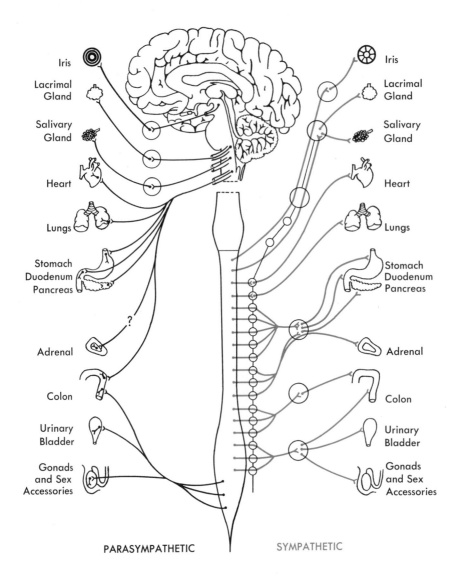

Fig. 18.17 The peripheral connections of the autonomic motor system. Parasympathetic pathways are shown on the left, sympathetic pathways on the right. One of the paired sympathetic trunks is shown to the right of the spinal cord. (After Turner, *Endocrinology*)

termed the autonomic system. These two divisions of the autonomic system are called the sympathetic and parasympathetic systems, and are motor networks that originate within the brain and spinal cord.

Neurons of the parasympathetic mechanism exit from the central nervous system either from the brain stem or from the lowest reaches of the spinal cord. Sympathetic neurons leave by spinal nerves attached to the cord's middle sections. These latter nerves are connected at this level with the sympathetic trunks, which are beadlike structures that parallel the cord from the lower back to the neck.

The picture is further complicated by the fact that neurons from the brain and spinal cord do not themselves connect the visceral effectors to the central nervous system. Rather, the former terminate in outlying clumps of neural gray matter, and are there synaptically related to neurons that lie completely outside the limits of the central nervous system. Massed cell bodies of these sympathetic neurons form the beads of sympathetic trunks, and their axons complete the relays to the visceral effectors. Peripheral neurons of the parasympathetic system tend, in contrast, to be short, and in some instances are buried within the walls of the organs they supply.

The antagonism of the autonomic system

We can make some sense of these complexities, but to do so we must first understand some properties of visceral effectors. We have said that skeletal effectors are wholly dependent on their motor nerve supply, and exhibit no activity whatever when deprived of neural signals. This is not the case with the heart or with an organ that has smooth muscle tissue in it; under some conditions, for example, hearts will beat when wholly separated from bodies. Hence the problem for the autonomic system is one of regulating these effectors, since they have intrinsic actions in the absence of the neural signals.

Generally speaking, if the actions of an organ are speeded up by sympathetic signals, these same actions are suppressed by a parasympathetic volley. Thus one-half of the autonomic system works as an accelerator, and the other half, for any given organ, operates to put on the brakes.

These antagonisms are partially achieved by the secretion of chemicals by outlying neurons. Generally, though not universally, the neurons of the sympathetic division produce one of two important chemicals, adrenalin and noradrenalin. The parasympathetic peripheral neurons mostly produce acetylcholine, a compound that is also probably released at many different central neural junctions.

665

The foregoing facts are of great importance, for they indicate that neurons must be thought of as partially glandular in nature. This becomes particularly evident when we study the relations between the neurons of the sympathetic system and the central core of the adrenal gland—a member of the endocrine system. Here, as in no other portion of the system, single motor neurons link the central nervous system directly to an outlying organ. This organ, furthermore, produces, as a gland, the chemicals also released by outlying sympathetic neurons. Clearly, then, the endocrine and nervous systems are extremely closely related, and events in one are likely to have repercussions in the other.

Roles of the autonomic divisions

There are marked differences between the roles of the autonomic divisions in providing what has been appropriately termed the background of behavioral support. A simple illustration of this fundamental fact is given by the way in which the systems operate to meet the body's needs for blood. Blood is actually in short supply (we can think of it as money), and demands for blood vary with the level of work to be accomplished by an organ. These demands can only be fulfilled through borrowing or by changes in the rate of blood flow, and both possibilities have parallels in ordinary economic life.

The principal competitors for the blood supply are the skeletal muscles and the digestive organs. During exercise, the muscles have to have it, and the stomach has to do without. The necessary shift is accomplished by an autonomic sympathetic discharge. When this occurs, the smooth muscles built into the walls of arteries that serve the stomach and intestines clamp down these vessels and force the blood into the vessels of the arms and legs. At the same time, sympathetic signals increase the output of the heart, and the working muscles thus are well supplied with the materials they need.

After exercise is over, parasympathetic operations dominate the general recuperative scene. Blood shifts back to the digestive tract, and movements of the stomach are resumed. Along with this activity, the glands of the tract resume secretion of digestive juices. But, at any moment, this can all be stilled should some emergency arise which requires a vigorous and prompt response. Then, once again, it is the muscles that are served, and served by sympathetic

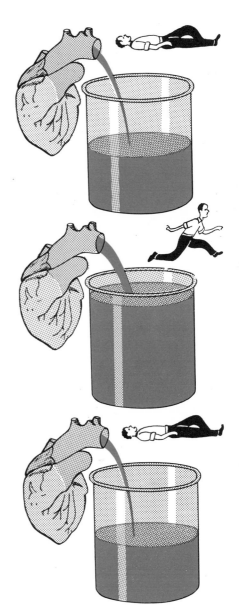

Fig. 18.18 Variations in the output of blood with changes in exercise. When we are at rest, as shown in the upper diagram, the amount of blood that is pumped by the heart is reduced. Under the stress of exercise, however, the output of the heart may increase from a base level of about 3 liters per minute to more than 30 liters. With the passing of the stress—and thus the demand—the output of the heart returns to the base level, as in the bottom diagram. (After Wickware, "Psychosomatic Medicine," © LIFE, Feb. 19, 1945)

integrations; parasympathetic processes abate for the duration of the action.

Autonomic changes in emotion

Sympathetic processes similar to those which appear in ordinary work are also very prominent constituents of patterns of fear.

In these patterns, autonomic changes mobilize the body for action, and it matters not a whit whether such an action actually ensues. This gives the basis for procedures that are known as scientific lie detection, the detector being nothing more than a set of instruments for measuring autonomic changes. Thus one instrument detects a sweaty palm by measuring electrical resistance; a blood-pressure cuff placed around an arm picks up the change in circulation. Sometimes a record of the heart rate is added, and can be conveniently obtained by measuring electrical changes that appear whenever this great muscle contracts.

The use of the autonomic indicators in detection of deception is a very old art indeed. One method, practiced in ancient India, was to feed a suspect a mouthful of uncooked rice. Presumably a man who was afraid when he answered would have a dry mouth in doing so, and so he would be judged a guilty party unless the rice was thereby moistened. The method is a crude one, but completely sound, for saliva does stop forming during sympathetic reactions. We have made some progress in the last few centuries, but the principle remains the same.

Learning and autonomic patterns

Autonomic patterns of response can be conditioned, and indeed a favorite tool of students of learning is the conditioned galvanic skin response. This response, a change in skin resistance, is generated by a sympathetic discharge to the sweat glands of the palms. Parasympathetic patterns also change with practice, and in fact the earliest experiments of Pavlov utilized secretion of saliva as the measure of the dog's behavior. Through these pathways, the central nervous system has control of most, if not all organs, and through the changes thus induced we have a basis for effects of learning upon a wide variety of basic physiological events. Sometimes learning leads, for example, to an ulcer, and these effects are the patterns we describe as psychosomatic disorders.

These disorders are treated in a great variety of ways. Thus, for example, drugs are used to block the chemicals that neurons release, and other chemicals are often employed to neutralize the products of glands. The better solution is, of course, to unlearn the underlying patterns of response—and this is what psychiatrists and clinical psychologists aim for in their counseling.

MECHANISMS OF RECEPTOR CONTROL[15]

Not too long ago, a few years at the most, we would here conclude our discussion of response mechanisms. It would seem that we have traced a pathway out to every possible effector, and surely this should mean that we have dealt with every kind of motor neuron. But we have abandoned this conclusion, and for rather startling reasons—not only are there motor neurons to effectors, but also motor neurons to receptors.

To say such a thing must surely make us wonder what we mean by "motor" neurons. Formally, the name applies to any type of neuron that originates within the central nervous system and terminates peripherally. And, in most instances, the motor neurons are indeed concerned with effectors, and hence with the production of mechanical or chemical responses. But this is not always so. Sometimes an impulse from the central nervous system does nothing whatsoever except to modify the signals being fed into it. As an example, striate muscles all contain receptors that are sensitive to being stretched. But how sensitive depends upon the signals being sent to such receptor organs, and a lot of stretch or a little stretch can—under varying conditions—lead to exactly the same number of inward-going signals from the muscles. It is just exactly as though all receptors have a kind of volume control, and that the central nervous system can either "turn them up" or "turn them down."

This same phenomenon is also illustrated by an experiment with cats, in which study the critical event was the appearance of a mouse. The experimenters first hooked a tiny wire electrode into a cat's brain at the point where auditory signals enter from the ear. They could then record the effects of clicking sounds upon the ear and auditory nerve; each click gave them a correlated burst of neural signals at this point. But, when the cat was confronted with a mouse, it "simply didn't listen" any more; the bursts of activity abruptly ceased, and stayed suppressed until the mouse's exit.

These discoveries have obvious relations to those psychological events that we term "attending to" or "not attending to" a stimulus. These events have been discussed before in the chapter on stimulus selection. Psychologists have long thought that

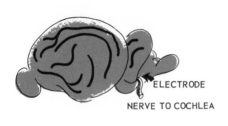

ELECTRODE

NERVE TO COCHLEA

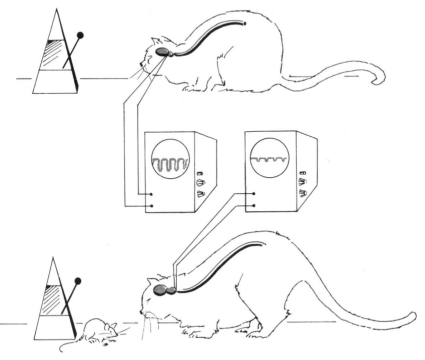

Fig. 18.19 An example of the central control of signals from peripheral receptors. An electrode buried in the brain stem of a cat, where the fibers from the ear connect, records an impulse every time a click is delivered to the ear. However, these responses are markedly reduced when the cat is shown a mouse.

whether stimuli will be effective in controlling behavior depends upon what happens to these signals after they arrive within the brain. Now, however, it is evident that the signals may not get that far, but rather be suppressed in the sense organs by receptor-motor neurons.

Receptor-motor neurons, like all motor neurons, are of course themselves controlled by the integrative networks of the central nervous system. How the networks operate to give us these effects is still not understood completely, but many of the most im-

670

portant links in the chain are being worked upon at the moment. In the chapters yet to come, we will be concerned with these and other questions that arise when we ask what goes on within the mechanisms that stand between receptors and effectors. What we have considered thus far are the tools with which the central nervous system works, and its working now becomes the prime concern of our analysis.

REFERENCES

[1] Pieron, H. *The Sensations,* Muller, 1952, pp. 120-123.

[2] Pieron, H. *The Sensations,* Muller, 1952, pp. 123-162.

[3] Willmer, E. N. *Retinal Structure and Color Vision,* Cambridge, 1946, Chapters 6 and 7.

[4] Rushton, W. A. H. Kinetics of cone pigments measured objectively on the living human fovea, *Annals N. Y. Acad. Sciences,* 1958, *74,* 291-304.

[5] Grant, R. *Sensory Mechanisms of the Retina,* Oxford, 1947, Chapter 19.

[6] Pfaffmann, C. In Stevens, S. S., *Handbook of Experimental Psychology,* Wiley, 1951, Chapter 29.

[7] Granit, R. *Receptors and Sensory Perception,* Yale, 1955, Chapter 1.

[8] Uttal, W. The three-stimulus problem, *J. comp. physiol. Psychol.,* 1960, *53,* 42-46.

[9] Bekesy, G. von, and Rosenblith, W. In Stevens, S. S., *Handbook of Experimental Psychology,* Wiley, 1951, Chapter 27.

[10] Schuknecht, H. F., and Neff, W. D. Hearing losses after apical lesions in the cochlea, *Acta Otolaryngologica,* 1952, *42,* 263-274.

[11] Woodworth, R. S., and Schlosberg, H. *Experimental Psychology,* Holt, Rinehart and Winston, 1954, Chapters 12 and 16.

[12] Wendt, G. R. In Stevens, S. S., *Handbook of Experimental Psychology,* Wiley, 1951, Chapter 31.

[13] Gelfan, S. In Fulton, J. F., *Textbook of Physiology,* Saunders, 1955, Chapter 8.

[14] Lindsley, D. B. In Stevens, S. S., *Handbook of Experimental Psychology,* Wiley, 1951, Chapter 14.

[15] Granit, R. *Receptors and Sensory Perception,* Yale, 1955, Chap. 7.

Chapter Nineteen

THE CENTRAL NERVOUS SYSTEM AND BEHAVIOR

THE ROLE OF THE CENTRAL NERVOUS system in behavior is the provision of linkages by which events initiating changes in receptors control the action of effectors. It is with these linkages that we will be concerned in this chapter and the next, with the channels of communication that have been provided by the neural networks of the spinal cord and brain. The bulk of neural elements, the interneurons, are involved in networks of this kind, and their operations are at the very heart of our adaptability. They provide, in essence, a complicated switchboard to which information is supplied and from which emerge the signals that endow behavior with its well-known patterning.

To study the events that underlie a pattern, we have first to specify the pattern. After this is done, we can then assess what its mechanisms are. When these mechanisms have been identified, we can next proceed with the assessment of the operations that the system performs in synthesizing patterns of response. In some areas, for some behaviors, we have gone a long way towards this goal; in some others, we are still frankly trying to identify the mechanisms. What we know the most about are the simple patterns generally described as reflexive; as we must expect, much less can be said about the most complex performances. But, as we shall see, excellent beginnings have been made upon the problems posed to us by virtually the whole gamut of observable behaviors.

MECHANISMS OF THE WAKING STATE

In most psychological experiments, the waking state is taken for granted. Some behaviors, such as breathing, do persist whether we are sleeping or not, but for most, a background of arousal is essential to elicitation of the pattern. It is thus appropriate that we begin our study of central integrative mechanisms by looking at the processes that underlie the daily sleep and waking cycle.

All of us are generally familiar with a number of the properties of both sleep and waking, and usually our diagnoses of these states is based upon a cue constellation. Evenness of breathing, closure of the eyes, and widespread relaxation of the muscles are, in most instances, convincing evidence that a given person is asleep. When we are in doubt, we may make some tests of sensitivity to stimulation; should the state alarm us because of its resemblance to coma or perhaps to death itself, we carry these assessments to the point where we are sure that what we see can be reversed.

Autonomic and neural indices of sleep and waking

Certain of the other characteristics of the patterns probably are less familiar. Sleepers also have a lower temperature than is normal for the waking hours, and both the blood pressure and

673

the heart rate are reduced in slumber. The skin's electrical resistance is high, and pupils are markedly constricted. However, the stomach, intestines, and their glands continue to carry on their functions. During arousal, the heart speeds up, and pressure of the blood increases; temperature goes up, and the pupils undergo dilation. This group of indices reflects the changes that take place in visceral effectors and complete the pattern so far as we can readily observe it by peripheral procedures.

Centrally, the shift from sleep to waking is reflected in changes in the brain's operations. These changes have associated with them some definite electrical events. These events, furthermore, can be detected at some distance from their origin, and because of this, can be recorded from the scalp. The pattern thus obtained is called the EEG, short for electroencephalogram. Popularly, it is termed the brain wave, and it is extremely complicated. Certain of its features are nonetheless related in a fairly simple way to the alternation we observe in organisms going through the sleep

Fig. 19.1 Brain-wave (EEG) changes that occur with the transition from the sleeping to the waking state. The records shown represent about three seconds of recording time.

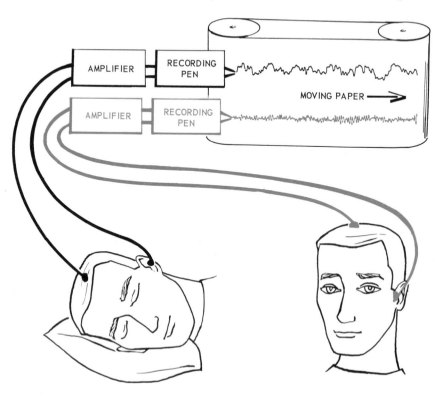

and waking cycle. In waking, the brain wave frequencies are low and the amplitudes are large, and just the opposite is characteristic of the sleeping state. Since these changes vary in a quantitative manner, the EEG is very useful as a tool for measuring the depths of sleep and the heights of waking.

The pacemaking function of the brain stem

With these observations of sleep and waking patterns, we can turn directly to the problem of finding the mechanisms crucially involved in the production of the cycle. The method of exclusion is the one that we begin with, and several kinds of evidence suggest that centers in the brain stem are particularly crucial for the sleep and waking states. This at first may seem to be unlikely. The whole body, after all, tends to be involved in the sleep and waking rhythm, and this implies that sleep and waking rhythms affect the whole central nervous system. However, experiments have shown that the brain stem serves a kind of pacemaker function, and that other portions of the central nervous system are driven by it in the cycle.

In the first such study,[1] we isolate a portion of the lower spinal cord by severing its normal connection with the rest of the central nervous system. This is done by cutting the spinal cord in two in the middle of the back; essentially, an animal that is thus prepared has two separate central nervous systems. Each subsystem is connected with a different group of receptors and effectors, and the isolated spinal cord is in connection only with the trunk and hind legs. Both components share, of course, the same circulation, but this is their sole communication (it could be important should the sleep and waking cycle have its source in changes in the blood).

Given such an animal, we next need methods for measuring the sleep and waking rhythm. So far as the head-end system is concerned, the cycle is easy to detect: most of the phenomena of sleep and waking are marked in this portion of the body. However, for the hind legs, we have only one straightforward behavioral procedure, and this is testing reflex movements to stimuli applied to the feet. Now, in normal animals, movements of this kind are harder to elicit during sleep than during waking. It would seem accordingly, that if this fluctuation were observed in dual-system subjects, then the spinal cord either has its own rhythm

675

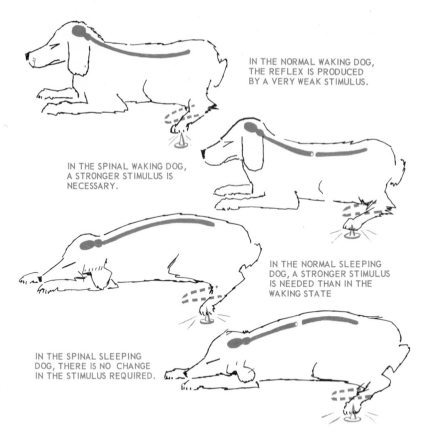

IN THE NORMAL WAKING DOG, THE REFLEX IS PRODUCED BY A VERY WEAK STIMULUS.

IN THE SPINAL WAKING DOG, A STRONGER STIMULUS IS NECESSARY.

IN THE NORMAL SLEEPING DOG, A STRONGER STIMULUS IS NEEDED THAN IN THE WAKING STATE

IN THE SPINAL SLEEPING DOG, THERE IS NO CHANGE IN THE STIMULUS REQUIRED.

Fig. 19.2 Reflex variations in the hindlimb of the normal and the spinal dog as a function of the sleep-waking cycle.

or is being driven by the blood stream. What we find, however, is that the reflex movements now are much the same in sleep and waking, and the spinal cord may thus be said to lack a rhythmic mechanism of its own. Furthermore, we see that its normal variations are not associated with the blood, and we can thus conclude that the severed linkages are crucial to the reflex fluctuations.

Sleep and waking rhythms in the isolated brain[2]

In the head-end system of such a preparation, sleep and waking rhythms still take place. This, at first, would seem to show that waking states do not depend upon the spinal cord. However, it is possible that, even though the brain is crucial to the rhythm, its mechanisms fail to work unless some information reaches them from spinal cord centers. We know, for example, that as we go to sleep, we first lie down and try to relax; as we start to sleep, we relax even further, and finally achieve the state of sleeping. It is very hard indeed to go to sleep while standing, and one reason why this might be so is that the brain is being continually bombarded by stimuli arising from effectors. Since the spinal cord is one avenue for incoming signals of this kind, it could be important that our first experiment was done with an animal whose brain was still connected with the upper spinal cord segments.

An answer to the question thus confronting us has been obtained in studies with cats. Here the brain's connections with the spinal cord were cut at the junction between the skull and vertebral column. Under these conditions, signals reach the brain only through the cranial nerves: these, by definition, are joined to the brain stem, and are in large part concerned with the receptors and effectors of the head.

The main complication in a study of this kind is that the procedure interferes with respiration by severing connections between the lower brain stem and the respiratory muscles. However, it is possible to keep such cats alive by artificial respiration, and when this is done the isolated head provides us with dramatic evidence for a sleep and waking rhythm. Thus, for example, the cat's eyes may close and its pupils undergo constriction, but this can be reversed if food is put before its nostrils, and the cat will lick its chops. At the same time, the EEG recorded from the brain is altered in the manner that, in normal cats, we associate with changes from the sleeping to the waking state.

If we now continue with the study of the head, but make the cut at somewhat higher levels, the sleep and waking rhythm is completely abolished. If we pick up brain waves under these conditions, the record very closely resembles the pattern that we would obtain from the cerebral hemispheres of normally sleeping animals. Since, from this, the hemispheres do not appear to have a sleep-waking rhythm of their own, the mechanisms crucially involved in the cycle must be between them and spinal cord. This leaves the brain stem and the cerebellum as our lone remaining choices, and the latter structure can be dismissed at once by studies that have shown that its removal is without effect upon the normal succession of the sleep and waking patterns.

677

SLEEP, WAKING AND THE CENTRAL BRAIN STEM

We have beeen regarding the brain stem as a unitary structure in the studies just considered, and properly so as an introduction to the problem. However, to proceed from here, we must recognize that while the brain stem seems to be a simple structure compared to other brain components, its interior is actually complex and highly differentiated. Basically, the plan is such that its internal core is made up of gray neural tissue, and this core is surrounded on the sides and bottom by bundles of sheathed neural fibers. It is therefore reasonable to ask what these components each contribute to the rhythm; both of them, of course, could be important, and this is what our studies must decide.

The classical theory of cortical bombardment[3]

Generally, we know that bundles of fibers relay signals in the nervous system, and that the bulk of integrative work is done in centers in the gray matter. Since it is obvious that sleep and

Fig. 19.3 Procedures in the isolation of the cerebral hemispheres in the cat from the spinal cord, the brain stem, and the receptors that connect to the central nervous system at the latter levels. Severing the central nervous system at *B* does not eliminate the waking state, but division of the brain stem at *A* produces irreversible sleep.

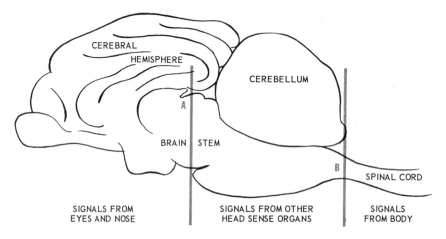

waking patterns involve processes of integration, these facts tempt us to emphasize the role of the central core of the brain stem. However, it could be that the brain stem itself is actually comparatively passive, and that its association with the cycle arises from the fact that its position makes it the channel of communication between all other major central nervous system structures. Perhaps, for example, both the spinal cord and the cerebral hemispheres would have the sleep-waking rhythm if they were provided with the data flowing inward over the nerves that serve the head. If so, then the gray matter of the brain stem's core could have different functions to perform, and would merely seem to be concerned with sleep and waking without being actually involved.

Consider, for example, the fact that hemispheres—when isolated from the brain stem—give an EEG that is similar to that observed in cats in normal sleep. We can think of this as a normal resting rhythm that is broken up, during waking, by the bombardment of neural signal volleys conducted over the brain stem's outer pathways. This would fit the notion that most of us accept, that sleep is passive, waking active; by walking, standing, or exposing ourselves to bright lights, noises, and the like, we maintain a high enough level of bombardment to keep the state of sleep away.

If we grant the concept long enough to test it, we should very readily be able to induce a state of sleep by severing the pathways which connect the hemispheres to all the different major sense organs. This should produce a lowered level of bombardment of the upper brain. In effect, we do this when we separate the brain stem from the cerebral hemispheres, but we still cannot be sure whether all the possible connections between these two divisions are important. In other words, must we make the cut complete, or can some connections remain without affecting the appearance of the sleep that follows severance of all connections?

The classical pathways of the brain stem[4]

Fortunately, many of the pathways to and from the hemispheres are accurately known. Some of them are so well known that we call them "classical" pathways. In their broader outlines, they were well defined half a century ago. The incoming pathways begin in sense organs and end within the cerebral cortex; they consist of neural fiber bundles linking neural centers together. To pick one example, the system that is crucial for touch sensitivity in fingers begins with receptors in the fingers and the nerves that connect them to the spinal cord. The fibers in these nerves are there joined by others and travel upward in the spinal cord until they reach a mass of gray matter near the junction of the spinal cord and brain stem. Here they are related synaptically to neurons whose cell bodies lie within this center, but whose fibers go on up the brain stem and end just before they reach the hemispheres. Then, in a region termed the thalamus, the second group

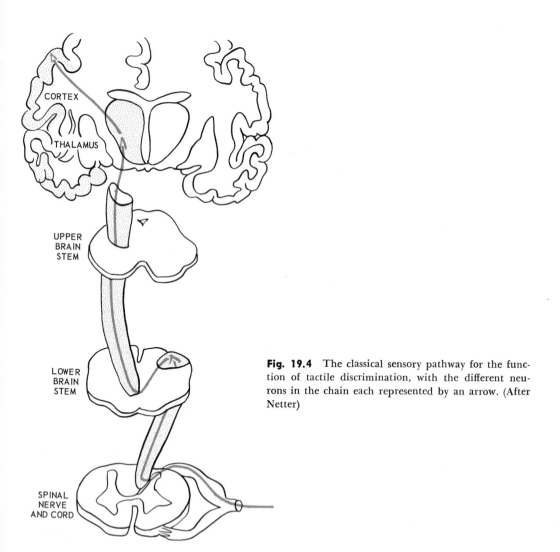

CORTEX

THALAMUS

UPPER
BRAIN
STEM

LOWER
BRAIN
STEM

SPINAL
NERVE
AND CORD

Fig. 19.4 The classical sensory pathway for the function of tactile discrimination, with the different neurons in the chain each represented by an arrow. (After Netter)

of neurons makes connections, and the third group of neurons in the pathway travels upward to the cerebral cortex.

Most of the distinct fiber bundles in the brain stem—they are also known as tracts—belong to pathways of this general character. Not all are sensory in function. Some that are similar in placement and construction link the centers of the cerebral hemispheres to the different classes of effectors. The ones that are, however, are the ones that interest us so far as our present problem goes, and the ones whose severance we will next attempt in studying the concept of bombardment.

The role of the brain stem in waking[5]

It is not convenient to cut all the pathways for, in some instances, this would damage both the central and peripheral components of the brain stem. However, we can sever groups of pathways that we know to be concerned with different stimuli, and then determine the arousing properties of such stimulation. The pathways for hearing and body sensitivity are best suited to the purpose. Their pathways travel in the brain stem's outer margins, and can hence be interrupted surgically by cuts that will not do any great damage to the central brain stem. Having done this, we must wait until the animal has recovered from the operation, and then we can assess the effects of sounds and touches as potential awakeners.

Such investigations have been carried out with cats, and with remarkable results. When the cat is sleeping, a sound will arouse it, even though the classical auditory pathways to hemispheres have been destroyed. The same is true of touches to the body, though their pathways also have been severed; hence, for waking, the classical pathways to the hemispheres can be dispensed with. To check out this conclusion very carefully, we measure changes in the EEG, and we find that animals without these pathways show the normal shift in the rhythm.

Somehow, then, the signals from the ear and body are finding their way into the cortex, and this implies that there is still some route leading upward from the brain stem to the hemispheres. Since the outer margins have been eliminated, our guess is that these routes are in the core, and so the next experiment is one which a cut is made between the upper levels of this core and the cerebral cortex. After this is done in an animal whose classical pathways remain intact, the behavioral result is wholly different. The cat is now asleep, and permanently so, by all of our criteria. We can thus conclude that classical sensory bombardment does not produce arousal, and that states of waking are dependent upon the integrative centers of the brain stem.

THE BASIC ARCHITECTURE OF THE BRAIN

These and other studies have led us to our modern concept of the way the brain is built. In its central core, we have an ancient group of mechanisms which, because of its relation to arousal, has been termed the *activating system*. The activating system is thought to be concerned with primitive patterns of behavior that involve the integration of responses of the organism as a whole. Other neural structures thus may be considered as additions or elaborations of the integrating networks of the central brain stem. The newer systems, presumably, are there to broaden the controls upon behavior, and to provide further mechanisms for the differentiation of responses.

We do not regard the activating system as the oldest system of all. This distinction seemingly belongs to mechanisms at the

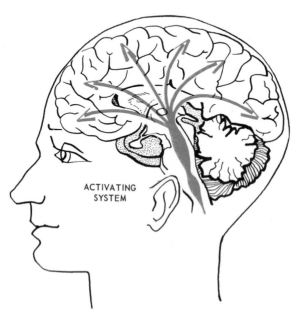

ACTIVATING
SYSTEM

Fig. 19.5 The activating system and its relationships to the newer systems of the brain.

level of the spinal cord. The activating system develops *pari passu* with the importance of the head, and with the importance of the head's sense organs in control of patterns of behavior. All such organs not only make connections directly with the two great hemispheres, but also with the older brain stem centers and the overlying cerebellum.

Phenomena of brain-stem activation[6]

The nature of the linkages between the brain-stem system and the older and newer systems has been systematically examined by combining techniques of recording from a center with techniques in which a shock is given directly to the central core of the brain stem. Thus, for example, we prepare an animal with one electrode buried in its brain stem; other electrodes are attached to varied regions of the cortex of the hemispheres. The surgical procedures involved in preparation are carried out before the study proper, and once again the animal most commonly employed is the ordinary house cat. After the animal has fully recovered from the surgical procedures, it becomes a fairly simple matter to connect the buried electrodes to equipment which will either give shocks or pick up the brain waves while the cat is behaving normally.

As we would expect from what has gone before, stimulation of the central brain stem rapidly awakens cats that were asleep at the time the shocks were given. More importantly, the brain waves change simultaneously in many regions of the cortex, which would indicate that connections are diffuse between the brain stem and the hemispheres.

The central brain-stem system has similar effects upon the centers of the spinal cord. This is indicated by experiments in which the effects of stimulation of the system are measured by means of reflex movements. Thus, for example, if we measure the knee jerk produced by a tap below the knee cap, such a tap combined with stimulation of the brain stem markedly increases the response. This result has been obtained in both cats and monkeys, and with other spinal-cord responses, for one can just as easily facilitate withdrawal of a limb from stimulating pin pricks. It should be apparent that these are the changes that give the spinal cord its daily rhythm, changes that apparently originate within the brain-stem activating system.

683

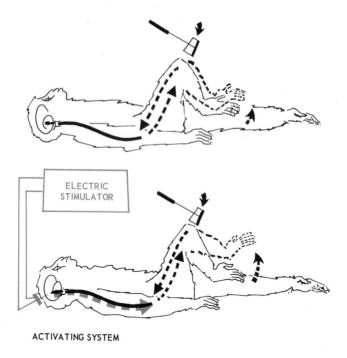

ELECTRIC
STIMULATOR

ACTIVATING SYSTEM

Fig. 19.6 The effects of stimulation of the knee alone, and of combined stimulation of the knee and the activating system. (After French)

PATTERNS OF BRAIN-STEM INTEGRATION

To describe the central brain-stem system as an activating mechanism is, in one sense, merely to ascribe to it important and well-established functions. As a prime determinant of the waking state, the system clearly activates behavior, and it is most tempting to think of it as being the neural mechanism for drive. The fact that its connections with the cortex are diffuse suit the system for this role, as do its largely unselective effects upon the centers of the spinal cord. As a drive mechanism, it would merely be concerned with the level of behavior, not with what, but rather with how much a response a situation would evoke.

The fault with this increasingly popular conception is that it obscures the basic fact that the central brain-stem system has been shown to have important qualitative functions. Certain quite specific patterns of behavior have their origins within the system, and the processes involved in their production are extremely complicated. Shocks to the brain stem tell us the truth about its function as an activator, but such methods have their limitations and have failed to tell us the whole truth.

Brain stem mechanisms and posture[7]

One important clue as to the kinds of behavior that depend upon the brain stem comes from the study of the brains of many different species. There are certain parallels between the brains of men and the brains of other vertebrates, but it is invariably the brain stems in which the resemblances are closest. On the general principle that function is reflected in the structure of a mechanism, we are led to guess that the brain stem is involved in rather common vertebrate behaviors.

Of the classes of response thus suggested, postures are prime candidates. Every vertebrate from fish to man comes equipped with top and bottom, and a large share of behavior is devoted merely to keeping topside up. Postures are the starting points for most of our responses, and we tend to take them for granted. However, just to stand is no mean achievement, and it grows

Fig. 19.7 The brains of the codfish, dove, alligator, and dog. All have been drawn to the same size to emphasize the changes in the relative prominence of various brain parts. (After Newman, ed., *The Nature of the World and of Man*)

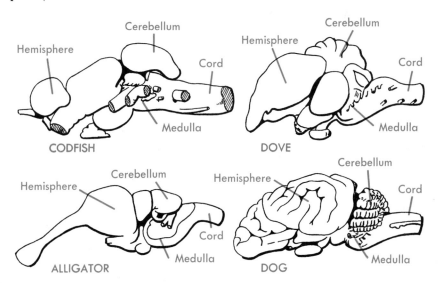

particularly impressive when it is combined with walking, running, jumping, dancing, and the like.

That the ancient brain-stem system is concerned with the integration of postures has been shown in many experimental studies based upon the isolation method. A first observation offered in this proof is a stance produced in mammals when the central nervous system is divided near the middle of the brain stem. A cat so prepared is extremely rigid, demonstrating what has been described as an exaggeration of the standing pattern. The muscles activated are those that counteract the work of gravity upon the body, and these generally, though not exclusively, are muscles that extend the joints.

In itself, this pattern of rigidity does not provide convincing evidence for a richness of detail in the responses integrated by the brain stem. However, we can modify a posture of this sort by certain fairly simple procedures, and the variations indicate a wealth of differentiation of the brain stem. If, for example, we twist the cat's head, its far-sided forelimb relaxes; this is the posture that a normal cat assumes when it turns to look at a mousehole. If, instead, we bend the cat's head downward, both of its forelegs quickly bend; this is the posture of a normal cat when it stoops to look into the mousehole. If we bend the cat's head upward, the opposite relations are produced; the rear legs bend, the forelegs extend, and we have the begging stance.

Some postural responses in man

Lest it be considered that these results apply to cats but not to human beings, we shall next examine the evidence that shows that this is not the case at all. In a human baby, the patterns just described can also be readily evoked, but are full-blown only in the period before the maturation of the newer systems. If, in consequence of accidents in men, the latter systems are destroyed, these reactions once again appear in the form that we see them in the normal infant.

Another interesting example of the kinds of patterns that the brain stem integrates can be seen in infants, six months old, if a toy is held above them. As the infant lifts its head, its arms and legs go upward, just as though the toy were a magnet; in some purely psychological descriptions, this is how the toy has been regarded.[8] That there are simpler ways of looking at this problem

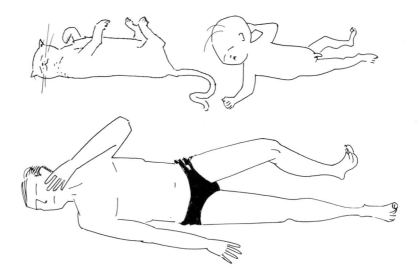

Fig. 19.8 Similarities in postural responses of the brain-stem cat, the human infant, and the adult with damage to the cerebral hemispheres. (After Walshe; Gesell and Armatruda; and McCouch, Deering, and Ling)

is suggested by experiments in which we take away the fore-brain of a cat and put it in the same position. Under these conditions, the cat's limbs are flexed until we bend its head slightly upward; when we do, the hindlegs and forelegs all extend as in "reaching" in the human baby. Further studies show that this phenomenon depends upon receptors in the inner ear; these are stimulated when the cat's head is lifted, or when the baby lifts its head in looking.

Fig. 19.9 Similarities between the reaching pattern of a human infant and the posture assumed by a brain-stem cat when its head is bent upward. (After Gesell and Armatruda; and Bell, Davidson, and Scarborough)

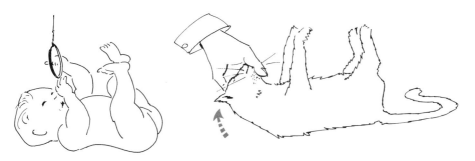

Ultimately, patterns of this kind disappear as the individual develops; for newer mechanisms of the nervous system broaden the control of posture. Then they are elicited only on condition of failure in the newer mechanisms, whether by their loss due to some disease or by circumstances in which the new systems are not stimulated properly. Of the latter, we can cite the pattern of responding that we see when grown human beings are subjected to an unexpected, quick deceleration. This, as we have noted, stimulates receptors in one portion of the inner ear. The result, as when a car has hit an unseen pothole, is for arms and legs to be extended, and, in the legs, this is likely to result in the flooring of the car's accelerator. In the arms, the consequence is poor steering, and at speed this leads to accidents.

But it is uncommon for the mechanisms of posture to fail an organism. Usually they operate reliably, and in a manner suited to the other movements that we organisms make. Here, as in no other area perhaps, vertebrate resemblances are clear; these resemblances apply both to mechanisms and to the behaviors they produce.

BRAIN-STEM MECHANISMS
FOR THE CYCLIC DRIVES

Differentiation of the brain stem, so far as we can judge from structure, reaches a maximum in its upper portions in a region termed the diencephalon. Here, many kinds of observations demonstrate, are centers related to such periodic drive states as hunger and thirst. Eating and drinking, for example, are controlled by stimuli delivered to these zones, and these behaviors can be eliminated by localized destruction of their centers.

The method of selective destruction[9]

We will first consider experiments in which particular centers are removed, for they serve to illustrate some new procedures for studying the central nervous system. One way of localizing mechanisms for a given set of functions is to study the behaviors that remain after systems have been isolated. A second possibility, however, is assessment of the changes that take place in behavior when a given mechanism is selectively destroyed. This approach has been employed extensively in studies of the drive mechanisms, where what has been looked for are behaviors that are lost, rather than behaviors that are spared.

In following this plan, we logically begin by studying the changes in behavior that follow the destruction of particular gray-matter zones or nuclei within the upper brain stem. However, to destroy a tiny group of cells that is buried deep within the brain is not as easy as the isolation or removal of a large neural segment. All too frequently the target is surrounded by unrelated masses of neurons, or even more importantly, will lie adjacent to a mechanism whose destruction could produce the very opposite effect. What we need, accordingly, is some procedure for making highly localized removals; a "magic bullet" as it were, that will hit the target and yet spare the other mechanisms.

Several different methods have been used to solve this problem, including radiation, treatment with ultrasonic waves, and bombardment of the brain with particles from nuclear accelerators. Presently, however, the usual technique utilizes fine electrodes; these are insulated except for their tips, and the tips are driven into buried nuclei with little damage to adjacent structures. Placement is, of course, a blind procedure—the experimenter guides the electrodes by measurements derived from other brains. When the electrode tip is finally in place, a strong electric current is applied, and the neurons near the tip of the wire are coagulated and destroyed.

It is possible, with this technique, to produce a rat, cat, or monkey that will continue to eat until it becomes so fat that it cannot even stand. Alternatively, zones exist in which such destruction leads to quite the opposite result: animals so treated do not eat at all and quickly become emaciated. And, in nearby regions, with this same technique, one can make a preparation that will seem completely normal except for the fact that it will not engage in sexual acts. These profound effects, furthermore, can be produced by extremely small destructions, for rarely does a center related to a pattern extend for more than several millimeters.

689

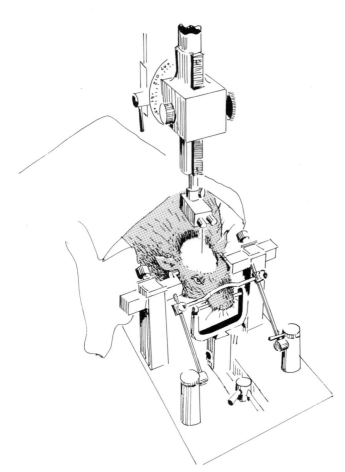

Fig. 19.10 Technique for production of small areas of damage deep within the brain. The head of the anesthetized animal is fixed within a calibrated framework, and the electrode is guided into place by means of calibrated scales. (Courtesy of David Gutzey)

Effects of diencephalic stimulation[10]

Buried electrodes have also been employed for work upon the drive mechanisms in conjunction with instruments for giving weak electric shocks to the centers. The typical effects of such stimuli are the opposite to those of destruction. In experiments conducted by this method, a socket is attached to the electrode, and the socket extends outward from the skull of the preparation. One can then attach a wire to the socket and deliver shocks to the brain while the animal is otherwise behaving in a "natural" situation.

Not only is it possible, with such stimuli, to produce both eating and drinking, but also defecation or urination at the experimenter's whim. But, when defecation is induced in cats, the cat

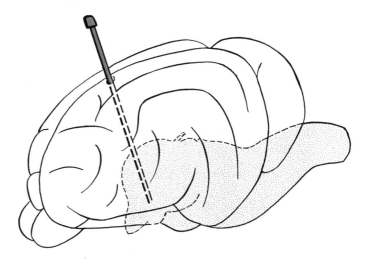

Fig. 19.11 The brain of a cat, with the brain stem shown in red, and with an embedded electrode in the diencephalon. Stimulation in this region through such electrodes can evoke many different states of drive.

may not defecate at once, but rather may first search for a sand box in which to perform the defecation. Similarly, there are zones which, when stimulated, lead a cat to go to sleep—but only after first seeking out a quiet corner and curling up in usual cat fashion.

However remarkable this all may seem, even more striking is the fact that in at least a number of these zones a stimulus can serve to reinforce a habit![11] In such experiments, the experimenter surrenders the "button" to the subject; the animal then can stimulate its brain electrically by pressing on the button. This is done with rats by giving them a lever that controls the stimulator, and it has been shown that with appropriate electrodes rats will press the lever several thousand times an hour. Why this works is still very poorly understood, as the finding is quite recent, but it seems apparent that systems have been tapped which normally operate in learning.

CONTROL OF HUNGER

If we grant that nuclei within the upper brain stem are related to the cyclic drives, there remains the question as to how these centers are controlled in everyday behavior. The pattern that we term "being hungry," for example, seemingly is put together by a group of cells contained within a highly localized portion of the diencephalon. But such patterns must have instigators, and the instigators must precede them; these are the events for which the shocks were substituted in the studies just considered.

If we disregard "specific hungers," cravings for particular foods, and think instead of hunger that might be satisfied by almost any kind of foodstuff, the group of changes that could serve as hunger stimuli is not so large as one might first suppose. Hunger is for most of us a short-term affair, and hence the crucial agent must be something that varies rather markedly within the body within the space of just a few hours. Stores of body fat and protein fluctuate but little within such periods of time, which would seemingly eliminate their levels as directly leading to hunger. But with carbohydrates, particularly sugar, such variations are substantial, and furthermore we store comparatively small amounts of sugar-yielding compounds.

From these facts, our first inclination is to think that hunger comes about when stimuli are somehow triggered off within the body when a certain level of reserves of carbohydrates has been reached. Until recently we thought we had an answer to the question as to what these are—namely, that the stimuli for hunger are produced by patterns of contraction in the stomach. It was then considered that the problem was to find the agent producing the contractions, and eventually the circumstance that led to the production of the agent.

Several flaws have been discovered in this argument, but perhaps the most important flaw has been shown to be related to procedures for measuring stomach contractions. The classic method is to have a subject swallow an inflatable balloon, which is then attached to instruments that measure the pressure of the stomach upon it. The problem with this method is that the balloon affects the behavior of the stomach, with that organ treating it as though it were a regular meal. That this is the case has been shown by measurements of stomachs that have no balloons within them, this being possible because the contractions generate electrical changes which can be recorded from the outer body wall.[12] Unfortunately for the theory just described, the empty stomach does not contract, and hence the crucial stimuli for hunger must be found somewhere else.

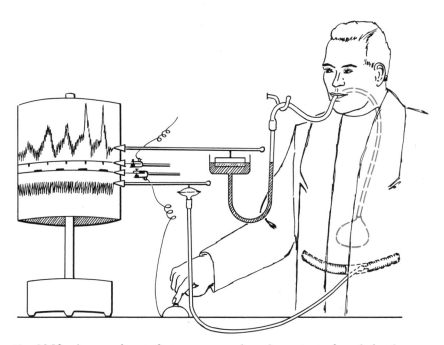

Fig. 19.12 An experiment that was supposed to demonstrate the relation between stomach contractions and the occurrence of hunger pangs. The tube leading into the mouth of the subject is connected with a balloon, as shown in red, and pressure of the stomach upon this balloon moves the upper pen of the recording device. The second pen marks off time intervals; the third is activated when the subject presses a button to signify the occurrence of a hunger pang. Note that hunger pangs occur whenever the balloon is strongly compressed and the upper pen moves up sharply. This effect is not related to respiration, for the fourth pen records such movements and they show no changes. The problem with this method is that the contractions depend upon the presence of a load within the stomach, which in this instance is the balloon with which the contractions are recorded. (After Cannon, *The Wisdom of the Body*)

It is wholly possible that there are no conventional receptors for control of hunger, but that centers in the brain stem are themselves sensitive to changes in the blood that come about through deprivation. Such a mechanism would be a parallel to the way in which carbon dioxide affects the breathing centers of the lower brain stem. According to this concept, the receptor neurons use blood sugar at a rate that is higher than for other groups of neurons, and this rate of usage in its turn depends upon the sugar content of the blood. When the level of the blood sugar falls, these neurons are the first to starve, and in being starved, release their normal braking action upon the "hunger centers."

The most important evidence for this assumption comes from experiments in which toxic compounds have been made of sugar, gold, and sulfur.[13] Such compounds are taken up by cells, which are thereafter poisoned by them. By feeding the compound, we can thus determine which cells in the brain die first, and hence which cells normally use sugar at high rates. Now, it has been shown that the giving of this compound to rats makes the rats extremely hungry, and that the areas destroyed by the compound are identical to those whose destruction by the passage of electrical current yields the overeating pattern. We deduce from this that the central mechanisms have their own receptors for sugar, and that an important natural control of the process of eating is the rate at which these receptors take their sugar from the blood.

CONTROL OF THIRST

The success of this analysis should lead us to wonder if some similar events underlie control of brain-stem mechanisms for drinking. For thirst, as for hunger, past emphases have been upon peripheral events, notably the dryness of the throat that comes about when we are deprived of water. As it has been pictured, thirst arises first because the cells of salivary glands become unable to maintain the throat membranes in their normal moist condition. These glands, in turn, are rendered inoperative because their source of water is in the blood, and blood presumably becomes less liquid as the body loses water.

All of these events have actually been shown to follow deprivation of fluids, and doubtlessly the dryness of the throat does constitute a source of stimuli for thirst. However, merely wetting down the throat does not suffice to eliminate all thirst, and the question then is one of what mechanisms supplement this signaling event.

Some means of instigating thirst

The first requirement for experiments designed to answer questions of this kind is some sort of method for inducing thirst at any time we please. Psychologists employ the "natural" procedure in most of their experiments; that is, they remove the animals from water for a certain period of time. However, there are other ways of generating thirst, and one way is to introduce solutions of salt into the circulating blood.[14] As the salt circulates, cells along the route lose their water to the blood, and are thus subjected to a set of circumstances which would also come from water loss.

A disadvantage of this general procedure is that the blood goes everywhere, and thus that every cell in the body can be thought of as a potential thirst-receptor. The question, then, is whether we can work out some technique for showing that certain body cells are much more sensitive to losses of their water than are the body cells at large. Very recently, this problem has been solved by the development of methods which permit us to inject small quantities of fluids into quite specific zones. These are in such quantities that were they to be mixed with and diluted by the blood, the effect of their injection would be negligible. However, if these quantities are given through a needle with its tip exactly where we want it, they are then effective and also localized stimuli.

The methods for implanting needles of this kind are the same as those for electrodes: The needles are placed in a calibrated framework, and then driven into the brain by means of scales attached to the framework. Now, if this is done so that the needle goes into the diencephalon, places can be found where injections of salt will promptly cause an animal to drink. Under such a stimulus, the animal imbibes enormous quantities of water, and the place in which the injection is effective is the place whose localized destruction will inhibit drinking behavior.[15]

MULTIPLE CONTROL OF CYCLIC DRIVES

This apparent proof that the thirst centers are, like those for hunger, susceptible to changes in the blood that bathes them is a most dramatic finding. But the fact remains that, as a general principle, behavior mechanisms are subject to multiple control. This was shown to be particularly true for the mechanisms of breathing, and experiments confirm it in the instance of drinking. Thus, for example, if one induces thirst by passing salt solutions into blood, the drinking that results can sometimes be suppressed by water put into the stomach. While it might appear that all that this implies is that needs have come and gone, it is also true that the suppression may result from loading of the stomach with a blown-up rubber balloon. That the suppression is achieved by stimulation of receptors is suggested further by the fact that drugs applied to the stomach will abolish this effect.[16]

Sexual behaviors provide us with another illustration. First, these behaviors, as thirst or hunger do, vary with the status of the blood, and it can be shown that there are sexual mechanisms sensitive to circulating agents. The proof of this assertion involves the introduction of needles into upper brain stem systems, and their use for the administration of small amounts of sexual hormones. There, in such small quantities that they would lack effects if given directly into blood, the hormones alter sexually related behaviors in a thoroughgoing manner. It is even possible, by this procedure, to induce a sturdy male rat to engage in such domestic femininities as building nests and herding young.[17]

But the sexual hormones have other roles as well, each related to the mating process. One such role is the maintenance,

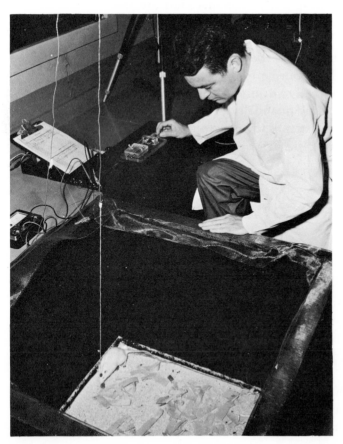

Fig. 19.13 In these experiments, a hypodermic needle is embedded in the diencephalon. One of the female sex hormones is then injected into the region. Such a stimulus leads the rat—a male—to build a nest and take care of newly born rats.

as shown in an experiment with rats,[18] of the receptors that endow the genitals with their sensitivity. Another is the role of these hormones in control of the development of body characteristics that encourage courtship and mating in a sexual partner. Finally, control of sexual behavior is, in human beings at least, subject to important social values that determine what is beautiful and what is proper.

PROSPECTUS

One does not exhaust the problems posed by hunger, thirst, and sexual behavior by showing that the brain stem contains mechanisms for integration of these patterns. Nor is it enough to demonstrate the simpler mechanisms of control. All of these are basic to behavior of men, but also that of vertebrates in general; what we have as yet to consider are the differences between us and the lower organisms.

We have talked of patterns of behavior that depend upon these mechanisms of behavior as differentiations of the waking state. But behavior obviously can be split into a vastly greater number of patterns. Such further differentiation is the function of the newer systems of the brain, and it is to these that we must turn at last as we conclude this section of the book.

REFERENCES

[1] Manaceine, M. de. *Sleep*, Scott, 1897, Chapter 1.

[2] Bremer, F. *Some Problems in Neurophysiology*, Athlone Press, 1953, Chapter 2.

[3] Kleitman, N. *Sleep and Wakefulness*, Univ. of Chicago, 1939.

[4] Gardner, E. *Fundamentals of Neurology*, Saunders, 1958, Chapters 11 and 12.

[5] Magoun, H. W. *The waking brain*, Thomas, 1958.

[6] Lindsley, D. B. In Stevens, S. S., *Handbook of Experimental Psychology*, Wiley, 1951, Chapter 14.

[7] Walsh, E. G. *Physiology of the Nervous System*, Longmans, 1957, Chapter 5.

[8] Lewin, K. *Dynamic Theory of Personality*, McGraw-Hill, 1935, Chapter 3.

[9] Stellar, E. The physiology of motivation, *Psychol. Rev.*, 1954, *61*, 5-22.

[10] Hess, W. R. *The Functional Organization of the Diencephalon*, Grune, 1957.

[11] Olds, J. Self-stimulation of the

brain, *Science*, 1958, *127*, 315-324.

[12] Davis, R. C., Garafolo, L., and Kveim, K. Conditions associated with gastrointestinal activity, *J. comp. physiol. Psychol.*, 1959, *52*, 466-475.

[13] Anliker, J., and Mayer, J. The regulation of food intake, *Am. J. Clin. Nutrition*, 1957, *5*, 148-153.

[14] Wayner, M. J., and Reimanis, G. Drinking in the rat induced by hypertonic saline, *J. comp. physiol. Psychol.*, 1959, *51*, 11-15.

[15] Andersson, B. The effect of injections of hypertonic NaCL solutions into different parts of the hypothalamus of goats, *Acta Physiol. Scand.*, 1953, *28*, 188-201.

[16] Montgomery, A. V., and Holmes, J. H. Gastric inhibition of the drinking response, *Am. J. Physiol.*, 1955, *182*, 227-231.

[17] Fisher, A. E. Maternal and sexual behavior induced by intracranial chemical stimulation, *Science*, 1956, *124*, 228-229.

[18] Beach, F. A., and Levinson, G. Effects of androgen on the glans penis and mating behavior of castrated male rats, *J. exp. Zool.*, 1950, *114*, 159-171.

Chapter Twenty

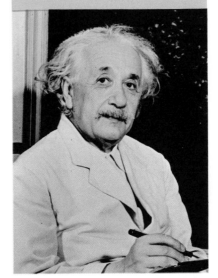

THE
CEREBRAL
CORTEX
AND
COMPLEX PROCESSES

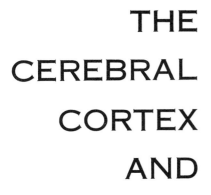

IN THOSE ANIMALS WHOSE PATTERNS of behavior are most similar to man's, enlargement of the forebrain is the most conspicuous of changes in structural endowment. It is no small wonder, then, that when we make assessments of our evolutionary gifts, a first place is given to these massive central neural networks. Man is not particularly favored in the kingdom with respect to eyes, ears, or muscles: birds see better, cats hear more, and elephants and whales are stronger. We are nonetheless the rulers of the earth, and because our forebrains make us so: in the last analysis, our very culture rests upon the workings of a three-pound organ.

699

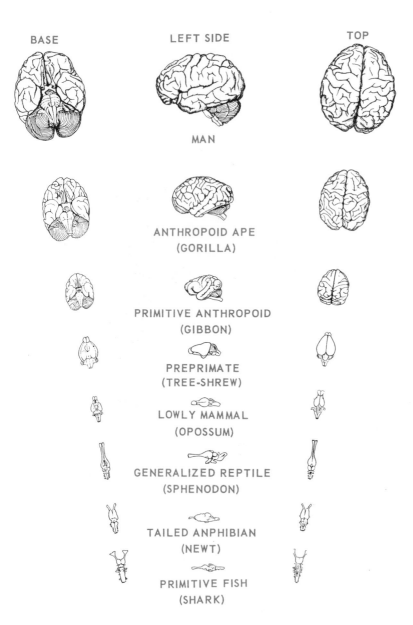

BASE LEFT SIDE TOP

MAN

ANTHROPOID APE
(GORILLA)

PRIMITIVE ANTHROPOID
(GIBBON)

PREPRIMATE
(TREE-SHREW)

LOWLY MAMMAL
(OPOSSUM)

GENERALIZED REPTILE
(SPHENODON)

TAILED ANPHIBIAN
(NEWT)

PRIMITIVE FISH
(SHARK)

Fig. 20.1 The growth of the brain from fish to man, showing the notable development of the cerebral hemispheres. (Courtesy American Museum of Natural History)

The cerebral hemispheres are not at all new, and even the lowly fishes have them. It is in their cortex or covering that the greatest growth has taken place, and this development is important only in the mammals. Reptiles have some of the new cortex, but the birds have virtually none; why the course of evolution went this way is largely a speculative matter.

THE ANCIENT FOREBRAIN AND

EMOTIONAL BEHAVIOR

In such simple forms as frogs and salamanders, the hemispheres appear to be involved in those behavior patterns to which odors make important contributions. Such functions seemingly are still related to the older portions of the human brain. In the human hemispheres, these are congregated in the region of the base, and are wholly overlain by the larger, newer forebrain mechanisms.

In relatively recent years, our concept of the functions of these portions of the forebrain has been broadened quite substantially by proofs of their involvement in the behaviors that we term emotional.[1] The story begins with experiments that showed that angry behavior in the cat—hissing, striking, arching of the back, and elevation of the hair—depends for its appearance upon the integrity of the upper brain stem mechanisms. A cat that lacks its diencephalon may give us any one of these component patterns, but never does one see in such a preparation the pattern of anger as a whole. Further, in an animal that lacks the whole forebrain, but whose upper brain stem is intact, angry behavior can be elicited by seemingly trivial events. Merely touching such a cat will lead to a behavioral explosion, but fortunately for experimenters, these attacks are not well-directed.[2]

The neocortex and placidity

A reasonable conclusion to be drawn from this result is that the forebrain holds in check the violent emotional behavior patterns that are put together by the brain stem. Thus, when the forebrain is surgically removed, so are mechanisms of restraint, and—in addition—the devices that direct the pattern of angry behavior. This is an attractive viewpoint. Presumably, the networks of the forebrain are there to broaden the controls upon behavior, and the experiment appears to show that such controls are readily removed.

701

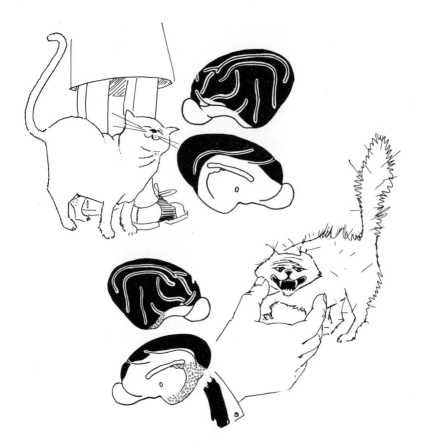

Fig. 20.2 Removal of the newer portions of the cortex yields a placid cat, but further removal of the older portions changes the state to savageness. (After Bard and Mountcastle)

Considered as an outline, the viewpoint thus expressed still seems substantially correct. But the fact that there is both an old and new division of the hemispheres of mammals leads us to inquire as to their separable roles in integrating patterns of emotional response. The newest tissue, or the neocortex, is in a position that makes it fairly easy for a surgeon to remove it, and yet not damage the older forebrain mechanisms. But when this is done, again with cats as subjects, the effect upon behavior proves to be entirely different from complete removal of the cerebral hemispheres. Now the cat, instead of being very fierce indeed, is actually a placid creature; one can handle such a preparation very roughly, yet it does not seem to mind at all.[3]

This result suggests that the neocortex, rather than suppressing anger, actually contributes to the angry behavior of the normal animal. We are left, accordingly, to wonder why removal of the whole forebrain leads to anger, and the suggestion is that older forebrain systems serve the role of checkreins. To show that this is so, we have merely to destroy certain portions of the older system, and when this is done the animal becomes a most unpleasant cat to be around. With little provocation, it will spit, snarl, and strike, and its aim is now unerring—to handle it, experimenters have to wear very heavy pairs of gauntlets. It is thus apparent that the older forebrain has the role suggested for it, and that its operations generally are different from those of neocortex.

SOME MECHANISMS OF THE NEOCORTEX

The foregoing studies have yielded us some facts of fairly general consequence. They show that the forebrain has separable systems with very different modes of operation, and it thus becomes of interest to inquire as to whether such a parcellation can be carried any further. Are we, for example, to regard the neocortex as a unitary organ, or is it an aggregate of separable organs—each with very special functions?

A superficial study of the human neocortex yields but little evidence in favor of its being differentiated into organs. To the naked eye, all of it seems very much alike. There is, of course, a folding of its surface which produces many different cortical zones, but within each zone the tissue looks alike, and many of the folds are variable. On the outer surface there are, nonetheless, two folds that are notably constant, and these folds are one criterion by which the hemispheres can be subdivided. These are the lateral and central fissures, and the subdivisions of the cortex are termed the frontal, parietal, temporal, and occipital lobes.

This parcellation can be carried further, but we need the microscope to do it. It then becomes apparent that the neocortex differs greatly in the different regions. Not only does it differ in its thickness, but also in the types and numbers of the neurons it contains. Furthermore, the different zones mature at different times, with some being nearly so at birth; others continue to develop even after we are in our teens. Such observations favor the concept of an aggregate of organs, but are not themselves sufficient proof of functional differentiation.

703

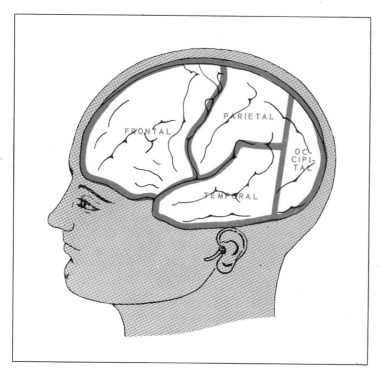

Fig. 20.3 The major subdivisions, or lobes, of the cerebral hemisphere of man. Except for the boundaries between the frontal and the parietal and temporal lobes, these division lines are somewhat arbitrary.

Fig. 20.4 The maturation of various regions of the cerebral hemisphere. The areas shown in red are the first to develop and include the well-known sensory and motor regions. The unshaded areas are the slowest to mature, and the shaded regions mature after the red but before the unshaded areas. (After Bailey and Bonin, *The Isocortex of Man*)

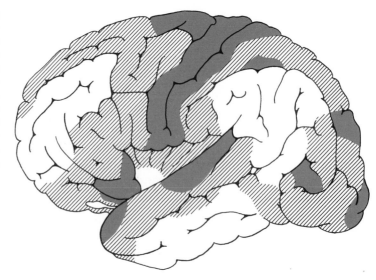

Effects of stimulation of the neocortex[4]

Fortunately, we can supplement the charts obtained through anatomical studies with certain observations of the consequences of local stimulation of the brain. This is now a routine procedure in the course of human brain surgery, and is of particular significance because the operations can often be conducted with patients under local anesthetics. The tissue of the brain itself is insensitive, and can thus be cut into and handled by the surgeon with no painful consequences. Accordingly, so long as the scalp, the skull, and the membranes of the brain are narcotized, the brain can be exposed and explored with electrodes while the patient is awake.

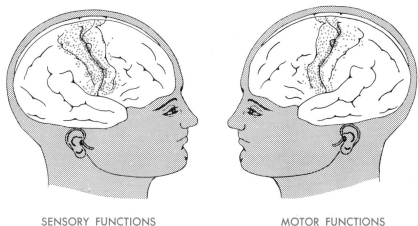

SENSORY FUNCTIONS   MOTOR FUNCTIONS

Fig. 20.5 The principal motor region of the brain, and the corresponding sensory region. The density of points reflects the prominence of each brain region in sensory or motor functions. (After Penfield and Rasmussen, *The Cerebral Cortex of Man*)

One of the first observations of this kind led to the identification of a region which, when lightly stimulated, yields movements of the body. This zone is mainly concentrated in the region of the central fissure, and the movements are most readily obtained when the electrode is applied to the fissure's forward bank. Twists of the wrist, flexions of the elbow—even simple vocalizations—are readily produced and reproduced by the activation of this zone. The zone, accordingly, is termed the motor cortex, which is not completely accurate; actually, within it, there are several motor systems, rather than a single mechanism.

If, alternatively, one applies a current to the fissure's rearward bank, movement may result, but it is much more likely that the patient will report a feeling localized somewhere in his body. This may be a numbness, a tingling, or a "feeling of electricity," and this feeling generally occurs in definite relation to the zone being stimulated. The higher on the brain, the lower on the body is the rule in such results, and a very similar relationship exists for motor cortex movements as well.

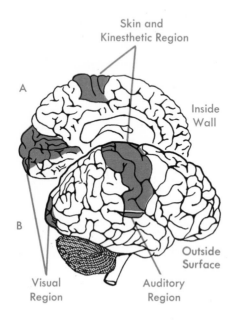

Skin and
Kinesthetic Region

A

Inside
Wall

B

Outside
Surface

Visual
Region

Auditory
Region

Fig. 20.6 Principal sensory regions of the human cerebral cortex. The right half of the brain has been displaced downward and to the right so that the inside wall of the left hemisphere can be seen. (After Dashiell, *Fundamentals of General Psychology*)

Corresponding areas for vision and hearing have also been identified. The area for vision is in the rearmost portion of the brain, and yields flashing lights, stars, and pinwheels when the stimulator is applied. The region for hearing, where a stimulus produces clicks and buzzes and noises, lies along the upper margins of the temporal lobes of the cerebral hemispheres. There is also an area for taste, but it is not upon the outer surface; rather, it is in a region of the cortex deep within the lateral fissure.

If we next examine these results in relation to the developmental chart, it becomes apparent that the regions correspond to the areas that first mature during individual growth. Once again, our working rule that structure and function go together has been verified, for where the brain differs in the way that it is built, it differs in the functions it performs. Furthermore, at least for simple forms of sensing, the cortex has specific zones, and the segregation of these zones parallels the segregation of our senses.

CEREBRAL FACTORS IN DISCRIMINATION

One of the outstanding common properties of sensory and motor regions is that the receptor and effector organs served are represented disproportionately. Thus, for example, in the major motor region bordering the central fissure, the area from which a movement of the fingers is produced by stimulating currents is as great or greater than the area supplying the entire trunk musculature. Similarly, what we term the face area is larger than that

Fig. 20.7 Spatial organization of the motor cortex. The parts of the manikin represent the body parts that move in response to stimulation of the corresponding motor areas. (After Penfield and Rasmussen, *The Cerebral Cortex of Man*)

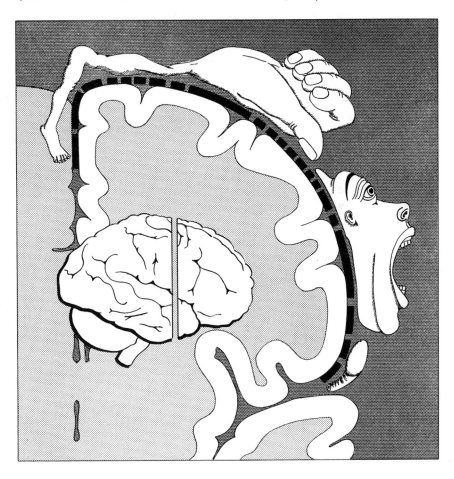

for legs and feet, and the tongue region by itself is much greater in extent than the zone for the arm.

Our problem now is one of trying to assess the meaning of such differences for movements as we see them in the behaving organism. One very obvious relation is that those portions of the body which engage in the most delicate of actions are the ones that have the largest motor regions in the cerebral cortex. In other words, the muscles with the smallest motor units have the largest central mechanisms, and we thus think of the expansion as a means for keeping motor pathways separated.

Relations of brain emphasis to sensory acuity[5]

Such a supposition has a parallel in terms of sensory discriminations, particularly for those processes in which the spatial arrangements of the receptors are important. As an example, we have seen that our ability to tell where we are touched upon our skins depends upon the fact that such stimuli produce conduction in particular neurons in the nerves connected with this great sense organ. If we now determine how accurately such discriminations

Fig. 20.8 Regional variations in the spatial acuity of the body surface as measured by the two-point method. (From Stevens, *Handbook of Experimental Psychology*)

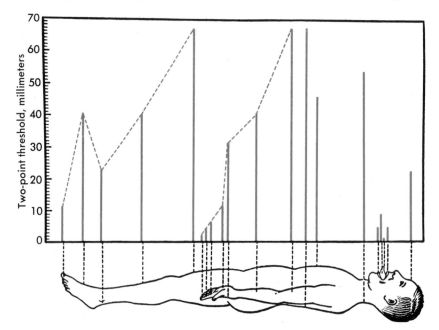

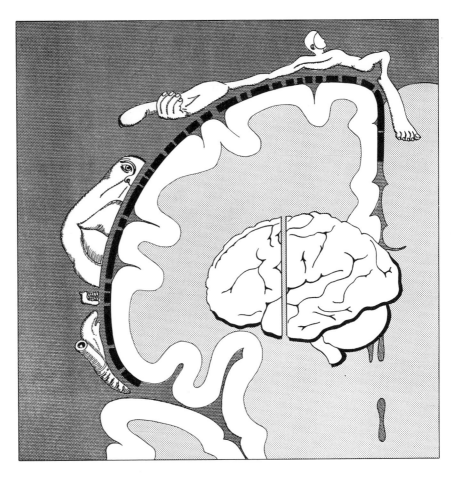

Fig. 20.9 Functional chart of the skin sensory area in the cerebral cortex. The inset shows the approximate location of the plane in the brain. (After Penfield and Rasmussen, *The Cerebral Cortex of Man*)

can be made—this is done by measuring how far apart two pinpoint contacts to the skin must be in order to be sensed differently from one—the resulting data show that surfaces may differ ten-fold in their acuity. Tongues, lips, and fingertips are the most acute, and the back and thighs the least.

If we next examine the brain region which, when stimulated, yields sensations in the skin, these variations in acuity can be related to the sizes of the regions devoted to the different surfaces. Experiments have further shown that areas for hearing and vision in the cerebral cortex contain very similar distortions which, again, can be related to acuity of spatial discriminations in these

709

senses. For the one, of course, such discriminations are those of patterned light stimuli, and these discriminations are best when light patterns fall upon the retinal regions that are relatively favored in the brain. For the other, such discriminations are of pitch, and vary with the frequencies involved, and pitch perception generally is best for stimuli that affect those portions of the cochlear partition for which the brain areas are largest.

Central mechanisms of quality and quantity[6]

That we have these parallels between the spatial layouts of brain regions and their sense organs leads us to wonder whether we can also find arrangements that can be related to the fact that we are able to make intensitive and qualitative stimulus judgments. Relatively speaking, these arrangements are but poorly understood, though in recent years there have been notable advances in the general area. These advances are, in turn, related to successes in the development of methods by which it is possible to make recordings from individual neurons in the cortex. This achievement is best appreciated if we consider that the brain is filled with blood vessels and can thus be jarred with each and every beat of the heart. Hence, it is essential that the method for recording be such that these pulses are abated, which they are so long as the skull cavity is maintained as one closed box. The technique, then, is to insert a fine electrode through a plugged opening in the skull, and under these conditions, the single elements "stay put" while the measurements are made.

In one experiment, responses were obtained from individual neurons in a region in the cat brain corresponding to the area that lies just behind the central fissure of the human brain. The stimuli included movements of hairs, pressure applied to the skin, and deformation of the deep tissues lying underneath the skin. In the vast majority of instances, individual neurons would be fired by one, and only one kind of stimulus. It was noted also that if an electrode encountered a neuron of a given type near the surface of the cortex, neurons of this same type were also encountered as the electrode was pushed into the deeper layers. These results indicate that each of the three classes of stimuli affect central neurons which, for each stimulus, occupy a tiny vertical cylinder of cortex. The cylinders for different stimuli are intermixed with one another, and, of course, vary in position with

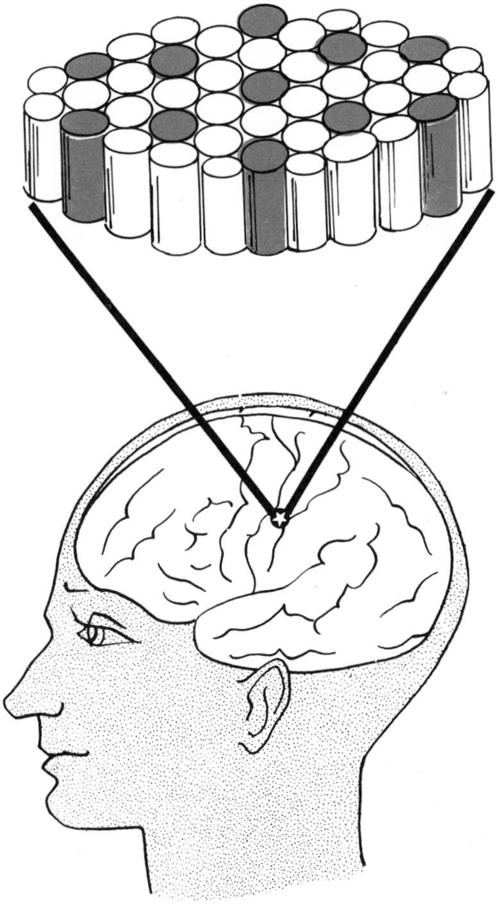

Fig. 20.10 Presumptive arrangement of neurons related to qualitatively different skin receptors in man. Within this tiny area, which we know to be primarily concerned with the thumb, qualitatively specific neurons are probably disposed as shown above.

respect to the related body part. Thus, instead of brains containing separate areas for qualities within modalities, the areas for major sense organs have internal qualitative differentiation.

At this writing, it has not yet been determined whether there are cortical neurons related to the different colors that we see. However, measurements are now available from cells that occupy the last synaptic station in the visual pathways prior to the cortex itself.[7] Of several results obtained with this technique, possibly the most fascinating is the fact that there are cells which prove to be selectively responsive to stimuli delivered to the eye that fall within the "yellow" portion of the visual spectrum. Thus, although the pigments of the retinal cones are not what one expects them to be from the primacy of red, yellow, green, and blue as colors in the band of the rainbow, the action of the neurons is. How it is that this occurs is not yet settled, although there are two interpretations: one is that at least some cones contain a pigment mixture, and that those for "yellow" have both the "red" and "green" pigments. Another possibility, and a bit more likely, is that the "yellow" cells are fed by systems that, within the eye, begin with separate "red" and "green" receptors.

The individual neurons studied by this method indicate their sensitivities by the rates at which they discharge their separate messages. This implies that, centrally, a similar device to that observed in nerves is used to represent the quantity of stimulation. Further, it appears that the other rule—that strong stimuli excite a larger number of neurons—equally applies to cells within the sensory regions of the brain. If, for example, a weak stimulus is applied to some sense organ, the brain area from which electrical changes are recorded is comparatively small. However, the area markedly expands when the stimulus is strong, and very strong stimuli may activate virtually the whole mechanism. Here, again, is evidence that our discriminations rest importantly upon the relative degrees to which receptive systems are excited. What is true for sense organs thus seems to be a characteristic of the whole of any given sensory mechanism.

ASSOCIATIVE MECHANISMS OF
THE NEOCORTEX

Sensory and motor zones, as we have now defined them, take up comparatively little of the neocortex of the human brain. This is not the case with other animals, particularly the lower mammals, but to show that this is so requires further methods that have not as yet been considered. There is no particular experimental problem so far as motor functions go; we can study animals in much the same manner as we have already studied men. But sensory functions are another matter, for we have to find a substitute for those most convenient verbal skills that only human patients can command.

One way of solving this dilemma is to train the animals in some performance, and then to make performance depend upon discrimination of a given stimulus. After this is done, a region of the brain can be removed, and a test given to the animals to see if the performance has been lost. This has been a widely used procedure, but it has a bootstrap quality: not only is the test being used to find the zone, but also to assess its functions.

An excellent alternative is provided by the method of evoked potentials.[8] This is the method that we first encountered in studies of the problem of sensory encoding in individual neural elements. Even when an animal is under anesthesia, we observe electrical changes in its cortex if and when a stimulus is applied to one or another of its major sense organs. It has thus been possible to work out charts of the brains of many different species, and to show what regions in their brains correspond to our own sensory and motor regions. If this is done in rats, we find that almost all the neocortex is devoted to them; in the cat and monkey, on the other hand, there is neocortex in excess. In the human brain, the latter kind of cortex is clearly the most dominant feature, and it would seem, accordingly, that man's superiority can be related to the fact that so much of the human neocortex is devoted to these extrasensory zones.

Fig. 20.11 The growth of the associative regions. The brains are all drawn to the same size to emphasize the comparative developments. Sensory and motor regions are shown in red, associative regions in white. The areas of the brain that are shaded are not cerebral cortex. (Courtesy C. N. Woolsey)

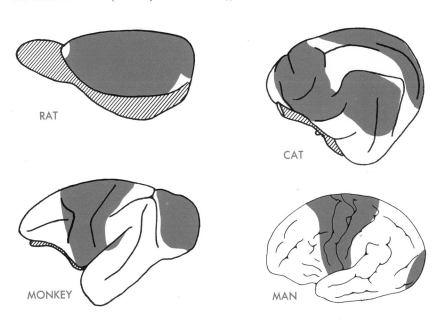

RAT

CAT

MONKEY

MAN

General characteristics of associative cortex

Quite a variety of names have been applied to these special regions of the cortex. Sometimes they are termed associative because of certain theories that presume that they perform synthetic integrative functions. Sometimes they are called intrinsic regions, and this is because they lack direct connecting pathways with receptor and effector mechanisms. In the past, the regions were termed the silent zones, for early workers in the field had failed to find the stimulation method as effective here as with the sensory and motor areas.

That these zones indeed contain specific mechanisms for extremely complex behaviors was initially suggested by the study of brain-damaged patients. An early observation of this kind indicated that, within the left frontal lobe, there exists a region crucially involved in speech. If it is destroyed, behavior is impaired, and quite specifically impaired: a person with this handicap may thus understand what he reads as well as anyone, and yet have a speaking vocabulary of no more than several words.

Fig. 20.12 Location of a region known to be involved in speech. Note that the area is outside the sensory-motor cortex but is near a region from which a stimulus will elicit vocalization. (After Penfield and Rasmussen, *The Cerebral Cortex of Man*)

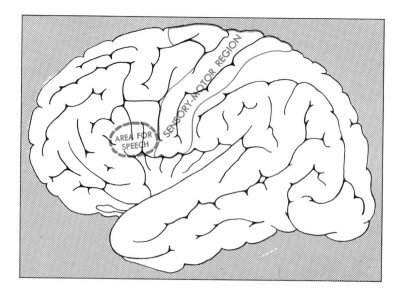

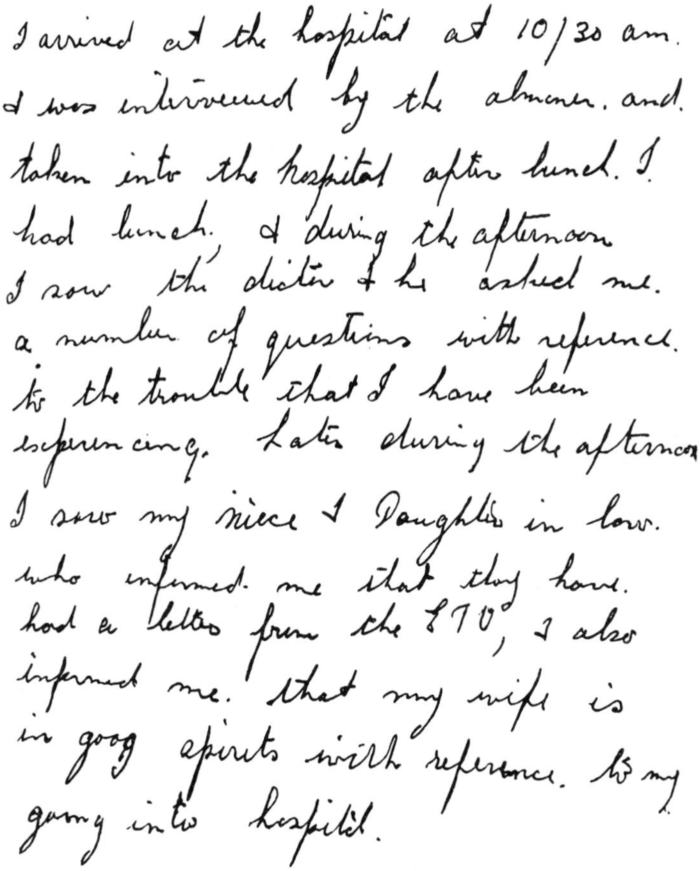

Fig. 20.13 This manuscript was written by a patient with a tumor in the left temporal-occipital region of the cerebral cortex. However, he was then unable to read what he had written. (From Critchley, *The Parietal Lobes*)

I arrived at the hospital at 10/30 am. I was interviewed by the almoner, and taken into the hospital after lunch. I had lunch, & during the afternoon I saw the doctor & he asked me a number of questions with reference to the trouble that I have been experiencing. Later during the afternoon I saw my niece & Daughter in law who informed me that they have had a letter from the £70, I also informed me that my wife is in good spirits with reference to my going into hospital.

This conclusion is supported by results obtained from special applications of the technique of stimulation during human brain surgery.[9] Even though a shock to associative centers usually does not produce responses, such a treatment seemingly impairs or blocks the normal operations of these systems. Thus, if a shock is applied to the region whose destruction gives impairment of speech, the talking patient slows down and stops no matter how the surgeon may urge him to continue in this way. Then, if asked later why he failed to do so, the patient replies that he could not —somehow the shock had "paralyzed his mouth" and left him unable to control his vocal cords.

Associative cortex, language, and learning

Such observations are but two of many which suggest that there is quite substantial differentiation of associative regions for

715

the complex integrative functions. These bits of evidence also indicate a number of the ways in which the systems are concerned with varying aspects of language and communicative behavior. As an example, there are instances in which patients suffering from brain damage in the regions behind the motor systems of the cortex seemingly have problems that are more receptive than expressive. Such a patient thus might be able to write a quite coherent paragraph, and then be unable to recognize the very words that he had written.[10]

Something very similar to this can also be produced by blocking stimulation; a waking patient treated in this manner can still talk, but is likely to use the wrong words in naming very common objects. If shown a hammer, he may call it something else, know that he is wrong, and be quite unable to correct it. These are clearly not simple functions, but rather are encroaching upon the types of learned behaviors that particularly distinguish human beings from their lower animal brethren.[11]

Fig. 20.14 At the points marked in red, a blocking stimulus interferes with the naming of objects. Thus, a patient shown a picture of a foot may say, "What you put in your shoes." (After Robb, *Res. Pub. Ment. Nerv. Dis., 27,* 1948)

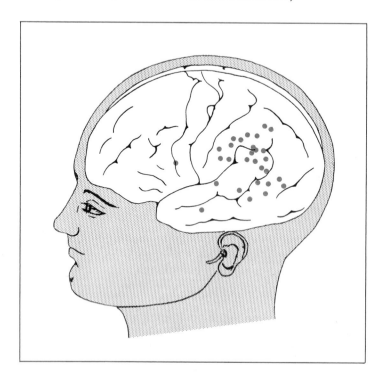

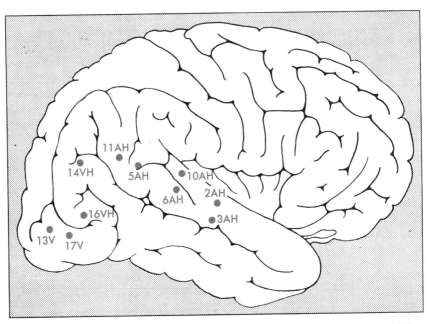

Fig. 20.15 In this diagram the symbol *V* indicates a simple visual response, *VH* a visual hallucination, and *AH* an auditory hallucination. The differences are best illustrated by several of the patient's responses to stimulation, which were as follows: *2AH*: "A lot of people shouting at me." *3AH*: "Yelling at me for doing something wrong." *3AH* (restimulated): "Everybody is yelling again. It is mostly my family. I can hear my mother and brothers." *11AH*: "Yelling." *16VH*: "I saw someone coming toward me as though he was going to hit me." The other *AH* areas produced similarly detailed responses. In contrast with the complexity of the foregoing replies, when the patient's visual area was stimulated (*13V* and *17V*) he stated that he saw "colored stars." (After Penfield and Erickson, *Epilepsy and Cerebral Localization*)

That regions between the motor, visual, and auditory areas are involved in some manner yet to be explained in processes of learning and retention, is indicated in an even more striking manner by results obtained with stimuli applied to these regions in the brains of patients suffering from epilepsy. Such stimuli produce hallucinations, usually extremely vivid ones, that the patient recognizes as an event that has occurred at some time in the past. These are sometimes visual, sometimes auditory, and upon occasion both, and the probability that visual or auditory modes will be produced depends upon just where the stimulus has been delivered to the patient's brain. In the regions bordering the visual cortex, visual responses are obtained; auditory images appear most often if the shock is given further forward.

Such results have many implications, and not only for the way in which we think of the brain as being put together. These

717

hallucinations are so vivid, for example, as to be a kind of evidence in favor of the notion that forgetting stems from interference. It has been suggested that within our heads are records, in magnificent detail, of everything that we have ever seen, heard, or felt from the day that we were born. How this is possible escapes us, but that it is possible is clear, and it is also clear that with a very simple stimulus—at times—samples can be taken from the record.

MECHANISMS OF HIGHEST-LEVEL

INTEGRATION

It must now be clear that we cannot think of the neocortex as a mass that works as a whole. We have found that it performs some quite specific functions in its different regions. But, in view of this, we must ask another question that would not concern us otherwise: if the brain is segregated into many parts, what ties the brain back together?

Many different concepts have been advanced as solutions to the problem. Each have their merits, but none appears to be an ultimate solution. One such view is that the neocortex, in addition to its parcellation, also has a common mode of operation in its many different regions. From another viewpoint, synthesis is by special synthesizing organs, and in human brains the vast frontal lobes have been said to do this work. It has also been proposed that synthesis is performed by the fibers of the central core, and lastly, that the brain stem mechanisms serve the final integrative function.

An experimental approach to integration

There are ways of testing these ideas, and one of them will serve as a general introduction to the kinds of methods and problems that have been used. Let us first suppose that we are interested in a simple human performance: a light comes on, and when it does, the subject responds by pressing quickly on a key. Sometimes this reaction must be made with one hand, and sometimes with the other hand, and the measure that we take of the behavior is the time required for the reaction. All of this seems perfectly straightforward, and surely here at least we should be able, more or less, to specify the series of events that will occur between the stimulus and the response.

There are complications in the layouts of the systems that will be involved in these responses that make such performances particularly relevant to studies of the integrative process. Let us first consider the details of the relations between the eyes and visual areas. As the fibers of the visual nerves come backward after exit from the eyeball, they are grouped together in a most extraordinary manner. Half of the fibers from each retina come together in a single bundle, and thereafter make connections only with a single cerebral hemisphere. A given visual area can thus be seen to be concerned with visual stimuli that fall in one or the other half of the external visual field. If, indeed, the left visual cortex is removed, a patient will see nothing to his right, and the converse finding appears when the right visual region is destroyed.

There is a similar, though not so complete, laterality in motor systems. For such a movement as pressing a key, the right hand is primarily controlled by the region found within the left side of the brain. Thus, if the signal light is to the right, and the reaction with the right hand, most of the events presumably go on within the left cerebral hemisphere. If, however, the signal light

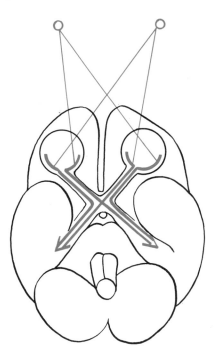

Fig. 20.16 The brain from its base, showing the arrangements of the fibers from the right and left eyes. Near the center, the two visual nerves come together to form a structure that is termed the optic chiasm and within it fibers from half the retinas of both of the eyes commingle to form the visual tracts. Note that the fibers from the left half-retinas proceed to the left hemisphere, and that the fibers from right half-retinas proceed to the right hemisphere.

is moved, or the other hand is used, the pathways presumably involve both hemispheres rather than a single hemisphere. Hence the problem raised is one of understanding how the hemispheres are linked together, since such linkages must surely be established somewhere in the central nervous system.

Now, a likely candidate for this kind of linkage is an enormous band of fibers which passes directly between the right and left hemispheres. This is termed the corpus callosum, and, in certain surgical procedures on humans, the corpus callosum has been severed. By studying patients both before and after brain operations of this kind, we can perform an experiment suggested by the previous discussion. Same-side reactions should not be affected by destruction of the band of fibers, but the crossed reactions should —that is, they should if the fibers of the corpus callosum are involved in the performance. Such a study has been done, and with

Fig. 20.17 These two diagrams illustrate the pathways hypothetically involved in a crossed (right) and an uncrossed (left) response to a visual stimulus. Note that in the crossed, but not the uncrossed, situation, both hemispheres presumably participate in the integrative process. In the crossed reaction, the normal time required is a few milliseconds longer than in the uncrossed reaction. If the differences were due to the inclusion of pathways passing through the corpus callosum in the crossed situation, we would expect the difference to increase with the cutting of these fibers.

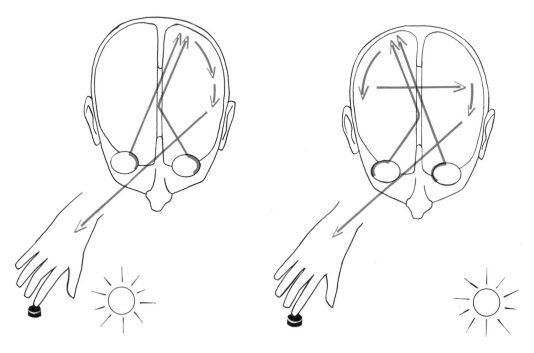

negative results; it makes no difference whether the reaction is a crossed or uncrossed reaction.[12]

The "vertical" theory of brain integration[13]

This result is very serious for one concept of synthetic processes, namely that which puts the burden on the fibers that we find within the hemispheres. And, indirectly, it supports that view that vertical connections are important, for after we have cut the corpus callosum, there is almost nothing left to link the hemispheres until we reach the level of the brain stem. Here the hypothetical communicative channels might be something like the following. Visual stimulation is transmitted upward to the visual areas, and perhaps initiates events in the adjacent portions of associative cortex. Then, from both regions, signals travel downward to the region of the brain stem, where they are mixed with signals that define the "test situation." Then, from the brain stem downward go the signals that accomplish postural adjustments, and upward "arousal" and specific motor signals, the latter triggering the motor cortex. This arrangement clearly gets around the problem that had been previously raised, and also fits in well with many different kinds of evidence on brain-stem functions.

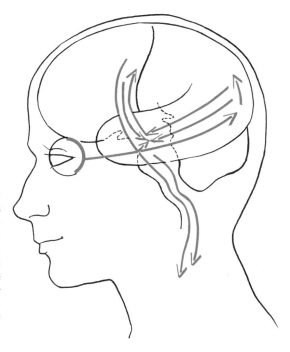

Fig. 20.18 The "vertical" theory of brain integration as applied to a simple visual reaction. In this scheme, highest-level integration is a brain stem function. We see that the pathways to and from the visual regions come together here, and that this zone initiates the action of the motor region.

721

SOME MECHANISMS OF LEARNING
AND RETENTION

So ready a solution to the crossed and uncrossed problem leaves us with still other quandaries. If, indeed, the corpus callosum has no role in interhemispheric integrations, why then does the brain contain this bundle? Recently, beginnings have been made upon this question, and with an ingenious technique: it involves the preparation of the so-called "split-brain" cat. Essentially, the split-brain cat is one in which two cuts are made in the tissue of the forebrain. The first such cut completely severs the fibers of the corpus callosum. The second cut is made within the visual pathways, and at such a level that all crossed connections between the eyes and hemispheres are gone. The left eye is connected only with the left hemisphere and the right eye only with the right hemisphere. There are still communicative pathways between the two separated hemispheres, but these are mostly by way of linkages between the brain stem and the hemispheres.

In the first experiments conducted with these cats,[14] one eye was completely covered. The animal was then taught a simple visual habit with the other eye. Now, we know that in ourselves it makes no difference which eye we might use to read with, and that we can recognize a passage we have learned with one eye when we use the other. But not so with a split-brain animal. What it learns with one eye is remembered with that eye, and with that same eye alone. If, however, either the crossing visual fibers or the corpus callosum is intact, a habit learned with one eye transfers almost wholly to the other.

This result has two implications. First, whatever changes underly the process of learning in these animals apparently go on within the two separated hemispheres. Second, the corpus callosum is concerned, not with momentary integrations, but with the establishment of learned alterations of the hemispheric tissue. One can split the brains after learning is complete, or split either pathways or callosum, without affecting transfer from one eye to the other in the least.

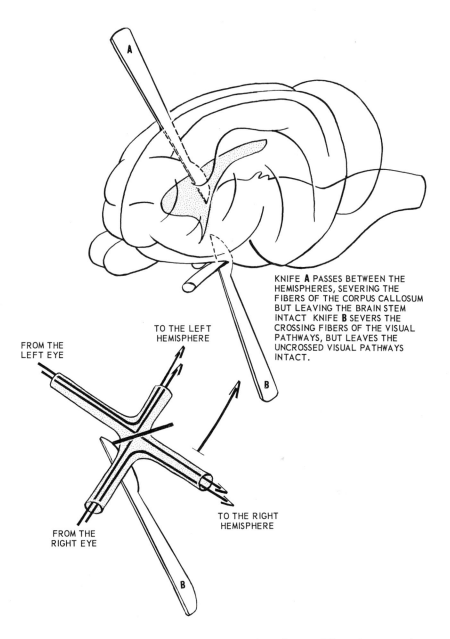

KNIFE **A** PASSES BETWEEN THE
HEMISPHERES, SEVERING THE
FIBERS OF THE CORPUS CALLOSUM
BUT LEAVING THE BRAIN STEM
INTACT KNIFE **B** SEVERS THE
CROSSING FIBERS OF THE VISUAL
PATHWAYS, BUT LEAVES THE
UNCROSSED VISUAL PATHWAYS
INTACT.

TO THE LEFT
HEMISPHERE

FROM THE
LEFT EYE

TO THE RIGHT
HEMISPHERE

FROM THE
RIGHT EYE

Fig. 20.19 Steps in the preparation of a split-brain cat. When they are taken, each eye has direct connections only with the same-sided cerebral hemisphere, and the fibers of the corpus callosum between the hemispheres are destroyed.

Some evidence for brain unity

Split-brain cats are also very useful in the study of another concept. This is that the neocortex has general integrative properties above and beyond its parcellations into separate systems. Suppose, for example, that we make a split-brain cat, one eye to one hemisphere. How much of the hemisphere will the cat require to learn a visual habit with this eye? If the neocortex is an aggregate of pieces, each with quite specific functions, we would think that

Fig. 20.20 The two hemispheres of a split-brain cat, in which the neocortex outside the visual region is removed from the right, but not from the left hemisphere. Such an animal can learn a visual habit with its left eye, but not with its right.

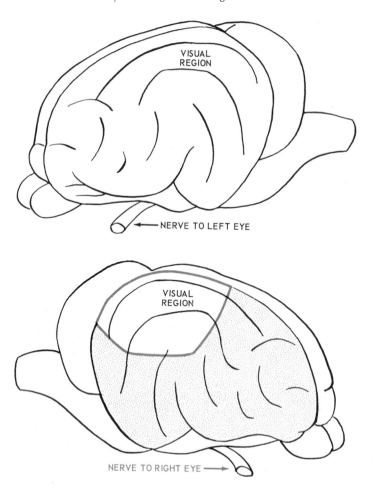

all that we would have to spare would be the visual regions of the brain. If, on the other hand, the learning process does involve the whole neocortex, destruction of tissue outside these areas should also be of some consequence.

What we do, accordingly, is first split the brain, and then remove all tissue from one hemisphere except that known to be involved in vision. We can then compare the rates at which the cat can learn a visual habit with each eye, the one of course connected with a whole hemisphere, the other only to a visual system. What we find from this is that the latter system simply does not seem to be enough; the animals can learn with the "half-brain" eye, but not with the eye with connections only to the "visual brain."[15] This suggests that much more of the neocortex is involved in learning a habit than would be suggested by the patterns we obtain when we use electrodes for mapping out the surface of the brain.

For reasons that we still do not fully understand, other kinds of habits can be learned just as well with portions as with whole hemispheres. Thus, for example, if an animal is trained in a habit that involves the sense of touch, almost the whole of its rearward cortex can be removed without there being an effect upon the rate at which it learns. It has even been reported that, when classical conditioning is used, the learning of a touch-dependent habit may be even faster after such operations than before them. Many problems must be solved before our answers to these queries will be complete, but the recent progress in solutions has been very promising.

THE NATURE OF THE TRACE
IN LEARNING

All such experiments as those just discussed concern themselves with finding out where learning goes on. They are not, accordingly, concerned with the nature of the basis of a habit. While we have yet much to learn about this process, a number of the more important issues now appear to be decided. There are two outstanding possibilities as to kinds of learning processes, and these are known as the dynamic and the structural trace hypotheses.

According to the first of these, the trace left by learning is a pattern of brain activity. Once established, it persists forever, maintained by continued excitation. The structural theory, on the other hand, regards the trace as some sort of change in the anatomical constituents of neurons or in the junctions between them.

Tests of the dynamic trace theory

Probably the most dramatic of techniques suited to the purpose at hand is one that was developed in experiments with rats.[16] It was first established that, with ice packs, one can lower a rat's body temperature to levels just above the freezing point, and in a few minutes thereafter warm them up again. Further, when the temperatures are at their lowest points, there is not so much as a heart-beat, and neither are there any electrical signs of continued brain activity. But, the rat recovered from "suspended animation" nonetheless remembers what he learned, and so we must conclude that the structure of the brain is altered by the process of learning.

A role for dynamic processes

These hypotheses have lent themselves to tests that have their basis in the supposition that dynamic traces can exist only if the brain is always working. The structural hypothesis would lead us to believe that, if we could "shut down" the brain, habits would remain intact if we had a method for starting it to work once again. So the basic problem is one of working out some sort of stop-and-start routine, such a routine to be invoked when we have trained an animal in some kind of habit.

There is nonetheless a possibility that some reverberations are essential in order for the anatomical events to take place in fixation of the habit. This suggestion has arisen from results of studies which, instead of using cooling, upset the ongoing workings of the brain by passage of strong electric currents. This procedure is an adaptation of a clinical technique used in the treatment of certain forms of severe behavioral disorders. When the current passes, the animal or person undergoes a violent convulsion, and the supposition is that the patterned brain activity cannot weather such a storm.

The first result pertaining to the question at hand was that whether such a treatment will affect retention of a simple habit depends upon the time that is permitted to elapse between a learn-

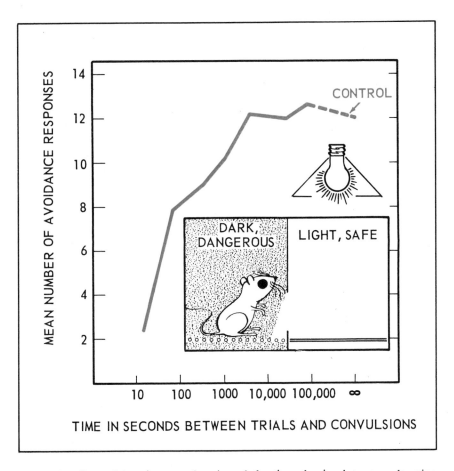

Fig. 20.21 Rate of learning as a function of the time elapsing between a learning trial and an electrically-induced convulsion. The rat's task, as shown in the inset, was to move from a compartment on the left when the one on the right was illuminated strongly, and in so doing to avoid a painful shock to its feet delivered to the grid at the left.

ing trial and the shock-induced convulsion.[17] In one situation, it was found that convulsions had no effect if they were given after a delay of one hour or more. If given twenty seconds after the trial, almost no learning was observed, and intermediate amounts of learning followed intermediate spacings. Thus, it seems important that something going on after the completion of a trial is critically important to the ultimate establishment of some sort of structural change.

This conclusion finds additional support from work related to the effects of deprivation of the oxygen supply to the brains of rats in training. In one experiment,[18] the rats were subjected to an

727

atmosphere equivalent to that at altitudes of 20,000 feet. This treatment was administered at intervals that ranged from thirty seconds to four hours after the rats had reached the criterion of learning. As in the experiments with convulsive shock, the greatest deficits were found in those groups whose treatments were given very quickly after training was complete.

In conclusion, then, we think of memory traces as involving structural change, but change that is established only if activity continues for some time after practice.[19] What the changes are is presently in doubt, but at least we know what to look for; where to look is still in many instances obscure, but the search is well on its way.

SOME FACTORS IN CEREBRAL EFFICIENCY

The variables that we have used in working on the problem of the nature of the trace in learning and retention are, in general, factors that reversibly impair the operations of the brain. Some of these are also factors that operate in everyday behaviors, albeit not necessarily for each and every individual. As a first example, it is not uncommon for pilots of high-performance aircraft to, through failures of their oxygen equipment, be subject to cerebral impairments. This can also happen when an individual drowns, and some time later is revived, or when workers—through electrocution—have had heart failure for a time. That such individuals are able to recover stems from the fact that the older neural centers are much less sensitive to oxygen depletion than the new.

Effects of alcohol and insufficiency of oxygen[20]

The effects of lack of oxygen in men have been quite extensively examined both during mountain-climbing expeditions and in chambers from which the air can be removed. Under such conditions, judgments grow progressively faulty with increasing oxygen lack; thus a pilot who ascends beyond 10,000 feet without an oxygen mask is likely to consider his performances to be substantially better than they are. Under these conditions, too, attending may be poor, calculations unreliable, and susceptibility to

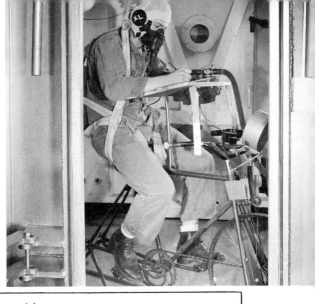

Fig. 20.22 Deprivation of oxygen, especially under conditions of physical exertion, can produce gross changes in behavior. Here the subject's handwriting shows progressive deterioration as he works under conditions of increasing oxygen deficiency. (Courtesy U.S. Air Forces and R. A. McFarland)

SEA LEVEL

18,000 FT ALTITUDE

20,000 FT ALTITUDE

22,000 FT ALTITUDE

25,000 FT ALTITUDE

28,000 FT ALTITUDE

upset by trivial frustrations substantially enhanced. All these factors have to be considered by leaders of mountain expeditions and by the designers of vehicles to carry man beyond his normal milieu.

Such deteriorations of behavior can also be observed at sea level, for in most respects they are duplicated by the symptoms of intoxication. This is thought by some investigators to be due to the fact that the effect of alcohol arises from an interference with the normal mechanisms by which oxygen is used by neurons. In keeping with this view, a rare atmosphere enhances the effect of a drink; those in Denver are more potent, for example, than the ones consumed in New York.

Some effects of other chemicals[21]

So radically do patterns of behavior change with changes in brain chemistry that it seems distinctly possible that certain forms of the behavior disorders will be proved to have their roots in changes in brain metabolism. The recent advent of tranquilizing drugs, well known now to almost everyone, has served to spur renewed interest in this point of view after many years of its denial.

Other observations that contribute to this interest have been made with drugs that produce, instead of alleviate, the patterns judged by some to be psychotic. One such substance, lysergic acid diethylamide, is of particular significance because the changes in behavior are produced with doses measurable in thousandths of a gram. It is thus apparent that changes need not be particularly massive for the symptoms that we see in, say, schizophrenia to make their appearance. How such changes come about, what the changes are, still have not been well analyzed, as indeed they cannot be particularly quickly because of the size of the task.

CONCLUSIONS

Solution of the riddles posed by these behavior patterns, as indeed by anything we do, requires the skills of virtually the whole gamut of biological researchers. There are biochemical reactions to be measured, modified, and analyzed; these are only partly meaningful, however, until we can determine in what systems they occur. Nor are the systems in themselves of much interest apart their roles in behavior, for it is with these that our problems have begun and with them that our task will end.

There are many ways, in summary, of studying the individual. Only some of these are the methods that have been developed in psychology. Everything that we have learned about our bodies strengthens our conviction of the merits of looking at ourselves as mechanisms built of parts whose functions can be identified. The job is one that has required—and always will require—the teamwork of many sciences, all of them united by a common interest in the phenomena of life. The fruits of past teamwork have been many; the promise of the future is a great one.

REFERENCES

[1] Brady, J. In Harlow, H. F., and Woolsey, C. N., *Biological and Biochemical Bases of Behavior,* Univ. of Wisconsin, 1958, pp. 193-236.

[2] Cannon, W. B. In Reymert, M. L., *Feelings and Emotions,* Clark Univ., 1928, pp. 257-260.

[3] Bard, P. In Reymert, M. L., *Feelings and Emotions,* McGraw-Hill, 1950, pp. 211-237.

[4] Penfield, W., and Rasmussen, T. *The Cerebral Cortex of Man,* Macmillan, 1950.

[5] Ruch, T. C. In Stevens, S. S., *Handbook of Experimental Psychology,* Wiley, 1951, Chapter 4.

[6] Mountcastle, V. B. Modality and topographic properties of single neurons of cat's somatic sensory cortex, *J. Neurophysiol.,* 1957, *20,* 408-434.

[7] DeValois, R. L., Smith, C. J., and Kitai, S. T. Recordings from single on-cells of macaque lateral geniculate nucleus, *J. comp. physiol. Psychol.,* 1959, *52,* 635-641.

[8] Woolsey, C. N. In Harlow, H. F., and Woolsey, C. N., *Biological and Biochemical Bases of Behavior,* Univ. of Wisconsin, 1958, pp. 63-81.

[9] Penfield, W., and Roberts, L. *Speech and Brain Mechanisms,* Princeton, 1959.

[10] Critchley, M. *The Parietal Lobes,* Arnold, 1953, Chapter 11.

[11] Robb, J. P. The effect of cortical excision and stimulation of the frontal lobe on speech, *Res. Pub. Nerv. Ment. Dis.,* 1948, *27,* 587-609.

[12] Smith, K. U. Learning and the associative pathways of the human cerebral cortex, *Science,* 1951, *114,* 117-120.

[13] Jasper, H. In Harlow, H. F., and Woolsey, C. N. *Biological and Biochemical bases of behavior,* Univ. of Wisconsin, 1958, pp. 37-61.

[14] Sperry, R. W. In Harlow, H. F., and Woolsey, C. N. *Biological and Biochemical Bases of Behavior,* Univ. of Wisconsin, 1958, pp. 401-424.

[15] Sperry, R. W. In Hutchings, E., *Frontiers in Science,* Basic, 1958, pp. 48-60.

[16] Andjus, R. K., Knoepfelmacher, F., Russell, R. W., and Smith, A. U. Some effects of severe hypothermia on learning and retention, *Quart. J. exper. Psychol.,* 1956, *8,* 15-23.

[17] Duncan, C. P. The retroactive effect of electroshock on learning, *J.*

comp. physiol. Psychol., 1949, *42*, 32-44.

[18] Thompson, R., and Pryer, R. S. The effect of anoxia on retention of a discrimination habit, *J. comp. physiol. Psychol.*, 1956, *49*, 297-300.

[19] Hebb, D. *The Organization of Behavior*, Wiley, 1949, Chapter 4.

[20] McFarland, R. *Human Factors in Air Transportation*, McGraw-Hill, 1953, Chapter 6.

[21] Rinkel, M. *Chemical Concepts of Psychosis*, McDowell, 1958.

Chapter Twenty-one

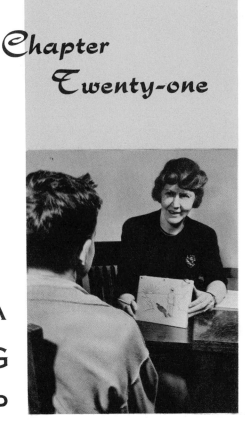

A
SUMMING
UP

AFTER YOU HAVE FINISHED THIS TEXT-
book and the course in which you used it, you will probably carry
away with you many items of specific information that may be useful and pertinent to your daily living. But more important than
your retention of factual data is your assimilation of something of
the psychologist's general approach and attitude toward the behavior of human beings.

THE SCIENTIFIC METHOD

AND BEHAVIOR

The basic position taken by modern psychology is that although man's behavior is wondrously complex, it is not eternally

obscured in mystery and there is no overriding edict that says that man can never understand himself. Modern psychology assumes that man's behavior is lawful and is determined by natural causes—and with diligence and patience the psychologist may discern the basic laws and discover some of the determinants of behavior.

The psychologist feels that these discoveries can be—and have been—made by the application to human behavior of the same basic methods of investigation that have led us to our present understanding of the physical world. Because living organisms are more complex and more variable than the materials with which the physical scientist deals, the psychologist must frequently modify the procedures that he has modeled after those of the physical sciences, and he must often devise some new investigating procedures of his own. Nevertheless, the essentials of the scientific method are as applicable to the investigation of human behavior as they are to the investigation of the physical world.

The discovery of the facts of behavior

The scientific method is, in essence, a set of rules for establishing truth—a kind of limitation we place upon ourselves. It first demands that we establish our facts of behavior beyond cavil, that we do not accept heresay evidence, that we set up our investigations so that our own prejudices and our own blindness will not lead us to see things as they are not or to disregard the things that are there. Sensible and obvious though this rule sounds, it is often violated in daily life. But by the use of certain careful experimental procedures we may sift the wheat from the chaff. And when we have done this and have ascertained what the facts of behavior are, then we must set about the task of explaining the behavior.

The interpretation of the facts of behavior

The task of explanation is made difficult by the fact that human behavior occurs in a complex environment, too complex for us to be able to discern with certainty the specific stimuli that are responsible for the behavior. Thus, to develop satisfactory explanatory systems and to determine adequately the degree to which a given condition influences our behavior, it is necessary to resort to precise experimental procedures. For this purpose we turn to the laboratory and contrive situations that are simpler than those we will find in everyday life. By making them simpler, we can identify the factors that make the behavior possible. In a certain sense our laboratory experiments are much like the wind tunnel employed by the aeronautical engineer. The plane that he flies in his wind tunnel is only the simplest model, yet these investigations aid him in predicting the actions of a real plane in a real sky. In much the same fashion our contrived laboratory experiments tell us something about the behavior of persons in the real world.

All in all, the task of understanding human behavior is both time-consuming and complex, and the wise student is wary of glib and oversimplified statements of the what's and why's of behavior. He learns to be critical both of statements of *what* occurred and of explanations of *why*. With this critical approach, he may free himself of or avoid acquiring many misconceptions and many superstitions.

SOME CHARACTERISTICS OF BEHAVIOR

Let us re-emphasize a few of the important generalizations based upon the many facts about behavior and the interpretation of these facts that we have presented.

The modifiability of behavior

Perhaps the most dramatic change that has occurred during the past half century in the psychologist's evaluation of behavior is his recognition of the great importance of learning as a determinant of behavior. Our researches during this period have led us to conclude that organisms—especially man—are born with relatively few inborn and fixed ways of reacting. They are, however, endowed with a tremendous capacity to learn new ways of acting under the appropriate environmental conditions. This statement implies not only that many of our actions have been learned but also that we are capable of unlearning that which is no longer adjustive for us, and that re-education in the direction of better living is always possible. What can be, and is, learned includes not only the ways of doing things but also many of the motives for our actions. This view inevitably emphasizes the extreme importance of the environment in shaping our behavior and, because so much of our environment is supplied by the presence of other organisms, it points to the significance of social forces in molding the behavior of the individual.

The fact that we seem to be able to account for so much behavior by reference to the mechanism of learning implies that society itself controls to a fairly large extent what its own future citizens may be like. It is a privilege and a responsibility, a responsibility that can be adequately met only if we continue to study and learn more about the facts of behavior in an objective and clear-eyed fashion.

Individual differences

Since every individual will differ from every other individual in his environment as well as in his genetic make-up, individuals will inevitably differ from one another in their behavioral characteristics. An awareness of how genetic and environmental forces operate upon individuals and cause them to differ in their actions may lead us to view these actions with a greater degree of tolerance. We need not condone these actions, but if we understand their origins we may be less inclined to reject the individual. This understanding and tolerance may lead us to take positive steps to re-educate that individual or perhaps ourselves, and it may inspire us to take steps that will eventually decrease the friction arising among us.

THE PRESENT AND THE FUTURE

We have attempted in this text to present the essential facts about behavior as we know them now, and also to present a systematic method of explaining behavior which seems to be the most fruitful, the most rigorous, and the most promising one today. In short, it is the method of analysis which, it seems to us, is able to make more accurate predictions about behavior in a variety of situations than any other method. We are under no illusion that we have presented a complete and final accounting of man's behavior—that is, a system which predicts with complete accuracy. Psychology is a young science, and there is still much that the future researchers—and perhaps the reader will be one of these—

must and will discover about its subject matter. As we learn more, we shall find new things to explain, and we are likely to find that some of our present principles of explanation are too simple in nature or too limited in scope, and perhaps even a few of them may be wrong. But such, of course, is true of any science, and we approach a deeper understanding of the world about us only gradually and through the products of continuing research.

GLOSSARY

Acetylcholine. A substance released during activation of nerves, and known to be involved in the excitation of *skeletal muscles** and some types of glands.

Adrenalin. A hormone secreted by the central portion of the adrenal gland.

Affective psychosis. A *functional* psychosis that is characterized by extremes of mood. The manic condition is characterized by elation and the depressive condition by sadness and misery. An individual may move from one to another of these extremes.

All-or-none principle. As applied to *neurons,* the statement that an impulse, if it is conducted at all, is of the same strength regardless of the magnitude of the initiating stimulus.

Anatomy. The study of the structure of living organisms.

* Words in italics are defined in their appropriate places in this glossary.

Anesthesia. Loss of sensitivity to stimuli.

Anger. An emotional reaction to a frustrating event.

Anxiety. The anticipatory reaction to stimuli that have been associated with events that produce *avoidant reactions*. The term implies that the reaction to the stimulus is learned.

Appetite. Preference for a certain incentive over others despite the fact that these others may be equally capable of satisfying the same need.

Approach-approach conflict. Type of conflict situation in which the individual is simultaneously attracted to two goals, with the attainment of either one precluding the attainment of the other.

Approach-avoidance conflict. Type of conflict situation in which the individual is attracted toward a stimulus object that also has characteristics that repel him.

Approach reactions. Behavior directed toward some stimulus event.

Aptitude. The degree of proficiency of performance in a specific and fairly narrow area of behavior.

Associative cortex. Synonym for the *intrinsic regions* of the cerebral cortex.

Ataracic drugs. Popularly known as tranquilizers, these drugs are used to reduce *anxiety*.

Autonomic system. A division of the nervous system whose chief function is the regulation of the heart, *smooth muscles,* and glands.

Atmosphere effects. Irrelevant characteristics of a problem situation that nevertheless influence behavior.

Attitude. A learned predisposition to react in a certain way to classes of objects, persons, or situations.

Avoidance-avoidance conflict. Type of conflict situation in which the individual is repelled by the consequences of one course of action and thereby directed into another course of action which is also repellant.

Avoidant reactions. Behavior directed away from some stimulus event that can be described as painful or unpleasant.

Axon. The long, slender, and relatively unbranched portion of some kinds of *neurons,* toward and through which signals are conducted.

Barrier. Any obstacle that stands, psychologically, between the organism and attainment of a goal.

Behavior. Any activity of an organism.

Binaural disparity. The difference in the sound patterns impinging on the two ears from a single sound source.

Biochemistry. The chemistry of living processes.

Biology. The study of living organisms.

Blind matching. A procedure in which one is given a description of each of several persons or events and required to select another of the same person or event from an independent set of descriptions.

Brain. The portion of the *central nervous system* that is enclosed within the skull and which includes the *cerebral hemispheres*, the *cerebellum*, and the *brain stem*.

Brain stem. One of the major divisions of the brain, lying between the spinal cord and cerebellum.

Brain wave. The fluctuating electrical activity of the brain, which is measured by the *EEG*.

Bunsen-Roscoe law. A quantitative statement of the fact that the apparent brightness of a visual stimulus is a joint function of the intensity and the duration of the stimulus.

Capillary. A minute blood vessel linking arteries and veins.

Cell. The structural unit of complex organisms.

Cell body. The central portion of a *neuron*, to which *dendrites* and the *axon* are attached.

Center. A network of neurons that integrates a pattern of behavior.

Central fissure. An indentation near the middle of the lateral surface of each *cerebral hemisphere* which divides the *frontal* from the *parietal lobe*.

Central nervous system. The brain and spinal cord.

Central tendency. A clustering of a large number of scores about some value, which is likely to be toward the middle of the range of scores. (See *Mean, Median,* and *Mode*.)

Cerebellum or little brain. One of the major divisions of the brain, attached to the *brain stem* just beneath the *cerebral hemispheres*.

Cerebral cortex. The surface layers of gray matter of the cerebral hemispheres.

Cerebral hemispheres. The largest portion of the brain of vertebrates; they surmount the brain stem within the skull.

Chemogenic theory. A theory that the functional psychoses are produced by toxics or chemical imbalances.

Chiasm. The place where the two *visual nerves* are intermixed and give rise to the visual tracts. In the chiasm, fibers from the nasal halves of the two retinas cross over to the opposite side before passing upward to the cerebral hemispheres.

Class. A subdivision of a culture. Classes differ from each other by the extent to which they possess the high-valued items of their culture.

Class interval. That span of scores which is treated as a unit in representing the distribution of scores.

Cochlea. A spiral bony tube within the *inner ear* which contains receptors for hearing.

Coefficient of correlation (r). A numerical expression of the degree of relationship between two sets of scores. The value of r has a maximum of 1.00 and a minimum of -1.00.

Color blindness. An organism, man or animal, is color blind if it is unable to differentiate between light stimuli of different wavelengths to the same extent that normal individuals do.

Color mixture. The simultaneous presentation to one area of the eye of two or more color stimuli.

Compensation. A reaction to frustration in one area of activity by successful participation in another activity.

Concept formation. The ordering or categorizing of sensory impressions by identification of the similar aspects of a group of stimuli.

Conditioned response. A learned response to a previously neutral stimulus (the conditioned stimulus). The response has been acquired as a result of the pairing of the conditioned with the unconditioned stimulus.

Conduction. Transmission of a neural impulse; also, the transmission of any change in energy from one place to another.

Conductive mechanism. That portion of a sense organ which spans the gap between receptors and the body surface.

Cones. Small structures within the *retina* that respond to the energy of light rays and stimulate attached visual neurons. Cones, in contrast to *rods,* are believed to be the receptors for color.

Conflict. An instance where the individual is motivated toward two or more goals that are mutually exclusive.

Conformity. The tendency for an individual's response to be determined by the responses of others.

Consummatory response. The response, such as eating, that eliminates the impelling force of the motive.

Control group. A number of subjects in an experiment that are exposed to all the features of a given experiment except the variable being investigated. The characteristics of the control group are matched as closely as possible to those of the experimental group.

Coordination. The working together of a number of parts, such as muscles in a movement.

Corpus callosum. A mass of white matter that links the two *cerebral hemispheres* together.

Cortex. The thin outer layer of an organ.

Counterconditioning. The process of extinguishing a previously *conditioned response* by conditioning a new and antagonistic response.

Cranial nerves. Twelve pairs of nerves attached, within the skull, to the *brain stem.*

Criterion. In learning situations, some chosen level of performance that the subject must reach to succeed in the task. In testing, a measure of the behavior in the situation which the test attempts to predict.

Cross validation. A recheck upon the *validity* estimate of a test or test items by repeating the validation procedure on another and independent population.

Culture. The common, shared ways of behavior that tend to be transmitted to succeeding generations.

Cutaneous receptors. *Receptors* in the skin.

Dendrites. The branched receiving fibers of a *neuron.*

Depressive reaction. Emotional behavior resulting from the complete elimination of attainment of highly desired objects or persons.

Developmental level. Any given level of competence in responding reached by an organism as a result of the interaction of maturational and environmental conditions.

Diencephalon. The lowest portion of the *forebrain* or highest portion of the *brain stem.* It includes the *thalamus, epithalamus,* and *hypothalamus.*

Discrimination training. A situation in which the occurrence of one stimulus is followed by reinforcement and the occurrence of another and similar stimulus is not reinforced.

Discriminatory response. Differential reaction to differences in stimuli.

Displacement. The directing of an emotional reaction toward an object or an individual that is similar to, but is not actually the agent responsible for, the reaction.

Drive or drive state. A physiological state that is the consequence of a need and that impels the organism to activity; the activity may or may not be specifically directed towards an appropriate goal.

Duplex theory. The theory that *cones* are color receptors, and *rods* have achromatic sensitivity alone.

Dynamic trace. A pattern of brain activity assumed to be left in the *central nervous system* as a result of prior activity.

EEG. Abbreviation for *electroencephalogram* or electroencephalograph.

Effector. A muscle or *exocrine gland;* an organ of response.

Ego. In psychoanalytic theory, the division of the personality that is in contact with the real world. Through its motor, perceptual, and intellectual activities it achieves release of the tensions that are produced by the *id.*

Electroencephalogram. A graphic record of the wavelike changes in the electric potential observed when electrodes are placed on the skull or on the exposed brain. The instrument by which the records are obtained is termed an electroencephalograph.

Emotion. A form of responding, characterized by high levels of psychological activation, which often results in disruption of the usual patterns of behavior.

Empiricist. One who believes that behavior is learned.

Endocrine glands. Glands that secrete their products (*hormones*) directly into the blood stream.

Epidermis. The outer layer of the skin.

Epilepsy. The name given to a group of diseases characterized by abnormal patterns of activity within the nervous system.

Exocrine gland. A gland that secretes through a duct that leads to a surface of the body.

Experimental group. A group of subjects in an experiment that is exposed to the variable being investigated, whose performance is to indicate the influence of that variable on behavior.

Expiration. The expulsion of breath from the lungs.

Extinction. The progressive reduction of a previously established *conditioned response* by means of repeated presentation of the conditioned stimulus without reinforcement.

Fear. An emotional reaction arising when the individual is unable to react to a strange or unexpected stimulus with a controlling response.

Figure-ground. The relationship between the stimulus event that is psychologically dominant (figure) and other stimuli existing in the total stimulating field (ground). The figural stimulus stands out psychologically from the ground.

Fixation. The process of establishing a stimulus → response connection in the organism.

Forced choice. A device by which the respondent is required to choose the one of each pair of characteristics which best describes the individual being rated.

Forebrain. Jointly, the *cerebral hemispheres* and the *diencephalon*.

Forgetting. A decrement in retention as a result of the passage of time.

Forgetting curve. A diagrammatic representation of the relationship of the passage of time to the amount of material of a previously learned task that is retained.

Frequency polygon. A graphic means of representing a distribution of scores by a series of dots in the midpoints of the class intervals, at heights determined by the frequencies. (See *Histogram*.)

Frontal lobe. The upper and forward half of a *cerebral hemisphere*.

Functional disorders. Psychotic or neurotic conditions that are not attributable to any physiological or organic cause.

Functional fixedness. The degree to which an object cannot be comprehended as functioning in a context other than in which it usually functions, or has recently functioned.

Galvanic Skin Response (GSR). An electrical reaction of the skin that can be detected with a sensitive meter.

Goal object. See *Incentive*.

Group tests. Tests, usually of special aptitudes, intelligence, or personality dimensions, that are designed to be given simultaneously to a number of individuals.

GSR. See *Galvanic Skin Response*.

Habit. A psychological construct accounting for the tendency for a particular response to be given to a stimulus as a result of previous associations of the stimulus and response.

Hallucination. A false perception that exists in the absence of stimuli for its production.

Heart muscle. The contractile substance of the heart of vertebrates, noted for its rhythmic contractions, which is *striated* and composed of fibers that are interlaced with one another.

Histogram. A graphic means of representing a distribution of scores by a series of columns, whose widths are determined by the class intervals and heights by the frequencies of scores within the intervals. Its purpose is essentially identical to that of the *frequency polygon.*

Homeostasis. A state of internal equilibrium about which the properties of body fluids tend to fluctuate.

Hormone. A chemical substance produced by one organ and carried by the blood to another, where it produces a change in function.

Hue. The characteristic by which the colors differ from white, the grays, and black—and from each other.

Hypothalamus. A group of nuclei, at the base of the brain, which forms one part of the *diencephalon.*

Hysterical reaction. The neurotic solution of a psychological problem by the development of some form of physical disability. Sometimes called a conversion reaction.

Id. In psychoanalytic theory, one of three divisions of personality. This division is the source of blind, amoral, and instinctive impulses that seek immediate gratification.

Illumination. The amount of light falling upon a surface.

Illusion. A disturbed or mistaken perception that does not agree with objective measurement and is brought about by conflicting sensory cues.

Implicit responses. Responses that are not perceptable to an observer without the aid of special instruments of measurement.

Incentive. Stimulus events that are capable of reducing a drive or satisfying a motive state. They are the events that terminate a sequence of motivated behavior.

Individual test. Tests, usually of special aptitudes, intelligence, or personality dimensions, that must be administered by the tester to a single person at a time.

Inhibition. The stopping of a process from continuing, or from starting, although its stimulus is present.

Inner ear. The innermost division of the sense organ for hearing, and the sense organ for perception of rotation and acceleration. It contains the *cochlea* and the *vestibular mechanism.*

Inspiration. Drawing in of the breath.

Instigator. That which initiates an action.

Instrumental acts or responses. Actions of the organism which achieve—are instrumental in obtaining—an incentive.

Integration. The bringing together of neural impulses in such a manner as to produce a coordinated pattern of behavior.

Intelligence. A construct that refers to the degree of proficiency with which the individual solves problems, deals with abstract materials, verbalizes, and learns new material.

Intelligence Quotient (I.Q.). The ratio of an individual's mental age, as obtained from a test, to his chronological age, times 100; symbolically, I.Q. $= (MA/CA) \times 100$.

Interneuron. A neuron of the *central nervous system* that is in synaptic relation to sensory neurons, motor neurons, or other interneurons.

Intrinsic regions. A fairly recent term for those regions of the *cerebral cortex* that classically were called associative, and that constitute the zones other than those described as sensory or motor.

Isolation method. A technique by which, through appropriate removals or severings of neural tissue, relatively simple integrative mechanisms can be studied without their being affected by other mechanisms.

Job analysis. A procedure employed in aptitude-test development in which the psychological abilities necessary for performance on the job are identified.

Kinesthetic receptors. Receptors located in the muscles, tendons, and joints by means of which we perceive the movements and positions of parts of the body.

Labyrinth. The structure in the *inner ear* that contains the receptors for hearing and *vestibular* sensitivity.

Latency. The time elapsing between the occurrence of the stimulus and the occurrence of the response.

Lateral fissure. The cerebral indentation that separates the *temporal lobe* from the *parietal* and *frontal lobes*.

Laterality. Sidedness.

Learning. The more or less permanent modification of the response or responses to a stimulus or to a pattern of stimuli that results from experience with these or with similar stimuli.

Lie detector. An apparatus for measuring the blood pressure, pulse, and respiratory changes, and the *GSR*, that occur when a subject is asked to answer questions.

Localize. To designate (to be aware of) the position of a sensory stimulus—such as sound and touch.

Loudness. That characteristic of a tone that is mostly closely related to tonal stimulus intensity.

Love. An emotional response associated with a strong positive attachment toward an individual or group of individuals.

Maturation. Structural changes in an organism that are paced primarily by its biological and genetic make-up and that are relatively independent of the psychological environment. The stage of maturation determines the profit obtainable from proper environmental stimulation. .

Mean. A measure of *central tendency* obtained by adding all the scores in a distribution and dividing by the number of cases.

Median. The score value above and below which there are an equal number of cases.

Medulla. The lowest part of the *brain stem;* also, the central core of the adrenal gland.

Membership group. A group to which one is formally attached, such as a church, college, club, or fraternity.

Mental age (MA). The mean chronological age for a particular level of test performance for the members of the standardization group of an intelligence test.

Middle ear. An air-filled space containing the auditory bones (hammer, anvil, and stirrup). It lies between the eardrum and the *inner ear,* or *labyrinth.*

Modal difference. A gross difference in kind of sensing, as, for example, between seeing and hearing.

Mode. The score which occurs most frequently in a distribution of scores.

Motivation. A general term referring to the operation of motives and their contributions to behavior.

Motive. The psychological mechanism that results in behavior that is directed toward a goal or incentive object. The term implies some background of learning on the part of the organism, either of what incentives are appropriate to the state or of the arousal of the state itself by some previously neutral stimulus.

Motor cortex. Those portions of the *cerebral cortex* that, when stimulated, yield prompt and specific movements of the different parts of the body.

Motor neuron. *Neuron* that terminates in an *effector* organ.

Myelin. The fatty material that surrounds the medullated nerve fibers, forming the myelin sheath, and that is responsible for the color of neural white matter.

Narcotize. To subject to the influence of a narcotic.

Nativist. Those who believe that behavior is directly inherited.

Needs. The chemical requirements of the tissues of the body. The term is sometimes, but loosely, used to imply the source of any behavior that is persistently directed toward any incentive object.

Negative transfer effects. The decreased adequacy in the learning of a task as a consequence of previous performance on another task.

Nerve. A bundle of *neurons,* generally encased within a sheath.

Nervous system. An inclusive term for the complex network of *neurons* in the body.

Neurology. The study of the form and functions of the nervous system.

Neuron. The structural unit within the nervous system, usually comprising a cell body and several fiber processes.

Neurosis. A form of maladjustment which is usually characterized by high levels of anxiety. The neurotic is not likely to require institutionalization.

Nondirective therapy. A form of psychotherapy in which the therapist offers a minimum of advice, guidance, or evaluative comments to the client.

Noradrenalin. A hormone secreted by the adrenal medulla during emotional reactions of rage.

Nucleus. A cluster of cells within the *central nervous system.*

Occipital. The back of head, as opposed to forehead.

Occipital lobe. The rearmost portion of each cerebral hemisphere.

Olfactory. Pertaining to smelling or to the sense of smell.

Optic. Pertaining to the eye, or to vision.

Optic nerves. See *Visual nerves.*

Organ. A part of an organism specialized for the performance of some specific function.

Organic disorders. Psychotic conditions that can be attributed to physiological causes, such as damaged brain cells, or the excess of certain toxics in the system.

Organism. A system capable of self-maintenance and reproduction.

Organismic variable. The capabilities and competencies that the particular individual brings to the task.

Outer ear. A part of the hearing apparatus that serves for the collection of sound waves and their conduction, within the *middle ear,* to the bones.

Overlearning. Practice on a task beyond that level necessary to attain the *criterion* level.

Overt responses. Responses that are readily perceptible to an observer.

Paired associate learning. Learning that requires a specific response term to a specific stimulus term. The order of presentation of the various stimulus terms in the total task is usually varied from trial to trial.

Paranoid. A characteristic of maladjustment in which the individual suffers from delusions of being persecuted or talked about.

Parasympathetic system. The cranial and the sacral parts of the *autonomic system.*

Paresis. An organic psychotic condition resulting from syphilis.

Parietal lobe. A major division of either cerebral hemisphere, lying between the *frontal* and *occipital* lobes and above the *temporal* lobe.

Partial reinforcement. The condition in which reinforcement does not follow the *S-R sequence* each time it occurs.

Perception. The grasping of the meaning of a stimulus by the use of a partial stimulus to predict the coming or the presence of the total stimulus complex.

Perceptual constancy. The tendency for the perception of objects to remain constant (in size, shape, brightness, etc.) despite changes in their stimulus characteristics.

Performance test. In the field of intelligence testing: a test that contains a minimum of symbolic material on both the question and answer side. It contrasts with a verbal test, in which emphasis is placed upon facility in language usage.

Peripheral nervous system. All those components of the nervous system that lie outside the brain and spinal cord, including the cranial and spinal nerves and the *autonomic* trunks and nerves.

Permissiveness. A term used to describe an important characteristic of the psychotherapy situation. It means that an atmosphere is established wherein the client feels free to speak of any personal matter regardless of how trivial or embarrassing it would be under normal conditions. Used more broadly to describe a nonrestrictive attitude.

Personality. All the factors that determine the total behavior of the individual. Of particular importance are those factors that make the behavior of the individual unique.

Physiology. The study of the functions of organs.

Phobia. An abnormal, dominating, and compelling fear.

Photochemistry. The study of chemical changes as produced or modified by light.

Pitch. The character of a tone as high or low. It is determined chiefly by the frequencies of sound waves.

Plasticity. The capacity for change as a result of experience.

Pleasure principle. In psychoanalytic theory, the demand for the immediate gratification of current needs. It is the governing principle of the *id*.

Positive transfer effects. The increased adequacy in the learning of a task as a consequence of previous performance on another task.

Posture. The position of the body with respect to the force of gravity, or of its members in relation to one another.

Power test. A test of intelligence or aptitude in which the time taken for completion is not a scoring factor.

Proactive inhibition. The fact that previously learned material interferes with the recall of material learned at a later time.

Probability learning. Learning to estimate the frequency with which a particular event follows a particular stimulus.

Problem solving. The process of selecting from a group of instrumental responses the response or responses that overcome some barrier to a goal.

Procedural variable. A psychological variable that influences learning or performance on a task, but that is extrinsic to the task itself.

Projection. The tendency to see in others the motive or motives that dominate one's own behavior.

Projective techniques. An unstructured but standard situation to which the testee is instructed to respond.

Psychoanalysis. The method of psychotherapy developed by Sigmund Freud. It involves numerous sessions in which the client talks without direction to the analyst about his past and present feelings and experiences.

Psychology. The study of behaving organisms.

Psychophysiology. The study of the relationships between physiological events and the behaviors of integrated organisms.

Psychoses. A group of severe mental illnesses that have in common serious distortions of reality. The psychotic is likely to require institutionalization.

Psychosomatic disorders. Disorders in physiological functions whose origins are attributable to psychological causes.

Psychosurgery. A *somatic procedure* used in treating certain behavioral disorders. It involves severing certain tracts or removing certain parts of the brain.

Psychotherapy. The treatment of behavioral disorders by psychological means. Usually the basis of the treatment consists of extensive interviews between the therapist and the client.

Purkinje shift or effect. The fact that the red-yellow end of the spectrum decreases in brilliance, with decreased illumination, more rapidly than does the green-blue end.

Random sampling. Selection of individuals for the sample by choosing them at random from the parent population.

Rating scale. A test used to obtain an estimate of an individual's status on any selected behavioral characteristic.

Rationalization. The interpretation of one's behavior as stemming from a socially and personally acceptable motive, whereas, in fact, it is primarily instigated by a motive that is unacceptable to the individual.

Reactive inhibition. The tendency to avoid repeating a response that has just been made.

Readiness. A composite of the level of maturation, relevant training, and adequate motivation that makes profitable engagement in learning possible.

Reality principle. In psychoanalytic theory, an awareness of the acceptable possibilities for action in the social world. It is the governing principle of the *ego*.

Receptor. A specialized organismic structure that is sensitive to specific forms of physical energy.

Receptor-motor neuron. A motor *neuron* that terminates in some sense organ and, by the signals it conducts, alters the sensitivity of that sense organ.

Reference group. The social group that is capable of serving as a source of motivation for the individual, whether positively or negatively.

Reflex. A stimulus-response sequence, demonstrably unlearned, that is observable in all members of a species.

Regression. Adoption of a previously learned, more childlike response following frustration. When used in the context of psychotherapy it means that the client has become more emotionally dependent on the therapist and more childlike in his attitudes. It was considered by Freud to be an essential stage in the psychoanalytic process.

Reinforcement. In classical conditioning: the occurrence of the unconditioned stimulus (UCS). In instrumental conditioning: the occurrence of an event that satisfies a current motivational state of an organism.

Reliability. The consistency of measurement of a test. In its simplest form it is measured by the correlation between performance on the test at once time and at a later time.

Remission. The disappearance of symptoms of maladjustment in the absence of treatment for the maladjustment.

Repression. The inability to recall highly significant personal events in which the individual has behaved in a manner that is unacceptable to himself.

Resistance. A psychoanalytic term referring to an attitude that develops during psychotherapy. Resistance takes the form of avoiding the scheduled therapy session, aggression toward the therapist, and similar negative reactions.

Resistance to extinction. The degree of persistence of a given response under conditions of nonreinforcement.

Response. An action of the organism made possible through contractions of the muscles.

Response generalization. The process by which a given stimulus becomes effective in eliciting responses similar to the original response with which the stimulus was specifically associated.

Response-produced cues. The internalized or implicit after-effects of responding to aspects of the stimulus structure of the environment. These after-effects then generate stimuli which serve as cues for making overt responses.

Retina. The innermost membrane or coat of the eyeball, having a complex and chiefly neural structure and containing *rod* and *cone* receptors.

Retroactive inhibition. A decrement in recall resulting from the fact that material learned at a later time interferes with the recall of previously learned material.

Reverberation. A periodically recurring event.

Rhodopsin. A substance in the *rods* of the *retina* that bleaches in white light.

Rods. Rod-shaped structures in the *retina,* which are believed to be receptors for gray or achromatic visual qualities at low intensities.

Role. The sum of those behaviors that the individual shows in response to the standards of the group.

Role playing. A technique by which an individual's behavior is observed as he acts out a role in a contrived situation.

Saccule. The smaller of two sacs in the vestibule of the *inner ear.*

Savings score. The ratio between the number of trials originally required to learn the material and the number of trials required to relearn it to the same *criterion* after some interval of time.

Scattergram. A graphic means of representing the relationship between two sets of data. The values of one set of scores are referred to the *X* axis and of the other to the *Y* axis.

Schizophrenia. A *functional psychosis* which includes a wide range of behavioral characteristics, especially withdrawal from reality, paranoid reactions, and hallucinations. The term "dementia praecox" has also been used to refer to this condition.

Secondary reinforcer. Stimulus events which have acquired a motivating or reinforcing property because they have been associated with another reinforcing stimulus.

Semicircular canals. Three tubes in each *inner ear,* which are set at nearly right angles to each other and contain receptors that are stimulated by rotation of the head.

Senile dementia. An *organic psychosis* resulting from old age.

Sense organ. A complex of receptors, conductive apparatus, and *neurons* specialized for the detection and transmission of signals belonging to a given class of stimuli.

Sensitivity. The degree to which an organism can be stimulated by physical changes of low intensity.

Sensory cortex. Any region of the *cerebral cortex* that is directly and specifically related to some sense organ of the body.

Sensory neuron. A *neuron* that begins outside the *central nervous system* and conducts its signals toward the central nervous system.

Serial learning. Learning that requires the organization of responses in an exact predetermined, list-like order.

Set. The tendency to respond to stimuli in a certain general way, the tendency being established by events preceding the stimulation. The term implies that alternate ways of reacting to the stimulus are present, but temporarily blocked by the set-producing event.

Shock therapy. A *somatic procedure* used in treating certain behavioral disorders. It involves the use of an electric current or of large doses of certain drugs.

Sigma. When this Greek letter is capitalized (Σ) it means to sum or add. The lower case letter (σ) is an abbreviation for the *standard deviation.*

Skeletal muscle. A muscle type whose fibers are distinct from one another and have prominent striations.

Skull. A group of bones that enclose the brain and form the face.

Smooth muscle. A type of muscle that lacks cross-striations in its fibers.

Sociogram. A graphic presentation of the interactions between members of a group.

Sociopathic personality. A pattern of abnormal behavior characterized by frequent and repeated transgressions of the codes of behavior of society. The term "psychopathic personality" is also used to refer to these behavior patterns.

Somatic procedures. The treatment of behavioral disorders by the use of drugs, surgery, or some other physical procedure.

Sound wave. Alternating changes in pressure propagated through a medium such as air or water in the range of frequencies between 20 and 20,000 cycles per second.

Space perception. Interpretation of the size, distance, or depths aspects of the environment by attaching meaning to sensory cues (sound, sights, touch, etc.).

Spectrum. A band of radiant energy which, after passing through a prism or being otherwise dispersed, is segregated so that its components are spread out in regular order.

Speed test. A test of intelligence or aptitude in which the individual's score is partly determined by the time in which he completes a test.

Spinal cord. The portion of the *central nervous system* that lies within the vertebrae.

Spontaneous recovery. The re-emergence of a previously extinguished response following a period of removal from the stimulus situation, but with no additional training.

S-R sequence. That unit of behavior composed of a stimulus and the response to it.

Standard deviation. A measure of the variability of a distribution of scores. It is obtained by squaring the difference between each score and the mean, summing all these values, dividing by the number of cases, and extracting the square root.

Standardization group. The *reference group* on which the norms of performance for a test have been established.

Stanford-Binet. A widely used *individual intelligence test,* heavily weighted on verbal ability; an American revision of the Binet-Simon test.

Stereophonic effect. A three-dimensional effect in hearing that is generated by the simultaneous and differential stimulation of the two ears.

Stereoscopic effect (stereoscopic vision). Perception of depth or solidity arising from the simultaneous and differential stimulation of the two eyes.

753

Stimulator. Any apparatus or instrument employed to generate or apply a stimulus.

Stimulus. A form of energy that activate the sense organs and results in a response.

Stimulus generalization. The tendency for a response to be given to other, similar stimuli as a result of being attached to a specific stimulus. In *primary* generalization the similarity dimension is within a particular sense field. In *secondary* generalization the similarity dimension has been acquired through prior learning.

Stimulus satiation. The tendency to avoid entering an environment with which the individual has had recent contact.

Stimulus selection. The fact that, although the environment is ordinarily rich in stimuli, the organism reacts only to a limited number of them.

Stratified sampling. The selection of individuals in a sample according to their membership in classes or groups in the population and the proportion that these groups represent in that population.

Striate muscle. See *Skeletal muscle.*

Structural trace. A structural alteration presumed to have been left in the nervous system as a consequence of prior activity therein.

Subliminal perception. Perception determined by stimulus cues of which the subject is not conscious.

Subliminal stimulus. A stimulus too weak for the subject to be aware of its occurrence.

Suggestibility. The extent to which one's perceptual reactions to a situation are biased by events that are not intrinsic to the stimulus situation.

Superego. In psychoanalytic theory, the division of personality that incorporates the parental values and taboos.

Sympathetic system. The thoraco-lumbar division of the *autonomic system.*

Sympathetic trunk. The chain of interconnected groups of sympathetic *neurons* that extend along each side of the vertebral column.

Synapse. The point at which two *neurons* are in contact with one another.

Systems research. The study of an entire group whose productivity is the consequence of the complex interactions of all its members.

Tachistoscope. An instrument that exposes, by means of a shutter, a visual stimulus for a short known duration of time.

Tactile. Having to do with touch.

Target organ. An organ that is affected by (is the "target" of) any specific hormone.

Task variable. A psychological variable that influences learning or performance on a task, is intrinsic to the task, and cannot be modified without changing the nature of the task.

Temperament. The biasing of behavior caused by the individual's genetic background.

Temporal lobe. That part of each *cerebral hemisphere* that lies below the *lateral fissure* and in front of the *occipital lobe*.

Test battery. A test composed of a number of subtests, each of which measures a different psychological variable.

Thalamus. A mass of gray matter in the *diencephalon* which is an important relay center between the various sense organs and the *cerebral cortex*.

Thinking. A stimulus-response sequence that is implicit.

Trait theory. Trait theory holds that there are a limited number of basic characteristics of behavior and that we may describe an individual's personality by his status on each of these characteristics or personality dimensions.

Transference. A psychoanalytic term describing the fact that clients in psychotherapy develop strong positive and negative feelings toward the psychotherapist.

Transfer of training. The field of inquiry dealing with the utilization of old habits in later, modified stimulus situations.

Type theory. A theory of personality which holds that all persons may be classified into one of a limited number of categories, each describing the organization and the direction of the individual's many response tendencies.

Unconditioned response. A response evoked consistently by a stimulus before training.

Utricle. A structure in the vestibule of the *inner ear* that contains the receptors stimulated by the inclination of the head.

Vagus. A descending bundle of fibers originating in the *brain stem* and supplying *parasympathetic* signals to many of the large internal organs of the thorax and abdomen.

Validity. The degree to which a test measures what it is supposed to measure. It is estimated by the value of the correlation between the test and the *criterion*.

Vascular muscle. *Smooth muscle* found within the walls of blood vessels.

Verbal test. See *Performance test*.

Vestibular mechanism (or vestibular apparatus). A division of the inner ear that includes the *utricle,* the *saccule,* and the *semicircular canals.*

Visceral muscle. A type of *smooth muscle* found within the walls of large hollow organs such as the stomach and intestines.

Visual nerves. The cranial nerves that run between the eyes and the *chiasm,* there undergoing rearrangement and forming the visual tracts that continue to the brain.

Visual purple. See *Rhodopsin*.

Wavelength. The distance, at any instant, between two adjacent crests of a series of waves.

Wechsler intelligence scales. Widely used *individual intelligence tests.* One of the scales is designed for adults, the other for children. They contain both verbal and performance sections.

INDEX

rage, 236-237, 238
  see also anger
random sampling, 496
range, 408
rating scales, 564
rationalization, 580-582, 585
Raynor, R., 232
reaction-time, variability in, 292
reactive inhibition, 288-289
readiness, 387-388
  developmental, prediction of, 392-394
reading, as perception, 336-338
reality principle, 550-551
recall, free, 130, 131
receptors, in breathing mechanism, 635-636
  characteristics of, 624-626, 627
  discrimination by:
    in hearing, 656-660
    in skin, 642-643, 654-655
    in smell, 653
    in taste, 643-644
    in vision, 646-653
  for internal changes, 627
  kinesthetic, 661
  motor neurons of, 669-670
  specialization of, 641-646
recognition, 131
recovery, spontaneous, 58-59, 83
reference group, 475
  and attitudes, 493
reflex, 391
  startle, 229
  sucking, 168-169
regression, in therapy, 611
reinforcement, 45, 70, 71, 196, 198, 283, 289, 515, 516
  of attitude, 488, 489-490, 493
  definition of, 81, 82*n*.
  delay of, 91-92
  and differentiation, 65-67
  of emotional reactions, 256-257
  partial, 63-65
  in verbal behavior, 82-83
reinforcer, 174, 175
relationship, statistical, measurement of, 414-419
relearning, 131
reliability, of tests, 464, 465

remission, in mental illness, 613
repetition, avoidance of, 287-290
  and learning, 94-95
  and stimulus selection, 271
repression, 589-593
research, basic, 26-27
  systems, 477
resistance, in therapy, 611-612
respiration, 635-638
response, correct, 36-37
  conditioned, *see* conditioned response
  conflicting, *see* conflict
  consummatory, 158, 170
  discovery of, *see* problem solving
  extinction of, *see* extinction
  fixation of, 37-38
    see also learning
  and habit, 61
  instrumental, 38-40, 72, 80, 158, 514-516
    and learning, 103
  learned, 38
  and learning, 105-106
  perceptual, *see* perception
  reinforcement of, *see* reinforcement
  to stimulus, 23-24
  unconditioned, 45, 52
  variability of, 284-292
    and set, 290
  see also stimulus-response *and* transfer
response generalization, 57-58, 71, 106
  and verbal learning, 86-87
response mechanism, skeletal, 661-663
  visceral, 663-667
  see also effectors
response-produced cues, 279-280
retention, 118, 134, 143, 151
  see also forgetting
retina, of eye, 646
  see also eye *and* vision
retroactive inhibition, 136, 591
  conditions influencing, 137-139
review, in learning, 143
  see also overlearning
reward, 193-194
rhodopsin, 616, 617
Rod-and-Frame Test, 519, 520
rods, in retina, 647, 651, 652